Impressionism James H Rubin

D0769802

ART&IDEAS

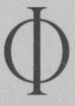

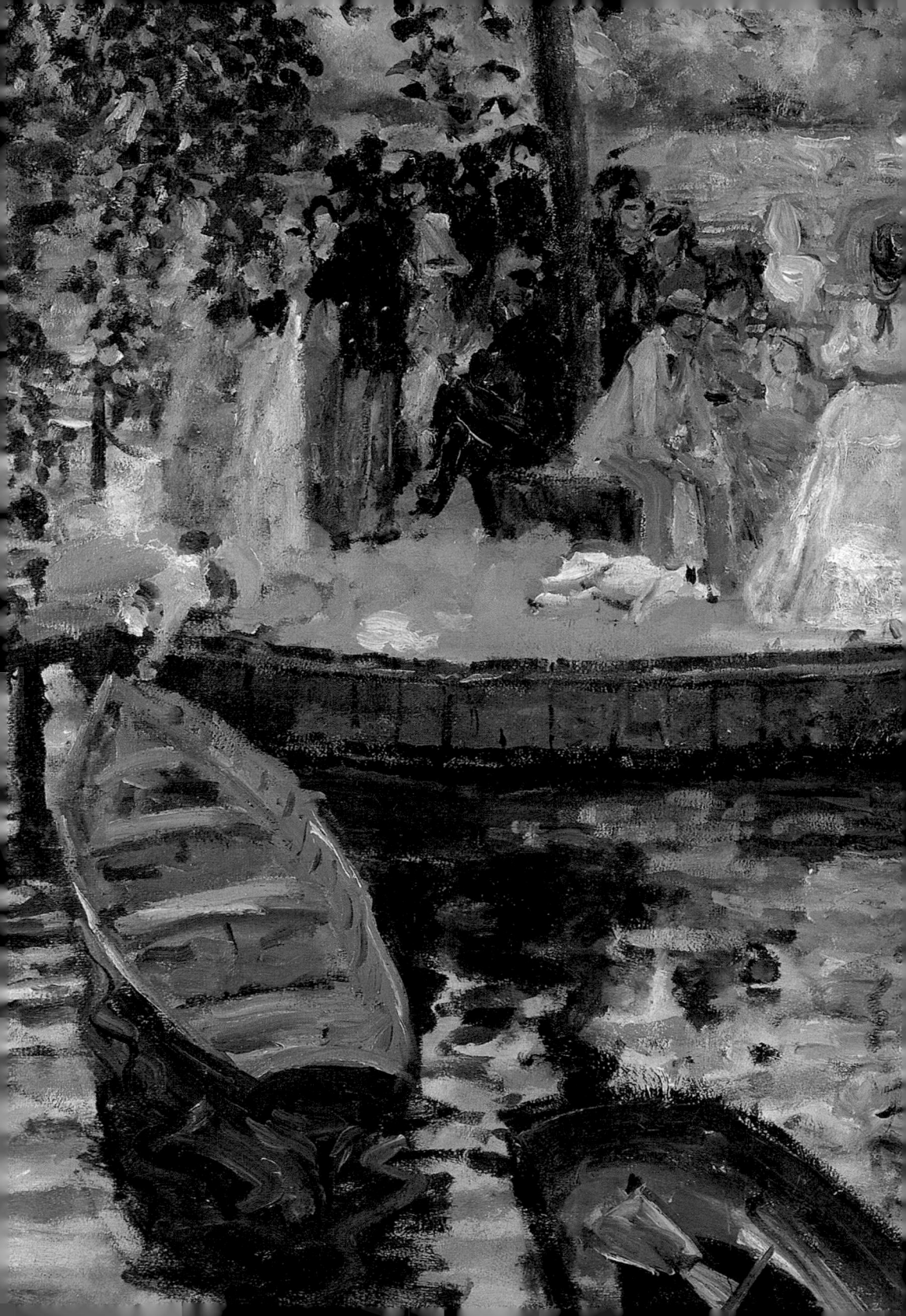

Impressionism

Opposite
Pierre-Auguste
Renoir,
La Grenouillère
(detail of 1),
1869.
Oil on canvas;
66 × 86 cm,
26 × 34 in.
Nationalmuseum,
Stockholm

No art form is so familiar and satisfying as Impressionism. No single movement better fulfils assumptions about the uplifting pleasures art is thought to provide. Whether refreshing vistas of countryside and seashore, glittering sites of fashionable entertainment, celebrations of modern city streets, or comfortable domestic interiors, most Impressionist scenes provide momentary access to a lifestyle that is widely admired (1). The paintings generally radiate bright decorative colours, have a private rather than museum scale, and employ a wilful, often experimental technique; they exemplify the culture of visual display that has come to characterize a prosperous and ostensibly progressive upper middle class. Indeed, it was through Impressionist paintings that urban life based on leisure, consumption and spectacle first acquired visible identity, one conveyed through forms that imply the free expression of the artist's personal vision. Moreover, Impressionism also provides us with a model for how artists act – independent of convention and true to self. If it still appears natural today, it is because its ideals continue to be so dominant that most people now take them completely for granted.

In representing what our society takes as a norm, Impressionism has generally escaped critical examination. Some have seen Impressionist paintings as essentially truthful renderings of an unproblematic world, or as concerned mainly with questions of perception. Yet beneath a seemingly natural surface, Impressionism raises deeper issues and begs serious questions. The present text incorporates diverse approaches and explores both pictorial evidence and underlying theories to present a complex whole, grounded in the historical context in which the works were made. It strikes a balance between a chronological narrative of the movement and exploration of the work of individual artists, respecting their wide diversity. In keeping with the concept of 'art and ideas' that motivates the present series, each chapter focuses on an issue central to Impressionism. For the sake of

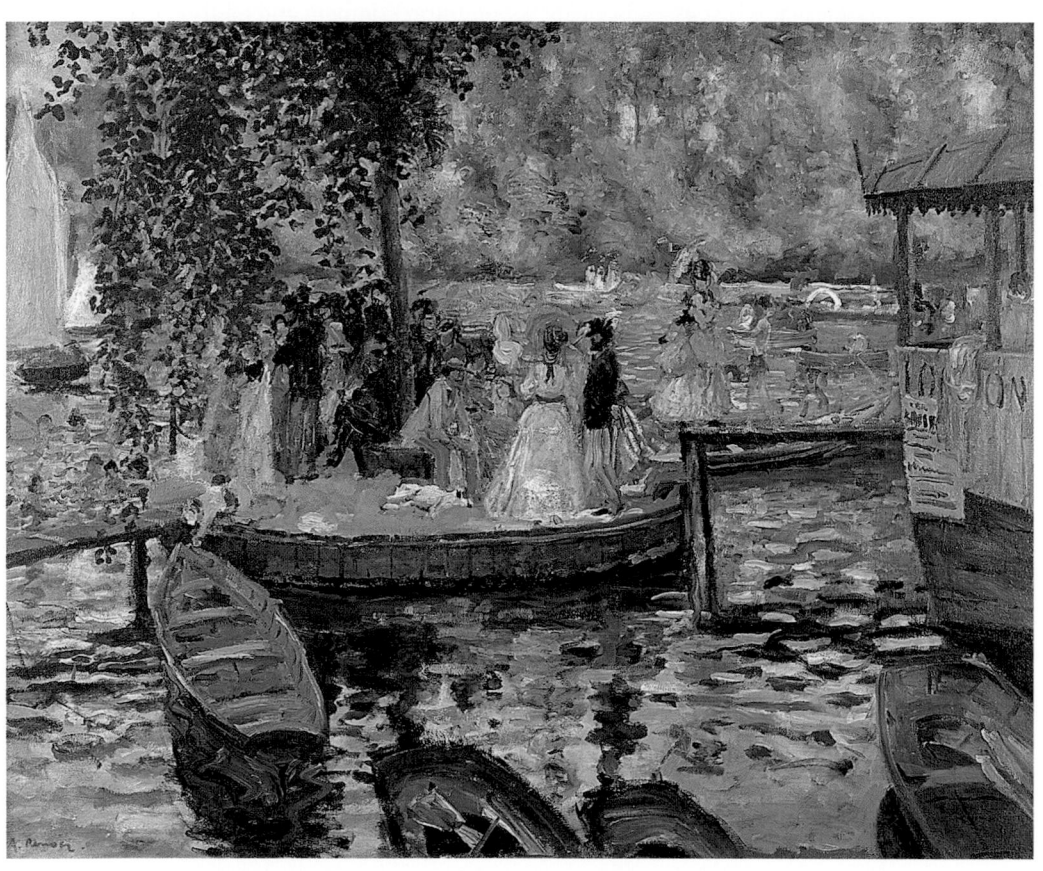

1
**Pierre-Auguste
Renoir,**
La Grenouillère,
1869.
Oil on canvas;
66 × 86 cm,
26 × 34 in.
Nationalmuseum,
Stockholm

clarity, these themes are organized within the framework of a roughly chronological development. Sometimes a chapter is devoted to a theme that is particularly relevant to a certain artist. Other chapters, such as one on politics and another on the marketing of Impressionism, may deal with further aspects of the same artist's work and other paintings not yet mentioned. Thus Édouard Manet's challenge to the contemporary Parisian art world is the theme of Chapter 2, but his famous painting, *The Execution of the Emperor Maximilian*, is discussed in Chapter 7 on Impressionism and politics.

This book is intended as a serious, up-to-date, reliable and stimulating overview for the general reader and student rather than an exhaustive reference work for scholars. The absence of footnotes streamlines the text for readability. While aiming for accessibility, the book nonetheless offers an introduction to current debates in art history. It is based on some twenty years of extensive travelling and avid looking, enthusiastic teaching and tracking of the most recent scholarly literature, as well as personal research and insight. Like any survey of such breadth, it is immensely indebted to many scholars who have invested their careers in making important factual discoveries and developing fundamental interpretations that allow us to see the work in newly meaningful ways. The book is therefore to a certain degree the product of shared conceptions, and I have tried to acknowledge debts, sources, alternatives and parallels through means other than the cumbersome apparatus of references. When textual indications themselves are not sufficient to lead the reader to original and secondary sources, the Further Reading list will do so. In the end, I hope the book will enrich the reader's experience of works that all of us will continue to admire, to probe and to enjoy.

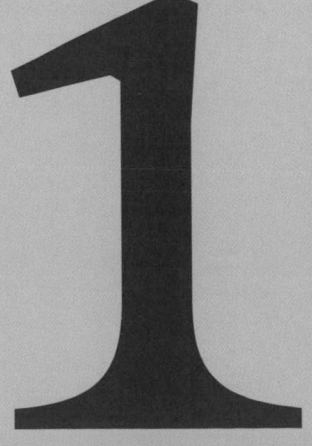

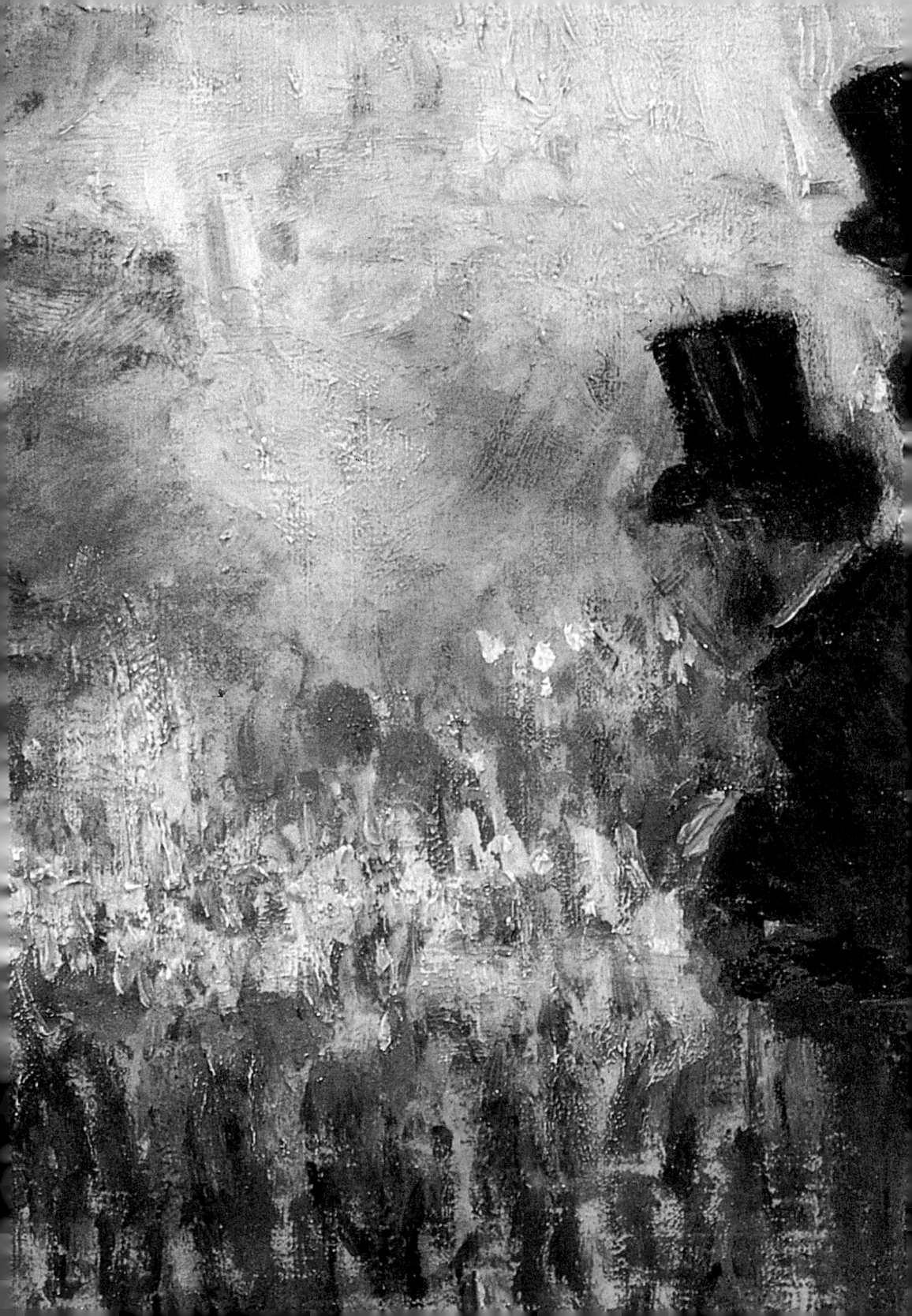

There are perhaps as many definitions of Impressionism as there are historians of art, but all are based on certain facts that never change. This chapter will explore them while introducing a background of social conditions and intellectual currents essential to understanding what follows. Most of the painters we associate with Impressionism today already shared a group identity well before they had their first independent exhibition in 1874. The term Impressionism was coined in 1874 in the satirical magazine *Le Charivari*, by one Louis Leroy. He mocked the loose brushwork of several paintings, especially Claude Monet's now famous *Impression, Sunrise* (3), a sketchy picture of the harbour of Le Havre, the Normandy port where Monet was brought up as a child and began his career as a painter.

2
Claude Monet,
*Boulevard des
Capucines*
(detail of 5)

In 1874, Monet (1840–1926) and other artist friends – including Paul Cézanne (1839–1906), Edgar Degas (1834–1917), Armand Guillaumin (1841–1927), Berthe Morisot (1841–95), Camille Pissarro (1830–1903), Pierre-Auguste Renoir (1841–1919) and Alfred Sisley (1839–99) – organized an exhibition in the former Paris studio of the notorious photographer Nadar (Gaspard-Félix Tournachon; 1820–1910) at 35 boulevard des Capucines. This group constituted most of Impressionism's core, and the event has come to be known as the first Impressionist exhibition. In the popular tone of journalistic humour, Leroy described the outrage of a (fictional) companion, the academician, M. Vincent. At the sight of Camille Pissarro's *Hoarfrost* (4),

the good man thought that his spectacles were dirty, and wiping them carefully set them on his nose ... He cried, 'What on earth is that?' 'It's a hoarfrost on deeply ploughed furrows,' I replied ... 'They look more like palette scrapings placed uniformly on a dirty canvas.' ... 'Perhaps, but the impression is there.'

As to the 'black tongue-lickings' of Monet's *Boulevard des Capucines* (5), M. Vincent exclaims: 'Is that what I look like when I am walking

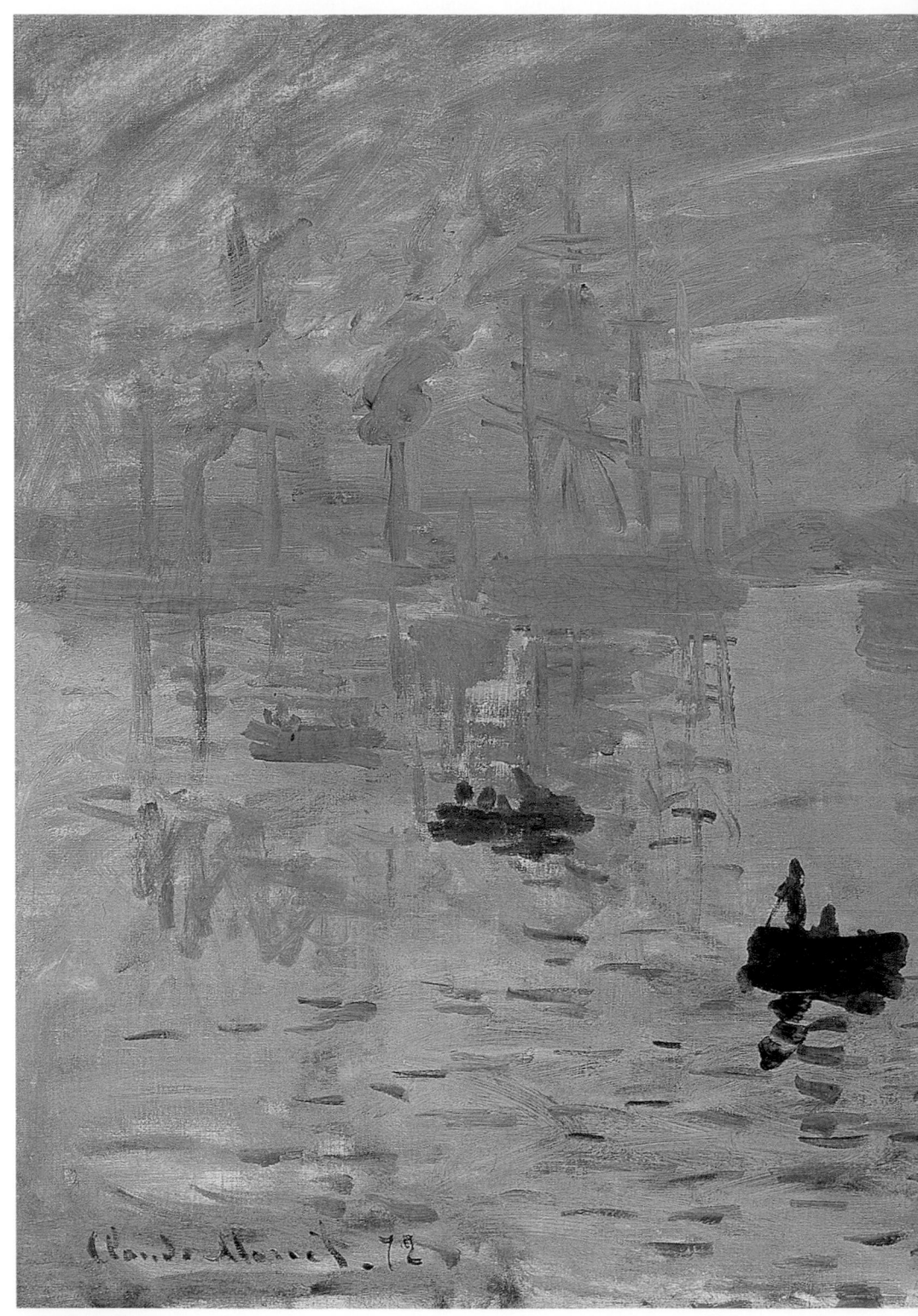

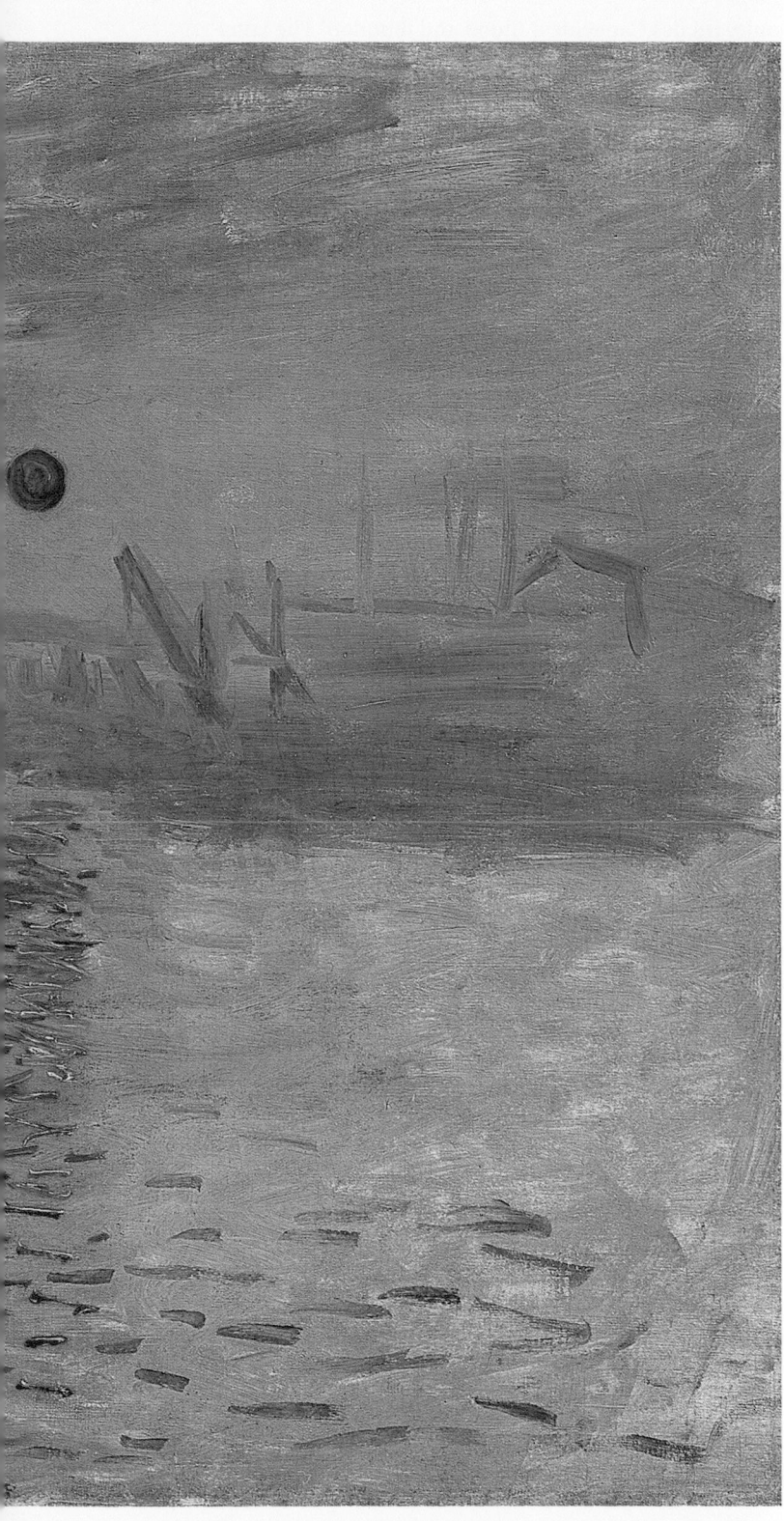

3
Claude Monet,
Impression,
Sunrise,
1872.
Oil on canvas;
48 × 63 cm,
18⁷⁄₈ × 24⁷⁄₈ in.
Musée
Marmottan,
Paris

down the boulevard des Capucines? Blood and thunder!' The latter showed a view from the third-storey window of the very place where the exhibition was being held. Leroy implied that such techniques spoiled the realistic effect that paintings of contemporary themes should have and took them as signs of shoddy crafting – a criticism that was often made. However, reactions to the exhibition were by no means universally unfavourable. Dissatisfaction with official art led some to praise such enterprising young artists. Other writers, sometimes admiringly, called them simply 'Intransigeants' – an allusion to the contemporary Spanish revolutionaries who were known by the same name. The painters' defiance towards established

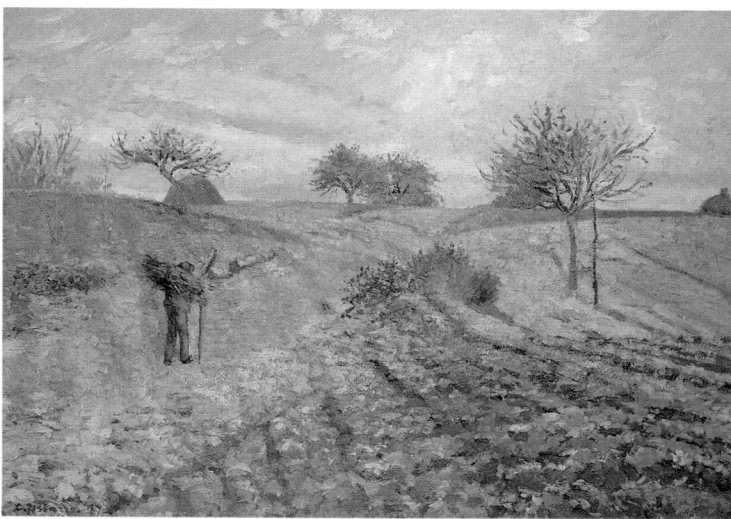

4
Camille
Pissarro,
Hoarfrost,
1873.
Oil on canvas;
65 × 93 cm,
25⁵⁄₈ × 36⁵⁄₈ in.
Musée d'Orsay,
Paris

authority seemed to have taken a lesson from politics. The Paris Commune of 1871, in which workers briefly ruled the city with a socialist government, was a recent memory, and Nadar, whose studio the artists used, was a known leftist sympathizer. This epithet, stressing the artists' adamant refusal of pictorial conventions and desire to start with a clean slate, focused less on the actual appearance of their art than on the rebellious conduct it implied.

Although the public and many of the painters soon accepted the Impressionist label, it was never undisputed. According to the critic Théodore Duret, writing in 1878, Monet was 'the Impressionist

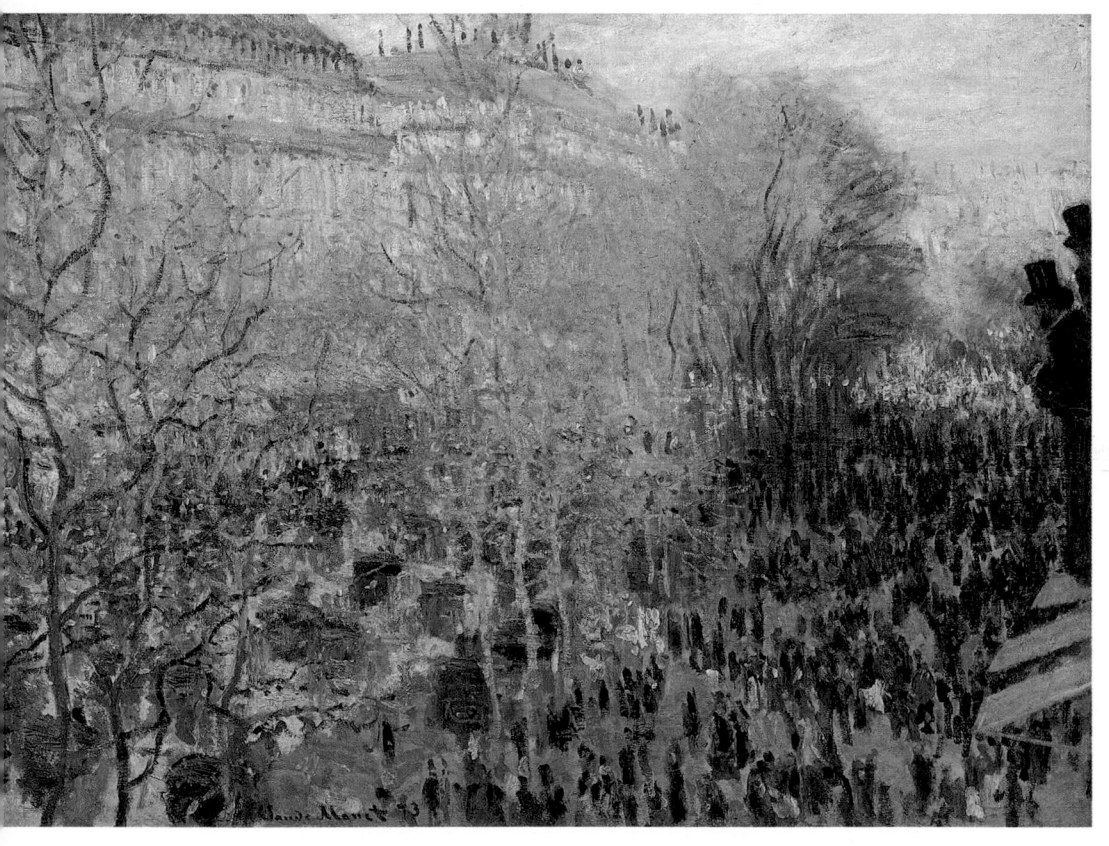

5
Claude Monet,
Boulevard des Capucines,
1873.
Oil on canvas;
61 × 80 cm,
24 × 31$\frac{1}{2}$ in.
Pushkin
Museum of
Fine Arts,
Moscow

painter *par excellence*', for his ability to capture fleeting and atmospheric effects so rapidly – an opinion that has generally survived to this day. But that characterization would surely not have included painters of interiors such as Degas, and there is no evidence that even Leroy intended to label all exhibitors with his epithet. In 1876, the Realist author and friend of Degas, Edmond Duranty, distinguished between colourists and draughtsmen in his essay *The New Painting*: Monet belonged to the former, Degas to the latter. Monet's bright style of short, vigorous brushstrokes and fragmented forms, which he developed with Renoir at the suburban bathing spot of La Grenouillère in 1869 (see 1), became the dominant idiom for only about half of the exhibitors. Although in 1876 Morisot (6), Pissarro and Sisley painted in a related manner, Degas, Giuseppe de Nittis (1846–84) and Henri Rouart (1833–1912) did not.

By the time of the third exhibition, held in 1877 across from Paul Durand-Ruel's gallery on the rue Le Peletier, the term 'Impressionism' was current, and the painters even discussed using it as the title of their exhibition. That year, a writer-friend of Renoir named Georges Rivière published a journal called *L'Impressionniste* to accompany the show as publicity. It is worth noting that rather than focusing on technique or landscape, Rivière insisted on the historical realism of pictures such as Renoir's large-scale *Ball at the Moulin de la Galette* (see 109) and Monet's *The Gare Saint-Lazare, Arrival of a Train* (see 71), albeit distinguishing them from other types of modern-life painting by their attention to colours and tones. The following year, Degas insisted that their title should include 'Independents, Realists and Impressionists'. From the beginning of their collaboration, Degas had envisaged an independent 'Realist' exhibition and preferred that or the more scientific-sounding 'Naturalism' as a more inclusive term. After 1879, Artistes Indépendents became the simple compromise title.

There is no definitive list of Impressionist artists, although certain names are regularly cited. In all, there were eight exhibitions of the so-called Société Anonyme des Artistes Peintres, Sculpteurs, Graveurs, etc., with a total of fifty-seven artists. Only Pissarro exhibited in all

6
Berthe Morisot, *Hide and Seek*, 1873. Oil on canvas; 45 × 55 cm, 17³⁄₄ × 21⁵⁄₈ in. Private collection

Dear Reader, Books by Phaidon are recognised world-wide for their beauty, scholarship and elegance. We invite you to return this card with your name and e-mail address so that we can keep you informed of our new publications, special offers and events. Alternatively, visit us at **www.phaidon.com** to see our entire list of books, videos and stationery. Register on-line to be included in our regular e-newsletters.

Subjects in which I have a special interest

☐ Art   ☐ Contemporary Art   ☐ Architecture   ☐ Design   ☐ Photography

☐ Music   ☐ Art Videos   ☐ Fashion   ☐ Decorative Arts   ☐ *Please send me a complimentary catalogue*

Mr/Miss/Ms   Initial   Surname

Name

No./Street

City

Post code/Zip code   Country

E-mail

This is not an order form. To order please contact Customer Services at the appropriate address overleaf.

Affix

stamp

here

PHAIDON PRESS INC

7195 Grayson Road

Harrisburg

PA 17111

PHAIDON PRESS LIMITED

Regent's Wharf

All Saints Street

London N1 9PA

Return address for USA and Canada only

Return address for UK and countries
outside the USA and Canada only

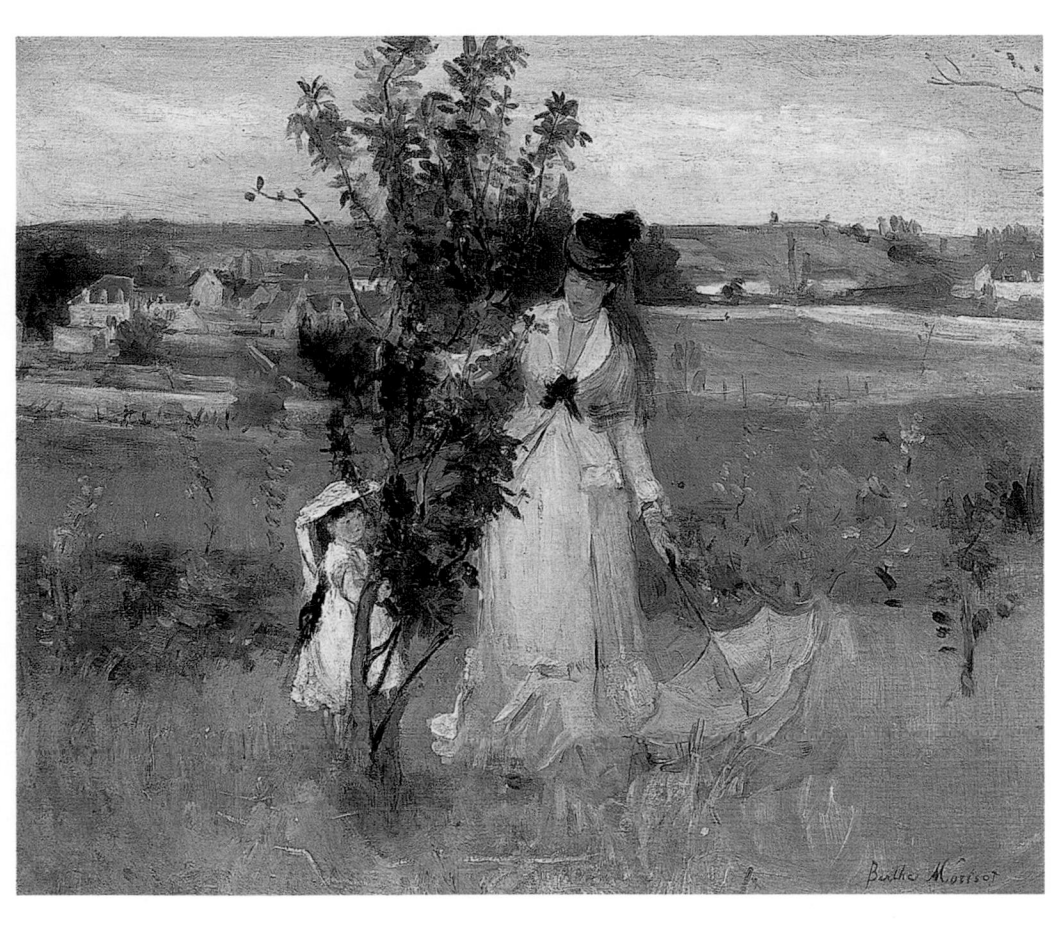

eight; Degas and Morisot showed more often than Monet; and Renoir participated in only four. Cézanne exhibited twice with the group, but until recently art historians have made him a pillar of Post-Impressionism. Paul Gauguin (1848–1903) exhibited five times, but his mature Symbolist art became quite opposed to the group. Edgar Degas's urban and often indoor imagery is the least like Monet's, yet he was one of the principal organizers and is as central to today's understanding of Impressionism as Monet himself. Along with Gustave Caillebotte (1848–94), he exemplifies a crucial urban dimension that Duret's conception (though not Rivière's) seemed to miss. They were joined by the American, Mary Cassatt (1844–1926). Édouard Manet (1832–83), whose subjects are also primarily urban, never exhibited with the group at all, but his work of the 1860s was seminal to the development of all the Impressionists previously mentioned, and he was intimate friends with several, who considered him their first leader. When Frédéric Bazille (1841–70) drew up preliminary plans for a group show as early as 1867, Manet was a central figure. Work towards the exhibition was interrupted by the Franco-Prussian War of 1870–1, during which Bazille himself was killed.

The idea of independent exhibitions was far from unprecedented, and Manet, in particular, knew something of them. The boisterous Realist painter, Gustave Courbet (1819–77), had set up his own pavilion opposite the grounds of the Universal Exposition of 1855 – the year Pissarro came to Paris from the Caribbean island of St Thomas. In 1867, Manet did the same, as did Courbet for the second time. Already in 1863, Manet's Le Déjeuner sur l'herbe (Luncheon on the Grass; see 30) had been the conversation-stopper at another special, though not private, exhibition – the Salon des Refusés (see Chapter 2). The idea behind the Impressionist exhibitions was to offer a liberal alternative to the official exhibition, called the Salon, for artists to display their work to critics and potential buyers. There would be no juries and no medals, awards or privileges. Those Salon practices seemed anti-democratic and pitted artists against one another. The Impressionists could choose which works to show, could mix recent items with earlier ones, and would have ample space between the paintings, rather than crowding them frame to frame and stacking to the ceiling as at the Salon. In the later 1870s some began using cheap white frames, others such as Pissarro and Cassatt began colouring them, to distinguish themselves from the Salon's traditional gilding.

The favoured location for the Impressionist exhibitions was always in the commercial heart of Paris, on or near the Grands Boulevards, and the exhibitions were financed by an economic cooperative – Société Anonyme means Limited Corporation – later with subsidies from the well-to-do Caillebotte. It benefited from a broad base of associates, all of whom were to share in any profits. The concept of mutual associations was in the air, and when a leftish writer-friend of Cézanne named Paul Alexis got wind of the plans in 1873, he extolled the 'powerful' idea as a model for reviving 'anaemic' institutions. Thus the exhibitions were never aimed at promoting an exclusive style but at gaining recognition and financial viability. Other artists, many unheard of today (from Édouard Brandon and Jean-Baptiste-Lèopold Levert in 1874 to Charles Tillot and Paul-Victor Vignon in 1886), joined the early exhibitions. Degas promoted painters such as de Nittis, Rouart and Federico Zandomeneghi (1841–1917). For the core Impressionists, whose friendships and styles had developed over the previous decade, the organization was a forum rather than a leap into the unknown. Rather than a beginning (other than for the name Impressionism itself), the exhibitions signalled maturity and confidence.

The painting by Henri Fantin-Latour (1836–1904) of *A Studio in the Batignolles Quarter* of 1870 (7) assembles the early Impressionist school for a group portrait. Manet is seated at the easel in his studio surrounded by friends who include the painters Renoir (in front of the picture frame), Bazille (the tallest), and behind him Monet, along with the novelist and critic Émile Zola (looking to our right), and the critic and poet Zacharie Astruc, posing for Manet. Critics had already begun wondering what to call them. In reviewing some of their paintings admitted to the official Salon, Zola ventured the label 'Actualists', praising their modern subject matter. The slightly reserved Duranty, who was more loyal to Realism (and whom Fantin-Latour left out of his picture because a dispute with Manet had led to a duel) tried 'Irregulars and Naïves'. In a caricature by Cham (8), they are called

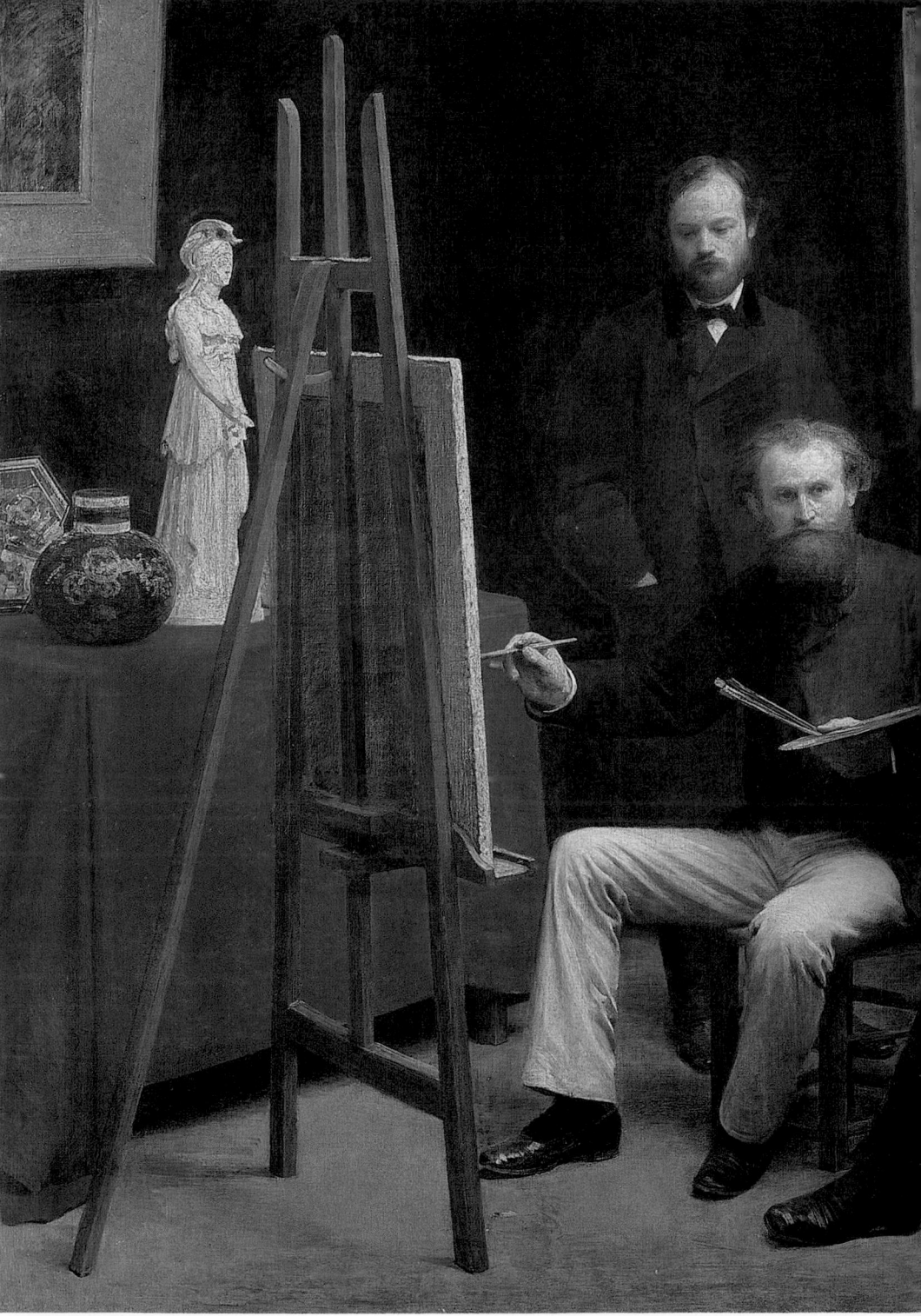

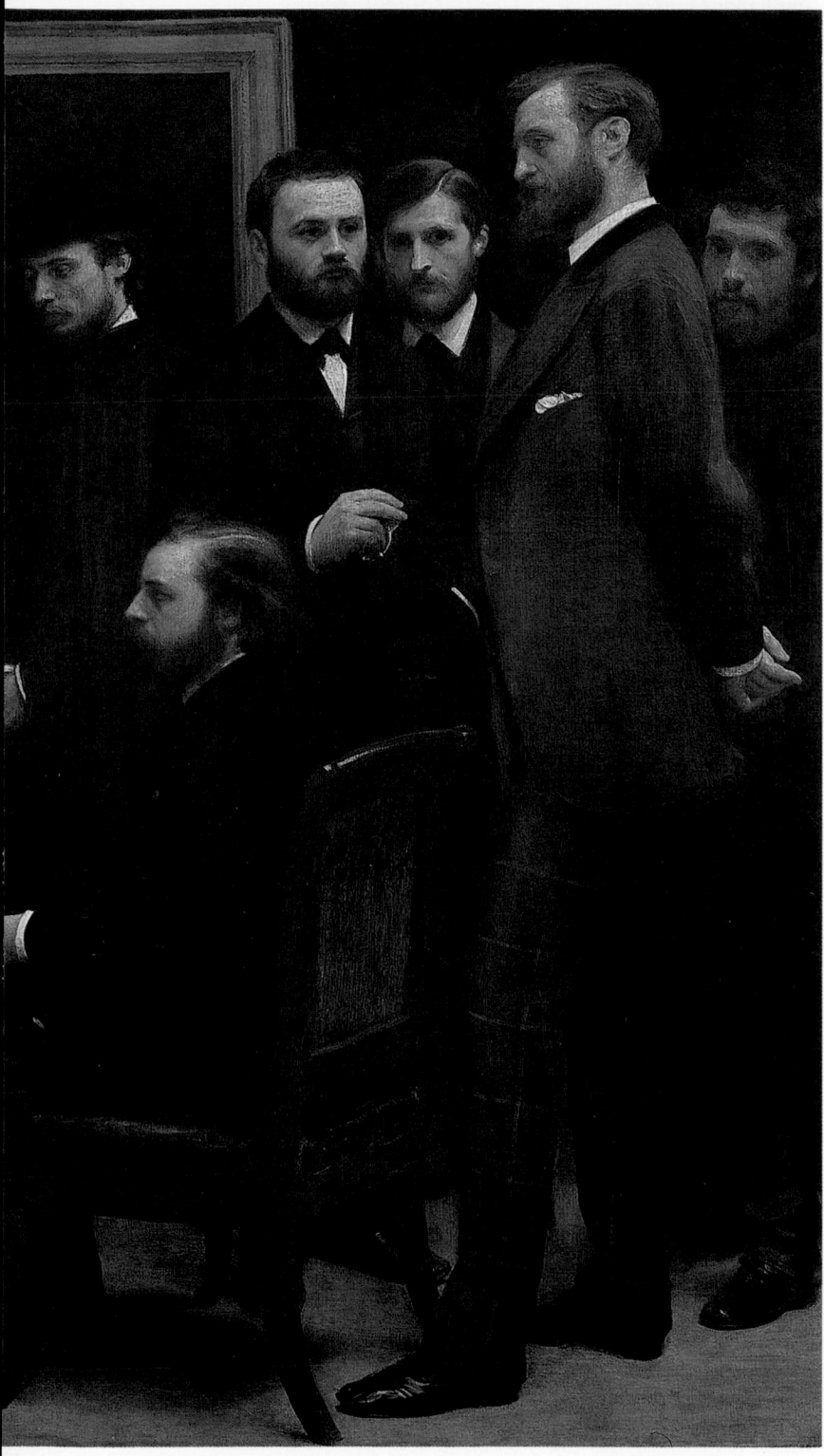

7
Henri Fantin-Latour,
A Studio in the Batignolles Quarter, 1870.
Oil on canvas; 204 × 273 cm, 80³⁄₈ × 107⁵⁄₈ in.
Musée d'Orsay, Paris.
l to r:
Otto Scholderer, Édouard Manet, Pierre-Auguste Renoir, Zacharie Astruc, Émile Zola, Edmond Maître, Frédéric Bazille, Claude Monet

simply (with mock outrage) 'Manet's Gang'. The more neutral expression, 'Batignolles School', came from the fact that Manet's leadership attracted others to the neighbourhood of that name north of the Saint-Lazare station – both Bazille and Sisley moved in at about the same time.

The wealthy Bazille could always afford spacious quarters, which became a centre of Impressionist activity in the late 1860s; companions such as Monet and especially Renoir often stayed with him and shared his space. In a painting of his studio in the rue de la Condamine (9), Bazille portrayed many of the same friends. The lanky Bazille himself (a figure painted by Manet) shows a picture to Monet and Manet, the

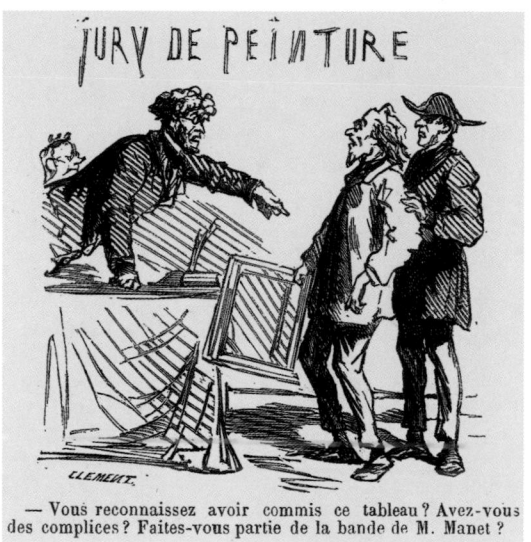

— Vous reconnaissez avoir commis ce tableau ? Avez-vous des complices ? Faites-vous partie de la bande de M. Manet ?

8
Cham,
Caricature of the Salon jury. The painters are asked: 'Do you admit having committed this painting? Are you accomplices? Are you part of the gang of M. Manet?' *Le Charivari*, 1868

9
Frédéric Bazille,
The Artist's Studio in the Rue de la Condamine, 1870.
Oil on canvas; 98 × 128·5 cm, 38⅝ × 50⅝ in. Musée d'Orsay, Paris.
l to r: Pierre-Auguste Renoir or Alfred Sisley, Émile Zola, Claude Monet, Édouard Manet, Frédéric Bazille, Edmond Maître

latter wearing a fashionable bowler hat. Zola is on the stairs looking down at Renoir or Sisley; the critic and musician Edmond Maître plays the piano. Historically, such camaraderie has often provided the social basis for avant-garde artistic movements, from the intense friendships of the Romantics to the American Abstract Expressionists at the Cedar Bar in New York's Greenwich Village. Our task will be to explore the characteristics shared by twelve artists – Bazille, Caillebotte, Cassatt, Cézanne, Degas, Guillaumin, Manet, Monet, Morisot, Pissarro, Renoir and Sisley – as well as the uniqueness of each. Every name stands for a special combination of techniques, attitudes and effects, all of which comprise today's notion of Impressionism.

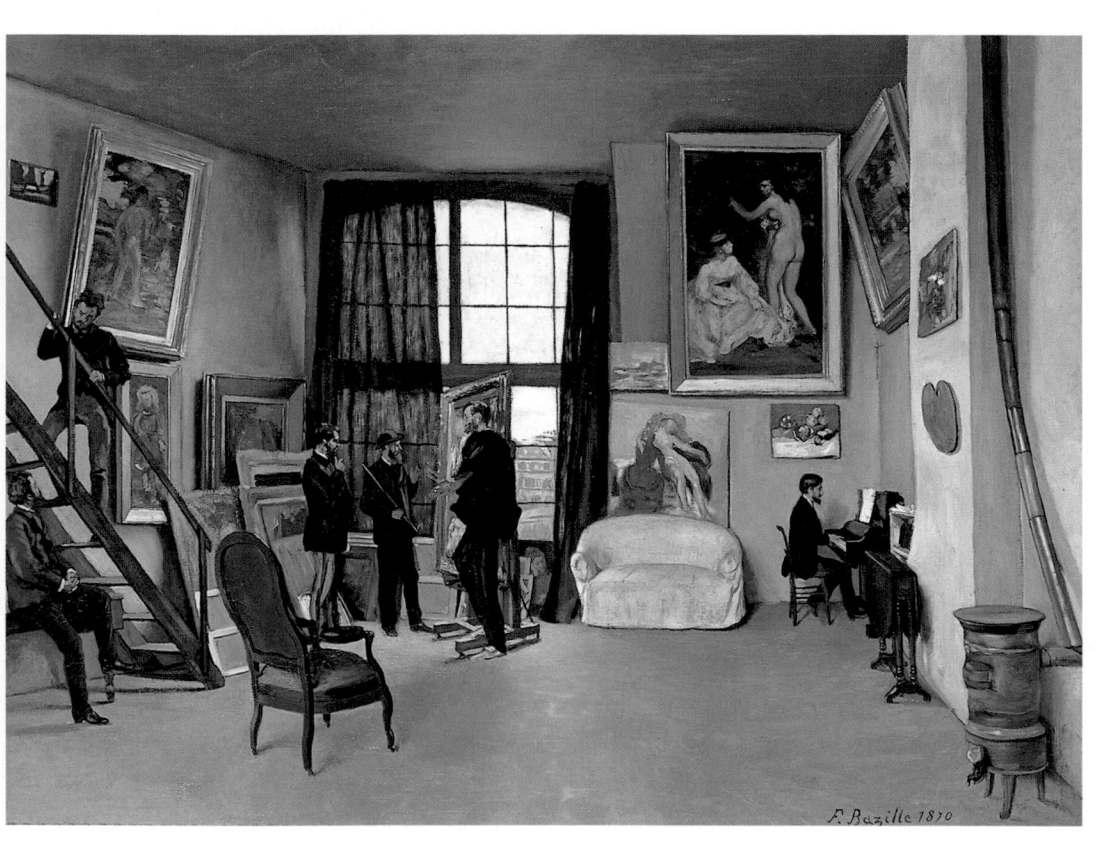

While acting as a group label and indicating a collective effort, the term Impressionism also stood for freedom and originality – hence the diversity within its recognizable parameters. To attract the attention of his or her contemporaries and to survive in the historical canon, an artist needed to create a personal identity rather than imitate a formulaic style, even if self-reliance and resistance to tradition were regarded as 'intransigeant'. True innovation demanded more than simply new choices of subject matter (which could be rendered in old-fashioned techniques): the fresh, novel technical processes were also the sign of their modernity. Uninhibited by academic procedures, the Impressionists also embraced the ready-mixed pigments in tubes and new colours – especially blues and purples – developed by French chemists and metallurgists since the beginning of the century.

When Monet wrote to Bazille from Fécamp in 1868, he warned of being preoccupied with 'what one sees and hears in Paris', preferring to produce work that would 'have the advantage of resembling no one else because it will simply be an impression of what I have experienced'. In this aim, Monet was following on the heels of Realism, whose leader, Gustave Courbet (Monet's friend at this time), advocated painting one's own time from one's own point of view: 'To be able to translate the customs, the ideas, the appearance of my epoch according to my own appreciation,' Courbet proclaimed in *The Realist Manifesto* of 1855. But Courbet's Realism was rooted in a kind of hardy provincial self-reliance and took its themes from rural and working-class life. Moreover, Realism had often been denigrated as no more than unimaginative reproductions of reality. To defend it, Realists felt forced to insist on their 'sincerity', meaning the authenticity of a personal vision derived from within themselves rather than from tradition, technical conventions or mechanistic reproduction. It was this 'subjective' element that the Impressionists would pursue.

Indeed, although the Impressionists certainly continued Realism's tradition of representing nature directly, responses to their work viewed the personal as having taken the upper hand. The unprecedented look of their paintings – whether in colour, paint handling or structure – was the guarantee that rather than repeating past recipes or copying nature slavishly, they were experiencing it anew and drawing on that experience for their techniques. Art historian Richard Shiff has stressed how the term Impressionism contains this duality of truth to nature as well as to subjective self. In today's vocabulary, as well as that of the nineteenth century, an 'impression' is both a physical imprint – implying an absolute and verifiable correspondence between the original (nature) and the image – and a more generalized conception, summary or recollection. In the eighteenth century, the word was used by the British philosopher David Hume to distinguish immediate sensations from ideas – the latter resulting from reflection – so that it referred to the often indiscriminate 'effects' of experience. In the nineteenth century, the word could refer to the traces of light on photosensitive surfaces as well as to records of the effects of certain sights on those who observed them. In art, brief sketches, for which the market was increasing, were sometimes exhibited as 'impressions'.

Painting of 'effects' was a common practice in the Barbizon School of landscape painters, some of whom, especially Jean-Baptiste-Camille Corot (1796–1875) and Charles-François Daubigny (1817–78), paved the way for, and overtly encouraged, the younger Impressionists (see Chapter 4). Daubigny was especially admired for his 'truth to the impression'. The sympathetic critic Jules-Antoine Castagnary wrote shortly after the satirical *Charivari* article on the 1874 exhibition: 'If one wants to characterize them with a single word that defines their efforts, then one would have to create the new term *Impressionist*. They are *impressionists* in the sense that they render not the landscape, but the sensation produced by the landscape.' He was referring to a personal process of internal perception. Sensation, he argued, lies in the realm of ideas; its reality exists within the mind of the individual, even though its reference is to the world. Hence, for friend and foe alike, the *subjective*, non-realist dimension of Impressionism was apparent from the outset – besides its derivation from experiences of external reality – and therein lay its novelty as a movement, the individual contributions of its practitioners and its difference from Realism.

The defences of Impressionism on grounds of objectivity thus need to be taken with a pinch of salt. Their purpose may have been to counter accusations of excessive subjectivity. For example, Castagnary had for years advocated 'naturalism' – his favoured term – meaning representations of modern life. The focus on subjective process in Impressionist painting was a cause for his concern. In *The New Painting*, Duranty praised the accuracy with which the painters rendered effects anyone could observe on 'sunny afternoon walks in the country', and he compared their angled views to glances out of city windows. For him there was no doubting Impressionism's naturalist premises, which he linked to Courbet and the Realism he had supported a decade before, as long as he used Degas as his standard. The new painting, he held, wanted to 'eliminate the partition between the painter's studio and everyday life in order to encounter the reality of the street'. Most agreed that the power of Impressionism lay in a correspondence between this modernity of subject matter and the originality of its means of representation. It is this combination – the performance of individual freedom in the production of truthful appearances – that has made Impressionism a paradigm for modern art.

The reality of the street to which Duranty alluded is for the most part a pleasurable one as seen in Impressionist paintings. Even the sharpest social observations of a subtle artist such as Degas are a far cry from the polemical political challenges made by Courbet's paintings of workers and provincials. That is to say nothing of Monet's luminous beach scenes, Sisley's limpid countryside vistas or Manet's dazzling cafés. Impressionism arose during a period of prosperity and rapid modernization, interrupted temporarily by the Franco-Prussian War, in which the French suffered a humiliating defeat, and the Paris Commune, which verged on a civil war and ended in a blood bath (see Chapter 7). In the early years of the Second Empire and through much of the 1860s, when the Impressionists began painting, France was in full industrial expansion, with the construction of bridges, roads and railways, the development of heavy industry (10), and especially the gigantic renovations and building projects for the city of Paris, the nation's hub. Perhaps at no period in French history had there been such an acute sense of the dawning of a new era. As the poet Charles Baudelaire (see 28) wrote in 1863, modernity meant rapid metamorphoses – 'the ephemeral, the fugitive, the contingent [and] the transitory'.

Signs of change were especially visible in Paris, where demolition, expansion and renovation took over the city for nearly two decades. Louis-Napoleon Bonaparte, nephew of Napoleon I (r.1799–1814), had been elected president of France following the democratic revolution of 1848. Prevented by the constitution from re-election in 1852, he seized absolute power by a *coup d'état* in December 1851.

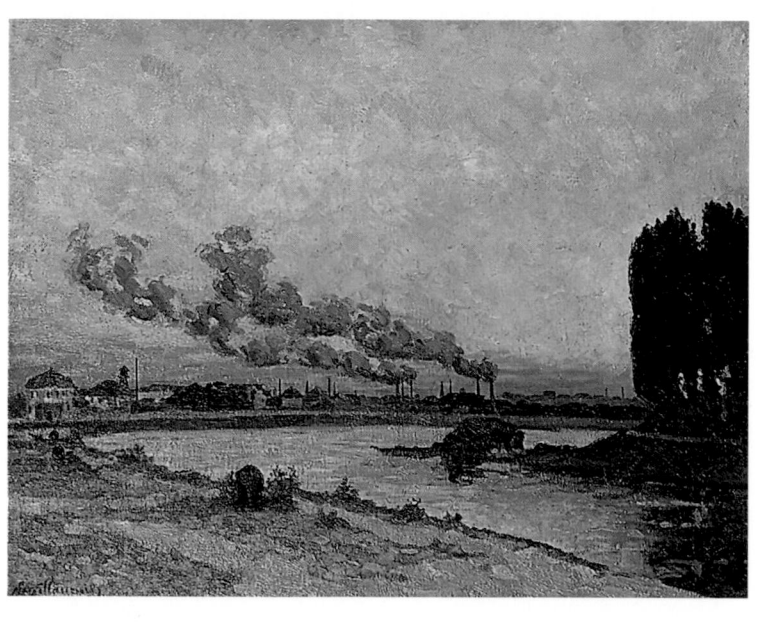

10
Armand Guillaumin, *Setting Sun at Ivry*, c.1869. Oil on canvas; 65 × 81 cm, $25\frac{5}{8} \times 31\frac{7}{8}$ in. Musée d'Orsay, Paris

(On proclaiming himself emperor, he took the name Napoleon III; r.1852–70) The new emperor hoped through economic growth and cultural politics to place France at the forefront of Europe and thus consolidate his popularity and power. These goals converged in projects for the modernization of Paris, which were implemented during the 1850s and 1860s by his Paris prefect, a ruthless bureaucrat of Alsatian origin, Georges Haussmann. Expenditures of more than forty times the city's usual annual budget were lavished on clearing thousands of buildings from congested, mainly working-class areas, displacing the inhabitants to less central locations.

Haussmann's aim was to 'tear open Old Paris, the district of riots and barricades, by a wide, central thoroughfare that would pierce this almost impenetrable labyrinth from one side to the other'. In 1860, Paris annexed its surrounding suburbs, so that neighbourhoods such as Les Batignolles (site of Manet's studio) and Montmartre (site of Renoir's studio) became a part of the city's tentacular urban extension. The gigantic whole was intended to function as an efficient centralized machine. Haussmann built new avenues, such as the rue de Rivoli, with its arcades; new parks, such as the Bois de Boulogne and the Parc Monceau; sewers, lighting and municipal buildings, including the Halles Centrales (Central Markets), designed by Victor Baltard in 1847; and the famous Opéra, designed by the young Charles Garnier in 1861, though not completed until 1874. A new style of architecture, based on cast iron and glass, was celebrated in buildings erected for the Universal Exposition of 1855, through which Louis-Napoleon intended to showcase French industry and art.

Hence progress and modernity were clearly identified with Paris, which attracted increasingly more people, from foreign tourists and aspiring artists to workers seeking higher wages after fallow years on struggling provincial farms. As a result the population of Paris nearly doubled during the Second Empire. Even without Napoleon III's visions of glory, sanitary conditions and traffic congestion had so deteriorated that urban renewal was long overdue. Paris had been an impassible warren of dingy and malodorous habitations that bred disease (19,000 cholera deaths in 1847) and crime. Hard as it is to believe today, the grand spaces surrounding the Louvre and even those inside its current bounds, as well as almost the entire Île de la Cité, where government edifices and Notre Dame Cathedral now have primary place, were densely packed with medieval buildings. In addition to a healthy opening up, the renovations of Paris facilitated the takeover of prime city centre sites from lower-class inhabitants by property developers and their middle- and upper-class clientele. The long straight avenues with their imposing perspectives and allusions to Imperial Rome cut right through old neighbourhoods. One of the streets eliminated was the rue Transnonain, scene of a brutally

11
Cross section
of a Parisian
apartment
building.
Woodcut from
a drawing by
Bertall,
from Edmond
Texier's
Tableau de Paris,
Paris,
1852

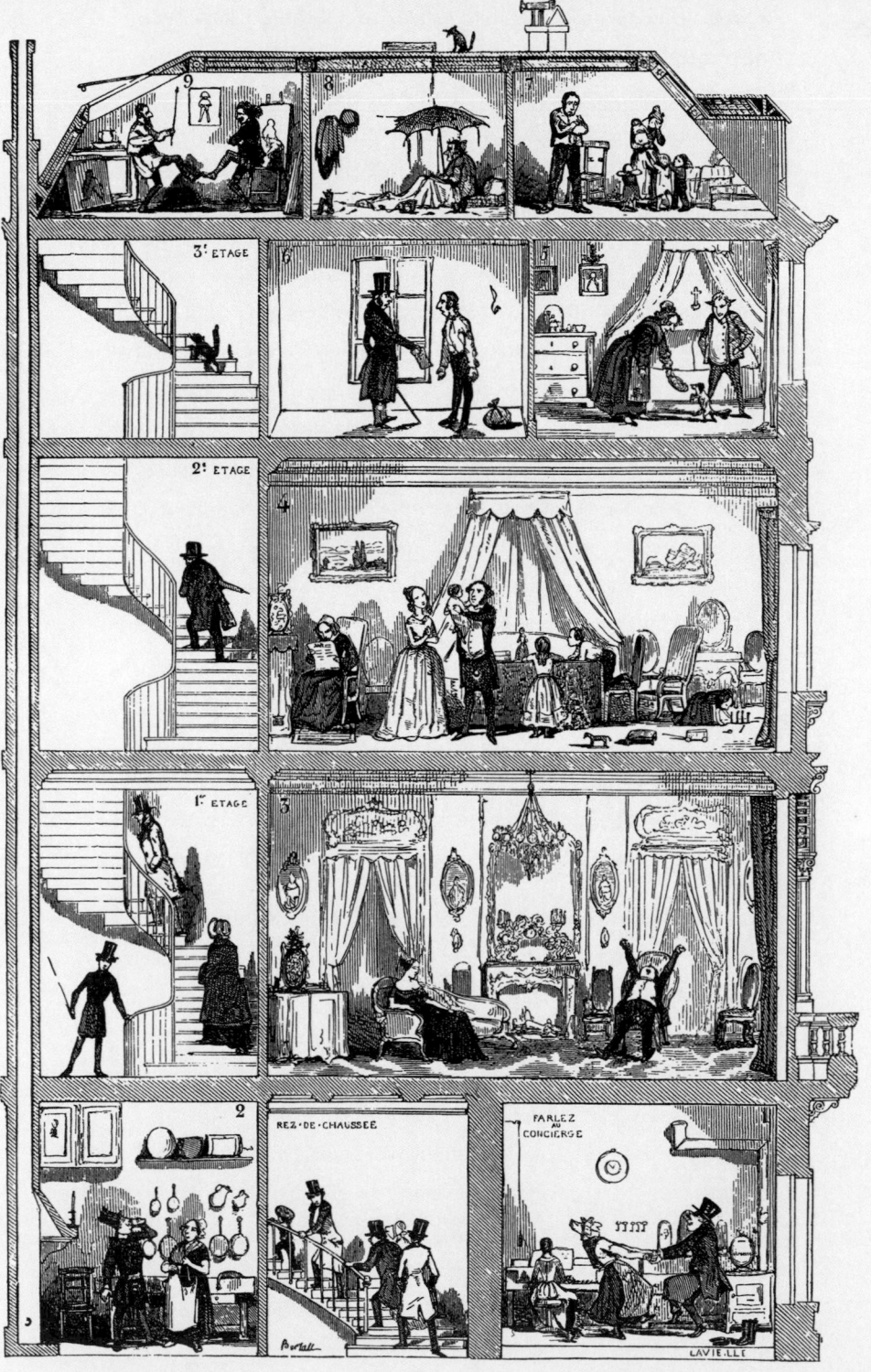

quashed uprising of 1834. To finance the construction, Haussmann granted concessions to builders, who would line the avenues with apartment houses with shops at street level and dwellings above. A typical cross section of such a house is reproduced in a humorous print from Edmond Texier's *Tableau de Paris* (11). Obviously, only a small percentage of the original residents could afford the higher rents, and wealthier families moved into the fashionably bright, airy and centrally located new flats.

Doubtless the liberal poet Victor Hugo and others were right that the new thoroughfares were made deliberately too wide for raising insurrectionary barricades and straight enough for artillery to fire easily at protest gatherings. The so-called 'dangerous classes' – workers and other disenfranchised who tended to take their complaints to the streets – were being exiled to the periphery. After all, Napoleon III's coup followed a series of uprisings, from the revolt of 1830, which led to the abdication of the Bourbon Charles X (r.1824–30) in favour of Louis-Philippe d'Orléans (r.1830–48), to the left-wing revolution of 1848 that put an end to the monarchy once and for all. Louis-Napoleon could argue that his authoritarian regime was the needed response to continuing instability. Indeed, plans for the new Opéra, built on its separate, easily defendable city block, were partly motivated by a bombing attempt on the Emperor's carriage that had injured hundreds in front of the old opera house on a narrower street.

What had the potential to serve military and political purposes, however, also introduced freedom of circulation – of air to dispel foul vapours, of waste drainage for better sanitation and of commercial traffic, which enhanced business efficiency and trade. Furthermore, at its height in the 1860s the enormous public works programme employed some twenty per cent of Parisian labourers; it was the engine of a prosperity that smoothed over social conflicts and laid the basis for industrial France. Property speculators and railway barons, such as the Pereire family and the Rothschilds, among others, accumulated vast riches under imperial financing. Even when favouritism and corruption were exposed prior to the regime's collapse in 1870, fortunes had been made. It was a gilded age.

This teeming but increasingly open, clean and well-lit metropolis – largely the one we so admire today – was not simply the subject matter visible in much Impressionist painting. The new urban experience it afforded was the context within which key ideas underlying Impressionism arose. Central to understanding this relationship is the core thinker behind what might be called Impressionist theory – the poet and critic Charles Baudelaire (see 28), author of the seminal essay of 1863, *The Painter of Modern Life*. Although Baudelaire died in 1867, just as the early group identity of the Impressionists was emerging, and years before the name, he was the first to argue cogently that modern life was the only worthy subject matter for the modern artist and that visual art could be the central medium for conveying its poetry. He was the first to identify the forms through which its representations would operate, for he saw how rapid execution and informal painterly technique expressed both progressive efficiency and personal leisure. No one else so deeply understood how the combination of naturalism and subjectivity we now take for granted in Impressionism was grounded in experiences of the modern city. As early as the 1840s, his writing celebrated the heroism of modern man suffering through an existence that placed material values above things of the spirit. The role of an art suitable to such new times – hence its moral worth and historical significance – would be to make the workaday experience of the newly ascendant bourgeois class harmonious by providing access to beauty and testifying to human freedom.

These ideals were embodied in Baudelaire's notion of the *flâneur*. This modern citizen-hero was an indigenous by-product of the new urban society. Baudelaire saw him as an enviable gentleman-dandy, whose financial independence allowed him to cultivate the aesthetic and rise above the crowd. He was the model for a new vision. The *flâneur* would stroll about the town, through the new parks or along the endless boulevards, purely for the purpose of enjoyment, as we might when taking a break from work, except that time off could last all day. The effect of infiltrating society in order to see up close, yet maintaining distance as if observing through a spyglass, is typical of the strange combination of anonymity and intimacy one experiences in a crowd. It may help explain the fascinating combination of directness and remove we often sense in Impressionist work. For Baudelaire, this detached but inquisitive gaze embodied the modern human condition because it originated in the need to maintain individual integrity against the threat of loss of identity in densely populated urban spaces. More pointedly, it was the attribute of certain superior beings boldly resisting through their indomitable bearing the rising tide of democracy, at a time when the old order was on the verge of collapse. This *flâneur*'s visual acuity is at the cutting edge of culture, for it is located at the point where change meets resistance – where co-existence in a dialectical relationship produces new forms. It would signal, he hoped, the emergence of a new class based on talent and merit whose production would be literature and art.

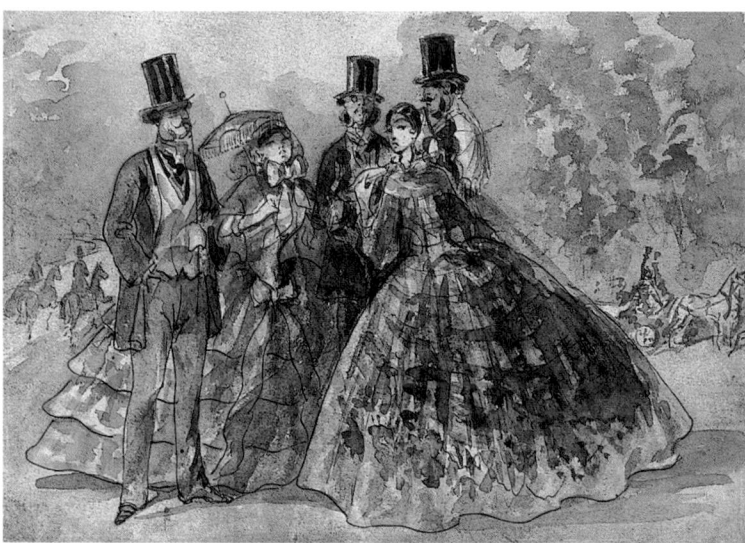

12
Constantin Guys, *Meeting in the Park*, c.1860. Pen and watercolour; 21.7 × 30 cm, 8½ × 11⅞ in. Metropolitan Museum of Art, New York

That Baudelaire exemplified the expression of modernity through an artist – his 'Painter of Modern Life' – highlights his belief in the pre-eminence of vision, hence visual art. The eye, it could be said, was at the centre of the 'I' – the self; the *flâneur*'s sharp insights reaffirmed individuality in a context where it was under siege. In addition, the rapid pace of urban existence made forms of contact other than the visual virtually impossible and made guesswork about the lives of others both a necessity and a fascinating adventure. A concern with distinctions and identities is evident in the proliferation of illustrated compendiums of social and economic types in mid-nineteenth-century France. One of the first and most extensive, *Les Français peints par eux-mêmes* (*The French Painted by Themselves*) of 1839–42, offered a 'moral and physiognomical' panorama of French society ranging from the grocer to the ragpicker, the street urchin to the landlord, the shopgirl to the lady of fashion. Even in our day, who has not strolled through the modern city speculating on the origins, status and perhaps character of diverse members of the population whose paths we cross? The painter of modern life, Baudelaire held, exercised these typological skills by making 'differences of class and breed … immediately obvious to the eye'.

The artist through whom Baudelaire exemplified his theories was the watercolourist and illustrator Constantin Guys (1802–92; 12). His quick, sketch-like style, Baudelaire claimed, embodied both the volatile passion and rapt fascination of the naïve observer (one unencumbered by outworn conventions) and the modern ideal of efficiency (the greatest effect with the most economy of means). No painter had yet grasped this connection. Baudelaire had for at least a decade been writing about the significance of illustrators and writers of the occasional piece – journalists like himself, for that was how he made his own meagre living. He knew at first hand, from the writer's point of view, that a certain short, rapid form of article, the *feuilleton* rather than the extended tome or pedantic dissertation, was required by modern publishing. The literate public, which increasingly meant the middle classes, demanded succinct, incisive and entertaining work. Agile summarization and expression of an author's wit were the manner for modern writing. In visual art he sought similar traits, discovering equivalents in graphic media – caricature and outdoor sketching – both of which are directly tied to the observation of reality. By the 1870s, in other words, the forms Baudelaire held to be modern were associated with naturalism.

For sketching, which takes on-the-spot notations derived directly from the motif, the relationship between a free style and natural effect seems obvious to us today. We forget that until Impressionism, the looseness and seeming lack of finish, in which brushstrokes and daubs of colour are easily visible, shattered the illusion of reality for all but the most progressive viewers and were only considered as preparatory to tighter, smoother final work. Even among supportive critics, Impressionism's technical characteristics were regarded as signs of artistic subjectivity that had a mitigating rather than reinforcing effect on realism. That had been Castagnary's concern, and indeed Duranty's defence of Impressionist naturalism praised its effects while excusing its techniques. How, then, can the ostensibly quick and fragmentary notations so familiar to a modern audience have become *both* signs of artistic subjectivity *and* signs of naturalism based on observation? The answer lay in the example of artists such as Guys and Honoré Daumier (1808–79; see 16 and 122). What Baudelaire saw in them was the connection between sure knowledge – caricature's biting essence of truth – and fugitive expression – its breathtaking shorthand. In his essay on caricature, Baudelaire wrote: 'the word "modern" refers to manner and not to date.' This concept would lie at the heart of Impressionism, too.

For Baudelaire, a process based on colour was inherently modern. It is often said that the Impressionist technique eliminated traditional drawing as the basis of form in favour of deriving it directly from colour. As taught at the academies, line was associated with reason, for outline defined form intellectually without materiality; colour, which is formed of matter itself, was connected primarily to the senses, for its use in modelling and its appeal to the eye created sensuous effects. To found artistic style on colour rather than line was an oppositional position, in which sensuousity and emotional charge – characteristics once denigrated as feminine – were substituted for the virile regime of reason. But it was also a position aligned both with nature and with modern technology, as evidenced through the important new representational medium of photography, the invention of which was announced in 1839 by Louis Daguerre (1787–1851) in France, though Henry Fox Talbot (1800–77) had been developing the process simultaneously in England. In photography, one could say that nature made its own impression, through the intermediary of light. Indeed, Talbot called it the 'pencil of nature'. Without the use of line, the images made by photographers of city streets or rural scenes

13
Eugène Cuvelier, *Forest of Fontainebleau in Mist,* c.1865. Salted paper print from glass negative; 19·9 25·7 cm, 7³⁄₄ 10¹⁄₈ in. Metropolitan Museum of Art, New York

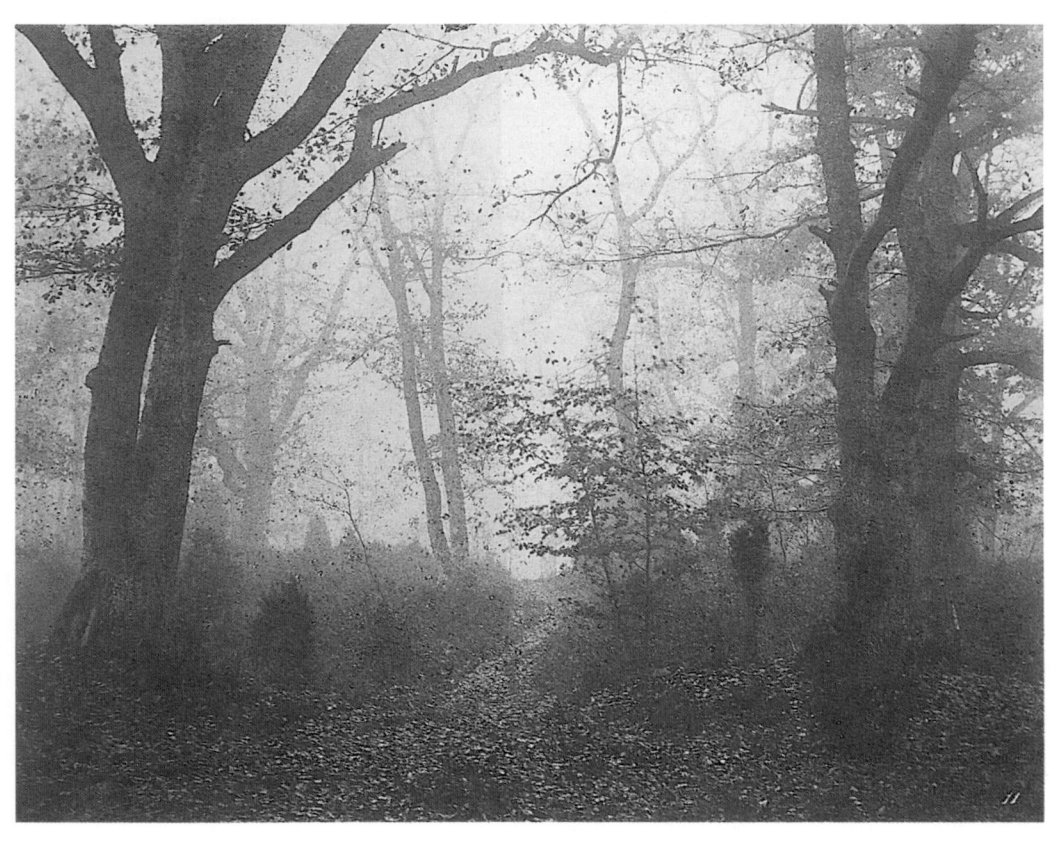

set standards for naturalism. The blurred edges and illegible areas of black and white, caused by technical limitations of exposure times or paper negatives (known as calotypes, photographic images produced on paper which replaced the metal-based daguerreotypes in the 1850s), were signs of a seemingly natural process made possible through technology. Photography transcended conventions of line and colour to produce images literally formed in and drawn by light, as indicated by the combination of the Greek words *photos*, meaning 'light', and *graphos*, meaning 'writing'. Photographers such as Eugène Cuvelier (*c*.1830–1900; 13) were as plentiful as painters in the Forest of Fontainebleau. When landscapists such as Corot (see Chapter 4) saw their work, they began to imitate their effects in painting; lack of definition could now be read both as signs of poetic evocation and naturalism.

By working directly in colour, the Impressionists thus emulated both reality itself and modern technology. Of course, Monet's use of patches or strokes of unmixed paints corresponds to the idea of drawing directly in colour. So too, however, does the later style of Degas – an artist obsessed with drawing – when, for example, he employed the method of modelling the bodies of his bathers from a gridwork of pastel hatch marks (see Chapter 5). The writings of Baudelaire give full significance to their orientation. The transcendence of opposition between line and colour was precisely what he found essential in the graphic arts. Thus, in praising Honoré Daumier's drawing as 'naturally *colourful* [his emphasis]', Baudelaire meant that it evoked the general demeanour of form itself. For Baudelaire, a colouristic approach to rendering form was the means through which artists could address the inner human consciousness, whether it was to bare the soul or to render more effectively the specificity of an individual or an object. Yet it did so while partaking of the material realm, since colour itself had material existence and appealed to the senses rather than the intellect. In this way it was the essence of an art of modern life, which must be rooted in the visible but also express something beyond it – something internal, in other words, as the response of intelligence to what Baudelaire felt was an epoch of increasing materialism and mechanization.

Prior to his writings on caricature, Baudelaire had eulogized the Romantic painter Eugène Delacroix (1798–1863). Baudelaire took the artist's loose handling of paint (see 19) and his links to traditions of colouristic painting – to the Flemish Baroque painter Peter Paul Rubens (1577–1640) and his eighteenth-century heirs – as signs of spirituality and imagination. Hence, in equating a rapid, colourist style with psychological or conceptual rather than exclusively physical expression, Baudelaire laid the ground for Castagnary's theory equating free technique with inner sensation and subjectivity (though without the Romantic angst). On Delacroix's death in 1863 – the year the painter was visited by Monet and Bazille, and the year Manet (who had visited Delacroix years earlier) showed in the Salon des Refusés – Baudelaire republished parts of his essays on Delacroix as a tribute to the master. Fantin-Latour painted a *Homage to Delacroix*, which showed Delacroix's famous *Self-Portrait* of 1838 surrounded by admirers, including Baudelaire, Manet, Duranty, Fantin-Latour himself and a number of other artists. When such newcomers as Monet, Bazille, Renoir, Sisley, Cézanne and the writer Émile Zola arrived on the scene, therefore, Baudelaire, Delacroix and colour were at the heart of progressive artistic thought.

Thus, the Paris of Haussmann was a city in cultural as well as physical transition. In literature and the social sciences, too, there were important transformations that can help us understand artistic developments. For example, there were two widely publicized literary scandals that sharply focused attention on new trends. In 1857, Baudelaire was tried and censored for obscenity in several poems from his collection *Les Fleurs du mal* (*Flowers of Evil*), published that year. Although set in contemporary Paris, his poetry transcended reality through imagination in precisely the way he argued for art. In the same year, Gustave Flaubert was acquitted of accusations of immorality for his recently published novel *Madame Bovary*, the meticulously descriptive story of adultery committed by a bored, delusional country wife. A literature of modern life was making celebrities of its proponents. The novels of the Goncourt brothers, Edmond and Jules, probably aroused as much interest as Flaubert's. *Germinie Lacerteux* (1865) was based on detailed observation of the lives of prostitutes; *Manette Salomon* (1867) is the story of an artist's model who becomes her employer's downfall. Émile Zola, the leading figure to promote Naturalism in literature, advocating detailed, factual description, was the boyhood comrade of Paul Cézanne, who introduced him to the circle of young artists when they were in Paris together. It was through the Goncourts that Zola got the idea of chronicling contemporary life in a way professed to be scientific. Science reached new heights of theory and discovery, with Louis Pasteur's work on bacteria, Gregor Johann Mendel's on genetics, Charles Darwin's theory of evolution and Hermann Ludwig Ferdinand von Helmholtz's theory of optics (see Chapter 8). Most of Zola's best-known works evoke contemporary Paris: *Le Ventre de Paris* of 1873 is set in the Central Markets; *L'Assommoir* of 1877 is about an alcoholic laundress; *Nana* of 1880 features a courtesan and the 1883 *Au Bonheur des dames* explores the modern phenomenon of Parisian department stores. In contrast to the aristocratic Goncourts, Zola's fiction – and his interest in Naturalism – stemmed from his sense of social obligation. And his journalistic style – he had begun his career doing reviews of books and art exhibitions – was far more accessible to the general reader than the more sophisticated prose of the Goncourts.

In 1866, in an essay on Realist painters at the Salon, Zola assessed the intellectual moment in French culture as one when 'the wind is blowing in the direction of science' and 'we are drawn in spite of ourselves towards the exact study of things ... The movement of the epoch is certainly realist, or rather, positivist.' Positivism was undoubtedly the dominant philosophy of the third quarter of the nineteenth century, permeating historical and critical writing as well as literature. Its founder, Auguste Comte, held that to be valid, knowledge must be verified through scientific examination. Replacing the religious faith of former times, empirical analysis would be the key to social harmony and progress. This popular theory had two important consequences for art and literature. First, it supported the Realist claim that art must be based on observation of one's times and that in doing so it would contribute to human freedom. Second, it meant that all art, past and present, must be evaluated in the context of its historical period.

Of direct interest to Zola, too, were the related aesthetic and psychological theories of Hippolyte Taine, a famous historian, philosopher and critic, who lectured at the École des Beaux-Arts during the 1860s. Taine believed that perception of reality was a biological process and therefore each artist would necessarily represent reality according to his personal way of seeing. Each of us views the world through a unique, personal 'screen', to use his term. Taine thus grounded in science the claims found both in Realism and Impressionism that art combines the objective and the subjective. In addition, Taine elaborated the contextual interpretation of art into a formula based on race, milieu (social and geographical) and historical moment, which he considered factors in every human biological profile.

Zola himself described his early novel of 1867, *Thérèse Racquin*, in related quasi-scientific language. Thérèse enlists her lover to murder her husband but is eventually given away by the lover's feelings of guilt. In defending the novel, Zola wrote: 'I have simply done on living bodies the work of analysis which surgeons perform on corpses.' His was a literature of forensic observation. We shall see that when he wrote about art he advocated a similar method for the artist and adopted a parallel critical approach.

Historical writing was based on the new positivism, too. The historian Jules Michelet had already grounded historical movements in the living conditions and democratic aspirations of the French people, rather than in individual leaders or élite groups (*Le Peuple*, 1846). Following this example, Ernest Renan attempted to found his history of religions on scientific method. His *Life of Jesus*, published in 1863, placed historical writing at the centre of public debate by linking Christ's exploits to the practical, human circumstances of his life and times rather than to spirituality and divine intervention. There was perhaps no better example of the progressive social purpose Comte had given to Positivism than Renan's effort to tie religion to conditions among the people, but his conclusions were understandably attacked by those whose vested interests lay in established institutions and practices. It was assumed that Manet's *The Dead Christ with Angels* (14), exhibited at the Salon of 1864, was the painter's homage to Renan's

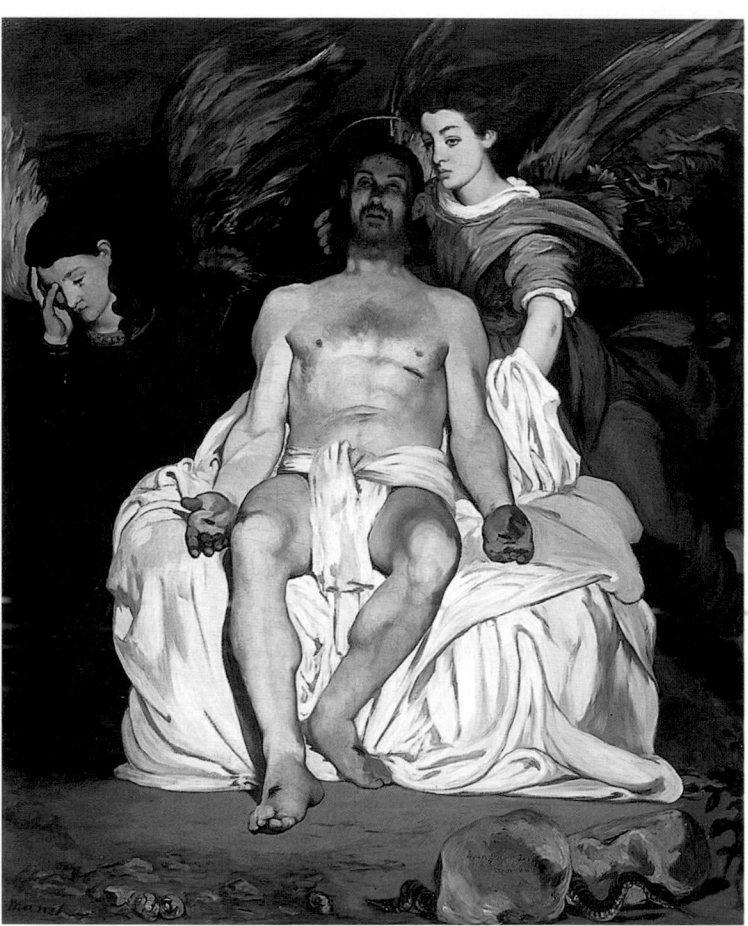

14
Édouard Manet,
The Dead Christ
with Angels,
1864.
Oil on canvas;
179 × 150 cm,
70¹₂ × 59 in.
Metropolitan
Museum of Art,
New York

historical and more humanizing view of Jesus. One critic wrote: 'Don't miss Manet's *Christ*, or *The Poor Miner Raised from the Coal Mine*, painted for Renan.' With his use of grey modelling and his blackening of the figure's hands, Manet insisted that the dead son of God should resemble a very human, perhaps working-class cadaver. Similarly, Manet made his angels look like boys in theatre get-ups, as if he was responding directly to Courbet's declaration a few years earlier that one cannot paint what cannot be seen concretely. By the time the Impressionists were emerging, the call of reality had become irresistible.

Indeed, the name of Gustave Courbet, although not an Impressionist, will run through any study of Impressionism for two important reasons. First, as noted earlier, Courbet's claim to paint directly from his own world in his own manner laid the ideological foundation for the Impressionist movement. Second, conflict had been a frequent theme in the visual arts since Courbet's provocations of the 1850s. The struggle of painters for recognition and access to the Salon, wherein lay the keys to patronage, had all been experienced by Courbet. His performance of the role of modern artist, with his one-man exhibitions and outspoken radical politics, was a powerful model. The central work of his 1855 Realist Pavilion, *The Studio of the Painter* (15), expressed the function of the painter as the chief interpreter and leading light of society. The rights of creative freedom and individuality that Courbet sought for artists exemplified more general rights that were being claimed for all humanity. His painting thus gave visual expression to notions we take for granted today – namely that artists must be free in order to create their work and that a society that values artists is one that values freedom. In the mid-nineteenth century, those freedoms were yet to be won. In 1861 some art students dissatisfied with the École des Beaux-Arts, conventionally known as 'the Academy', petitioned Courbet to open a studio where they could learn and practise Realism. Courbet agreed, but he insisted on collaboration and cooperation rather than the traditional master–student relationship. His friend, the critic Jules-Antoine Castagnary, ran the workshop for a few months before it closed, a failure.

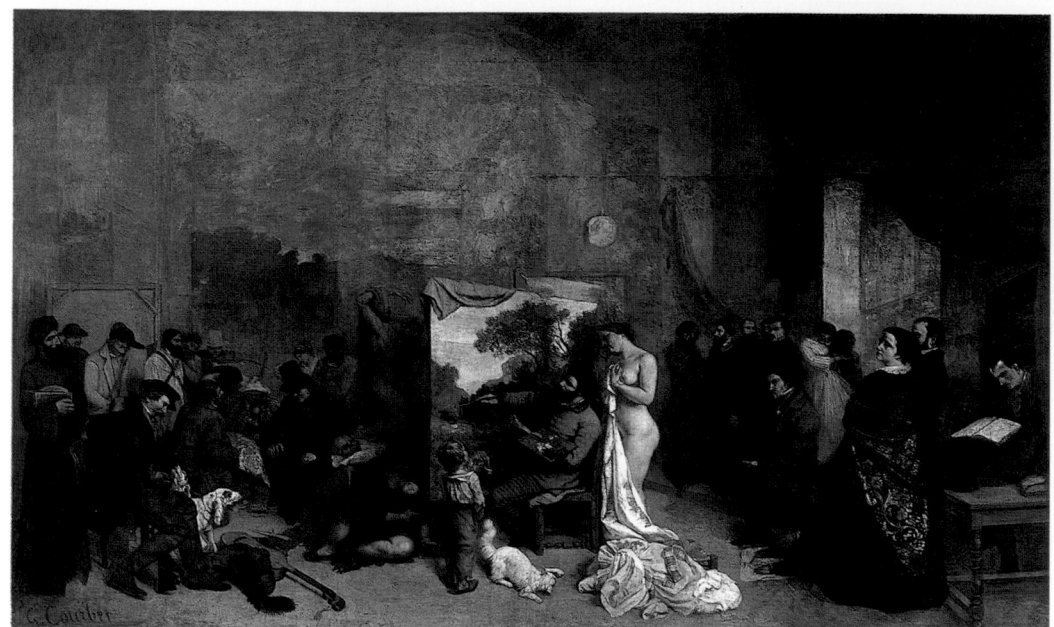

Other alternatives to the Academy existed, too: by the 1860s there were several active independent studios. Degas was enrolled at the École des Beaux-Arts but did most of his training under a follower of Delacroix's great rival, the arch-conservative Jean-Auguste-Dominique Ingres (1780–1867). A painter named Thomas Couture (1815–79), politically liberal and artistically middle-of-the-road, had a successful school that Manet attended for a few years. As recent arrivals to Paris, the young Monet, Renoir, Sisley and Bazille met in the studio of Charles Gleyre (1808–74), where they worked from 1862 to 1863. Fantin-Latour also studied there. A deeply conservative painter, Gleyre was nonetheless a permissive teacher, and his charges were minimal. There also existed a drawing class run for years by an artist's model named Suisse (first name unknown) whose studio, the so-called Académie Suisse, was a frequent rendezvous during the 1860s. Finally, there was the Louvre itself, the former royal palace long devoted to the visual arts and by far the most comprehensive museum in the world, where one could register to make copies. Fantin-Latour often took his friends there; Monet would look solely at landscapes, while Bazille and Renoir seem to have worked quite seriously. It was here, too, that they met Berthe Morisot.

15
Gustave
Courbet,
*The Studio of
the Painter*,
1855.
Oil on canvas;
361 × 598 cm,
142¼ × 235⅝ in.
Musée d'Orsay,
Paris

The government-run exhibition known as the Salon took place
annually at the large glass and masonry-covered cast-iron exhibition
hall called the Palais de l'Industrie, which had been built near the
Champs-Elysées for the Universal Exposition of 1855. The Salon had
become a gigantic marketplace: in 1859 there were nearly four thousand paintings, sculptures, drawings and prints, representing some
seventeen hundred artists. Admission was by vote of a jury composed
of various government officials and artists with connections to the
École des Beaux-Arts; among the few notable exceptions were
Delacroix, Corot and Daubigny. The artists on the jury were elected
by previous award-winners – a system intended to guarantee stability
and which perpetuated conservatism.

From 1859, artists began organizing public demonstrations and
proposed reforms, to which the administration responded fitfully.
In 1863, anxious to curry favour with the intelligentsia, the emperor
Napoleon III intervened to allow refused works – particularly numerous that year – to be shown in a Salon des Refusés, which became a
landmark event. In other years, many artists including the young
Impressionists exhibited in their own studios or those of friends,
while continuing to petition. Liberalization was gradual, but given the
direction the juries were moving towards, it should not be surprising
that most of the Impressionists had at least something accepted at the
Salon during the 1860s. They also had many rejections and resented
the unpredictable outcomes. For example, Monet, who had had a
number of works exhibited and received a few good notices since
1865, saw both his submissions refused in 1870. As a result, he did
not apply again until 1880, which was to be the last time. Following
the path of Corot and the Barbizon School, the landscapists Morisot,
Pissarro and Sisley were frequently admitted in the 1860s and did not
shock, though their paintings were poorly displayed in back rooms
known euphemistically as 'le dépotoir' ('the dump'). A photograph of
the Salon of 1861 (17) shows how works were hung edge to edge,
sometimes in four registers from slightly below eyelevel to high up
near the skylight. Yet government exhibitions nevertheless exerted an
inevitable pull. They brought publicity and discussion (16), and the
public turned out in the tens of thousands rather than mere hundreds

at other venues. After the fall of the Second Empire in 1870 and the Commune in 1871, however, a timid and deeply conservative Third Republic began backpedalling on Napoleon III's art reforms. The Impressionists responded by reviving an earlier idea of holding exhibitions of their own to promote their work. Thus the first Impressionist exhibition of 1874 was planned in a context where artists made continued efforts to redress grievances that they experienced within the official art structure, while at the same time seeking independence from it.

As the occasional acceptance of Impressionist neophytes at the Salon demonstrates, officially sanctioned art was by no means uniformly academic or moribund. The pre-eminence of Courbet in the public eye

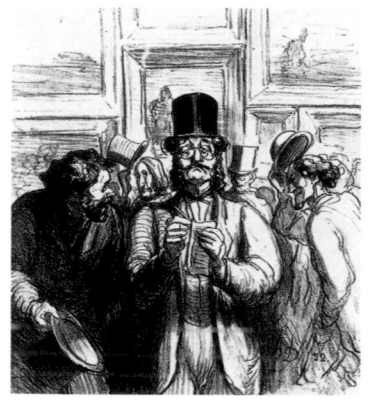
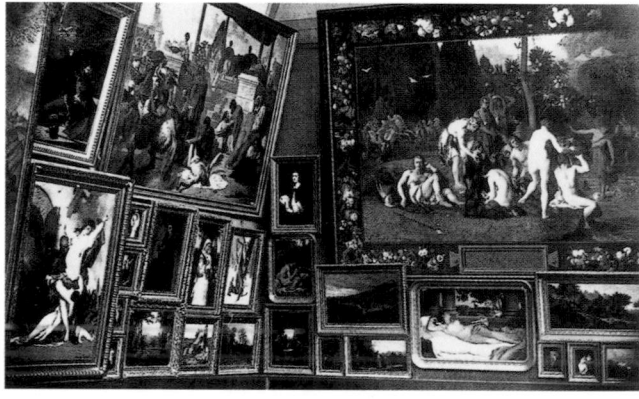

16 Above
Honoré
Daumier,
*The Influential
Critic at the Salon.*
Lithograph in
Le Charivari,
24 June 1865

17 Above right
The Salon of
1861, showing
Pierre Puvis
de Chavannes'
Concordia,
Michelez album

and the frequent appearances of Manet at the Salon from 1865, despite sporadic refusals, suggest a considerable diversity. The complaint of Achille Fould, Louis-Napoleon's minister of state, is an indication that the official edifice was crumbling. At the Salon of 1857, he exhorted artists to ignore public taste and stay faithful to the 'elevated regions of ... the great masters' rather than 'the new school of realism [with its] servile imitation of the least poetic and least elevated aspects of nature'. Fould bestowed public awards on history painters in order to stem the tide. That year's medal of honour went to one Adolphe Yvon (1817–93), whose military subjects served the Second Empire's propaganda. First prizes went to Paul Baudry (1828–86), Isidore Pils (1813/15–75), and Adolphe-William Bouguereau (1825–1905; 18). In today's current rage for kitsch, Bouguereau has become something of a hero among collectors and revisionist historians. That he was taken seriously in 1857 indicates the desperation of official art policy, ready to reward traditional craft regardless of originality. The works of prize winners were purchased for the Musée du Luxembourg, which was dedicated to contemporary French art. (An artist had to be dead ten years to be eligible for the Louvre.)

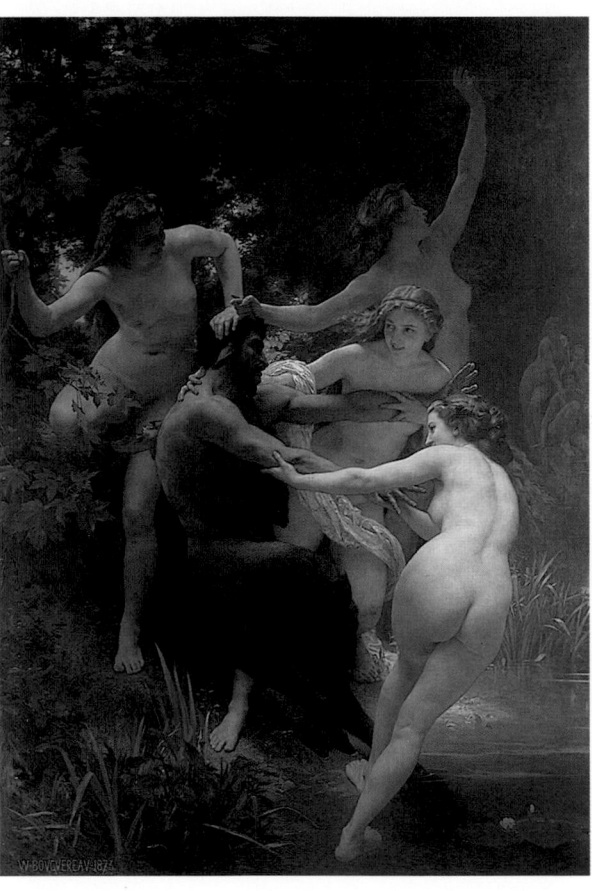

18
William Bouguereau, *Nymphs and Satyr*, 1873. Oil on canvas; 260 × 180 cm, 102⅜ × 70⅞ in. Sterling and Francine Clark Art Institute, Williamstown

Despite Fould's efforts, many already saw a crisis. Landscape – an inherently naturalist genre – seemed to be taking over, outnumbering history, religious and genre paintings, as well as portraits. In the academic 'hierarchy of genres', subject matter with human content, preferably historical, was considered superior. In 1859, Delacroix (19) and the Barbizon painters Daubigny, Jean-François Millet (1814–75; see 95) and Étienne-Pierre-Théodore Rousseau (1812–67) were all represented at the Salon by major landscapes. Castagnary remarked in 1866 on 'the great army of landscape painters' trooping across France. Yet very few were painters of modern life. Even works showing some forward-looking technical brio, as in the late paintings of Corot, evoked timelessness and nostalgia, as in his subtle and poetic *Souvenir of Mortefontaine* of 1864 (see 83). The comical cartoons by Jules Renard Draner (1833–c.1900; 20) show how startling the Impressionists' works must have been to a contemporary audience. Resolutely modern subject matter was rendered with adamantly artificial means – strong colours, choppy brushwork or bold structures – means that embody visual modernity as personal and

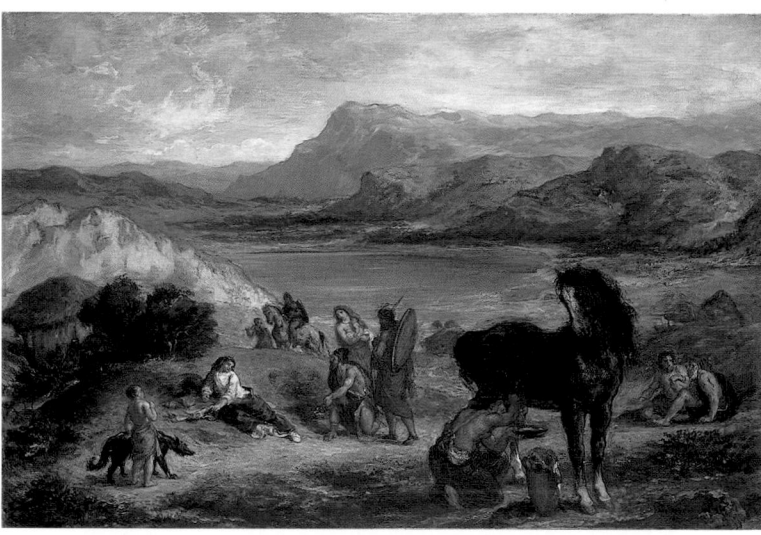

19
Eugène
Delacroix,
*Ovid Among
the Scythians*,
1859.
Oil on canvas;
87·6 × 130·2 cm,
$34^{1}2 \times 51^{1}4$ in.
National Gallery,
London

20
Jules Renard
Draner,
Selection of
details from
At the Independents.
Le Charivari,
23 April 1879.
Captions loosely
translated from
the French

self-conscious rather than conventional or mechanical. As Baudelaire argued, modernity resided in manner, not date. A single comparison may serve as an example. Gustave Caillebotte's *Paris Street: A Rainy Day* (21) of 1877 is relatively moderate by Impressionist standards. But in contrast to Jean Béraud's slightly later *Sunday near the Church of St Philippe du Roule* (22), one is struck by the fresh luminosity and compositional boldness of the Caillebotte, compared to Béraud's already passé, photographic literalism. Hence, there is no mistaking Impressionist painting for the more traditional works of officially sanctioned contemporaries even when, by the late 1870s, certain Salon pictures began to betray their influence. Moreover, such influence was strictly technical, as in the loosely painted landscape setting of the otherwise anecdotal and tightly handled *Haymaking* by Jules Bastien-Lepage (1848–84; 23).

In saluting the direction French culture was taking towards science, Zola must surely have had in mind Baudelaire's recent attack on positivism as the bane of art. Baudelaire advocated an art derived

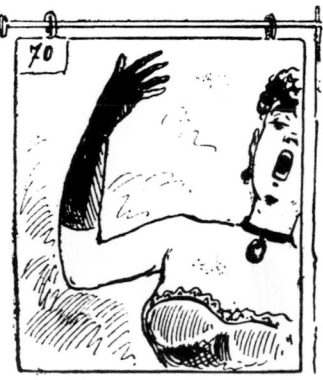

CAFÉ SINGER.
fr7·50 a pair! Eight buttons! What an excellent sign for a glove shop!

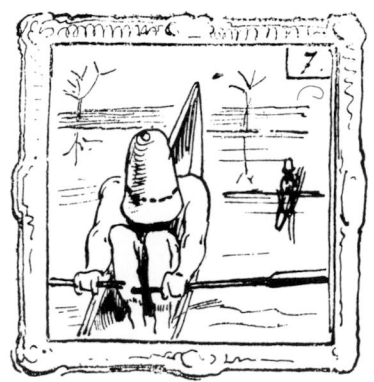

ROWERS.
What can he be doing?

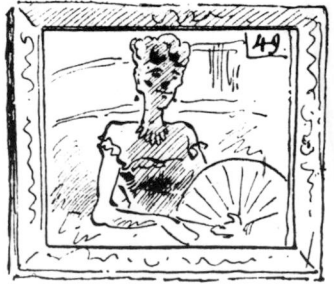

WOMAN IN A LOGE.
Wouldn't she be better in the upper gallery?

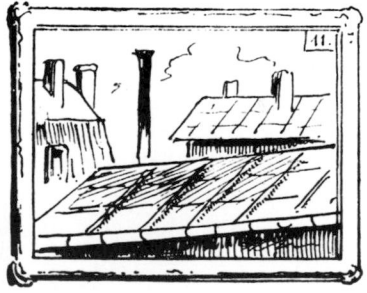

VIEW OF ROOFS.
Sentimental zinc roofs full of poetry. Inspired by *L'Assommoir*.

from imagination, which he believed testified to artistic and moral worth. He feared Realism for what he thought were slavish and mechanistic reproductions, like photography. In his article 'Salon of 1859', he railed: 'the "positivists" ... say, "I want to represent things as they are, or rather as they would be supposing that I did not exist." In other words, the universe without man. The others, however, the "imaginatives" say, "I want to illuminate things with my mind, and

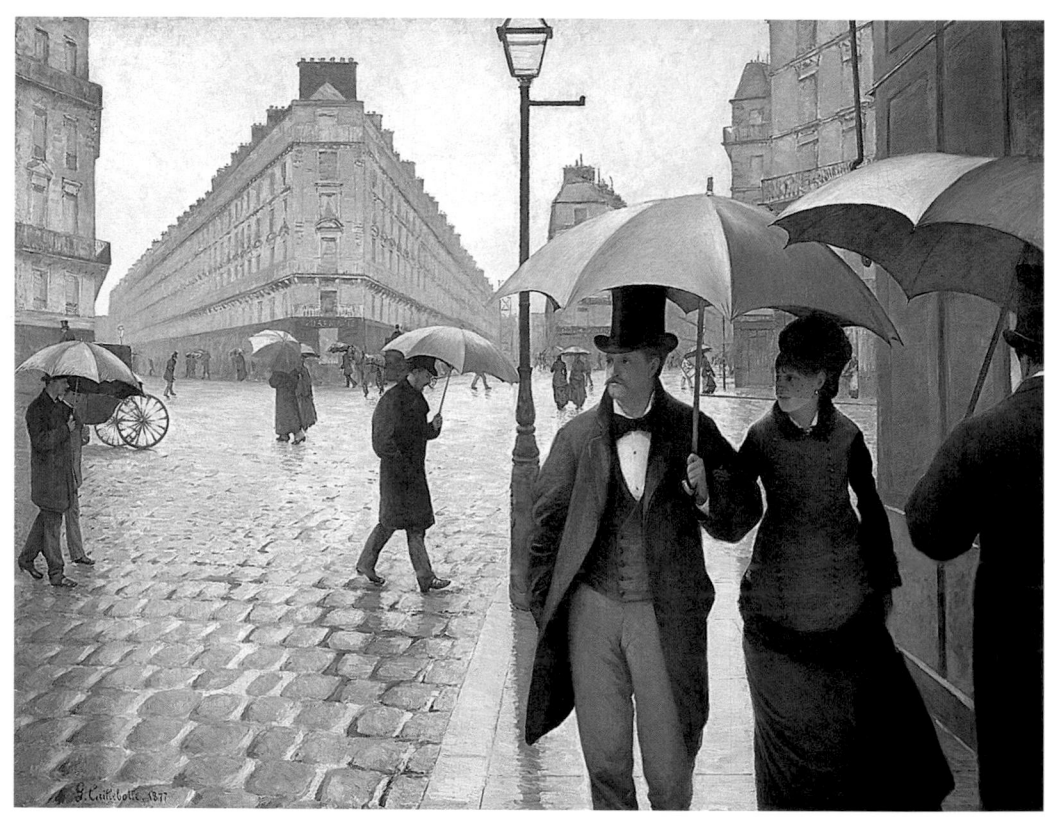

21
**Gustave
Caillebotte,**
*Paris Street:
A Rainy Day,*
1876–7.
Oil on canvas;
212·2 × 276·2 cm,
83¹⁄₂ × 108³⁄₄ in.
The Art Institute
of Chicago

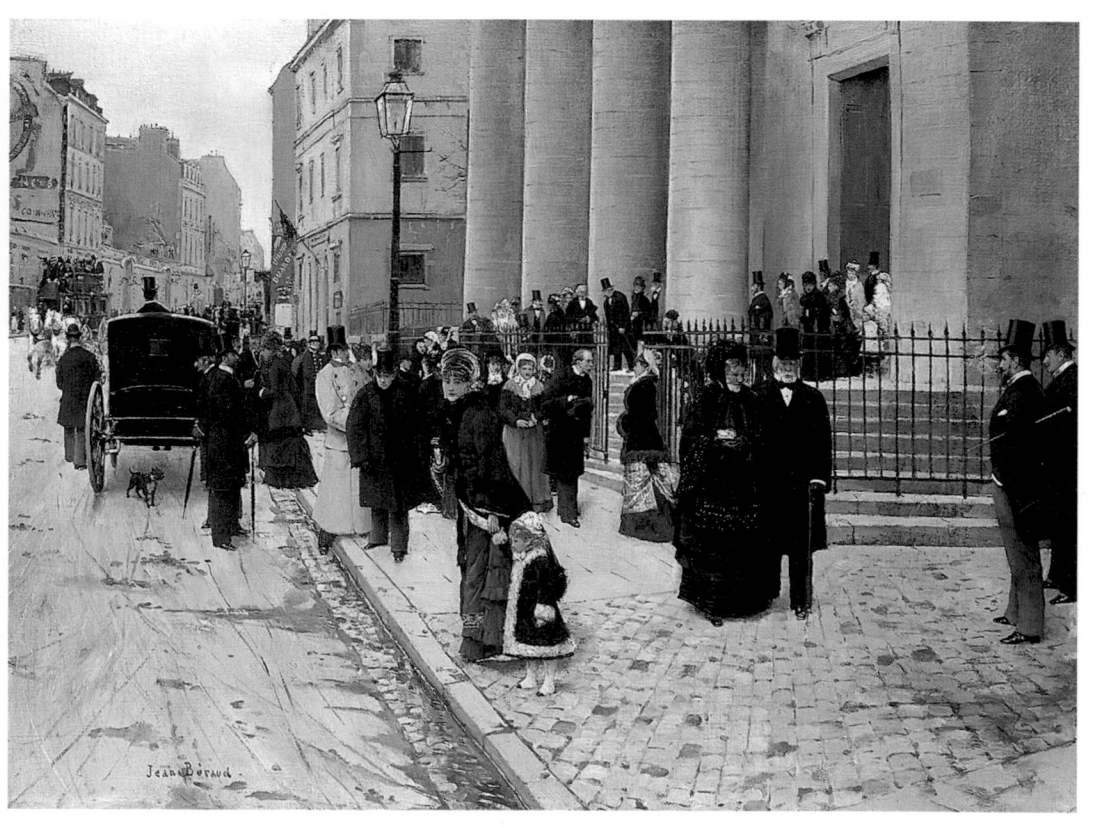

22
Jean Béraud,
Sunday near
the Church of St
Philippe du Roule,
c.1878–82.
Oil on canvas;
59·3 × 80·9 cm,
23⅜ × 31⅞ in.
Metropolitan
Museum of Art,
New York

to project their reflection on other minds.'" But Baudelaire's concept of positivism was grossly oversimplified. Its followers had actually laid the foundation for an art far more sympathetic to Baudelaire's defence of personal expression. When Zola defined painting as 'a corner of nature seen through a temperament', a formula quite suitable to Impressionism, he was relying on the notion derived from recent science (especially from the work of Taine) that all forms of human perception were biologically imbricated with traces that express the individual self.

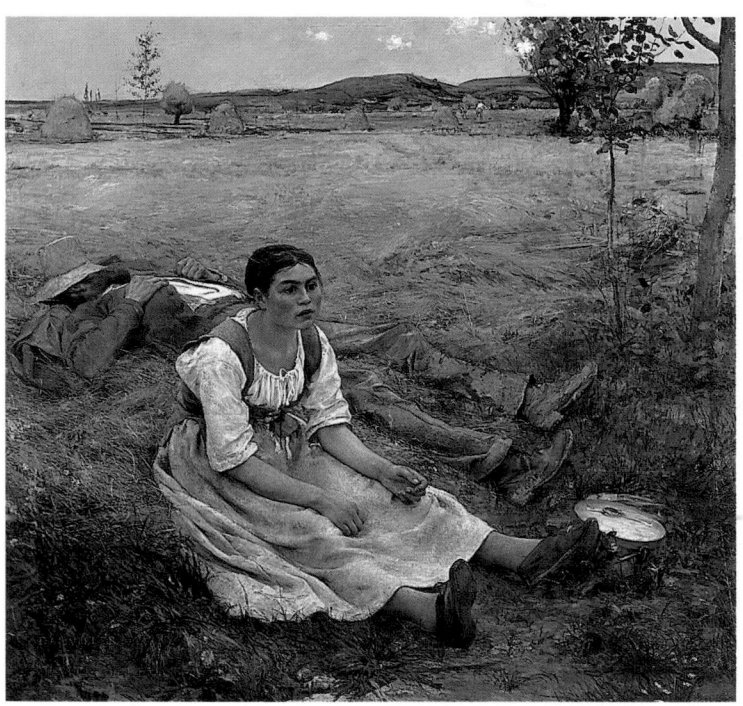

23
Jules Bastien-Lepage,
Haymaking,
1877.
Oil on canvas;
180 × 195 cm,
70⅞ × 76¾ in.
Musée d'Orsay,
Paris

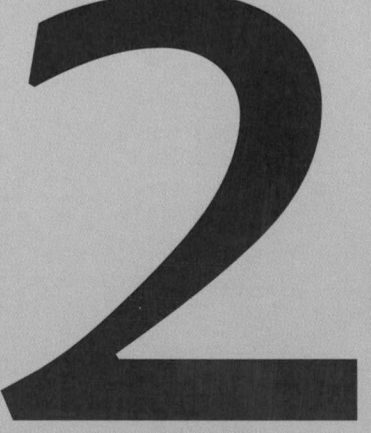

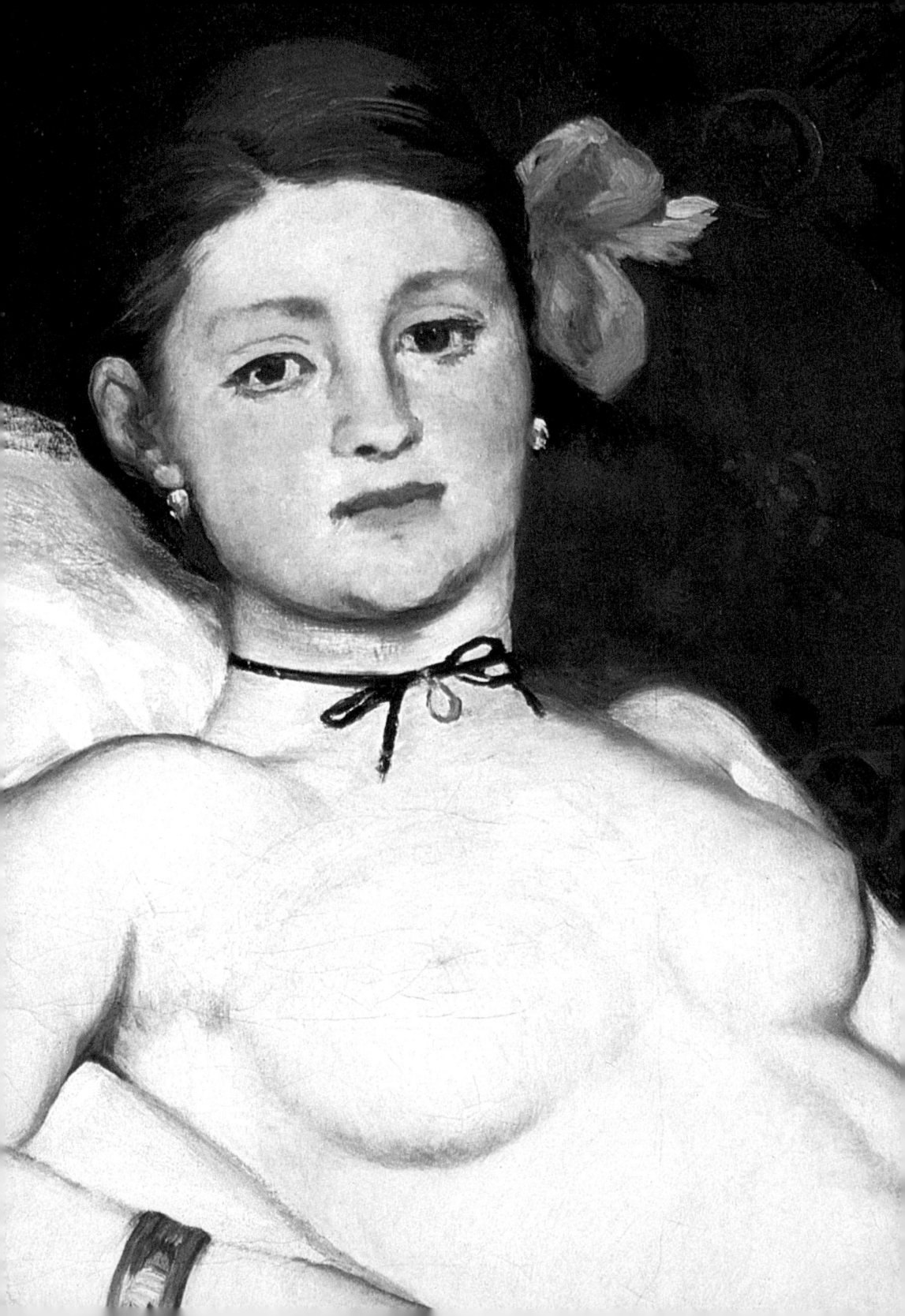

No discussion of Impressionism can begin without Édouard Manet, the sophisticated Parisian whose scandal-provoking challenges to tradition lay the basis for modern art and the avant-garde conception of the artist. As we saw in Chapter 1, he was the acknowledged leader of the group in its earliest years, when it was sometimes known as the Batignolles School. Even though his ambitious projects of the 1860s are more involved with the past and lack the spontaneity we often associate with Impressionism, they gave preliminary form to Impressionism's principal pictorial combination – naturalistic representations of modern life produced through visible artifices. Moreover, Manet's public reputation – based on an individualism, self-consciousness and irony that ranged from the merely disconcerting to the shocking – provided a new role model for the serious artist. By the end of the decade, his work would embody the group trends towards colouristic immediacy and an assertive artistic posture. In the 1870s he remained a central figure, as evidenced in the 1876 essay 'Édouard Manet and the Impressionists' by his poet-friend Stéphane Mallarmé. In 1877, Caillebotte included Manet with those (Degas, Monet, Pissarro, Sisley and Renoir) he invited to his home to organize that year's exhibition. Manet continued in his refusal to join, insisting the Salon was where the public should be confronted.

Born to comfort and status – his father was a judge in the Imperial administration; his mother, the daughter of a diplomat – Manet acquired impeccable manners and self-assurance, debonair taste and wry reserve. This persona was as important to his art as his Parisian subject matter. He studied in the independent studio of Thomas Couture, visited the Louvre frequently and made early trips to the Netherlands, central Europe and Italy. Thanks to his secure social position, he needed no popular approval for his painting, even though he may have hoped for public success. His attitude was closer to that of the enlightened amateur than the career professional. He felt free

24
Édouard Manet,
Olympia
(detail of 34)

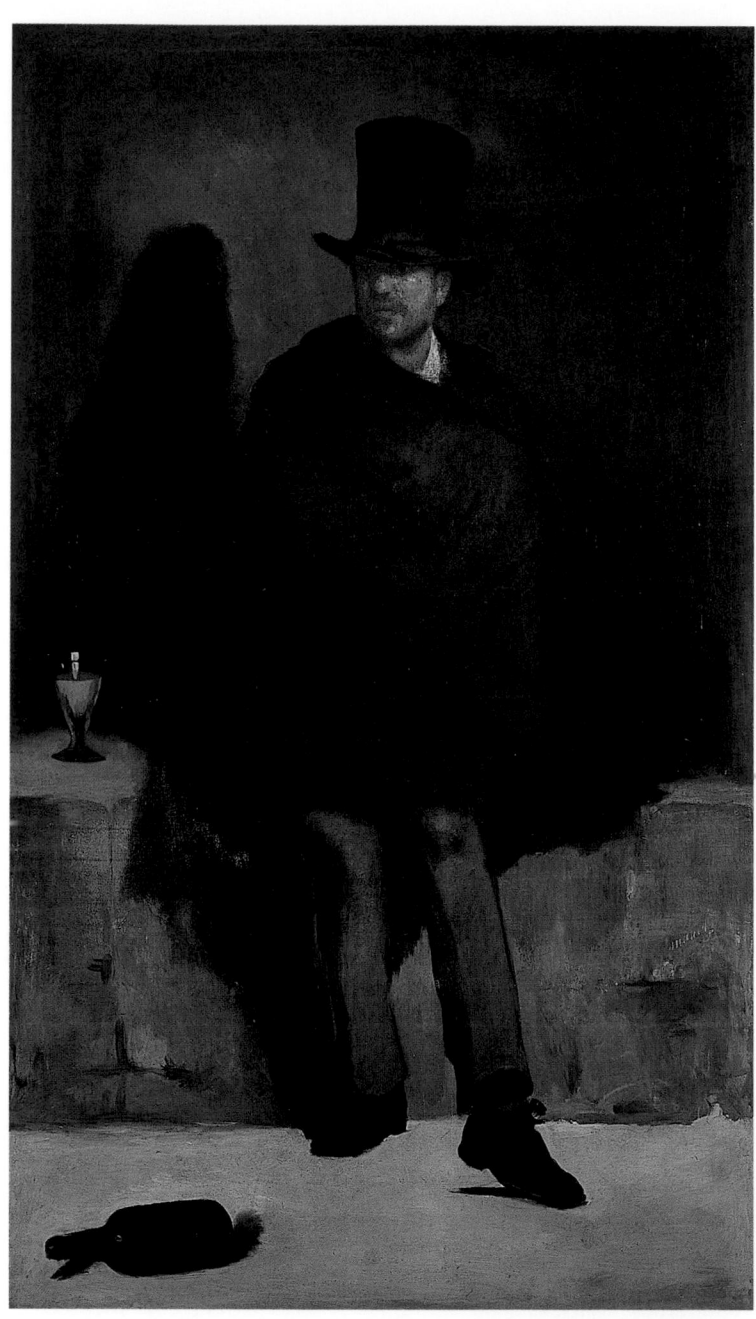

25
Édouard Manet,
The Absinthe Drinker,
1859.
Oil on canvas;
180.5 × 106 cm,
70$\frac{1}{2}$ × 37 in.
Ny Carlsberg
Glyptothek,
Copenhagen

to explore the latest ideas and to experiment. Building on Courbet's insistence that artists represent their epoch and on his friend Baudelaire's celebrations of modern life, Manet took figures from his own world rather than the historical or literary heroes most ambitious painters before him used. Furthermore, he painted in a loose, open manner – not waiting until his brushstrokes dried before painting with other colours – a technique that offended academic expectations of linear design and polished workmanship. Yet, especially in the first decade of his career, Manet was still deeply concerned with tradition, as a man of his social origins would naturally be. His attitude was to engage it through a positive critique. The combination of these factors – modern life and dialogue with the past – defined an early series of choices and projects that would change the history of art forever.

From the beginning, Manet was preoccupied with his own position in relation to the culture and society of his times. His initial predilection for the Realist repertory of low life was a way to challenge conservative beliefs in what was suitable and dignified for art. His earliest effort on a large scale, *The Absinthe Drinker* (25), dealt with important social and literary issues through a subject most considered degrading. The down-and-out denizen of the streets was based on a ragpicker named Colardet from Manet's neighbourhood, but posed to echo a famous eighteenth-century painting, *The Indifferent One* by Jean-Antoine Watteau (1684–1721).

Alcoholism was a serious problem in nineteenth-century Paris, especially among the working classes. It would be the topic of Zola's famous novel *L'Assommoir* (1877), which records the descent into drink of a laundress, Gervaise Macquart, mother of the courtesan-to-be, Nana. Absinthe, distilled from the plant wormwood, was a particularly noxious potion, cheap and so poisonous that it was banned in the early 1900s. However, Colardet was the sort of character Baudelaire celebrated as a 'street philosopher', familiar with the hardships and frustrations of modern life. His poem 'The Ragpicker's Wine' from *Les Fleurs du mal* proclaims alcohol's ability 'To drown out the bitterness and cradle the indolence/Of those elderly outcasts who pass away in silence.' So Manet's subject, ostensibly a genre figure, had specific

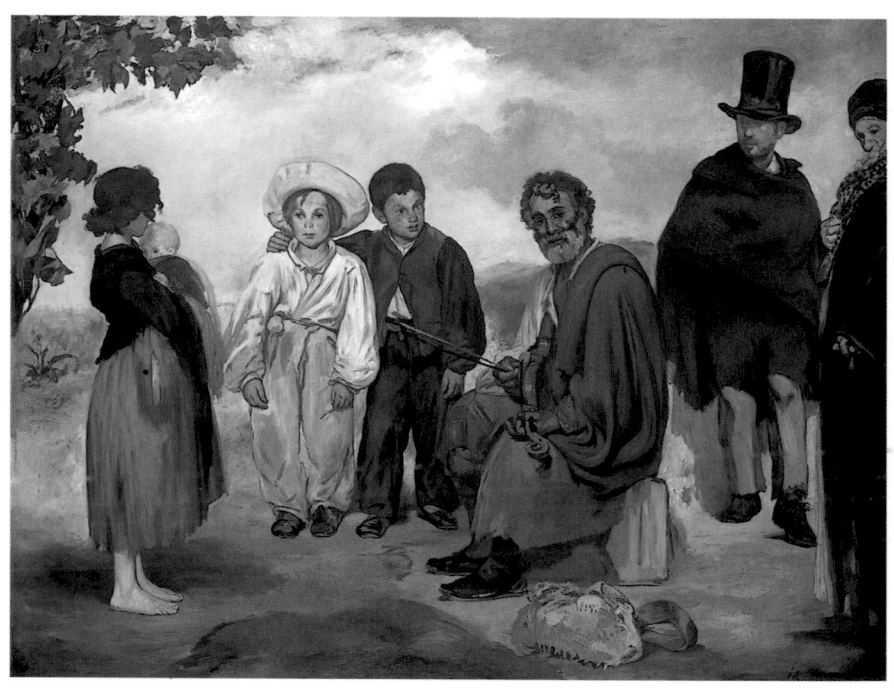

26
Édouard Manet,
The Old Musician,
1862.
Oil on canvas;
187·4 × 248·3 cm,
73³⁄4 × 97³⁄4 in.
National Gallery
of Art,
Washington, DC

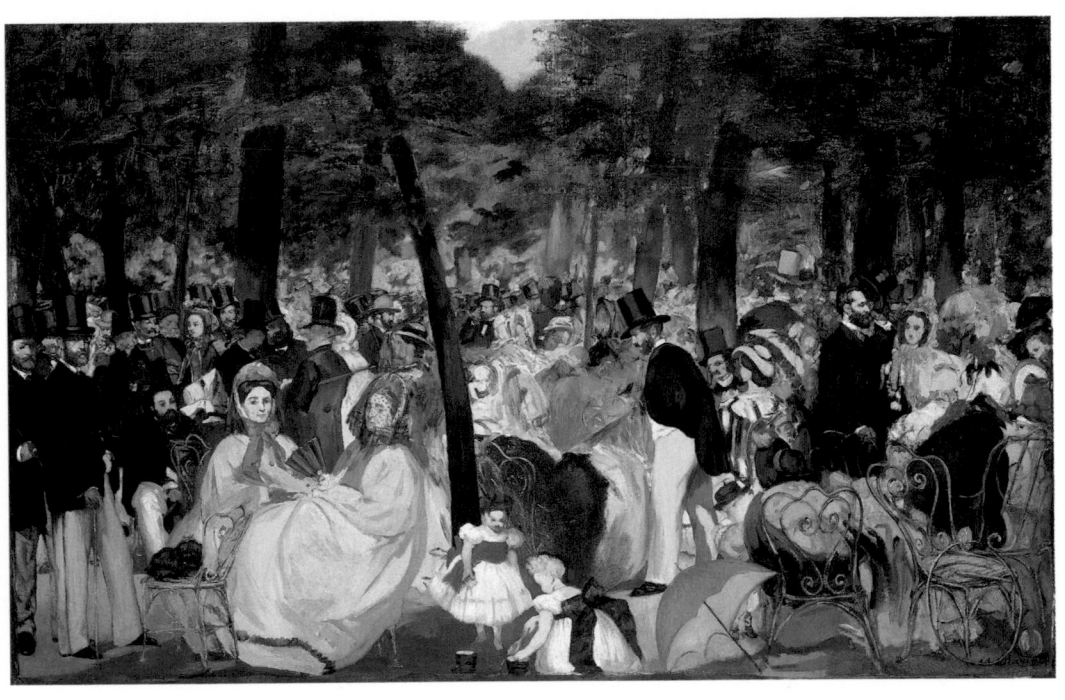

27
Édouard Manet,
Music in the
Tuileries Gardens,
1862.
Oil on canvas;
76·2 × 118·1 cm,
30 × 46½ in.
National Gallery,
London

social and literary associations. The 1859 Salon jury's rejection of the awkwardly painted and thematically distasteful work, despite Delacroix's defence of it at the Jury deliberations, was Manet's first encounter with official disdain.

There is an important shift between two paintings Manet worked on simultaneously and exhibited together in 1863 at the cooperative gallery of the art dealer and engraver Louis Martinet (1810–94). They are The Old Musician (26) and Music in the Tuileries Gardens (27). Both assemble multiple figures in a horizontal format. The Old Musician is like a catalogue of types from the bohemian world, characters more likely to appear in illustrated journals than in so-called high art or, for that matter, in Manet's own society. Prior to The Old Musician, Manet had done several images of entertainers, one of which, The Spanish Guitar Player of 1860, was accepted by the Salon. Through them, he evoked the tenuous relationship of artists to their world. The cast in The Old Musician includes Manet's absinthe drinker; a street entertainer based on a gypsy named Jean Lagrène who lived in the Batignolles area; a Jew referring to the Wandering Jew theme (the ultimate outsider, portrayed in a novel by Eugène Sue serialized in 1844–5 and echoed in certain paintings by Courbet); and others from magazine prints of vagabonds or based on reproductions of French and Spanish Realist art. The two boys could be from Bartolomé Esteban Murillo (1617/18–82) or Watteau.

The barren landscape in which the figures are located may be all that remained of their demolished slum behind the Saint-Lazare train station, which was a site of vast urban expansion and new construction near where Manet's apartment building had been erected. Much has been made of The Old Musician, therefore, as an evocation of the displacements caused by renovations under Haussmann. As an artist new to the area, Manet may have felt some sympathy with such persons. He may still have thought his career choice made him, like them, marginal and bohemian. Yet his presence was also an intrusion, foreshadowing demographic shifts in places that grow fashionable after artists discover them. Moreover, rather than deriving from direct observation, the figures of The Old Musician have been rounded up from a variety of sources and staged in the studio as modern heirs to the art of the past. Thus Manet's populist solidarity is belied by self-conscious artistic knowledge and aims as well as by the link between his class and the powers behind his characters' dislocation. The inevitable result is ambiguity and psychological distancing – signs of conflicts (familiar to our own society) between nostalgia for an unfettered 'bohemian' way of life, with its Baudelairian sensibility, and the reality of poverty and brutal change.

One must wonder if such contradictions led Manet towards what for him would be a more authentic form of Realism. For in *Music in the Tuileries Gardens*, he gathered together the bourgeois artistic and literary intelligentsia of 1860s Paris, which included his own family, peers and friends. A series of portraits (from left to right) gives us an introduction to this world. Manet begins with himself, half in and half out of the picture – an early example of the artist's self-positioning as marginal *flâneur*, that is, as both part of a world and yet its objectively distant observer. Next to Manet, with a monocle and walking stick, is his aristocratic friend and studio mate Albert, comte de Balleroy (1828–73), a painter of animals and genre scenes; seated nearby is another friend, the bearded poet and critic Zacharie Astruc. Behind them are recognizable writers and critics (Jules Champfleury and Aurélien Scholl), along with Manet's recently deceased father, with grey beard and a red hat, and Suzanne Leenhoff, Manet's piano teacher and future wife.

The younger of the two prominently seated women in the foreground is Madame Lejosne, who was married to the commandant in whose house Manet had met Baudelaire and the fledgling painter Bazille, who appears as the tall, bearded figure with a grey hat. The older woman in the foreground was the wife of Jacques Offenbach, composer of both the opera *Tales of Hoffmann* (1881) and dance-hall music, who is himself seated (wearing spectacles and a moustache) further to the right, between Manet's brother Eugène (turned to the left) and the painter Charles Monginot (1825–1900) doffing his hat.

The most important group is that near the large tree above Madame Lejosne. Next to it and facing us is Henri Fantin-Latour, a member of this post-Courbet Realist circle and, as we know, its portraitist, who also did flower still lifes and was renowned for lithographic illustrations of Richard Wagner's *Tannhäuser*, the opera which had recently shocked Paris, to Baudelaire's great delight. In the group of three engaged in conversation to Fantin-Latour's left is, at the left, Baron Taylor, a Frenchman despite his British name, who was involved in early Realism as the editor of illustrated travels through Spain and France, and had acquired Spanish art for state collections. To Taylor's right is Théophile Gautier, the Romantic author and critic, whose open-mindedness often gave younger artists their first press exposure. Equally important, Gautier was a chief proponent of the theory of art for art's sake. In the preface to his novel *Mademoiselle de Maupin* (1836), he rebutted theories of the social utility of art espoused by Romantic utopians, arguing that art's sole purpose was its creation of aesthetic experience. Beauty could not exist when tied to baser human interests, for it was to be their disinterested antidote.

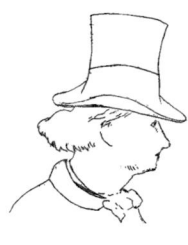

This theory, reviled by Courbet, was expanded and transformed by Baudelaire, who stands in profile between Gautier and Fantin-Latour. Baudelaire had been Manet's friend for several years and was probably the greatest single intellectual resource for him in the early to mid 1860s (28). Indeed, this very painting embodies ideas from Baudelaire's recently completed *The Painter of Modern Life*. It obviously represents the *flâneur* society Baudelaire extolled and which was Manet's own. It also employs an accurate yet rapidly economical style appropriate to modern vision, akin to that Baudelaire had attributed to Constantin Guys, the illustrator-protagonist of his essay. The children playing in the foreground are actually painted in a sketchy manner that resembles Guys's style translated to oils. Not only does this method express the fleeting glance of the strolling dandy, it also expeditiously summarizes its subject matter so that it retains a sense of the painter's bravado and superiority over the objects of his gaze. His respect for reality is not so great that it subjugates the signs of artistic individuality to rendering detail, even though he exquisitely captures the essence of observed form. With this painting, then, a Baudelairian and urban Manet took up both the themes and style that would define mainstream Impressionism. It both documents the world from which

28
Édouard Manet,
*Charles
Baudelaire,*
1862.
Etching

Impressionism emanated and embodies ideas that gave it life. Modernity and the expression of self-consciousness were inseparable.

In taking his own world as the subject matter for painting, Manet was certainly declaring a social position and artistic attitudes, much in the same way that Courbet, constantly referring to his hometown of Ornans in the Franche-Comté, always put his origins and loyalties on display. Another self-promoting strategy Manet adopted from Courbet was deliberate provocation – although unlike the overtly political Courbet, Manet stuck primarily to moral and aesthetic controversy in his exercise of artistic freedom. Two pictures from 1862–3, *Le Déjeuner sur l'herbe* (30) and *Olympia* (see 34), caused a huge uproar and definitively clinched his fame. In both, Manet's

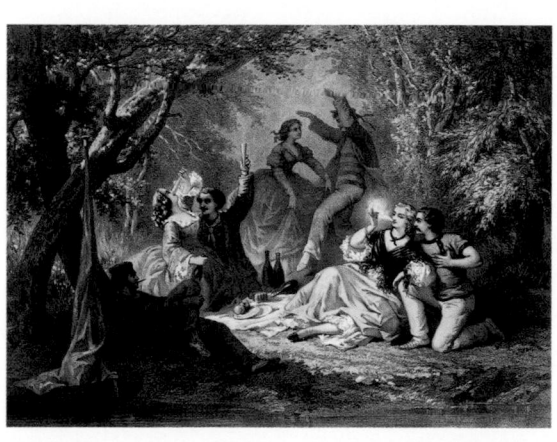

29
A Morlan,
*Boating Party
on the Banks
of the Seine,*
1860.
Lithograph

studio model, Victorine Meurent, was shown unclothed – naked rather than nude, for the latter implies idealization – and, combined with the free paint handling he had already developed, brought such outrage and disgust, except on the part of a few personal supporters, that his name has henceforth been associated with radical, avant-garde destruction of tradition. (Victorine's lesbianism and belated artistic ambitions are recent discoveries, completely unknown at the time.) *Le Déjeuner sur l'herbe* was originally called *The Bath* (Manet changed the title for his 1867 show) and alluded to the increasing popularity of summer outings along the banks of the River Seine in locations not far from Paris. The spread of leisure to the urban middle classes and the increasing freedom, especially for women,

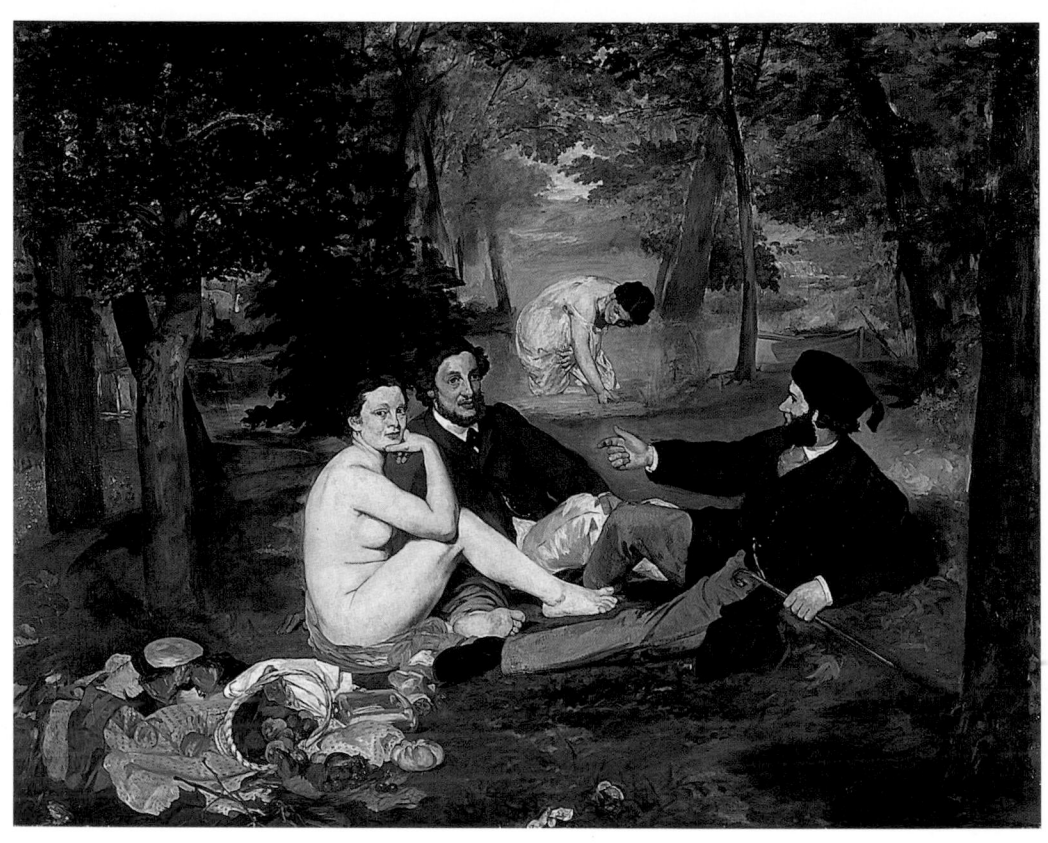

30
Édouard Manet,
Le Déjeuner sur l'herbe,
1862–3.
Oil on canvas;
208 × 264·5 cm,
82 × 104½ in.
Musée d'Orsay,
Paris

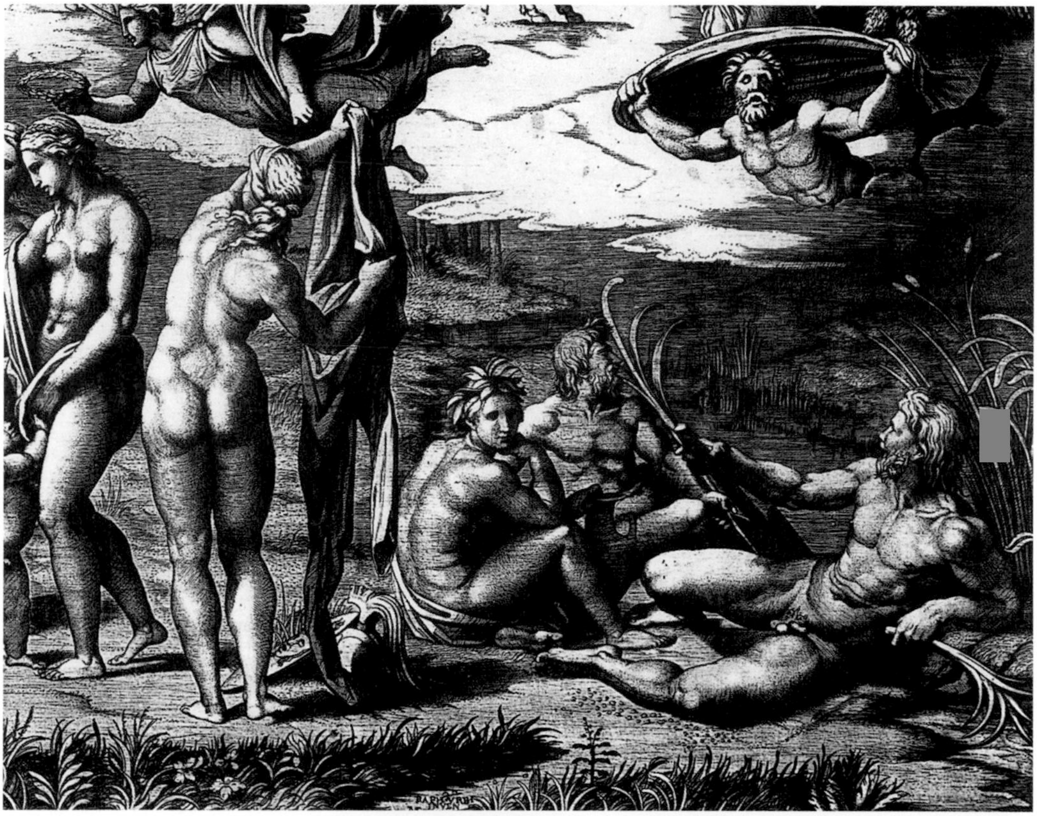

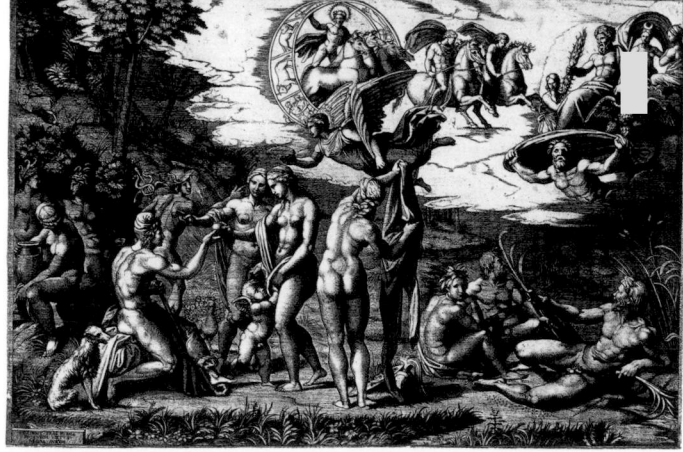

31–32
Marcantonio
Raimondi,
The Judgment
of Paris,
c.1517–20.
Engraving after
a lost cartoon
by Raphael;
29·2 × 43·3 cm,
11$\frac{1}{2}$ × 17 in
Above
Detail

embodied by public bathing are hallmarks of mid-nineteenth-century change. Bathing and riverbank scenes had already been subject matter for popular prints (see 29). Manet went much further in *Le Déjeuner sur l'herbe*, which parodies the new customs as much as it reflects them. One is immediately confronted by the fixed gaze (opposite of the *flâneur*'s discrete glance) of a woman whom most assumed to be a prostitute lounging with youths dressed as students or artistic bohemians. One outraged critic cried: 'A common whore, stark naked at that, lounges with two [boys] ... on a holiday misbehaving to prove themselves men.' Indeed, so awkward and cryptic are the attitudes and expressions that the painting seemed like an oversized student prank.

A few of Manet's contemporaries knew that the composition was based on part of an engraving by Marcantonio Raimondi (c.1480–after 1527; 31, 32) after a lost cartoon by Raphael (1483–1520). But here Manet's 'up-dating' of a classical prototype is done with the irony of an inside joke. Many more recognized the *Déjeuner*'s allusion to a famous painting in the Louvre, the *Concert Champêtre* or *Pastoral Symphony* by Giorgione (c.1477–c.1510; 33). Again, differences are more remarkable than the superficial similarity of nude and clothed couples in a natural setting. They stem principally from the lack of contact between Giorgione's figures and the viewer, preserving the fiction of a world apart from our own, in which literary or symbolic meanings could explain the anomalous juxtaposition of nude and clothed figures. The women in the Giorgione function as timeless muses – one playing a flute, the other dipping into a wellspring – and with the landscape setting so revered by Venetian artists, they surely allude to the inspiring effect of nature upon art. Manet, on the other hand, refused any such narrative or symbolic framework. The connection he forced between the viewer and Victorine's gaze tied the painting to the world of their own day. Centuries of experiencing art prepared Manet's public to read paintings as equivalents of works of literature, a concept the artist ruthlessly challenged. The viewer is here thrown back without explanation on to strictly visual appearances, and is therefore forced to react to the model's blatant nakedness.

In creating this uneasy situation the painter clearly raised the question of intentions – placing himself in the forefront as the person who would be taken to account. His wilful command of the performance is confirmed by the gesture of the figure based on Manet's two brothers directing our eye towards the woman, and by the evidence of her clothing on the ground showing that she has stripped for the purpose of posing. (Along with the accoutrements of the picnic, her dress and straw hat constitute a lovely still life.) In parodying and deflating traditional art with a staged contemporary tableau, Manet called attention to the enormous gap between reality and convention – and

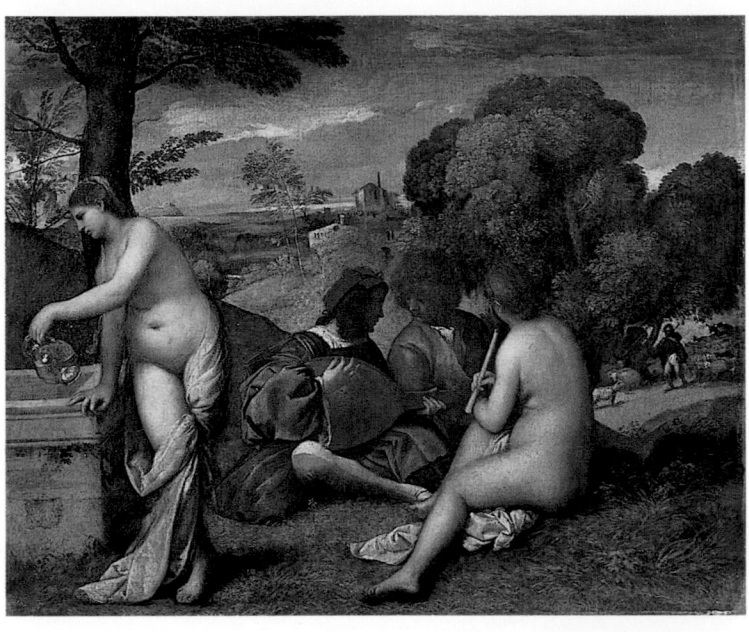

33
Giorgione,
Concert Champêtre,
c.1510.
Oil on canvas;
110 × 138 cm,
43³⁄₈ × 54³⁄₈ in.
Musée du Louvre,
Paris

to himself as the agent of that exposure. It was as if for Manet the representation of the present day must be a blow against tradition mindlessly revered, but a challenge registered also with an irony that mediates insistent realism. This is another self-conscious posture, therefore, which distances his composition from the more straightforward, rural world of Courbet, while achieving for his generation a similar sense of liberation from worn-out formulas.

Naturally, the *Déjeuner* was rejected by the Salon jury, but it was shown at the Salon des Refusés. Manet's picture attracted more attention than

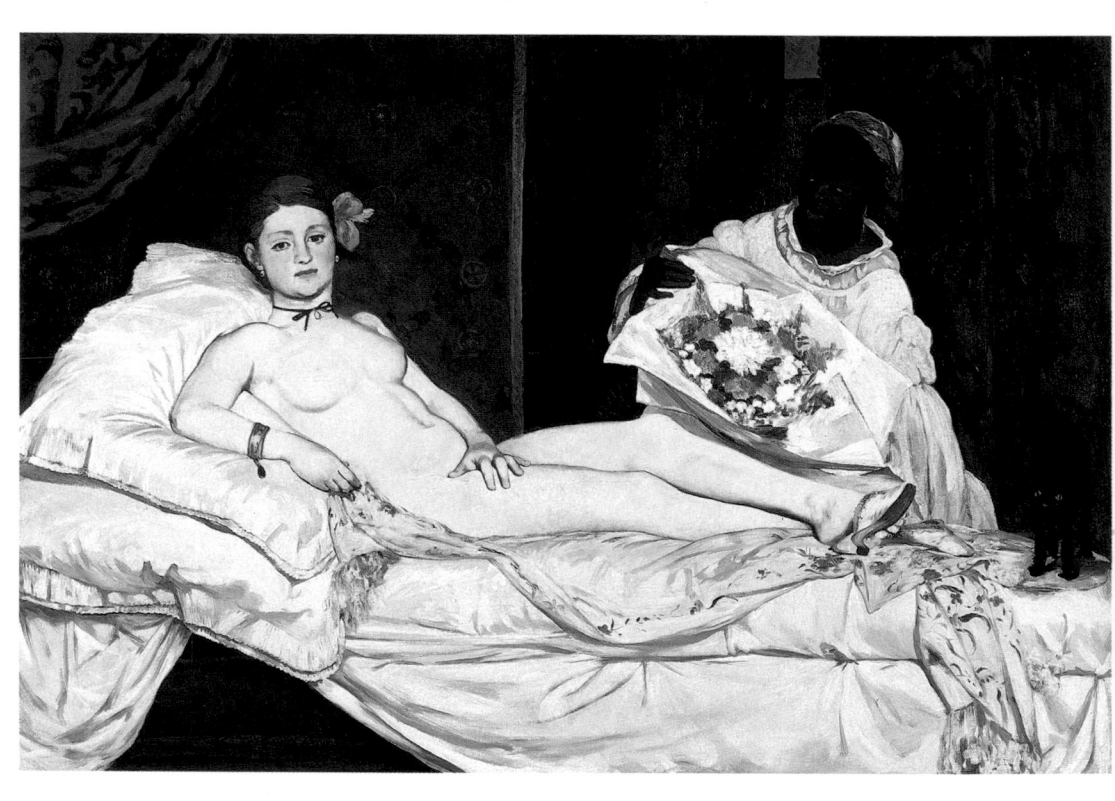

any other, especially from the most adventurous young painters of the time. With the liberalization of admission rules in time for the Salon of 1865, he was able to exhibit another scandalous painting, completed just after the *Déjeuner*, alongside the work of mainstream artists. The effect was even more shocking than in 1863. Manet's *Olympia* (34), posed again by Victorine, was a naked woman whose identity as a prostitute was now left in no doubt. It was evident from her pretentious name (with literary derivations of the sort affected by *cocottes*), her minimal attire – she has kept on slippers, a velvet choker and her bracelet – and the position of her hand, which both

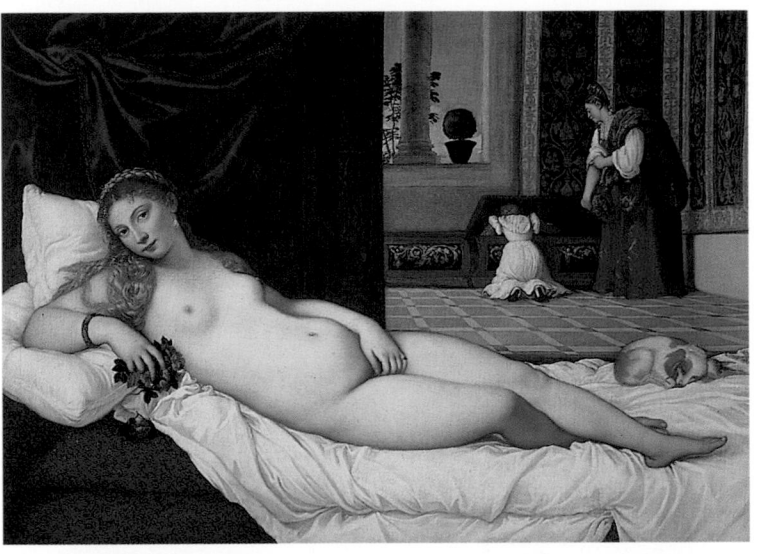

34
Édouard Manet,
Olympia,
1863.
Oil on canvas;
130·5 × 190 cm,
51³⁄8 × 74⁷⁄8 in.
Musée d'Orsay,
Paris

35
Titian,
Venus of Urbino,
1538.
Oil on canvas;
119 × 165 cm,
46⁷⁄8 × 65 in.
Galleria degli
Uffizi,
Florence

covers up yet calls attention to the commodity for sale. An African servant (France had colonies in West Africa and the West Indies) brings flowers from an admirer, while Olympia is accompanied, at the end of her bed, by a black cat. Again, Manet cast daring subject matter from modern life in a traditional mould, for the *Olympia* was a brazen remake of the famous painting by Titian (c.1487–1576), *Venus of Urbino* (35), showing the Duke of Urbino's mistress, which Manet had copied twice during a trip to Florence. Rather than disguising the courtesan as a goddess, making her warmly submissive and reminiscent of classical statuary as Titian had, Manet made her cold and domineering, a career woman on glaring display. For the lap dog of Venus, a symbol of fidelity, Manet substituted a cat, a symbol of freedom – one might say of self-possession.

In France, prostitution was an old and widespread if not respectable profession. Paris in particular was famous and appreciated by many male *habitués* for its wide choice of available young women, who were known by as many different names – *filles*, *cocottes*, *grisettes*, *lorettes* – as there were different steps on the social scale from streetwalker to

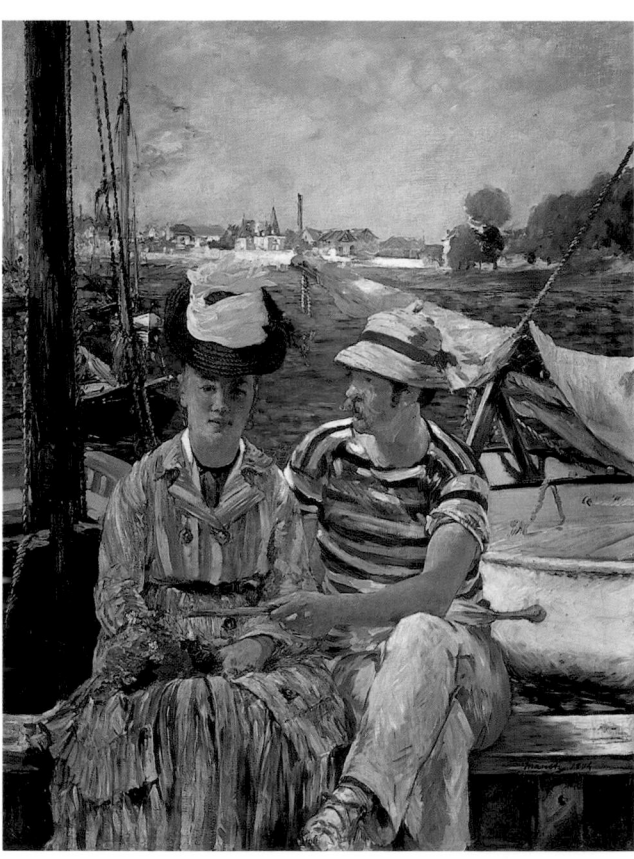

36
Édouard Manet,
Argenteuil,
1874.
Oil on canvas;
149 × 115 cm,
58⅝ × 45¼ in.
Musée des
Beaux-Arts,
Tournai

courtesan. Early in the nineteenth century, the government had recognized the inevitability of the practice and, under the rationale of public health, tried to regulate it through a system of official brothels known as *maisons closes*. As the migration to Paris of working-class women from the provinces increased in the 1830s, however, open, unregistered prostitution proliferated, and the number of authorized houses declined from over 250 in 1840 to about seventy in 1880.

In 1878, Paris had 3,991 registered prostitutes, or approximately forty-five for every 10,000 women aged fifteen to forty-nine, but that is taking no account of independents, courtesans or the occasional fling. Men could meet them at a variety of entertainment or recreational venues, many of which were built as part of the Parisian embellishments supported by the government. Among the higher-class establishments, which painters also frequented, were the Café des Ambassadeurs on the Champs-Elysées, and the nearby Folies-Bergère, as well as many brasseries. A pastel by Edgar Degas of *Women on a Café Terrace, Evening* (see 132) shows prostitutes having a nip at a café on a well-lit boulevard. In a less commercial vein, Manet's *Argenteuil* (36) shows a boatman waiting for a woman to decide if she will go with him for a row. Famous as a sailing spot on the Seine near Paris, Argenteuil was a place where unattached women might be encountered. One cannot know if this lady will turn out to be one, but that the man has approached her suggests the activities one could expect in such locations.

Prostitutes had become important subjects in literature, from Alexandre Dumas *fils*'s *La Dame aux Camélias* (1852) to the Goncourt brothers' *Germinie Lacerteux*. The former had a character named Olympe and was turned into the memorable opera *La Traviata* (1853) by Giuseppe Verdi. But perhaps the most significant literary association underlying *Olympia* was Baudelaire's parallel between art and prostitution in *The Painter of Modern Life*. Baudelaire's theory suggested that, since art is communication that requires an audience, the artist must, like the prostitute, exhibitionistically attract his clientele by means of artifice. It may not be too far-fetched to see Olympia as both a metaphorical self-portrait and alter ego for Manet, a notion confirmed by the recent discovery that the bracelet she wears belonged to Manet's mother and contained a lock of the artist's hair. Returning to Olympia's cat, we note that Champfleury had recently produced a book documenting feline promiscuity. Manet did a lithograph publicity poster for it, and, with several other artists, contributed an illustration. Baudelaire associated the mores of the cat to those of artists, and Courbet even placed a cat in the foreground of his controversial *The Studio of the Painter* (see 15).

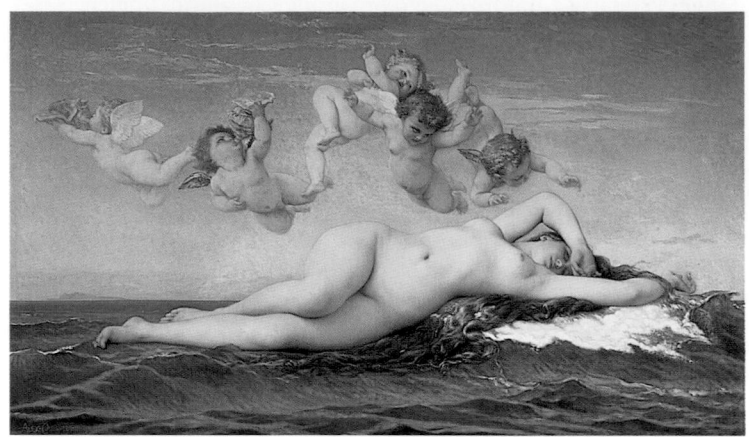

37
Alexandre
Cabanel,
*The Birth
of Venus*,
1863.
Oil on canvas;
130 × 225 cm,
51⅝ × 88½ in.
Musée d'Orsay,
Paris

However complex and self-conscious were the ideas underlying the
Olympia, it is evident that Manet's demythologizing of the female
nude was foremost a timely reminder of modern realities. However,
it is also certain that Manet's interest was more sociological and
psychological than erotic. In avoiding the seduction theme, he focuses
on the woman's power over the commercial transaction. Her almost
rubbery flesh is purveyed matter-of-factly, like abalone in a fishmonger's
window. Her unflinching gaze insists that the fantasy of male
domination is nothing more than business-as-usual as far as she is
concerned. She exemplifies the commodification of human relationships one experiences in the modern world (to be discussed later in
this chapter). No seductive use of paint is evident either. Academic
painters created rich transluscent effects with glazes – diluted oils
used thinly and allowed to dry before additional coats were added.
The sheen and glow of such surfaces, like the polish of fine furniture,
could sensualize virtually any form, to say nothing of the female body.
The *Olympia* is often compared to Alexandre Cabanel's *Birth of Venus*
(37) shown in 1863, for the latter is a far more sexually appealing
work, despite its mythological guise. Manet's dry handling and thick
strokes call attention to surfaces rather than roundness and depth;
they spoil the illusion of reality – hence of sexual attraction – by
reminding us of the technical processes underlying representation.
The majority of critics attacked the painting with unmitigated disgust,
equating the low morality of its subject matter with the seeming lack

of skill in its production: 'What is this odalisque with the yellow belly, ignoble model dredged up from who knows where?'; 'The flesh tones are filthy ... Shadows are indicated with strokes of shoe polish ... '; or 'There is an almost infantile ignorance of the basic elements of drawing [and] the painter's attitude is one of inconceivable vulgarity.' The government was forced to post guards!

Through his friend Cézanne, Émile Zola joined Manet, Degas, Monet, Astruc and others at the Café Guerbois (38). Annoyed by what he regarded as the public's unjust contempt for Manet, he took up the painter's defence, trumpeting what he regarded as his naturalism. Zola's simple formulation of Manet's aims (which we know to be complex) became the first coherent, if narrowly limited, interpretation of Impressionism. In several articles, Zola claimed the artist's intention was simply to see honestly, with regard neither for convention nor for moralizing:

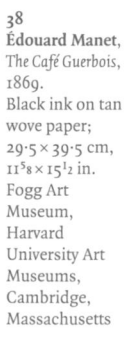

38
Édouard Manet,
The Café Guerbois,
1869.
Black ink on tan
wove paper;
29·5 × 39·5 cm,
11⁵⁸ × 15¹₂ in.
Fogg Art
Museum,
Harvard
University Art
Museums,
Cambridge,
Massachusetts

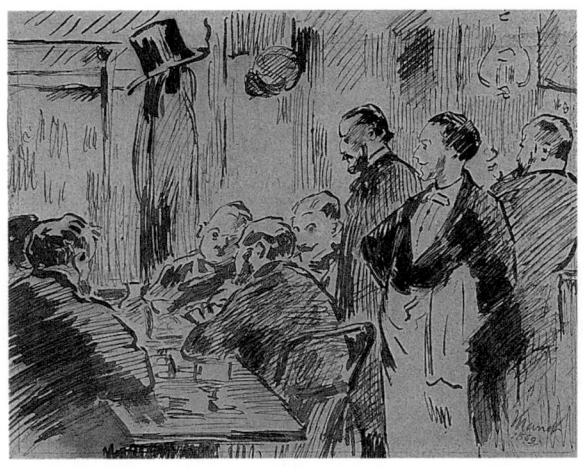

I cannot repeat enough that we must forget a thousand things in order to taste this talent ... The artist paints neither story nor sentiment; dramatic composition does not exist for him, and the task he has set himself is not to represent some idea or some historical act. That is why we must not judge him as a moralist or a writer but as a painter. He treats figure paintings in the same way as in art schools one may treat still life; I mean that he groups figures before him, somewhat by chance, and that his only concern is then to fix them upon the canvas as he sees them … Ask no more than an accurate and literal translation. He knows neither how to sing nor to philosophize.

We saw in Chapter 1 how Zola believed that Positivism and science represented the progressive direction of modern French culture. Here his approach to Manet is tied directly to his belief that naturalism was modern. For Zola, Manet's method of picture-making was based on observation and description; he worked directly from nature. In a discussion of *Olympia*, Zola observed that Manet saw in terms of spots or areas of colour, a process he claimed, echoing Baudelaire on Delacroix and Daumier, imitated nature itself:

Lying on her white sheets, Olympia makes a great pale spot against the black background … Moreover, the details have disappeared. Look at the girl's head: the lips are two thin pink lines, the eyes are reduced to a few black strokes. Now look at the bouquet, and closely, I ask: touches of yellow, blue and green … The accuracy of the eye and simplicity of the hand have created this miracle: the painter has proceeded like nature itself, by way of clear masses and broad planes of light.

For Zola, then, Manet's colourist approach paralleled nature and was free of academic formulas. He quoted the artist as saying in quasi-scientific language that he could do nothing without nature: 'I know not how to invent … If I am worth something today, it is thanks to exact interpretation and faithful analysis.' Manet, Zola exclaimed, was 'above all a naturalist'.

Today, Zola's theories seem limited for their refusal to discuss seriously the subject matter that was as shocking as Manet's style. Yet Zola's purpose was probably to divert attention from that subject matter by claiming it to be like any other object of naturalistic scrutiny – a defence similar to that he made for his early murder novel *Thérèse Racquin* (see Chapter 1). Thus for Zola, the look of Manet's paintings was a reflection of a way of seeing tied to the operation of the painter's eye working from nature without the intermediary of learned conventions. He thought Manet fitted perfectly the definition of art he had summarized as 'nature seen through a temperament' – a combination of the objective with the subjective – and better than anyone, Zola articulated what the new generation of artists would see in Manet's work. The appeal of his conception lay in the justification it provided for following one's intuition, validating youthful rebellion via the logic of contemporary philosophy. We might say it made the 'content' of art the artist himself – his artistic personality and freedom as expressed through a unique way of seeing the world. As with Courbet, Manet's persona and challenges to tradition, as much as what his paintings looked like, made him the leader of his generation.

In his *Portrait of Émile Zola* (39) Manet paid homage to his new defender, who would become a life-long friend. He used the painting to confirm important aspects of Zola's analysis, but he went so much further that we also sense his desire to maintain the upper hand. Although Zola is the *subject matter* of the painting, Manet has made himself very much the *subject*, meaning the active agent, as in the grammatical structure of a sentence where the subject performs the action of the verb. Of course, in that sense, all artists are subjects in their works, since they are the creators. We tacitly admit this fact when we so often refer to a painting by the name of the artist (*eg* a Manet) rather than by its subject matter. But that is a particularly modern way of interpreting art for which Manet, above all, has become the model. Manet's paintings so clearly display the artist's activity, through brushwork, clever juxtapositions and other devices, that the presence of the artist often eclipses that of his subject. A similar effect is found in the watercolours of Constantin Guys, where we experience the work not only as a representation of reality but as aesthetic form created by the artist's specific talents. Manet demonstrates that artistic imagination, not mechanical copying (as if such a thing were possible), is essential to the production of what is 'real'. In making the case for creativity in an art of the real, then, Manet made it possible for later artists to take it for granted. His efforts led directly to the dualism – of truth to nature as well as truth to subjective self – implicit in the term Impressionism, when it came into use.

Manet's portrait of his defender thus contains numerous references to himself. Zola is seated at his desk, on which are piled books and pamphlets, one of which prominently displays Manet's name.

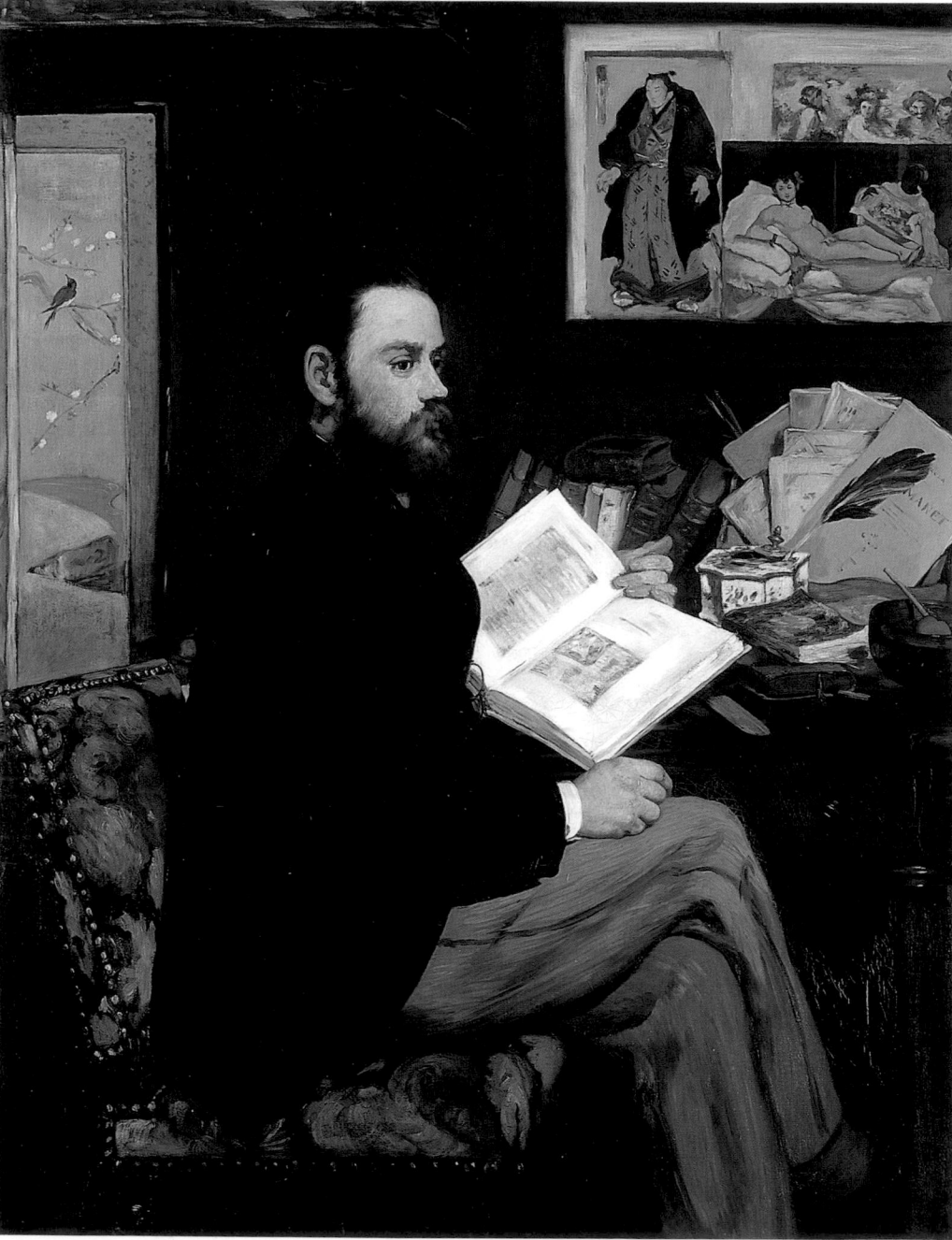

Alluding to the article Zola had written, the name also serves as the painter's signature. On the wall behind the critic is a frame containing three images, one of which paraphrases the *Olympia*, which Zola so vigorously championed. Instead of being domineering here, the prostitute (alter ego for the artist) looks out kindly towards the man who metaphorically became the lover who sent her (or him) a critical 'bouquet'. The two other images stand for important resources that Manet called on for his paintings of the time. One is an etching by the Spanish painter Francisco Goya (1746–1828) after his predecessor Diego Velázquez (1599–1660), which reminds us of Manet's admiration for Spanish Realism. This particular work, *Bacchus*, or *The Drunkards* (c.1629), stages its realist effect in an especially dramatic manner by having one of its characters, who anticipates the bohemians Manet had painted in *The Old Musician*, look directly out of the painting to offer the viewer a glass of wine. Manet's paintings, including the *Olympia*, often asserted their connections to the real world through similarly disarming gazes and gestures.

39
Édouard Manet,
Portrait of
Émile Zola,
1867–8.
Oil on canvas;
146 × 114 cm,
57¹₂ × 45 in.
Musée d'Orsay,
Paris

The other image, a colour woodblock of a Sumo wrestler by Kuniaki II (1835–88), refers to the recent discovery of Japanese prints by painters of Manet's generation. Both stylistically and in their subject matter, such works appeared to the Western eye to be free from the burden of traditions weighing upon European painting (forgetting that the Japanese certainly relied on their own traditions). Unaffected by demands for Renaissance illusionism or classical prototypes, Japanese prints embodied the possibility of an alternative visual culture. They treated subjects from contemporary life with bold lines and colours that expressed a joy in the aesthetic possibilities of their medium. The Japanese artist's method thus exemplified Zola's criteria that an artwork be above all a combination of fine lines and colours done according to the artistic personality of the creator. In addition, as with the wrestler, the themes were often taken from realms devoted to pleasure or entertainment. The many Japanese prints of courtesans fall into this category and might have encouraged Manet's decision to paint the *Olympia*, too, as well as to accentuate the painting's flatness, which Courbet (a proponent of full-bodied women) compared to a playing card.

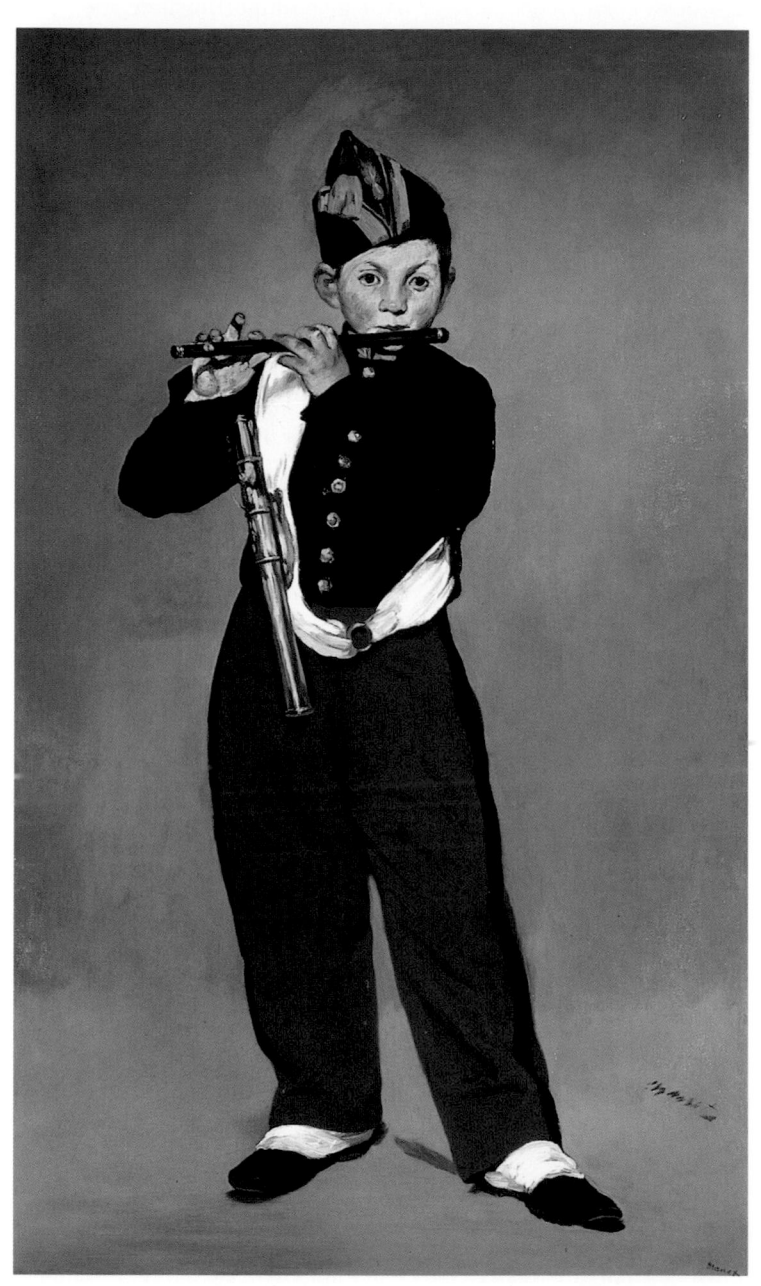

In a painting such as *The Fifer Boy* (40), we see how Manet assimilated many of the characteristics of Japanese art. The frontal pose, bold colours, flatness and strong outlines (particularly those emphasized by the stripes of the trousers) are all hallmarks of what is known as Japonisme, a French word that has become part of art-history terminology. In addition, the careful observer will notice some features whose interference with the illusionistic effect of the image stress the degree to which Manet's conception of art is self-referential. At

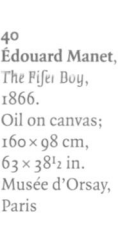

40
Édouard Manet,
The Fifer Boy,
1866.
Oil on canvas;
160 × 98 cm,
63 × 38½ in.
Musée d'Orsay,
Paris

41
Katsushika
Hokusai,
Wild Horses,
c.1833.
Colour
woodblock
print

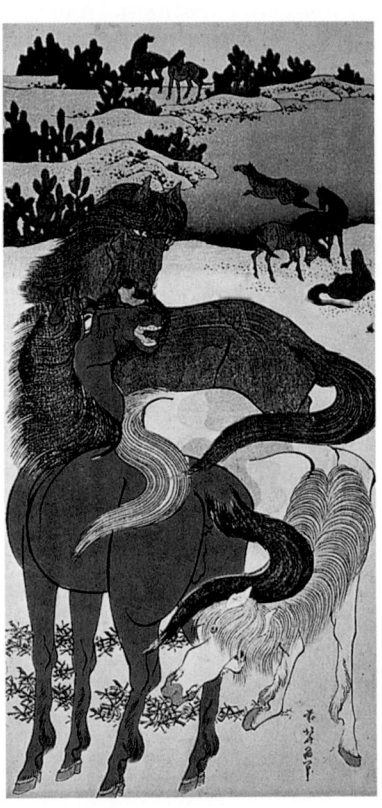

the place where the fifer's left trouser leg overlaps his spats, the white paint representing the spats has in fact been laid over the red, even though real spats must go under the trousers. Behind the foot is a brushstroke that continues its diagonal. At first glance this form suggests something like a shadow; but there is nothing it can be the shadow of, and there is other shading, for example under the shoes, that suggests a frontal light source. These anti-illusionistic effects negate any interpretation that does not focus on the work's status as a record of the act of painting. Such visual puns can be found in Japanese prints, as in the overlapping tails and bodies in *Horses* by Katsushika Hokusai (1760–1849; 41). Their psychological impact is to declare and revel in the artifice of the artwork, to confirm its distance from nature as the condition of our immediate experience of it. That experience is governed by aesthetic and subjective rather than by naturalist principles.

Manet listed fifty-three works at the pavilion he erected near the fairgrounds of the 1867 Universal Exposition. From the brochure accompanying that display, we have a rare public statement that summarized his position at that point. Complaining that his opponents, 'because [they] have been brought up to believe in [traditional] principles will admit no others', he protested the 'sincerity' of his own work, which aimed 'only [at] rendering his own impression'. He persisted in a personal approach to painting over the conventions taught in schools, and the result of his elaborate efforts forced people to take his commitment seriously.

By the late 1860s, however, Manet was less apt to define himself through audacious challenges to the past. His provocative ironies gave way to more subtle vehicles, which would increasingly have the look and freer execution of the recognizably Impressionist painting of modern life. His colours and compositional arrangements now conveyed the intensity and presence of modern visual consciousness. Yet Manet never quite abandoned certain traditional aspirations, for along with many small pictures, he continued to work on a large scale and to exhibit at the Salon. Increasingly, his work followed the tendency of his younger colleagues in representing friends in domestic or outdoor settings. *The Balcony* (43), which he exhibited at the Salon of 1869, shows a group of Parisians looking out from an apartment. Manet got the idea at the Channel resort of Boulogne-sur-Mer, where the artist and his wife often spent the summer, though the painting seems equally Parisian and was posed in his Paris studio. In the shadows to the left is Léon Leenhoff – once thought to be the artist's son, though born before his marriage to Suzanne. (New evidence suggests the father was Manet Senior, since Léon was never

42 Right
Francisco Goya,
*Majas on
a Balcony,*
*c.*1808–12.
Oil on canvas;
194·8 × 125·7 cm,
76³⁄₄ × 49¹⁄₂ in.
Metropolitan
Museum of Art,
New York

43 Far right
Édouard Manet,
The Balcony,
1868–9.
Oil on canvas;
169 × 125 cm,
66 ¹⁄₂ × 49¹⁄₄ in.
Musée d'Orsay,
Paris

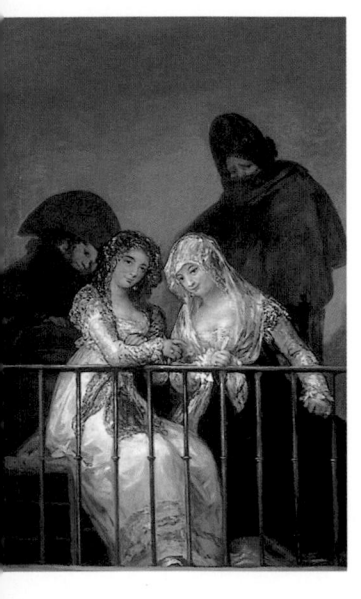

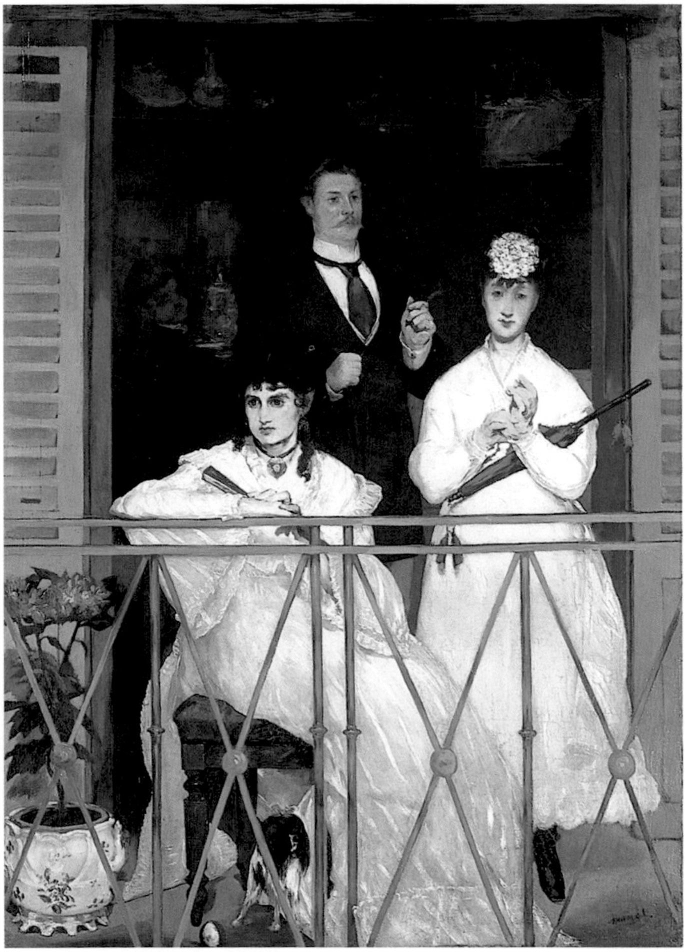

legitimized and used his mother's maiden name.) The others are friends of the Manet family: the violinist Fanny Claus stands to the right holding a parasol; to the left is Antoine Guillemet, a landscape painter who exhibited at the Salon but supported the Impressionists. The woman seated in the foreground is the painter Berthe Morisot (see Chapter 6), whom Manet had met at the Louvre through Fantin-Latour in 1868. Morisot and her sister became constant companions of the Manets, and Berthe married Manet's brother, Eugène, in December of 1874.

The painting is striking for its combination of taut formality in compositional design with technical looseness in rendering individual forms, particularly in areas of hair, clothing and accessories, most notably Fanny's gloves. The painting also harbours a reference to a famous painting by Goya, *Majas on a Balcony* (42), which Manet could have seen in various versions either in Paris or on his trip to Spain. The reference was both art-historical – Manet's perennial dialogue with the art of the past – and ironic – for Manet's friends were nothing if not outwardly respectable, compared to the courtesans and their companions in the Goya. Such expressions of self-consciousness and strong artistic personality, within the framework of painting contemporary life, are precisely what signalled Manet's vision as so resolutely modern.

During the 1870s, Manet did a number of compositions featuring couples in which psychological distance and ambiguity go beyond those features of *The Balcony*. Both *Boating* (44) and *In the Conservatory* (45) partake fully of what we immediately recognize as Impressionism through their conspicuous naturalism, their fashionable and leisure-oriented setting, their brilliant colour and loose brushwork. Moreover, their flattening and break-up of solid form, especially evident in the dress of the woman in the foreground of *Boating*, are typical of paintings by Monet, whom Manet knew well by this time (see Chapter 3). Yet unlike many of the Impressionists, whose works so often appear innocent and uncomplicated, Manet was still mulling over the traditions he had worked to engage and transform. For Manet knew that juxtaposing two figures inevitably raised the question of a relationship

44
Édouard Manet,
Boating,
1874.
Oil on canvas;
97·2 × 130·2 cm,
38¼ × 51¼ in.
Metropolitan
Museum of Art,
New York

45
Édouard Manet,
*In the
Conservatory*,
1879.
Oil on canvas;
115 × 150 cm,
45¼ × 59 in.
Nationalgalerie,
Staatliche
Museen,
Berlin

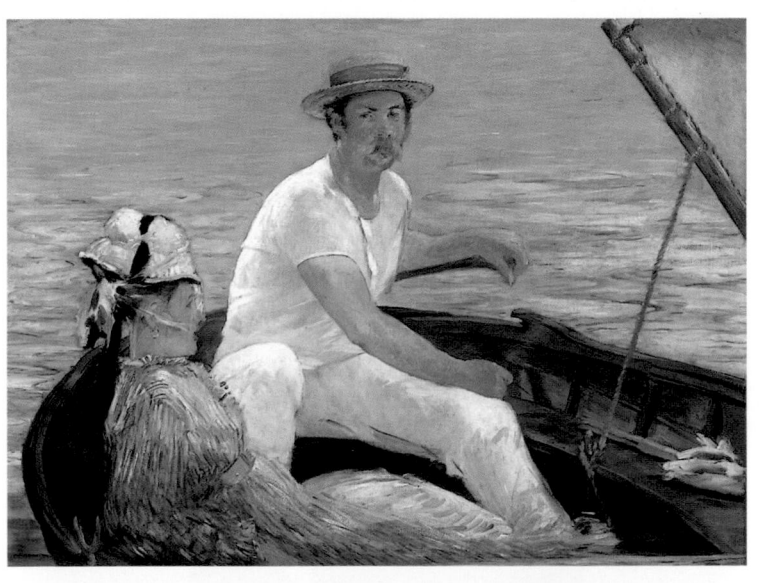

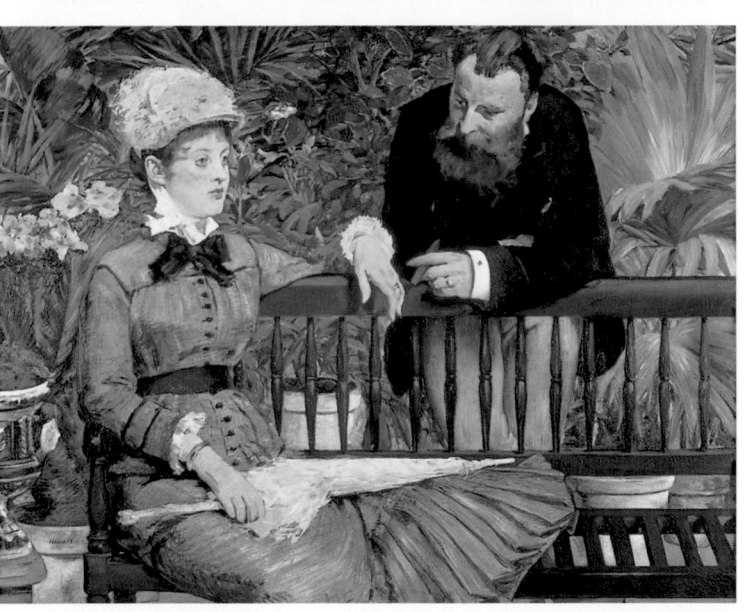

between them. His friend Degas was a master at exploring subtle psychological interactions in similar groupings (see 112, 113). Yet Manet has given no clues to the thoughts of his figures here; rather, there is a sense of detachment, estrangement even. In *Boating*, the woman's mind seems as suspended and adrift as the sailing boat.

On one level this strategy is that of the artist who, as Zola said, paints 'neither story nor sentiment'. It is worth remembering that by the standards of the Salon, where Manet was exhibiting, these themes would be associated with genre painting and its strong reliance on

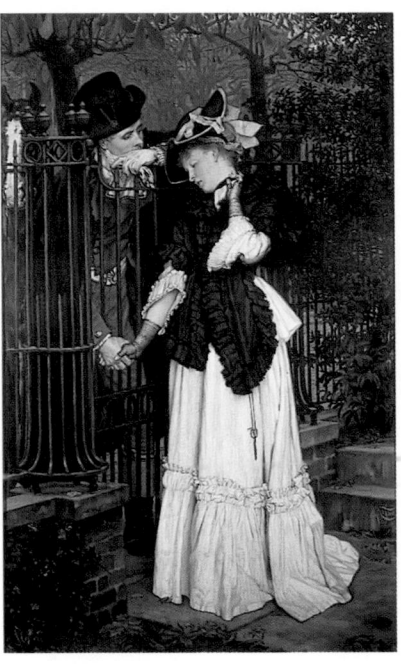

46
James Tissot,
The Farewell,
1871.
Oil on canvas;
100·3 62·6 cm,
39^1$_2$ 24^5$_8$ in.
City of Bristol
Museum and
Art Gallery

narrative. Yet one has only to compare Manet's works to those of contemporaries such as Ernest Meissonnier (1815–91), Alfred Stevens (1823–1906) or even his friend James Tissot (1836–1902; 46) to understand his purgative effect. Gone are the cloying anecdotalism and ingratiating stylistic references to 'little Dutch masters' and the Rococo. Manet's concentration of our attention on visual surfaces, as opposed to inner life, is amply accomplished through bold, dazzling and seductive passages, of which the hypnotically shimmering blues of *Boating* are the most extraordinary example. Yet it is certainly impossible not to respond to the figures' emotional blankness as an aspect of Manet's theme. Even within the context of such aesthetic beauties as the images generously supply, the figures' psychological remove is disconcerting.

The figures in *Boating* have not been identified. *In the Conservatory* shows Manet's friends, Monsieur and Madame Jules Guillemet, who owned a shop on the fashionable rue Saint-Honoré. For both pictures, one may justifiably ask whether the sitters' psychological state is one of reverie induced by their surroundings, or of ennui. Manet's painting raises the unanswerable question of the connection in real life between alienation and aesthetics in modern culture: is leisure necessary as compensation for solitude and vacuity or is it the underlying cause?

One can only answer such questions through theories. For example, we can return to Baudelaire, for whom the anonymity of urban life gave rise to the aesthetic gestures of dandies and courtesans. Through love, art or stimulants – or maybe just trips to the country – one could escape the solitude and triviality of everyday life. A somewhat more complex theory, first proferred by the Marxist sociologist Georg Simmel in the early 1900s and often introduced in this context, holds that under capitalism, the modern city dweller, who is rootless and traditionless compared to his country ancestors, places his faith in economic and scientific values. Thus alienated by the 'commodification' of the 'citizen-stranger's' existence, the modern gaze is self-preserving and neutral rather than gregarious and warm. Modern urbanites maintain relationships based primarily on money and justify their dispassionate judgements by observable facts and quantitative measures. Clearly this pessimistic theory corresponds in important ways to both Baudelaire and to Positivism. However, it fails to account for the friendships and family relationships that are so central to Impressionism's coherence and vision of the world. Moreover, it underestimates the role of art in fulfilling our yearnings at the same time as it expresses them. Indeed, as art historian Jonathan Crary has suggested, there is a positive way to characterize many of these features – through the notion of autonomy or self-possession, of which alienation is inevitably the obverse. The pleasurable experiences of the fashionable and idyllic surroundings of *In the Conservatory* and *Boating* may be the antidote to Simmel's alienation. It is worth noting that the environments of both paintings are artificial. In the former, plants have been brought inside a specially dedicated room; in the latter, the couple has travelled to Argenteuil, where rental boats await them, and the man has dressed up in yachtsman's clothes. So our own experience of Manet's pictorial display of lush colours and of the material exuberance of his richly painted surfaces parallels the sensuousness experienced by his figures in their chosen environments. If Manet's art has captured something of a modern consciousness, then, it may well be because that consciousness was Manet's own. Visual and social experience are coextensive: Manet's vision embodies the detachment and emotional reserve, as well as the immersion-in-the-aesthetic of his painted protagonists, who are quintessentially urbane, like himself.

The Parisian social meaning of Manet's imagery is perhaps most apparent in his last large work, *A Bar at the Folies-Bergère* (47). It was painted in 1881–2, just after he developed neurological complications from gangrene that would worsen until his death in 1883. The careful, monumental construction looks back to works of the 1860s, but the composition is also the culmination of a series of paintings of cafés and other scenes of urban leisure stemming from the 1870s. *A Masked Ball at the Opéra* of 1873–4 (48), for instance, presents an élite crowd in an elegant setting. With its several not-quite-identifiable representations of men who presumably belonged to Manet's circle, this composition looks back also to *Music in the Tuileries Gardens* (see 27). Like this predecessor, it defines a social class through cultural activities, although here those activities are less innocent – the solicitation of sexual favours from masked women who seem willing to grant them. In the world of Paris entertainments, masquerade – the unreliability of outward appearances – is an important theme. Closer to *A Bar at the Folies-Bergère*, though less complex, are pictures in the group including the unaccompanied woman smoker of the exquisite *The Plum* (see 159) and the brilliantly coloured and broadly painted bourgeois couple of *At the Café* (see 160), paintings which recall the many hours Manet spent with friends in such places as the Café Guerbois, La Nouvelle-Athènes and the Café-Concert de Reichshoffen.

In *A Bar at the Folies-Bergère*, we are met by a barmaid, named Suzon, whose counter is arrayed with one of the most scintillating still lifes in nineteenth-century art. Painted with broad brushstrokes in vibrant colours are aperitif, champagne and cordial bottles, aligned with fruit, crystal and flowers as an unmatched foretaste of the consumable pleasures offered in a major establishment for entertaining the rich and aspiring. Who knows whether the barmaid herself, with her wooden posture and gaze which almost avoids the viewer's, might also be an available commodity? Or whether Manet, who signed his name on one of the cordial bottles, was consciously comparing his painting to one (and hence himself to the barmaid) as well? Waitressing was at the time a suspicious profession, almost like the role of artist's model; and, as in *A Masked Ball at the Opéra*, things are not always as they appear, especially in establishments where access was based on looks and money rather than on clearly defined social origins. Typical of the ambiguities in Manet's art, the mirror behind the barmaid both deepens and flattens the space. It is the medium through which we witness the vast cabaret hall filled with light, smoke, acrobatic spectacle above the stage, and the fashionably dressed crowd. Many of Manet's contemporaries commented on the mirror, which is also the crux of many recent theories about the painting (including the proposal that the barmaid herself is looking in a mirror, hence the viewer is construed as female), for one could hardly fail to notice how its reflection both encompasses a vast society and defies physical possibility. Yet the psychological effects of its optical anomaly are fully consistent with Manet's sensibility. Even though the barmaid does not look directly at the viewer of the painting, she so strongly centres the composition that there is a clear sense that the viewer's position should be directly in front of her. At the same time, the mirror reflects figures and the objects on the counter as if the viewer were standing considerably to the right. Only from such a position could one see the reflection of the barmaid's back and of the customer she is serving (the viewer himself?). In Manet's own sketch for the painting, or in a café scene with mirrors by Caillebotte (see 161)

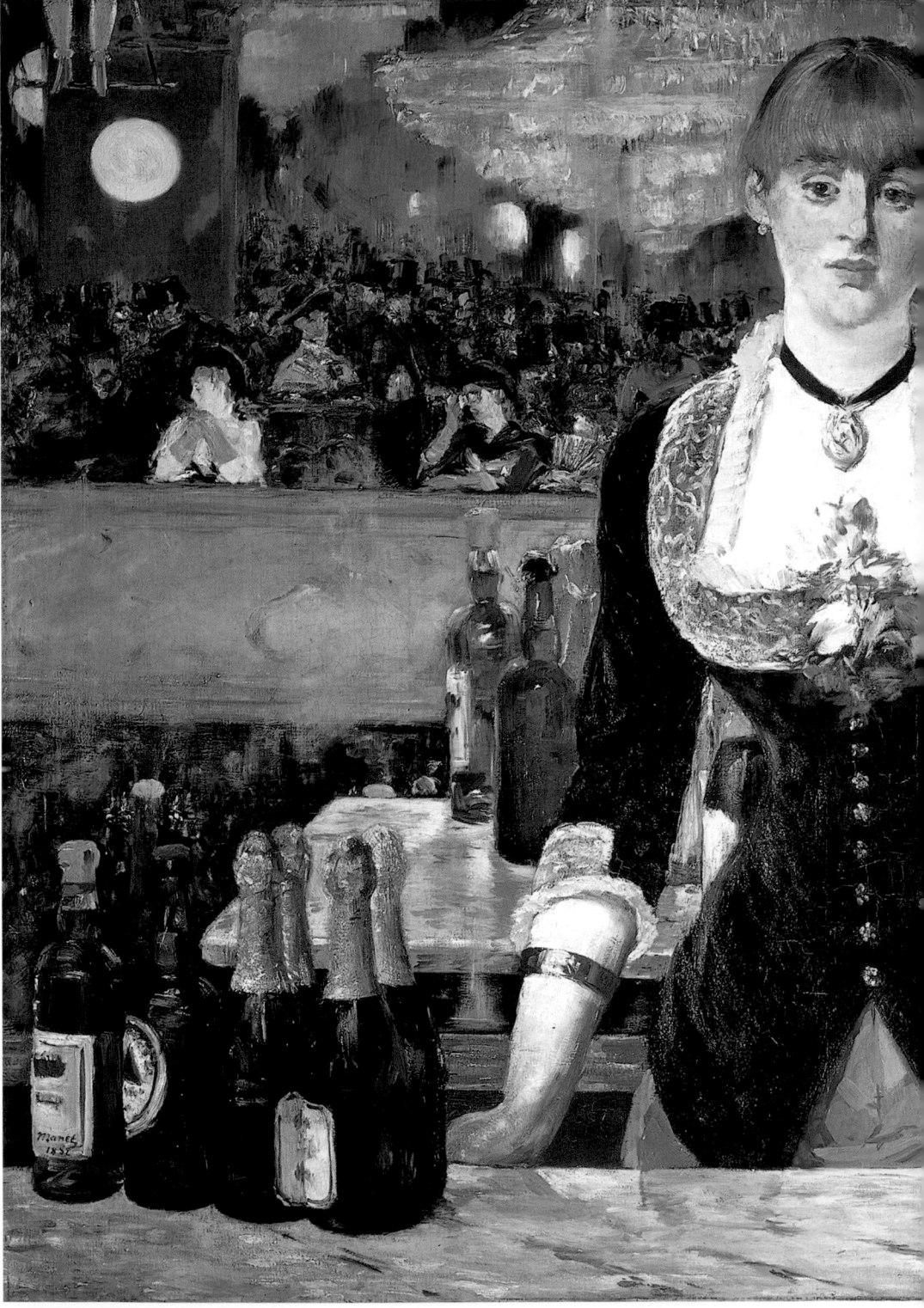

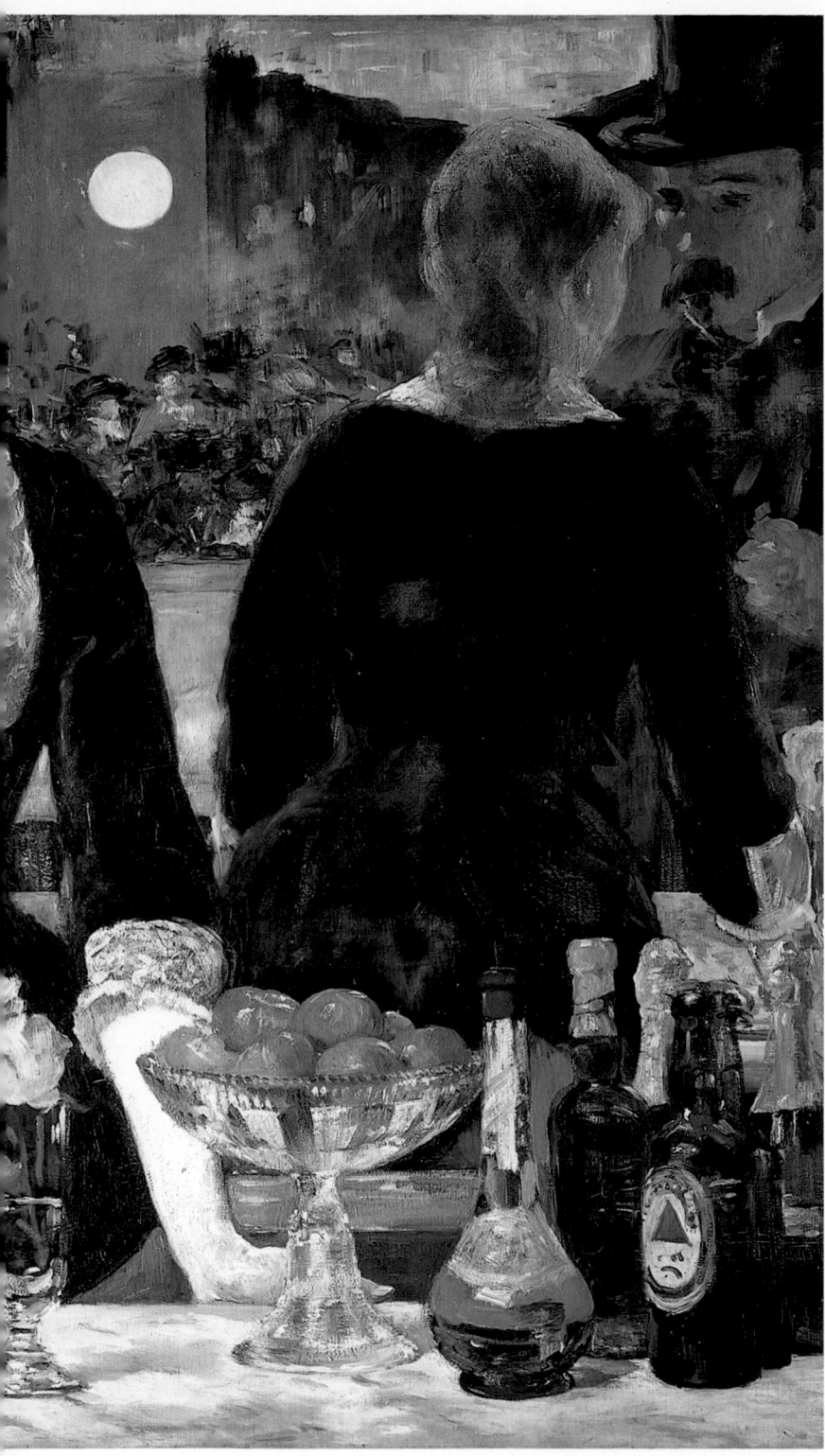

47
Édouard Manet,
*A Bar at the
Folies-Bergère*,
1881–2.
Oil on canvas;
96 × 130 cm,
37³⁴ × 51¹⁸ in.
Courtauld
Institute
Galleries,
London

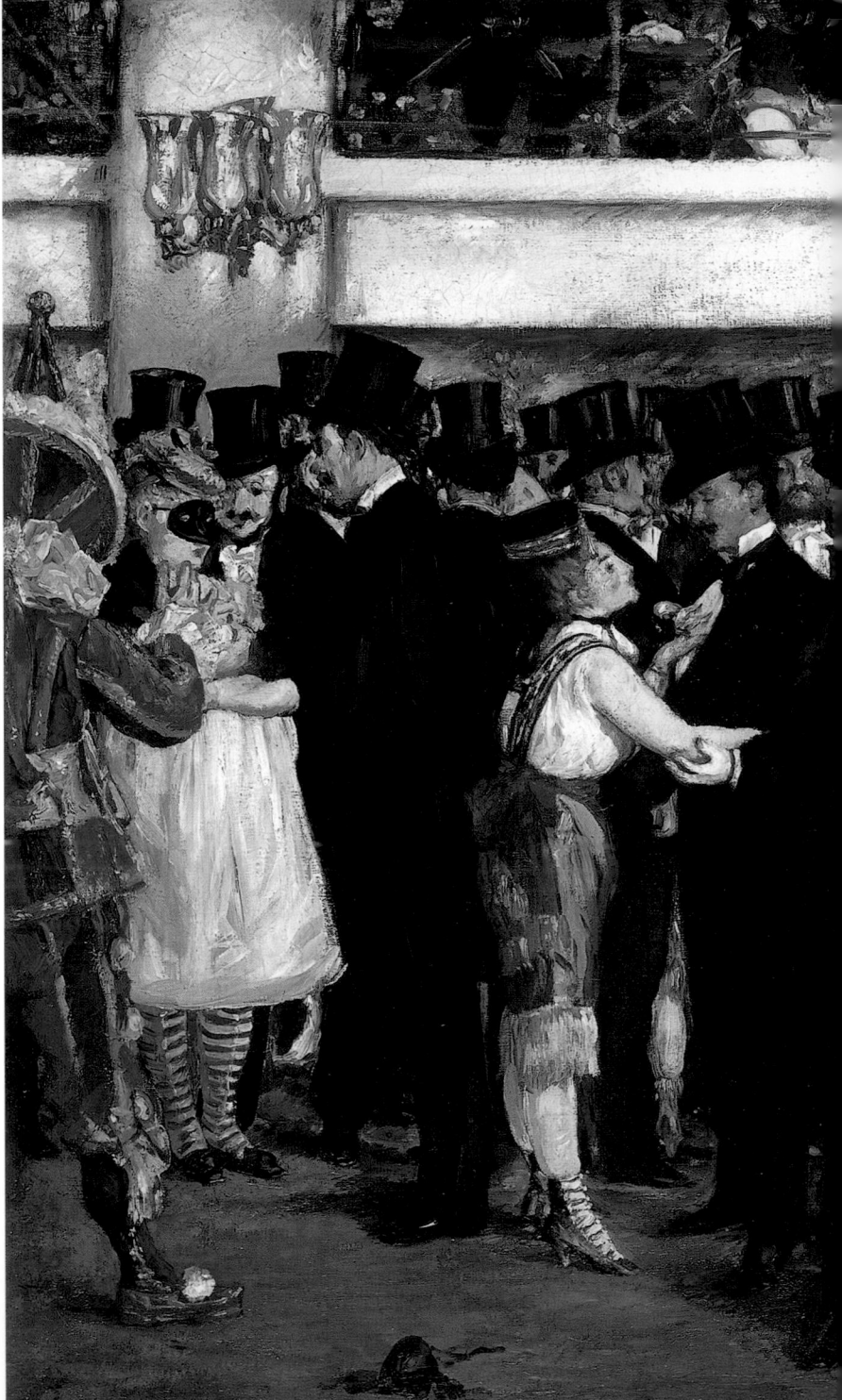

48
Édouard Manet,
A Masked Ball
at the Opéra,
1873–4.
Oil on canvas;
60 × 73 cm,
23⁵⁸ × 28³⁴ in.
National Gallery
of Art,
Washington, DC

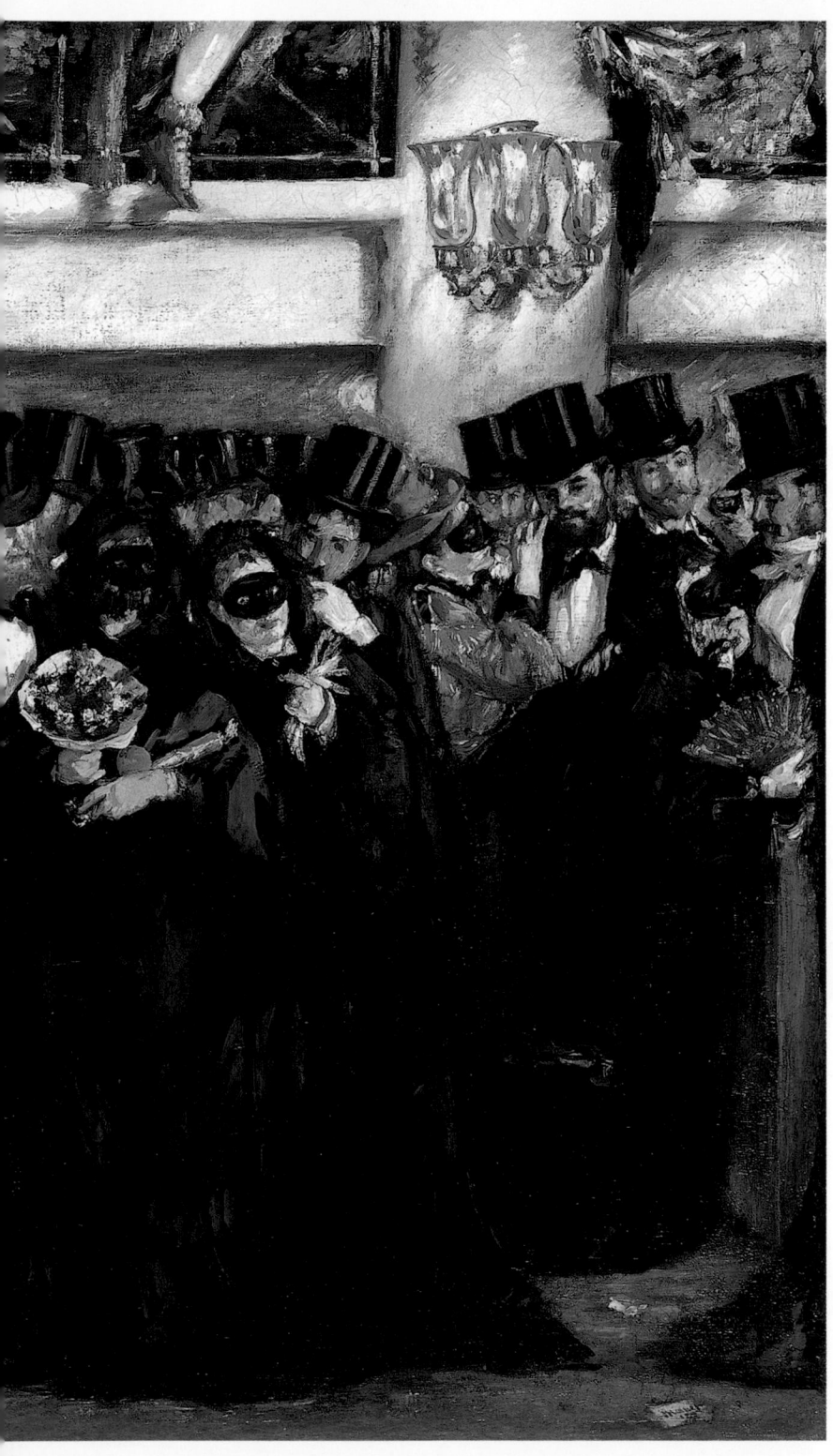

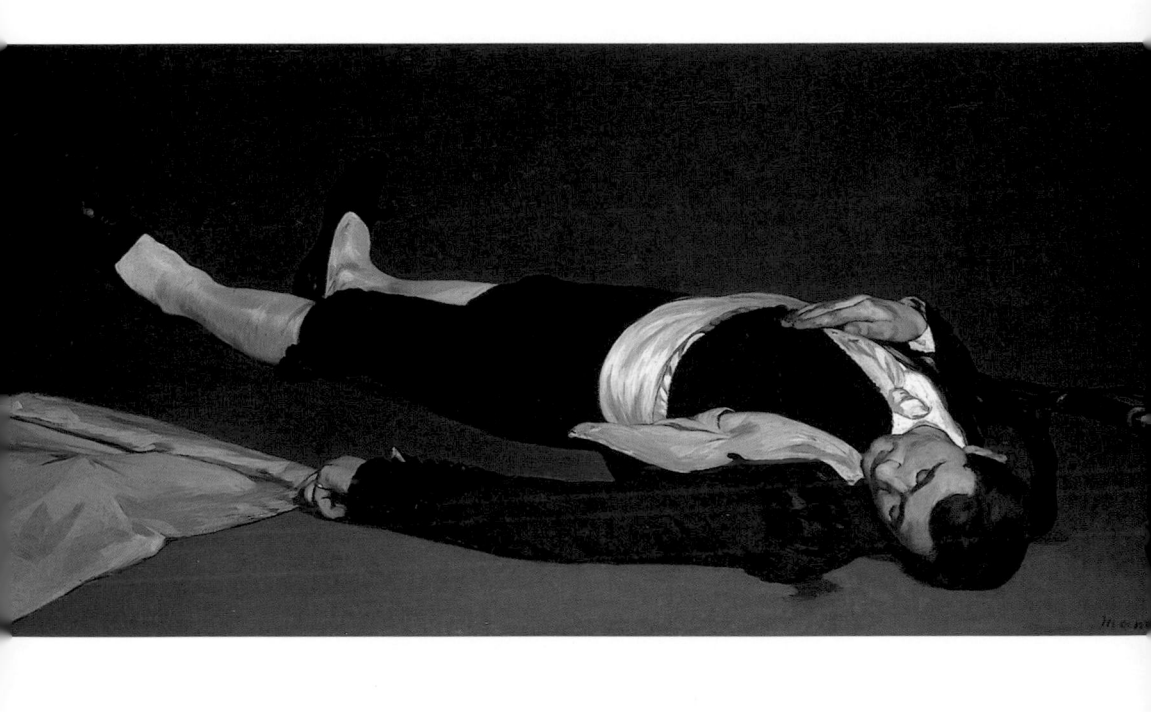

which Manet probably knew, it is easier for us to imagine a coherent viewpoint. So Manet's finished work deliberately placed the reflection in tension with normal viewing. It might almost be said that A Bar at the Folies-Bergère has presented the aesthetic of the *flâneur*'s detached gaze as a surgical operation, in which the eye has been removed (figuratively speaking) from its location in the body and placed further to the right. The detached eye, so-to-speak, concentrates us wholly on signs of artifice, such as the artist's compositional counterpoint of alternating forms and rhythmic repetition, his treatment of surfaces – especially textural where the chandeliers are reflected in the mirror – or the still-life objects of consumption, which ultimately include the painting itself. The painting's unstable 'reflection' of this space embodies the social ambiguity of its world. Both produce a sharpening of attentiveness and self-consciousness. Manet had often flaunted the artist's staging of reality, and he had certainly raised questions of social psychology through indefinable relationships he could create between two figures – one of them now the viewer. Yet in no other painting have both the foundations of reality and social identity together become so problematic.

49
Édouard Manet,
The Dead Toreador,
c.1864–5.
Oil on canvas;
76 × 153·3 cm,
29⁷⁸ × 60³⁸ in.
National Gallery
of Art,
Washington, DC

In conclusion, it may be fitting to return to an earlier work by Manet for clues to the continuity of his art. The Dead Toreador of c.1864–5 (49) was cut out from a larger painting called Episode from a Bullfight. Manet must on some level have viewed the fragment as the more satisfactory version in both compositional and psychological terms, as it confronts us with its single poignant and inescapable fact – the stillness, yet physical beauty of the corpse. As he often did in the 1860s, Manet played off sources from past art: a dead soldier once attributed to Velázquez (now Italian School) that was in a well-known collection, and Goya's bullfight etchings. He defied conventional expectations, however, by emptying the painting of elements of dramatic and emotional commentary that, for a viewer reared on Romantic painting, would have once constituted the expected 'content' of art. But it is not enough to say that by ridding his painting of these elements Manet eliminated narrative simply to favour silent realism. While that may be the psychological impact, so that the toreador's death looms brutally immediate and stark, the vacuum left by the real surgical operation –

the cutting of the painting to leave only the non-narrative fragment –
is gradually filled by one's perception of the graphic signs of art.
The emotional chasm is counterbalanced by the aesthetic – by effects
of deft handling and deliberate brushstrokes that stand for the shimmer
of silk, the polish of leather or a trickle of blood. The Realist reading
and its accompanying emotions are held in suspension with our
consciousness of artifice: the beauties of representation have the
potential to poeticize the concrete facts of nature, including death.
Conversely, death lurks even at the heart of pleasure. As for Baudelaire,
unpleasant realities could be transcended through the aesthetic; or
ostensible pleasures might be fraught with unease, as in *A Bar at the
Folies-Bergère*. Through it all, the artist, imposing his private vision on
the world, fashions a modern subjectivity, shaped by the conflicting
conditions, perceptions and aspirations of the new Parisian culture.
As such, Manet's art appears today not only as the powerful first stage
of Impressionism, but as a paradigm of modern art.

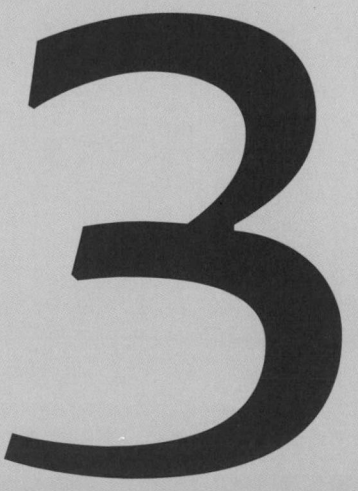

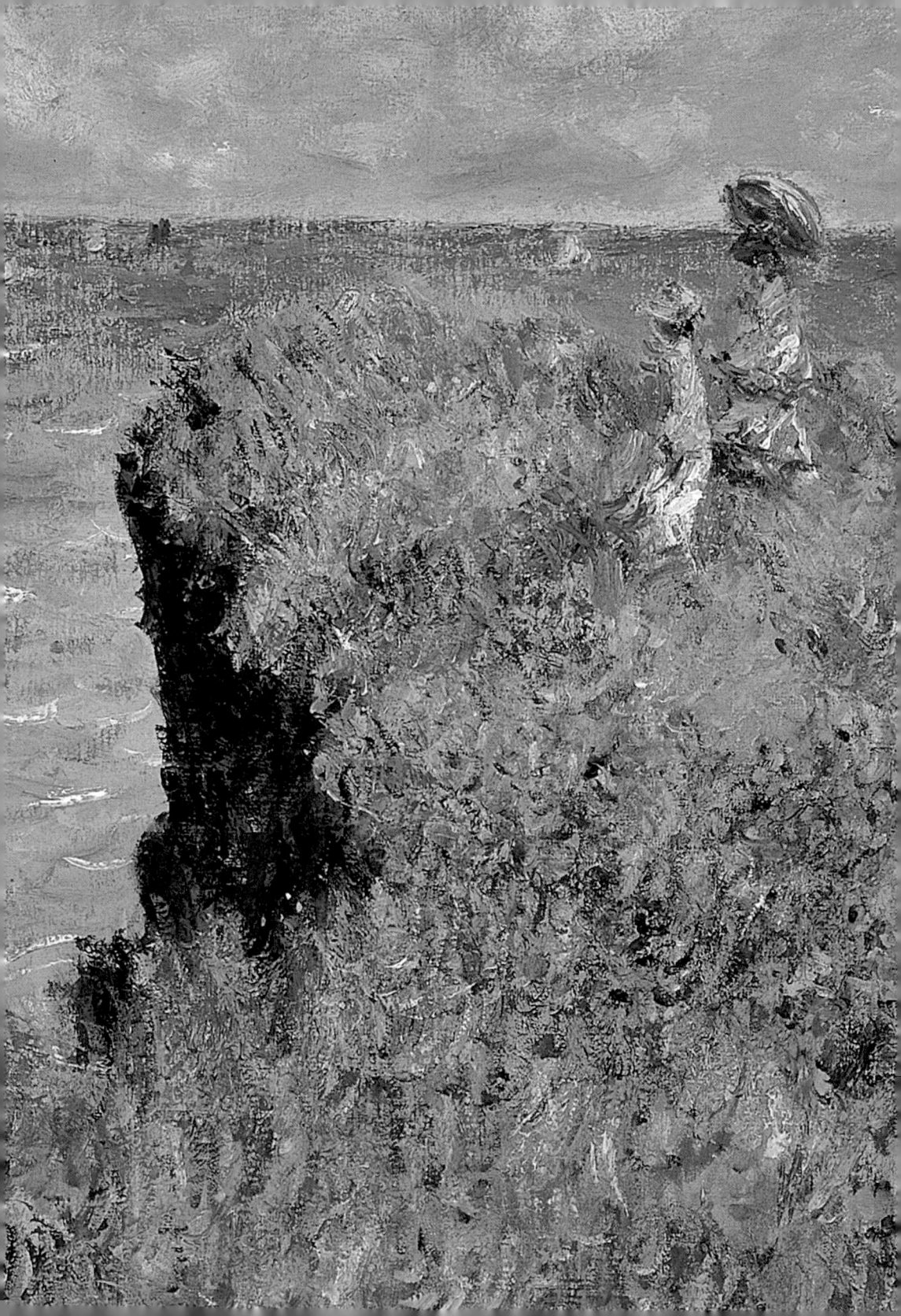

Claude Monet's commitment to painting directly from nature formed a second path, compared to Manet's urban inspiration, in the development of Impressionism. Though born in Paris, Monet was brought up in the booming Channel port of Le Havre, and his attitudes to art were formed in the coastal environment of Normandy, a considerable distance from the capital. However, as for any painter expecting to be taken seriously, Parisian culture would have a profound effect on his conception of what serious art should be. Monet was primarily a landscapist, and as such we often think of him as more straightforward than his urban peers. Yet his concentration on that genre was forged against the continuing prestige of figure painting, which for Manet and Baudelaire was the primary vehicle for representations of modernity. The first part of Monet's career shows a resolve to integrate assumptions about painting he brought from the seashore with the practices he encountered in Paris. From very early on, working directly from nature was central to his self-definition. As time went by and he did more work in the studio, preserving the myth that he painted completely out-of-doors and on-the-spot became more important to him than actually doing so. His travels, his studio boat and other strategies combine with the look of his paintings to construct an image of art as a *plein-air* ('open-air') practice.

The story of how the young Monet met the painter of Normandy beaches, Eugène Boudin (1824–98), has often been told. Monet had shown his skill and wit in caricatures, a popular contemporary form requiring incisive observation and confident shorthand to summarize succinctly and capture essentials. These abilities would serve Monet well throughout his career. The two became acquainted when Monet's drawings were exhibited in a local stationery and art supply store, alongside Boudin's modest oils of vacationers on the beaches (51). Monet later claimed Boudin had opened his eyes to nature. There was a well-established tradition of painting on the Normandy coast by

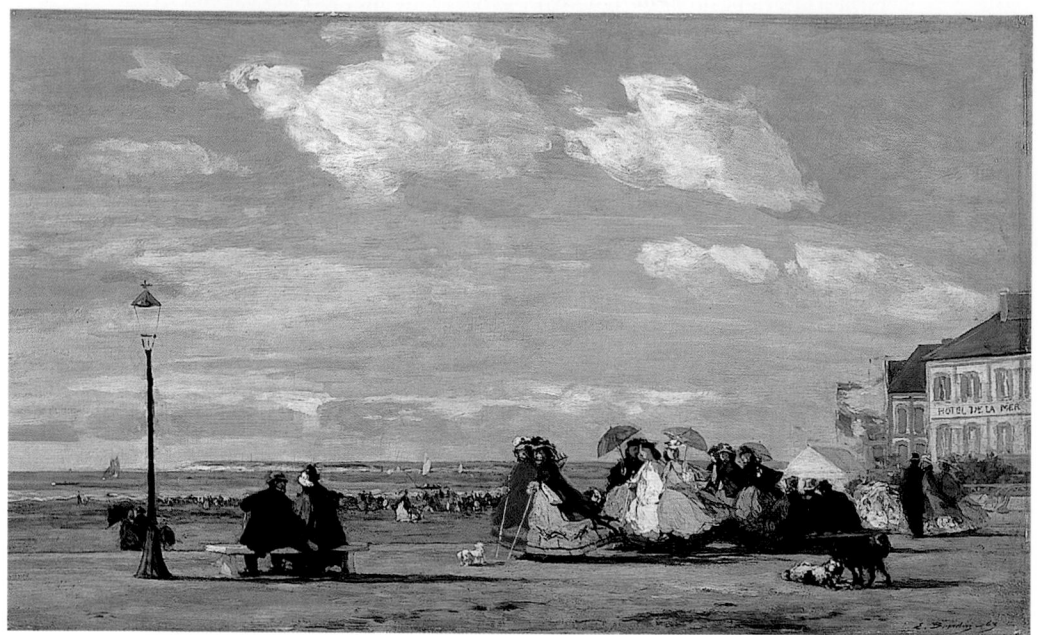

Monet's time, as many British landscapists, such as Richard Parkes Bonington (1802–28), crossing the Channel to tour the Continent, stopped first in Normandy. Their preferred medium for recording the scenic fishing villages and sleepy harbours was watercolour, in which they freely brushed semi-transparent colours (pigment suspended in water) over white sketchbook pages. Dutch artists, including Monet's friend Johan Barthold Jongkind (1819–91), came too, along with the French themselves, among them Delacroix, who learned watercolour from the English and sketched the famous Étretat cliffs long before Monet. *Plein-air* painting was also practised by French landscapists such as Corot. Like him, Monet would use light-hued grounds to prepare his canvases – so-called *peinture claire* (light or clear painting). A close look at Boudin's oil technique of the 1860s shows that his patches of colour and relatively loose handling emulate the freedom of watercolour sketches, although he was producing paintings he considered finished. He preferred vibrant contrasts to the mellower effects of closely related tones which Corot and his woodland followers of the Barbizon School were using. In addition, Courbet befriended Monet in the mid-1860s when he made several trips to Normandy to paint freely handled seascapes, a genre that sold well.

51
Eugène Boudin, *Empress Eugènie and her Suite at Trouville*, 1863. Oil on wood; 34·2 × 57·8 cm, 13½ × 22¾ in. Burrell Collection, Glasgow

Hence, the environment in which Monet began was already known to many artists and was associated with working *en plein-air*.

Throughout the 1860s, Monet travelled back and forth between Le Havre and Paris, where he first went in 1859 at the age of eighteen, determined against his family's judgement to pursue his art. After joining the Académie Suisse and then spending a year in military service in 1861–2, he enrolled at the atelier of Charles Gleyre (see Chapter 1), a more respectable school which satisfied his father. There he met Renoir, Sisley and Bazille. In Paris, he discovered that landscape painting was just one of many genres and that modest views with sketch-like handling were not usually considered worth exhibiting. His letters show him sceptical about much of what he saw, with the exception of Corot, Rousseau and Daubigny, Barbizon painters who were more committed to the direct study of nature than most of their contemporaries. The most advanced painters in the public eye, however, were Courbet and Manet. Monet's first major effort was, therefore, to position himself with a large painting, conceived on the scale of public exhibition (though never actually shown), for which he took a subject related to both Manet's *Déjeuner sur l'herbe* (see 30) and Courbet's woodland scenes, yet different from both. Monet worked from his own experience, representing summer day-trippers at Chailly, near Fontainebleau, including his mistress Camille Doncieux, his painter-friend Bazille (whom he bombarded with requests to come), both of whom posed for three or four figures, and the bearded Courbet himself stretched out in the foreground. He offered an outdoor corrective to Manet's studio-staged realism, both in terms of composition – with less historically redolent poses – and in his treatment of sunlight filtering through trees. Meanwhile, the technique on the tree trunks and foliage resembles Courbet, who had been urging Monet to loosen his handling even further. Only a large sketch survives in full (52). Monet ambitiously tried to aggrandize it to a scale that would have outdone Manet; but he gave up on the project, probably because he was unable to finish it satisfactorily before the 1866 Salon deadline. The large canvas was removed to a cellar and eventually cut up (53). The enlargement of spontaneous brushstrokes to Salon scale made them clumsy. More importantly,

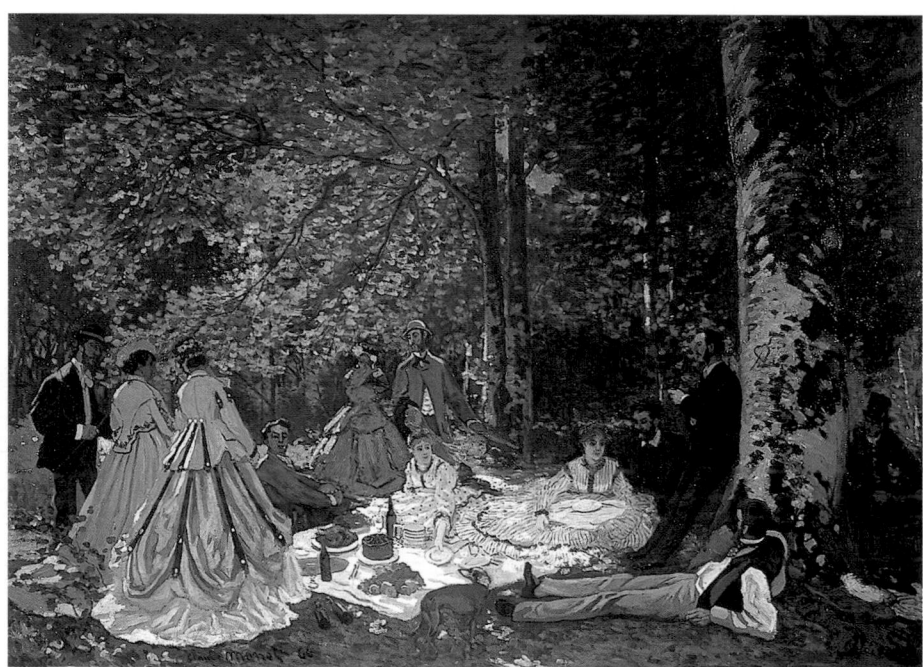

52 Left
Claude Monet,
Sketch for
*Luncheon on
the Grass*,
1865.
Oil on canvas;
130 × 181 cm,
$51^{1}4 × 71^{3}8$ in.
Pushkin
Museum of
Fine Arts,
Moscow

53 Opposite
Claude Monet,
*Luncheon on
the Grass*
(central
fragment),
1865.
Oil on canvas;
248 × 217 cm,
$97^{3}4 × 85^{1}2$ in.
Musée d'Orsay,
Paris

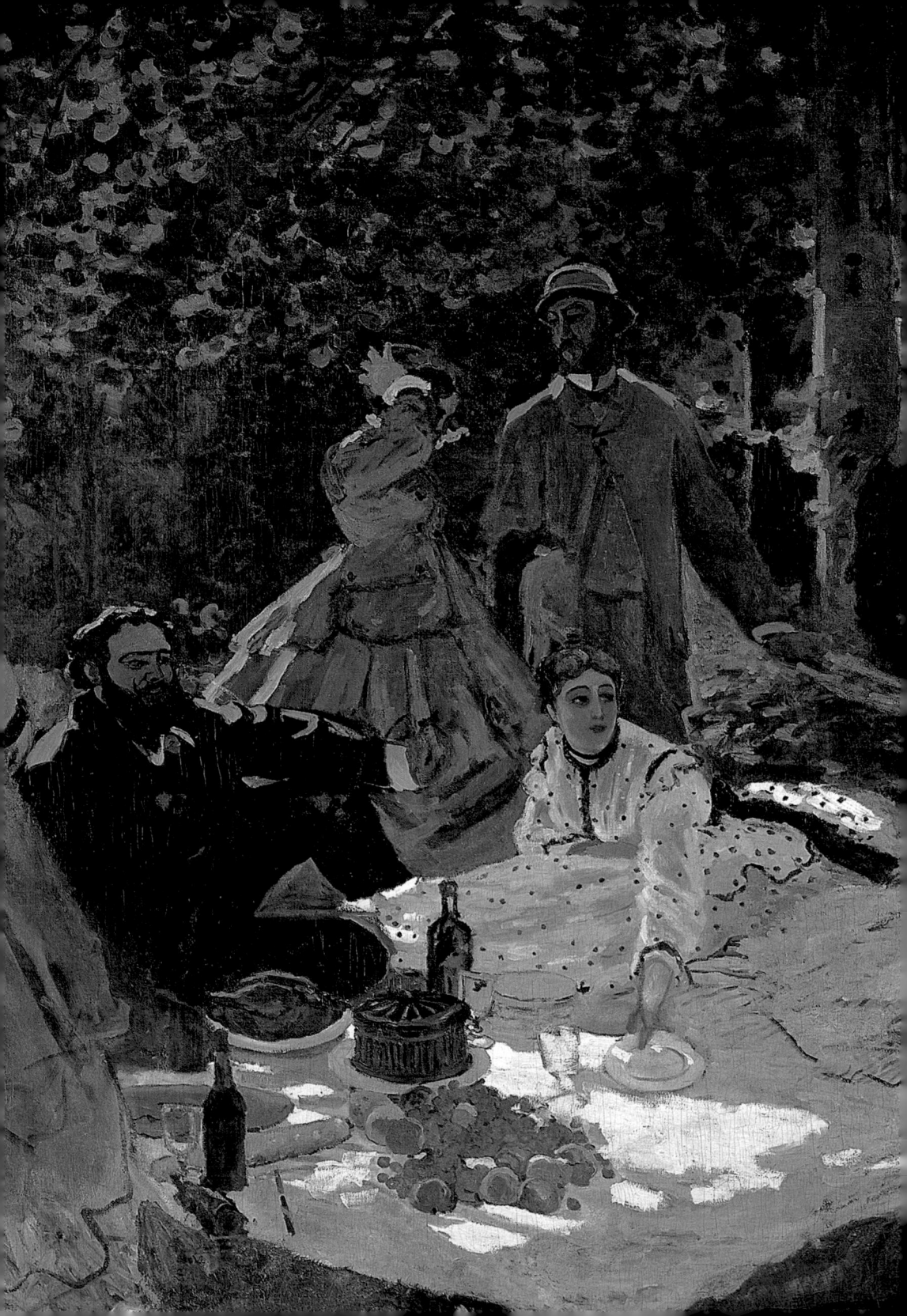

in working from the outdoor sketch to a large studio version, he compromised the very commitment to *plein-air* painting this *Luncheon on the Grass* had been conceived to proclaim.

Apparently Monet's friends dragged him off to the Louvre, where he hated looking at anything but landscapes. At certain times, painters could sign in with their easels and equipment, for it was assumed they would copy the great museum masterpieces. Instead, in early

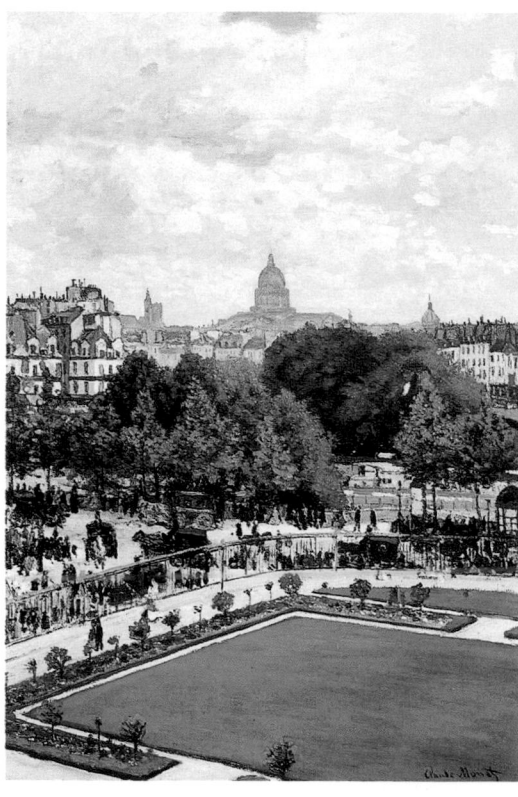

54
Claude Monet,
The Garden of the Princess,
1867.
Oil on canvas;
91·8×61·9 cm,
36¹⁸ × 24³⁸ in.
Oberlin College,
Ohio

55 Opposite
Paris from
Tour Saint
Jacques,
1867

1867, Monet made a view of the Princess's garden and the newly constructed quays bordering the Seine (54) by looking out from the balcony of the Louvre's famous colonnade. The view is much like that in many photographs of the city (55) that were proliferating. It is not that Monet was directly influenced by photography, but that for a picturesque view of central Paris, his vision paralleled the photographic works that were setting the standard for naturalism (see Chapter 1). The sense of his window-like frame is similar to the moveable frame of the camera viewfinder. Setting his sight, so to speak, on the bustling scene of carriages and *flâneurs* across the garden and along the river, Monet captured the attractive life of leisure enjoyed by tourists and the upper-middle classes. However, Monet adjusted his perspective and probably the foliage to reveal skyline, with the Pantheon prominently in the background, framed by Notre-Dame to the left and the domed church of Val-de-Grace to the right. Historic Paris is thus the background for activities of modern life. Similarly, though Monet turned his back to the world's greatest collection of art, he was certainly conscious of it behind him. While continuing to make traditional Normandy scenes whenever he went back there, Paris, its pleasures and its art world were increasingly on his mind.

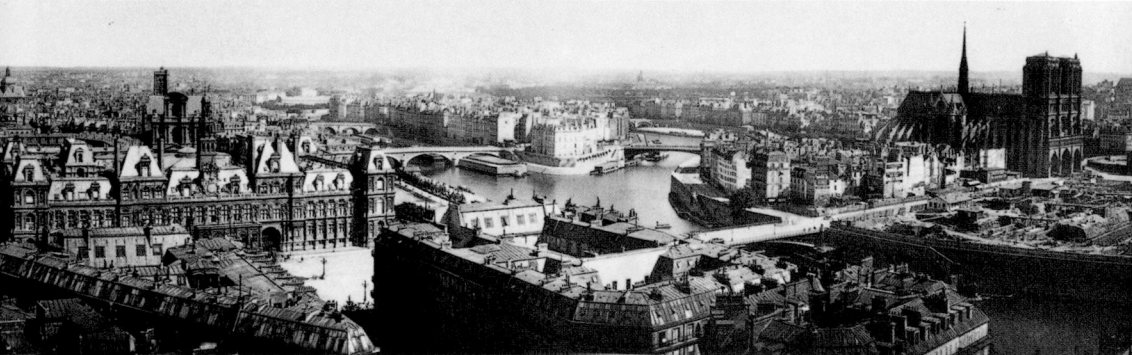

Monet moved quickly to reconceive as a true *plein-air* painting his abandoned project for a large-scale landscape. Of course, he would often work on landscapes in his studio, but from that point on they were always begun and considerably developed out-of-doors. *Women in the Garden* (56), painted in the spring and summer of 1866, affirmed that practice. In the studio, painters would have used a ladder to reach the top of a 2·5 m (8½ ft) canvas without stretching. Monet claimed to have dug a trench, into which he lowered the canvas, in the garden of the house he rented in the Paris suburb of Sèvres, presumably so he could have freedom of movement on the ground. The painting does have the authentic feel of the outdoors (even though it was finished in the studio), with its emphasis on spring embodied by bouquet-making and the ladies' appreciation of the scented flowers. But it is also

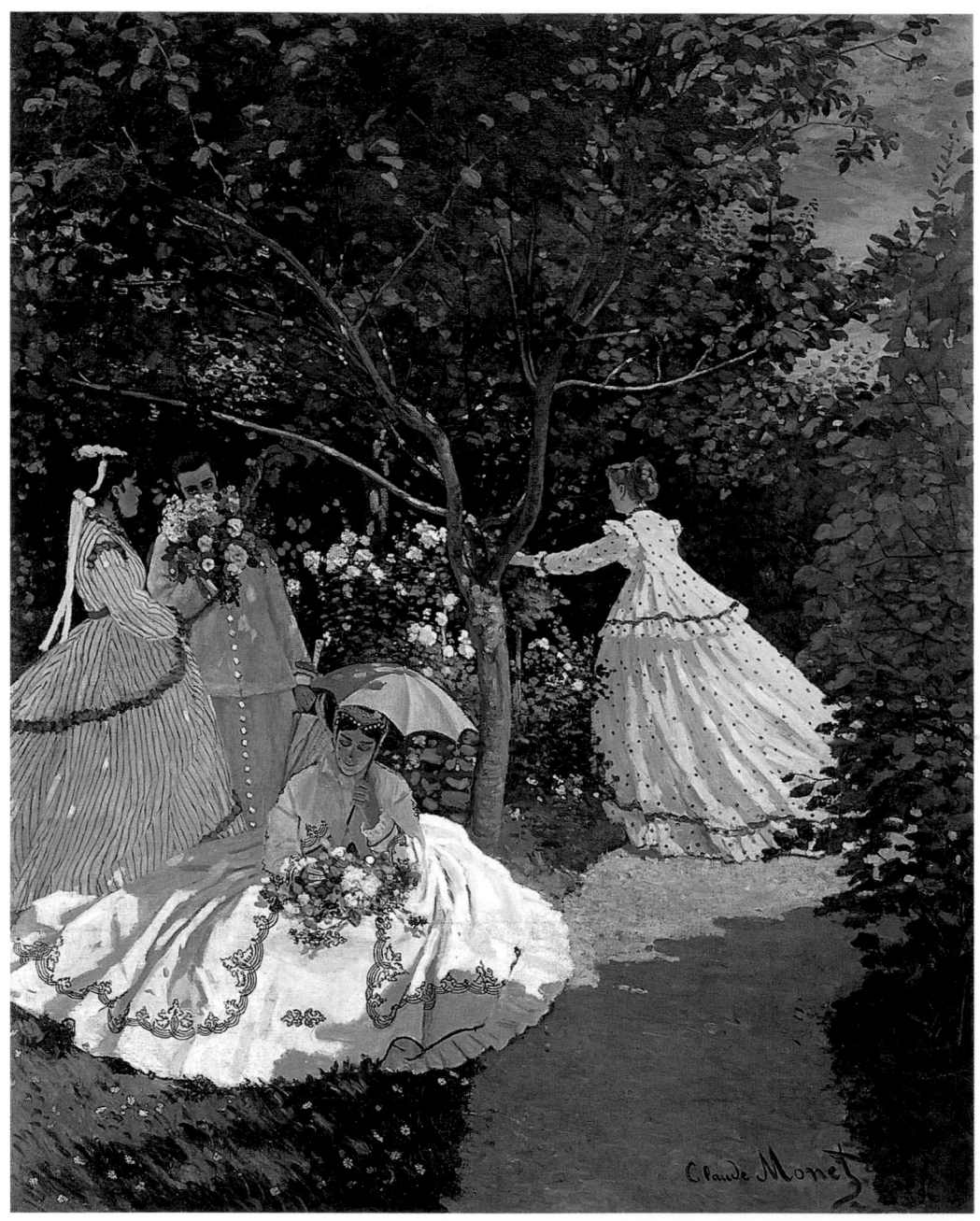

a systematic exposition of Monet's skills and ambitions at the time, for the piece is not without contrivance: Camille posed for all four figures, and the fashionable dresses were surely taken from designs in magazines rather than purchased with the couple's meagre income. The grouping of the figures and the combination of poses is less fluent (the emphasis on pattern reminding us of Manet) and less natural than other Monets, including the earlier *Luncheon on the Grass* sketch. The sharp contrast of sunlight and shade crossing the foreground, while quite successful, is a conspicuous statement of the *plein-air* principle, as is the reflection of sky blue on the face of the seated figure, though it is so forced that it produces a mask-like effect. Unlike academic painters, who would mix grey with their colours to indicate shadow, Monet represented it through a shift in hue. It is from such procedures that Impressionists earned the reputation of having banished black from their palette, a hyperbolic reference to their refusal to use it for modelling in light and dark. Despite its rejection by the 1867 Salon jury, *Women in the Garden* established Monet as a leader of the emerging school of painters dubbed 'Actualists' by Émile Zola. With Baudelaire and Manet in mind, Zola linked Monet's image of leisure and fashion to contemporary Parisian culture and the increasingly popular migrations to the countryside; he was also impressed by Monet's 'exact sense' of nature. Outdoing Manet's scale, *Women in the Garden* is indeed the first monumental painting of modern suburban life.

56
Claude Monet,
*Women in
the Garden,*
1866.
Oil on canvas;
256 × 208 cm,
100⅞ × 82 in.
Musée d'Orsay,
Paris

Monet had been living with Camille in the face of his family's strenuous objections, his allowance from his father never entirely secure. In the summer of 1867, he left the fully pregnant Camille in Paris (their son Jean would be born in August), in order to make a conciliatory stay at home. (The couple did not marry until 1870.) Adolphe Monet had originally moved to Le Havre to work in his brother-in-law Jacques Lecadre's wholesale grocery business. When Lecadre died in 1858 (a year after the death of Claude's mother when he was sixteen), Adolphe Monet and his widowed half-sister Sophie took over the company. The commerce of France's premier port – Le Havre had outstripped the Mediterranean port of Marseille – provided a comfortable life. It was to his aunt Sophie's waterside villa in the wealthy suburb of

Sainte-Adresse north of Le Havre that the painter returned. Again looking out from an upstairs window, he executed the deservedly famous *Terrace at Sainte-Adresse* (57), a painting that has come to define early Impressionism.

It is again a scene of leisure, with his father and aunt in the foreground of the flower garden, while his well-dressed cousin, Jeanne-Marguérite, and a respectable suitor chat near the boundary fence. Beyond them lies the Channel, near the mouth of the harbour (a few kilometres off to the left), with its traffic of clipper ships, merchant steamers

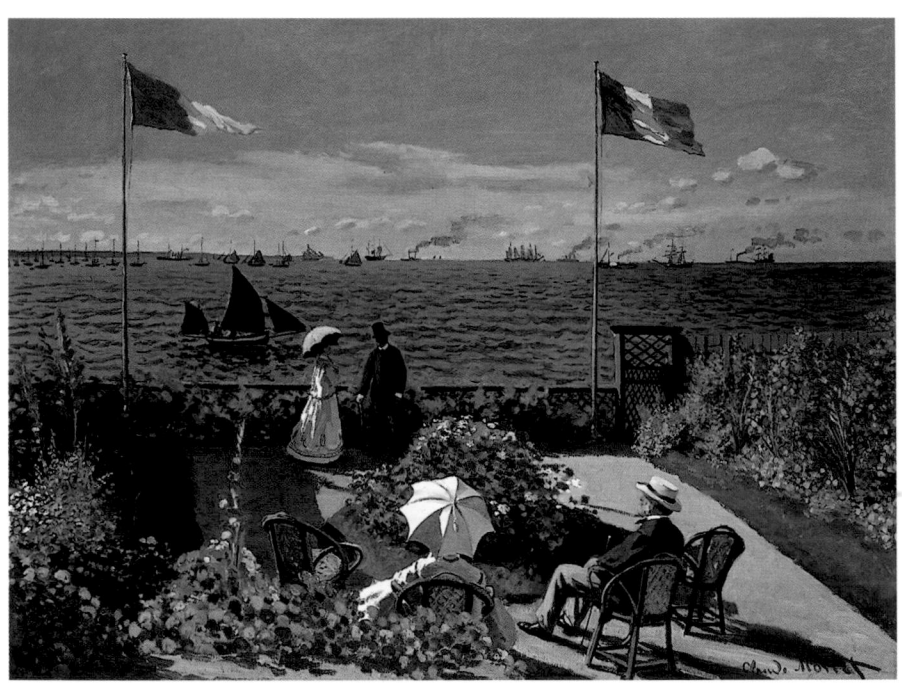

(one of which bears national colours), fishing boats and moored pleasure craft. The bright afternoon light is accompanied by a brisk southern breeze which flutters the flags in the same direction as it blows the steamboats' smoke. One feels able to set a watch and tell the season, so specific and convincing is the sum of Monet's effects. Yet coexisting with the freshness of spontaneous naturalism is a sharp sense of artifice. For example, even without approaching the painting too closely, we are conscious of the flowers as dabs of contrasting coloured paint lying on the canvas surface rather than receding into space. Moreover, one can hardly fail to notice the rigorous geometry of the parallel flagpoles, the crisply defined edges of the grass both left and right, and the circular parterre. It has often been observed that the Impressionists abandoned traditional perspective, treating the canvas as a surface on which to transcribe observations of colour. Monet used simple geometric patterns as a substitute for the coherence provided by the imposition of a mathematical scheme denoting space. The flagpoles and the meeting of the sailing boat with his cousin's parasol (a device similar to the tree connecting the two right-hand figures in *Women in the Garden*; see 56) flatten the picture in a manner probably inspired by Japanese prints. (Monet called this his 'Chinese painting' – the terms 'Japanese' and 'Chinese' were freely interchanged at the time.) Thus Monet's painting expresses a coherent vision of his day by uniting the prosperity of modern commerce with the leisure it procured into visual forms that have the clean lines and practical legibility of the most advanced taste, to say nothing of their appealing colours. He unwittingly produced an updated, mercantile version of the kind of commemorative and congratulatory picture that once showed landed gentry posing before bountiful farming estates.

Although *Terrace at Sainte-Adresse* is a substantial easel-sized canvas, it was essentially a private work, smaller than those Monet had submitted to the Salon. Yet Monet had not abandoned his ambition to produce works of public note. In the late spring of 1869, he moved near to the popular village of Bougival, only 12 km ($7^{1}2$ miles) along the Seine from Paris. With Renoir, who was living nearby, Monet went to paint at La Grenouillère (58, 59), a swimming, eating and drinking spot, called by one contemporary observer both 'indecent and refined', yet so popular that Napoleon III and his wife visited it that very summer. It is not known whether the name, meaning 'the frog place', refers to the habitat of amphibians or to the easy women – also known as *grenouilles* – who could be found there, too. In his novel of 1880, *La Femme de Paul*, the prudish Guy de Maupassant wrote condescendingly: 'One senses there, even through one's nostrils, all the scum of the world, all the most distinguished riff-raff, all the motliness of Parisian society.' Working side by side with Renoir, Monet, according to his testimony, made 'some bad sketches' for a

57
Claude Monet,
Terrace at Sainte-Adresse,
1867.
Oil on canvas;
98·1 × 129·9 cm,
$38^{5}8 × 51^{1}8$ in.
Metropolitan Museum of Art, New York

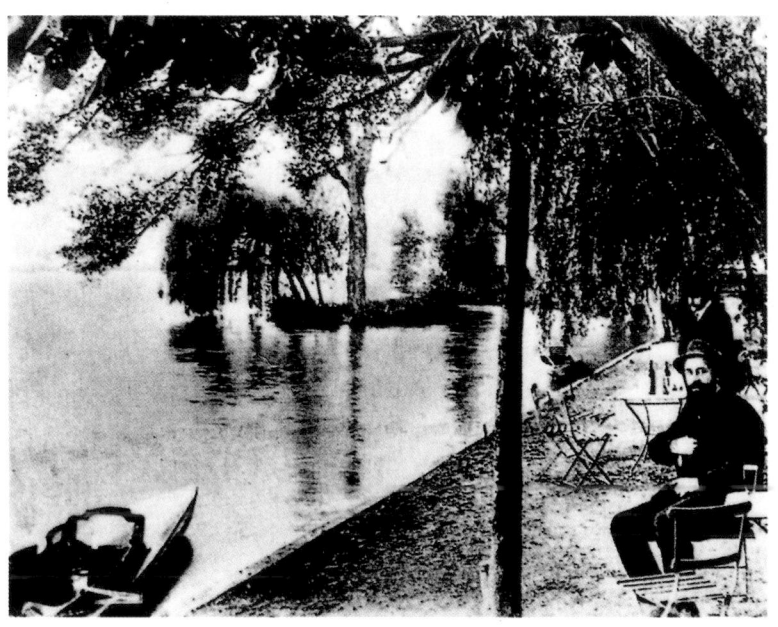

58
Claude Monet
and Pierre-
Auguste Renoir
at La
Grenouillère,
c.1869

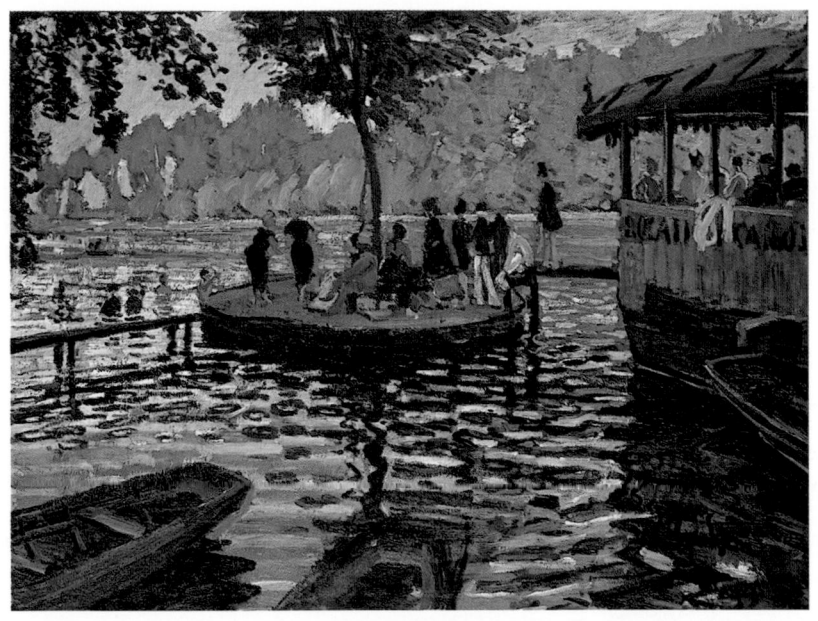

59
Claude Monet,
La Grenouillère,
1869.
Oil on canvas;
74·6 × 99·7 cm,
29³⁄₈ × 39¹⁄₄ in.
Metropolitan
Museum of Art,
New York

large painting intended for the Salon of 1870 (again never carried out). It is not clear how seriously we should take Monet's remarks about his 'sketches', for he did submit one of them, now lost, to the Salon. Most likely he discovered the contradiction between finished Salon painting and *plein-air* practice, deciding that, as the most effective vehicle for his intentions, his open brushwork deserved a place at the Salon. After the jury's refusal, he abstained from submitting for ten years, putting his energies towards the independent exhibitions with his friends.

The so-called 'sketches' that survive – one at the National Gallery in London, the other at the Metropolitan Museum of Art in New York (59) – are among the first masterpieces of Monet's mature style. They are indeed far more boldly brushed and seem less artificially composed than his previous work, although the New York version does somewhat redeploy the geometric scheme of *Terrace at Sainte-Adresse* (see 57). But it seems now that Monet wanted to disguise that structure in favour of a more spontaneous appearance. With a bravado exceeding the flowers of his *Terrace* painting, the broad strokes signifying reflections seem to float on the painting's surface in a way that emulates the visual effects of water. The figures are handled summarily, and the trees in the background are virtual abstractions. A comparison with Renoir's painting of the same site (see 1) is revealing. The gregarious Renoir places us closer to the people, who are treated with more detail, giving a greater sense of sociability than in Monet's quieter work. The trees in Renoir's background are more clearly identifiable as poplars, with their spindly trunks and delicate leaves. Yet in the foreground, where Renoir tries his hand at Monet-like summarization of ripples and reflections, the result is murky and dead. This juxtaposition affords an understanding of what will become Monet's tendency to view scenes for their overall pictorial effects rather than for description of specific detail. Yet he was obviously still committed to painting modern life, especially the suburban scenes we see emerging as his specialty in the 1870s.

When he returned to Normandy in 1870, Monet was attracted by the grand, recently built resorts on the other side of the Seine estuary from Le Havre. Vacationing at the seashore was a relatively new phenomenon, encouraged by a growing belief in the healthy effects of bathing and made easily accessible by train. With his new family, Monet spent the summer at Trouville, and although his hotel was a less expensive one off the beach front, his paintings showed the principal establishments, such as the Hôtel des Roches-Noires (60), frequented by international visitors, as indicated by the American flag rendered sketchily in the foreground of a brightly lit, balanced composition. Among other pictures from his summer stay is a scene of Camille – a parasol held aloft to protect her skin from the tanning associated with fishwives and outdoor labourers – on the beach at Trouville (61). This painting actually has windblown sand embedded in its surface – testimony to his working *en plein-air*. These paintings clearly reveal aspects of Monet's process. Working in the tradition of *peinture claire*, he prepared both canvases with a ground of lead white mixed with a little yellow and black to produce a warm grey. In the *Hôtel des Roches-Noires*, this ground shows through as a large patch on which the stripes of the flag are lightly indicated. The same colour shows through in the sky and dominates the overall tonality of *Beach at Trouville*. Yet despite the effect of sketch-like rapidity and bravura brushstrokes, including the casual, initialled signature, the beach picture – with Monet's familiar device of objects touching one another to create planes – is carefully constructed and framed.

In retrospect, Monet hardly seems to have missed a beat during the Franco-Prussian War, in which the French suffered defeat in 1871. Impressionist responses to the Paris Commune, which immediately followed the surrender, will be a topic of Chapter 7. Monet fled to London, where he painted with Pissarro and met the dealer Paul Durand-Ruel. He then travelled to Holland, before returning to Paris in the autumn of 1871. In January 1872 he moved to Argenteuil, some 15 km (9 miles) away, with a 22-minute train journey to Saint-Lazare station. The family remained there until 1878. More than any other Parisian suburb, Argenteuil has come to be identified with Impressionism. Its attractions were many – fresh air, affordable rents, picturesque neighbourhoods and a site along the Seine where the widening of the river into a basin afforded excellent sailing and

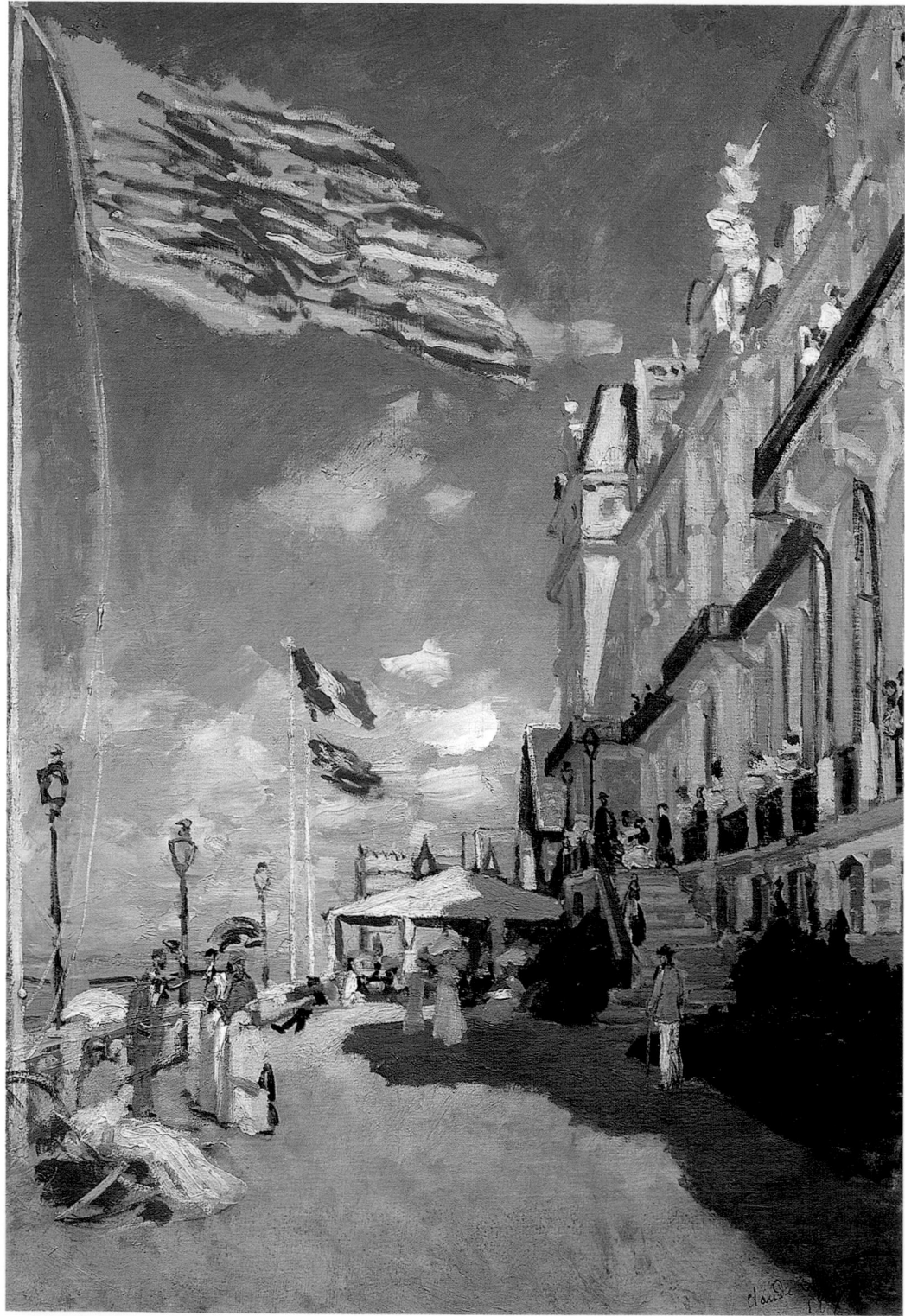

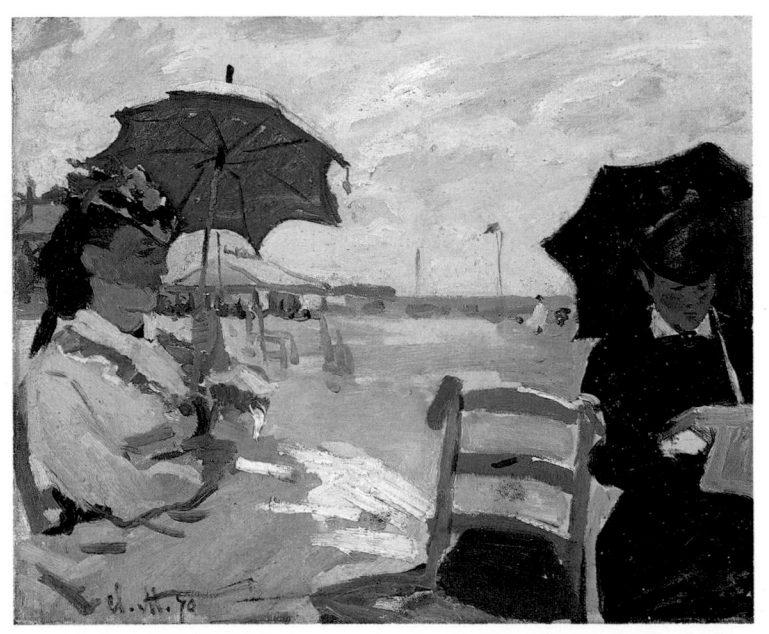

60
Claude Monet,
*The Hôtel des
Roches-Noires*,
1870.
Oil on canvas;
80 × 55 cm,
31¹₂ × 21⁵₈ in.
Musée d'Orsay,
Paris

61
Claude Monet,
*The Beach
at Trouville*,
1870.
Oil on canvas;
38 × 46 cm,
15 × 18¹₈ in.
National
Gallery,
London

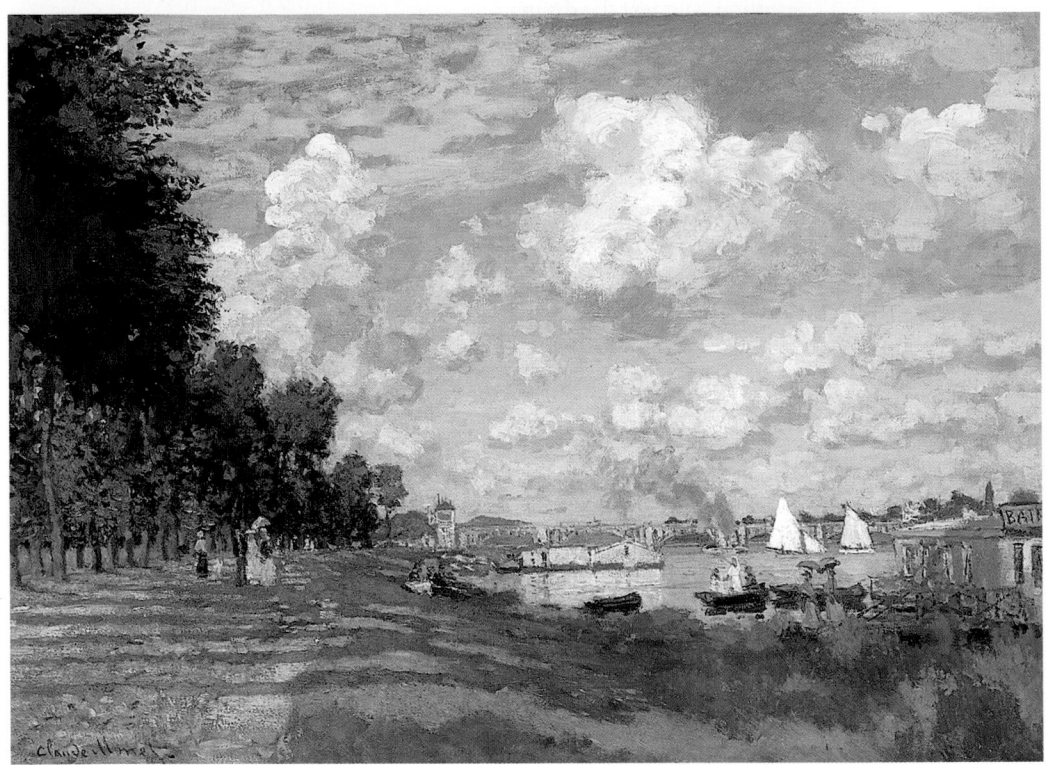

rowing. The prosperity of the village was based both on the tourism associated with pleasure boating and on industrial establishments, including a tannery, a distillery and an iron forge, which used the river for transportation and for the expulsion of waste. In a painting made shortly after Monet's arrival, *The Basin at Argenteuil* (62), one sees people strolling or sitting along the riverbank with some ladies in a rowing-boat near the shore framed by two boat sheds. Further out, against the road bridge leading to Paris, a steam-driven barge shares the waterway with two sailing boats. As in Monet's paintings at Trouville, the outdoors is a setting for socializing. In *The Hôtel des Roches-Noires* (see 60), a man in the group to the left doffs his hat to two ladies. In *The Basin at Argenteuil*, there are groups of three, probably couples with an older female chaperone. Paris customs have been transferred to leisure spots. The light coloured dress for both men and women, often greys on whites, connote the informality of country holidays. Darker colours were reserved for more staid occasions in the city, at night, in winter or for business.

62
Claude Monet,
*The Basin
at Argenteuil*,
1872.
Oil on canvas;
60 × 80·5 cm,
23⁵⁸ × 31⁵⁸ in.
Musée d'Orsay,
Paris

In the many paintings Monet executed during these highly productive years, no single motif is more ubiquitous than the sailing boat, which symbolized Argenteuil's appeal to the middle classes. Yet despite his frequent depictions of boats, the compositional and technical variety of Monet's work is such that it rarely appears repetitive. Monet himself experienced life on the water directly from his studio boat (63), which he launched in 1873, following the example of his older friend, Daubigny. Usually appearing utterly intuitive, but just as often highly planned, Monet's pictorial strategies are as changing as reflections on the water. His paintings of sailing boats, done within the relatively confined area between the basin and the bridges, precisely because of these limitations, often reveal a greater sense of framing and structural play between foreground and background than do pictures of poppy fields and promenades. Where Monet had more space to roam and greater choice, he seems to have painted with more conventional, less self-concious, structures.

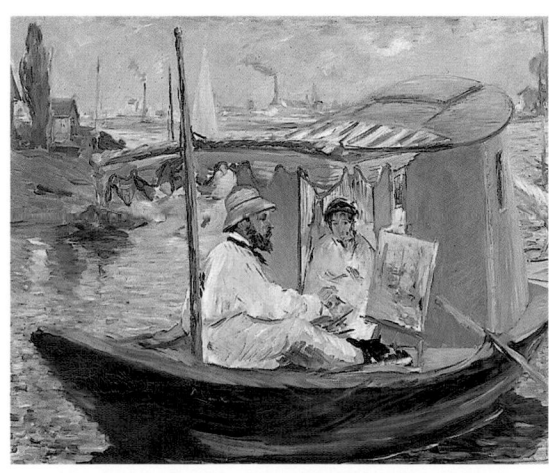

63
Édouard Manet,
Claude Monet in the Studio Boat,
1874.
Oil on canvas;
81·3 99·7 cm,
32 39¼ in.
Neue
Pinakothek,
Munich

The brushstrokes of *Regatta at Argenteuil* (64) are broad and separate in areas conveying calm waters or broad sheets of sail; the painting's bold, contrasting colours are appropriate for bright sunlight. In comparison, the brushstrokes of a second version of *The Basin at Argenteuil* (65) are short and closely spaced, combining with the deep blue water and the steel-blue sky to suggest the sweltering heat of a summer's day. The range of greens, dominated by pale yellow-greens with occasional darker tones in the foreground, suggest the drying effect of intense sunlight on high summer grass. In each of these pictures, brushstrokes change direction, length and width with the forms they represent. In this version of *The Basin at Argenteuil*, the sails are treated in a manner akin to *Regatta at Argenteuil*, even though the rest of the painting is entirely different. In *The Bridge at Argenteuil* (66), the boats are held together in a taut geometry created by their parallel masts, overlapping rope stays and halyards, and are framed by the road bridge to the right. Similarly, another 1874 view of *The Bridge over the Seine at Argenteuil* (67), this time face on, frames a complex arrangement of at least eight boats within the wooden-beam construction of the bridge.

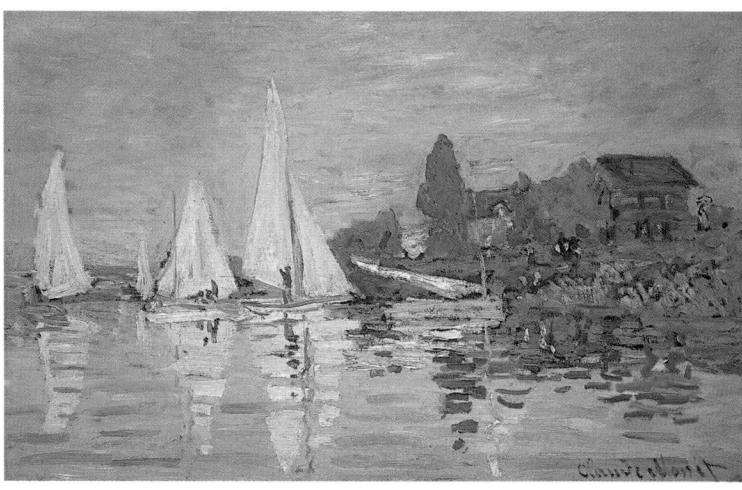

64
Claude Monet,
Regatta at Argenteuil,
1872.
Oil on canvas;
48 × 75 cm,
18⁷⁸ × 29¹² in.
Musée d'Orsay,
Paris

65
Claude Monet,
The Basin at Argenteuil,
c.1874.
Oil on canvas;
54 × 74¹⁴ cm,
21¹⁴ × 29¹⁴ in.
Rhode Island School of Design,
Providence

Comparing Monet's handling of reflections in some of these pictures is highly instructive. In *The Bridge over the Seine at Argenteuil* in Munich, it is the canvas ground preparation showing through, with thin, semi-transparent applications of black, that stands for the reflection of the bridge pier to the right, extending its framing function to the bottom of the canvas. In *Regatta at Argenteuil*, the reflection of a mast, house and tree to the centre-right are indicated in fragmented strokes of red and green, tied together with a large vertical squiggle of yellow-white, all drifting on top of the grey-beige ground colour of *peinture claire*. The reflection of the guardian's house in *The Bridge at Argenteuil*, which supplies the vertical visual frame closest to the boats, is

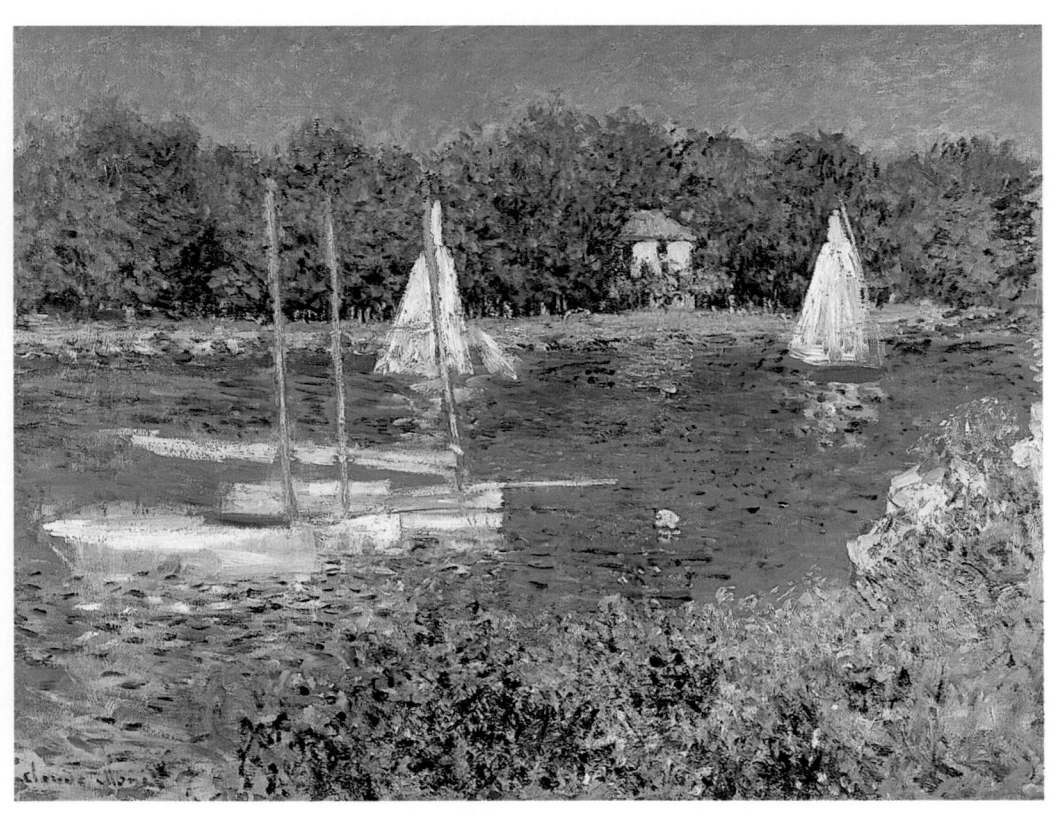

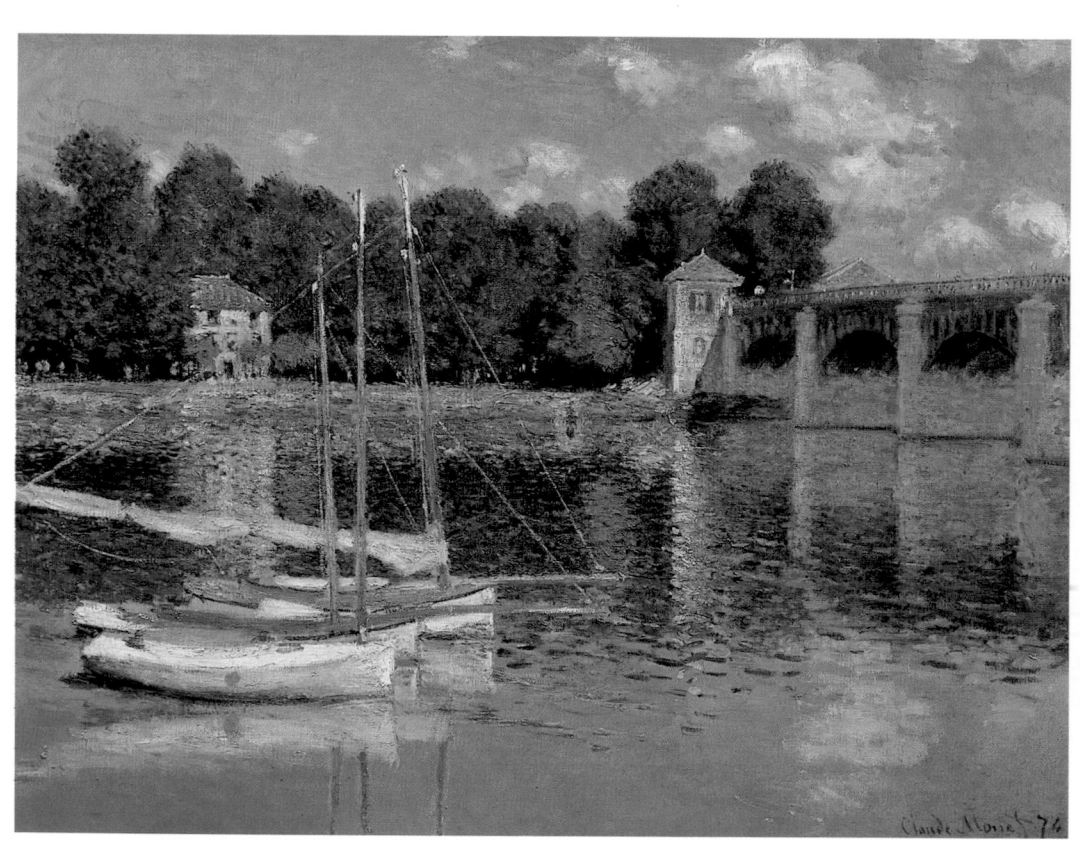

perhaps the most thickly painted passage in the picture, despite having no mass or weight in reality, since it is nothing but reflected light. In each case, Monet's techniques concentrate on purely visual phenomena to create a fascinating interplay between presence and absence – an interplay that calls attention to representation and illusion. While asserting the *plein-air* origins of his works through specifics of light, clouds and water, he simultaneously displays strategies with which he records sensations and produces them as visual spectacle. Surely the pleasures to be derived from his artistry are no less than those we experience vicariously through that art – the pleasures of a sun-filled Argenteuil day.

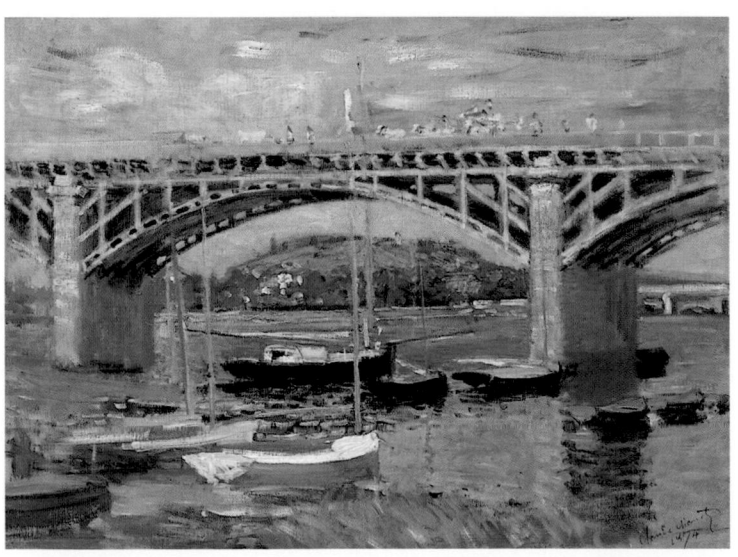

66
Claude Monet,
The Bridge at Argenteuil,
1874.
Oil on canvas;
60 × 80 cm,
23⅝ × 31½ in.
Musée d'Orsay,
Paris

67
Claude Monet,
The Bridge over the Seine at Argenteuil,
1874.
58 × 80 cm,
22⅞ × 31½ in.
Neue
Pinakothek,
Munich

During the early and mid-1870s, then, Monet was certainly the leader of Impressionist *plein-air* painting, which was centred in the suburbs along the Seine. Sisley had worked at Argenteuil in 1872 and continued to work at nearby Bougival, Louveciennes and Marly (except for a visit to Hampton Court near London in 1874). Pissarro and Cézanne were farther out at Pontoise. Occasionally, Monet was joined in Argenteuil by Renoir, who came over from nearby Chatou, and Manet, who had a country house across the river at Gennevilliers. Manet's carefully constructed compositions of *Argenteuil* and *Boating* (see 36 and 44), were obviously studio pieces that concentrate primarily on figures and on issues associated with them, though he also did less formal works, such as the picture of Monet in his studio boat (see 63), as did Renoir. Sisley's suburban images (see 92) were stylistically dependent on Monet, but they are usually less focused on leisure and have the softer echoes of Corot.

Indeed, if one were to extrapolate some concept of nature from *plein-air* painting of these years, it would have to be tied to the flux and flow of water and weather at places like Argenteuil. Monet's predilection for liquids and the effects of light and atmosphere,

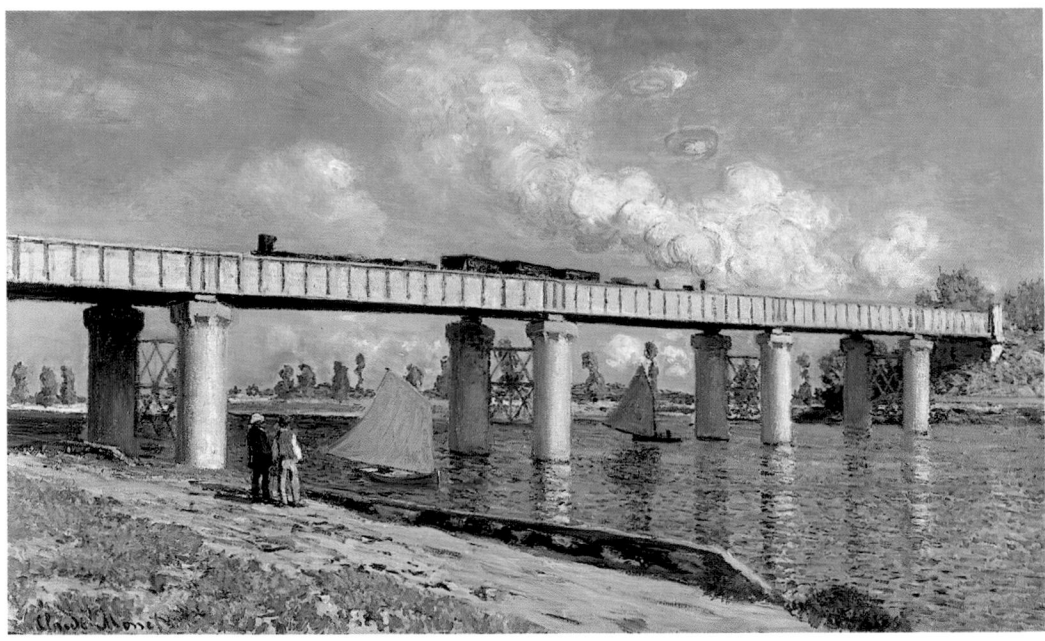

rather than for the solid forms predominant in classical art, embody a philosophy of nature as ever-changing surface rather than inner law, or perhaps the law of duration has given way to that of change. In his quite unscientific manner, Monet thus shares the Positivism of his times – a faith in the empirical data of immediate observation. This faith coincides with the assumption his paintings also express that the pleasure of the moment is the ideal goal of life. Indeed, the continuing presence of figures in his Argenteuil landscapes (though often diminished in scale from the 1860s), to say nothing of his frequent representations of his family in their garden, or the presence of objects such as sailing boats that directly allude to human pleasures, distinguishes Monet from *plein-air* peers such as Pissarro and Sisley. Their plainer images of a less fashionable life bespeak a greater sense of solitude and, in the case of Pissarro, reflect his radical anarchist views, highlighting by comparison Monet's upwardly mobile commitment to the leisure ethos.

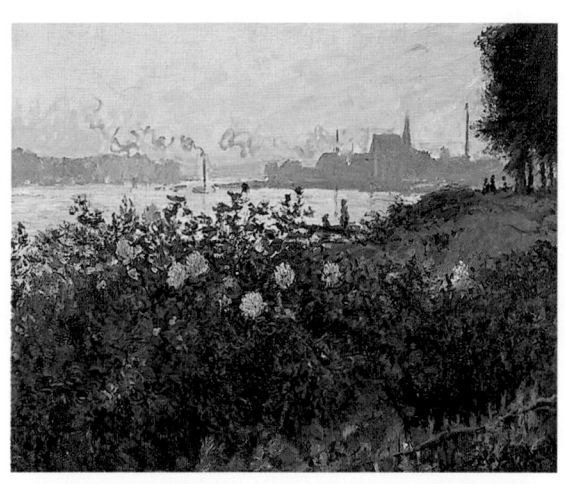

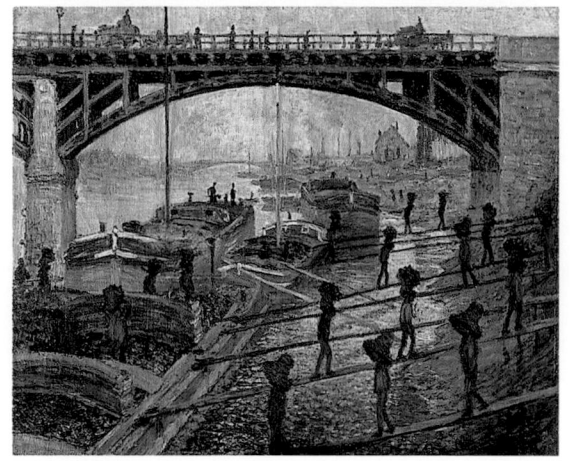

68 Opposite
Claude Monet,
The Railway Bridge at Argenteuil,
1873.
Oil on canvas;
60 × 99 cm,
23⁵⁄8 × 39 in.
Private collection

69 Above right
Claude Monet,
Argenteuil, the Bank in Flower,
1877.
Oil on canvas;
54 × 65 cm,
21¹⁄4 × 25⁵⁄8 in.
Private collection

70 Below right
Claude Monet,
Men Unloading Coal,
1875.
Oil on canvas;
55 × 66 cm,
21⁵⁄8 × 26 in.
Musée d'Orsay, Paris

However, in a seminal study of Monet's productivity at Argenteuil, Paul Tucker has suggested that the painter gradually, almost unwittingly, discovered the coexistence in Argenteuil of leisure and industry – the two sides of the coin of modernity – and became increasingly uneasy. Although Monet continued to be known as a proponent of modernity, it seems he was less and less sympathetic to its presence in

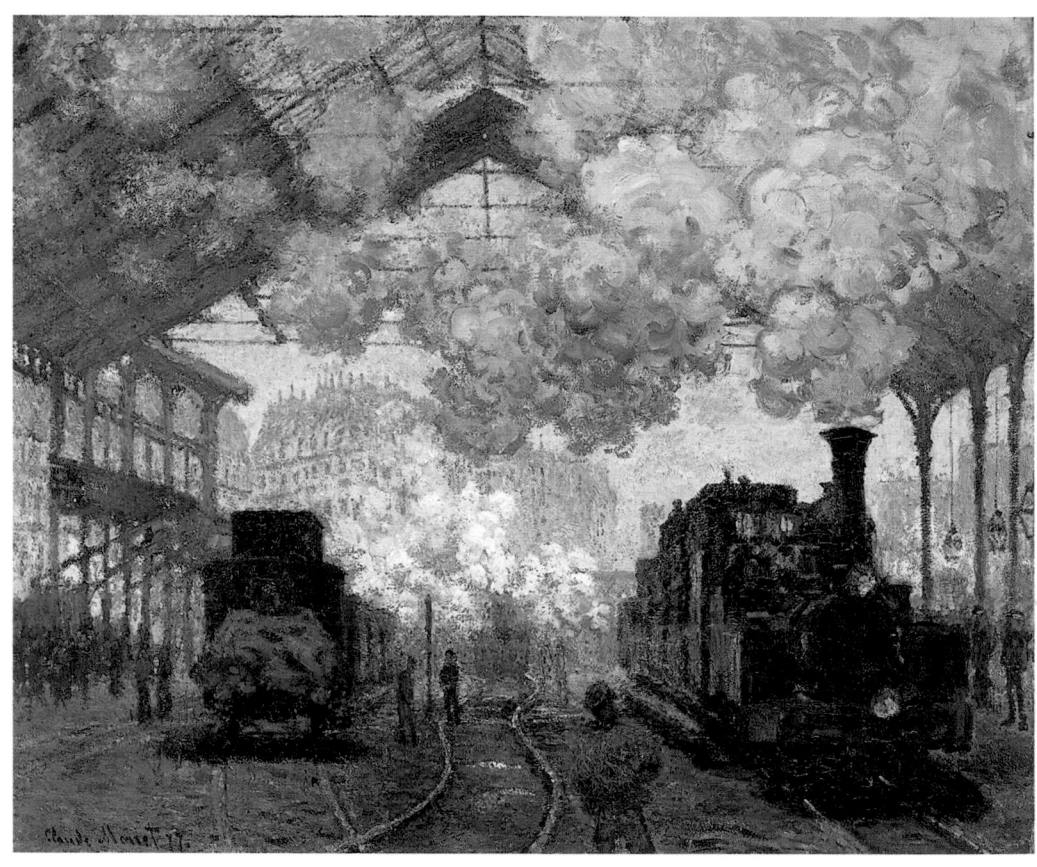

71
Claude Monet
The Gare Saint-
Lazare, Arrival of
a Train,
1877.
Oil on canvas;
80·3 × 98·1 cm,
31⁵⁸ × 38⁵⁸ in.
Fogg Art
Museum, Harvard
University Art
Museums,
Cambridge,
Massachusetts

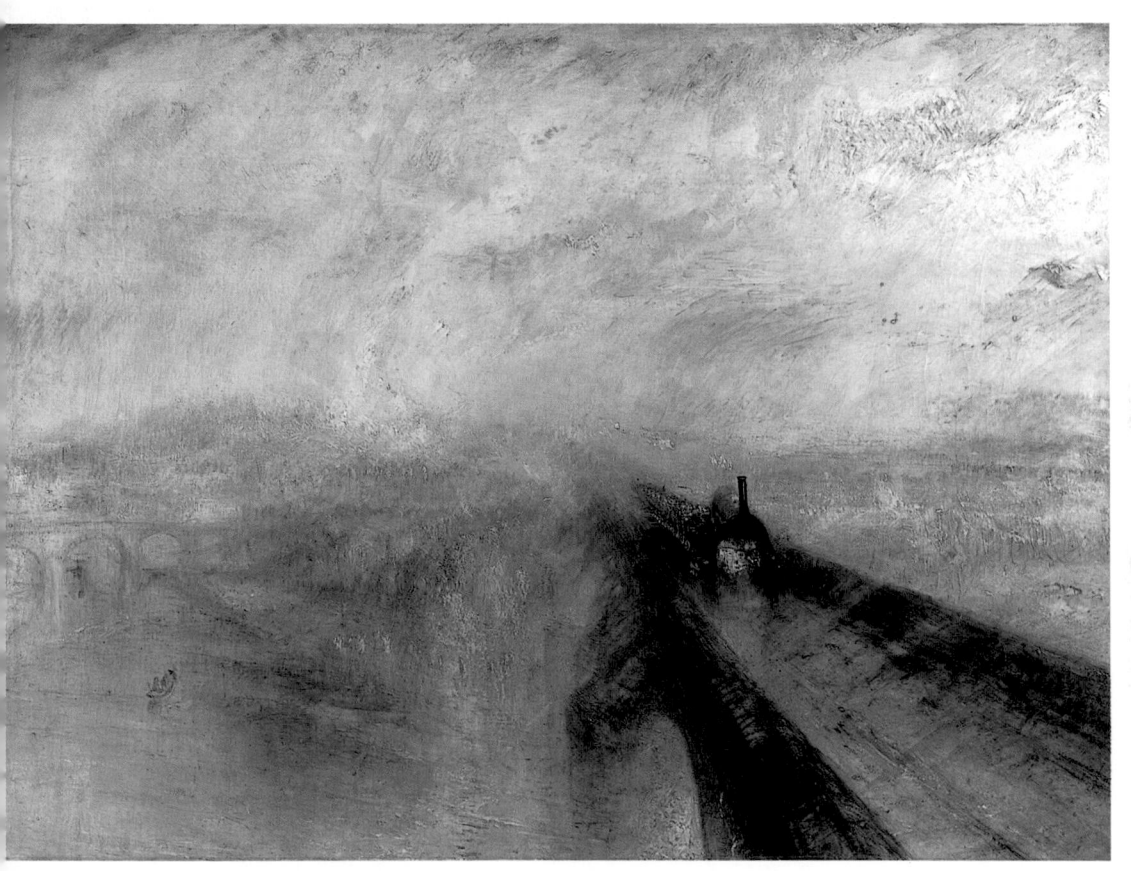

72
J M W Turner,
Rain, Steam and
Speed: The Great
Western Railway,
1844.
Oil on canvas;
90·8 × 121·9 cm,
35³⁄₄ × 48 in.
Tate Gallery,
London

his own back yard. In the early 1870s we sense a certain pride in the clean horizontal gleam and bold cylindrical piers of the sturdily rebuilt (after wartime destruction) railway bridge at Argenteuil (68). Yet by the later 1870s, Monet put at a distance the factories and smokestacks he had placed matter-of-factly in earlier paintings, and he consistently travelled away from Argenteuil for scenes celebrating labour or modern industry. In most paintings of the area after 1875, such features simply disappeared, or, as in his *Argenteuil, the Bank in Flower* of 1877 (69), a high, thickly painted wall of dahlias and peonies, through its very pictorial vigour, separates the viewer physically and psychologically from the river path, at the end of which a new factory has been erected. Smokestacks and a steam barge are subsumed in atmospheric effects along with a villa and its dependencies. Already in 1875, Monet had done a marvellously evocative and rhythmic scene of men unloading coal, but that was at the inner ring suburb of Clichy (70). Restless by nature, Monet spent much of the second half of 1876 at Montgeron on the estate of a new patron, department store owner Ernest Hoschedé (whose wife, Alice, Monet would later marry), painting large decorative panels (see 219) for the château dining room. Then in January of 1877, Monet set up a studio in Paris, rented for him by Gustave Caillebotte, to paint twelve views of the interior and railway yards of the nearby Saint-Lazare station (71).

Monet knew the Saint-Lazare station well, for not only was it located near where he had also previously lived in Paris, but he (and 13 million other passengers annually, equal to forty per cent of all Parisian rail traffic) passed through it to take the train to Argenteuil, as well as to Le Havre. Its gabled glass and cast-iron structure, designed by the engineer Eugène Flachat, opened the station to sunlight and air, fulfilling the most advanced ambitions of contemporary architects. The critic and novelist Théophile Gautier hailed such unusual constructions as 'new cathedrals of humanity', while Courbet and Flaubert saw railways offering challenging opportunities to the arts. The station had drawn other painters to work nearby, such as Manet and Caillebotte, to whose efforts Monet may well have been responding. Yet by comparison to what the art historian Robert Herbert has called the 'ruthless urban geometry' of Gustave Caillebotte's view of the bridge directly behind the station, *Le Pont de l'Europe* (see 171), Monet's steam-filled pictures celebrate light and vapours that make the station's architecture and the massive block of buildings in the background seem to float in defiance of gravity. The critic Georges Rivière's laudatory review of the eight Gare Saint-Lazare paintings Monet showed at the third Impressionist exhibition of 1877 described the locomotives as 'monsters' and the railway workers as 'pygmies'. His hyperbole responded no doubt to the sense of theatre that Monet's stage-like compositions created. Another writer thought he heard the 'din' and 'clamour' of the station, concluding that Monet had created 'a pictorial symphony'. Indeed, with their patterns of criss-crossing beams and cables, signal stanchions, pillar posts, suspended lamps and tracks, overlaid with a lattice-work of light and shadow, Monet's views dramatize vision itself as the spectacle produced by uniting modern industrial forces with modern artistic techniques. In this regard, Monet was preceded by a famous work by the visionary British painter Joseph Mallord William Turner (1775–1851). Turner's *Rain, Steam and Speed: The Great Western Railway* (72), painted in 1844, was said to be based on the painter's experience of holding his head outside the window of a speeding train for several minutes. A close look suggests those impressions were not altogether pleasant, as the sinister, squat, coal-black, fire-brimming machine barrels over a trestle-bridge, terrifying a fleeing hare. Monet's vision, by contrast, is celebratory.

However firm any artist's commitment to *plein-air* naturalism, his or her consciousness will always modify nature (assumed for this argument to be external to consciousness) as it is transformed into art. Even *plein-air* painting is a dialogue between nature and self, as Castagnary and others recognized. It is therefore important to define what patterns underlie Monet's particular consciousness. One feature we certainly find in this artist is the distancing effect of rendering the world as visual spectacle. In the Saint-Lazare paintings, we are given variations on a theme, so that contrasts between viewpoints, framings, dominant colour tonalities and placement of figures and machines flaunt the artistry derived from their industrial subject matter, which thus becomes aestheticized. In his review, Rivière had stressed how 'despite the aridity of the subject', Monet had displayed one of his 'master qualities', namely the 'knowledge of arranging and distributing elements'. The same is true for *Men Unloading Coal* (see 70), where the counterpoint of Monet's placement of the workers, perhaps responding to Degas, compares to choreography (see Chapter 5).

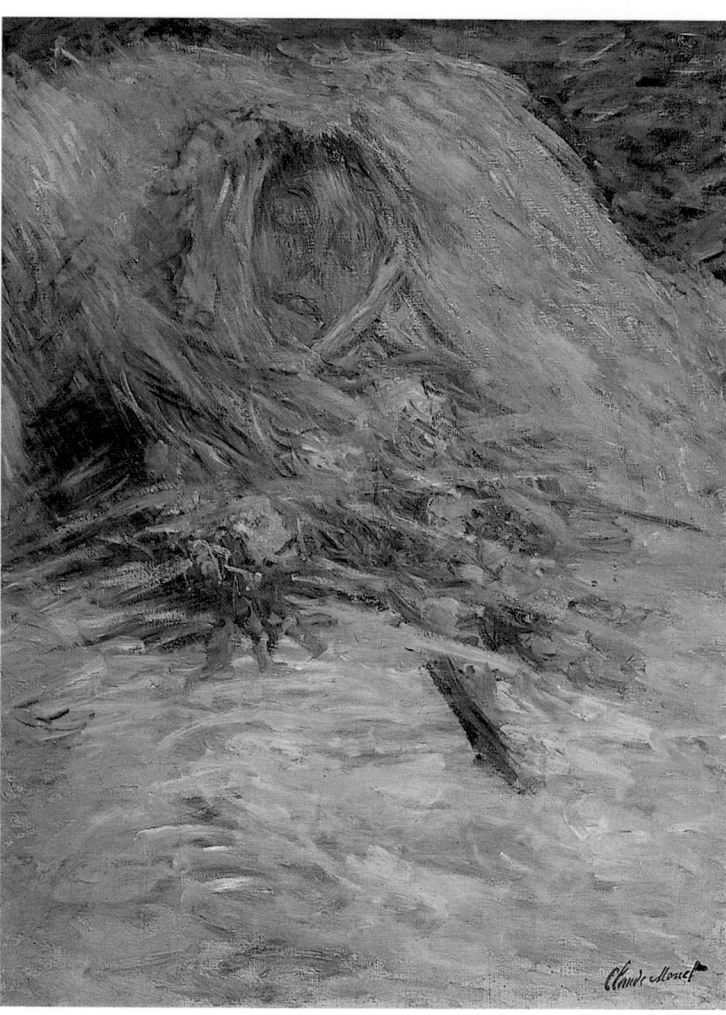

73
Claude Monet,
*Camille on
her Deathbed*,
1879.
Oil on canvas;
90 × 68 cm,
35^{1}2 × 26^{3}4 in.
Musée d'Orsay,
Paris

Attention to pictorial values explains the variety within Monet's Argenteuil pictures, too. The ability to visualize from many different angles, to organize the same elements repeatedly into arrangements that hold our interest, as if one were composing still lifes, and to amaze the viewer with signs of rapidity and summarization is what sustains both artist and viewer when returning to a motif. It is a manifestation also of a selective vision – one that made it possible for Monet to respond creatively to violations of his suburban idyll, until, finally, the breaking point was reached. For in spite of his quite natural practice of various pictorial artifices, Monet's commitment to *plein-air* painting was strong enough that when the spirit of Argenteuil had been exhausted he had no choice but to move on.

Vétheuil was 45 km (28 miles) farther down the Seine from Argenteuil, near Mantes and half-way to Rouen, all served by the same train line so that Monet did not give up access to Paris or Normandy. It was in fact much closer to Giverny, where he would eventually purchase property, than to Argenteuil or Paris. Although Vétheuil had the calm and isolation Monet thought he needed, particularly with a second child (Michel, born in 1878) and the now ailing Camille, it was a plain place that ultimately provided him with only modest visual stimulation. Though by 1880 Monet had for nearly fifteen years stood for the concept of *plein-air* painting it was in Vétheuil that he began most consciously to formulate his practice as a theory or ideology. Knowing his tendency to dissatisfaction, we should not be surprised that he became self-critical and in need of reaffirmation, but certain events of the 1880s, both personal and artistic, encouraged a more self-conscious attitude, as well. In 1879, Camille died a painful death from what is thought to have been uterine cancer at the age of thirty-two. Monet's account of the deathbed picture he made (73) is a famous description of his method:

I caught myself watching her tragic forehead, almost mechanically observing the sequence of changing colours which death was imposing on her rigid face. Blue, yellow, grey, and so on. This is the point I had reached. Certainly it was natural to wish to record the last image of a woman who was departing forever. But even before the idea had occurred to me to record those features to which I was so deeply attached, my organism was already reacting to the sensation of colour, and my reflexes compelled me to take an unconscious operation in spite of myself, one which was the daily course of my life – just like an animal turning his mill.

Stated to Monet's friend the politician Georges Clemenceau some forty years later, this description needs to be understood in context. In all likelihood, it transformed into artistic concerns an emotional ambivalence Monet had towards Camille, whom he had felt honour-bound to marry after her first pregnancy. Had he already begun a relationship with Alice Hoschedé in the late 1870s? After the debacle of Ernest Hoschedé's bankruptcy in 1877, Monet invited the Hoschedés, including their six children and three servants, to join him and the bedridden Camille in establishing the household at Vétheuil. Shortly after Camille's death, Ernest Hoschedé left Vétheuil, while Alice continued to live with Monet and all the children. (After Ernest died in 1891, Monet and Alice were married.) Yet Monet's account of his pictorial process nonetheless seems in perfect conformity with his paintings, despite ulterior motives it may have served.

Dating his artistic self-consciousness to this period corresponds to other facts, as well. For example, having abstained from the Salon for ten years, Monet decided to submit two large landscapes for 1880, showing ice floes on the Seine during the terrible winter. Only one painting was accepted, yet Monet was disqualified from the Impressionist exhibition of that year. Some accused him of betrayal; perhaps he was also saving work for his first solo exhibition, to be held at Paul Durand-Ruel's gallery. In an interview for the June issue of *La Vie moderne* (owned by publisher and Impressionist patron Georges Charpentier, in whose offices Monet exhibited), the artist made his feelings public. Declaring 'I am and I always will be an Impressionist,' he went on to assert a proprietorial claim on the label, since 'I'm the one who coined the word, or at least, through a painting I had exhibited.' But, he continued, 'I see my companions-in-arms, men and women, only rarely. Today the small band has become a banal school, opening its doors to the first dauber who comes along.' It so happens that the Impressionist exhibition of 1880 was dominated by Caillebotte, Degas, Pissarro and many friends of Degas's, most of whose work had little to do with the suburban *plein-air* painting Monet and Renoir (the latter, along with Sisley, having dropped out two years before) had been practising. For his part, Monet proclaimed, 'I have never had a studio, and I do not understand shutting oneself away in a room.' However exaggerated his claim – for we know he sometimes finished works indoors – it is an aggressive reaffirmation of his *plein-air* principles.

It was at this point that Monet began travelling a great deal, primarily to the Normandy coast, but also to the South of France. Through the diversity of scenery he visited, Monet acted out ever more ostentatiously the role of *plein-air* painter he had made his trademark. Just as he was drawn to the unusual ice formations on the Seine, he sought scenes out of the ordinary through tourism. No longer content with landscapes of suburbia, which would seem plain by comparison, he either discovered beauty in isolated parts of France where he was invited by friends, or he followed well-worn paths to dramatic sights along the coasts. One cannot overestimate the volume of tourist literature in mid-nineteenth-century France. Books such as *Voyage d'un Parisien* (1865) by Jules Claretie and *Les Environs de Paris illustrés* (1878) by Adolphe Joanne guided the middle classes through a countryside newly accessible by train. It is from this period that the mass exodus from cities during summer months dates. Indeed, for the ordinary traveller, tourism perfectly embodied the new freedom made possible by technological advances. In a newspaper of 1860, one writer exclaimed: 'Travelling is to live; it is to feel disengaged from all social restraint and prejudice.' What could be more enlightened? Normandy in particular drew Monet's attention, for the territory was familiar enough to him, and was extremely popular among Parisians. And from Vétheuil, then from Giverny, where he moved in 1883 and would thenceforth stay, the Channel coast was not far. The names of many of the places he painted – most of all Étretat, but also Pourville and Varengeville, near Dieppe, and Bordighera and Antibes on the Mediterranean – are probably as famous now because of his paintings as they were in his time as tourist destinations.

Robert Herbert has shown how Monet's choices of motif and vantage point conform closely to those of contemporary sightseers who were following the guidebooks, using paths or even steps carved into rock in order to attain the best views. So, despite the increasing absence or diminished size of figures in most works after 1880, Monet's vision of the landscape was still socially constructed rather than naïve. Though

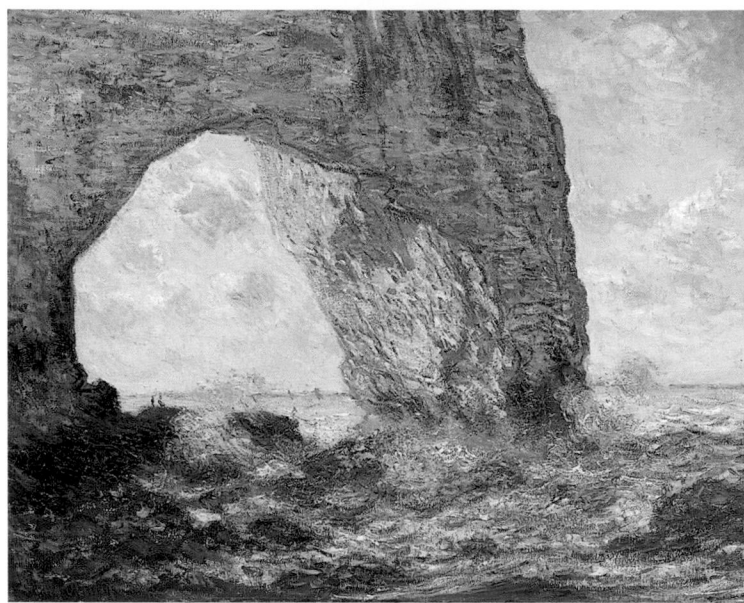

74
Claude Monet,
The Manneporte
(Étretat),
1883.
Oil on canvas;
65·4 × 81·3 cm,
25³⁄4 × 32 in.
Metropolitan
Museum of Art,
New York

75
Dieudonné
Auguste
Lancelot,
The Porte d'Aval
and the Needle
of Étretat.
Engraving by
August Trichon
from Eugène
Chapus's *De*
Paris au Havre,
Paris,
1855

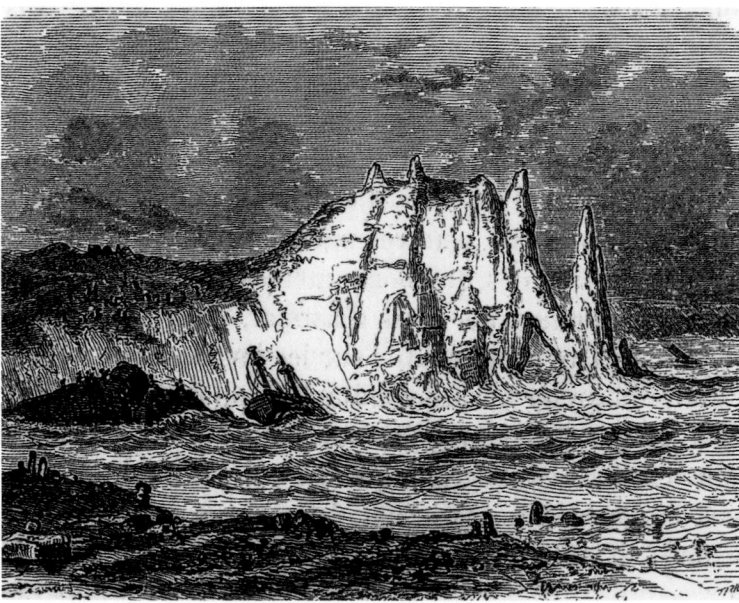

painting out-of-doors, with all the commitment to truth and freedom that implied, Monet acted within pre-existing perceptions, which his extraordinary images reaffirm and legitimize. Even effects of solitude before the grandeur of the cliffs at Étretat, for example, correspond to a romantic search for pure and direct experiences of nature pursued by urban dwellers with the time and means. There are tiny figures below the archway in the picture (74) of The Manneporte (Étretat), witnesses to the bright sunlight on eroded limestone and to the crashing waves – forces of nature that carved out the great gap in the ponderous hulk. Yet their experiences are vicarious: they are temporary visitors who always concentrate on unusual formations, desirable because they were 'picturesque'. That word, which means 'worthy of being made into a picture', originated in eighteenth-century Romanticism and indicates how nature could be removed from context and rendered as fragments judged by their value as visual spectacle.

Monet's pictures now generally focus on the motif to the exclusion of topographical surroundings or nearby villages. These developments were accompanied by his increasingly conspicuous practice of outdoor painting, in which he directly engaged with nature from spectacular vantage points, sometimes taking risks and battling against the elements. (He said the tide nearly drowned him when he was trying to paint the Manneporte.) Indeed, Monet's commitment to the outdoors became a sign of authenticity at the same time as his assumptions about what motifs made significant pictures (and good sales, an issue that will be discussed in Chapter 9) led him to rely less on everyday surroundings and personal discoveries than on places that were consecrated by tourist routes and had well-established artistic associations. Étretat was just such a place, with its famous cliffs that had lured Delacroix, Courbet and others, and were reproduced in illustrated travel literature (75) that predated Monet's stays, sometimes by as much as half a century.

Yet Monet certainly believed himself a more authentic observer than the tourists, whose company he shunned by choosing small hotels or renting a villa for his family, as he did near Pourville in the summer of 1882. It was there that he began developing increasingly bold techniques in order to convey both the intensity of nature's impression and the immediacy of his responses. *Cliff Walk at Pourville* of 1882 (76) is an excellent example of how Monet could pose as the isolated spectator of a dramatic scene, yet include indications of leisure such as sailing boats in the distance and the two women, probably Alice Hoschedé and one of her daughters. The composition is balanced between near and far, mass and void; it is animated by asymmetry and punctuated by figures – the same contrapuntal strategy which is key to the stability

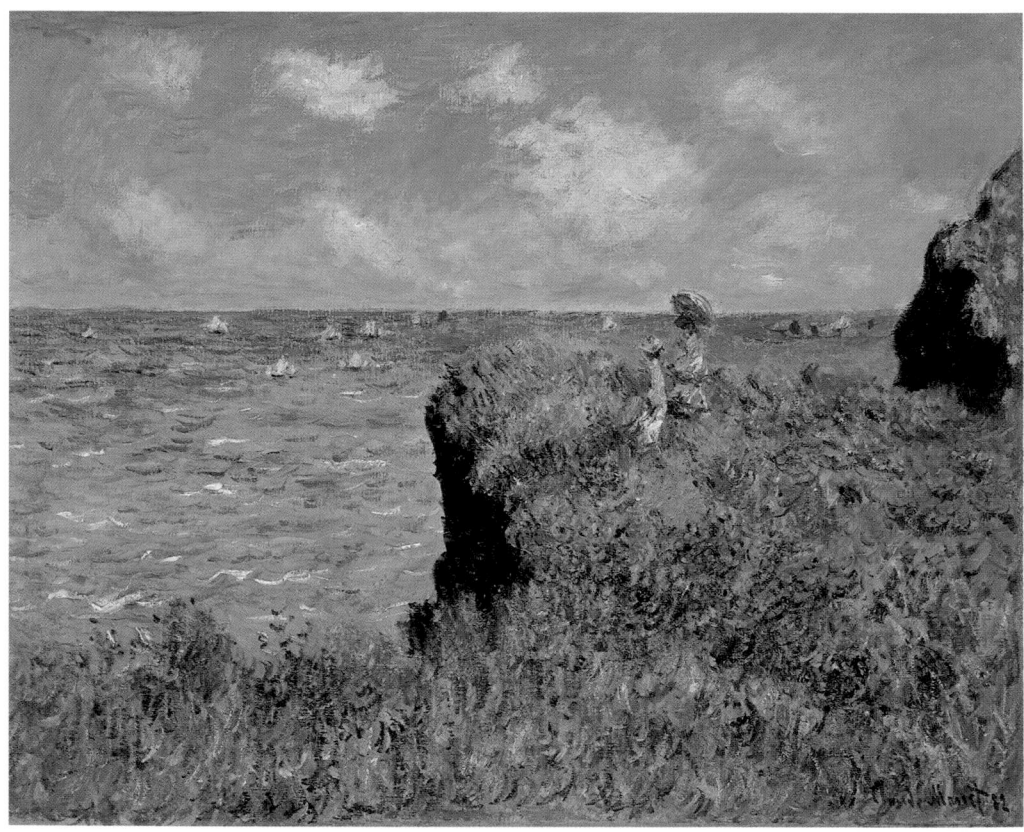

and natural harmony we feel in so many of his compositions. However, Robert Herbert, probably the keenest observer of Monet's methods, shows that even Monet's techniques for representing the interaction of light and form that presumably correspond to the artist's direct inner experiences reveal a certain formula. Monet began by lightly dragging a relatively dry brush across the canvas so that the more protruding vertical threads pick up the paint. Then, over that initial coat, he used a mixture of hues, sometimes contrasting (as the reds), sometimes closely related (as the greens), often with slightly curved or comma-like strokes. In the painting of the Manneporte, he used horizontal strokes that refer conceptually to the striations of its layers but which correspond more to the ineffable play of shadow over it than to the gritty texture of the stony surface. The paintings could take an average of ten or twelve sessions, and he might work on more than a single painting in a day. Lacking reference to specific and singular objects, his energetic and free-form technique suggests the visual excitation that are signs of direct experience –

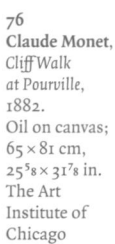
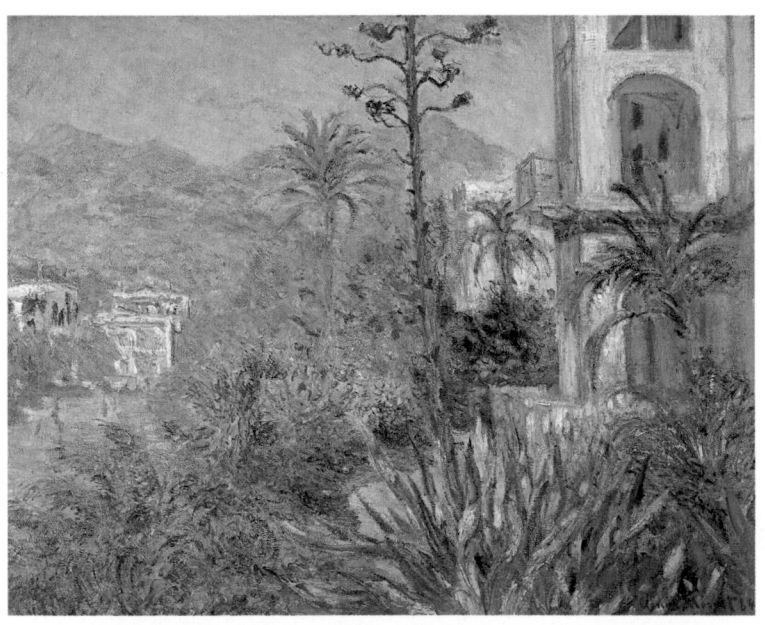

76
Claude Monet,
*Cliff Walk
at Pourville,*
1882.
Oil on canvas;
65 × 81 cm,
25⁵⁸ × 31⁷⁸ in.
The Art
Institute of
Chicago

77
Claude Monet,
*Villas at
Bordighera,*
1884.
Oil on canvas;
73 × 92 cm,
28³⁴ × 36¹⁴ in.
Santa Barbara
Museum of Art

evidence all the more necessary as the counterbalance to his dependency for themes and viewpoints on the conventional picturesque.

Other trips to places farther afield testify to a quest for originality. Even though the principles underlying that quest were no different from those of adventurous travellers seeking places away from the crowds, at least the relative remoteness of places such as Belle-Île in Brittany or Bordighera on the Italian Riviera gave his paintings the stamp of novelty. American and British travellers had begun holidaying in warm southern climates, and some fashionable homes were being built, such as one he included in *Villas at Bordighera* (77), which the architect of the Opéra, Charles Garnier, had designed for a wealthy Parisian. Monet's remarks on encountering the strange vegetation and brilliant Mediterranean skies show that, for him, the area held significant new challenges. He complained about the densely tangled foliage, for, as he said, he was 'a man for isolated trees and broad spaces'. In other words, Monet began by seeking ways to fit what he saw into familiar patterns, but his respect for nature and commitment to working from observation prevented him from simply inventing compositions that would satisfy that urge. The 'confused mass of foliage' was 'extremely difficult to render', that is, he was struggling to develop formulas for his new experiences. Thus, his art is shaped both by the commitment to respond directly to what he sees and the desire to render its effects coherently. For certain works, he adopted Renoir's high-keyed palette, which sometimes verged on pastel tones. In the lower left of *Villas at Bordighera*, however, one senses his scrambled sensory overload.

With *Storm, Coast of Belle-Île* (78), Monet was also on distant, if northern terrain. Here, the quest for renewal led to experiments with ever freer brushwork, stimulated no doubt by the sight of bizarre rock formations lashed by storm-driven waves. As art historian Steven Z Levine has proposed, these effects coincided with Monet's increasingly 'narcissistic' reflection of an inner, poetic self, encouraged by contemporary poets and critics from the burgeoning Symbolist literary movement, who favoured subjective expression over the naturalism expounded by Zola (see Chapter 8). Again, Monet was a follower, since Gustave Flaubert's travel writings, containing an account of walks on the Belle-Île cliffs, had been published in the very year of Monet's trip, and the artist owned a copy of the book. In addition, two literary critics, Gustave Geffroy, who would become Monet's biographer, and Octave Mirbeau, a close friend who also wrote about him, were in residence nearby. In Normandy, Monet had begun to paint in all kinds of weather, but at Belle-Île he became especially conscious of persisting in the face of nature's apparent fury. Geffroy described him dressed like a fisherman, 'booted, covered with woollens, enveloped by an "oilskin" with a hood' and setting off to battle.

78
Claude Monet,
Storm, Coast of Belle-Île,
1886.
Oil on canvas;
65 × 18 cm,
25⅝ × 31⅞ in.
Musée d'Orsay,
Paris

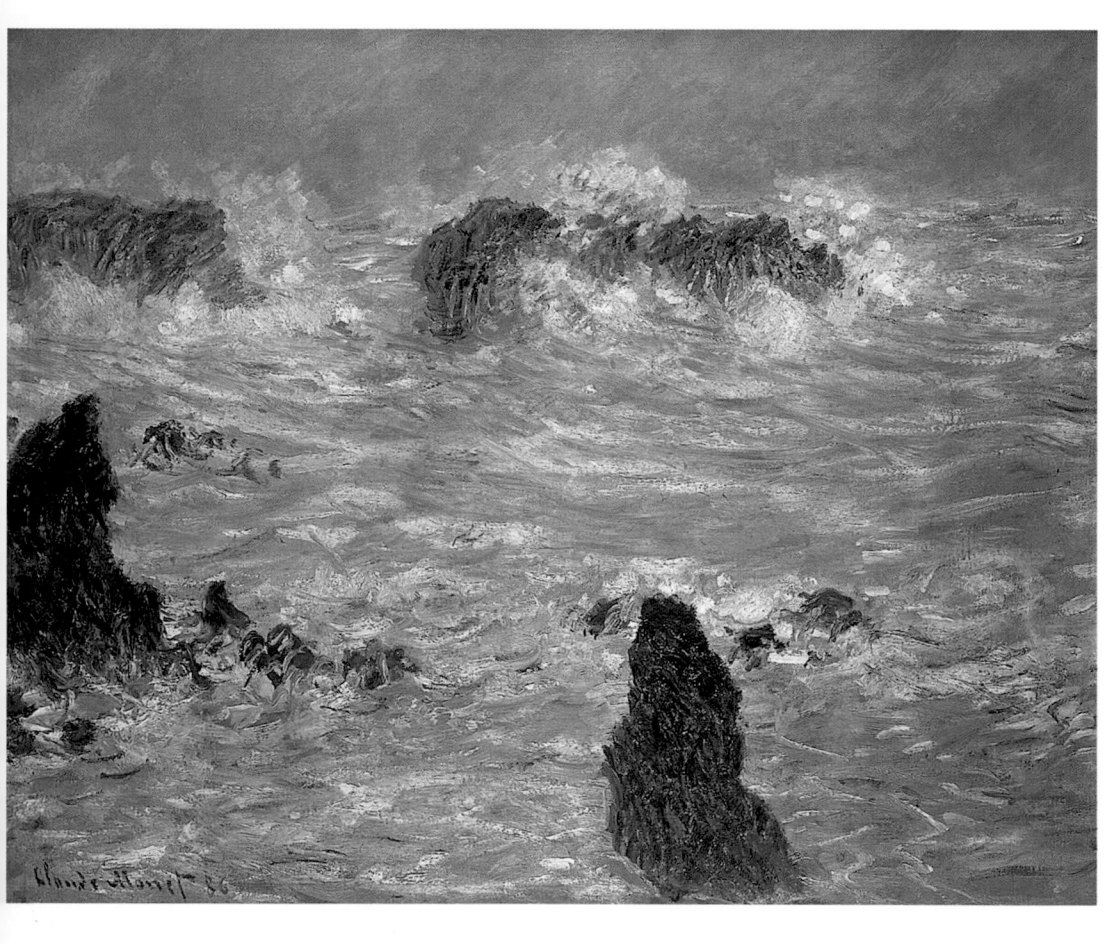

Now the performance of the artist's commitment to nature became almost more important than the resulting representation. Monet's letters to Alice Hoschedé, who impatiently awaited his return to Giverny, tell of the passion and frustration he experienced in sudden squalls, unexpected views and, especially, the endless guises of the sea. His accounts describe it as 'savage', 'diabolical', 'terrifying', 'unbelievable' and 'fantastic', while revealing his unmistakable pride as the modern-day successor to a heroic tradition of sea painters, including Turner.

This attitude illuminates Monet's willingness to paint feverishly to express his feelings, even at the expense of finish and specificity. Indeed, he lamented that he had ruined many canvases and that he would have to contemplate them in the calm of his studio once he returned to Giverny. Here, then, is more evidence that Monet's direct response to the original outdoor stimulus was not the end-point of his art. What is more, of the forty-odd canvases he made during this campaign, many, sometimes up to half a dozen, repeated the same motif, almost as if he had been making multiples. In this process lies the origins of his series paintings (see Chapter 9). Subtle differences between renderings of the same composition became the theme of his exhibition when he showed eight Belle-Île pictures at the Galerie Georges Petit in 1887. With nature now emerging as the vehicle for expressing personal sensitivity – that is, with the personal now eclipsing literal accuracy and the pretence to objectivity – Monet's art was verging towards the efforts of Neo-Impressionism (see Chapter 8) and Cézanne (see Chapter 10). As such, he relaxed his compulsive search for unusual sights. He could use motifs more accessible to the Giverny estate he purchased in 1890, such as poplar trees along the nearby Epte River, grainstacks made by local farmers or, eventually, the lily pond and gardens he would lovingly cultivate until his death in 1926 (see chapters 7, 9 and 11).

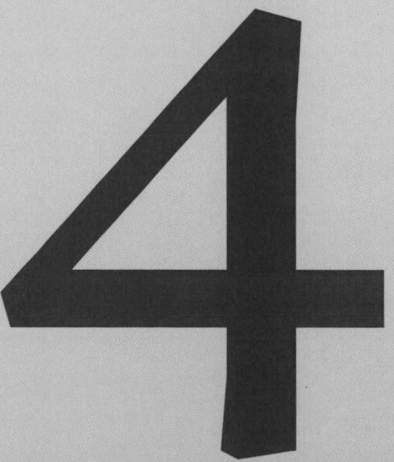

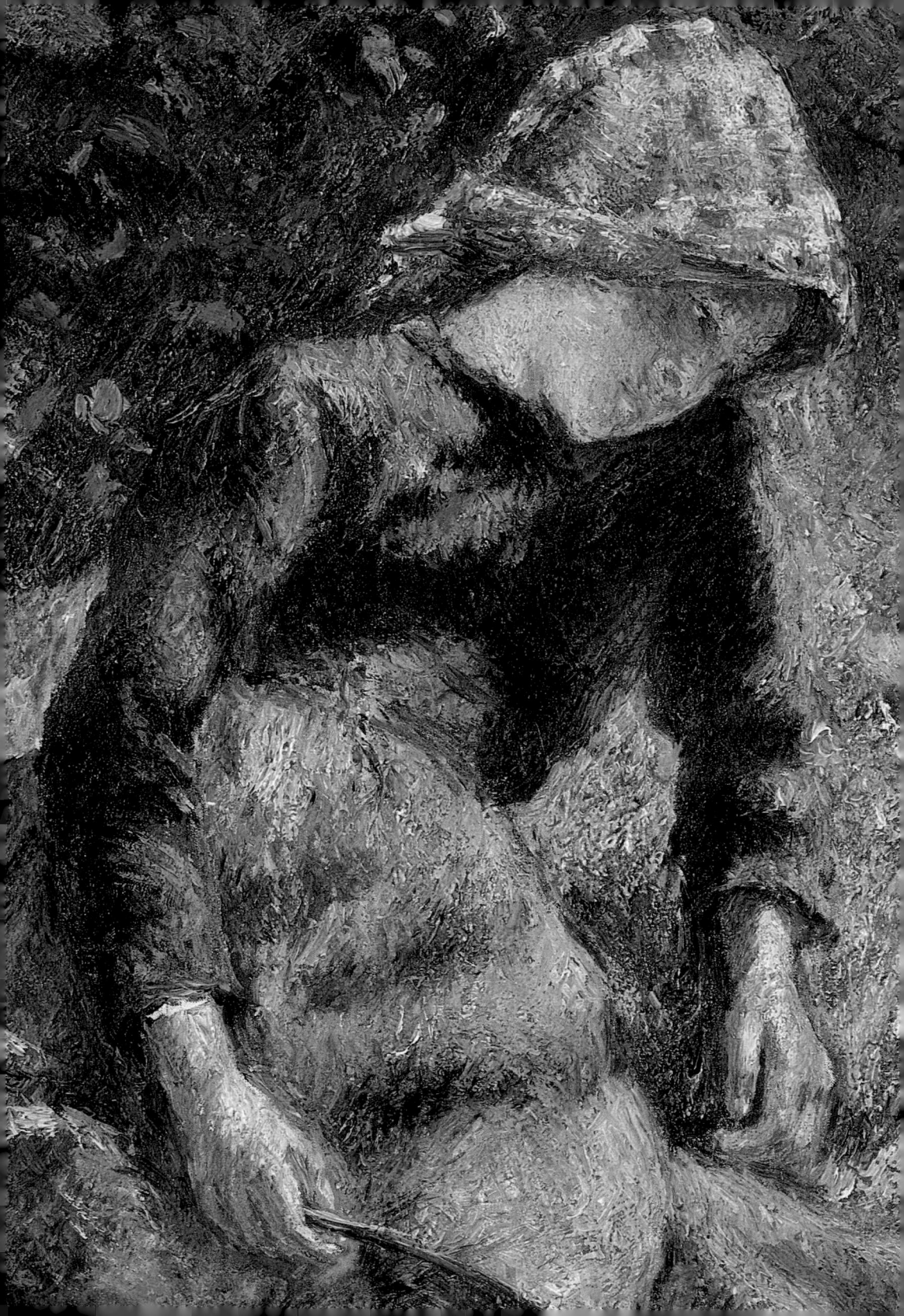

79
Camille
Pissarro,
*Peasant Girl
with Stick*
(detail of 97)

Impressionism produced visions of places and people that tell us much about the artists and their world. Yet even in the most realistic paintings, artists choose their scenes and shape their representations according to many different assumptions and desires. This chapter brings together three Impressionists who are not usually associated – Bazille, Pissarro and Renoir. Behind the diversity they represent, there is an important link. All three produced a synthesis of the modern idiom we find in Manet and Monet with more past art elements. Of course, no artist can abandon the past entirely, and Manet's engagement with it was self-conscious. In the work of Bazille, Pissarro and Renoir, these traditional elements were a means to integration and self-fashioning for artists who felt less empowered than their leaders. Each was in his special way marginal – an outsider. None was originally from Paris. Bazille was the scion of a prominent southern family and his intimate friendships with his comrades have fuelled claims that he was homosexual. (In the nineteenth century, homosexuality was still regarded as so deviant it was almost universally repressed.) Renoir was just the opposite – working class and lustfully pursuing female companionship as much as income. Yet Renoir often shared Bazille's studio (see Chapter 1) and at times their aims overlapped, as in their brief exploration of Oriental themes. The Jewish Pissarro was brought up in the Caribbean by merchants who were outcasts in their community. He fitted no clear category save that of an outsider, yet because he was older and a strong family man, he became an example to other Impressionists and their most faithful collaborator. His attraction to the traditional countryside was informed by his acceptance of modern change.

Although Frédéric Bazille was killed in 1870 during the Franco-Prussian War, for which he patriotically enrolled, he deserves to be counted as a central figure among the Impressionists during their formative years, when he had important friendships with Manet,

Monet, Morisot, Renoir and Sisley, and his studio was a gathering place. Émile Zola's 1868 review that had hailed Monet's *Women in the Garden* (see 56) as a new form of outdoor figural art, also drew attention to Bazille's *Family Reunion* (80). When Berthe Morisot saw Bazille's stunning *View of the Village* at the Salon of 1869, she commented on his success in 'what we have so often attempted, to place a figure in the open air'. This appeared to be a unifying goal of the group.

Family Reunion portrayed Bazille's extended family on their country estate, named Méric. He descended from the old Protestant bourgeoisie of Montpellier, near France's southern coast, but he had been raised in a progressive environment exceptional for that conservative milieu. Although he went to Paris to study medicine, his interest in painting was encouraged by his Parisian cousins, the Lejosnes, who were friends of Manet and Baudelaire and introduced him to advanced art. Much like Monet, however, Bazille's career did not have the full approval of his parents. Combining group portraiture with *plein-air* painting can be viewed as his negotiation between the two poles of family and friends, producing a modernized version of a traditional world. Bazille placed his self-portrait at the extreme left edge (behind his father), echoing Manet's position as both participant in and observer of the scene in *Music in the Tuileries Gardens* (see 27). That reference to a painting, in which he and his cousins had appeared, expressed his own work's legitimacy to his parents and his modern outlook to his friends. The scale was nearly as grand as Monet's *Women in the Garden* (see 56), and, painted just after Monet's *Terrace at Sainte-Adresse* (see 57), it may have served similar purposes – expressing the serious ambitions of Salon-scale art while displaying respectable social origins to a Parisian audience to whom he was unknown. Yet the painting's brilliant colour has a richness and intensity exceeding even Monet's at that time. Rather, it looks to Courbet's colouristically prophetic *Bonjour, Monsieur Courbet* or *The Meeting* (81), which was owned by the Bazille family's banker neighbour, the famous Courbet patron, Alfred Bruyas. Bazille would have known Courbet as they were both friends of Monet in the 1860s and had posed for Monet's *Luncheon on the Grass* (see 52, 53). Bazille's tighter

80
Frédéric Bazille, *Family Reunion*, 1867.
Oil on canvas; 152 × 230 cm, 59³⁄₄ × 90¹⁄₂ in.
Musée d'Orsay, Paris

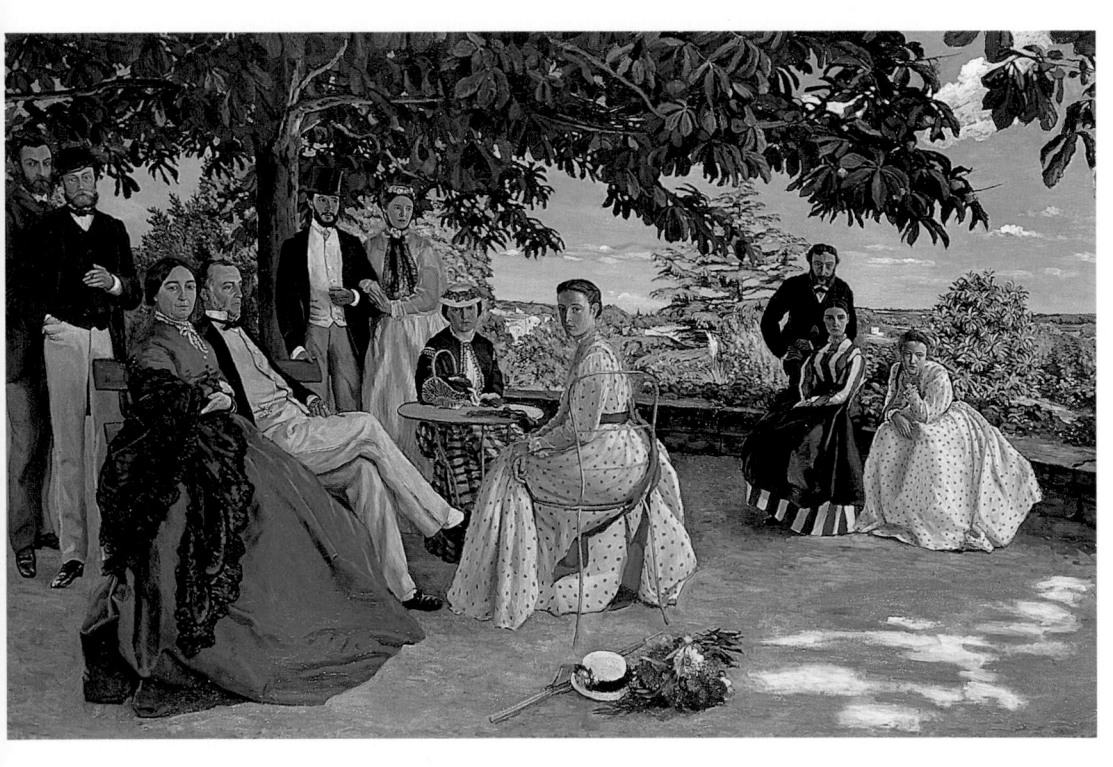

draftsmanship and higher degree of finish than Monet's correspond to both the more conservative expectations of his milieu and the more overtly descriptive demands placed on portraiture. However, his feeling for the physical bulk of forms is closer to Courbet than to the flattening effects found in Manet and Monet. Here was a bright and robust Impressionist-Realism of the south.

Yet Bazille's large works from the end of the decade are symptomatic of the difficulties of reconciling figure painting with *plein-air* practice, for the traditions underlying the two modes were in many ways opposed. Conflicts that would later emerge between Impressionist painters themselves were foreshadowed in his *Summer Scene (Bathers)*, which was accepted to the Salon of 1870. The painting (82) is surely a personal fantasy, with its group of young male swimmers dressed in

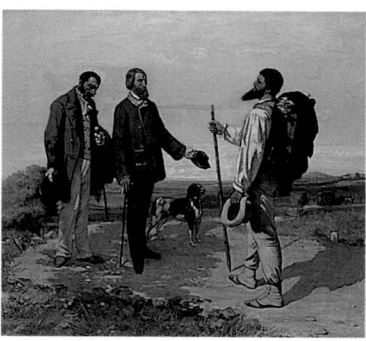

modern swimsuits, alluding to nudity without depicting it. One of them, who strongly resembles Bazille himself, helps another from the water. Bazille's strong homosocial impulse (male bonding without necessarily including sexual relations) is evident from his correspondence with Monet, with whom he at times shared his first studio and whom he helped financially.

Summer Scene sets male camaraderie in a utopian realm (in contrast to his painting of his studio; see 9). It was a vehicle through which Bazille wrestled with the problems Morisot described as a group concern. Despite all its freshness and the clarity of a true *plein-air* work, the painting self-consciously casts its bathers into historicizing poses, reminiscent of the work of the group's conservative teacher,

81
Gustave
Courbet,
*The Meeting
or Bonjour,
Monsieur Courbet,*
1854.
Oil on canvas;
129 × 149 cm,
50³⁄₄ × 58⁵⁄₈ in.
Musée Fabre,
Montpellier

82
Frédéric Bazille,
*Summer Scene
(Bathers),*
1869.
Oil on canvas;
160 × 160·6 cm,
63 × 63¹⁄₄ in.
Fogg Art
Museum,
Harvard
University Art
Museums,
Cambridge,
Massachusetts

Gleyre, or even Corot in his more classical moments. Bazille had done drawings in his Paris studio from models, which he later transferred to canvas when he went south for the summer. The outdoor setting was executed along the banks of the River Lez, adjacent to Méric. His family might have recognized that the reclining figure paraphrased

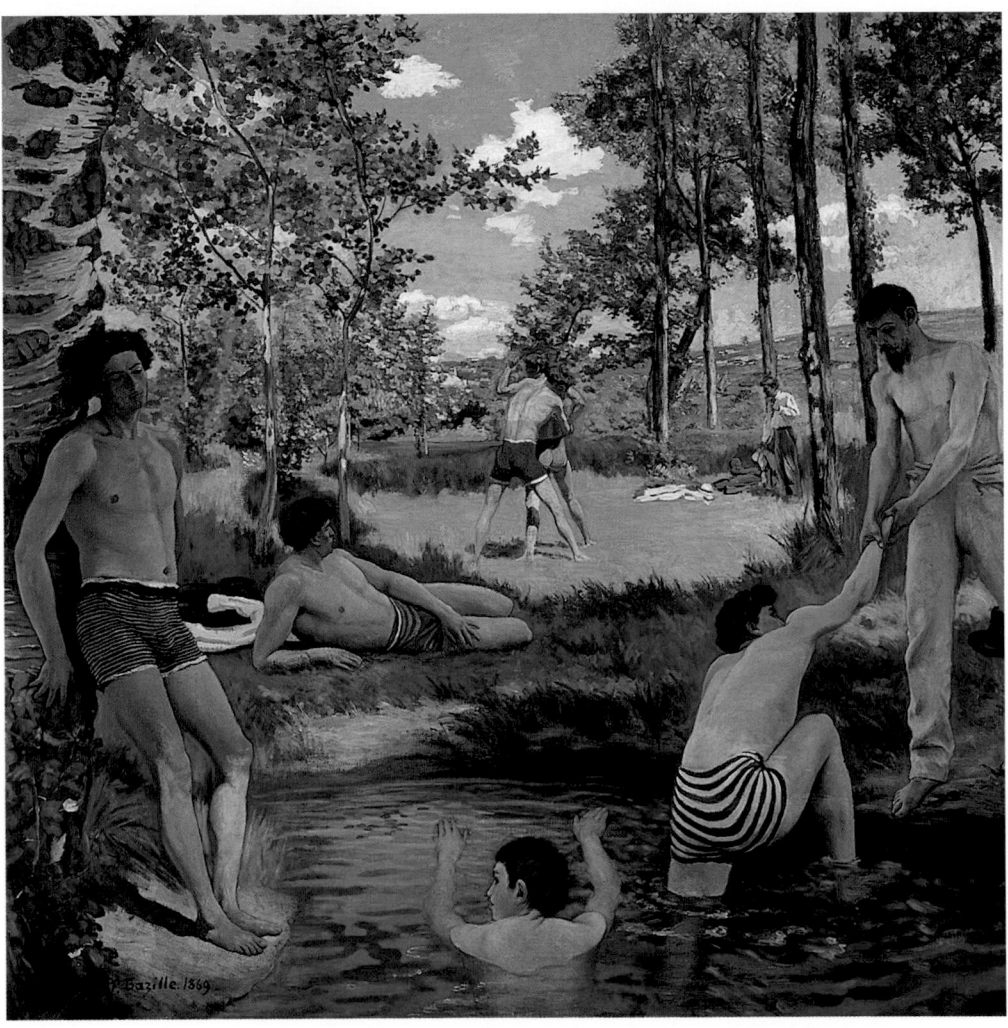

one by the seventeenth-century painter Laurent de la Hyre (1605–56) exhibited in their local museum; the bather leaning against the tree resembles a Saint Sebastian. But both also echo in reverse Monet's *Luncheon on the Grass* (see 52, 53). A close look at Bazille's surface reveals inconsistencies between the smooth handling of his figures and the freer landscape. Furthermore, Bazille's lack of spatial clarity is not a wilful emulation of Japanese geometries, as in Monet's *Terrace at Sainte-Adresse* (see 57), but a discontinuity produced by conflicting loyalties and procedures. Still, it is not entirely fair to judge Bazille on criteria derived from later Impressionism. Bazille's *Summer Scene* also echoes Manet's dialogue with tradition, though with the advantage of sunlight and brilliant colour, and minus the strangeness of Manet's heterosexual innuendo. Interweaving family and friendships through the interplay of styles and places, Bazille's paintings embody his struggle to find a space of personal security and artistic identity. The strength and intelligence of his effort, despite its lack of resolution, make his untimely death unfortunate for the history of art.

Older than most members of the group by ten years or so, Jacob Camille Pissarro is not included in either of Fantin-Latour's group portraits of their generation (see 7). Less of a leader in artistic matters than his companions, Pissarro was nonetheless regarded as reliable and solid, and during the 1870s he served as a mentor for some of his younger friends, especially Cézanne and Gauguin. He was staunchly progressive without being controversial and the group exhibitions offered a way to gain exposure while fulfilling his political ideal of mutual cooperation. Pissarro was a French Jew of Portuguese Sephardic origin, born on St Thomas in the then Danish (now US) Virgin Islands, where his family had set up business. He trained with the late Rococo Danish genre/landscapist Fritz Melbye (1826–96), with whom he travelled to Venezuela, before coming to Paris to study art in 1855. There he saw the work of Courbet and visited the eminent Corot, listing him as his teacher when he later showed at the Salon. Pissarro's landscape thus developed from a different, slightly earlier and more conservative tradition than Monet's. The latter's vision of nature was that of the urban holiday maker; for Pissarro, the countryside was both ideal and home. Pissarro the outsider was drawn to the enduring traditions of rural productivity; Pissarro the progressive accepted the inevitable transformations it brought about.

Corot's role in the history of Impressionism is widely recognized but not always fully understood. He was generous with younger painters who sought his tutelage, but devotion to their generation did not always extend to support when they submitted to the Salon. In the art-historical literature, Corot's undeniably progressive advocacy of *plein-air* study and his practice of *peinture claire* have overshadowed his profoundly conservative view of nature, which Impressionism was to reject. Until late in his career, Corot's *plein-air* studies were subordinate to large finished works in which landscapes were inhabited by classical or literary figures, with nature constructed as a timeless utopian realm. In *Souvenir of Mortefontaine* (83), landscape provides a serene alternative to the disharmonious and crowded urban spaces that defined everyday middle-class lives. In the tradition of the Swiss

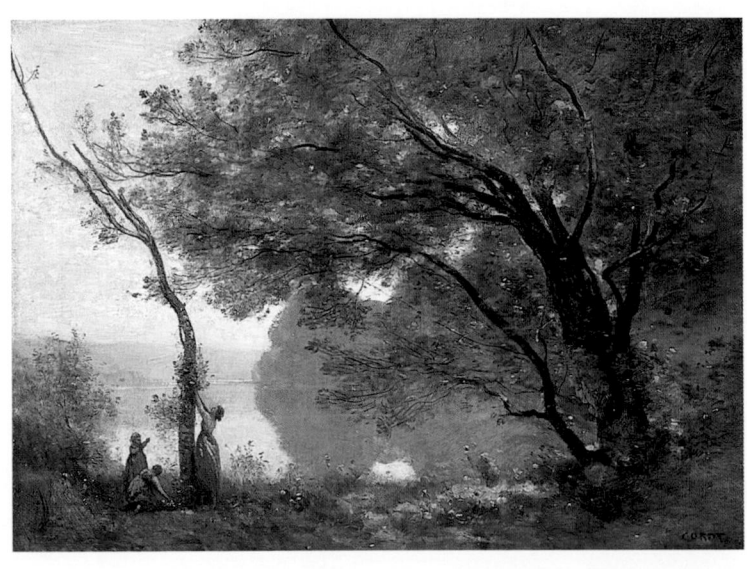

83
Jean-Baptiste-
Camille Corot,
*Souvenir of
Mortefontaine,*
1864.
Oil on canvas;
66 × 90·4 cm,
26 × 35⅝ in.
Musée du
Louvre,
Paris

philosopher Jean-Jacques Rousseau, Corot's world is an unspoiled realm of purity and virtue where one can experience freedom, if vicari-ously. This 'return to nature' proffered by Romantic landscape is thus a denial of the present and a search for lost innocence. Even when pictorial techniques give Corot's 'nature' convincing presence, their function is to make its ideal refuge seem materially available. Corot's delicately impastoed buds, blurred edges and supple branches mitigate feelings of specificity and substitute the sensuousness of paint for that of nature's physical forms so as to appeal to aesthetic connoisseurship. His silvery atmospherics provide a generalized sense of season, as compared to the temporal precision of Monet's *Terrace at Sainte-Adresse* (see 57). Not only Corot's sophisticated technique, then, but his reassuring vision lay behind his reputation as the foremost landscape painter of his time.

Pissarro had been studying at the Académie Suisse, where he met his future Impressionist colleagues. In keeping with a vision of the countryside based on Corot and the Barbizon School, he soon established his residency well beyond the Parisian suburbs. For most of the period

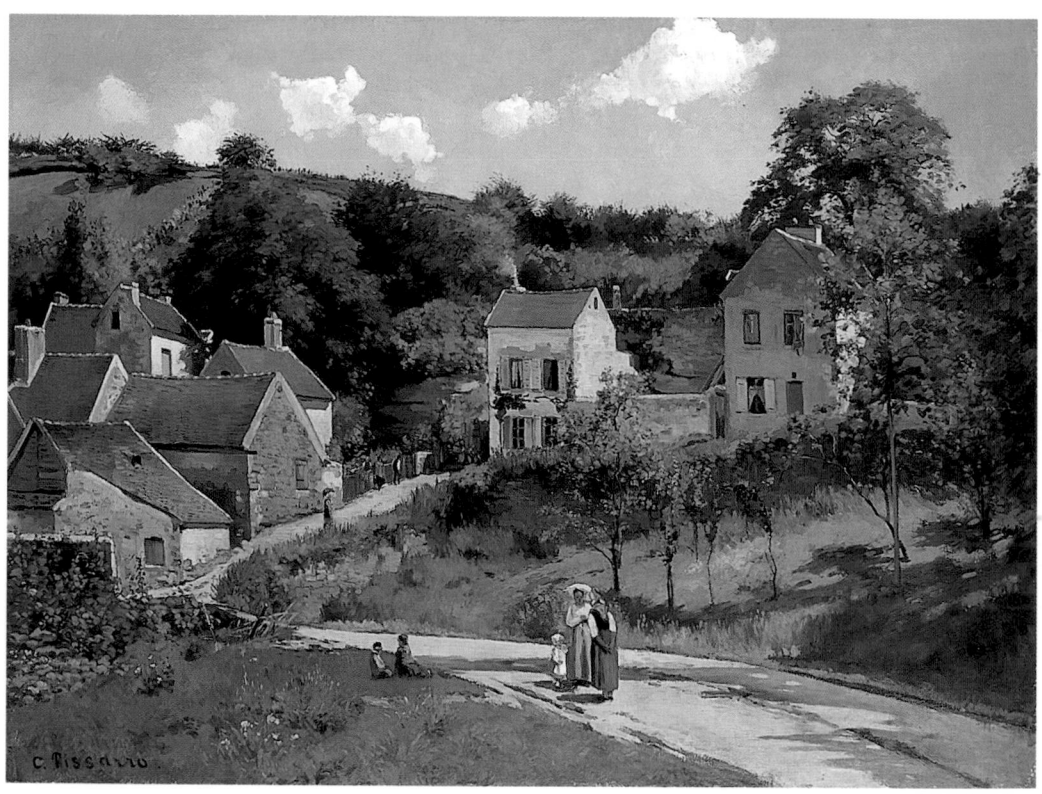

from the late 1860s until the early 1880s, he lived mainly in Pontoise, near where some other artists, including Daubigny, were established. Pontoise (meaning bridge on the River Oise) was a modest but ancient market town along a tributary of the Seine that was being dredged to connect it to France's northern canal system. That put him about an hour and a half from Paris by train, more than three times as far as Argenteuil. Like the association between Argenteuil and Monet,

Pontoise is now intimately connected with Pissarro and the friends (sometimes called School of Pontoise) who frequently painted with him there – among them Cézanne, Guillaumin and, a few years later, Gauguin. In most important respects, however, Pontoise was very different from Argenteuil. A seminal study by Richard Bretell shows how the town was largely untouched by suburban growth; it remained primarily an agricultural community with just a few factories, the most important of which was built during Pissarro's residency.

Pissarro felt a strong sympathy for the rural working classes and adopted certain left-wing political attitudes associated with anarchism (see Chapter 7). His native St Thomas, which was once in the heart of a slave-trading region, had been a hotbed of radicalism on questions of race and emancipation. Additionally, Pissarro's parents had lengthy skirmishes with the St Thomas Synagogue over their unorthodox marriage (they were related as aunt and nephew), so they sent young Camille to a Moravian church school, where he was one of very few whites. His early drawings show mainly blacks and workers. Throughout his life he was uneasy with the bourgeoisie, although he referred to himself ironically as 'a bourgeois without a penny'. The in-between existence of the landscapist – an outsider to both the rural society he depicts and the urban society to which he sells – was an ideal choice for a painter who did not easily fit standard social categories. Pontoise, far enough from the city to maintain the simple life so many perceived as socially harmonious, was a place where such categories mattered less. (Not the least among his distinctions was to have belatedly married his mother's cook, a young Catholic named Julie Vellay, after the birth of two children and with a third on the way.) The subtle tension in Pissarro's work between a willingness to challenge convention and the desire for security and belonging mirrors aspects of his personal history and social circumstances.

For most of his time in Pontoise, Pissarro resided in a hilly hamlet called L'Hermitage, which was more rural and presumably less expensive than the centre of town. It became the subject of several large paintings, including works exhibited at the Salon. *L'Hermitage at Pontoise* (84) mixes simple villagers and more prosperous residents.

84
Camille Pissarro,
L'Hermitage at Pontoise,
c.1868.
Oil on canvas;
151·4 × 200·6 cm,
59⁵⁄₈ × 79 in.
Solomon R Guggenheim Museum,
New York

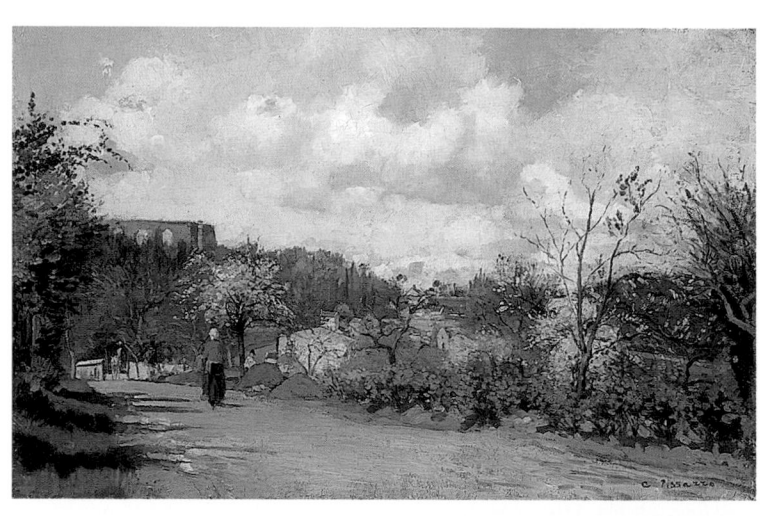

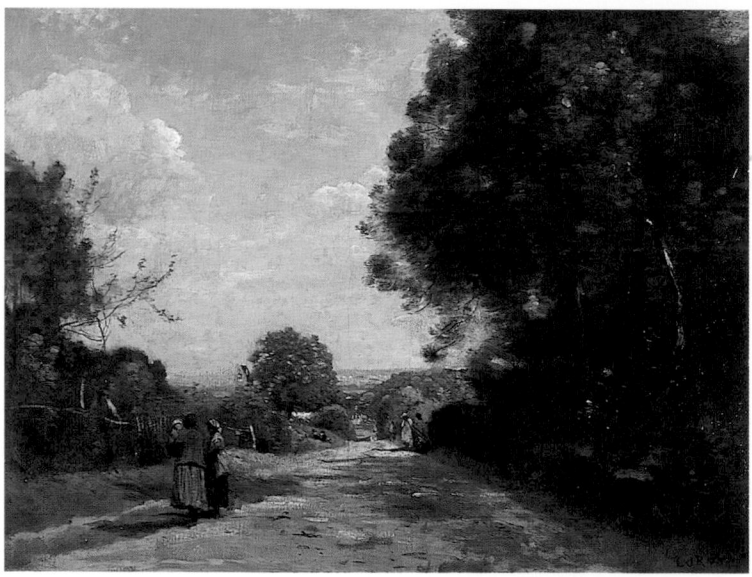

A well-dressed mother carrying a parasol is out walking with her daughter; both are dressed for the summer season. They converse with a village lady, perhaps the mother of the children seated near the edge of the road. Figures going to or from work are in the background. There is no sense either of discord or social segregation – or that such distinctions are significant, as they certainly would have been for an urban *flâneur*. The boldest indication of Pissarro's interest in modern developments is aesthetic: his sharp contrast between shadow and sunlight on the road recalls Monet's *Women in the Garden* (see 56) of the previous year. Zola labelled a similar picture 'the modern countryside', referring to the sense of workaday normality that defined Pissarro's vision. Compared to Monet's pictures of Argenteuil, there is no tension between the natural countryside and modernity, as might be evidenced by unpleasant sights or social hierarchies. With their high horizons, richly painted, geometrically circumscribed fields and solidly constructed houses, Pissarro's L'Hermitage landscapes combine the classical clarity of Corot's Italian studies with the new geometry and flattening of Monet – an ideal rendered palpable through the vocabulary of colouristic immediacy.

Until the 1880s, the large paintings of L'Hermitage with figures are as close as Pissarro came to the outdoor figure-painting problems tackled by Monet and Bazille. However, in 1869, Pissarro did move closer to the suburban painters and reflected their interests in modernity by relocating briefly to Louveciennes, near Bougival, where Renoir and Monet had been working together. From there, he was able to go to Paris to participate in the Thursday gatherings of the Batignolles group at the Café Guerbois. A picture of *c*.1868–9, *Road at Louveciennes* (85), clearly reveals the stylistic influence of Monet in its bright lighting, sharply delineated shadows and impastoed foliage. Yet it retains a certain loyalty to Pissarro's more pastoral vision evocative of Corot, to whom the painting owes a compositional debt. (Compare Corot's *The Sèvres Road*; 86.) For example, in the background Pissarro used the aqueduct of Marly, built to bring water to the château of Louis XIV (r.1643–1715), as an evocation of past grandeur; and his figure facing down the road continues a device used by Corot to domesticate his scenes while preserving a sense of privacy.

85
Camille
Pissarro,
*Road at
Louveciennes*,
c.1868–9.
Oil on canvas;
52·7 × 81·9 cm,
20⁵⁸ × 32¹⁴ in.
National
Gallery,
London

86
Jean-Baptiste-
Camille Corot,
The Sèvres Road,
1855–65.
Oil on canvas;
46·4 × 61·6 cm,
18¹⁴ × 24¹⁴ in.
Baltimore
Museum of Art

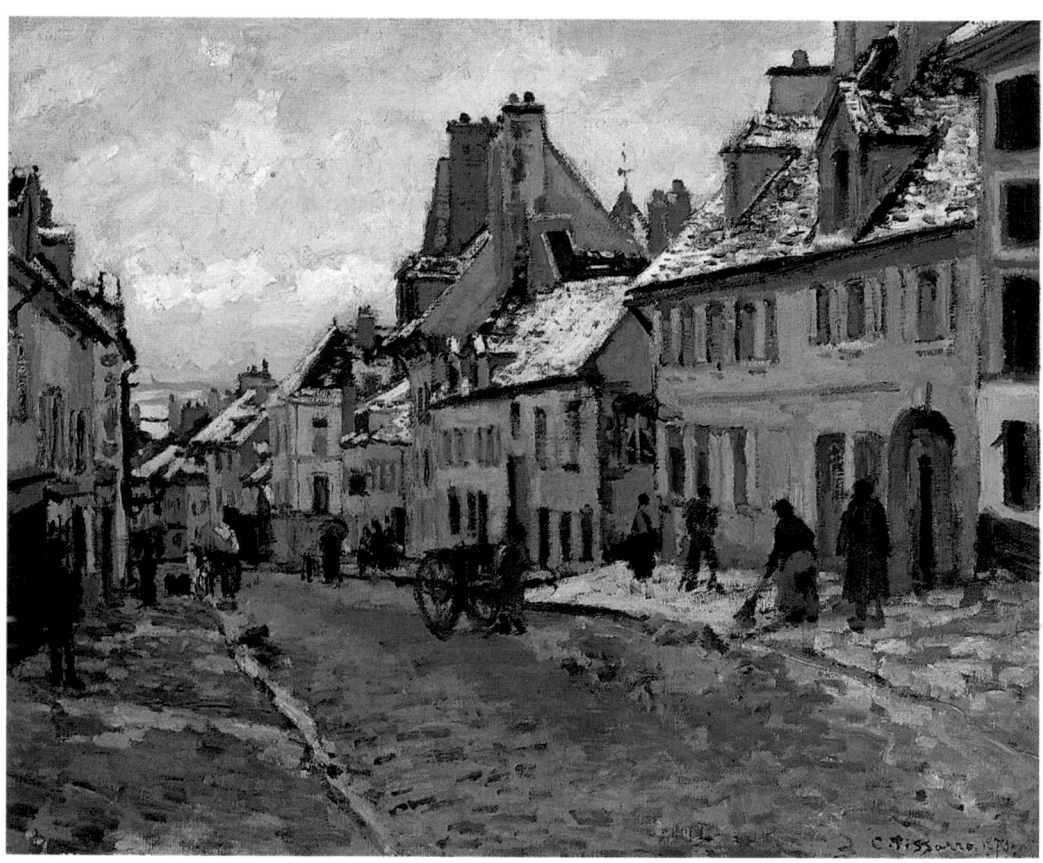

91
**Camille
Pissarro**,
*Route de Gisors
at Pontoise
in Winter*,
1873.
Oil on canvas;
59·8 × 73·8 cm,
23¹₂ × 29 in.
Museum of
Fine Arts,
Boston

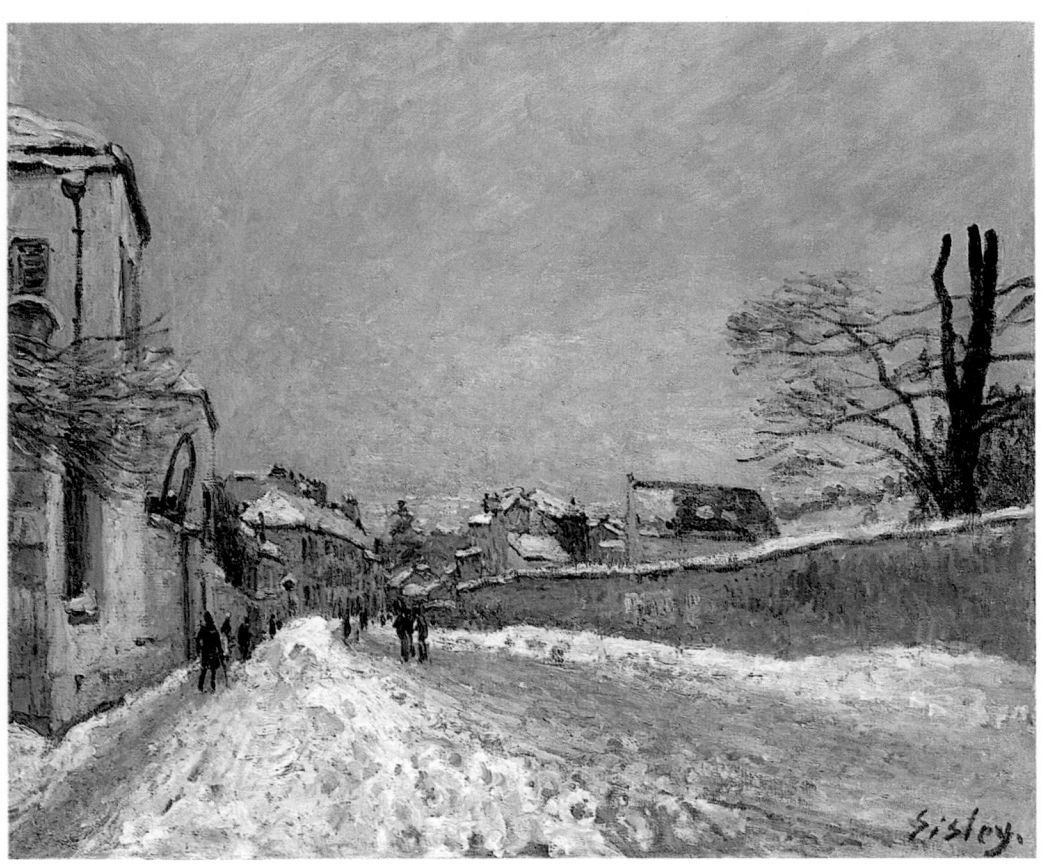

92
Alfred Sisley,
Rue Eugène
Moussoir at
Moret: Winter,
1880.
Oil on canvas;
46·7 × 56·5 cm,
18³⁸ × 22¹⁴ in.
Metropolitan
Museum of Art,
New York

the structure dwarfs the slender houses to the left, its smokestacks, peaked roof and nearby poplar trees form a harmonious descending diagonal. In partly cloudy weather, the dark smoke gradually blends with the sky, and the painting's general greyishness picks up the colour of the distillery walls to produce an overall tonal unity. The factory was an everyday sight for the artist and parallels the interest in steam barges and commercial river traffic we saw in his pictures of Port-Marly from the previous year (see 87). We should hardly be surprised to find Pissarro concentrating on it in several paintings, or showing it as part of the Pontoise environment in others. Its presence was a logical outgrowth of the agricultural market community at a

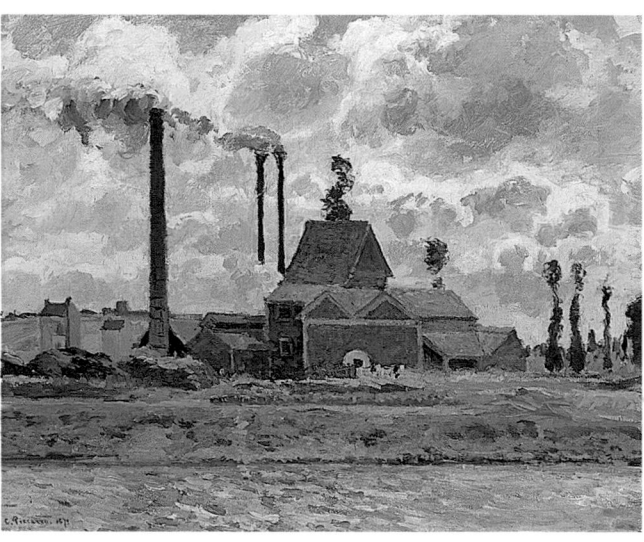

93
Camille
Pissarro,
*Factory near
Pontoise,*
1873.
Oil on canvas;
45·7 × 54·6 cm,
18 × 21¹₂ in.
Museum of
Fine Arts,
Springfield,
Massachusetts

secondary transportation crossroads. It is not so much within Pissarro's work that such pictures are exceptional as within Impressionist landscapes as a whole. For Pissarro, the factory was neither a matter for celebration nor regret. Unlike the avant-garde architecture of the Saint-Lazare station in Monet's group, the Chalon factory was a plain, square, styleless building reflecting modest and practical economics. For Pissarro, who had worked for five years in his family's business before deciding to become a painter, productivity and labour – agricultural or industrial – rather than leisure, were essential. Even though he lived from his parents' allowance in his early years – perhaps indeed because he did – he seems always to

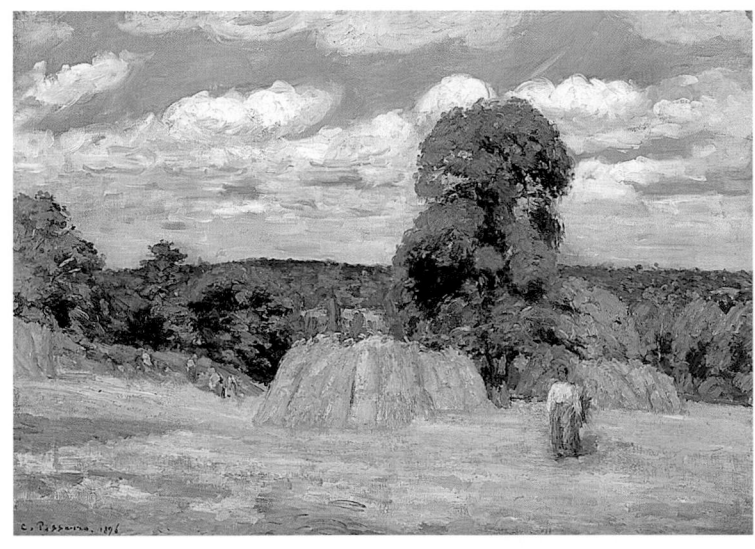

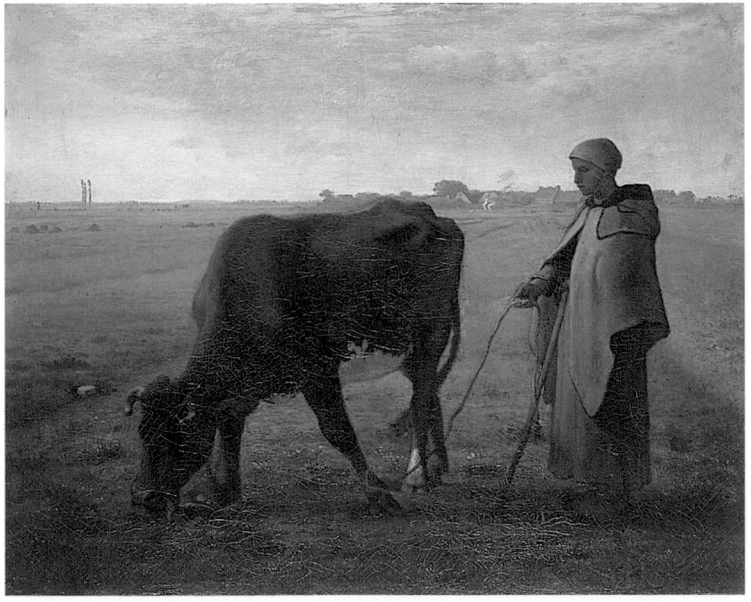

94
Camille
Pissarro,
The Harvest at
Montfoucault,
1875.
Oil on canvas;
65 × 92 cm,
25⁵⁄₈ × 36¹⁄₄ in.
Musée d'Orsay,
Paris

95
Jean-François
Millet,
Woman
Pasturing her
Cow,
1858.
Oil on canvas;
73 × 93 cm,
28³⁄₄ × 36⁵⁄₈ in.
Musée du
Brou,
Bourg-en-
Bresse

value industriousness, a quality he exemplified without fanfare in his persistent and methodical practices as a painter. Unlike Monet's equivocations before the industrial evidence of modernity, Pissarro's treatment of such motifs is a sign of an unsentimental commitment to rendering progress as a natural part of rural development.

It was late in the year of the factory series that Théodore Duret, friend of Courbet and Manet, supporter and future historian of the Impressionists, wrote to encourage Pissarro to specialize in paintings of rural life and 'rustic nature with its fields and animals'. He could tell Pissarro was sympathetic to this subject matter, even though it was different from that of most of his associates. In the mid-1870s, Pissarro made annual trips from Pontoise to the property at Montfoucault of his friend Ludovic Piette (1826–77), a gentleman farmer and painter who exhibited with the Impressionists. Some 225 km (140 miles) to the west of Paris, in the 'breadbasket' region of Mayenne in eastern Brittany, Pissarro encountered more traditional and purely agricultural motifs than in the small-holding market town of Pontoise. As guest of the owner of the local manor, Pissarro may have felt more authorized to study labouring figures directly than he had in Pontoise (where he was known to complain of the lack of models). He made many charcoal sketches and oil studies of figures, primarily women who worked closer to the farmhouse and were probably more docile than the men. They are engaged in tasks such as carrying water from the well, tending cattle or untangling wool. One result of Pissarro's efforts was *The Harvest at Montfoucault* (94), which shows women haymaking in a field, a painting he chose for the third Impressionist exhibition of 1877. The most prominent figure poses near the foreground holding her bunch of hay, while others are reaping in the background. The grainstack in the centre consists of hand-gathered bales leaned together. But lest we compare Pissarro's attitudes too closely to Millet's nostalgia for a pre-modern world and his redemptive attachment to the soil (95), we should note that Pissarro rejected such comparisons. However much he admired the work habits of the countryside, he hated sentimentality and considered Millet too 'biblical', wryly remarking that 'For a Hebrew, there is not much of that in me.' Moreover, at the same time as he created images

96
Camille Pissarro, *Côtes des Boeufs at L'Hermitage*, 1877.
Oil on canvas; 114·9 87·6 cm, 45¼ 34½ in.
National Gallery, London

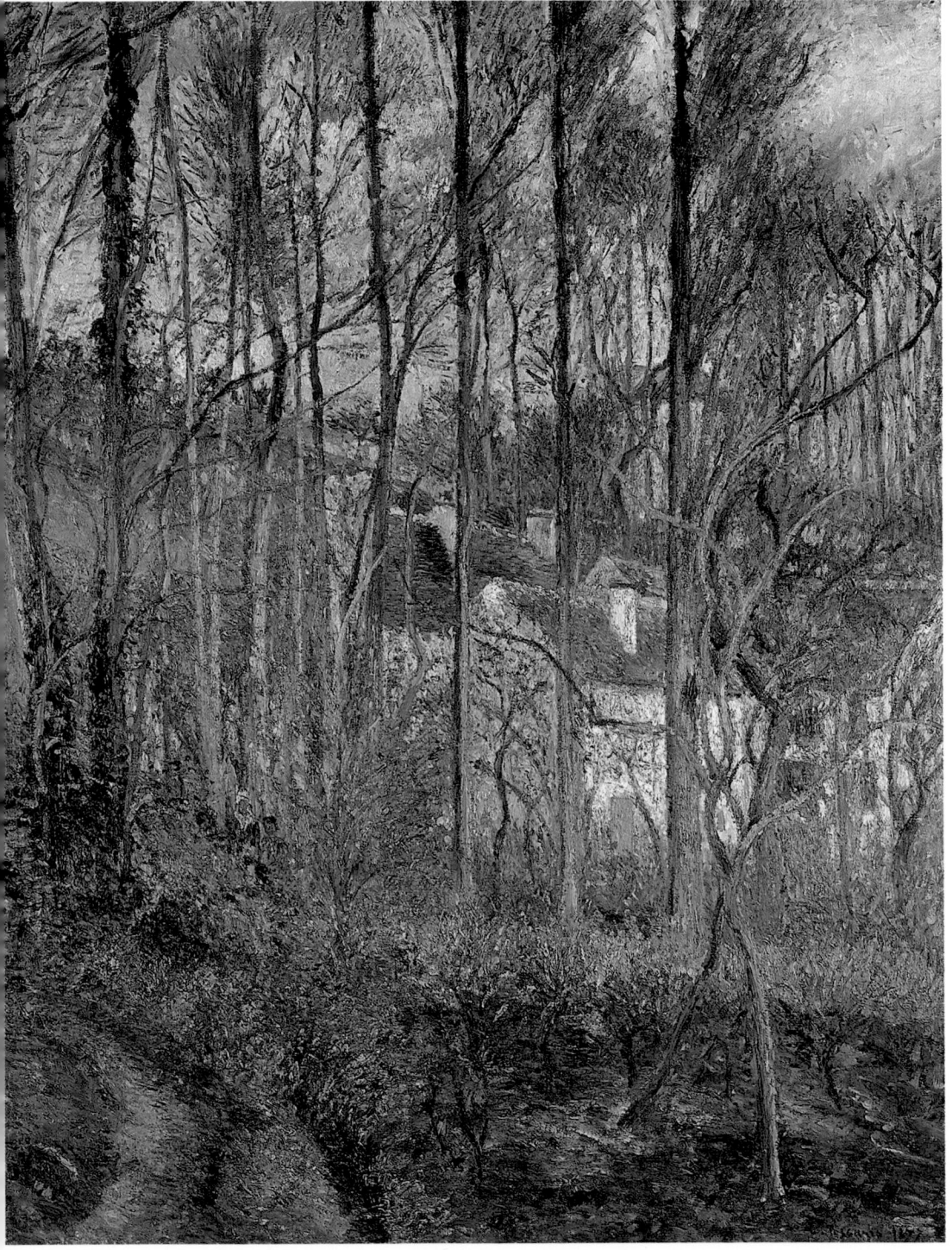

of hand labourers, Pissarro did paintings of Piette's modern threshing machine, a device that would have been rare on the smaller farms of Pontoise – even though those farms themselves were products of modern commerce with Paris. His attraction to enduring traditions was framed within a commitment to modernity that he shared with his Impressionist peers.

Pissarro's brushwork, though unlovely compared to the more ingratiating fluidity and brighter colours of Monet and Renoir's, powerfully conveys the materiality of form and the immediacy of what he

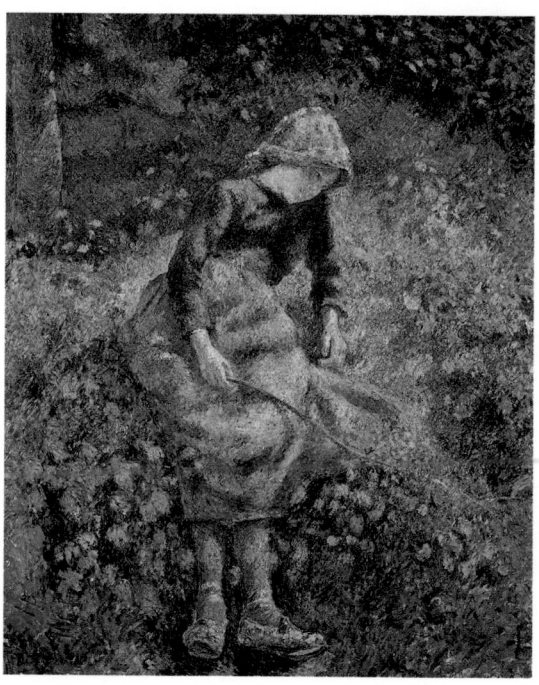

97
Camille Pissarro, *Peasant Girl with Stick*, 1881. Oil on canvas; 81 64·7 cm, 31⅞ 25½ in. Musée d'Orsay, Paris

constantly referred to as 'sensation'. In one of his masterpieces, *Côtes des Boeufs at L'Hermitage* (96) – a favourite he kept for many years – these elements attain a crescendo. In an exceptional effect, a peasant woman and her daughter stare back at the painter from a stand of trees behind the village houses, again, near L'Hermitage. The bolder and more saturated colours of Pissarro's later 1870s style convey an energy and tension beyond that of his earlier work. The whole is nonetheless unified by the systematically worked surface, which combines with the screen of trees to compress the composition into flattened pictorial coherence. A vertical format contributes to the sense of both isolation and concentration. It is unclear whose intimacy has been violated, but the question of Pissarro's presence seems to drive his pictorial response, as if throwing himself into the world of paint and surfaces can resolve the tensions this painting reveals.

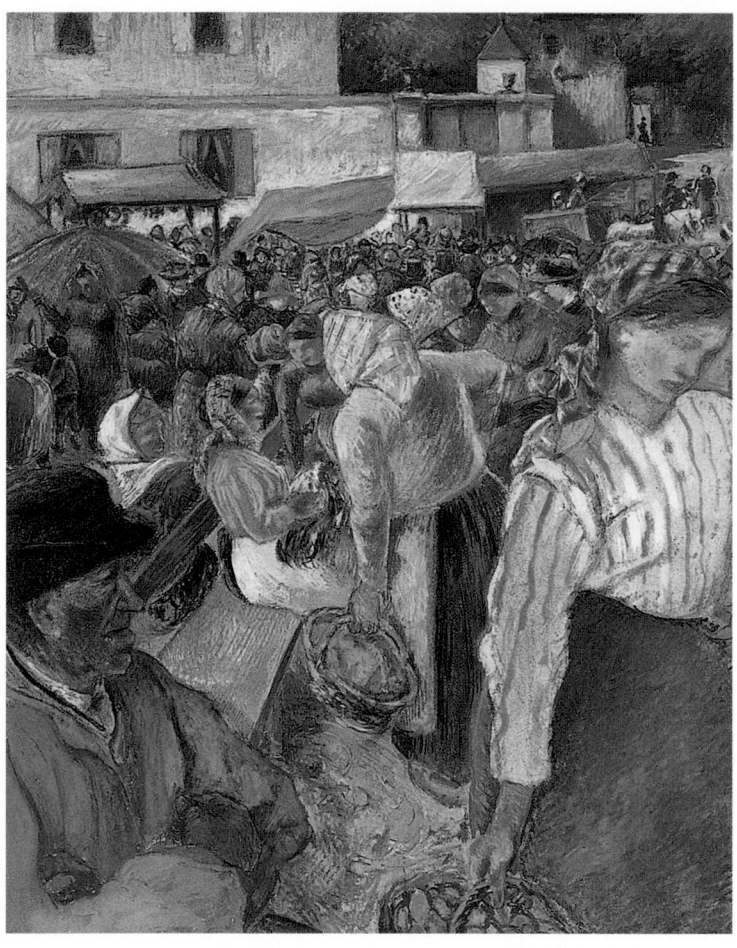

98
Camille Pissarro,
Poultry Market at Pontoise,
1882.
Tempera and pastel;
81 × 65 cm,
31⁷⁄₈ × 25⁵⁄₈ in.
Private collection

Eventually, Pissarro put greater emphasis on figure painting, conducted more privately no doubt than his depictions of village spaces, yet facilitating a dialogue with other painters in the circles of advanced art. *Peasant Girl with Stick* (97) is typical of many studies of single figures or groups of young women who must have posed for him. Their characteristic blue skirts and red and white checked kerchiefs brighten the compositions and contribute to his sense of an unhurried, peaceful life. Pissarro thus transposes the contemporary leisure ethos of Parisian Impressionism – with greater reference to Renoir (the antidote to Millet) than is generally recognized – into his own personal rural form. He deliberately avoids the nostalgic and picturesque mythologizing of rural subjects he abhorred in Salon painters such as Bastien-Lepage (see 23).

From this period Pissarro also began his market compositions, which run through much of the rest of his career. Here was a modern rural topic *par excellence*: the combination of different social classes – peasant vendors and domestic servants or bourgeois buyers – at the market place, the most urban spot in a country town. Pissarro thus brings the pictorial ambitions of figure painting together with unsentimental, commercial activities of the present time. An increasingly efficient transport system and the insatiable appetite of Paris meant that the agricultural economy of Pontoise was centred on providing produce for the capital. The discovery of such motifs gave Pissarro's career a new impetus and was accompanied by extraordinary experimentation as well. *Poultry Market at Pontoise* (98) of 1882, has a compact figure composition with cropping effects at the edges, ambiguous exchanges of glances and insightful social observation that reflect Pissarro's recent association with Degas. The latter had become a leading force in organizing the Impressionist exhibitions, and Pissarro collaborated with him and others in 1879 on a print journal that was never actually realized (see Chapter 8). Like Degas, Pissarro used an elaborate system of preliminary studies for these compositions, and he essayed novel media, such as tempera and pastel, yet on a scale comparable to oil painting. His figure subjects, done in bright colours and with lively surfaces achieved by the new techniques, brought Pissarro closer to the mainstream Impressionism of his colleagues, while maintaining the rural basis of his art. Indeed, in a letter of 1883 he reminded his son Lucien that 'my temperament is rustic, melancholic, coarse and savage ... I will only please in the long run'. When we return to Pissarro in the mid-1880s (see Chapter 8), we shall see him using Neo-Impressionist techniques to create a contemporary rural world he then would call the 'true poem of the countryside', implying both its artistic fiction and an affection for country life.

The most compelling *plein-air* figure painter of the original Impressionist group was certainly Pierre-August Renoir. It may seem odd to discuss an artist so central to Impressionism's popularity, and so seemingly opposite from Pissarro, in the context of marginality and compromise. But although Renoir's imagery was for the most part insistently bourgeois, leisure-oriented and Paris-centred, he was always uneasy about his working-class, provincial origins, referring to himself even late in life as 'a workman among painters'. In the middle-class Impressionist milieu and that of their wealthy patrons, he was reportedly tense and nervous, despite building successful relationships with almost all of them. As the art historian John House has pointed out, Renoir's upward mobility and social ambition can be gauged by the fact that, for a decade, he kept secret even from close friends his liaison with Aline Charigot, a pretty seamstress eighteen years his junior, whom he married five years after the birth of their first child. In the world to which Renoir aspired, such a humble spouse of reputedly awkward manner might not have served his aims. Renoir's father was a tailor who brought his family from Limoges to Paris when Pierre was three years old, hoping to improve their prospects. However, prosperity eluded them, and the children went to work at a tender age. The future painter was apprenticed at thirteen to a porcelain-decorating firm, the Lévy Brothers, where he learned to copy in miniature after the Old Masters, mainly in the Rococo style of the eighteenth century. From there he progressed to painting fans and blinds.

When Renoir enrolled in 1861 to study with Gleyre, he stepped up from craft to the higher status of academic professionalism. (He was also admitted to the École des Beaux-Arts.) The friends he met were of higher social standing, too. Yet the delicate techniques and bright colours, pleasurable aims and unproblematic world implied by his earliest artistic practice stayed with him for life, for it required little effort to adapt them to *plein-air* methods. Indeed, Renoir's ability and willingness to serve uncritically the artistic tastes of the leisured classes helped him by the late 1870s to establish a position mediating between Impressionism and more conservative art. In 1878, after expressing doubts about some of his friends, he dropped out of the Impressionist exhibitions to rejoin the official Salon.

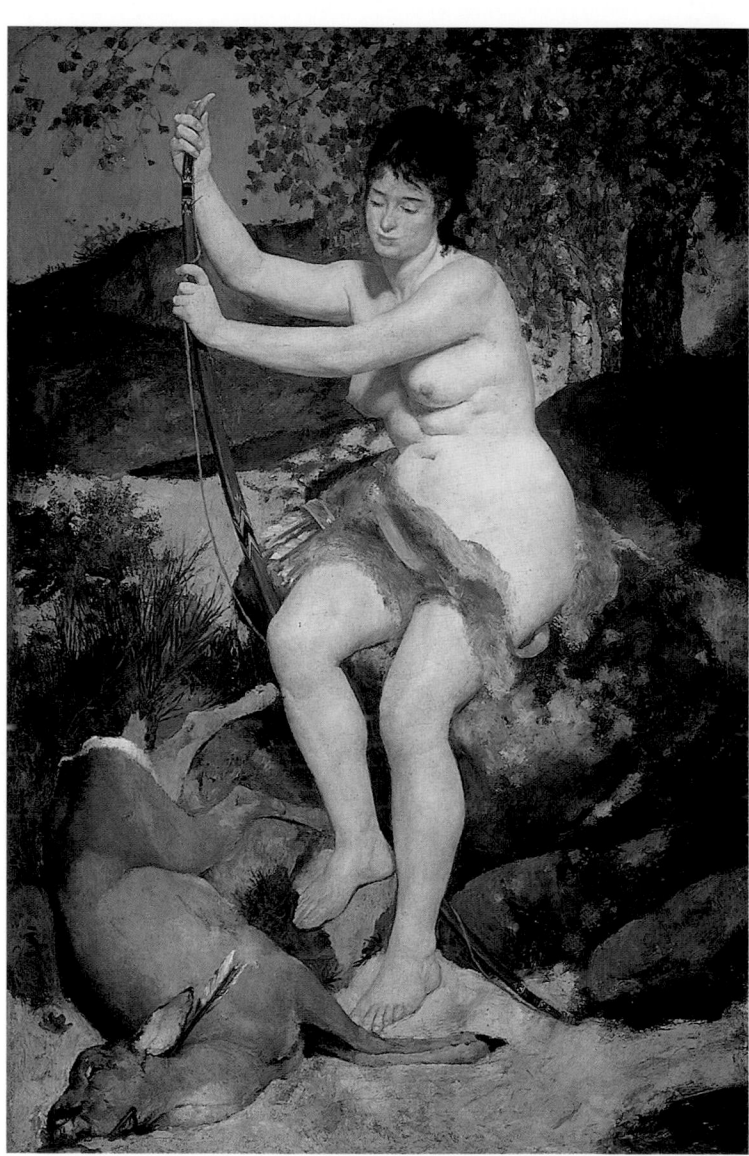

99
**Pierre-Auguste
Renoir**,
Diana,
1867.
Oil on canvas;
199·5 × 129·5 cm,
77 × 51¼ in.
National Gallery
of Art,
Washington, DC

Perhaps more than the work of any other Impressionist, including Bazille, Renoir's early paintings are records of friendships, relations with supporters and patrons (see Chapter 8), and comings and goings in various Paris locales. There was also a wide stylistic range and versatility in Renoir's work, as he sought a manner that would be both up-to-date and pleasing. He painted near Fontainebleau with friends, including Sisley and the amateur Jules Le Coeur (1832–82). And like the companions he had met at Gleyre's, Renoir hoped to show at the Salon. To this purpose in 1867 he made a large nude posed by his mistress Lise Tréhot. Called *Diana* (99), it showed the goddess of the hunt seated on a rock in the woods unstringing her bow, with a slain deer at her feet. Diana was a popular figure in

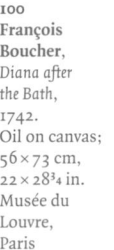

100
François
Boucher,
*Diana after
the Bath*,
1742.
Oil on canvas;
56 × 73 cm,
22 × 28³⁄₄ in.
Musée du
Louvre,
Paris

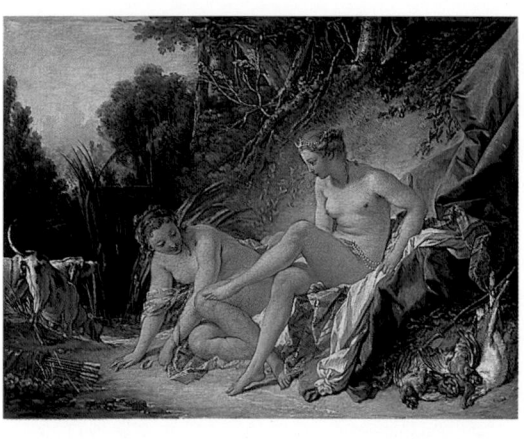

Rococo art, as in the famous painting in the Louvre by François Boucher (1703–70; 100) of the goddess bathing with her nymphs. Renoir's *Diana* both updates the Rococo tradition with which he was so familiar and uses it to legitimize his theme for the Salon. The form of his modernization was, as in the work of Bazille, to evoke Courbet. Both the hunting theme and the nude's voluptuous physicality referred to the latter's paintings shown at the Salon of 1866 the previous year: *The Covert of the Roe Deer* and *Woman with a Parrot*. Yet Renoir's imitations of Courbet's palette-knife technique were clumsy, and his treatment of his model as a nude portrait may have made his Realist effect too brazen for the jury, which in any case rejected most works submitted by the Impressionists in 1867.

With Parisian life increasingly on his mind, Renoir converted to a more modernist and socially up-market aesthetic, inspired by Manet and Monet. *The Pont des Arts* (101), a masterpiece of 1867, shows to what degree Renoir could assimilate the urban *plein-air* practice and themes of leisure which Monet had convincingly captured in his *Garden of the Princess* (see 54). The latter was done earlier the same year, and Renoir's painting echoes it technically, though perhaps with less daring. By comparison to Monet's radically compressed, window-like composition, Renoir adopted a traditional, balanced structure reminiscent of Corot's compositions featuring bridges over the River Tiber in Rome.

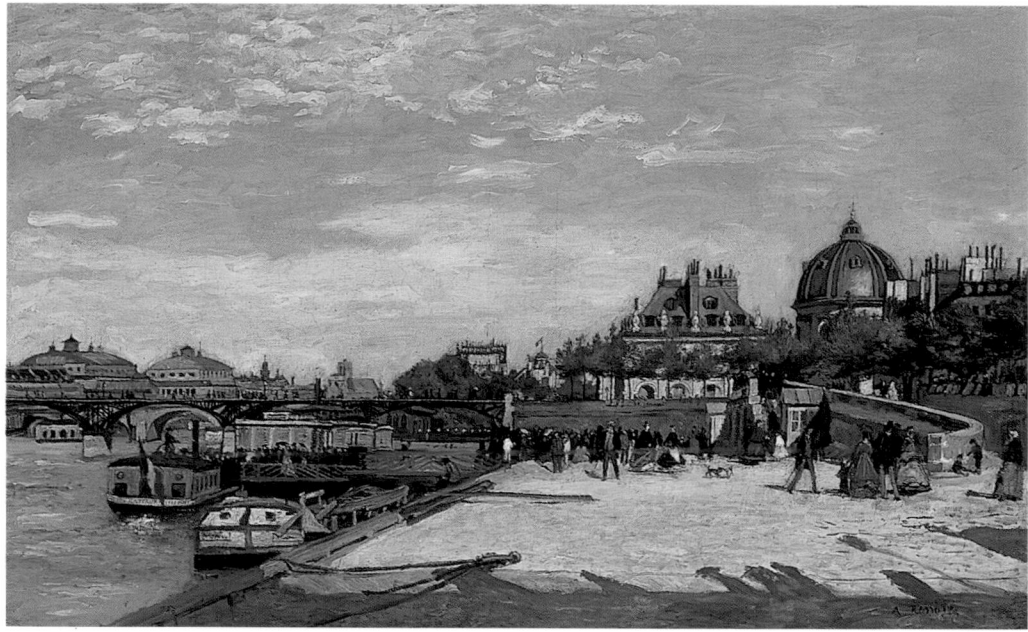

Like Monet, Renoir places us at the heart of modern and artistic Paris. We look down the Quai Malaquais, recently cleared by Haussmann's renovations, which created vistas to major monuments such as the Palais Mazarin, with its elegant cupola, to the right. The Pont des Arts ('Bridge of the Arts'), a cast-iron pedestrian bridge, linked the Louvre on the right bank of the Seine with the left bank, at a spot across from the École des Beaux-Arts. Both landmarks are outside the picture's field of vision, yet the well-informed viewer would have perfectly understood their relationship to the scene, indicated by the name of the footbridge. Thus against the absent framework of these hallowed institutions – echoing Monet's device of placing the Louvre colonnade at his back – Renoir overtly declared his *plein-air* position. Fashionably dressed tourists (contrasted to a less prosperous mother and daughter and idle boys to the left, who may have been begging) queue up to take the open air on excursion boats that cruise the Seine. Renoir paraphrases Monet's contrasting line of sunlight and shadow, actually going a step further by suggesting the image of a painter at his easel. By placing these motifs along his picture's bottom edge, we can say Renoir framed his composition within the signs of *plein-air* practice.

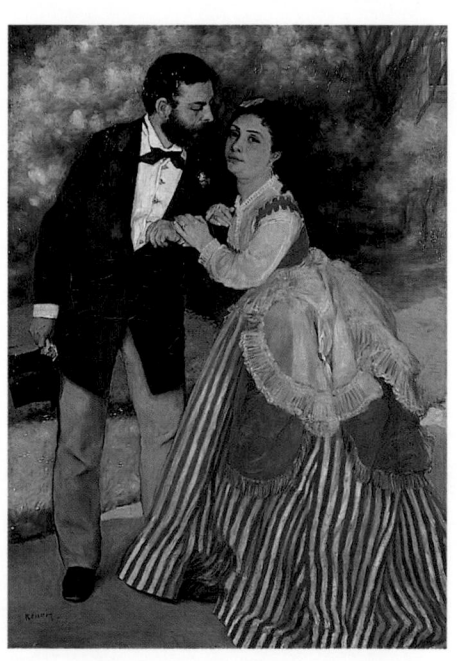

101
Pierre-Auguste Renoir,
The Pont des Arts,
1867.
Oil on canvas;
62 × 103 cm,
24¹₂ × 40¹₂ in.
Norton Simon
Museum,
Pasadena

102
Pierre-Auguste Renoir,
Alfred Sisley and Lise Tréhot in the Garden,
1868.
Oil on canvas;
105 × 75 cm,
41¹₂ × 29¹₂ in.
Wallraf-Richartz
Museum,
Cologne

In figure painting, Renoir's 1868 double portrait of *Alfred Sisley and Lise Tréhot in the Garden* (102) – until recently thought to show Sisley and his wife – is worth comparing to Monet's *Women in the Garden* (see 56) of 1866, for its indication of Renoir's distinct direction. Whereas Monet used his mistress, Camille Doncieux, for all four of his figures, posing her abstractly and anonymously, Renoir's practice was to cast the painting of large figures as portraits. His couple's compositional dominance and strong flattening patterns now evoke Manet – Sisley's stiff and strongly outlined trousers echo those of

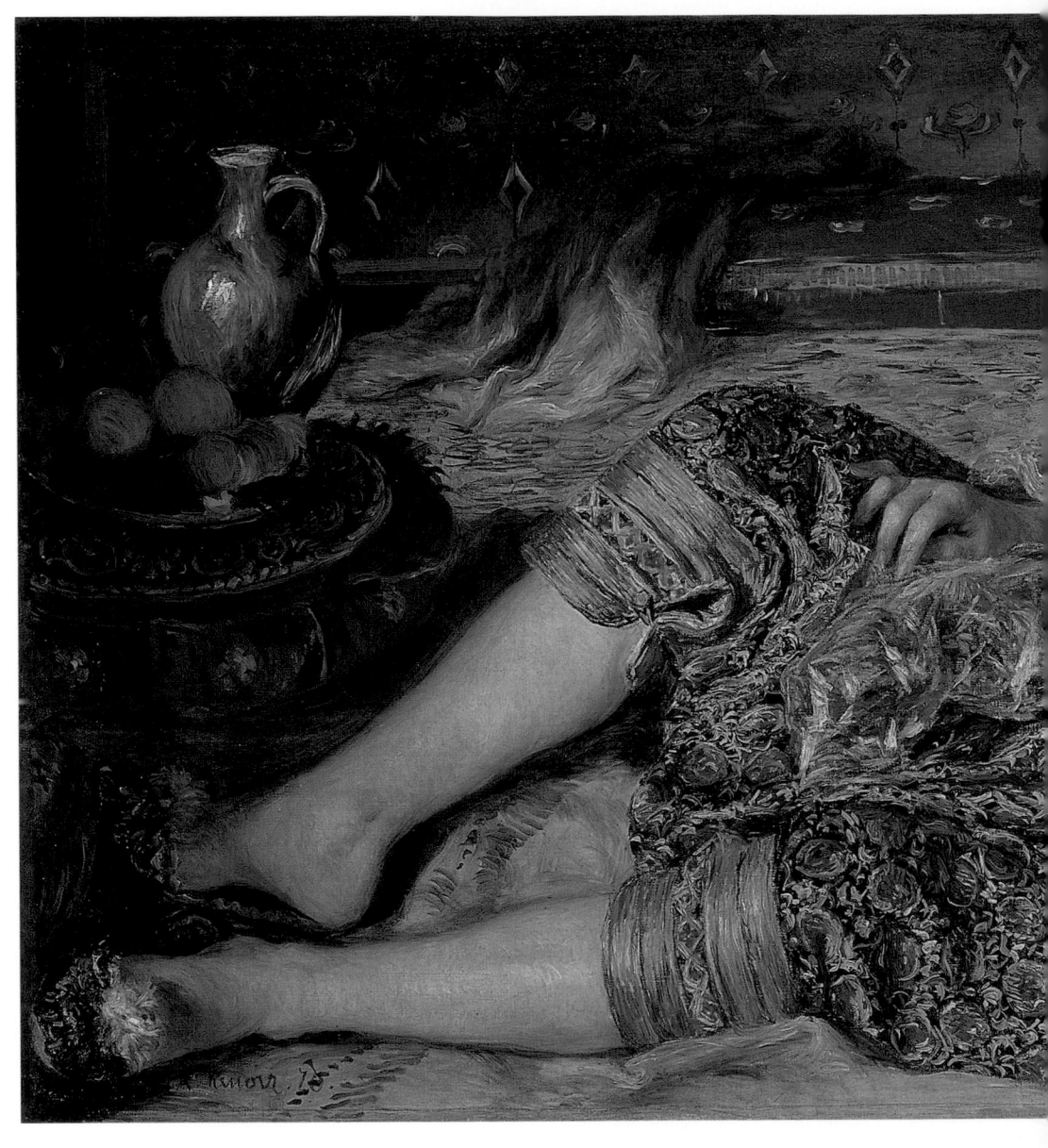

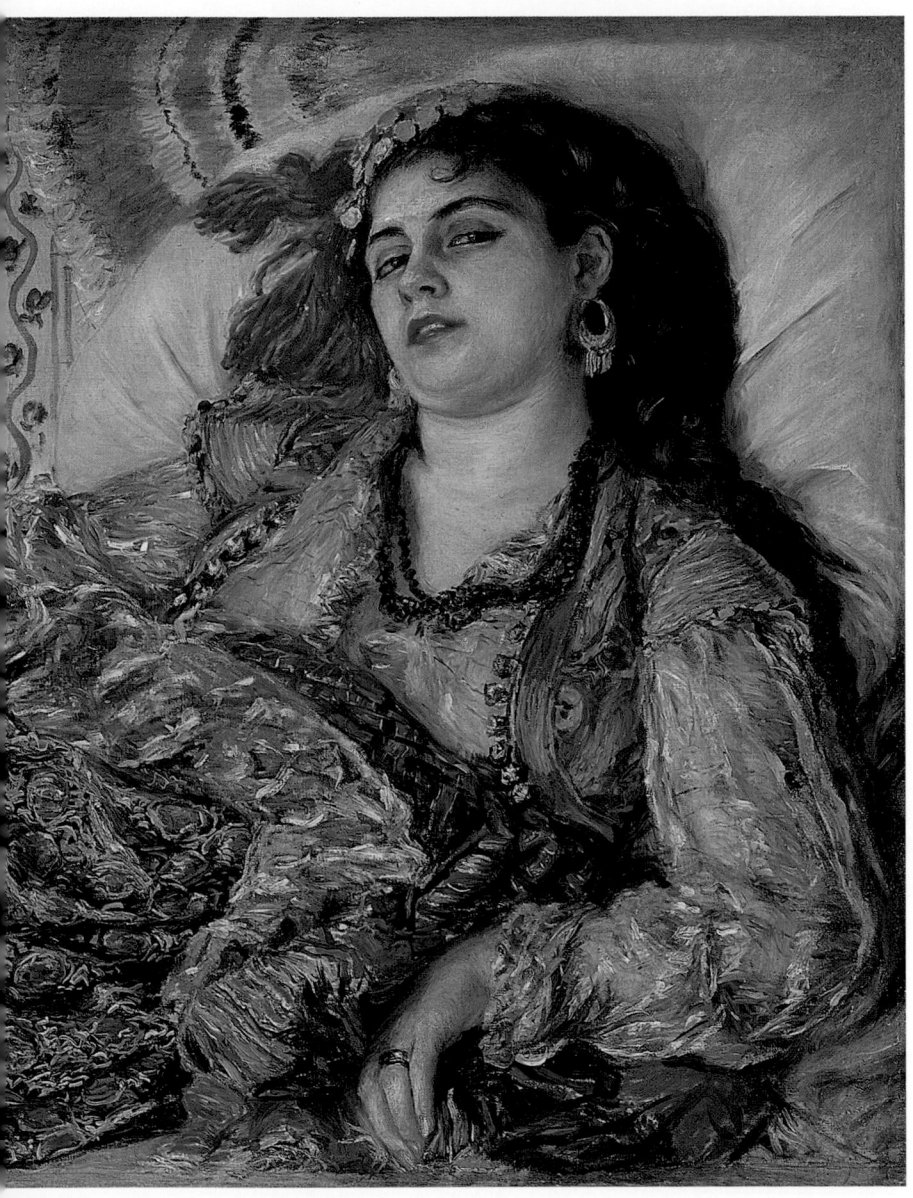

103
Pierre-Auguste Renoir,
A Woman of Algiers,
1870.
Oil on canvas;
69·2 × 122·6 cm,
27¹₄ × 48¹₄ in.
National Gallery of Art,
Washington, DC

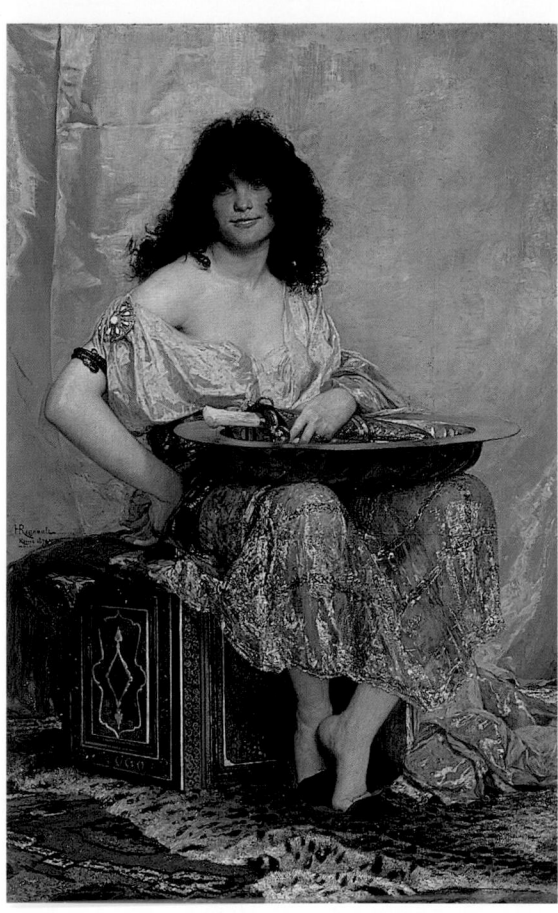

104
Henri
Regnault,
Salomé,
1870.
Oil on canvas;
160 × 102·9 cm,
63 × 40⅛ in.
Metropolitan
Museum of Art,
New York

The Fifer Boy (see 40). Renoir now seems indifferent to the contrasts of light and shade on which Monet had focused and which he used in *The Pont des Arts*. Rather, his joy in the bright colours, silky textures and shimmering patterns of Lise's dress – to which he adds the semi-transparency of her ornamental apron – suggest his attraction to decorative surface effects of things rather than to effects of light upon them. He was again drawing on sensibilities developed during the employments of his youth. In the background of the Sisley–Tréhot portrait is the embryonic version of Renoir's signature brushwork – a softened and fluid version of Manet's vigorous handling transformed into a Corot-like blur. The demands of portraiture, from which Renoir primarily made his living, and his friendship with Monet would lead him to use smaller brushes, but the liquid, fuzzy effects of soft bristles would remain.

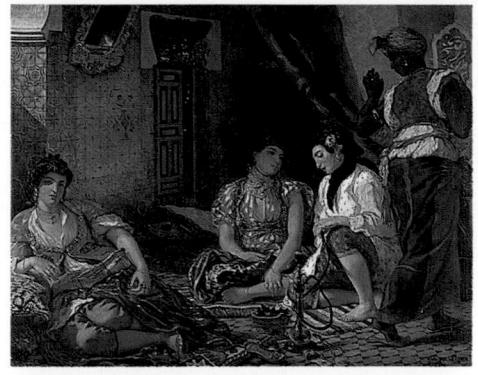

105
Eugène Delacroix,
Women of Algiers in their Harem,
1834.
Oil on canvas;
180 × 220 cm,
70⁷⁄₈ × 90¹⁄₈ in.
Musée du
Louvre,
Paris

106
Frédéric Bazille,
La Toilette,
1870.
Oil on canvas;
132 × 127 cm,
52 × 50 in.
Musée Fabre,
Montpellier

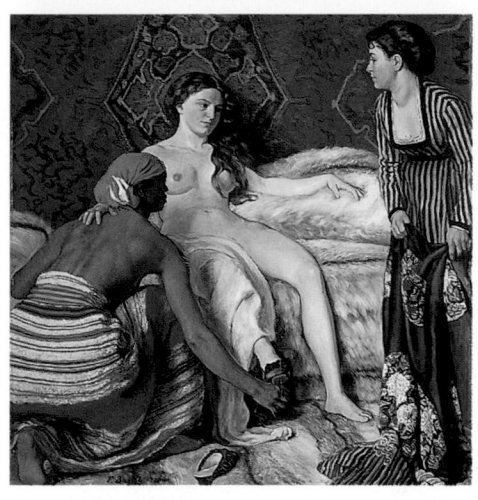

Renoir was the only major Impressionist not to rely heavily on subsidies from his parents for income at the beginning of his career. From an early age, he was used to finding any kind of work. Through Sisley and Le Coeur, he found commissions for portraits and, through Le Coeur's architect brother, for a ceiling decoration (now destroyed) in the Paris house of Prince Georges Bibesco. He also made a large panel of a clown as a commercial circus decoration, which evoked Manet's pictures of entertainers. In 1870, the Salon accepted *Woman of Algiers* (103), posed by Lise reclining in lavishly painted exotic costume and exploiting the fashion for Orientalism. (This tendency in nineteenth-century art drew inspiration from the Arab and Islamic cultures of North Africa, which were under French colonial rule, and Islamic centres such as Constantinople, the Ottoman capital at the eastern edge of Europe.) Seeming to evoke Delacroix, whose *Women of Algiers*

in their Harem (105) was widely known, Renoir's interpretation was in fact markedly different. In contrast to the melancholy created by Delacroix's subtle lighting and atmospherics, languid poses and blank expressions, Renoir overwhelms the viewer with complex material surfaces and brilliant colours. His background is but a perfunctory evocation of a harem. Both works embody contemporary fantasies about an alien culture; but if Delacroix's image of the Orient was to some extent a vehicle for psychological introspection, Renoir's made the Orient a spectacular utopian site for visual gratification. The heavily worked surface and variety of colour combinations is unprecedented in his work thus far, from the gold and black embroi-dered pantaloons, the ostrich-feather and tiara of gold coins, to the blue, red and black shawl and delicate blouse. Surely Delacroix's reputation for loose brushwork and colourism helped legitimize Renoir's pictorial pyrotechnics, so the younger painter's innovations read as the outcome of a tradition rather than a rupture with it. The erotic – enhanced by the supine Lise's sultry gaze and ample breasts, visible through the diaphanous chemise – was a common feature of Rococo painting, which had experienced a revival under the Second Empire, too. But rather than locating his woman's sexuality in the world of goddesses as he had in the *Diana* (see 99), Renoir transferred it to the more contemporary realm of a foreign culture of imagined sexual submission. *Woman of Algiers'* seductive pose and visual brilliance compares to *Salomé* (104) by the academic painter Henri Regnault (1843–71) from the Salon of the same year. Nor was Renoir alone in trying to reconcile Impressionist commitments with Salon promiscuity. But Bazille's conception in *La Toilette* (106), by contrast, is far less erotic in its matter-of-fact suggestion of both a scene in an artist's studio (Lise Tréhot is the model to the right) and a vignette from an Oriental-theme bordello (echoing Manet's *Olympia*; see 34). Success at the Salon continued to be a powerful lure, and through exoticism, Renoir could draw on examples ranging from Delacroix to Manet, while catering to utopian fantasies about the Orient.

In 1870, Renoir was drafted into the army; he soon fell ill and saw no action. He returned to Paris in 1871, where he stayed with his parents or friends (Bazille having been killed the previous year) until he found

107
Pierre-Auguste
Renoir,
*Road at
Louveciennes*,
c.1872.
Oil on canvas;
38·1 × 46·4 cm,
15 × 18¼ in.
Metropolitan
Museum of Art,
New York

a place of his own in a working-class neighbourhood near Notre Dame de la Lorette rather than in the newer area of Les Batignolles. Renoir's friendships with Pissarro and Monet took him to Louveciennes, where his own parents had retired, and Bougival, where he joined Monet at La Grenouillère. We saw him visiting Monet and his family in Argentueil, as well, but it is unlikely he ever went as far out as Pontoise. Renoir's *Road at Louveciennes* (107) shows the same general site as Pissarro's painting of 1868–9 (see 85), but it obscures most of the village with foliage to make it seem like a Sunday outing for the well-dressed family located at the centre, and the aqueduct is a blur. As we saw

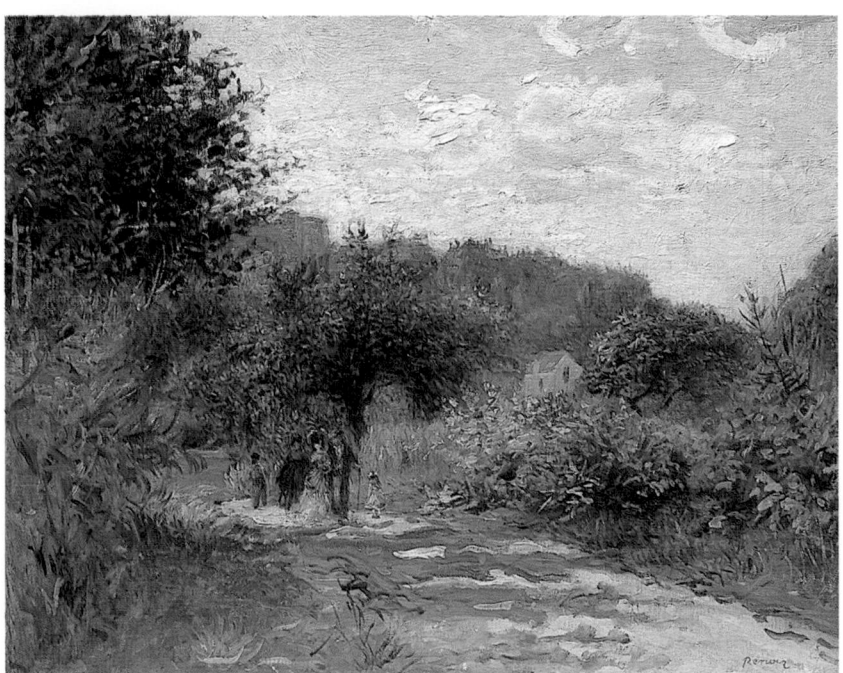

when comparing images of La Grenouillère, Renoir's world was more psychologically extrovert and immediate, less anonymous or remote, than either Monet's or Pissarro's.

Renoir took sustenance from social energies, to the point where he once exclaimed: 'I need to feel all the excitement of life around me, and I always will.' His almost compulsive need to be accepted is hardly surprising in one for whom ambition combined with humble background. But Renoir's social climbing was first and foremost entrepreneurial. There was no Impressionist who sought patronage for portraiture more avidly or who so instinctively adjusted his style in order to please. Hence, Renoir's interest in exhibiting with the Impressionists probably stemmed more from a search for exposure than from heartfelt opposition to the Salon or a firm commitment to modern principles. The overwhelming majority of the works he exhibited were of young women, as in his famous *The Loge* (see 156) from the first Impressionist exhibition. Most were portraits even when not identified as such. From the second Impressionist exhibition, many of Renoir's pictures were listed as owned by collectors (see Chapter 9), primarily the modest customs official Victor Chocquet and Zola's publisher, Georges Charpentier. By 1876, the dealer Paul Durand-Ruel had bought two paintings, and the artist was a regular guest at Madame Charpentier's literary salon – a sure way to make useful acquaintances and find important sitters, among them the ravishing actress Jeanne Samary, whose portrait Renoir painted in 1877. There, Renoir also befriended the writer Alphonse Daudet, with whom he stayed in September 1876; and by 1877 he was attending the Wednesday dinners at the restaurant of Eugène Murer, a pastry chef with literary interests who was a friend of Guillaumin and Dr Gachet, the homoeopathic physician and art collector. Thus, the tailor's son and one-time artisan-apprentice, who lived in humble quarters near workers, maids, concierges and *lorettes*, had a social life to rival almost any successful artist or progressive intellectual.

As early as 1873, Renoir met the writer Georges Rivière, who founded the journal *L'Impressionniste* in 1877. With Rivière and other acquaintances, Renoir began frequenting the recently annexed village of Montmartre, on the heights directly north of his studio on the rue Saint-Georges. One especially active meeting place was the indoor-outdoor café-cabaret named the Moulin de la Galette (108), after one of the two windmills that stood on the site. According to Rivière, Renoir not only enjoyed the conviviality of working-class socializing, with dancing, drinking and flirting, he also kept his eye open for models, since he felt ordinary girls posed more naturally than professionals. In 1876, Renoir decided to do a painting there on the theme of locals relaxing in their Sunday best. With Rivière's help, he set up a studio in the outbuilding of a crumbling folly in the rue Cortot. Renoir made studies of models in the dappled sunlight of its garden, following the lead of Monet, who had been painting in the Parc Monceau. Perhaps Renoir's gradually improving circumstances gave him the freedom to devote considerable time and expenditure of canvas to a large painting on an outdoor theme. The resulting masterpiece, *The Ball at the Moulin de la Galette* (109), was shown in the third Impressionist exhibition in 1877. Although not Renoir's largest picture to date, it was by far the most complex. In number of figures and their identifiability as portraits, it rivals Manet's *Music*

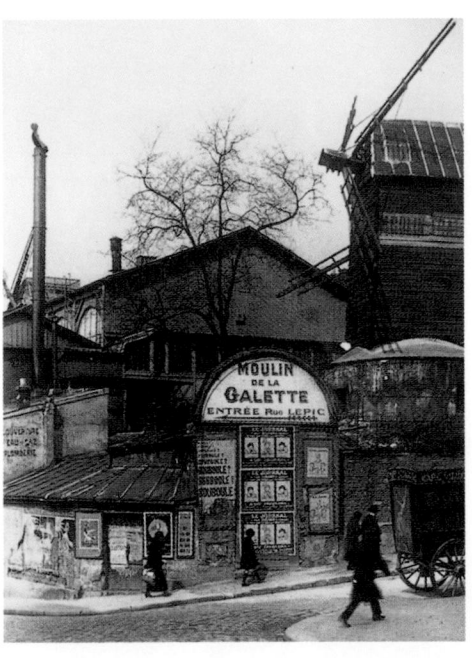

108
The Moulin
de la Galette,
Montmartre,
Paris,
late nineteenth
century

in the Tuileries Gardens (see 27). It also looks to Manet's *A Masked Ball at the Opera* (see 48), but if we are to believe Georges Rivière, amusements and courting at the Moulin were far more innocent. Rather than the public figures of Parisian intelligentsia, Renoir's painting shows close friends, most of whom were artists and their female companions. In the lower right corner sit Rivière (with pipe), along with Pierre Franc-Lamy (1855–1919) and Norbert Goeneutte (1854–94), painters in their twenties. They are drinking grenadine and chatting with one of Renoir's models, Jeanne, a seamstress,

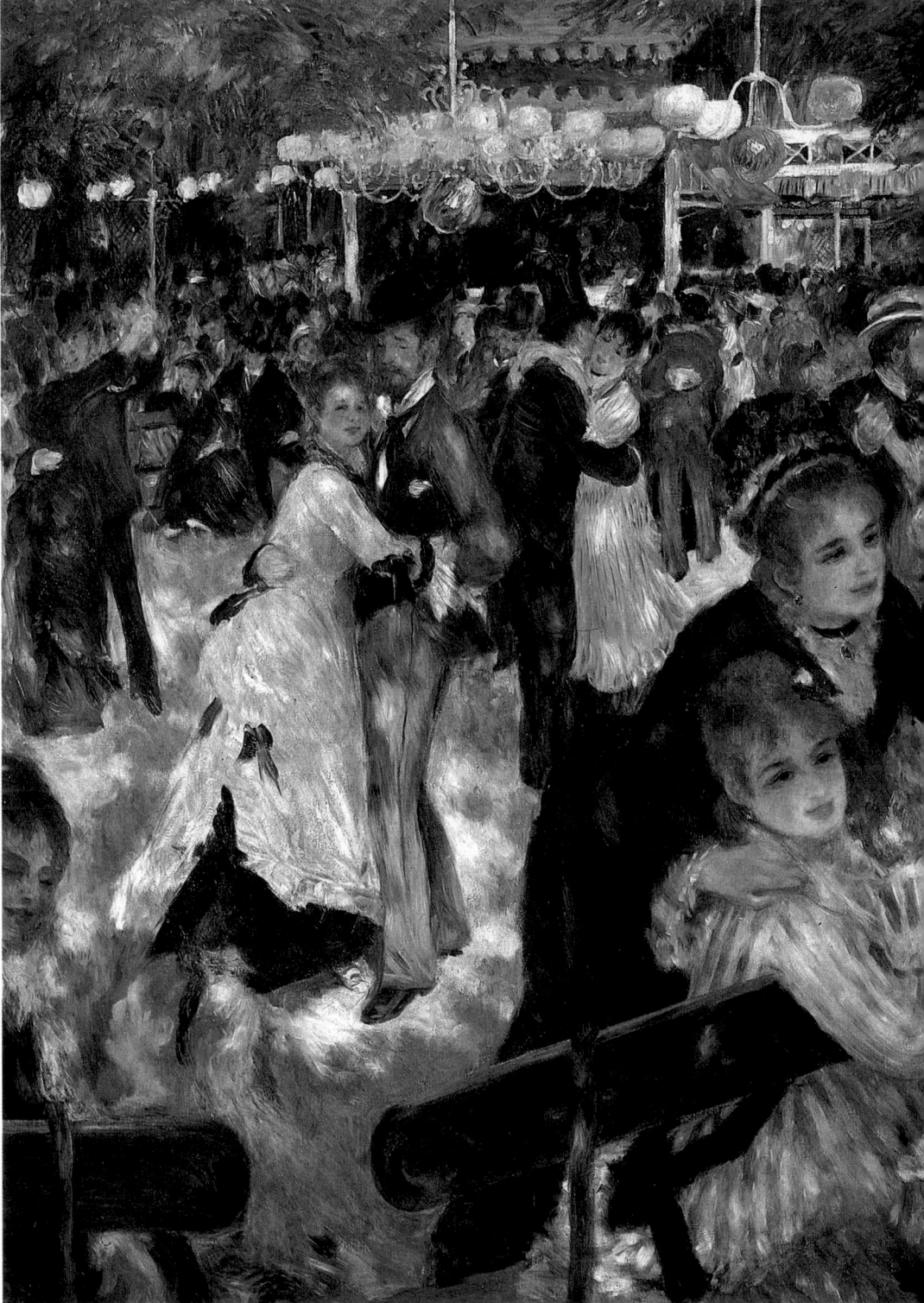

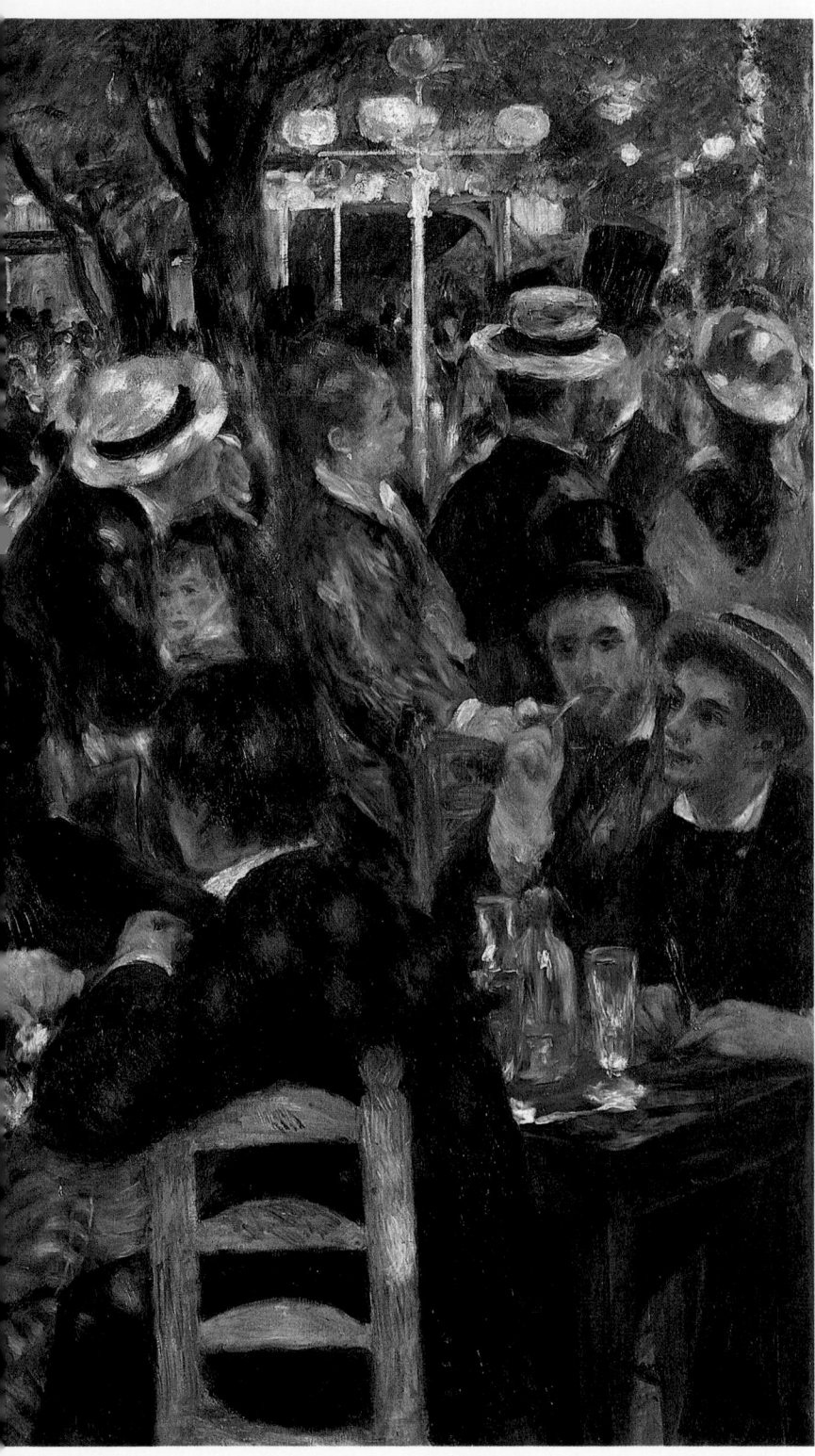

109
**Pierre-Auguste
Renoir**,
*The Ball at
the Moulin
de la Galette*,
1876.
Oil on canvas;
131×175 cm,
$51^1\!2 \times 68^3\!4$ in.
Musée d'Orsay,
Paris

who leans over her younger sister Estelle, seated on the bench. More Renoir models are seen dancing with other friends of the artist. If these figures represent a slice of Parisian society, it is the slightly marginal and bohemian world of male artists come to find models and mistresses among the working class. More likely, it is a fiction. In any case, its lack of articulation of social differences is quite unlike what we expect from the other urban Impressionists, Manet and Degas, with their ironic detachment and questioning of appearances. Though not himself represented in the picture, Renoir is clearly the dominant presence – older and admired by the women who posed for him. Montmartre – crowded, youthful and raucous; unaware of its future fame – is rendered in his own version of the most modern Parisian pictorial technique.

Although Renoir in fact used sketches and surely painted this large canvas in his studio, the painting displays its outdoor origins by incorporating contrasts of light and shade, rendered even more complex by suspended gas lights. Yet there is a significant nod to the eighteenth-century *fête galantes* of Antoine Watteau, with delicate tones and feathery brushstrokes that mitigate those contrasts into soft-focus harmony. The result is a fairy-tale transformation of a reputedly shabby setting, which from the outside, seems grimy and forlorn. Renoir's vision represents not quite a harem utopia, but a congenial urban paradise of pretty women to which almost any man would willingly belong. Oddly enough, in its production of a harmonious modern order, the integrative effect of Renoir's techniques and social choices parallels (with obvious differences) Pissarro's. In its rendering of desire into a combination of Realism and allusion to past art, it parallels Bazille, however different it may look.

Just after exhibiting this painting which so defines the Impressionist world as one of pleasure, what Renoir considered his real breakthrough finally came. It took the form of a relatively conventional portrait commission from the publisher Georges Charpentier. After Renoir's Impressionist success of 1877, he returned to the official Salon for the 1878 show. Writing several years later to Durand-Ruel, he justified himself by arguing that Paris had 'barely fifteen collectors capable of

110
Pierre-Auguste Renoir, *Madame Charpentier and her Children*, 1878. Oil on canvas; 153 × 189 cm, 60½ × 74½ in. Metropolitan Museum of Art, New York

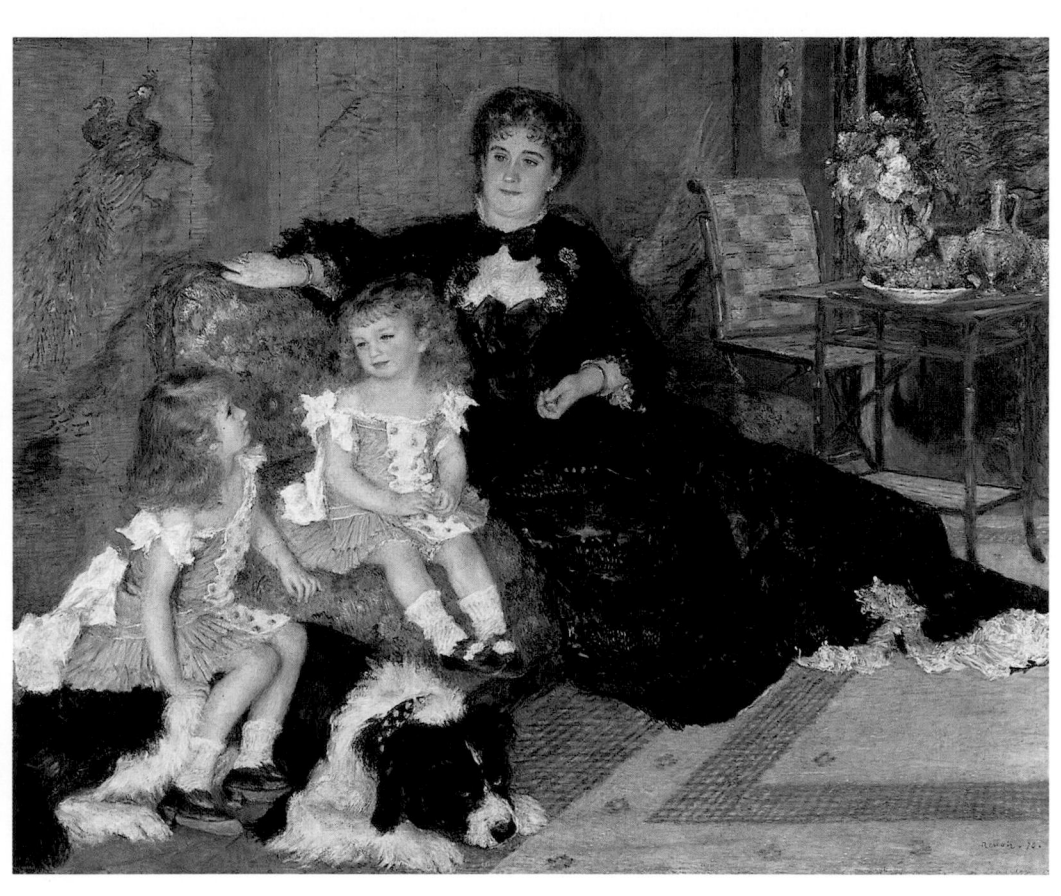

appreciating a painter unless he had exhibited at the Salon'. With the large portrait of *Madame Charpentier and her Children* (110), shown at the Salon of 1879, Renoir was prominently hung and had major if not universal acclaim. For the occasion, he adjusted his painting to traditional art, for example with the strong pyramidal composition of the figures – a Renaissance device – and the conventional articulation of space through the pattern of the Chinese rug. In his treatment of the expensive clothing, Charpentier's up-to-date Japanese screens and the latest bamboo furniture, Renoir aligned himself with current fashion. The three-year-old son, Paul, sitting nearest his mother, and his six-year-old sister Georgette are dressed in the matching outfits of pampered children. With their exchange of glances and the watchful look of their huge but cuddly Newfoundland dog, Porto, Renoir plays skilfully on sentiment and humour. Yet setting the picture in the patron's home corresponded to Impressionism's naturalist aesthetic, as opposed to the formal settings of society portraiture, redolent of Old Masters. Through its appropriation of tradition, the painting embodies domestic stability, in which is vested Renoir's trademark approach to surface colour and texture rendered through open yet graceful brushwork. So now Renoir's integration to the official art world was complete, sanctioned by the rich and prominent in the progressive mileu of arts and entertainment, whose preferred painter he would increasingly become. It is ironic, then, that at this very point when he had achieved his ambition he had a crisis of confidence. As we shall see in Chapter 8, he began to reformulate his style in questionable ways. In the meantime, Durand-Ruel began regular purchases, and Renoir would exhibit with the Impressionists only one more time.

Choreography and Science　Performances by Edgar Degas

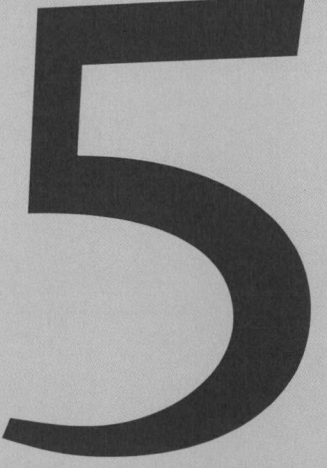

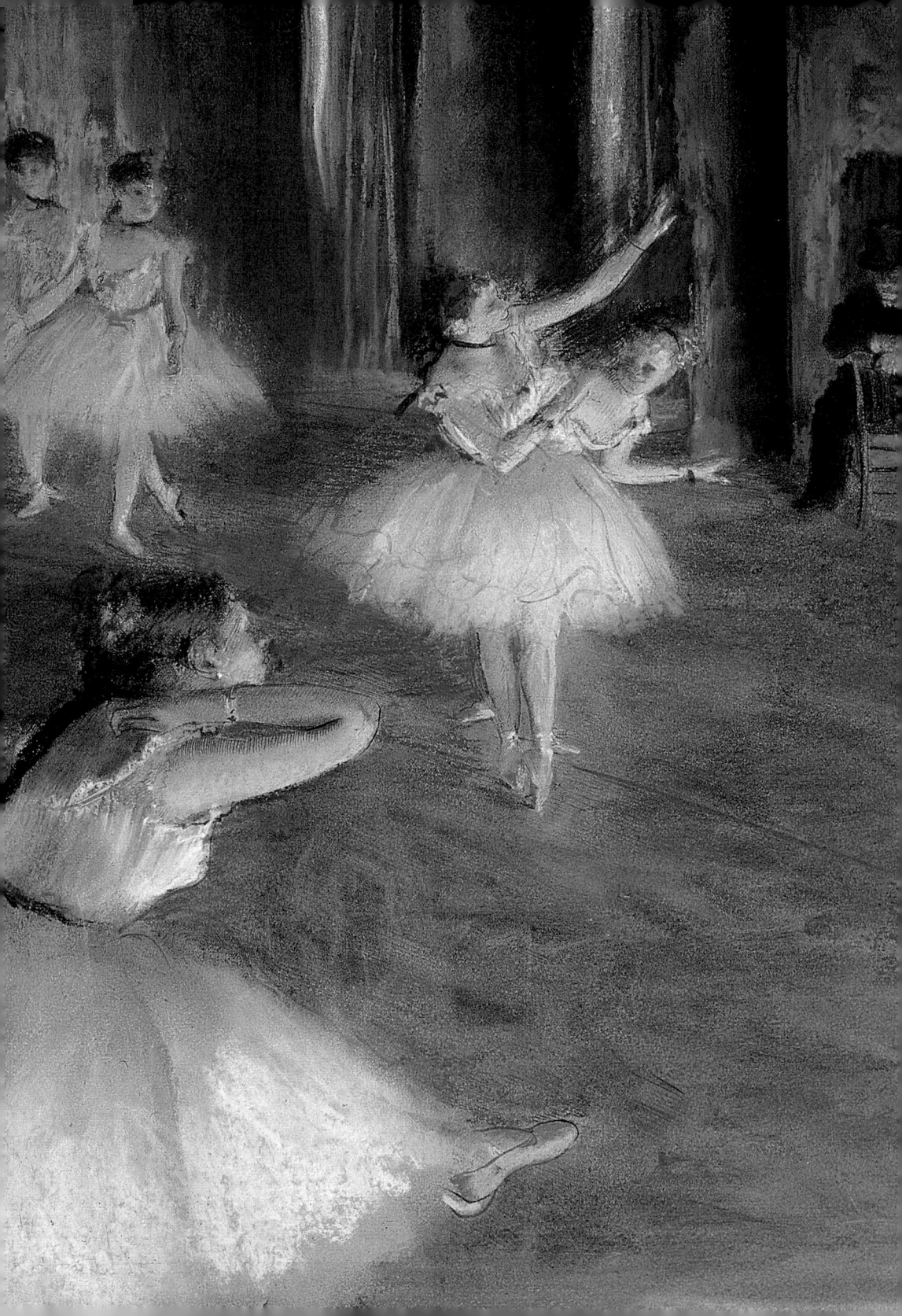

111
Edgar Degas,
*The Rehearsal
of the Ballet on
the Stage*
(detail of 124)

Edgar Degas's relationship to Impressionism has always been problematic. Although he knew both Fantin-Latour and Manet well in the 1860s, he was not included in Fantin-Latour's group portraits of those years, nor in other representations of the group. In many ways, except for his purchases of their work and participation in their exhibitions, Degas remained aloof from and even critical of his Impressionist peers, a position that led to quarrelling among them when he tried to bring in more conservative painters. His conversation at the Café Guerbois was often peppered with acerbic remarks and provocative theories. He was an exceedingly private person, too, scornful of the publicity and opportunistic business relationships through which others advanced their careers (he once said he wanted to be both 'famous and unknown'). Yet, along with Manet, to whom he was socially closest, Degas defined Impressionism's urban dimension based on sharp observation of contemporary leisure. Innovative structures and experimental techniques gave his work a self-consciously intellectual twist by insisting on the deliberate and artificial means underlying his naturalist effects. He valued drawing, copied past artworks and, like traditional artists, made many studies prior to painting – all of which placed him ostensibly in opposition to the *plein-air* ideology of spontaneity and directness. Indeed, Degas once facetiously proposed that outdoor painters should be lined up and shot; and after a series of pastels done on the Normandy coast in 1869, he refrained from landscapes until the 1890s. He claimed: 'No art is less spontaneous than mine. What I do is the result of reflection and study of the great masters; of inspiration, spontaneity, temperament, I know nothing.' (Art historian Carol Armstrong aptly characterized his position as the 'odd man out' of Impressionism.) Yet, precisely because this man of tradition accepted the need to represent modernity, he had to develop unique strategies to reconcile the two. His efforts eventually informed developments in the work of other Impressionists, as well.

Degas's insistence on careful studio craft constituted a moralistic and conservative defence of values and practices to which he felt bound by his aristocratic status, especially as that position was being undermined by the dissolution of the Second Empire, the death of his father in 1874 and the failure of the family fortunes. The family's wealth came from banking, and the name De Gas (his father's spelling – Degas changed it to appear more common), signalled claims to nobility (though it has recently been discovered that those claims were fabricated in the 1830s). In keeping with his social origins, Degas's education and artistic training were the most respectable available. He attended the élite Lycée Louis-le-Grand; then he took art classes at the École des Beaux-Arts, and studied with Louis Lamothe (1822–69), a disciple

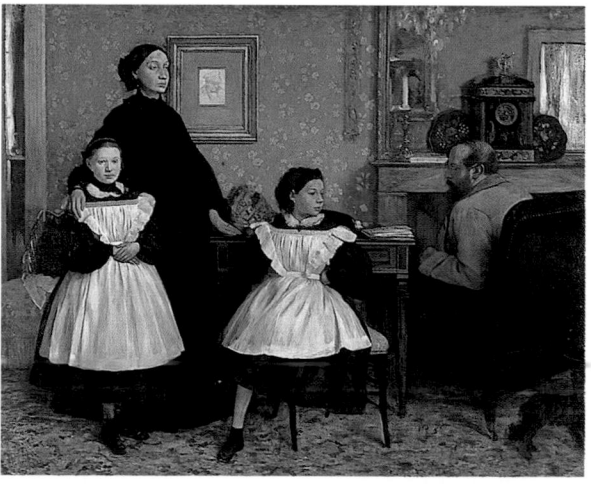

112
Edgar Degas,
The Bellelli Family,
1858–60.
Oil on canvas;
200 × 250 cm,
78¾ × 98½ in.
Musée d'Orsay,
Paris

113
Edgar Degas,
The Interior,
1868–9.
Oil on canvas;
81·3 × 114·4 cm,
32 × 45 in.
Philadelphia
Museum of Art

of Ingres and the Ingresque emphasis on drawing. In the 1860s, Degas tried his hand at history painting having earlier viewed master works of Renaissance and Baroque art in Italy. Like Manet, he was also deeply interested in the realist example of Dutch painting. Against this background he formed many assumptions that persisted through-out his career and made him, in relation to his associates, both anachronistic and radically forward-looking.

During a stay in Italy from 1856 to 1859, Degas lived mainly in Florence with his aunt Laura, who had married the exiled Neapolitan aristocrat Gennaro Bellelli at her father's insistence. *The Bellelli Family* (112), which commemorates that visit, reveals Degas's ability to combine subtle compositional structure and incisive physiognomic observation to produce psychological tension. In the painting's shallow space, divided geometrically into sections by the shapes and positions of the Bellelli apartment's furnishings, the figures are arranged in the horizontal, frieze-like disposition common to narrative historical painting. Degas's aunt is dressed in black for her recently deceased father, Degas's grandfather, whose portrait, in a drawing imitating the Northern Renaissance style, hangs on the wall.

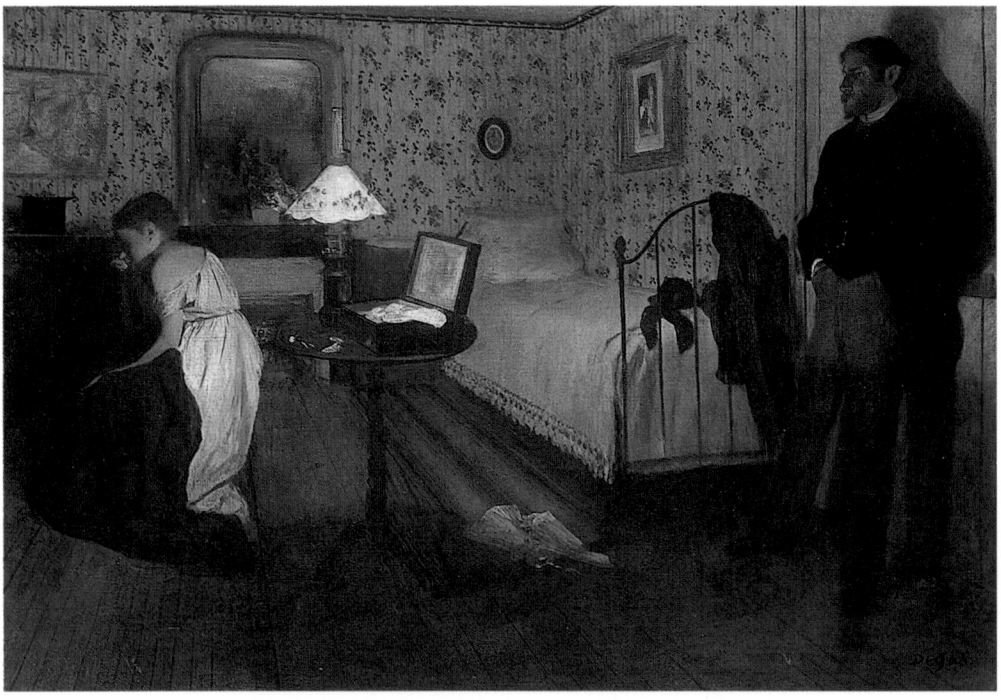

Standing firmly with her is her older daughter, cousin Giovanna. The younger Giulia provides the link to Degas's uncle by turning tentatively towards him from her chair. The idle aristocrat, 'without any occupation to make him less boring to himself', in Laura's words, is ensconced in a stuffed armchair, avoiding the stoic gaze of his domineering spouse by reading a newspaper. The position of his chair suggests the separateness of his world, reinforced by the mirror's illusion of a different space – a device worthy of the Dutch masters Degas had been studying. It may also indicate his reluctant

116 Below
A family in
a carriage,
c.1860

117 Right
Edgar Degas,
*A Carriage at
the Races,*
1869.
Oil on canvas;
36·5 55·9 cm,
14³⁄₈ 22 in.
Museum of
Fine Arts,
Boston

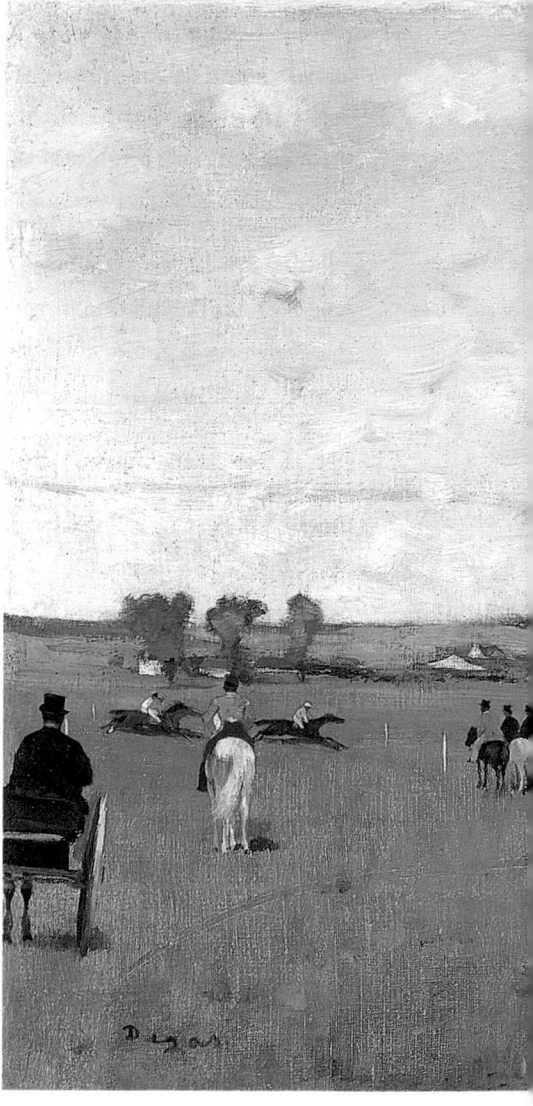

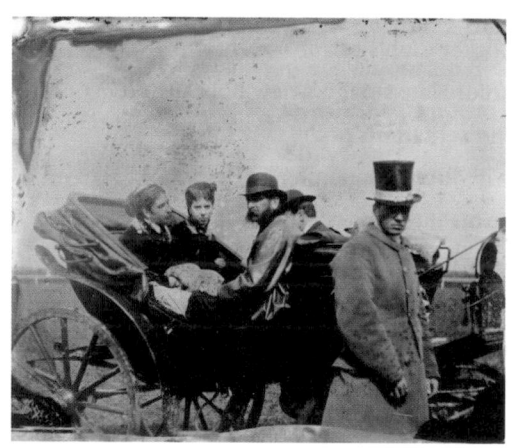

A Carriage at the Races records an outing to the nearby racecourse at Argentan. Tents, corrals, riders and some spectators are seen across the field in the distance. Against this background, we witness a touching domestic story, in which the baby Henri Valpinçon dozes off, leaving his wet nurse's breast dangling. His attentive mother checks the situation, and the pet bulldog and father look on from their proud perch. Degas makes some astute observations of social class: the intimacy of the mother, child and nurse displays the degree to which a bourgeois family took their domestic staff for granted –

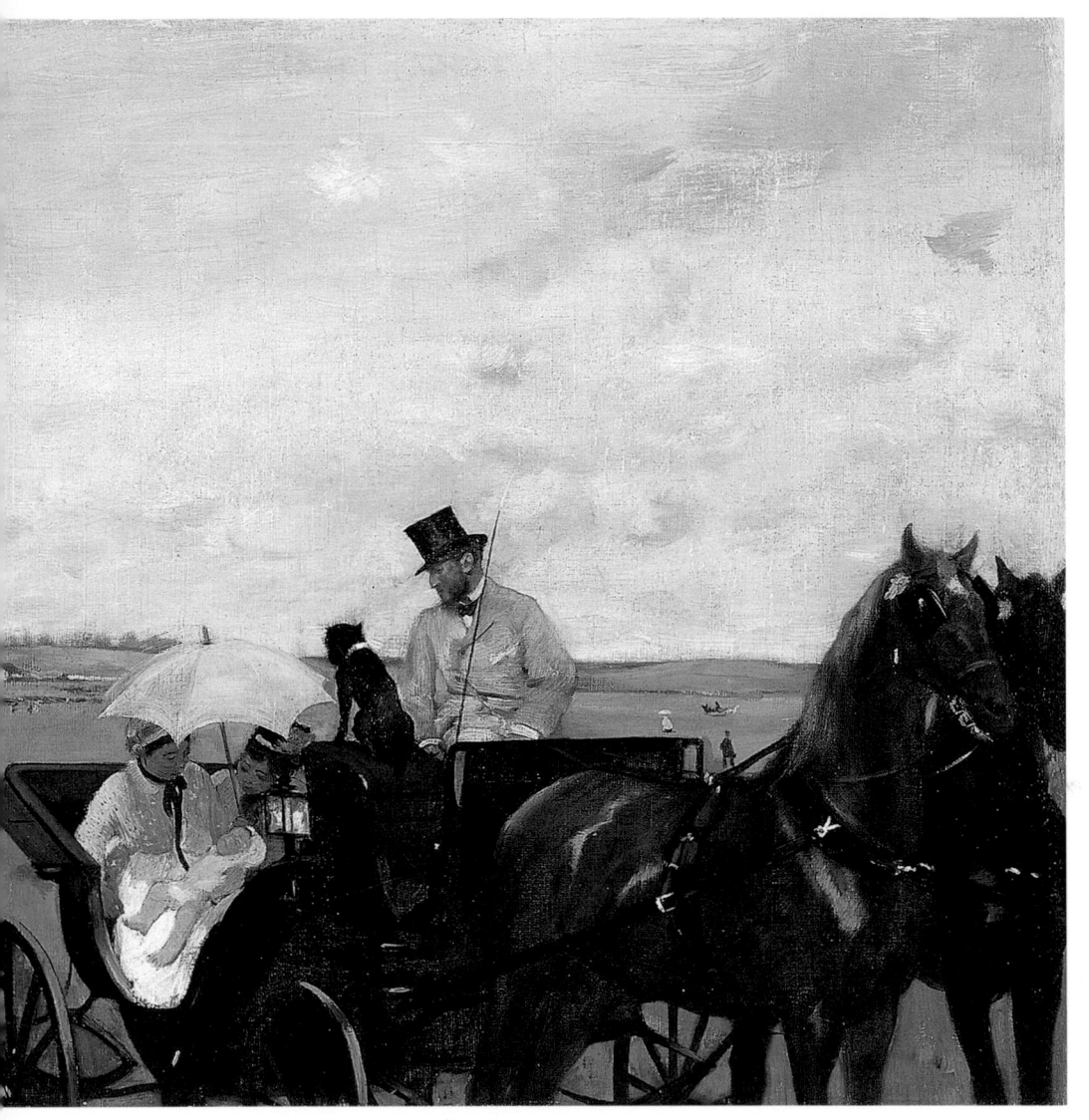

the nurse's exposed breast in broad daylight (rarely in the history of art had a breast drooped so realistically low) is no disgrace, for propriety among women of her class is a function of utility rather than sex. The father's dominant position and formal dress signify his circulation in the social world, while women and children remain in protected comfort.

The right-hand and bottom edges of this painting have attracted much comment. They derive most clearly from contemporary photography,

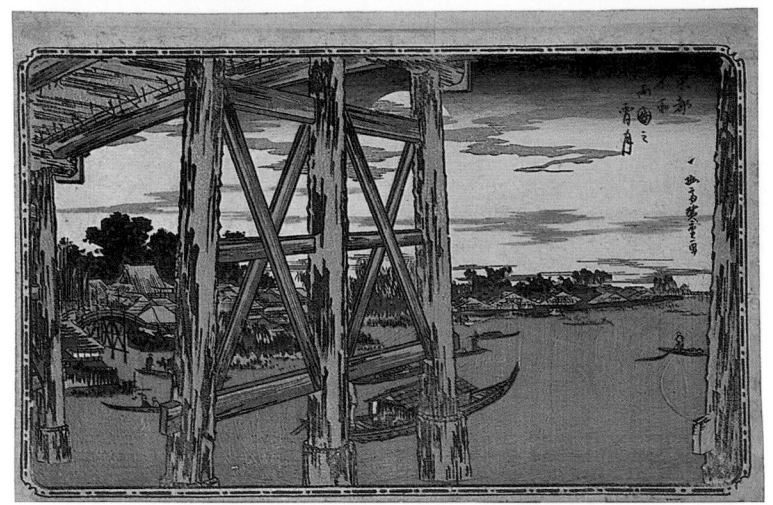

118
Andō
Hiroshige,
*Twilight Moon at
Ryogoku Bridge*,
c.1830.
Colour
woodblock
print;
24·2 × 36·5 cm,
9½ × 14⅜ in

as comparison with an anonymous family portrait reveals (116). The
cropping of wheels and horses in the latter are a result of the mobile,
tripod-based box camera viewfinder, which the photographer has
focused quite conventionally on the figures, much as in Courbet's *The
Trellis* (see 115). In a photograph such effects are regarded as incidental;
when they merit attention at all, it is as a sign of a technology associated with modernity and scientific objectivity. By transposing those
signs to painting, however, Degas has done the unexpected; they
demand attention precisely because they signify the new naturalist
vision. With his slicing effect at the left-hand edge – the carriage seen
from behind seems to balance precariously on a single wheel – Degas's
'cropping' becomes a declaration of modernity comparable to Monet's
foregrounding of contrasting shadow in *Women in the Garden* (see 56).
Degas's device is not without irony, though, for in producing a disjunc-
tive effect any other painter would certainly have avoided, he reveals
how calculated personal decisions – the subjective element – underlie
purported naturalist effects. In formal portraiture, for instance, no
artist would have allowed Paul Valpinçon's whip to cut across his body
or the parasol's point to cut into the nursemaid's head. Such signs of
casual naturalism are consciously affected against age-old habits.

Although it is unlikely that a specific Japanese print inspired Degas's
work, the unexpected cuttings, asymmetries and jarring juxtapositions

of foreground and background can be found in many works by the famous nineteenth-century woodcut makers Hokusai and Hiroshige (1797–1858), where they are essential aspects of a consistent and sophisticated aesthetic. For example, in *Twilight Moon at Ryogoku Bridge* (118), Hiroshige used the system of Western perspective, which Japanese artists had discovered relatively recently, to an aestheticizing rather than a solely realist end. Similarly, Degas used the framing edge, the close-up view and the overlapping of objects to call attention to the haphazard nature of reality as well as to his novel and clever recognition of it. If Monet can be considered the purveyor of light and colour, Degas may be called the master of space and formal arrangement. Like Monet, he is attentive to specific visual phenomena found in nature (and captured through the medium of photography), which he then used to produce effects perceived as 'natural'. Today, we have accepted Monet's fragmentation of forms, flattening and contrasting colours, which were disturbing to his contemporaries, as signs of a natural process of recording actual appearances, even though we are always conscious of looking at a painting while we do. Although the traditionally trained Degas avoided harsh criticism by handling his paint more tightly than Monet, the dynamic balance he produced between naturalism and artifice was related. With subtle irony, Degas appropriated effects from photography, but he made sure his results were far from photographic.

Rather, the effect of his off-centred objects extending beyond the frame is that of the casual vision of a passer-by – a *flâneur* on horseback or in a carriage in this case. There was no such thing as a 'snapshot' in his day. For his portrait (119) of *Vicomte Ludovic Lepic and his Daughters (Place de la Concorde)*, Degas used a layout nearly identical to that of *A Carriage at the Races* (see 117). Ludovic-Napoléon Lepic (1839–89), a watercolourist and printmaker friend whom Degas brought into the Impressionist circle, seems to wander aimlessly across the most splendid public space of Paris. The glorious, tree-lined avenue des Champs-Elysées is behind us; the garden of the Tuileries provides the painting's backdrop, with the beginning of the arcaded rue de Rivoli to its left. As in *A Carriage at the Races*, the slicing effect at the left-hand edge suggests a random, glancing view. His

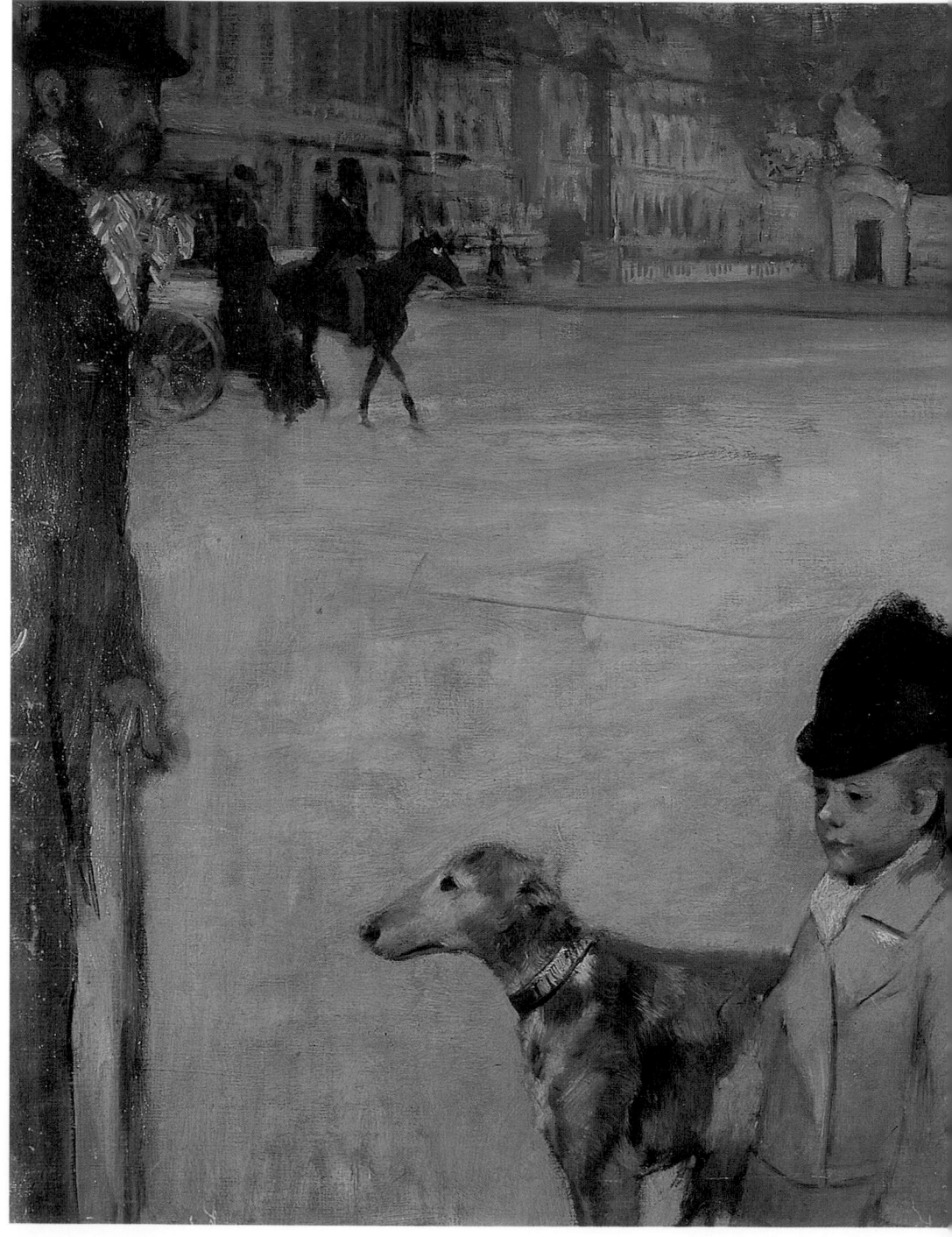

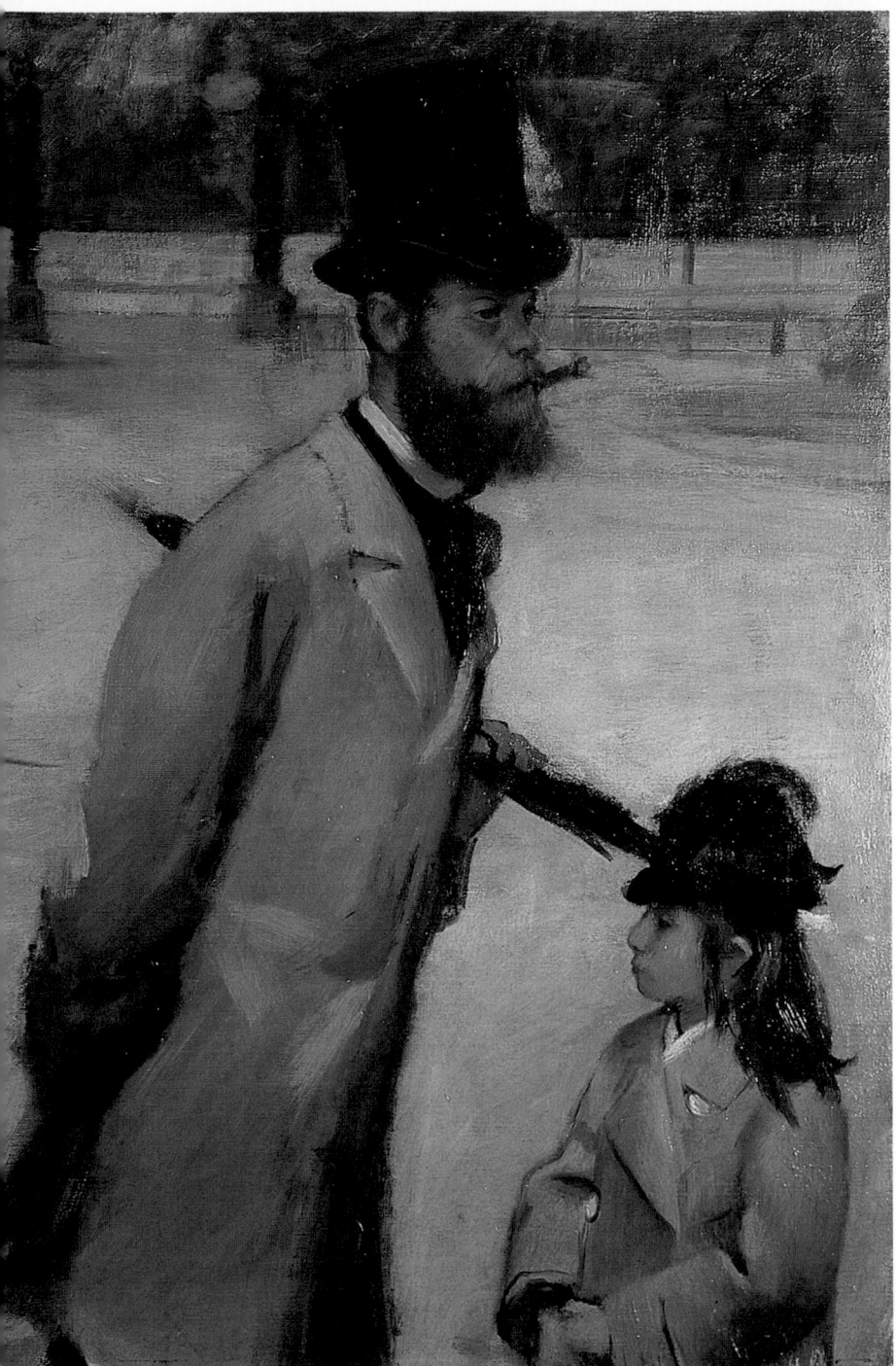

119
Edgar Degas,
*Vicomte Ludovic
Lepic and his
Daughters (Place
de la Concorde),*
1875.
Oil on canvas;
79 × 118 cm,
$31^1\!/_8 × 46^1\!/_2$ in.
State
Hermitage
Museum,
St Petersburg

principal figures are amputated at the knees to make them seem to float across the surface against which they are flattened, so that they appear weightless. Lepic's body language suggests a leisurely pace, with his right arm behind his back and his left arm squeezing his umbrella; biting jauntily on his cigar, he seems lost in thought. The figure to the left is a bystander momentarily distracted by the family but noticed only by Lepic's greyhound. To be out in place de la Concorde in the afternoon, he would presumably belong to the class whose leisure permits such pleasure strolling. As an artist, then, Lepic's attitude seems to be that of the amateur or even the dandy – like Baudelaire, we can see leisure as such a man's 'profession'. And placing his painted scenes at the races or on the boulevards, Degas implies that his own attitudes are similar. Lepic's was a posture Degas certainly admired, though following his father's death he could not afford to practise it quite so easily.

Another man whose ideas Degas emulated was the novelist and critic Edmond Duranty, whose portrait he made in 1879 (120). We already know Duranty as a supporter of Realism who saw the Impressionists, especially Degas, as its successors. In his essay on *The New Painting*, Duranty held that artists 'will no longer separate the figure from the background of an apartment or the street … Instead, surrounding him are the furniture, fireplaces, curtains and walls that indicate his financial position, class and profession.' Degas followed exactly that practice for Duranty's portrait, placing him at his cluttered desk before a wall of stuffed bookshelves. Duranty's contemplative pose is derived from the Romantic cliché of artistic insight commonly used for representations of poets, painters and musicians. However, the tension in his left hand – emphasized by a line of blue pastel – with its fingers pressing on the left eye, energizes the gaze and narrows its focus, thereby echoing the critic's theories of naturalist observation and seconding Degas's emphasis on vision. In the materials of the portrait – pastel and tempera – Degas echoed Duranty's fascination for specialized tools and techniques. Degas's art, too, we may deduce, flowed from a similar combination of dispassionate scholarly pursuit and heightened perception.

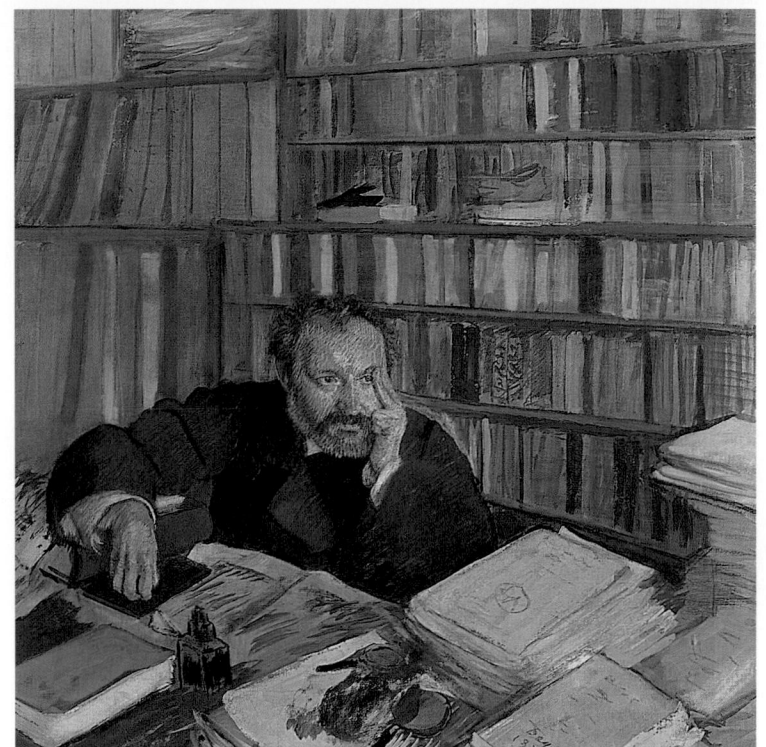

120
Edgar Degas,
*Portrait of
Edmond Duranty*,
1879.
Pastel,
watercolour
and tempera
on linen;
100·9 × 100·3 cm,
39³⁄₄ × 39¹⁄₂ in.
Glasgow Art
Gallery and
Museum

No group of works better embodies Degas's dual concern for sharp
observation and diffidence than his representations of the ballet.
Indeed, dance and stagecraft in general parallel Degas's artistic
efforts, for what the choreographer does to produce beautiful art by
means of his performers – who are real, quite often homely beings –
serves as a paradigm for how the painter draws from reality for
results that both clarify its effects and go beyond it. From his earliest
ballet scenes, Degas was preoccupied by what he believed was the
superiority of art to nature. He once told another Impressionist: 'For
you, natural life is necessary; for me artificial life.'

The Opéra, where ballets were performed, was a privileged site,
frequented by members of the upper classes. Degas's pictures speak
authentically, therefore, of his station within an exclusive world.
Members of the Jockey Club had season tickets to performances and
passes that admitted them to rehearsals and the back rooms where
dancers dressed and trained. Degas was also an insider through his

family connections – his father Auguste De Gas was an amateur musician who knew intimately several members of the orchestra, whom he invited to Monday gatherings at his home.

In *The Musicians in the Orchestra* (121), the composition is boldly divided in a way that echoes popular magazine illustrations, where artists practised eye-catching strategies and cutting wit, both of which were signs of modernity. Daumier, particularly, was a master of both (122). In the Degas, a broad view of the orchestra is blocked by the large heads of three musicians, a violinist, oboist and cellist, which seem to

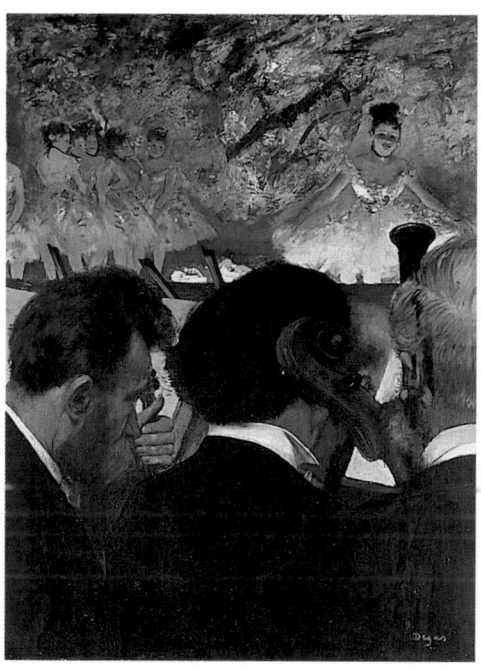 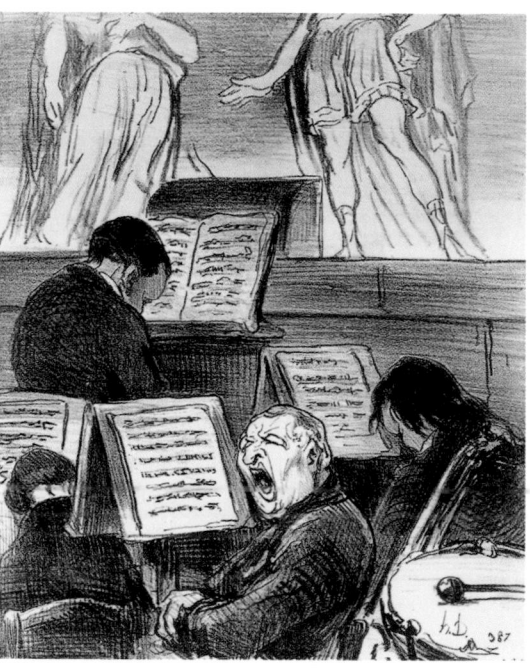

be portraits from the rear but have yet to be identified. Directly above them, the prima ballerina takes her bows, brightly illuminated by gas footlights from below. Other dancers stand to the side against loosely sketched flats of forest scenery. The radical juxtaposition of foreground heads with the stage above them makes it seem as if the view is taken from the front row of the audience. It is from this authoritative standpoint that we discover the spectacle to be a production combining multiple forms of art. The dancers shed their roles as characters to become professionals acknowledging applause; the musicians await the final curtain, holding the instruments they have finished playing. Degas has here assembled the various elements of the ensemble without actually showing the result, thus deconstructing theatrical illusion. In a parallel manner, his own pictorial construction brazenly displays its artifice, with its brutal division, flattening, and free handling of the upper register.

In paintings of dancing classes in rehearsal rooms done in the early 1870s, Degas systematically explored ballerina training, while structuring his spaces and playing on mirror reflections in ways that reveal his own self-conscious processes. Some of these paintings, for example *Dance Class at the Opéra* (123), have the feel of Dutch genre pictures, with their small size, muted tones and relatively conservative

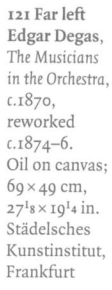

121 Far left
Edgar Degas,
The Musicians in the Orchestra,
c.1870,
reworked
c.1874–6.
Oil on canvas;
69 × 49 cm,
27¹⁄₈ × 19¹⁄₄ in.
Städelsches
Kunstinstitut,
Frankfurt

122 Left
**Honoré
Daumier**,
*The Orchestra
During the
Performance
of a Tragedy*,
1852.
Engraving

123 Right
Edgar Degas,
*The Dance Class
at the Opéra,
Rue Le Peletier*,
1872.
Oil on canvas;
32·3 × 46 cm,
12³⁄₄ × 18¹⁄₈ in.
Musée d'Orsay,
Paris

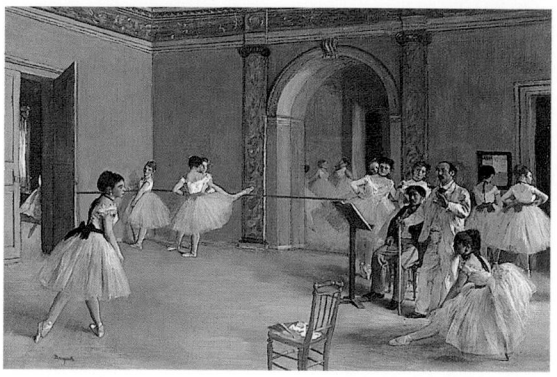

handling, and they sold fairly well. Their naturalism was always enhanced by his use of recognizable ballerinas and teachers. Although Degas probably visited the rehearsal rooms in both the old opera house in the rue Le Peletier and, after 1875, the Palais Garnier, he actually orchestrated his compositions in the studio. Indeed, despite the authentic look of his paintings, Degas wrote to his friend Albert Hecht in the 1870s to request a pass for a ballet examination class, confessing, 'I have done so many of these dance examinations without having seen them that I am a little ashamed.'

Within a few years of his first ballet compositions, Degas was exploring a whole series of complex and inventive structures. Many of them exist in several variants, testimony both to his interest in getting the

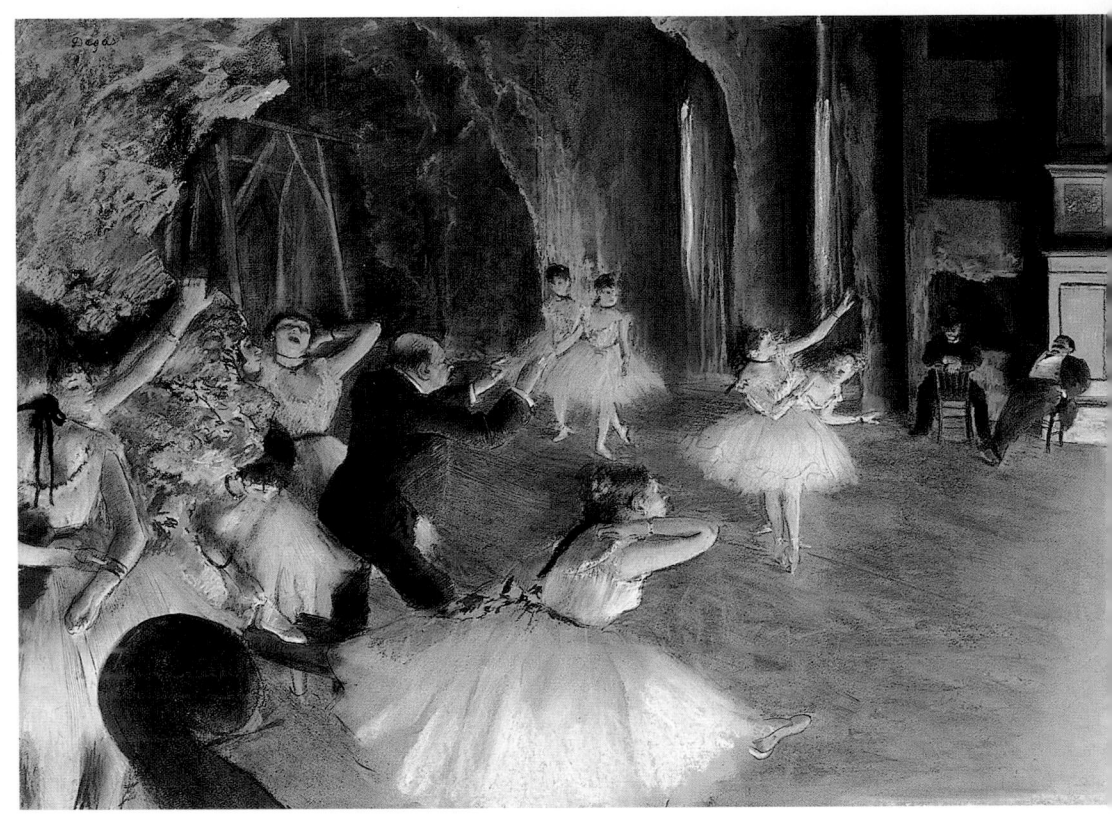

124
Edgar Degas,
*The Rehearsal
of the Ballet on
the Stage*,
c.1874.
Pastel over
brush and ink
drawing on
cream-coloured
paper, mounted
on bristol
board;
53 × 61 cm,
21 × 28½ in.
Metropolitan
Museum of Art,
New York

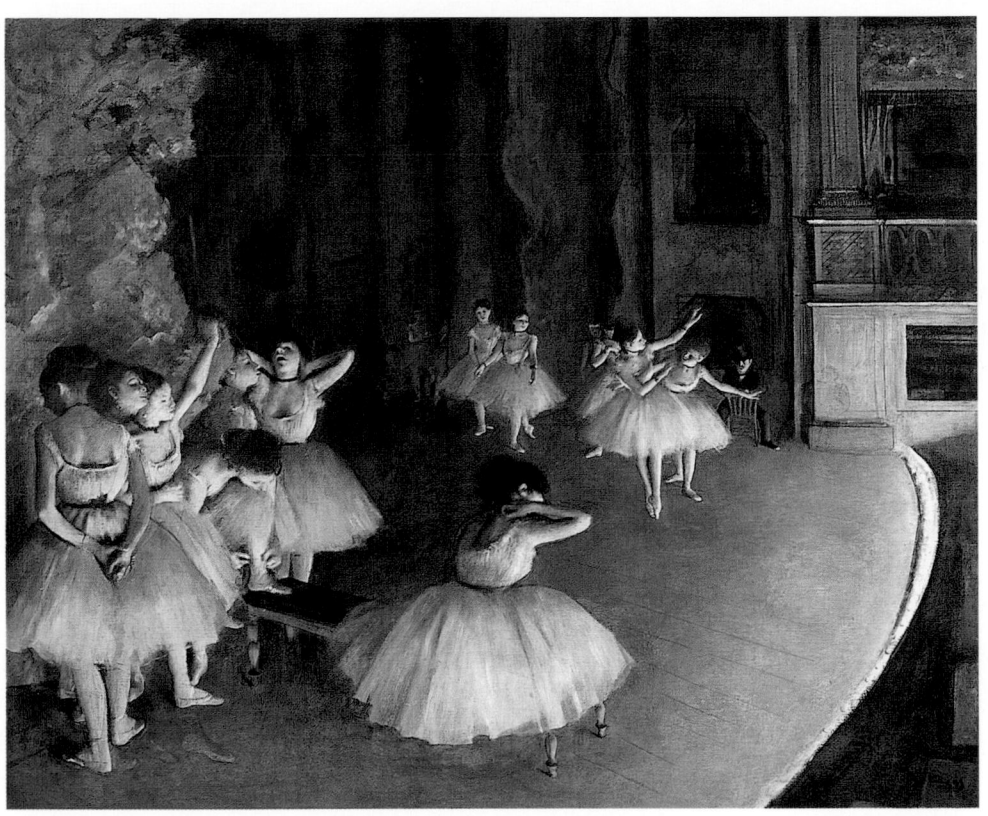

125
Edgar Degas,
*Ballet Rehearsal
on the Stage,*
c.1874.
Oil on canvas;
65 × 81 cm,
25⅝ × 31⅞ in.
Musée d'Orsay,
Paris

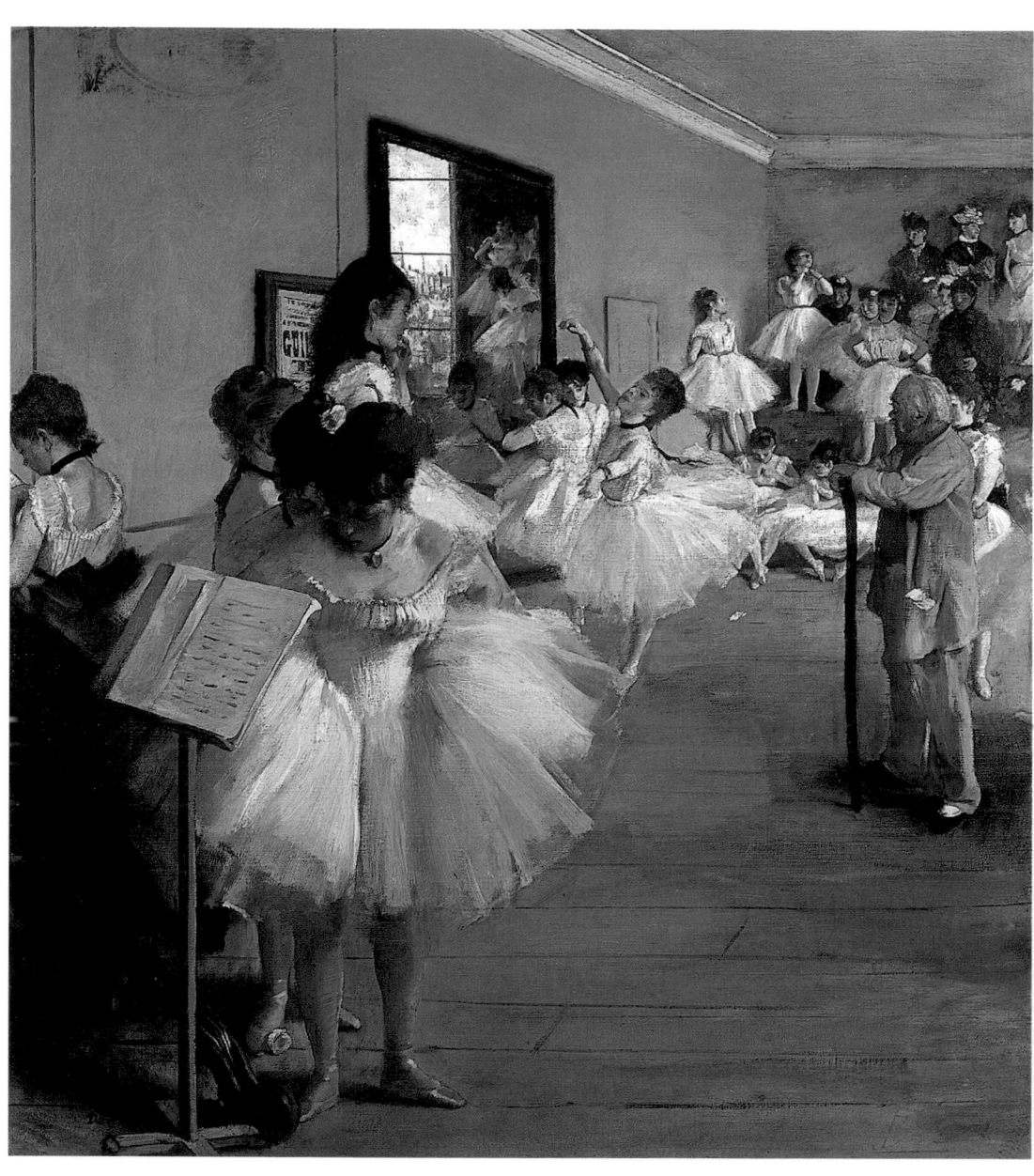

most from an idea and to a persistent experimentation that sometimes prevented him from finishing. *The Rehearsal of the Ballet on the Stage* (124) coexists with two other versions in different techniques, one of which is of slightly larger size. The latter, known as *Ballet Rehearsal on the Stage* (125), is painted in oils on canvas but is virtually monochromatic. It shows the rounded edge of the stage, but one of the gentlemen spectators to the right was painted out, the dance master is absent and there is no scroll of a double bass poking into the field of vision from below. These are significant elements, however, for they complicate the composition, distance it spatially and psychologically, and place the dancers' movements across the sweeping stage under watchful male eyes and direction. They expound a more complete statement of Degas's interest in the ballet as a scrutinizing and discriminating amateur. An important element of such pictures is the contrast between the graceful artifice of dancing positions, as for the two ballerinas at centre stage, and the awkward yawns, back-scratching and multifarious other gestures of the girls awaiting their turn. The view of the stage from the side reveals the structure of the scenery, like an anatomy lesson of the theatre's skeleton. To the left, it can almost be read as a sylvan setting; to the right, it looks like a series of ribs, with openings for entry from the wings.

126
Edgar Degas,
The Dance Class,
1876.
Oil on canvas;
83·2 × 76·8 cm,
32³⁴ × 30¹⁴ in.
Metropolitan
Museum of Art,
New York

It has often been observed that Degas's ballerinas are not necessarily pretty. An especially good example of what has been variously called Degas's cruel observation or misogyny (a much disputed term among art historians) is the stocky figure seen from the front in *The Dance Class* (126). Many theories have been offered in explanation of what may be simply a reflection of the mundane truth that dancers are real people and that it is their art, rather than their actual appearance, we admire. Yet the fact that Degas felt entitled to practise unvarnished naturalism on ballet dancers implies a position of both social and sexual power. Degas's representations of women, and dancers in particular, are therefore a much debated topic among Degas scholars. The question of sexuality and gender will be dealt with more extensively in Chapter 6. Here, we will examine the discourse of 'scientific' naturalism within which Degas's representational practices must be placed.

One of the most interesting case studies for this issue is Degas's sculpture of *The Little Fourteen-Year-Old Dancer* (127). Clearly a crucial piece in Degas's presentations at the Impressionist exhibitions – the only sculpture he ever exhibited publicly – he announced the work for 1880, when a glass case, like those used for anthropological or natural history exhibits, was set up in the middle of the gallery. (One critic referred to it as a cage.) For reasons unknown, he withheld the work until the following year, and, even then, he did not deliver it until two weeks after the opening. The model for the sculpture was one Marie van Goethem, who turned fourteen in 1878. Degas's use of wax was probably in part related to the revival in France of interest in ancient techniques and the discovery that ancient statues were painted. (The bronze casts of this work, like all Degas bronzes, are posthumous editions done in cooperation with the Degas estate.) With the wax, he combined other elements, such as a real cotton tutu, hair obtained from a doll-maker, and a satin ribbon – materials more closely associated with wax museum exhibits than high art. Indeed, the most remarkable effect of the statue was its realism. Responses to the work concurred in seeing the little girl as a 'blossoming street urchin', with a 'pug-nosed, vicious face', and 'brutish insolence'. 'Why is her forehead, as are her lips, so profoundly marked by vice?' one critic asked.

Degas had in fact been studying the physiognomy of vice. In 1880, he exhibited some pastels of criminals observed in the courtroom during the well-publicized murder trial in 1879 of Émile Abadie and members of his gang. These studies are perhaps the most sensational examples of Degas's attention to theories of physiognomy, racialism and criminality that were widespread in scientific circles of the nineteenth century. Relevant writings range from Johann Caspar Lavater's *Physiognomical Fragments* of the late 1790s, to Charles Darwin's *The Origin of Species* (1859) and Césare Lombroso's *The Criminal* (1876). Scholars Anthea Callen, Douglas Druick and Peter Zegers have amply demonstrated Degas's interest in illustrations that depicted human moral character through the degree to which an individual resembled animal ancestors. It was a concept so common, even before Darwin, that by the 1840s it was taken up by caricaturists

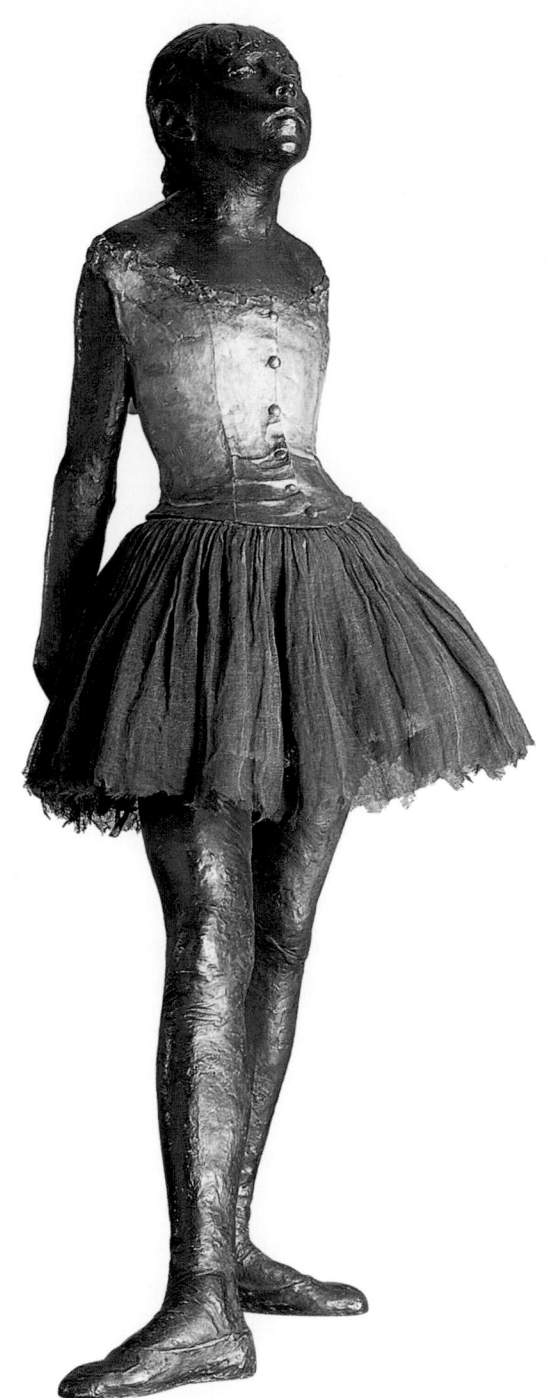

127
Edgar Degas,
The Little
Fourteen-Year-Old
Dancer,
1879–81.
Wax, cotton
skirt, satin hair
ribbon;
h.95·2 cm,
37¹₂ in.
Private
collection

such as Daumier and Grandville (128). In 1867, Degas's friend Duranty published an essay on physiognomy in which he called criminals 'savages of the civilized world', alluding to their relationship to so-called 'inferior' races. In the same essay, he advocated close observation as the means of judging character and cited the novelists Zola and the Goncourt brothers as masters of the technique. In *The New Painting*, he used similar criteria in support of Degas. For such an artist, he wrote, even a view from the back could reveal 'a temperament, an age, a social condition ... A physiognomy will tell us that one fellow is certainly an orderly, dry, meticulous man, whereas another is carelessness and disorderliness itself.'

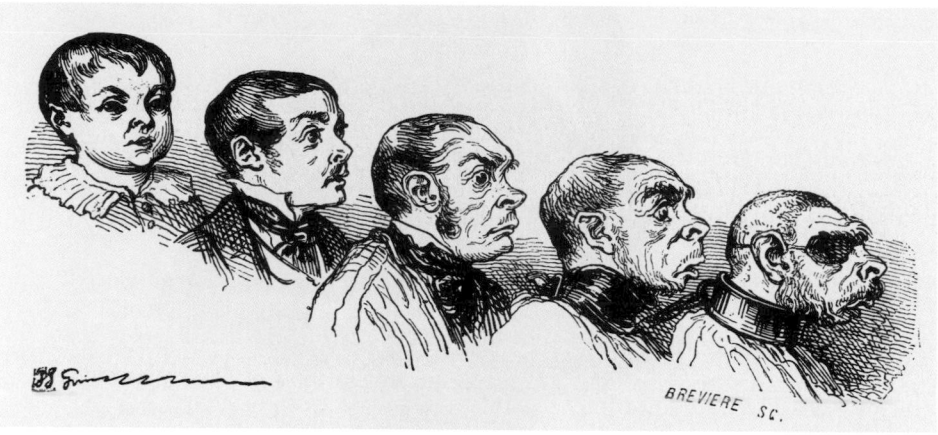

In a study of Mademoiselle Hughes for *Dance Class at the Opéra* (129), there is a line paralleling the dancer's nose and forehead which, if Degas had used it for the outline of her profile, would have given her the face of a monkey. In a notebook drawing (130) for *The Song of the Dog* (131) of c.1877 Degas sketched the singer's profile with ape-like features. In *The Little Fourteen-Year-Old Dancer*, Degas gave the young Maria van Goethem a far more simian look than in his first studies for the piece. Anthea Callen has shown how intermediate studies gradually transformed the dancer's physiognomy into its final form. Cracks in the neck of a maquette and fingerprints left in its modelling clay reveal that Degas pushed the girl's head back so the forehead would seem flatter and the ear would appear below the line of the mouth, attributes associated in nineteenth-century scientific theories with stupidity.

In recognizing these elements in Degas's art, his audience was confirming their preconceptions about dancers. The novelist Joris-Karl Huysmans acknowledged that Degas had 'implacably rendered' the 'terrible reality'. Although not all dancers came from the ranks of the poor and uneducated, most Parisians assumed they did. The ballet was often a means of upward social mobility, through the earnings it provided and the contacts girls could make with upper-class men. During the very period that Degas was producing his ballet paintings, his boyhood friend Ludovic Halévy was publishing his stories of *La Famille Cardinal* (1880), which recounted the foibles of two young dancers and their ambitious yet protective parents (see below). The inner world of opera and ballet were of intense public interest not only because of the artistic insights one could acquire but because of its allusions to sexuality. In the most basic terms, the ballet consisted of young girls using their bodies to entertain men. Ballerinas were considered available and were patronized by wealthy opera-goers who had access to the rehearsal rooms in a form of clandestine prostitution. When the new Garnier Opéra opened in 1875, a large foyer behind the main stage served as a meeting place (although Degas's paintings continued to represent the older spaces). Degas's ballerinas were therefore both objects of the male gaze and of sexual exploitation. His attitudes towards them combined fascination and distaste. Indeed, the ballerina embodied exactly that modernity Degas both feared and yet accepted as the necessary subject matter he would 'choreograph' into art.

128
Grandville,
*Man Descending
towards the Brute*,
1843.
Wood
engraving

Some observers felt Degas's sensational subject matter and radical constructions were deliberate affronts to bourgeois conventionality. But if his attitude towards the middle class may have been contempt, there is no sign he considered its members subhuman. Accompanying his 'scientific' explorations of ballerina physiognomy, however, one senses just such an assumption of superiority that allowed him to regard people of lower station as specimens for examination. Prominent among the Parisian phenomena that most fascinated such men was prostitution. In 1876, Huysmans published a novel about a prostitute entitled *Marthe*. In 1877, seven years after the death of his brother Jules, Edmond Goncourt published his novel *La Fille Élisa* (*fille* could mean prostitute as well as girl), which seems to have inspired Degas to make some sketches in his notebook. The artist later acknowledged Goncourt's profound influence on his work. In *L'Assommoir* (1877), Zola introduced the character of Nana, who would become the courtesan of his novel by that title of 1880. She was well-enough known that one writer referred to Degas's *The Little Fourteen-Year-Old Dancer* as 'little Nana' in 1881. Prostitution brought sexual fantasy and frustration together with contemporary debates on hygiene, female psychology, the family and criminality. In addition, Degas's virtual obsession with the theme raises questions about his own sexual ambivalences that must add complexity to the issue. Many of Degas's contemporaries believed prostitutes provided an

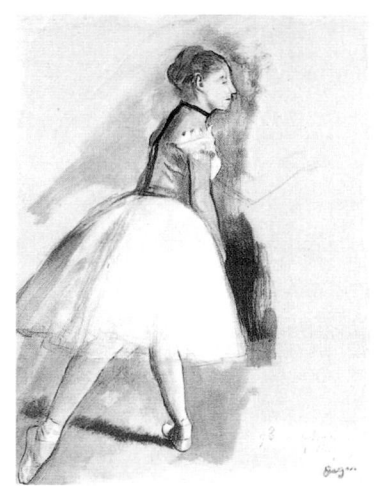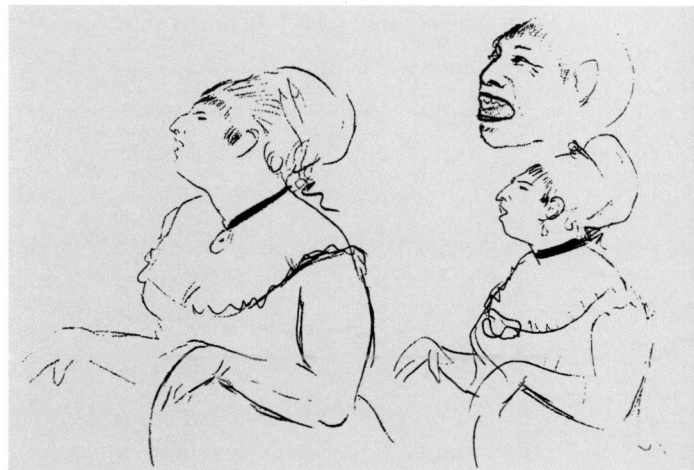

outlet for natural male drives and that they actually helped preserve the family. Prostitutes thus held the contradictory position of being tolerated as a social necessity and being condemned for contributing to depravity. Degas rarely showed prostitute pictures at public exhibitions or in oil paintings – a technique he generally reserved for formal and finished works.

One exception to Degas's reticence about exhibiting pictures of prostitutes was his *Women on a Café Terrace, Evening* (132). Unlike numerous monotypes of naked prostitutes in brothels which he made but did not display (see below), this picture showed them fully clothed at a

129 Far left
Edgar Degas,
Study for *Dance
Class at the
Opéra, Rue Le
Peletier*,
1872.
Essence and
pencil on
paper;
27·1 × 21 cm,
10⁵⁸ × 8¼ in.
Private
collection

130 Left
Edgar Degas,
Page of a note-
book with
sketch for *The
Song of the Dog*,
c.1877.
Private
collection

131 Right
Edgar Degas,
*The Song
of the Dog*,
c.1878.
Gouache and
pastel over
monotype
on paper;
57·5 × 45·5 cm,
22⁵⁸ × 17⁷⁸ in.
Private
collection

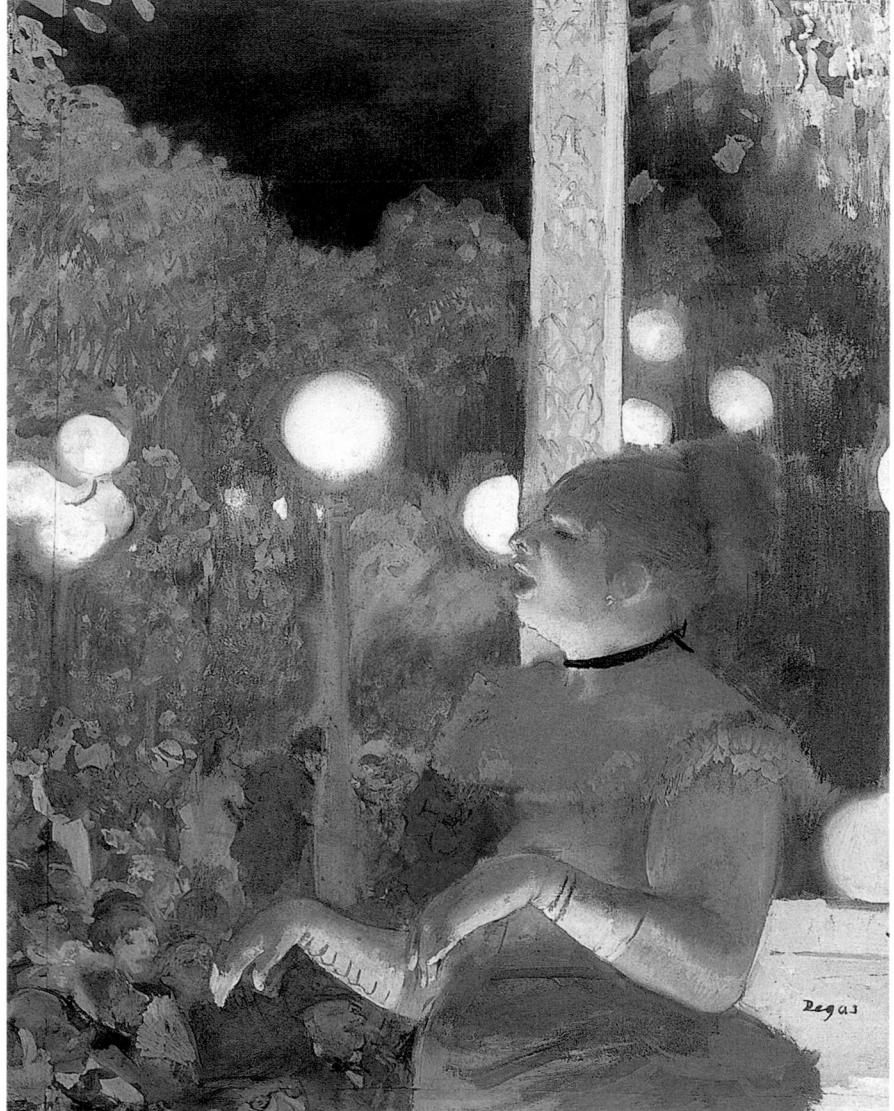

café. Whether they are just relaxing or awaiting clients is ambiguous. One makes a vulgar gesture of contempt with her thumb against her teeth. Has she just refused a proposition by the passer-by moving off along the boulevard to the right? Another is either sitting down or getting up; we can be sure of comings and goings but unsure of the reasons why. When this picture was shown at the Impressionist exhibition of 1877, critics recognized the 'painted, faded creatures, exuding vice, who cynically tell each other about their day's activities and accomplishments'. But a close look at their features reveals Degas's tendency towards caricature. The picture thus belongs with his other views of urban entertainments, such as *The Song of the Dog* (see 131),

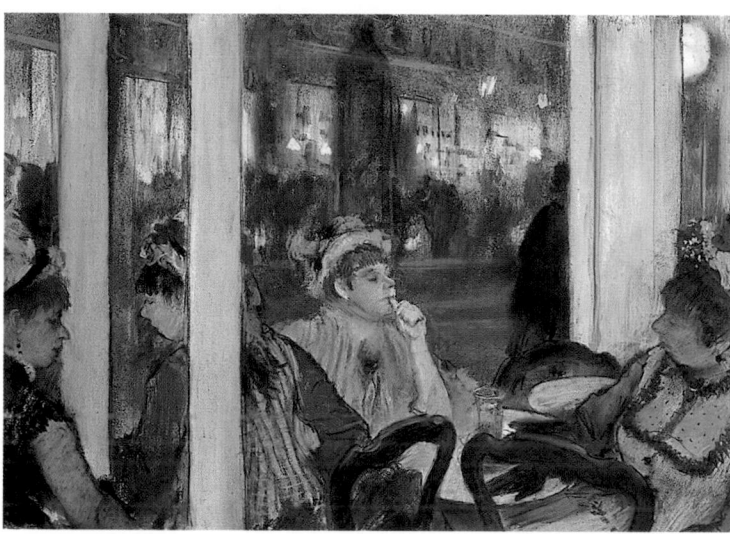

132
Edgar Degas,
Women on a Café Terrace, Evening,
1877.
Pastel over monotype;
41 × 60 cm,
16⅛ × 23⅝ in.
Musée d'Orsay, Paris

133
Edgar Degas,
Café-Concert at Les Ambassadeurs,
c.1877.
Pastel over monotype;
37 × 27 cm,
14½ × 10½ in.
Musée des Beaux-Arts, Lyon

with the canine gesture of the singer's arms, or *Café-Concert at Les Ambassadeurs* (133) – also shown in 1877 – in which the chanteuse reaches out to the audience while in the lower left-hand corner, a male spectator ogles some of the women nearby. Like the Folies-Bergère, the Café des Ambassadeurs was a crowded venue where members of different classes, Parisian and foreign, mixed fluidly and often sought encounters. Located in the heart of Paris, among the trees and prolific gas lamps where the Champs-Elysées meets the place de la Concorde, the Ambassadeurs and its sister establishments received a new lease of life during the 1860s by the lifting of restrictions that had privileged indoor theatres over outdoor cafés. The Ambassadeurs's ambitious

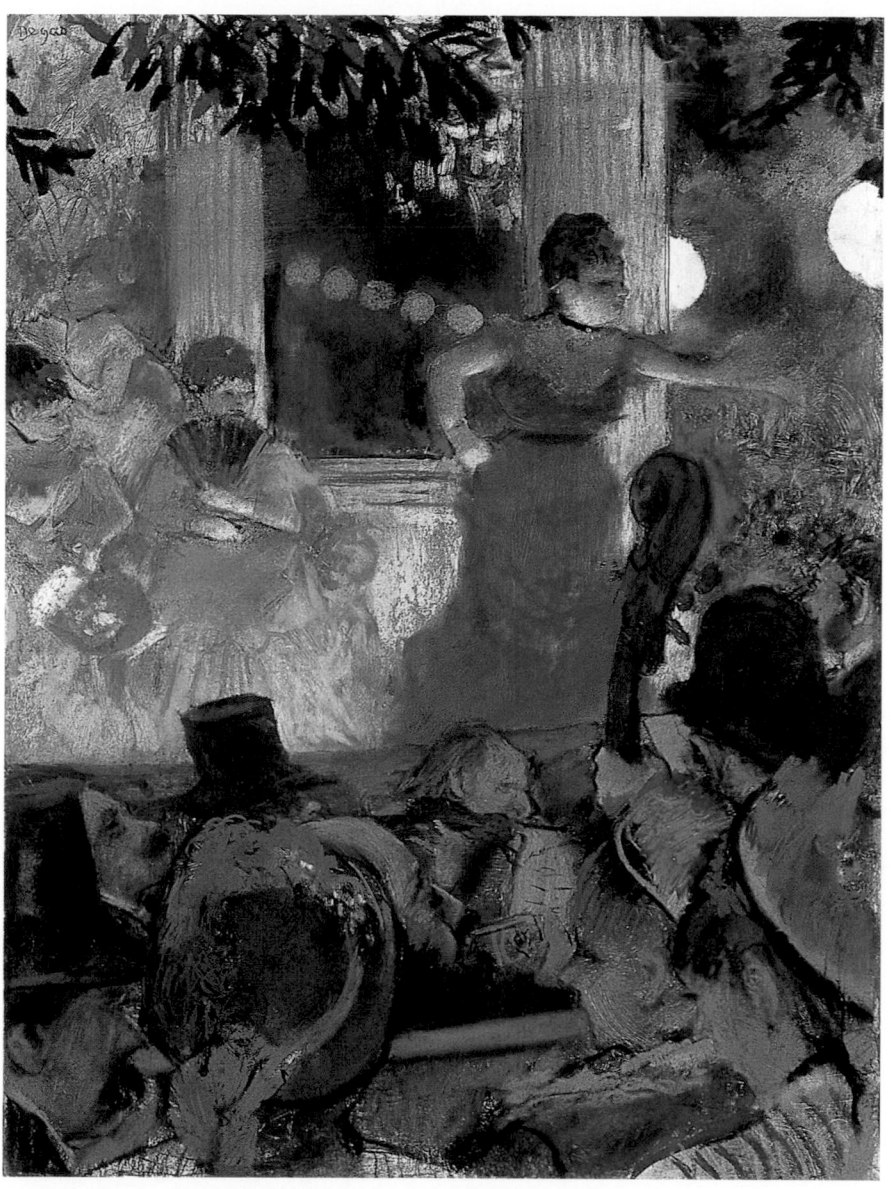

manager was, by his own account, 'always on the lookout for novelties, for original creations, for unexpected talents'. Cafés specialized in more popular entertainments, and, as Robert Herbert has pointed out, their acts were inevitably filled with sexual innuendo, working-class slang and coarse body language. Degas's images of nightlife, ostensibly at the other end of the artistic spectrum from ballet, certainly evoked this new world of class ambiguity and commercialism that defined the modern.

The technique of these images – pastel over monotype – was both novel and modern, yet with origins in traditional artistic craft. Degas learned monotype with his friend Lepic (most printmakers eventually discover it through trial and error), and gave it significant new status. A monotype is made by running an inked metal plate through a press with dampened paper. Degas might draw directly with the heavy printer's ink, wipe through areas covered with ink to produce the image, or draw through such areas with a stylus before taking the impression. Unlike traditional prints, where multiples are possible, only a single accurate impression of quality could be produced. The plate was never permanently marked by etching or engraving. To emphasize the uniqueness of his monotypes, Degas preferred to call them printed ink drawings. However, he often made a second, much fainter proof, which he then worked up with pastels. Pastels were pure pigments molded into stick form with a binding medium. They were considered extremely delicate (since the pigments easily flake off the paper surface into powder) and were associated with the elegant eighteenth-century Rococo style and with draughtsmen of the greatest refinement such as Jean-Baptiste-Siméon Chardin (1699–1779) or Maurice-Quentin de La Tour (1704–88). Pastel obviated the traditional distinction between line and colour by offering the opportunity to draw with colour directly. Degas's novel combinations were thus original, ephemeral and intimate – qualities which corresponded to the ideal of the fleeting moment and the rapid glance; yet they preserved his self-conscious relationship to historical methods. His dark, coarse foundation images overlaid with brilliant surfaces certainly parallel his subject matter of shady dealings and socially risky glitz.

Monotype alone was a natural medium for illustrations and for brothel images (134), both of which were intended for private viewing. Among the earliest works in Degas's nearly decade-long campaign in the medium were scenes from his friend Halévy's stories about the Cardinal family, which overlapped themes of the ballet with clandestine prostitution. For such scenes, the blurriness and lack of definition in monotype embodied both the discretion that a man of Degas's position would have brought to such conduct and his ambivalence about its coarseness – delicacy and unpleasantness combine in the aestheticizing 'heavy-handedness' of the unusual technique. Having made contemporary pastimes his specialty, brothel scenes were a logical step, impeded only by conventional propriety, to which he conceded by keeping most of the fifty-odd works for himself and friends. Naturally, the number of images of frontal nudity, onanistic gestures and grotesque postures raise questions about Degas's personal sexual attitudes. He never married, and there is slight evidence of an unfortunate rejection in his youth. Some have claimed he was celibate, but from an early letter we do know of his experience with prostitution. Whether the brothel scenes, located in state-regulated *maisons closes*, reveal his own proclivities or those of his social class to which he was a voyeur, seems less important than that he felt entitled to enter such spaces with the clinical eye of a detached observer. Many images seem like awkward experiments, but some of the bizarre poses parallel illustrations in Jean-Martin Charcot and Paul Richer's contemporary psychiatric treatises on hysteria, which was considered a female affliction. Others, such as the exceptionally large and coloured *The Name Day of the Madame* (135), are accomplished narrative compositions – this one an artful parody of bourgeois domesticity. In general, they appear neither unsympathetic to the women nor overtly judgemental.

Degas's more widely exhibited images of bathers were also derived from the theme of prostitution. The earliest ones were done in monotype and were part of the brothel series. Eunice Lipton has explained in her pioneering work that the form of bathing Degas depicted was certainly connected to prostitution. Bourgeois women did not bathe as often as prostitutes, who did so prior to intercourse

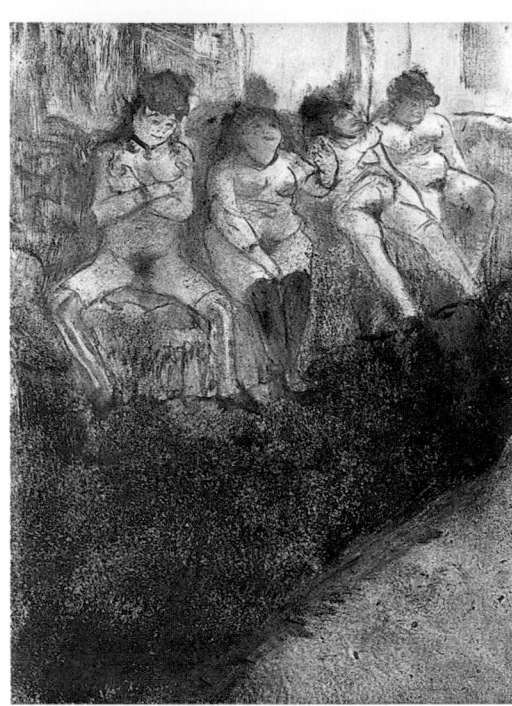

134
Edgar Degas,
Waiting,
1876–7.
Monotype in
black ink on
china paper,
2nd state;
21·6 × 16·4 cm,
8¹₂ × 6³₈ in.
Musée Picasso,
Paris

135
Edgar Degas,
*The Name Day
of the Madame*,
1876–7.
Pastel over
monotype on
white paper;
26·6 × 29·6 cm,
10¹₂ × 11⁵₈ in.
Musée Picasso,
Paris

in order to preserve the illusion of hygiene and ward off the dreaded
syphilis and other sexually transmitted diseases. In higher-class
establishments, which Degas's images reflect, maids often helped
with the bathing and prepared the room. Nor did 'respectable'
women generally bathe entirely naked (136), whereas for prostitutes,
nudity could be part of the ritual of arousal. In several of Degas's
bathing scenes there is a fully clothed male spectator. Yet, Degas's
bathers themselves are rarely shown from overtly titillating vantage
points (although after Degas's death, his brother is known to have
destroyed a number of images he regarded as obscene). In other
words, whether the viewer's position is that of the client or a disinterested third party remains ambiguous. Degas's friend George
Moore claimed the artist wanted to represent women who did not
know they were being observed, as if 'through a keyhole'. (Degas
himself admitted that in earlier times, he would have been painting
the story of Susanna and the elders, in which two older men cannot
resist spying on a beautiful young bather.) The odd angles and the
unconventional positions in the bather images suggest an unprivi-

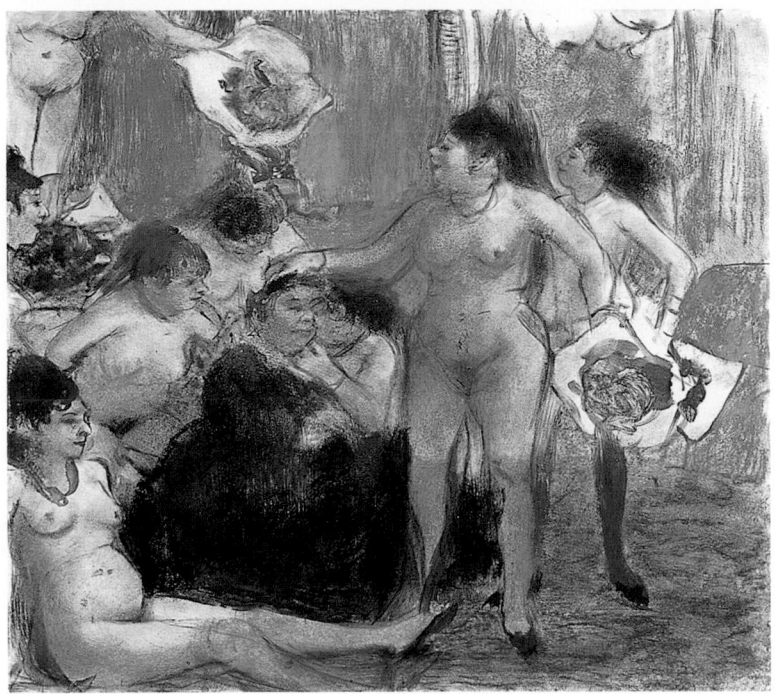

leged, haphazard view, like that of the opportunistic voyeur. Yet each
was carefully calculated; one model recalled how excruciating were
the poses the irascible artist demanded. Ironically, the end result in
certain cases may evoke a woman's private pleasure – her own self-
absorption apart from any dependency on men.

In the last Impressionist exhibition of 1886, Degas exhibited a series
of large pastels of bathers. His compositions were simpler than
before and closer up, with the figure tightly framed and dominating
the field of vision, yet psychologically removed by looking away or
posed from the side or rear, as in *The Tub* (137). Despite the obvious
beauty and technical finesse of the works, many in Degas's audience
continued to focus on who was represented. One writer compared
the bather reproduced here to a frog, alluding no doubt to her dubi-
ous profession (see Chapter 3). Another, one J M Michel, lamented
that the Venuses of old had been chased away by 'the Impressionist
ideal' – 'Nana washing, sponging and caring for herself, arming
herself for combat, that is. Don't forget that the exhibition is only
two steps from the corner of the boulevard [where prostitutes could

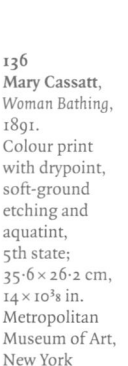

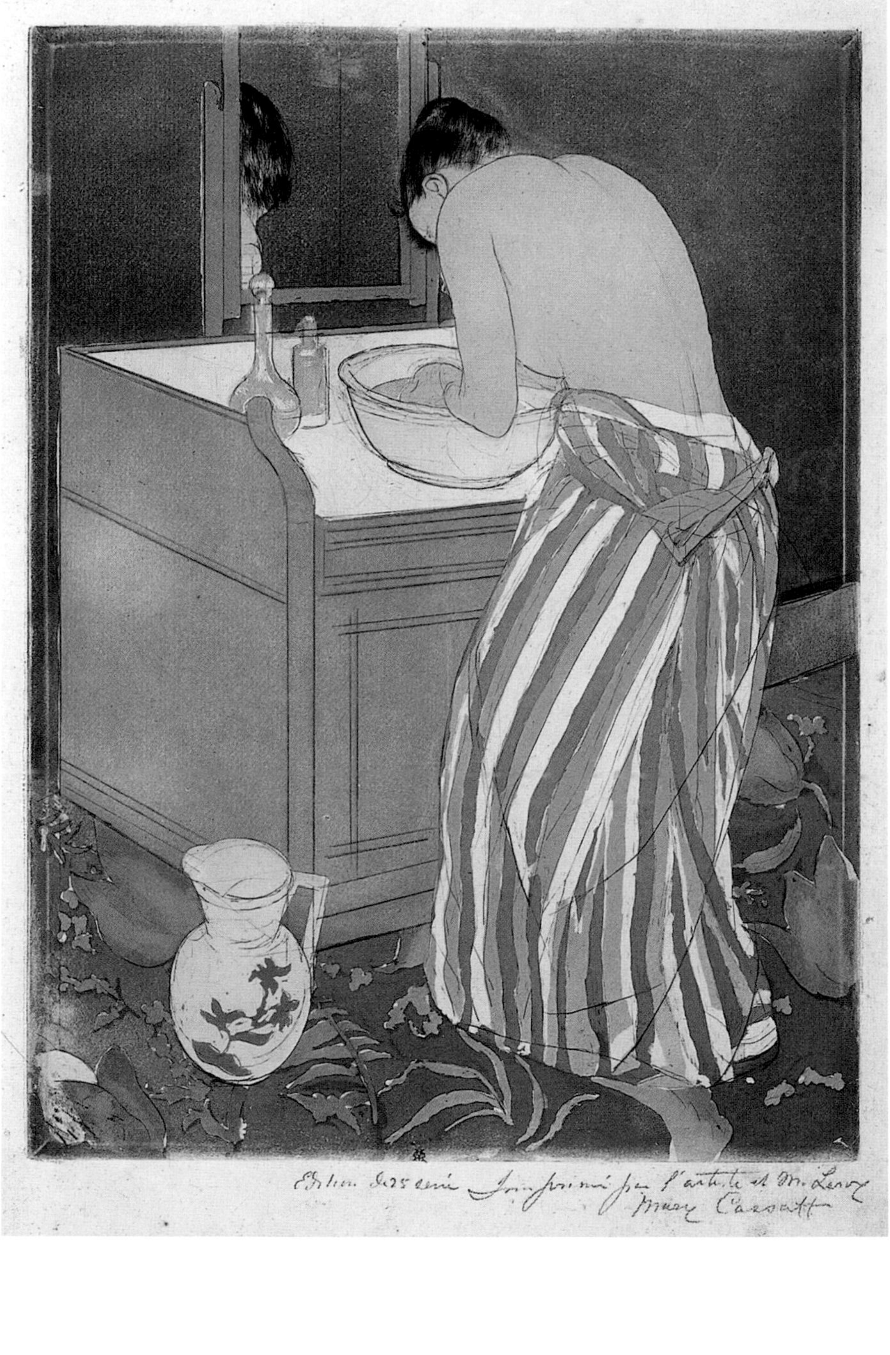

136
Mary Cassatt,
Woman Bathing,
1891.
Colour print
with drypoint,
soft-ground
etching and
aquatint,
5th state;
35·6 × 26·2 cm,
14 × 10³⁄₈ in.
Metropolitan
Museum of Art,
New York

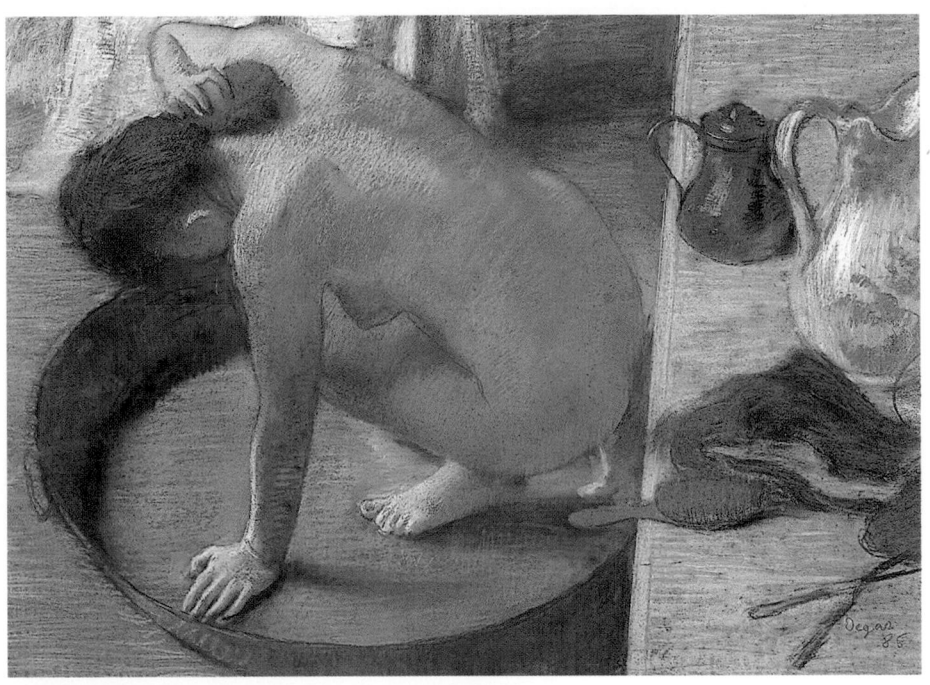

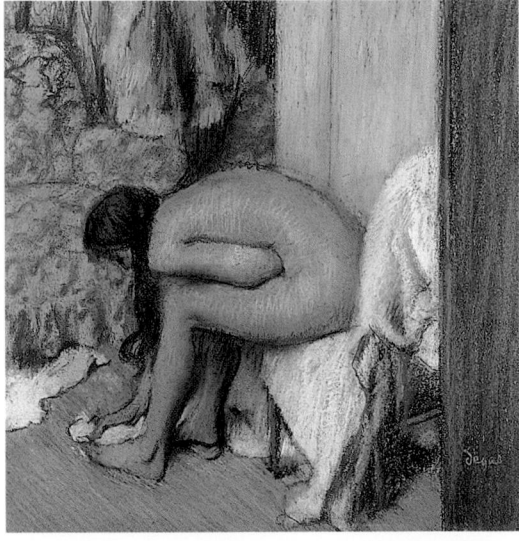

137 Above
Edgar Degas,
The Tub,
1886.
Pastel on paper;
60 × 83 cm,
23⅝ × 32⅝ in.
Musée d'Orsay,
Paris

138 Left
Edgar Degas,
*After the Bath,
Woman Drying
her Foot*,
1885–6,
Pastel on card;
54 × 52 cm,
21¼ × 20½ in.
Musée d'Orsay,
Paris

be found].' Yet the mention of Venus acknowledged kinship between Degas's bathers and Old Master works. Whether it was an ancient crouching Aphrodite, *Bathsheba* by Rembrandt van Rijn (1606–69), or *Diana after the Bath* by Boucher (see 100), all in the Louvre, there were plenty of respectable prototypes for Degas's up-dated subject matter. Not only was the location in a contemporary dressing room appropriate, Degas's method of representation was utterly modern, too. There were at least four pictures of the bather in a shallow tub, from different vantage points of approximately the same height, as in a pre-cinematic sequence of views rotating around the figure. Degas had made some notes to try such effects as early as 1879 or 1880. He probably read about the early experiments in America of Eadweard Muybridge (1830–1904) with sequential photographs. Degas himself was an amateur photographer and later used Muybridge's book, *Animal Locomotion* (1887), for studies of galloping horses. Looking back, he once confided to a biographer: 'Perhaps I looked on women too much as animals.'

Some measure of Degas's distinctiveness may be taken by his preoccupation with vision as a physical phenomenon. It is not that he read scientific treatises on the matter, but rather that he recorded the impact of vision as if it were physical. For example, his vigorous use of pastel in *After the Bath, Woman Drying her Foot* (138) appeals to our sense of touch, while maintaining the vicariousness of experience by producing it through hatchings that are obvious signs of art. Despite the remove of Degas's keyhole vantage point, his materials heighten sensuality, maintaining its location on the woman's body and the objects of her environment, yet displacing the erotic to the aesthetic. The viewer is made physically conscious of vision in ways comparable to Monet or Renoir's transpositions of light and colour into the materiality of paint. Degas's play of presence versus distance may certainly embody some deep-seated personal conflict between desire and self-abnegation, but it also embodies the nature of contemporary spectacle as experience at one remove.

Degas actually thematized that concept in a series of studies of a *Woman with Field Glasses* (139), made for a painting of the racecourse.

Lorgnette, the precise French term for the binoculars, contains the word *lorgner* – 'to ogle'. Anyone who has looked through such glasses will recognize the effect of a close-up view held curiously distant and disconnected by optical sensation. Their compressions of space and decontextualization of objects reduce our experience of them to the visual while simultaneously intensifying them. This figure is all the more disturbing because though her eyes are hidden from us, we sense her probing gaze, usually a prerogative of the male. That she

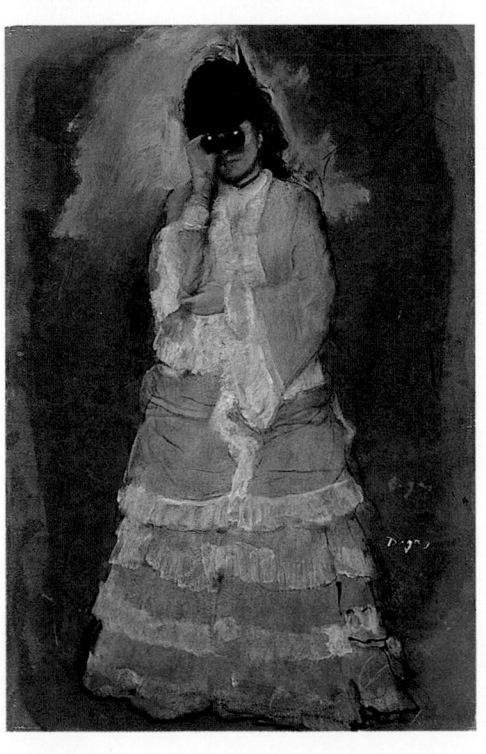

139
Edgar Degas,
Woman with
Field Glasses,
c.1875–6.
Oil on cardboard;
48 32 cm,
18⅞ 12⅝ in.
Staatliche
Kunstsammlungen,
Dresden

is a woman, therefore, heightens the (presumed male) viewer's sense of exposure and vulnerability resulting from the subversion of traditional hierarchies.

In numerous paintings, Degas emulated the close up/distancing effect produced by binoculars with startling results. One is the extraordinary *Miss La La at the Cirque Fernando* (140) of 1879, inspired by the daring of acrobats as well as by the appearance a few months earlier of Edmond Goncourt's novel *Les Frères Zemganno* (*The Zemganno Brothers*). Here the view from below a circus star hoisted by her teeth

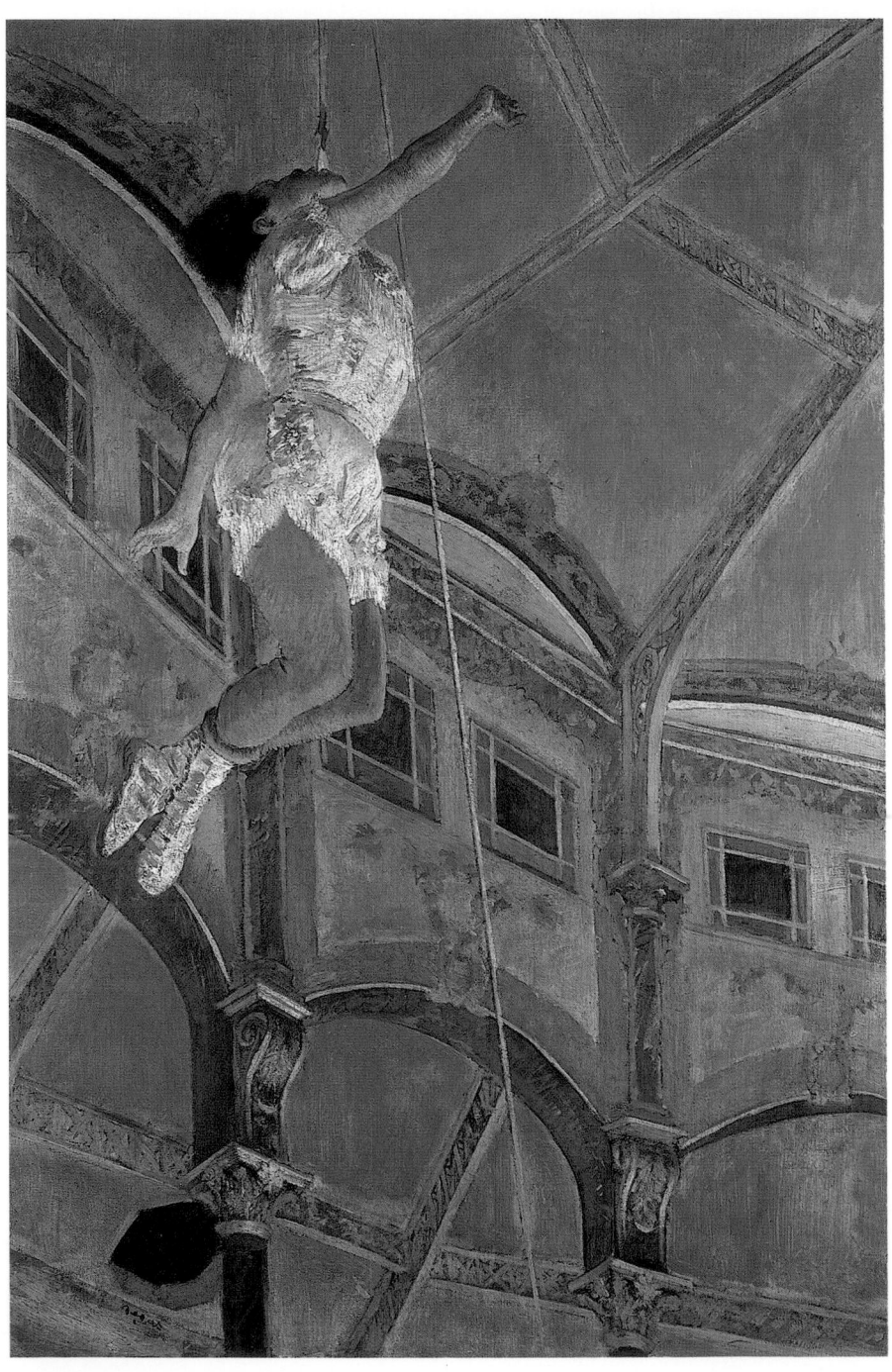

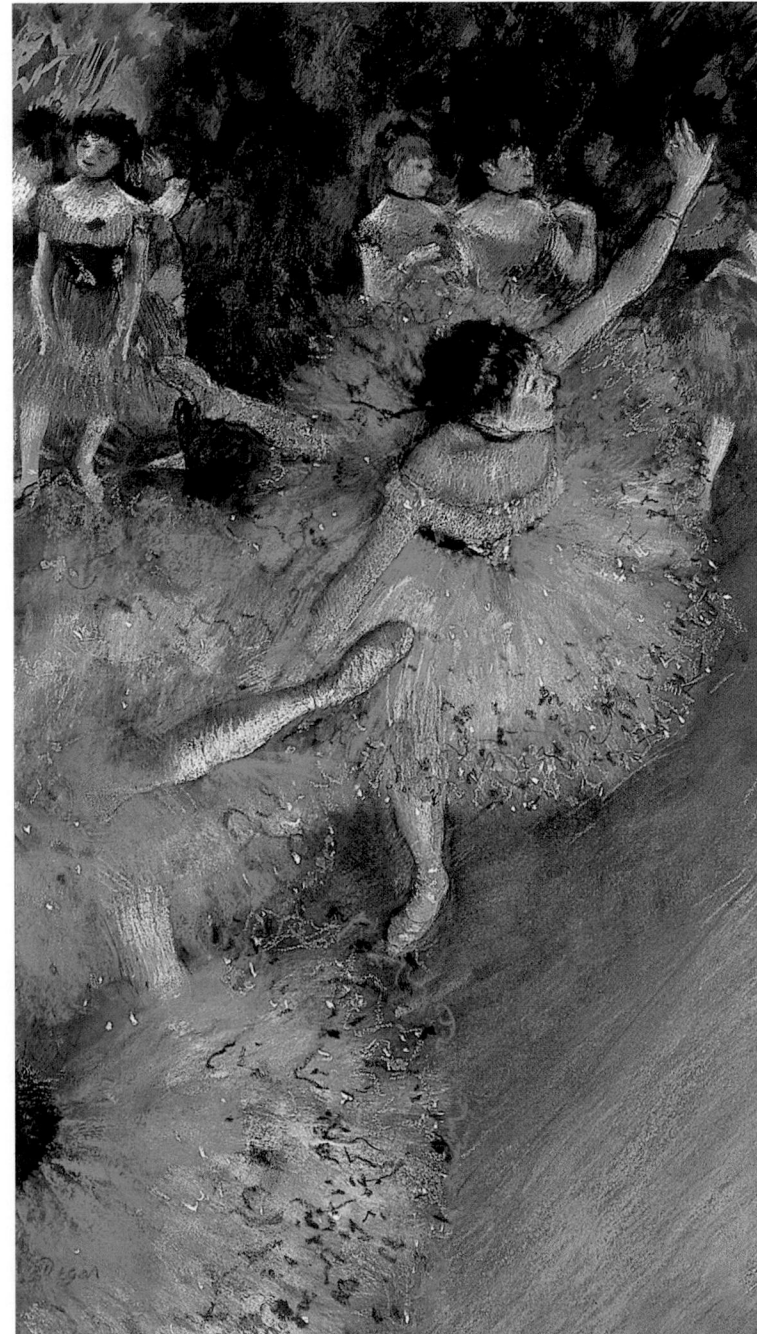

140
Edgar Degas,
*Miss La La at the
Cirque Fernando*,
1879.
Oil on canvas;
116·8 × 77·5 cm,
46 × 30$\frac{1}{2}$ in.
National
Gallery,
London

141
Edgar Degas,
The Green Dancer,
1877–9.
Pastel and
gouache
on paper;
66 × 36 cm,
26 × 14$\frac{1}{8}$ in.
Museo
Thyssen-
Bornemisza,
Madrid

to a dizzying elevation is precisely the kind of image one would have through binoculars. Besides the picture's brilliant lighting from below and unusual colours, the fragmentary viewpoint increases a physical impact which is already intensified by the performer's exciting execution of the physical feat. The parallel between Degas's daring and the art of acrobatics is obvious, but it is also linked to the Goncourt brothers' admiration of artifice.

Another example is Degas's *The Green Dancer* (141), in which the flattened rounded forms of the dancer's costumes, done in green pastel, become supports for an abstract tracery of brilliant colour. The spatial compression is such that a view of the stage from a nearby box seat is abruptly combined with that of dancers awaiting their entry in the wings. The cropping of figures in the foreground is matched only by the fragmentation of their bodies – a protruding limb here, a hidden leg there. Degas made several experiments with similar compositions, at least three of which have the front of the box in the foreground, with a woman's arm holding opera glasses. Because the viewer sits so close to the stage, we are forced to imagine her using the *lorgnette* to scrutinize other members of the audience. That spyglass view of the unsuspecting object is precisely what Degas's vision is about. In probing the reality of the other seen close up, Degas performs a kind of violence. He implied as much when he once observed: 'A picture calls for as much cunning, trickery and vice as the perpetration of a crime.' Even when it is transposed to the aesthetic – through fragmentation, ephemeral effects and lush handling – the act of vision is nevertheless an exercise of power. However loudly Degas's work proclaimed modernity, even while affecting detachment and impassivity, its underlying impetus was, as for Baudelaire's dandy, resistance to modernity's levelling effects.

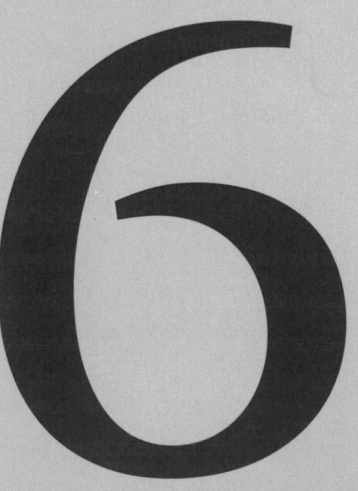

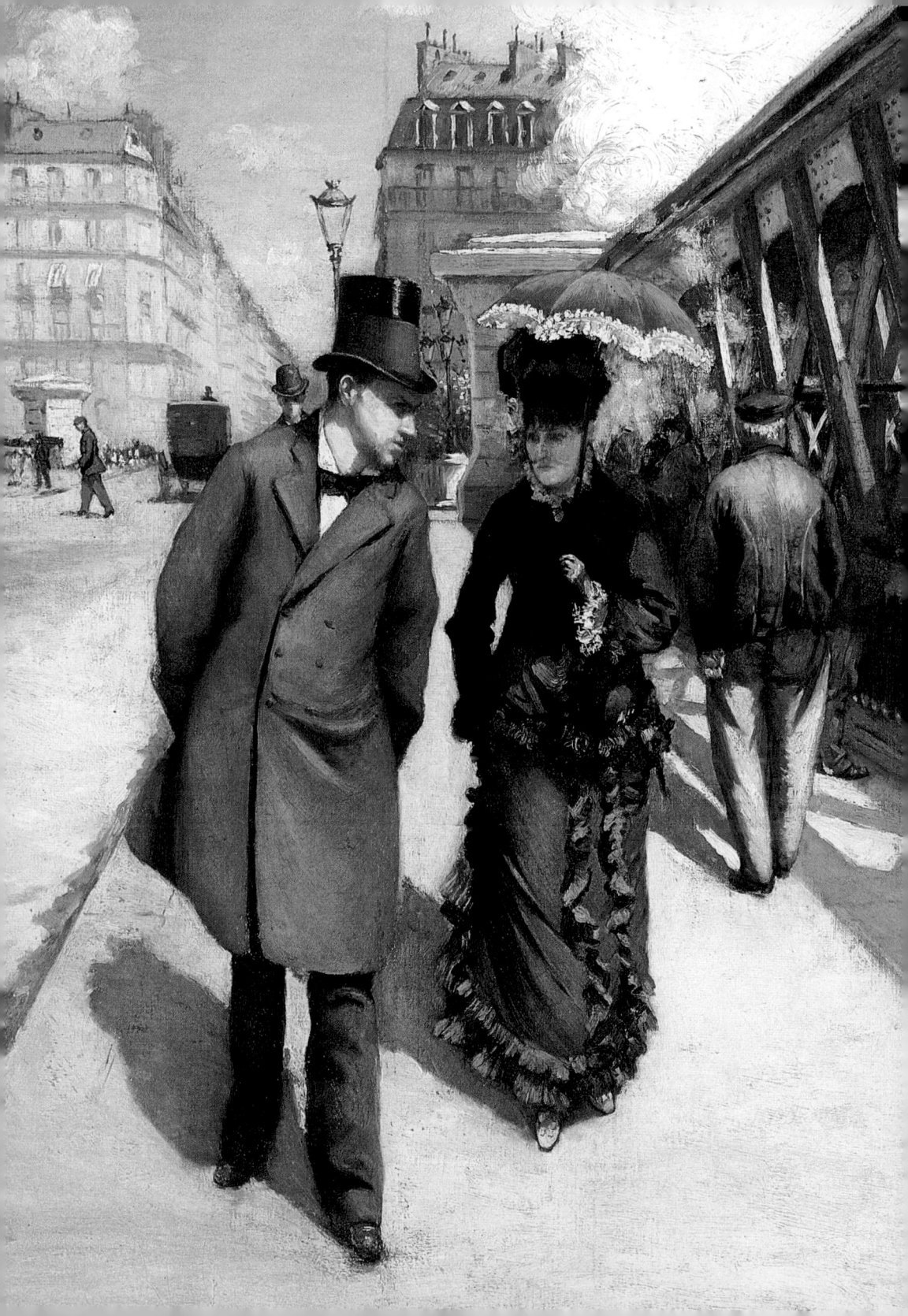

Few movements offer such opportunities as Impressionism for examining assumptions about relations between the sexes. Among the nearly sixty artists who exhibited with at least one of the eight exhibitions, there were three prominent women: Berthe Morisot, who participated from the beginning; Mary Cassatt, an expatriate American and friend of Degas; and Marie Quiveron Bracquemond (1840–1916; see Chapter 8), wife of the etcher Félix-Auguste-Joseph Bracquemond (1833–1914). Another gifted woman, Eva Gonzalès (1849–83), studied with Manet and painted in a related style (see 164), though she exhibited at the Salon, not with the Impressionists.

142
Gustave
Caillebotte,
*The Pont de
l'Europe*
(detail of 171)

Women were often the subject matter of Impressionist painting, perhaps more so than in previous periods, when narratives had greater importance than portraiture, landscape and interiors. Under the guise of objective representations of modernity, Impressionist imagery tended to legitimize roles into which women were socially cast. It thus participated in the construction and perpetuation of gender stereotypes and ideals. In addition, aspects of Impressionism, especially its basis in colour, were associated with femininity. Charles Blanc's influential *Grammar of the Arts of Design* (1867) reiterated the traditional association of drawing with masculinity and colour with femininity, including the assumption that the former must rule. Furthermore, the language used to describe Impressionist paintings was charged with terms associated with women, such as delicacy, spontaneity and charm. The Impressionists' painterly emphasis on surfaces and transcribing optical sensation played into the same gendered framework, so that certain critics would dismiss it as appropriate mainly for women. Feminist art historian Norma Broude has argued that defences of landscapists such as Monet, Sisley and Pissarro on grounds of scientific Positivism were attempts to 'masculinize' what was at heart a Romantic art of sensibility. In this chapter we shall first discuss the female Impressionists, the conditions they worked under and their portrayal of 'women's spaces'. We shall then move to male artists' representations of women and finally to Gustave Caillebotte's construction of the masculine.

Certain writers considered Berthe Morisot the quintessential Impressionist, characterizing her art as one of seductive colour and instinctual technique. Berthe and her sister Edma worked with Corot in the early 1860s. At the Louvre in 1867, Fantin-Latour introduced Morisot to Manet, though she is not included in Fantin-Latour's portrait of the Batignolles school. (Similarly, women were excluded from official arts institutions and committees until the last years of the century.) In 1874, Morisot married Manet's brother, Eugène; they were of similar backgrounds – both had fathers who were high government officials. It was an alliance that secured Morisot's position socially and financially, while offering a sympathetic setting for her to continue painting. Prior to her marriage, like any respectable single young woman, she had to be accompanied by an older female chaperone; it would have been considered improper for her to partici-pate in the fraternal life of cafés and studios. In 1874, Manet tried to dissuade Morisot from showing with the Impressionists, whom Degas had invited her to join. Unlike many of the others, she had been reasonably acceptable to the Salon juries. Yet following the inclusion of her work in the Impressionist exhibition, critics listed her as a disciple of Manet and an authoritative member of the new association. At the auction of works organized by Impressionists at the Hôtel Drouot the following year, her *Interior* (143) brought the highest price, paid by Monet's future patron, Ernest Hoschedé. Impressionism was diverse and flexible enough that there was never a question of Morisot's centrality or quality. And while some called her commitment to Impressionism the mere instinctual fulfilment of feminine nature, it resulted no less than for her male colleagues from conscious choice and opportunity, as well as limitations.

Morisot certainly recognized the constraints of being a woman, and she operated entirely within the woman's sphere and conventional propriety. There was no reason for her to challenge what that meant in her culture or to affect a 'masculine' style of precise draughtsmanship

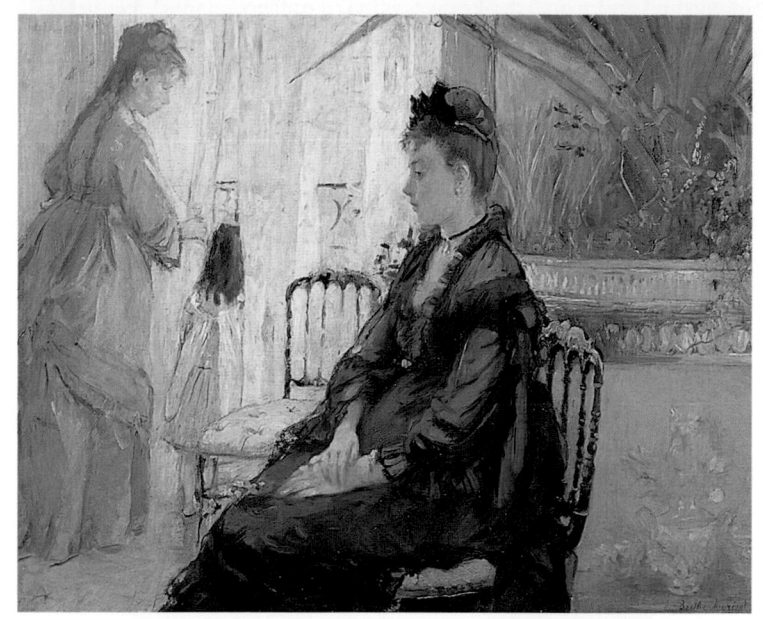

143
Berthe Morisot,
Interior,
1872.
Oil on canvas;
60 × 73 cm,
23⁵⁄₈ × 28³⁄₄ in.
Private
collection

and high finish. Her boldest belief was that her work deserved equal recognition to that of men, not that it was the same. One reason for this attitude, as Anne Higonnet has shown, is Morisot's relation to the tradition of the female amateur – equivalent in the visual arts of a well-bred young lady having music lessons. (On her Paris census form, Morisot implied her amateur status by recording herself as 'without profession'.) Since formal art instruction was unavailable from the state, women had to enrol with private teachers; and, as Marie Bracquemond recounted of her experience with Ingres, they were assigned 'only the painting of flowers, fruits, still lifes, portraits and genre scenes'.

That women fit so well into Impressionism suggests how expectations and practices were changing. Opposed to the official emphasis on grand historical compositions, Impressionism accommodated private, portable, informal and naturalist art, features corresponding to the amateur culture. It is true that Morisot's subject matter was almost exclusively domestic, hence of a domain bourgeois society defined as feminine. And her visualizations remained more or less within conventions of contemporary imagery except for her handling of paint. Yet even the latter had precedent, for Morisot's high-keyed colours and free brushstrokes were linked to Rococo masters such as Boucher (see 100) and Jean-Honoré Fragonard (1732–1806), artists who favoured images of women and were supported by eminent female patrons such as Madame de Pompadour, mistress to Louis XV (r.1715–74). Besides, the informality of sketchiness was an attractive quality that made pictures for one's intimate circle seem personal rather than official. At her death, Morisot was known in artistic circles but she lacked the wider fame of Monet, Degas, Pissarro or even Renoir, whose work most closely resembled hers. She herself gave their pictures pride of place in her living room, rather than her own.

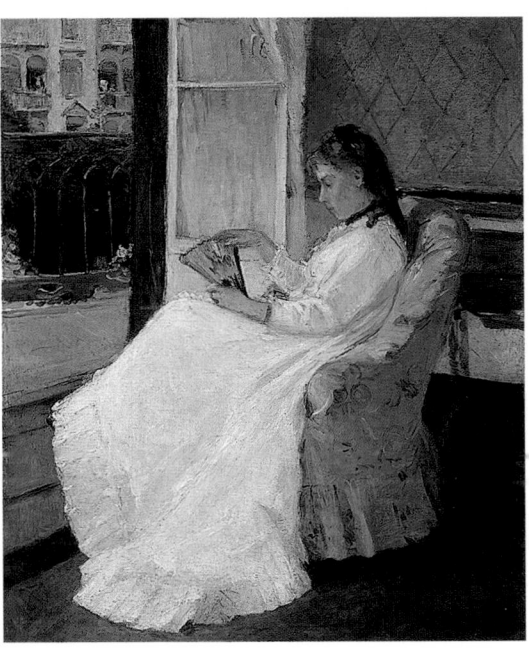

144
Berthe Morisot, *The Artist's Sister at a Window*, 1869. Oil on canvas; 54·8 × 46·3 cm, 21⁵⁄₈ × 18¹⁄₄ in. National Gallery of Art, Washington, DC

Through Corot, Morisot learned *peinture claire* and discovered her interest in outdoor painting, but she discarded other aspects of his influence and destroyed almost all of her early work in the late 1860s, after meeting Manet, Bazille and Degas, who encouraged a modern approach. Her painting *The Artist's Sister at a Window* (144), showing Edma Pontillon, her recently married sister, seated in the light of an open window, is an example of her resolve. Its palette may reflect the tonal unity of Corot, but its handling of paint has moved closer to Manet and Monet. Edma's informal *peignoir* afforded an opportunity to explore the play of light over white, a pictorial problem with which other Impressionists had been grappling. Following the announcement of her pregnancy, Morisot's sister returned, as was the custom in upper-middle-class families, to await the birth at her maternal home in the peaceful neighbourhood of Passy. Idleness and boredom, whether Edma's own or that projected on her by the still independent Berthe, are reflected by her absent-minded fondling of the fan. The boundaries of their world are suggested by the balcony railing and the cut-off view of buildings across the street. The previous year, Berthe had been the subject of a portrait taken from the other side of the railing, *The Balcony* (see 43) by Édouard Manet. There, in a similar though fancier gown, she was like a mysterious object of elegance

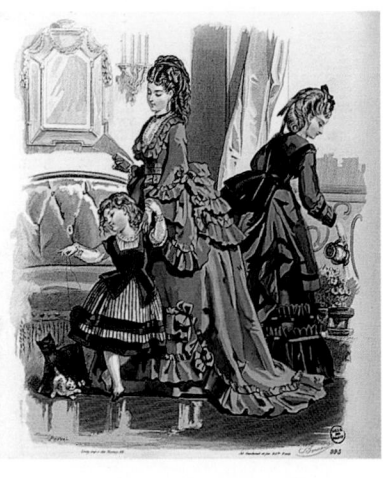

and beauty on display to the outside world. In her own painting, that world is remote; Edma sits back from the window and her gaze avoids encounters. In the background are figures on the balconies opposite: to the right is a maid probably watering flowers; the other is a gentleman staring down at the street.

A painting by Gustave Caillebotte (146), who was also interested in views from apartment windows, clearly contrasts the searching gaze of the male, aimed at a woman crossing the street, with Edma's reticence and introspection. Morisot's more muted colours make the interior if anything a refuge from the city, a modern equivalent to the nostalgic landscapes of Corot, where women embodied the ideal

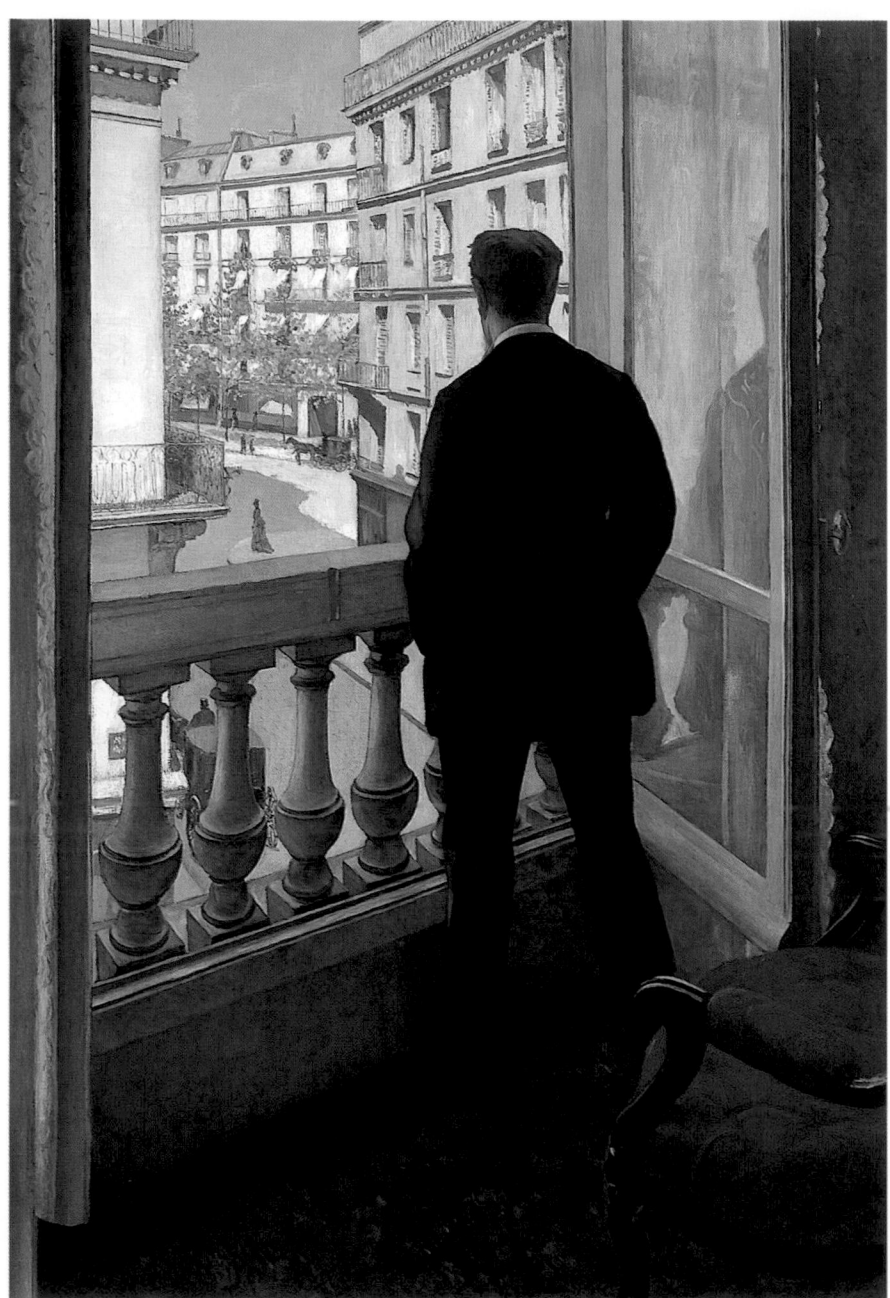

146
Gustave
Caillebotte,
Young Man at his Window,
1875.
Oil on canvas;
116·2 × 81 cm,
45³⁄4 × 31³⁄4 in.
Private
collection

of inner life and sensitivity. Indeed, the relationship between what Griselda Pollock calls the 'spaces of femininity', as depicted by Morisot, and modernity turns on the increasing emphasis in society on private pleasures, domestic and aesthetic, as antidotes to the demanding transformations of the urban industrial world. For reasons of social class and gender, but with no loss of self-respect, Morisot appropriated this aspect of modernity for her work.

Morisot showed a variety of pictures at the Impressionist exhibitions, which she helped to organize and in which she consistently participated except during 1879, following her daughter's birth. In addition to interiors, they included landscapes, such as *Hide and Seek* (see 6), which was shown at the first exhibition of 1874. Along with *Interior* (see 143), *Hide and Seek* invites comparison with other Impressionists. One is tempted to see it as a combination of Pissarro's tonalities and Monet's facture, or handling of paint, with the domestic subject matter considered appropriate to women. Similarly, *Interior* combines elements from her male colleagues – the cropping effect of Degas with Manet-like brushstrokes softened and liquified *à la* Renoir.

But such an analysis focuses too much on moments of male invention, rather than on shared vocabulary, and tends to render Morisot's own innovations secondary by their association with the feminine. Those innovations, however, were real. For example, Anne Higonnet has shown how *Interior* echoes fashion plates (see 145) – an important resource for up-to-date female culture, which had been used by male painters of modern life as well (see Chapter 3). In the Morisot, the apartment glows through muslin curtains, and the gilded accessories add a sheen that creates a halo around the contemplative figure in her fashionable dress. While it is true that women were associated with beauty and elegance in their personal grooming and attire, Morisot makes those characteristics a vehicle for expression of psychological vitality. Her attention to the setting confirms its importance as a sign of status, character and taste. This is a public but intimate reception room; the mother is seated on a light chair used for receiving friends while her daughter, attended by a nanny, watches for the guests. The mistress wears not the daily white house gown, but a more formal

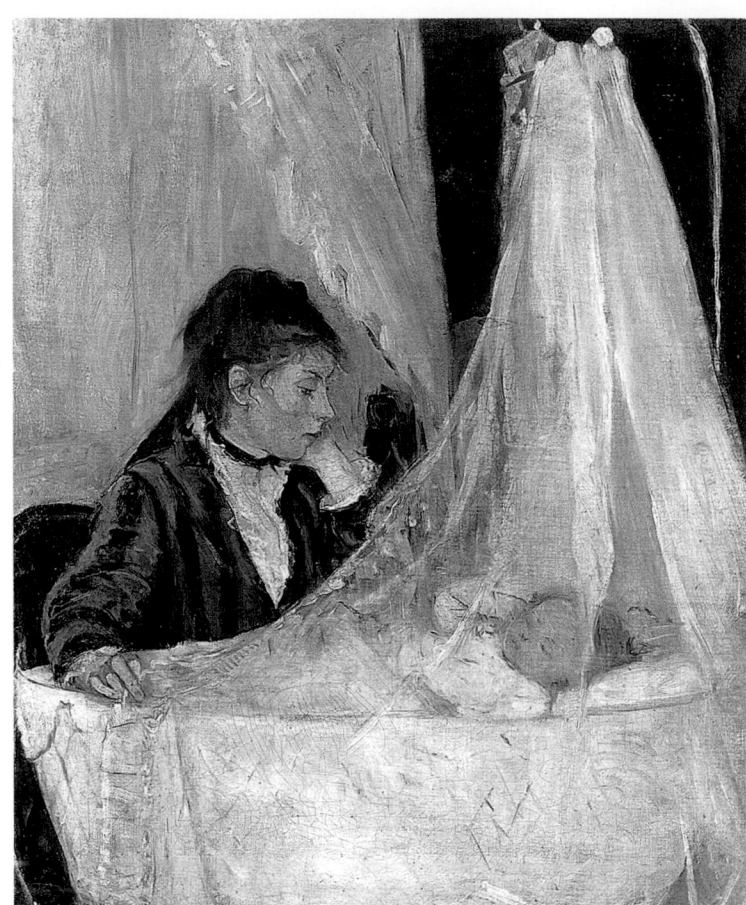

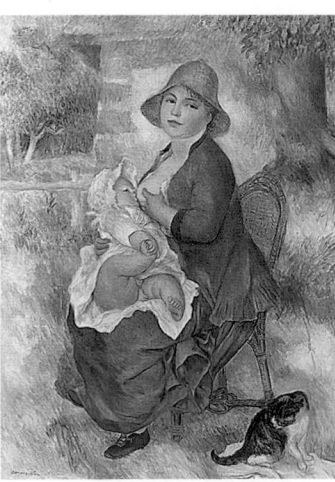

147 Left
Berthe Morisot,
The Cradle,
1872.
Oil on canvas;
56 × 46 cm,
22 × 18¹⁸ in.
Musée d'Orsay,
Paris

148 Below left
Pierre-Auguste
Renoir,
Maternity,
1886.
Oil on canvas;
73·7 × 54 cm,
29 × 21¹⁴ in.
Private
collection

149 Opposite
Berthe Morisot,
Eugène Manet
and his Daughter
at Bougival,
1881.
Oil on canvas;
73 × 92 cm,
28³⁴ × 36¹⁴ in.
Private
collection

and elaborate afternoon dress in black chiffon. Such attention to fashion expressed Morisot's commitment to modernity. In *Hide and Seek* (see 6), against the suburban background of Morisot's sister's summer house, the garden amusements of mother and child fill with specific activity the family life so generalized in pictures by other male Impressionists. *Hide and Seek* contrasts with the paucity of family imagery in Pissarro's output of the same years, despite his ample brood of children and a loving wife.

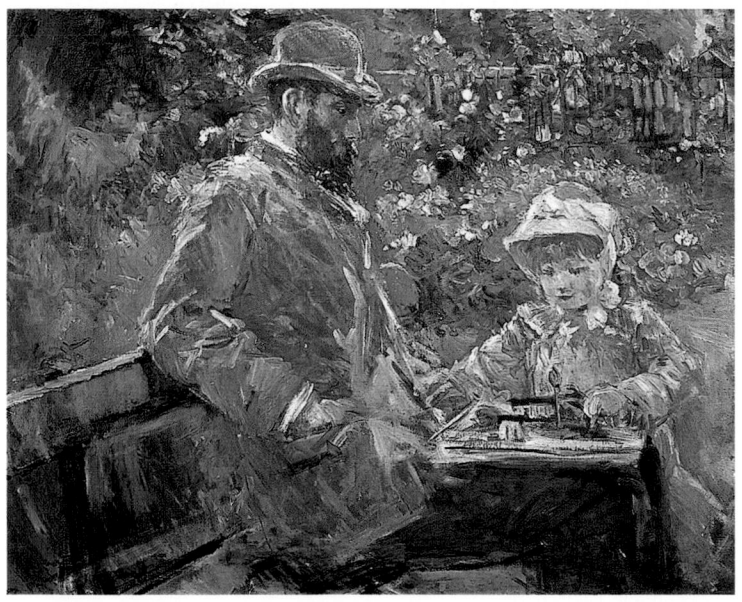

Even in popular imagery, there is little precedent for Morisot's bold compositional focus in *The Cradle* (147). Degas's vision of motherhood in *A Carriage at the Races* (see 117) was secondary to other social and formal concerns of that painting. By contrast, Morisot expresses her sister's tender feelings through soft handling and delicate colours. Normally, such pictures of parenthood would give equal honour to the child, as heir to the father's lineage and proof of his virility. Here, the baby is rendered as virtually anonymous: the mother opens the curtain part way, shielding her from our view. Echoing the cradle, the window curtains press in and forward to confine and flatten the mother's shape. Edma missed her family, and she had given up painting once she married; Berthe wrote to console her with the

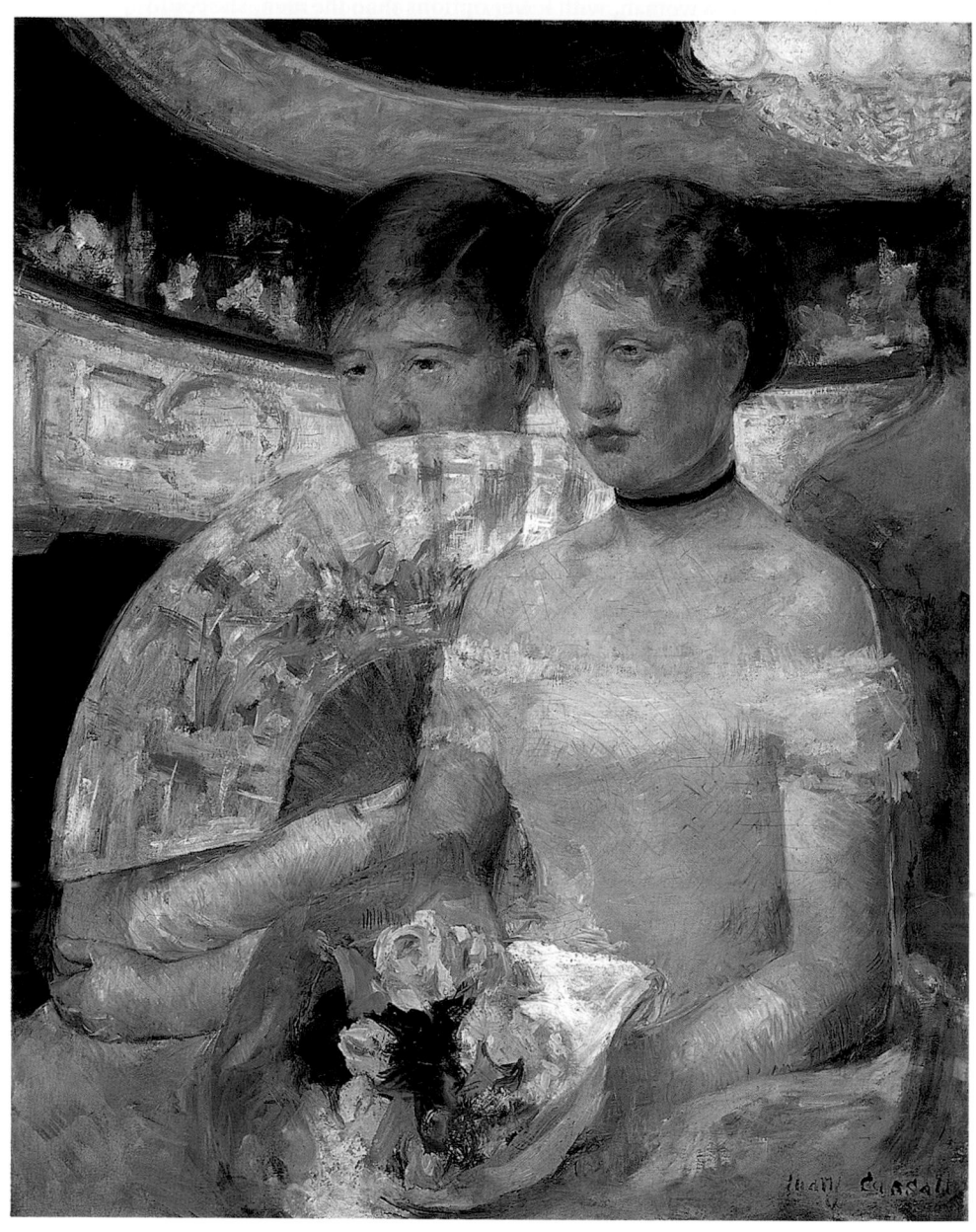

151
Mary Cassatt,
Two Young Ladies
in a Loge,
1882.
Oil on canvas;
79·8 × 63·8 cm,
31³⁄₈ × 25¹⁄₈ in.
National Gallery
of Art,
Washington, DC

Katherine Cassatt was fluent in French, which she had taught her children, and she regularly kept abreast of current events. Rather than reading a woman's magazine, she is absorbed in a mainstream daily normally associated with men, recalling Cézanne's *Portrait of Cézanne's Father Reading 'L'Evénement'* (see 235). Cassatt structured her composition to underscore the point by having the mirror reflect the newspaper rather than the other side of her mother's face. It is a back-handed tribute to traditional portraitists such as Ingres, who frequently used mirrors to include supplementary angles on his female subjects. Nor does Cassatt portray her mother as an intellectual spinster. Her wedding ring is prominently displayed, and her chintz chair and ruffled *peignoir* testify to traditional roles and creature comforts of the home. That she served as the primary model for her daughter is utterly believable.

Cassatt became a regular at the Impressionists gatherings, and though she would not have mingled with her colleagues at cafés, like Morisot she certainly attended Alfred Stevens' Wednesday dinners and Madame Manet's Thursdays. She adopted several Impressionist themes to which her experience gave her access. In *Two Young Ladies in a Loge* (151), the teenagers Geneviève Mallarmé and Mary Ellison (to the left) could be attending their first performance at the Palais Garnier. Their shyness, demonstrated by the open fan hiding Mary's expression, and the miming of adult propriety with their rigid posture, coexist with the obvious frisson of appearing publicly in formal gowns and white gloves. It is an image at the psychological heart of female socialization, contrasting to Renoir's *The Loge* (see 156), whose woman defers demurely to surface spectacle and its pleasure for the male. Indeed, in another opera box scene, Cassatt abruptly flouted masculine norms by placing a woman, dressed asexually in black, as the proprietor of the probing gaze. *A Woman in Black at the Opera* (152, 153) is masked not only by her clothing but by opera glasses – a favoured theme of Degas. Behind her, a few boxes down the graceful curve of the tier, a man is engaged in precisely the same activity, but directing it across the open space towards her (or the viewer, constructed as female)! The woman's fan – generally employed as an instrument of coquetry and discretion – is firmly

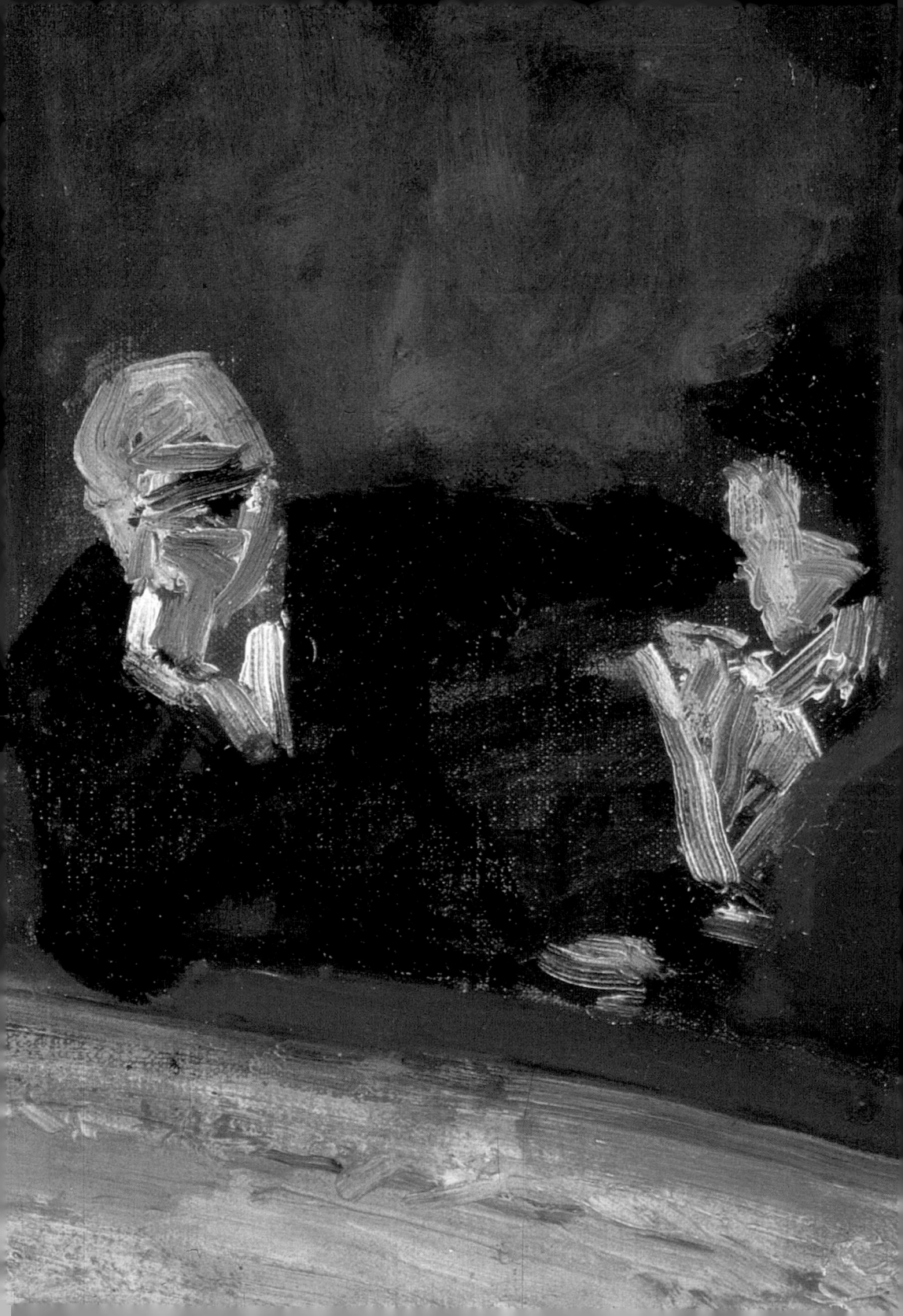

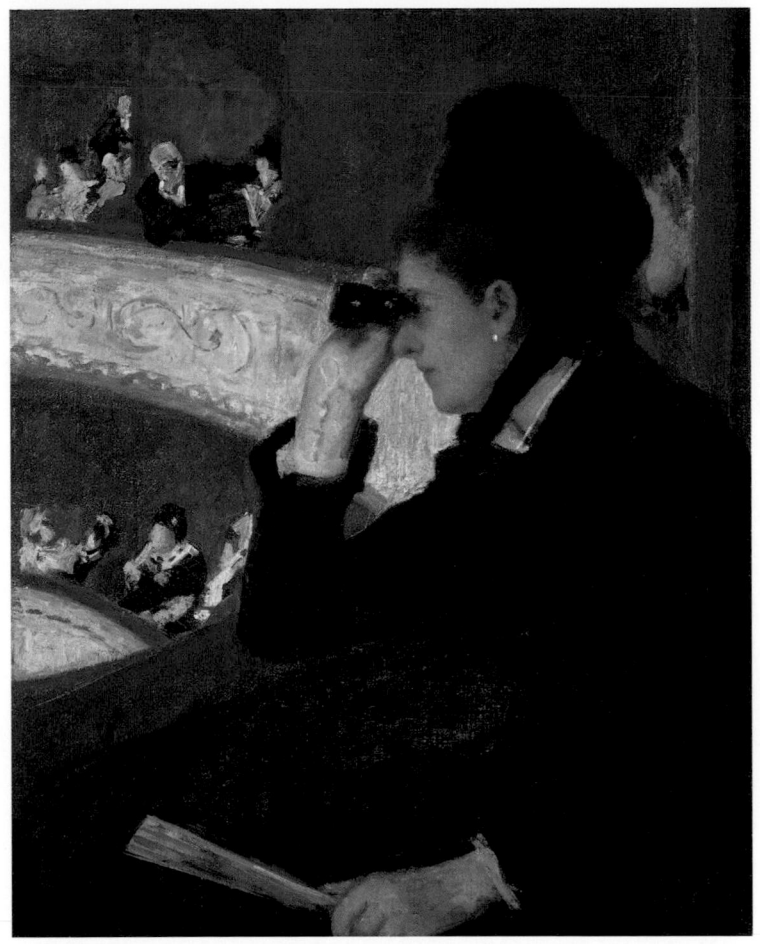

152–153
Mary Cassatt,
*A Woman in Black
at the Opera,*
1880.
Oil on canvas;
80 × 64·8 cm,
31^{1}2 × 25^{1}2 in.
Museum of Fine
Arts, Boston
Left
Detail

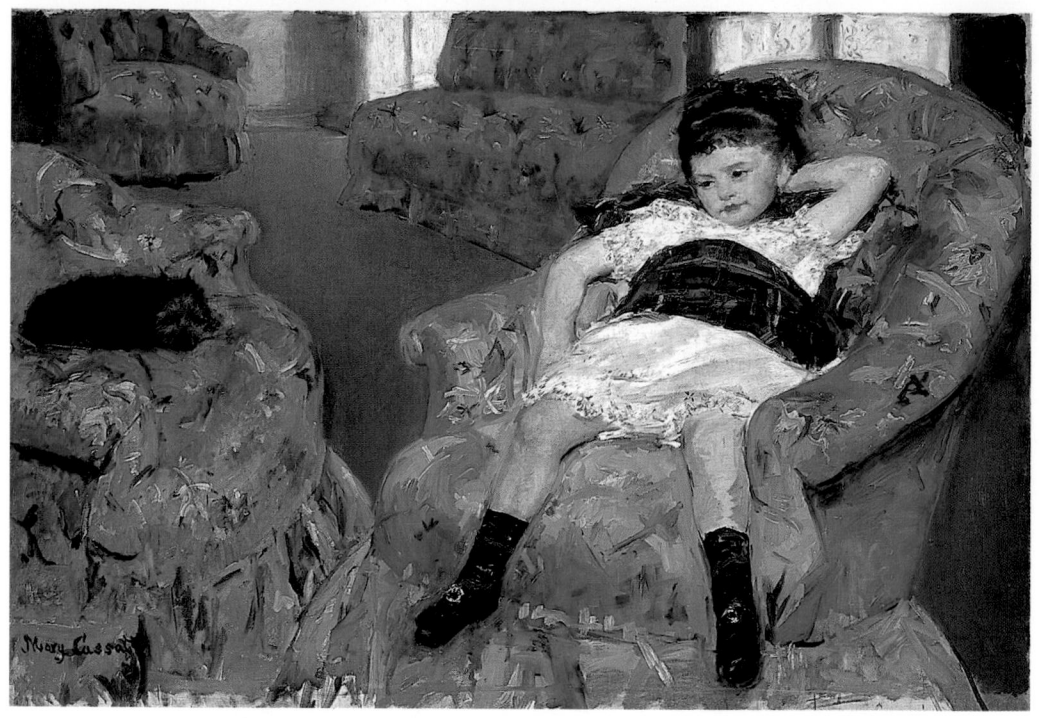

closed. Her angular body defies the presumed norm of female passivity to seize the prerogative of visual inspection.

Despite being unmarried and childless, Cassatt was one of art history's greatest observers of children. *Little Girl in a Blue Armchair* (154) catches the unselfconscious ease of a young girl, limbs akimbo lounging on an overstuffed chair in a comfortable family room. A little lapdog is having a nap on the facing chair. The sense of casual observation and intimacy, combined with a wilful use of blue and sloping space, speak loudly of Cassatt's modernity. But as her career evolved, her equally innovative observations of mothers and infants, for which she was especially renowned, became less openly audacious. In *The Family* (155), for example, Cassatt echoes monumental madonna-child-saint compositions to evoke the sanctity of motherhood. Yet the goofy gestures of the pudgy baby and the affections of adoring mother and big sister seem so natural one would never call the painting preachy. Cassatt's images of motherhood are therefore far from the anti-feminist ideals evoked by Renoir's Raphaelesque *Maternity*

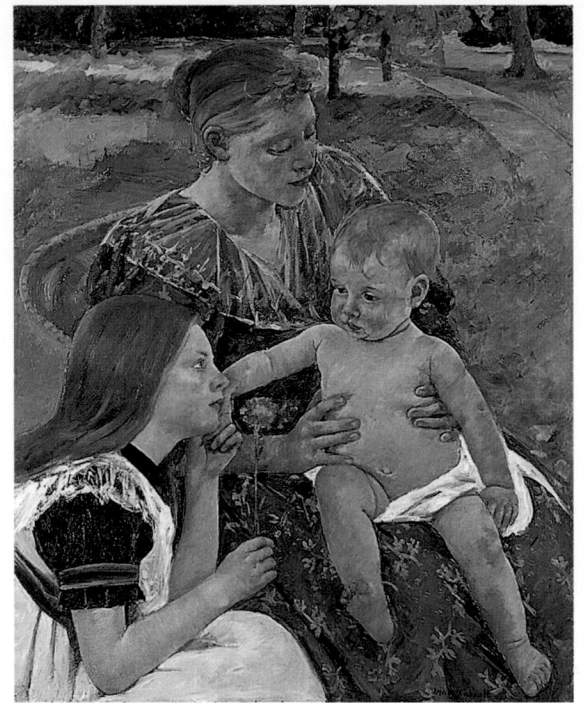

154
Mary Cassatt,
Little Girl in a
Blue Armchair,
1878.
Oil on canvas;
89·5 × 129·8 cm,
35¹₂ × 51¹₈ in.
National Gallery
of Art,
Washington, DC

155
Mary Cassatt,
The Family,
c.1886.
Oil on canvas;
81·9 × 66·3 cm,
32¹₄ × 26¹₈ in.
Chrysler
Museum,
Norfolk, Virginia

(see 148), even though they ultimately do accept a traditionalist
emphasis on the unitary family. Cassatt's outdoor setting contributes
to the sense of relaxation, and her close attention to fashions, especially
the mother's unusually bright lilac-coloured dress, confirms its
utterly contemporary feel. Outlining the mother's hands in red
where her fingers clasp the baby emphasizes the quasi-erotic physical
bonding of early childhood. Though a staunch supporter of many
women's causes, Cassatt did state later in her life that 'Women are
after all meant to bear children.' Accepting the family-oriented
ideology with which many of its proponents hoped to keep women
in the home, Cassatt interpreted such values as keys to bliss and
self-fulfilment. Nor is there any sense of the simplistic mother-versus-
prostitute dichotomy that pervaded polemics on gender during the
period. So one can only speculate whether Cassatt's detachment as
artist-outsider was infiltrated by some inner longing, or how much
the support of wealthy female patrons, such as her lifelong friend
Louisine Havemeyer, encouraged the production of these acute and
seductive paeans to motherhood.

If women's representations of their worlds are conditioned by their assumptions, then certainly male artists' paintings of women are tied even more to projection and desire, since men lack the insight of actually experiencing life from a female perspective. Baudelaire recognized this operation of fantasy, as he explained with a certain irony the centrality of women for a modern art. Through their fashion, coiffures and make-up – all calculated to attract the male gaze (which he takes for granted) – women exemplified current ideals of beauty. In *The Painter of Modern Life*, Baudelaire wrote that the world is a 'vast picture gallery' filled primarily with women, for they embody the 'approximation to an ideal for which the restless human [meaning male] mind feels a constant, titillating hunger'. Woman was, he argued, 'accomplishing a kind of duty, when [devoting] herself to appearing magical and supernatural; ... as an idol, she is obliged to adorn herself in order to be adored ... She is a divinity, a star, which presides at all the conceptions of the brain of man ... through whom artists and poets create their most exquisite jewels.' The principle that woman defines herself through male attention and is a vehicle for his creativity is presented as being rooted in the natural order itself.

Renoir is known as one of the greatest painters of women, and his delicate tones, bright colours and soft brushstrokes are as much associated with femininity as are the stylistic traits of Morisot. Perhaps in compensation for such associations, however, Renoir attributed this femininity to his subject matter rather than to himself. Morisot's paintings were called the result of 'delicious hallucinations', terminology that echoed Charcot and contemporary psychiatry's image of woman as lacking control (see Chapter 5). Renoir's famous assertion that he painted 'with his prick' stated his belief in male self-fulfilment through artistic processes, even though it also confessed its instinctual (and erotic) rather than intellectual basis. Renoir took for granted the male dominion over nature, with which woman was generally identified. Therefore, the male prerogative included representing women in their natural state, as in the unfettered availability of the harem (see Chapter 4), or the nude. Women in landscapes of course abound in the history of art. Such imagery was central to Renoir's commitment to naturalism and, later in his life, nostalgic nudes in tropical settings became a leitmotif, facile fantasies to sustain an exhausted imagination (see Chapter 8).

For the quick, ambitious Renoir of the 1870s, there is no better example of the avant-garde version of the feminine than his famous *The Loge* (156) from the first Impressionist exhibition. A ravishing and fashionably attired young woman is seated in a plush opera box with a male companion behind her. The opera was one of the few forms of public leisure accessible to bourgeois women. Dressing up was part of the ritual, for a woman displayed her status and that of her husband through such appearances. Unmarried women were present, too, some as part of their education, others who might be courted by eligible men, as well as many who were kept rather than courted. The spectacle of female beauty, whether of mistresses, wives or daughters, surely rivalled that of the opera or ballet performances. Renoir's painting stages both his model's beauty and her accessories. Whatever his figure's considerable personal endowments, they are heightened by the arts of make-up and *haute couture*, which were considered attributes of femininity. The stripes of her luxuriant gown outline her bosom and lead the eye to a richly cream-coloured face, rouged at the cheeks, set off at the neck by sumptuous pearls, topped with flowers, and framed symmetrically by sparkling earrings. The red in both corsages brings out her lips and the reddish highlights in her ears and the corners of her eyes – effects straight out of the Rococo tradition. Renoir once said that he hated the word 'flesh', which sounded like 'meat' (the French word *la chair* can mean both). What he liked was 'a young girl's skin that is pink and shows that she has a good circulation'. The erotic overtones of such opinions are scarcely hidden.

Certainly the generosity with which Renoir applied his paint appeals to appetite as much as the objects it represents – icing-like pinks for flowers; impasto like frothy egg-white for her pearls. The painted object is as much a luxury item as its referent; desire for the painting and for the woman converge. The artifice underlying Renoir's seductive strategy is revealed by our knowledge that he produced these effects in a studio with a model named Nini Lopez. But it is also embodied by the special vantage point. One would have to be suspended in mid-air to glimpse the couple so close in – unless observing them through opera glasses from across the hall. Since the man in the background is holding binoculars, such an idea may have occurred to Renoir. Having conquered the beauty at his right, the male companion seems absorbed in the quest for more. Though the woman also holds a set of glasses in her gloved hand, with her gold

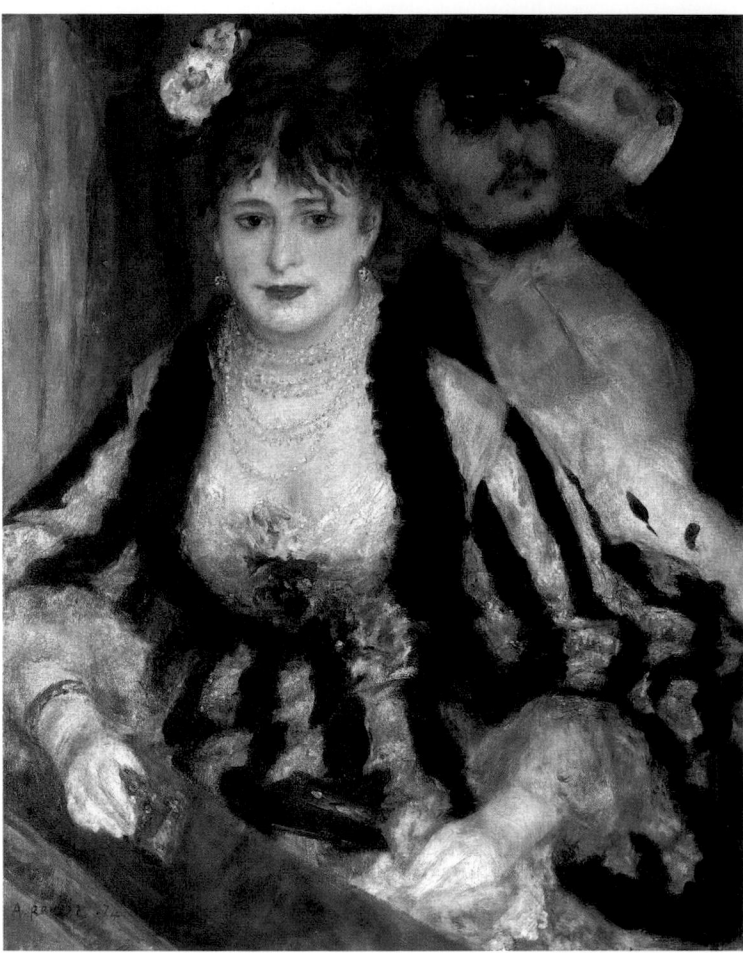

156–157
Pierre-Auguste Renoir,
The Loge,
1874.
Oil on canvas;
80 × 63.5 cm,
31¹⁄₂ × 25 in.
Courtauld Institute Galleries, London
Right
Detail

bracelet it is more part of her toilette than utilitarian. Colluding with the viewer – though we must remember this is a fantasy of complicity produced by the painter – she discretely accepts her role as visual object, holding her fan closed in her lap rather than opening it for privacy and propriety. So the image is framed at top and bottom by the instruments of sight – those *lorgnettes* used for social spying –

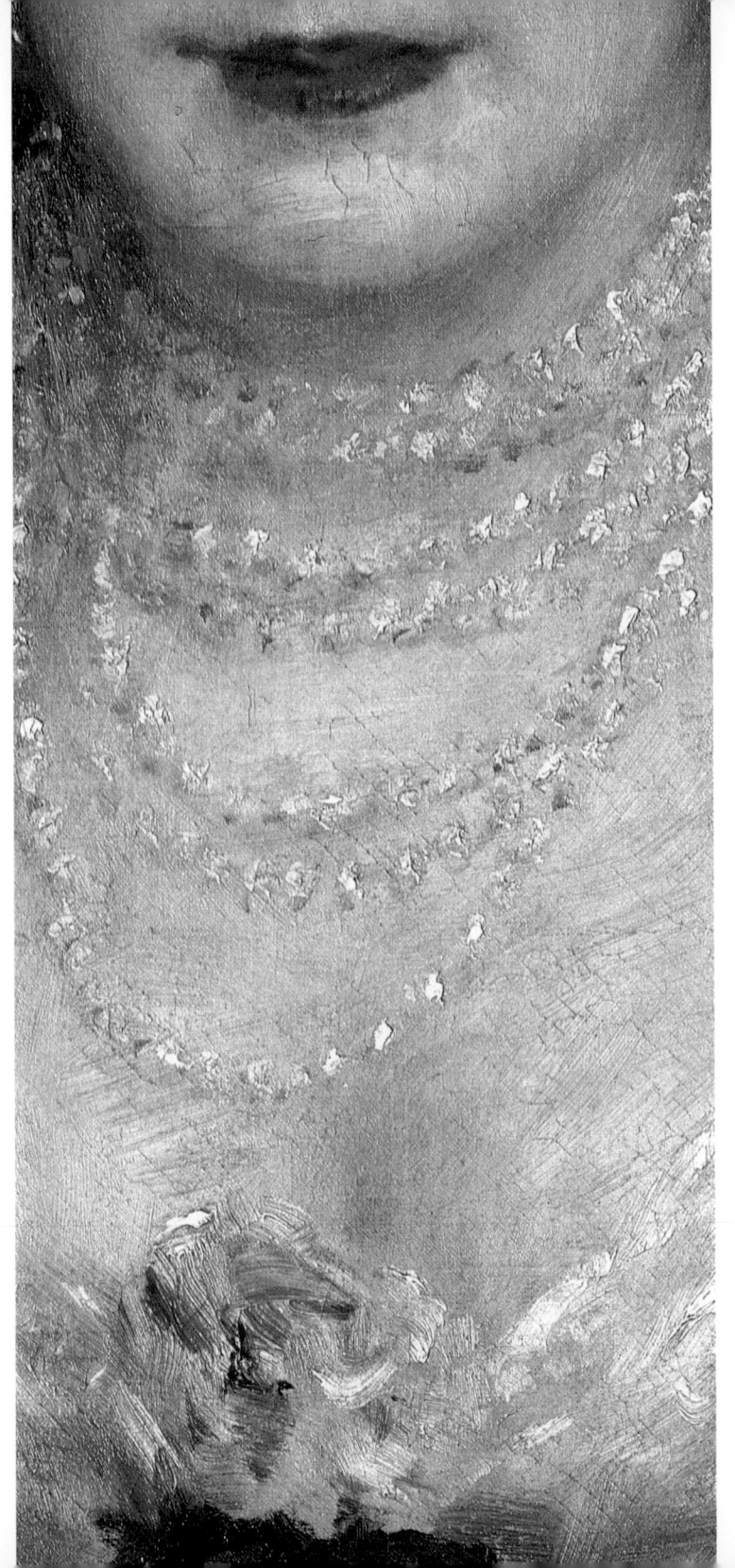

while the painting overall embodies its sensual motivations. One easily surmises that, with her casually kempt hair and excessive string of pearls, she is unlikely to gain respect for much more than her appearance, even though Renoir gives her an air of innocence.

At this juncture in his career, visual gratification is what Renoir's art aimed for – its appeal to the eye advertising his ability to satisfy contemporary desire. His conception of art was in tune with prescribed gender roles of the time: the pleasures proffered by paint are comparable to those provided by women. As Tamar Garb has pointed out, the pure pleasures of looking are hardly value free. The gendered economics of consumption and sexuality are inseparable when a woman is the object of the desiring masculine gaze.

That Renoir's attitudes towards women were reactionary will come as no surprise, but the explosion of feminist demands during the French Commune may have provoked increasing rigidity. Following a short hiatus, in 1878 the first French Congress for Women's Rights was convened by Maria Deraismes and Léon Richer; in 1880, the French Republic finally instituted public education for girls. On hearing of a woman lawyer, Renoir exclaimed: 'I can't see myself getting into bed with a lawyer ... I like women best when they don't know how to read, and when they wipe their baby's behind themselves.' He was echoing anti-feminist views held by even some advanced social thinkers, such as Pierre-Joseph Proudhon, and going back to Jean-Jacques Rousseau. Their arguments referred to biological differences, which current medicine and psychiatry corroborated, as we saw in Chapter 5. But Renoir's brand of 'science' was far less subtle. According to his son Jean, he thought housework, especially bending down to 'scrub floors, light fires or do the washing' was good for women because 'their bellies need movement of that sort'. Renoir had little use for the company of women unless they could somehow serve him; he even feared their seductive powers. He made exceptions for patrons like Madame Charpentier; and his long friendship with Morisot must, similarly, have been based on respect for her superior social standing. Renoir was as insecure in his masculinity as he was socially; a woman's femininity had to be the foil for his sense of self.

158
Edgar Degas,
Absinthe,
1875–6.
Oil on canvas;
92 × 69 cm,
36¼ × 27¼ in.
Musée d'Orsay,
Paris

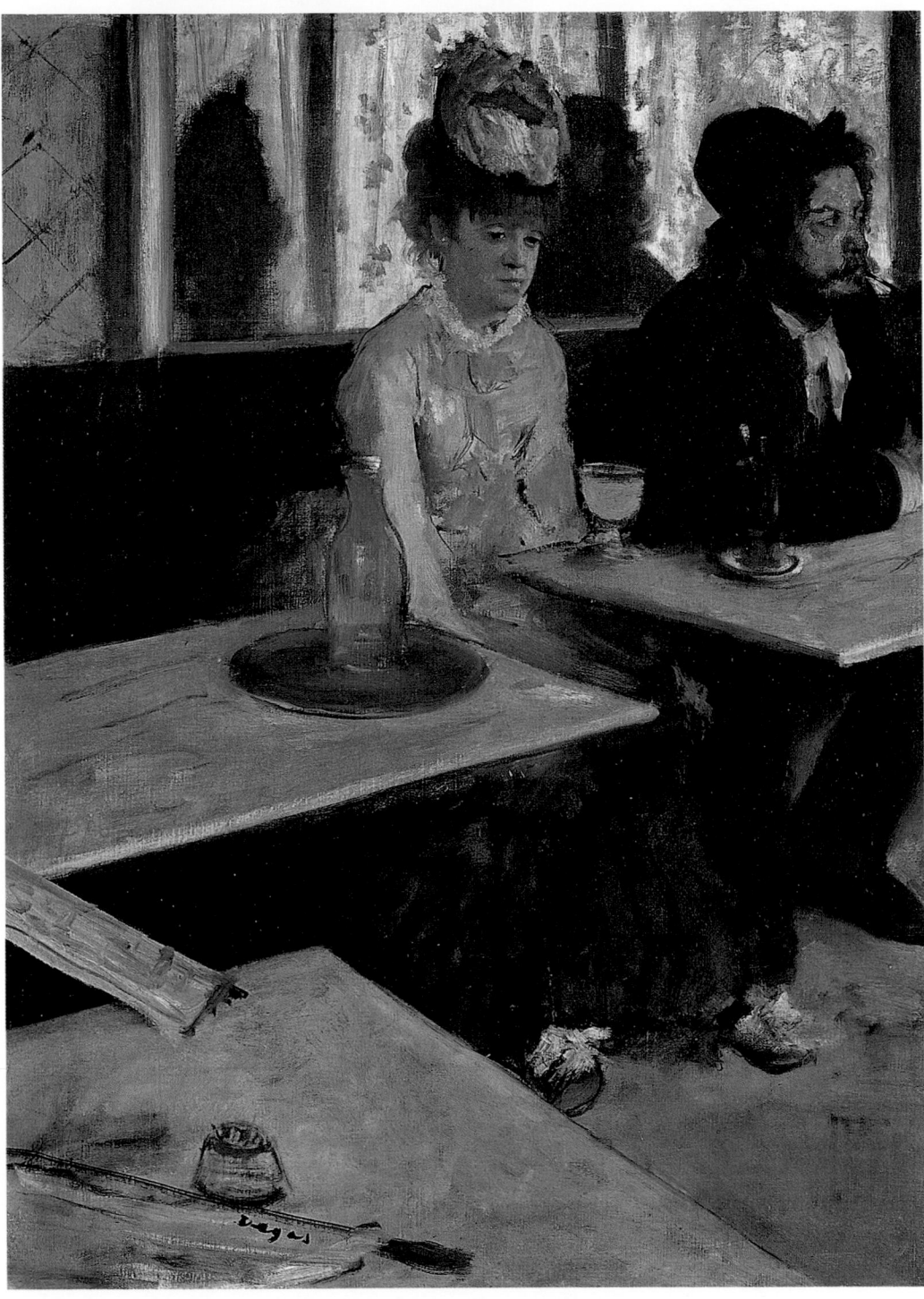

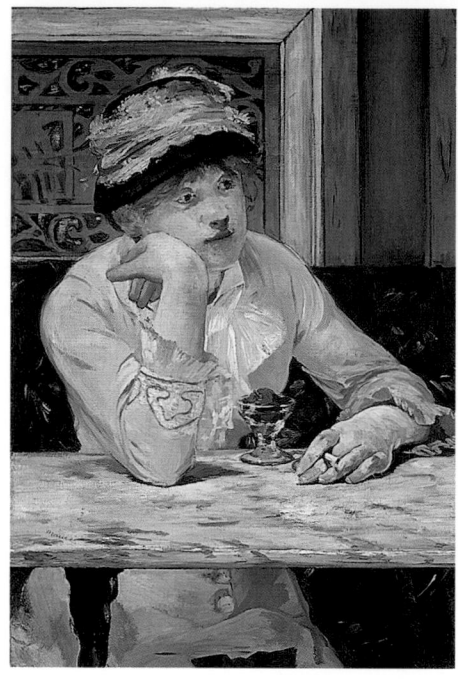

159 **Right**
Édouard Manet,
The Plum,
c.1878.
Oil on canvas;
73·6 × 50·2 cm,
29 × 19³⁄₄ in.
National Gallery
of Art,
Washington, DC

160 **Opposite**
Édouard Manet,
At the Café,
1878.
Oil on canvas;
77 × 83 cm,
30¹⁄₄ × 32³⁄₄ in.
Oskar Reinhardt
Collection,
Winterthur

In Degas's *Absinthe* (158) we see male and female in the public setting of a café, the Nouvelle-Athènes, where Manet, Degas and others migrated from the Café Guerbois. The artist Marcellin Desboutin (1823–1902), who exhibited with the Impressionists in 1876, and the actress Ellen Andrée pose as a couple of down-and-out bohemians killing time on a morning after. Like Manet's *Absinthe Drinker* (see 25), the painting reflects the alcoholism that was rampant in nineteenth-century Paris. Robert Herbert has described the drinks here as a coffee-based chaser for the man (though in real life Desboutin did not drink) and the cloudy addictive potion absinthe for the lady. He is no doubt right that the time is breakfast – hence the implied indictment of a dissolute woman starting so early. The viewer looks over from an adjacent table, where the morning papers, in which the couple take no interest, are scattered. (Degas's signature on one of the papers is a reference to his ideal of visual reportage.) The picture can also stand for certain truths about gender comportment which are tied to the reality of Desboutin and Andrée's lives beyond their assigned roles. More centred and sheltered from the window, Ellen Andrée is the primary object of our observation and moral judgement;

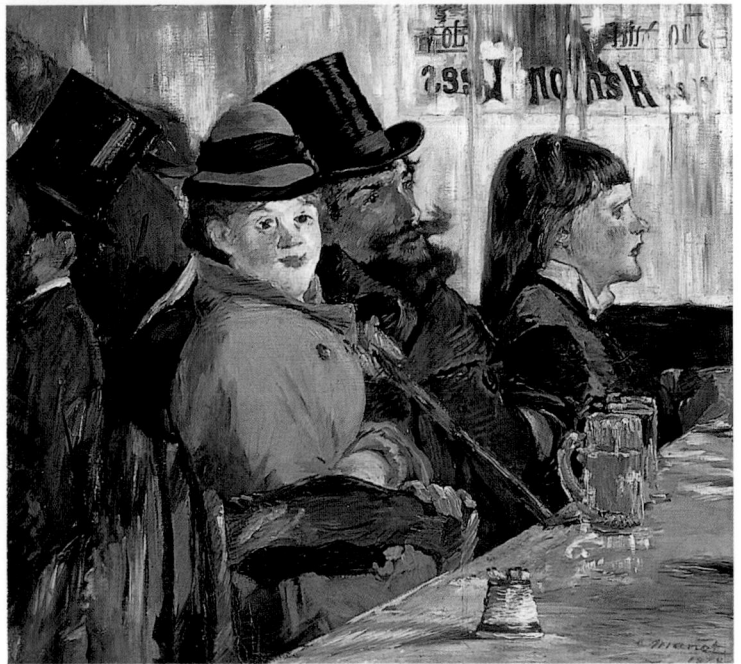

her gaze downcast in her sorry state, the actress responds as the object of spectacle – for, as an actress, to be watched is her *métier*. Similarly merging professional and painted persona, Desboutin's gaze as both *flâneur* and artist is unselfconscious: his line of sight away from the table, beyond the frame and towards the street, mirrors our empowered gaze (presumably masculine) over towards him.

Unaccompanied women in cafés were especially liable to catch the eye, and often they positioned themselves to do so. The woman in Manet's ravishing *The Plum* (159) sits on her own and is smoking, too. Alone in public and flaunting a male habit are signs of independence that to some might signal a modern feminist but to others were sure signs that she is up to no good. (For most nineteenth-century men, one equalled the other.) Manet's arresting pinks and the mouldings of the background emphasize a framing of the woman as his self-conscious work of artistic seduction, less innocently disguised than in Renoir's *The Loge* (see 156). Women's activities were so circumscribed that one could generally deduce their circumstances from the places they appeared and whether they were accompanied or by whom. In

Manet's *At the Café* (160), Ellen Andrée is now posing as a wife, held closely by her husband who taps his cane officiously against the bar for service. The unrelated and younger woman behind him gazes blankly, maintaining psychological distance amid the crowding. One wonders for whom the husband is showing off? Women are indeed a focus of attention in every Impressionist café painting except one – Caillebotte's *In a Café* of 1880 (161), which, in its play on mirror reflection, was an inspiration for Manet's *A Bar at the Folies-Bergère* (see 47). This contrast confirms our general rule.

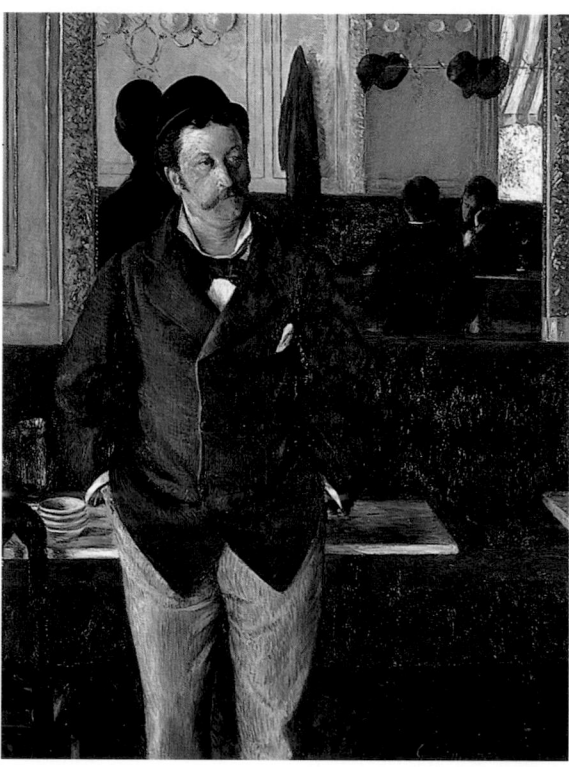

161
Gustave
Caillebotte,
In a Café,
1880.
Oil on canvas;
153 × 114 cm,
60¼ × 44⅞ in.
Musée des
Beaux-Arts,
Rouen

Compared to these paintings, *Absinthe*'s self-referential narrative is revealing in relation to the woman artist. Where Desboutin, as presented in the painting and as an artist in real life, like Manet and Degas, felt free to observe others in public surroundings, women were restricted in their freedom to practise what for men was the essential basis of modernity. The painter Pauline Orell, alias Marie Bashkirtseff (1858–84), complained to her diary in 1879:

What I long for is the freedom of going about alone, of coming and going, of sitting in the seats of the Tuileries, and especially in the Luxembourg, of stopping and looking at the artistic shops, of entering churches and museums, of walking about old streets at night; that's what I long for; and that's the freedom without which one cannot become a real artist. Do you imagine that I get much good from what I see, chaperoned as I am, and when, in order to go to the Louvre, I must wait for my carriage, my lady companion, my family.

Although shopping provided some new freedom, it was in Degas's pictures of hat shops that this women's space was recorded rather than in the work of Morisot or Cassatt. The painful paradox is that modern women who had leisure to be artists were the ones socially discouraged from practising in the modern *flâneur* mode. Compare Degas's representations of laundresses (163) to Morisot's (162). The former are public figures, ironing and starching men's shirts in one of hundreds of similar Parisian boutiques, undoubtedly in a bourgeois neighbourhood. The latter are integrated with the landscape of the village of Maurecourt, seen from her sister's house afar. In Morisot's picture, the spectacle of the linen itself is of greater interest than the laundresses. Cleanliness and neat clothing were aspects of the bourgeois obsession with health and appearances, attitudes Morisot and Degas certainly shared. The thought of representing members of the profession in a setting that could invite suspicion would certainly never have entered her decorous mind.

By contrast, for Degas's subsistence labourers, the heat of heavy irons and the strain of pressing take their toll, and they try to make the day more tolerable with a handy bottle of wine. (A similar bottle accompanies Caillebotte's floor-scrapers; see 170). What struggling young woman would not be tempted to improve her lot through a rendezvous on the side, especially if alcohol has lowered her defences? The ironer's light blouse thus served a dual purpose; and while her red cheeks speak of physical exertion, they mimic make-up. Eunice Lipton has shown that the contemporary discourse on laundresses associated them with coquetry and flirtation. She also discovered a stereoscopic photograph of an ironer whose dress hangs down to

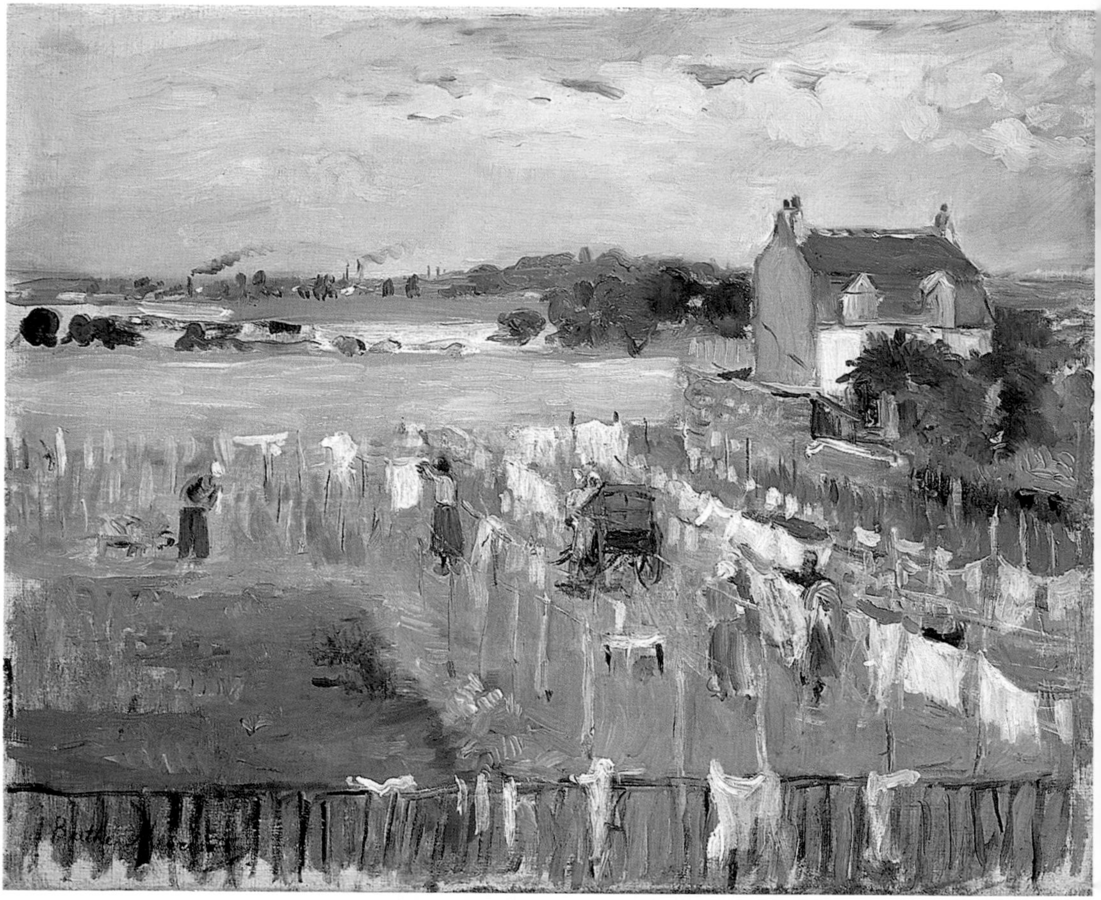

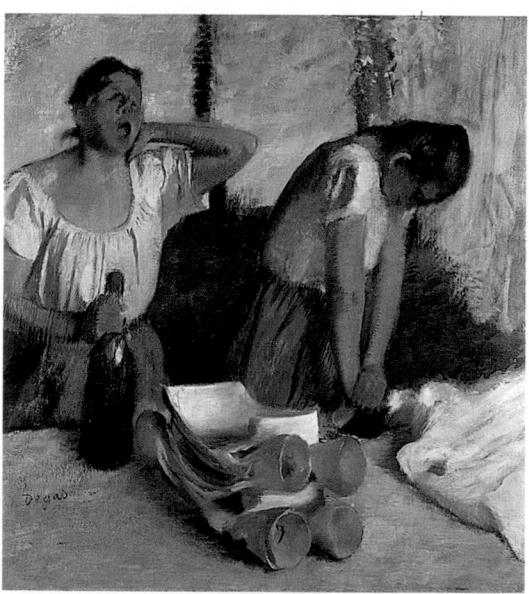

162 Above
Berthe Morisot,
Hanging the
Laundry Out
to Dry,
1875.
Oil on canvas;
33 × 40·6 cm,
13 × 16 in.
National Gallery
of Art,
Washington, DC

163 Left
Edgar Degas,
Women Ironing,
c.1884.
Oil on canvas;
82·3 × 75·5 cm,
32⅜ × 29¾ in.
Norton Simon
Museum,
Pasadena

reveal a breast, though we should remember that even such a document is more likely fiction catering to fantasy than fact. Like ballet dancing and waitressing, then, laundering was certainly among those women's professions considered 'dangerous'. By sexualizing his ironers, Degas masks their genuine labour and caters to appetites solicited by his own performances of the brush.

One area in which the limitations placed on women became especially apparent was in representations of the female artist. For instance, Degas made numerous pictures of Mary Cassatt, but none shows her at work. Manet's many portraits of Berthe Morisot represent her in mourning, as *femme fatale*, and as *grande bourgeoise*, but never with the tools of her trade. Only Morisot's sister ever showed her at the easel; and even in Berthe's own self-portrait of 1885, the brushes and palette are suggested cursorily by no more than a few strokes in the canvas's lower corner. Manet's *Portrait of Eva Gonzalès* (165) does present the artist at the easel, though the way she holds her tools speaks far more of a pose than of actual practice, as does her sumptuous dress. Her need to retouch a canvas already framed, which had been covered to keep the paints from drying, leaves doubt about her ability to get things right the first time round. Elsewhere, the painting is filled with bravado effects declaring Manet's mastery rather than his student's – especially the flowers strewn about the floor which inevitably compare to Gonzalès's flower still life. Finally, was it fair for Manet to show Gonzalès as a flower painter in the same year she exhibited and sold to the state her powerful *The Little Soldier* (164), a full-length Realist figure echoing his *Fifer Boy* (see 40)? It is true that Manet's painting was done before Gonzalès had established a career, and Manet himself had his own predilection for still life. (Also, who knows what role Gonzalès had in Manet's conception?) But we may certainly recall Marie Bracquemond's complaint that her training with Ingres was limited to flowers – and wonder if Manet's teaching was any different.

If Manet may have been uneasy about an ambitious female artist, one can imagine what rhetoric surfaced in less liberal quarters. The Morisot sisters' early drawing master feared 'catastrophe' (social, of course) if his charges pursued their considerable talents professionally.

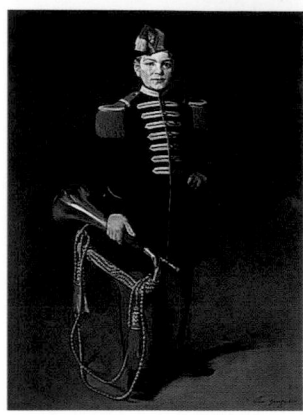

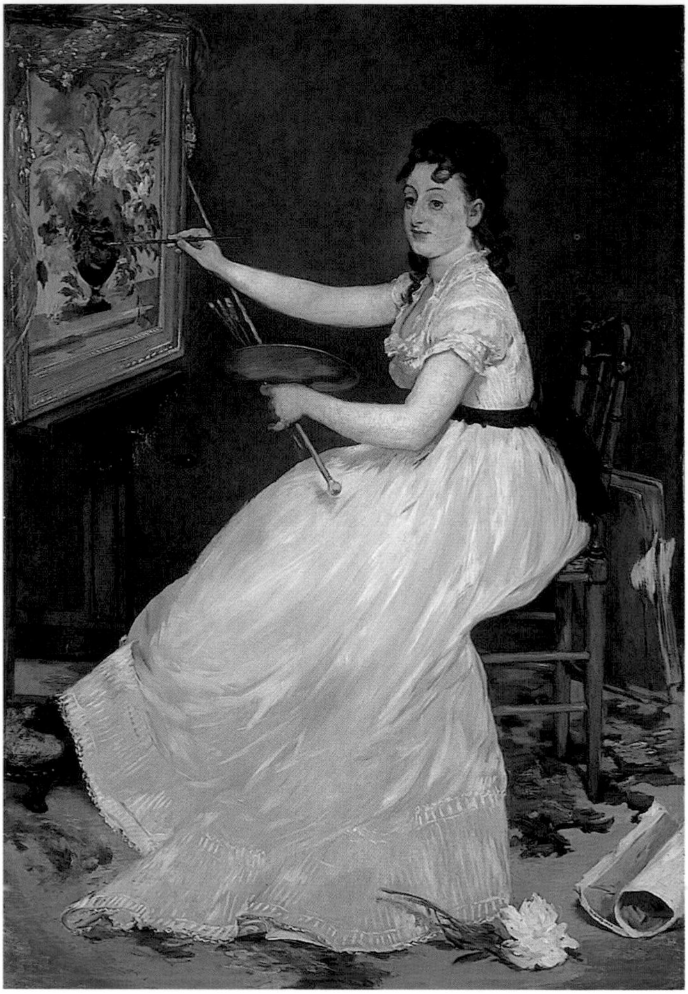

164 Above
Eva Gonzalès,
The Little Soldier,
1870.
Oil on canvas;
130 × 98 cm,
51 × 38¹⁄₂ in.
Musée de Gajac,
Villeneuve-sur-Lot

165 Right
Édouard Manet,
*Portrait of
Eva Gonzalès*,
1870.
Oil on canvas;
191·1 × 133·4 cm,
75¹⁄₄ × 52³⁄₈ in.
National Gallery,
London

Renoir echoed that attitude when, apparently forgetting his friendship with Morisot, he said, 'I consider women writers, lawyers and politicians ... as monsters and nothing but five-legged calves. The woman artist is merely ridiculous.' Art was the domain of the male. Thus, in 1896 the critic Roger Marx referred to Cassatt as 'that masculine American woman'.

The evolution of Degas's variants on his *Mary Cassatt at the Louvre* (167) may shed some light on these problems. His respect for Cassatt was secure, and in representing her in the hallowed spaces of the Louvre, which he might consider his own terrain, he certainly conceded to her artistic intelligence. Representing her from behind

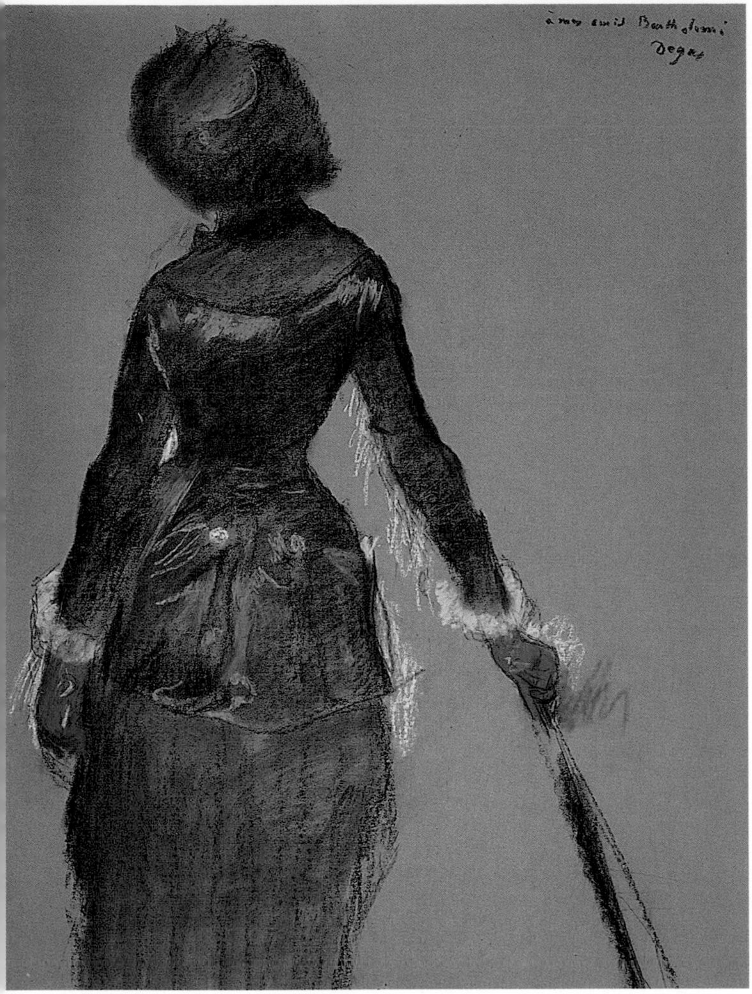

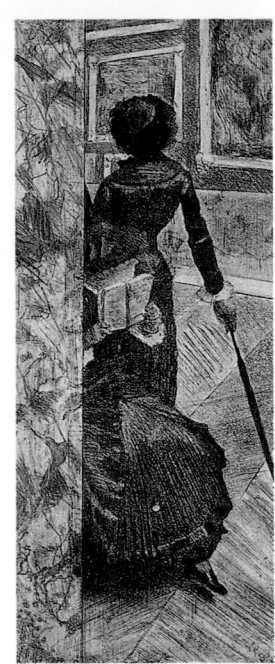

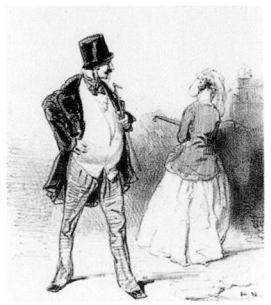

**166 Above
Edgar Degas**,
Study for
*Mary Cassatt
at the Louvre*,
1879–80.
Pastel on paper;
63·5 × 48·9 cm,
25 × 19¹⁴ in.
Philadelphia
Museum of Art

was a strategy perfectly within his naturalistic aim of revealing a character through views from different angles, and it was done at the same time as his portraits of Duranty (see 120) and the critic Diego Martelli. In one of Degas's most famous studies of Cassatt (166), she has an erect, alert presence, umbrella thrust firmly to the side, head cocked in rapt examination of paintings on the wall. Yet what dominates our view is nevertheless the shapely figure of a woman, all the more privately available in its presentation from the rear. In fact, watching women from behind seems to have been a national male preoccupation, judging by a cartoon of 1846 by Paul Gavarni (1804–66; 168); its caption translates freely as: 'Close enough to

**167
Edgar Degas**,
*Mary Cassatt at
the Louvre*,
1879–80.
Etching on
paper, 16th state;
33·7 × 17 cm,
11³⁴ × 6⁵⁸ in.
The Art Institute
of Chicago

**168
Paul Gavarni**,
*Balivernes
Parisiennes*,
'A portée de
lorgnon',
1846.
Lithograph in
Le Charivari, 1846

inspect.' In the final composition, Degas overlays on to Cassatt's figure that of her sister Lydia, who is reading from a guidebook and serves as chaperone. Her presence neutralizes any prurient reading to focus on the intellectual activity with which Degas intended to endow his artist friend.

One always makes exceptions for friends, for whom social solidarity has priority over prejudice. But despite Degas's efforts on their behalf and the great strides made by Cassatt and Morisot, when it came to women in general, including women artists, attitudes were slow to evolve. The statement of one C Bonheur, writing in the anarchist journal *La Chronique moderne* in 1889 about an exhibition organized by the Union of Women Painters and Sculptors (created in 1882), brutally reminds us of this point:

Woman is the ideal which dominates art, the eternal source of inspiration, but just as the artist could not aspire to attain this ideal – that is, supreme perfection in his reproduction – woman herself is not able to descend into the arena of the fight. She inspires, she encourages; she dominates, that is her role – but she cannot execute.

169
Alfred Stevens,
In the Studio,
1888.
Oil on canvas;
106·7 × 135·9 cm,
42 × 53½ in.
Metropolitan
Museum of Art,
New York

Although Cassatt and Morisot most certainly proved this critic wrong, a painting called *In the Studio* (169) by Alfred Stevens shows how ambivalent even friends could be. The work shows three women in an artist's workshop – a model, a visitor and another woman we suppose to be a painter. The studio looks almost like a drawing room, with artworks on the wall, including fashionable Asian objects, and a freely painted animal skin on the floor. A model poses as Salome in an exotic negligée and open kimono, her street clothes discarded at the opposite end of the sofa where she sits. The visitor, quite properly attired and precisely painted, examines drawings from a portfolio and maintains an air of kind superiority as she leans forward, contemplating the attractive but coarser-looking model. The third woman is dressed in a simple but fashionably bohemian gown, tastefully fastened at the waist with a lavender sash matching a knotted scarf. She holds a palette and maulstick with one hand while leaning on the canvas and looking over towards the model.

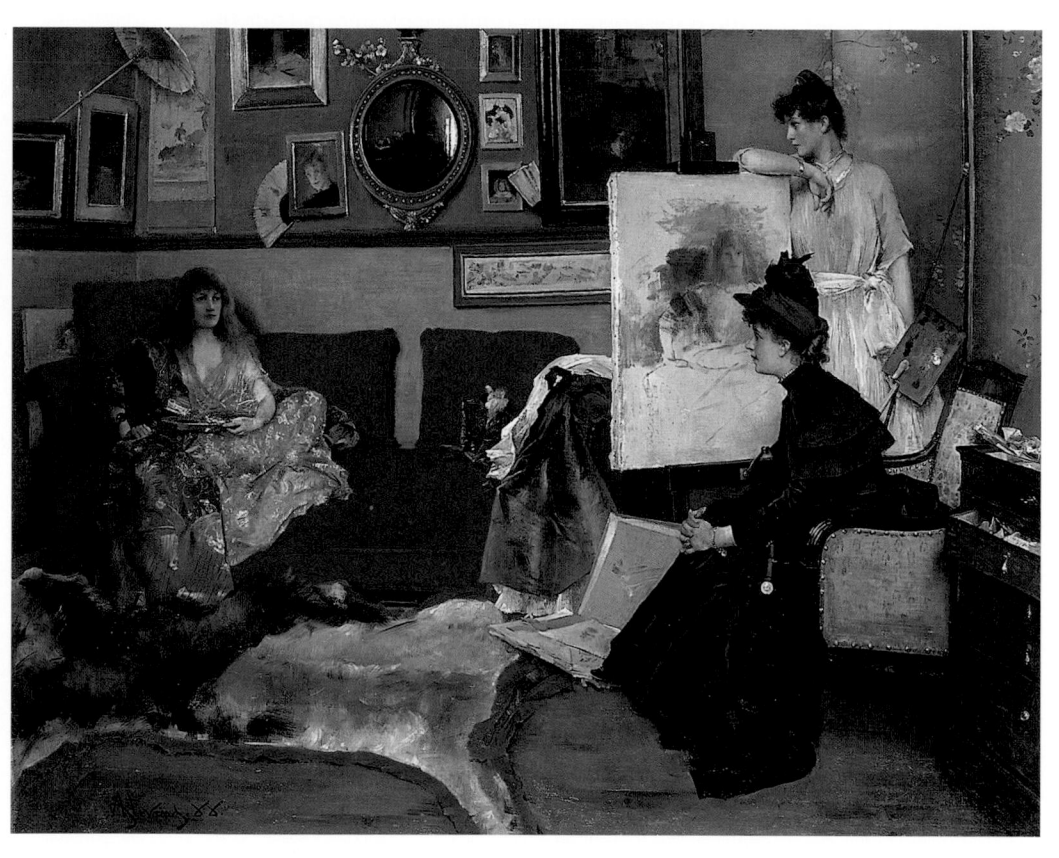

Today's viewer easily assumes she is the artist, but another interpretation is equally possible. A mirror on the wall at the composition's centre reflects a darker, more authentic studio, with a proverbial pot-belly stove. It reminds us that the mirror is an age-old reference to the interplay of illusion and reality produced by art. For on the easel, after all, is the *ébauche*, or sketch, of Stevens' own *Salomé* – an Orientalizing theme connected to sexual fantasies. It was executed in 1888, the same year as In the Studio, as many viewers would certainly have known. Who is the artist, then? Is it Stevens, here outside the picture representing his studio, or is it the woman holding a painter's tools? Is she his assistant or his muse? We must admit that even in a picture that appears at first to represent a woman painter, the male artist continues to be in control.

The association between control and masculinity is at the heart of the work of Gustave Caillebotte. He was several years younger than most of the Impressionists and did not join them until 1876, when he was invited by Renoir and Degas's friend Henri Rouart. From then on, however, he became one of the group's driving forces, from persuading those who were reluctant to participate, to buying frames and helping hang the shows. Secure in his personal wealth, inherited from his father's textile fortune in 1874, and generous to his friends, whose art he purchased in the early years, he was so completely committed to their cause that he was frustrated when others began defecting and became angry when Degas tried to pack the group with artists Caillebotte deemed unworthy. In 1879, the satirical cartoonist Bertall (Albert, vicomte d'Arnoux, comte de Limoges-Saint-Saens; 1820–82) said Caillebotte had used his wealth to save Impressionism from foundering and called him its new leader. A more marked contrast with Morisot and Renoir is hardly possible. Caillebotte never married, and women were secondary in his compositions. Rather, he defined himself through sport and male camaraderie, succeeding to Bazille's role. Caillebotte liked to have his way and could afford to. When he was elected to the town council of Petit-Gennevilliers (just across the Seine from Argenteuil), where he had purchased property, he paid for improvements to local amenities out of his own pocket rather than deal with state bureaucracy.

Caillebotte trained with the conservative Realist Léon Bonnat (1833–1922), and after rejection from the Salon of 1875, he exhibited his early masterpiece, *The Floor-Scrapers* (170), with the Impressionist group. Traditional in its relatively dark palette, finish and firm drawing, the painting made some critics wonder what it had to do with the loose facture, bright colours and outdoor scenes of Impressionism. Even its theme of manual labour seems closer to Courbet than to Impressionist scenes of leisure. Yet Caillebotte's labourers are planing and refinishing a floor in a bourgeois apartment – perhaps his mother's or one next door, according to a family tradition – and thus they are as much a part of the bourgeois world as Degas's *Women Ironing* (see 163), an early version of which was shown in the same year.

A relationship to Degas can be established through the latter's *Portraits in a Cotton Office, New Orleans* (see 217), which was shown in 1875 and has a similar treatment of space. And as in Degas's *The Dance Class* (see 126), Caillebotte uses a rigorous perspectival structure, with the vanishing point pushed far over to one side. One notes the receding street view through the open window and balcony railing. Indeed, the painting's foreshortening attracted the most critical attention. While some found it 'bizarre' and 'just too original', the painting had the optical perfection of photographs or the camera obscura. And wide-angle lenses were now available to produce the effects he desired. Although photographs of interiors were rare, Caillebotte worked with preparatory drawings, some squared off for transfer, that seem to have been traced and were the same size as photographic plates used by his brother.

Yet Caillebotte's traditional methods do not contradict his profound interest in optical sensation – in this case primarily spatial rather than colouristic or textural. Through those concerns, he appeared thoroughly modern, the back-lighting of his figures and the subtle play of the reflection over the floor paralleling the interests of his less traditional comrades. For a similar attempt to reconcile draughtsmanship and the theme of the male figure with a commitment to capturing optical experience, we might recall Bazille's picture of male bathers (see 82). But specific to Caillebotte is a peculiar psychological effect. The

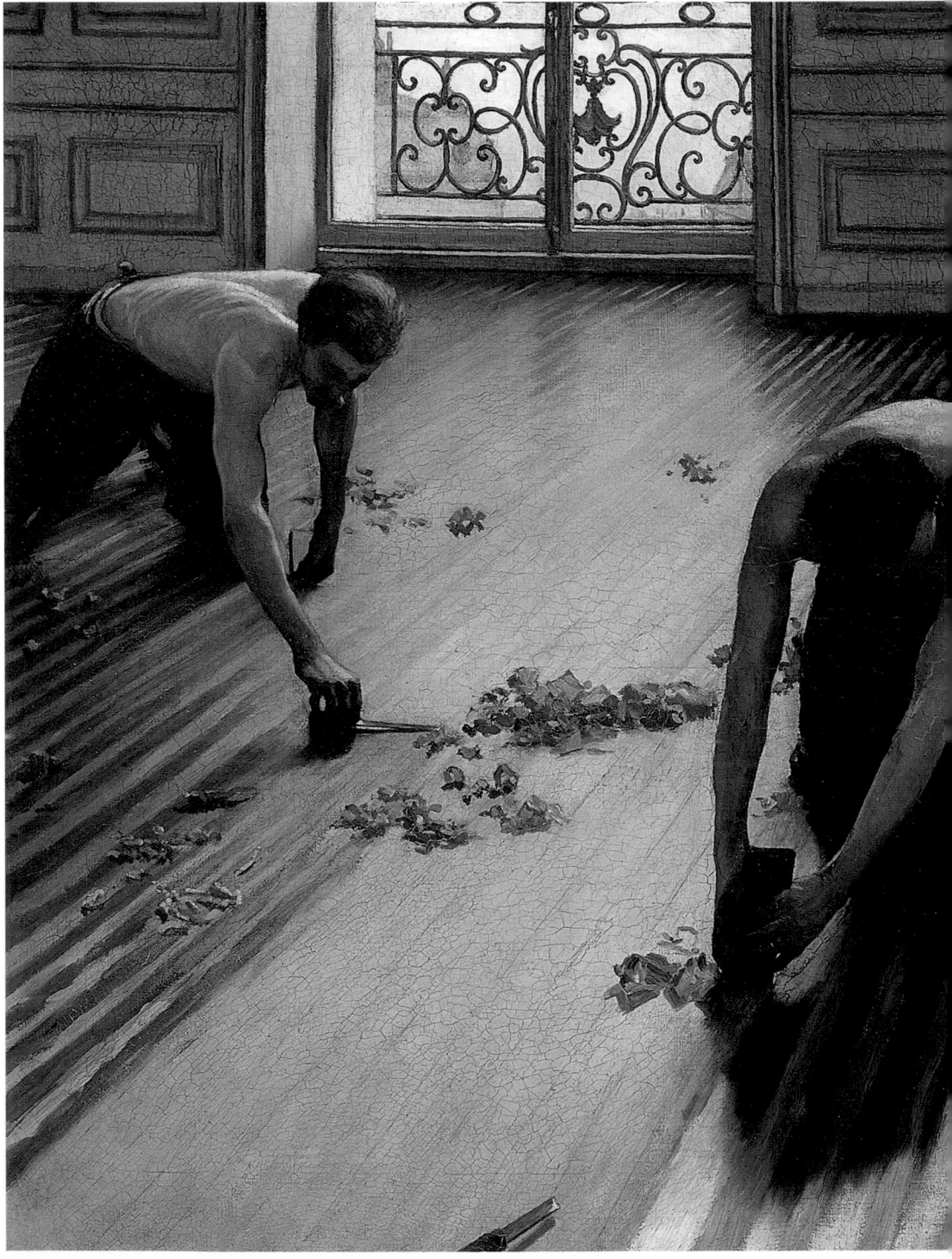

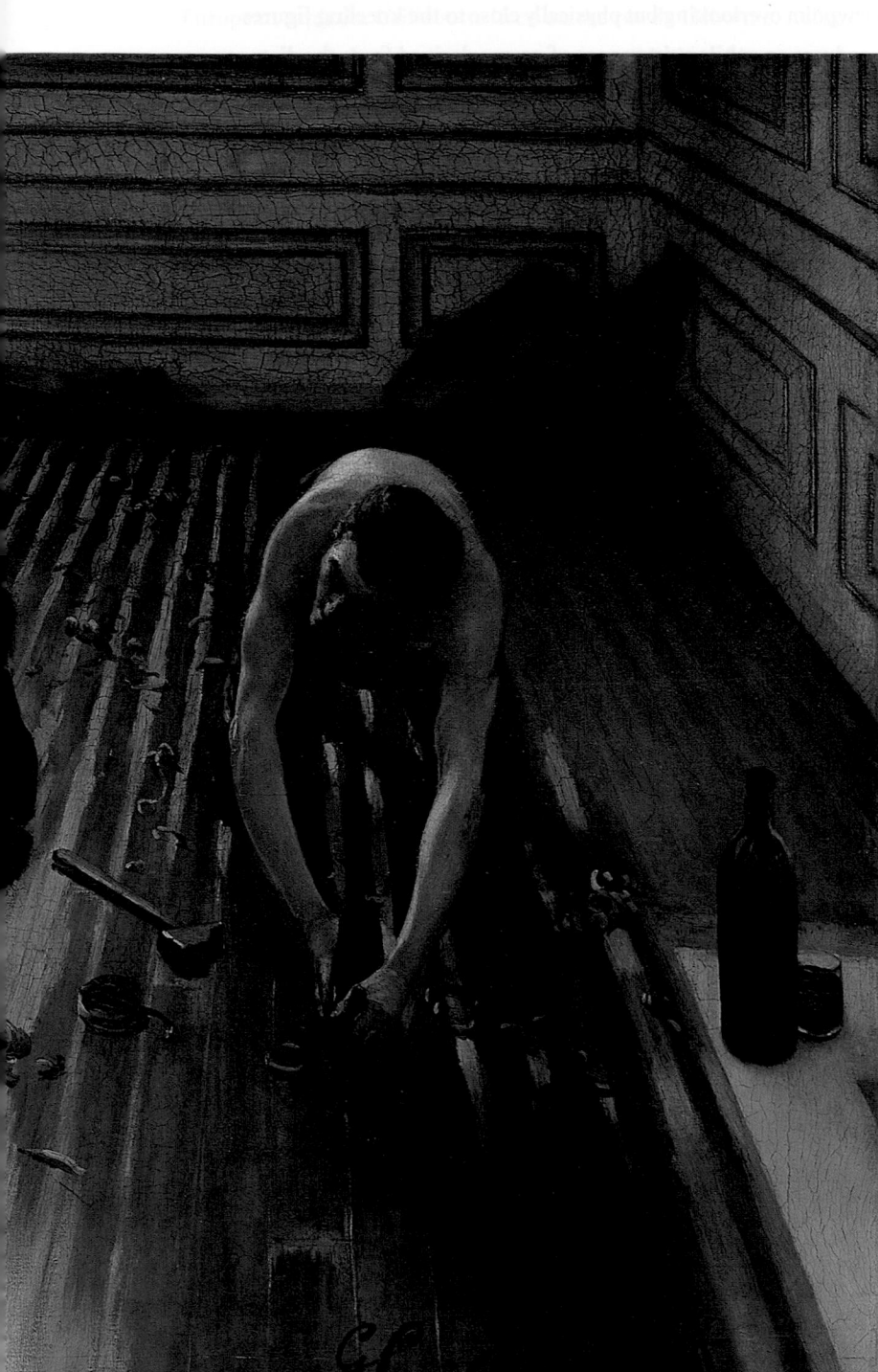

170
**Gustave
Caillebotte**,
The Floor-Scrapers,
1875.
Oil on canvas;
120 × 146·5 cm,
40⅛ × 57⅝ in.
Musée d'Orsay,
Paris

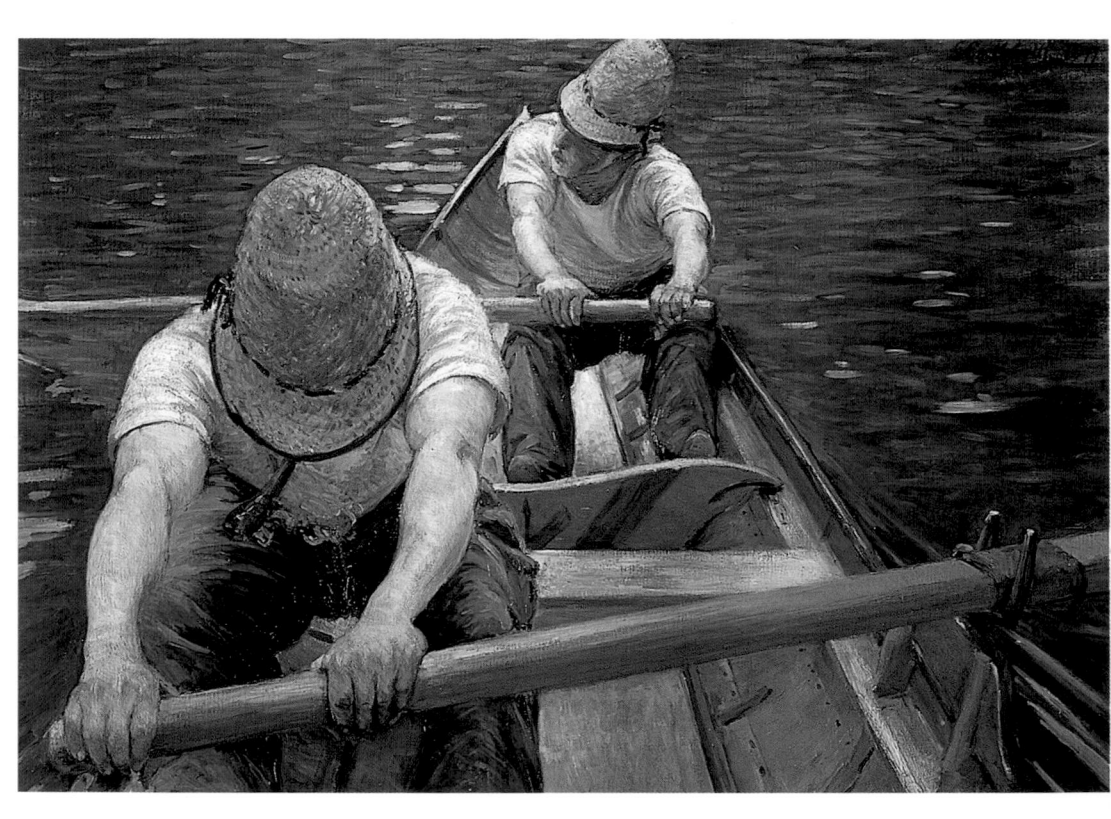

from other Impressionists might explain his preoccupation with the world of men. But, as implied within *The Floor-Scrapers* (see 170), there is an intensity and presence to his figures that creates tension with modernist detachment.

This ambiguity is especially noticeable when we compare his *Rowers on the Yerres River* (172) of 1877 to Manet's *Boating* (see 44). The latter celebrates the relaxing pleasures of open-air leisure, which Manet associates with the heterosexual couple. Caillebotte's figures, by contrast, are relentless sportsmen, rowers, boxers and sailors; he was himself fond of such sports (173). His family's imposing summer

172
Gustave Caillebotte, *Rowers on the Yerres River*, 1877.
Oil on canvas; 81 × 116 cm, 31⁷⁄8 × 45⁵⁄8 in.
Private collection

173
Gustave Caillebotte boxing, c.1880

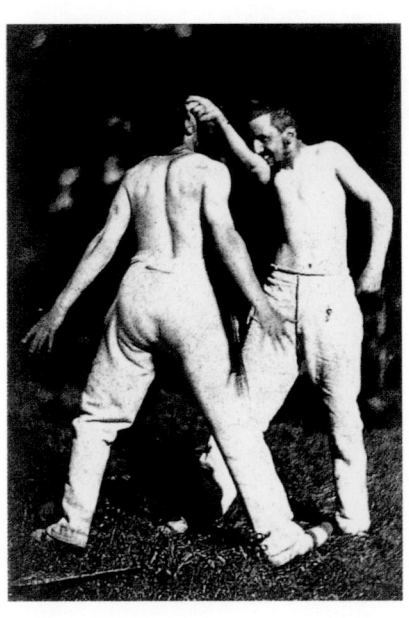

house stood along the bank of the river, a tributary of the Seine just south of Paris, and he possessed a number of skiffs and rowing shells. *Le rowing*, as the French called it, was part of the sporting rage imported from Britain. But this particular physical activity had further connotations, for the ideal of fitness became associated with military readiness and national service along the British and Prussian model, especially following the Franco-Prussian War. (Caillebotte was proud of his years as an army officer.) The painter places the viewer within the boat and tightly frames his rowers. The effect is so airless there is little chance for enjoyment of the riverscape. The foreground figure is uncomfortably close; both are absorbed in athletic exertion, relieved only by the foreground rower's smouldering cheroot. Caillebotte revels in the pleasures of the male physique. A man of slight stature but with military bearing, he produced art that leads us to speculate on his self-confidence and sexuality. Most male artists gave form to their masculinity through their ideals of women. Caillebotte measured himself against other men. His pictures leave no doubt that he wants his man's world to be a manly one.

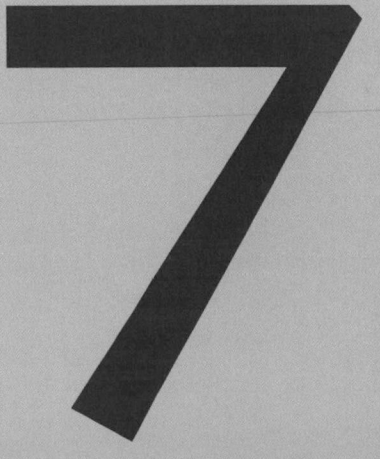

There is a theory that holds all art to be political because it is produced within systems of power that it on some level either accepts or opposes. Impressionism raises the problem of reconciling its overwhelmingly apolitical subject matter with its antipathy towards the artistic and sometimes the political establishment. There are a few exceptional works that openly express the political opinions of their makers – for example, Manet's Republicanism and Pissarro's anarchism. But artists' intentions are just one aspect of the politics underlying art. Political inferences can be made from what artists avoid doing as well as from what they do, from what they do not represent as well as what they paint. And some forms of politics, such as patriotism or nationalist pride, are so widely shared that they may be taken for granted by both artist and viewer. Beyond politics, ideology is a related but not identical issue. If politics is a field of action, ideology is the belief or value system that supports it. Even when it governs the most ordinary conduct of a person's life, by giving such everyday acts significance, ideology forms the grounding for political structures. To the extent that Impressionism implicitly celebrates or criticizes a way of life and legitimizes or undermines its assumptions, it participates in political debate.

174
Claude Monet,
*Rue Saint-Denis,
Festival of
30 June 1878*
(detail of 185)

There are several instances of political themes in Manet's work. How he reconciled them with his ethic of detachment provides a case study to compare with other Impressionists. The relationship between art and politics in France has a long history, for example, the role of Jacques-Louis David (1748–1825) in the French Revolution and Delacroix's famous image of French liberty (see 181) to Courbet's politicized challenges to prevailing taste and institutional authority. Manet was a staunch Republican, contemptuous of the autocratic government of Napoleon III, who had overthrown the Second Republic in 1851 when he could no longer rule as president (having served the maximum term of office). Yet Manet's political gestures, if they can be called that, were understated and often couched in irony. As a painter of modern life, he encountered manifestations of political power in daily events. For example, *The Balloon* (175) shows an imperial festival – a balloon launching on the Second Empire's national holiday – which transparently diverted public attention from the rapacious profiteering and population displacements that accompanied the regime. In bitter contrast to the well-dressed crowd admiring recent scientific progress, a crippled beggar sits in Manet's foreground. Could he be a wounded veteran of one of the emperor's disastrous foreign campaigns?

Particularly lethal were Napoleon III's Mexican adventures that, designed to extend French influence in the new world, ended in France's ignominious withdrawal in 1867. After a French, British and Spanish expeditionary force deposed the liberal Mexican president, Benito Juárez, on the grounds that he placed a moratorium on debt payments (because of Mexico's economic difficulties), the 32-year-old Archduke Maximilian, younger brother of Emperor Franz Joseph of Austria (r.1848–1916), was installed as puppet ruler in 1864. However, Mexican guerrillas, armed by the United States, eventually forced withdrawal of the French army, Maximilian's sole means of support. Refusing abdication, Maximilian was taken prisoner and with two of his generals, Miramón and Mejía, was executed on 19 June 1867.

175
Édouard Manet,
The Balloon,
1862.
Lithograph;
40·3 × 51·5 cm,
15⁷⁸ × 20¹⁴ in

Manet began working on *The Execution of the Emperor Maximilian* (176) shortly thereafter. He was first inspired by Goya's famous *The Third of May 1808* (177), a painting he could have seen in reproductions, if not in the Prado while visiting Spain. Then he used news accounts and photographs (178) for the uniforms, the grouping of the firing squad, and the wall behind the figures. Although Manet had never emulated academic history painting, he was, as we know, committed to confronting it with reality – to deflating heroic conventions by adhering to visual fact. Whatever Manet's political agenda in painting the event, it allowed him to depict its tragic human cost. His own comments stressed the painting's 'absolutely artistic' values. Indeed, Manet's attitude to Mexico is unclear: he had family relations and connections on both sides of the military and political establishment.

Impressionism

But even if one approved of France's foreign policy, one could be shocked by its cowardly conduct, as were many of the French élite. For example, Commandant Lejosne was willing to march an infantry squadron over to model at the painter's studio. A close examination of the outfits in *The Execution of the Emperor Maximilian* shows that Manet did not follow the photographs completely. The firing squad came from Juárez's regular army, but Manet's uniforms are closer to those of the French. He gave them white spats, like those in *The Fifer*

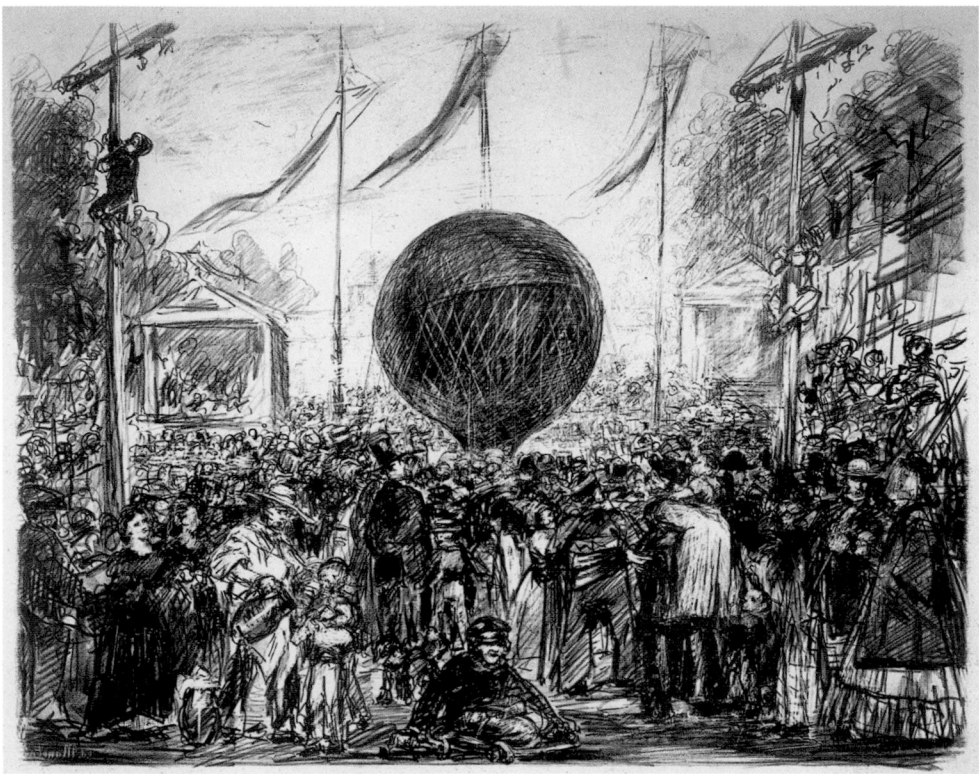

Boy (see 40), and, as Juliet Wilson-Bareau has pointed out, he dressed them up with the ceremonial swords used by French gendarmes. The end result, as Zola observed, was a 'cruel irony' in which it looks like 'France is shooting Maximilian'.

Goya used facial expressions, dramatic body postures and light to create distinctions between guilt and innocence, between brute and martyr. Manet's painting looks like a dispassionate, journalistic

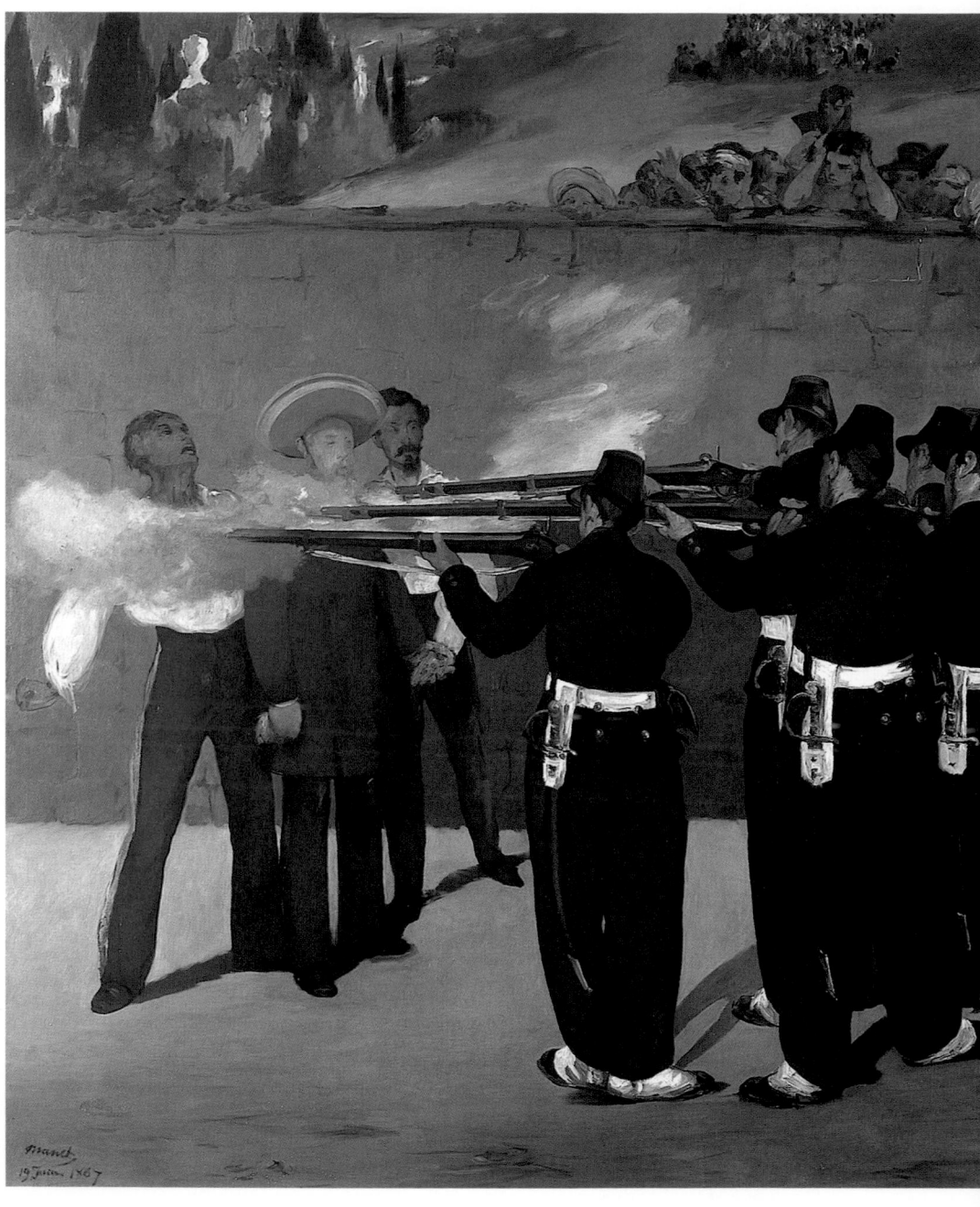

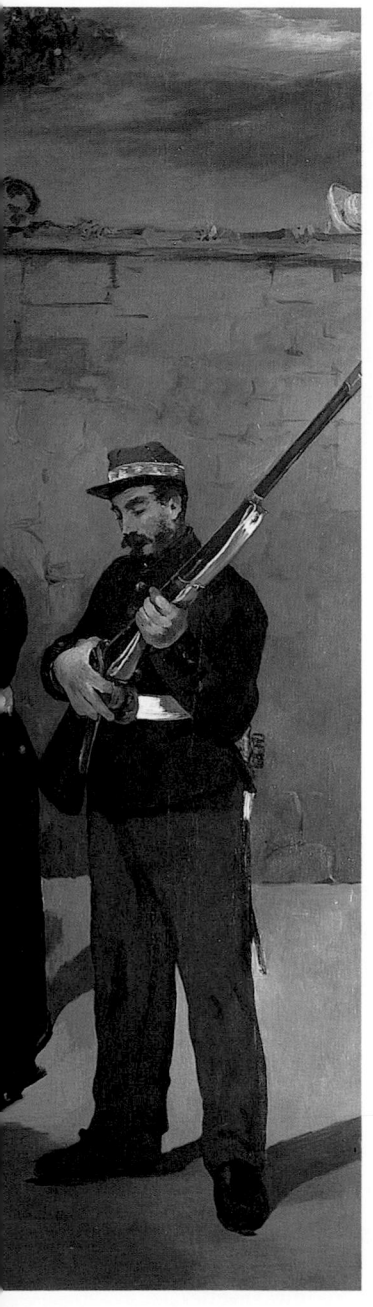

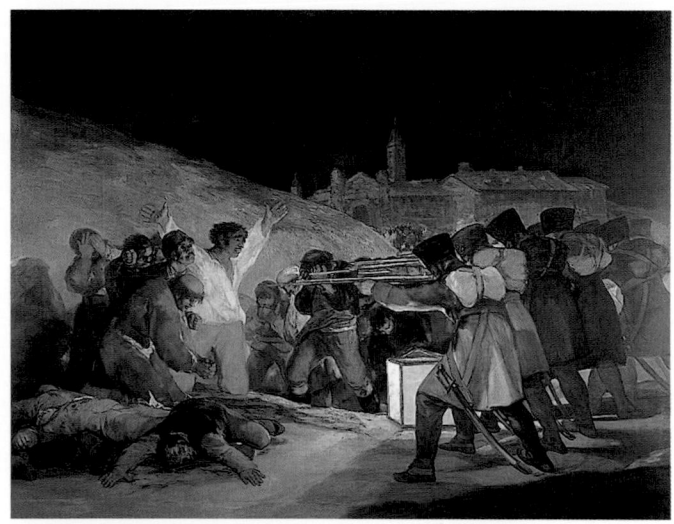

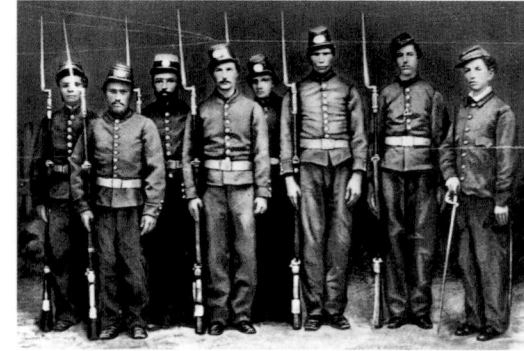

176 Far left
Édouard Manet,
*The Execution
of the Emperor
Maximilian*,
1867.
Oil on canvas;
252 × 305 cm,
99$\frac{1}{4}$ × 120$\frac{1}{8}$ in.
Städtische
Kunsthalle,
Mannheim

177 Above
Francisco Goya,
*The Third of
May 1808*,
1814.
Oil on canvas;
266 × 345 cm,
104$\frac{7}{8}$ × 135$\frac{7}{8}$ in.
Museo del
Prado,
Madrid

178 Left
The firing
squad used in
the execution
of the Emperor
Maximilian,
19 June 1867

account, with slack gestures, awkward poses and apparent indifference among spectators leaning on the wall (except for one shouting at the victims). The picture's non-narrative structure, stripped of drama, refrains from inducing overt emotional bias. Manet preferred to play on the soldiers' impassivity and our knowledge that the victims' deaths are foregone conclusions. Such features themselves provide a shocking commentary on the cheapness of lives trapped in an international power struggle. The spectators leaning on the wall reinforce the sense of apathy, for they are paraphrased from bullfight etchings by Goya, where boredom and detachment testify to the predictable outcome of the event, in the face of which victims acquit themselves with dignity. While Mejía reels in pain, the firm handclasp between Maximilian and Miramón suggests brotherhood in their fate.

It can certainly be argued that the same principle that underlay his *Déjeuner sur l'herbe* (see 30) is here brought to bear on contemporary history painting. Suppression of narrative and avoidance of the traditional indicators of emotion preserve artistic identity as a dispassionate, observing eye, the artist as *flâneur*, whose only evident interest is reportage of visual spectacle. Yet is not this affectation of indifference itself a form of political statement – one in which the dirty world of politics is rejected? Manet's attitude would then be similar (though less extreme) to that of Baudelaire's artful dandy, whose philosophy of disdain was a defence, however futile, against the rise of ineptitude and banality in public life. For him, the private and aesthetic were the only reasonable refuge and the only solid ground. It is an apolitical politics, with the cynical outlook of the alienated and solitary modern individual at its core. Yet merely treating the theme of Maximilian's execution made Manet's project suspect to the government, which kept the painting out of the Salon of 1869 and forbade publication of a lithograph after it. Such works could only remind people of issues the emperor hoped would be forgotten. Censorship therefore also explains the relative lack of political themes in Impressionist art.

Impressionist paintings give little hint that one of the bloodiest events in modern French history, the repression of the Paris Commune of 1871, took place at the time of the movement's formation. Following the deposition of Napoleon III during the Franco-Prussian War, a provisional National Assembly was established. The government was led by Adolphe Thiers, who signed an armistice on 16 February 1871 that ended the war. However, many of the workers and artisans of Paris refused to submit to the Thiers regime and, with the Parisian National Guard, forced the National Assembly to withdraw to Versailles. The Parisians elected a socialist municipal council, known as the Commune, which they hoped would be the first step in establishing revolutionary government throughout France.

The city had been largely abandoned during the war by its more prosperous inhabitants, who could afford to go to the country. For the same reason, right-wing propaganda was free to make unchecked accusations and attribute the direst intentions to the Communards. Under pressure from authoritarian politicians and the Royalist party, Thiers's Republicans prepared an all-out attack that would leave no doubt about its ability to exercise control. The 'Bloody Week', which lasted from 21 to 28 May, and subsequent executions produced a death toll of nearly 30,000 (far more than the just-ended war), with many more arrests and deportations to penal colonies overseas.

The impact of the war and the Commune have been variously evaluated. On the one hand, they can be seen as a profound break in French society, one which made the Second Empire seem like a golden age of prosperity and self-confidence. On the other, the Commune in effect permitted the re-establishment of the discredited bourgeois hegemony that had surrendered to the Prussians. In giving the bourgeoisie a battle they could win, the Communards contributed with their defeat to a revival of (middle-class) French self-respect, marred only by a gnawing guilt among the victors over its cost. Forgetfulness and erasure therefore became the unstated national policy. A letter from Zola to Cézanne on 4 July 1871 sums up the irony: 'Now I find myself quietly at home again in the Batignolles quarter as if I'd just awakened from a bad dream. My little house is the same as ever, my garden is untouched ... and I could almost believe the two sieges were bad jokes invented to scare children.' Only Pissarro's house and belongings in Louveciennes were damaged in the upheavals.

Most of the Impressionists were out of Paris during these events, either because, like Bazille (who was killed), Renoir, Degas and Manet, they enlisted for the national defence and were posted elsewhere, or like Monet and Pissarro, who both went to London, they fled the city altogether. Sisley stayed with his family in Louveciennes; Cézanne hid with his mistress at L'Estaque, a fishing village just west of Marseille. During the Commune following the war, Manet joined his family in the southwest; Degas visited the Valpinçons in Normandy. Among those who exhibited with the Impressionists, only Félix Bracquemond and Auguste Ottin (1811–90) were active Communards, elected to its Federated Council. But among artists there was a famous leader, Gustave Courbet, who was arrested for masterminding the destruction of a Napoleonic monument, the Vendôme Column, after wild press exaggerations of his role. His trial and persecution into exile typified official vengeance. One could not overestimate the importance of symbols in such unstable times. Understood as a branch of Realism, Impressionism in its first years was associated with Courbet. To the degree its opponents assumed it had a politics, they were considered left-wing, hence the name Intransigeants (see Chapter 1).

Following the Commune, then, overtly political art would have been singularly ill-advised. Moreover, almost everyone could agree that rebuilding France both physically and psychologically was the only path to healing. The succession of Prussian bombardments, the ravages of the artillery used against the Communards, and the latter's destruction of symbols of power and torching of buildings in defence of their positions, left Paris and its western suburbs in shambles. In Paris, the Hôtel de Ville, Tuileries Palace, Palace of Justice, Palais Royal and many other official buildings, including parts of the Louvre, were destroyed or severely damaged (179).

179
The rue de Rivoli after the Commune, 1871

Of all the Impressionists, only Manet alluded directly to the Commune. He produced two lithographs, one called *Civil War* (180), in which a corpse in the foreground – absent the glorious fighters of Delacroix's *Liberty Leading the People* (181) – implies futility, and another called *The Barricade*, which re-used some figures from the

firing squad in *The Execution of the Emperor Maximilian* to show
Versaillais soldiers executing their proletarian brethren. Most artists
were determined to put the past behind them, whatever their attitudes
towards political and social reform. Very few paintings showed any
of the destruction. In four pictures Monet made of the Tuileries
gardens from collector Victor Chocquet's flat overlooking the site
(182), there is barely a suggestion of the burnt-out royal residence
(183), although it was left uncleared for twelve years as a reminder
of the awful past. More direct evidence of war destruction and the
reconstruction that followed is found in Monet's several paintings of
Argenteuil bridges. During the Franco-Prussian War both the railway
and highway bridges were destroyed. By the time Monet moved
to Argenteuil, rebuilding had begun (see 68). His painting thus

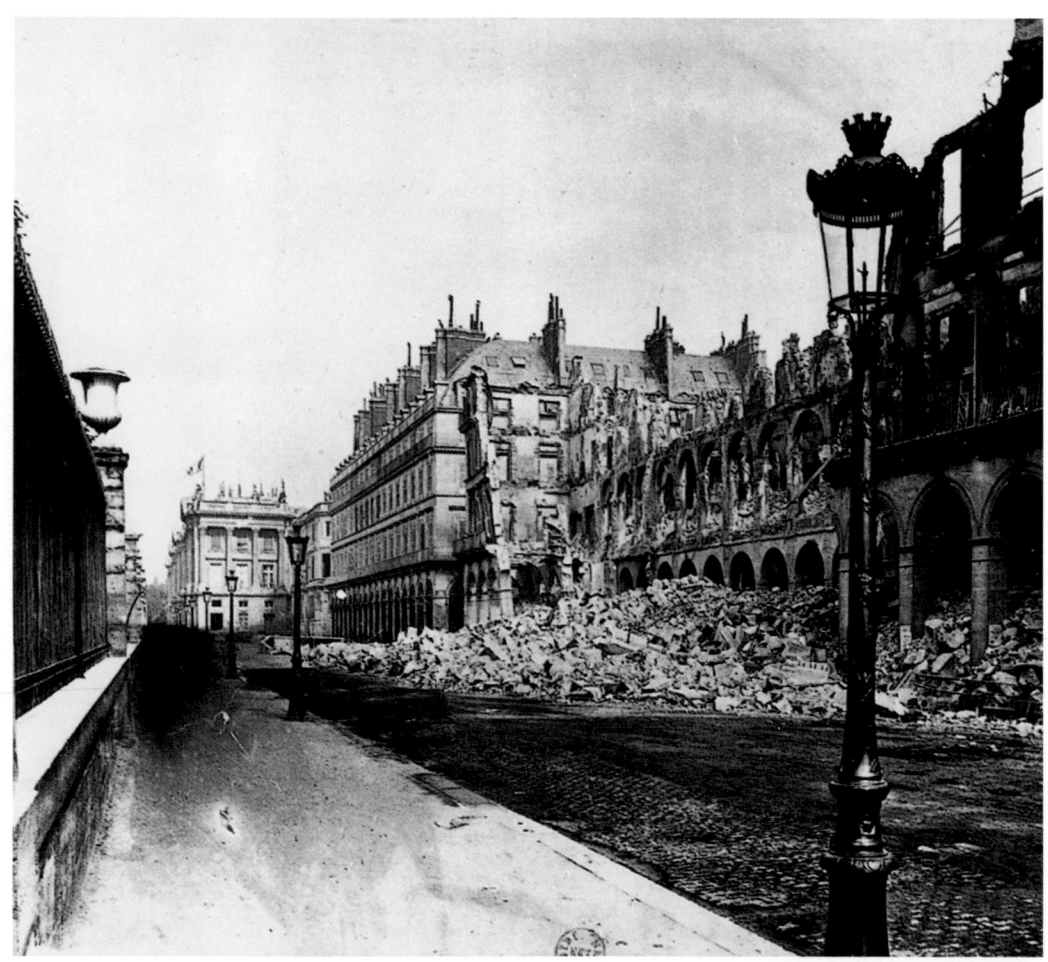

acknowledges the effort to get France back on its feet and implicitly propagates the agenda of national revival, a unifying goal which all political parties shared.

It has been suggested that paintings such as Caillebotte's street scenes and Degas's *Vicomte Ludovic Lepic and his Daughters* (see 119) embody a 'psychic recuperation' by the bourgeoisie of urban spaces once heavily occupied by the Commune. Representing them in peaceful normality emptied them of political memories. Lepic was a staunch Bonapartist – Napoléon was his middle name. In Degas's painting, his hat screens out the statue of Strasbourg, capital of the eastern French province of Alsace, which the victorious Prussians annexed to Germany. Feeling sold out by the Thiers government, which had signed a humiliating

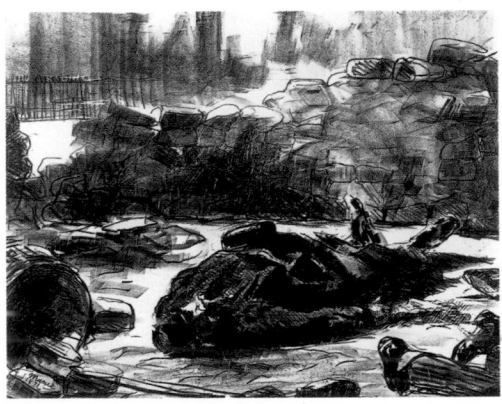 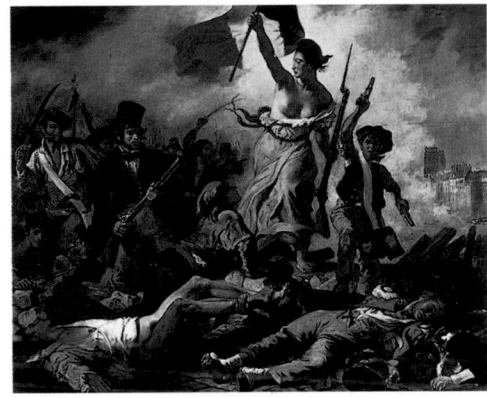

armistice and agreed to heavy reparations, Communards made the statue a rallying point in Paris's most central and open public space. Hence Degas's bitter nationalist irony may be coupled with nostalgia for the Second Empire, a feeling one need not have been a Bonapartist to share. In its different way, Renoir's *Ball at the Moulin de la Galette* (see 109) helped redefine Montmartre, a working-class neighbourhood that was reputedly the Commune's headquarters, as a place of carefree relaxation. Finally, Berthe Morisot, whose family enjoyed relative safety in the suburban area of Passy, painted *Summer's Day* (184), which shows two women boating in the nearby Bois de Boulogne. During the events of 1870–1, thousands of its trees had been systematically levelled to make way for troop bivouacs and

180 Above left
Édouard Manet,
Civil War,
1871.
Lithograph;
39·7 × 50·8 cm,
15⁵⁸ × 20 in

181 Above
Eugène
Delacroix,
*Liberty Leading
the People*,
1830.
Oil on canvas;
260 × 325 cm,
102³⁸ × 128 in.
Musée du
Louvre,
Paris

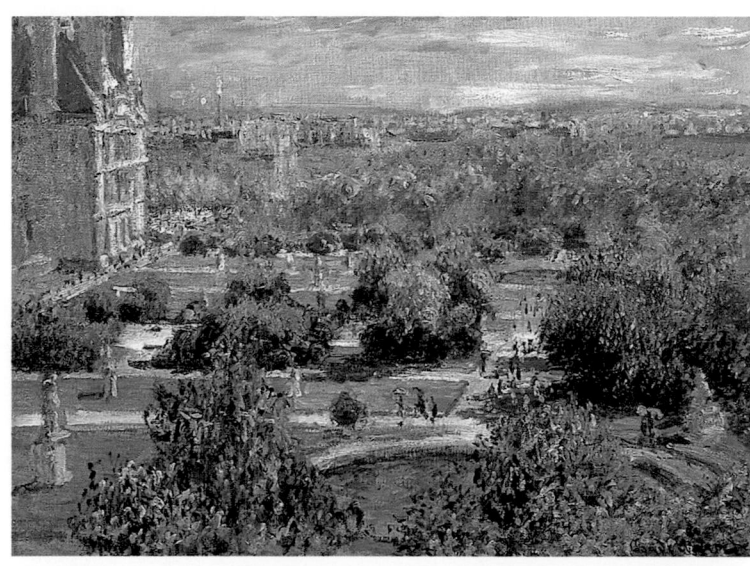

182
Claude Monet,
*The Tuileries
Gardens*,
1876.
Oil on canvas;
54×73 cm,
21^{1}4×28^{3}4 in.
Musée
Marmottan,
Paris

183
View of the
Tuileries Palace
after being
burnt during
the Commune,
1871

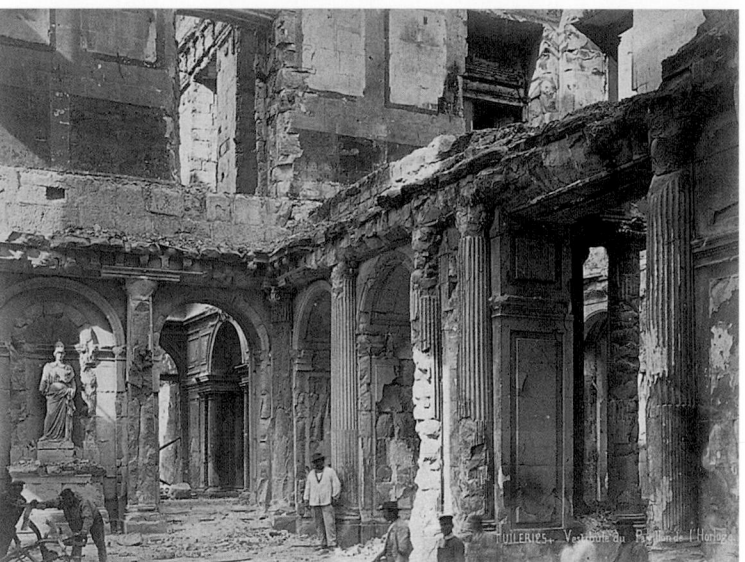

prison camps, and to provide firewood. By 1879, the park's bucolic setting had been restored. In that very year, British observer George Sala published a volume entitled *Paris Herself Again*.

Such paintings tell us little about the political instability that haunted the early years of the Third Republic, despite its repression of the Commune. The three major political parties – Monarchists, Bonapartists and Liberal Republicans – each claimed legitimacy based on historical antecedents, blaming the others for past failures. Some liberal election victories galvanized right-wing opposition to President Thiers, whom they were able to replace with the repressive

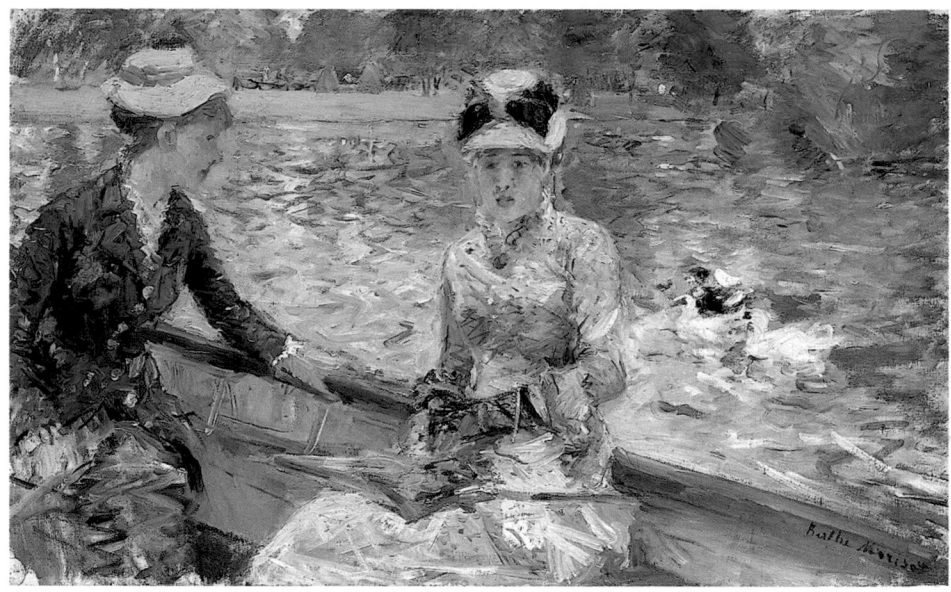

Marshal MacMahon, former leader of the anti-Commune troops. A Royalist uneasy with his authority, MacMahon was anxious to turn government over to the comte de Chambord, heir to the eighteenth-century throne. Skirmishes over symbols often embodied the struggle between Left and Right. In the early 1870s, when they were strong, Royalists tried to substitute the ancient fleur-de-lys of monarchy for the Republican tricolour flag. A similar dispute informs some paintings of 1878 by Monet and Manet, as Jane Mayo Roos has shown. The right-wing coalition had outlawed commemorations of 14 July, the revolutionary Bastille Day. By 1878, however, liberal gains in legislative elections strengthened challenges to these restrictions. As a compromise, the innocuous date of 30 June was chosen to celebrate the Republic. (In 1880, 14 July was re-established and remains France's national day.)

In Monet's *Rue Saint-Denis, Festival of 30 June 1878* (185), located in a working-class neighbourhood, the flags and 'Vive la France' banner hang across the street in a genuine outpouring of enthusiasm in which all French citizens could join. Judging by press accounts, this and a similar painting of the nearby rue Montorgueil were the hits of the Impressionist exhibition that year. The more sceptical Manet, by contrast, in his privately shown *Rue Mosnier with Flags*, placed in his foreground a one-legged figure with crutches, echoing the ironic motif from his early lithograph *The Balloon* (see 175). Manet's sombre note questioned the charade of unity, implicitly accusing Republicans of selling out to compromise; he refused what Roos has dubbed the political 'zone of silence' in which Monet was willing to participate. Her point is that Monet's ostensibly apolitical painting ultimately supported the political agenda of passing over responsibilities in silence – whereas Manet's more caustic commentary continues to reject politics as a corrupt and cruel hoax.

Is it too much to see Monet's famous *Impression, Sunrise* (see 3), with its evidence of resurgent industry, as an image of national pride, as Paul Tucker has suggested? Surely his pictures of the Saint-Lazare station (see 71) are tinged with similar spirit. Such patterns lead to inferences about Monet's later paintings, particularly those for which he chose significant motifs. For example, poplar trees, because they are so ubiquitous in France, are natural motifs for one of Monet's series (see 231). What could seem more politically innocent? Even when reminded that the poplar was the chosen Tree of Liberty during the French Revolution (in French *peuplier* means people's tree), with plantings of thousands across the nation, we find no overt indication of such memories in any Monet. Perhaps Monet chose the poplar for the same reason as the revolutionaries – there is no tree more typically French. Yet through that very choice, both may express an underlying pride in Frenchness, a glorification of that which makes one feel

184
Berthe Morisot,
Summer's Day,
1879.
Oil on canvas;
45·7 × 75·2 cm,
18 × 29⅝ in.
National
Gallery,
London

To exhibit with Pissarro, Gauguin and Guillaumin would be like exhibiting with a common socialist. The next thing you know, Pissarro would invite the Russian Lavrof [an anarchist] or another revolutionary to join. The public does not like what smacks of politics, and at my age I do not want to be a revolutionary. To associate with the Jew Pissarro means revolution.

Renoir favoured the restoration of the monarchy as a cure for instability. He thought Durand-Ruel, a Catholic traditionalist with strong monarchist sympathies, would agree with his opinion. Pissarro, by contrast, had briefly joined an overtly anti-bourgeois artists' union founded by one Alfred Meyer (1832–1904). In 1878, Cézanne persuaded him to leave in order to continue exhibiting with the Impressionists. In a rare instance of politically charged imagery, Pissarro commemorated his friendship with Cézanne in a portrait (186) against a backdrop of caricatures with anti-authoritarian themes. One of the images shows Courbet, the artist-nemesis of the Third Republic, with a palette in his left hand raising a beer glass with his right. The other shows Thiers paying off the Prussians. The title of the newspaper, *L'Eclipse*, might allude to the exclusionary tactics of the government. Courbet, who fled to Switzerland after his trial, was proscribed from all French exhibitions. Cézanne's outdoor clothing suggests the painting was done in winter, just before the first Impressionist show. A recent landscape by Pissarro himself is partly hidden by Cézanne's arm. Through their collaboration and participation with the Impressionists, both sought access to public view. Pissarro saw the group as a form of worker cooperative, like those advocated by leftist theories.

186
Camille
Pissarro,
*Portrait of
Paul Cézanne*,
1874.
Oil on canvas;
73 × 59·7 cm,
28³⁄₄ × 23¹⁄₂ in.
National
Gallery,
London

In expressing hope for the future through cooperation among artists, Pissarro reflected a broader political idealism that had a long history in France. Courbet's prominence in the portrait of Cézanne suggests continuity between Pissarro's political vision and that of Courbet. Courbet's Realism pavilion had launched the practice of self-financed exhibitions to rival those organized by official bodies. His project had a specific political conception underlying it, which was publicly linked to Courbet's friend, the notorious anarchist Pierre-Joseph Proudhon (who had died in 1865). For Proudhon, individuals in a

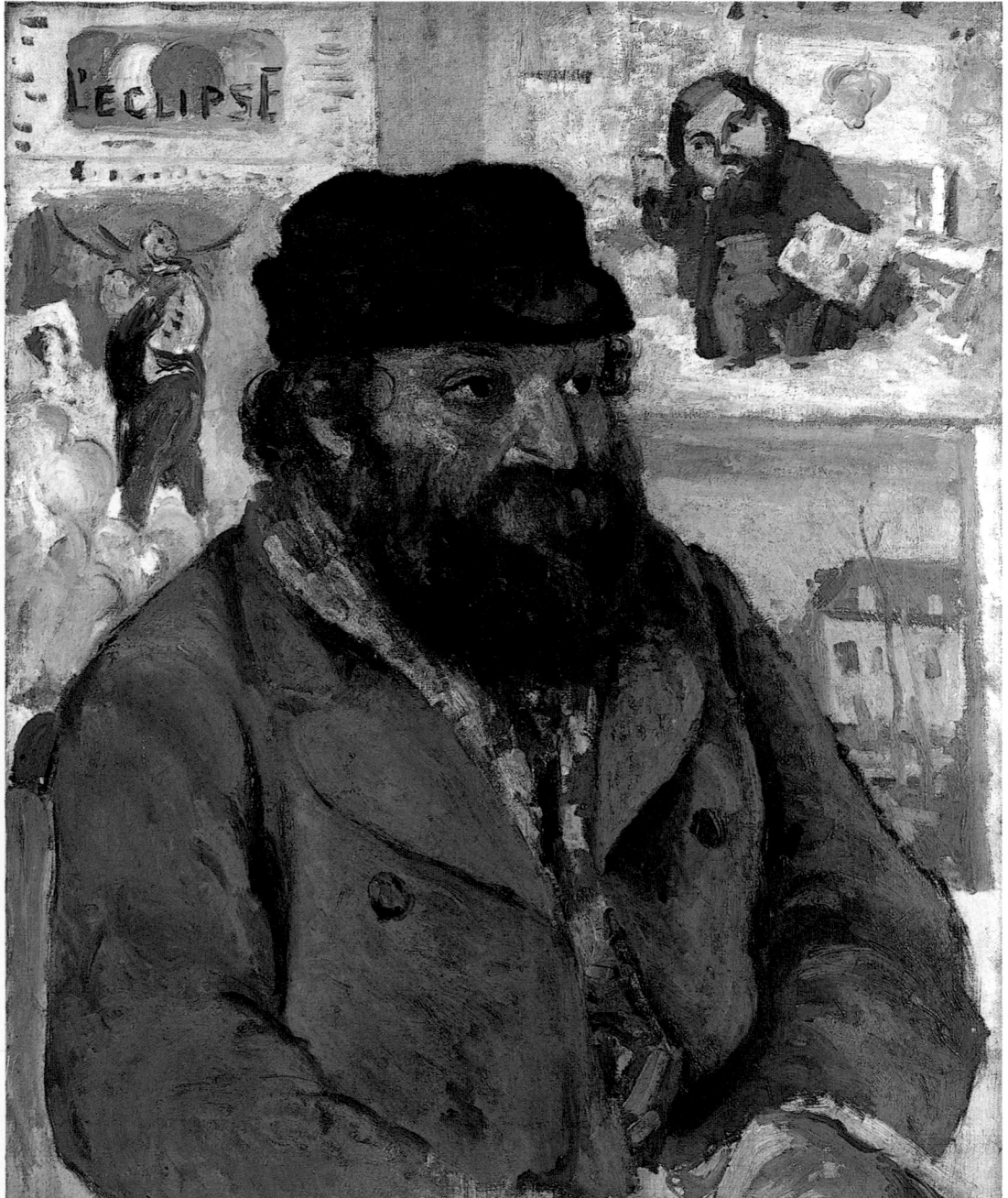

just society would establish mutual economic cooperatives, a system modelled on archaic rural practices that crossed class barriers and reinforced regional community and pride. However inadequate to the industrial realities of the new capitalism, this utopian vision was a powerful source of hope for those left behind in the race to modernization. But anarchism (meaning no central authority) was only partly nostalgic; Proudhon and his followers believed that science and logic would overcome the injustices of capitalism. During the Commune, many such ideas were put into practice, with elected municipal councils and initiatives for women's rights rather than government from the top. The Third Republic's violent riposte was motivated as much by fear of the Commune's success as from a compulsion to regain control. In defeating the Commune, however, the Versailles troops cut short its social experiment before disillusionment and failure might have undercut its seductive call.

Pissarro was attracted to Proudhon's theories. By 1876, he had subscribed to the principal radical journal of his time, *La Lanterne*, which contained writings by Proudhon and his followers. In paintings of the 1870s we saw Pissarro portray a countryside in which industry and traditional labour, worker and bourgeois coexist. To the degree that painting reflects desire as much as it records reality, Pissarro's political vision was already present. By the 1880s and 1890s, his politics became more explicit, though still obliquely translated by imagery and always non-violent. It was manifest in Pissarro's temporary conversion to the quasi-scientific techniques of Neo-Impressionism (see Chapter 8), and in letters to his sons. Pissarro saw optical theory as the basis for an objective vision – objective meaning not only scientifically accurate but socially just. Science would democratically afford everyone access to visual representation, whose images would be untainted by the social prejudices inherent in academic practice. In an epistolary outburst hypothesizing the destruction of museums, Pissarro echoed Proudhon, who aimed at freeing artists from tradition.

Pissarro's later imagery continued to idealize the countryside, though with less reference to modernity than before. In moving to the village of Eragny just north of Gisors in 1884, he headed into rural farming country about twice as far from Paris as Pontoise. There, market scenes and images of communal labour, such as *Peasant Women Planting Pea Sticks* of 1891, reflect the rural nostalgia lying behind the utopian dream. We know he had been reading (and sometimes disagreeing with) the Russian anarchist Peter Kropotkin, many of whose writings, which include *Modern Science and Anarchism* and *The Conquest of Bread*, were published in French in the early 1880s. In 1889–90, for the edification of his London nieces Alice and Esther Isaacson rather than for public viewing, Pissarro made a series of twenty-four drawings with a definite political bite. Called *Social Turpitudes*, they catalogue, in Pissarro's words, 'the shameful ignominies of the bourgeoisie'. The album cover (187) shows a melancholy philosopher, in sandals and beard, looking a bit like Pissarro himself. He holds a scythe, symbol of death, and beside him stands an hourglass, symbolizing time. The figure contemplates the Paris skyline replete with factory smokestacks and the new symbol of modern engineering, the Eiffel Tower. He is illuminated by the rising sun of anarchism on the far horizon, offering hopeful resolution to the evils the drawings adduce. Among Pissarro's topics were *Capital* (188), *The Arranged Marriage*, *The Temple of the Golden Calf*, *The Exchange Brokers*, *The Saint-Honoré Prison*, *The Hanged Man*, *The Beggar* and so on. Opposite each drawing was a quotation from the French Communist Jean Grave.

A few years later, Pissarro contributed some illustrations to Grave's journal *Les Temps nouveaux*. One showed a homeless family wandering the countryside. Another, done as a cover for an 1897 reprint of a lecture by Kropotkin, shows a farm worker tilling the soil – an image so redolent of Millet, it might seem frankly reactionary were it not for its association with the anarchist text. Indeed, it raises the question of the relevance to modernity of Pissarro's political beliefs at that time, and of his imagery to political reality. For while embodying principles Pissarro considered political, they participate neither aesthetically nor in terms of narrative in recognizable contemporary debates. They evoke an old-fashioned and simplistic politics quite distant from practical action, though maintaining the artist's sense of engagement.

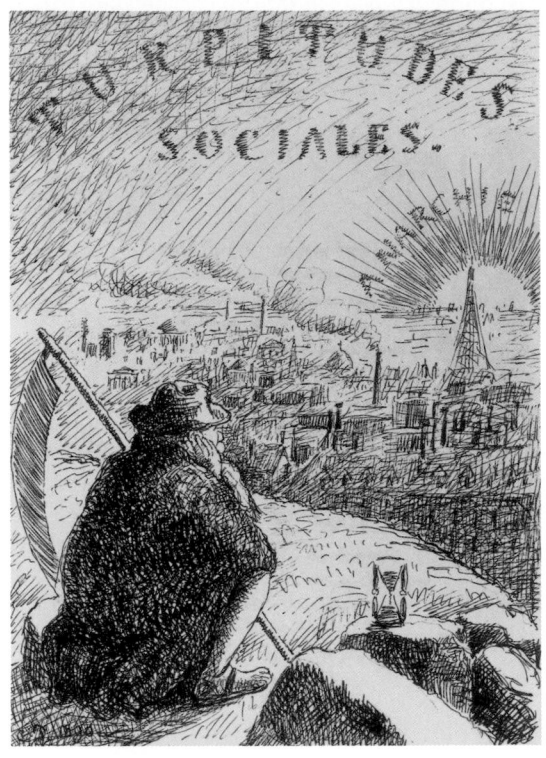

187
Camille Pissarro, Cover of *Social Turpitudes*, 1889. Pencil, pen and ink on paper; 31.5 × 24.5 cm, 12⅜ × 9⅝ in. Private collection

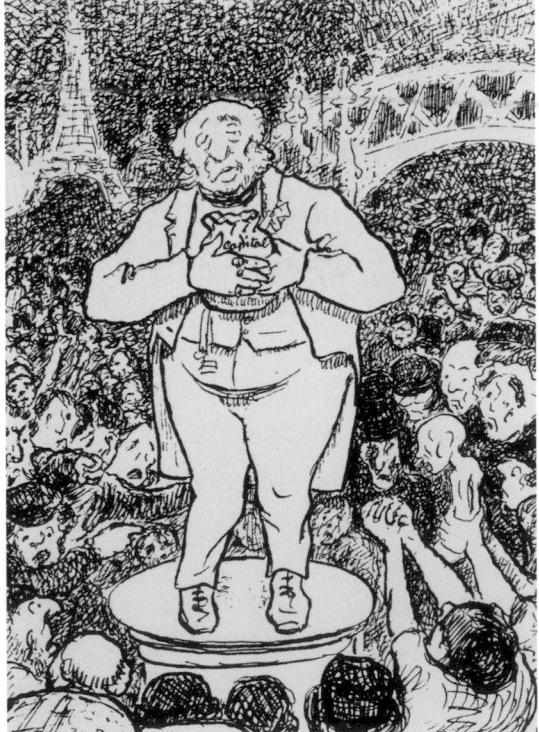

188
Camille Pissarro, *Capital*, 1889, Pencil, pen and ink on paper; 31.5 × 24.5 cm, 12⅜ × 9⅝ in. Private collection

One cannot close a discussion of Impressionism and politics without considering the position of Degas. Pissarro referred to him affectionately as 'Such an anarchist, in art of course, without knowing it', thinking of Degas's disdain for artistic authority. Indeed, Pissarro and Degas shared a dislike of bourgeois hegemony wherever they found it, though Degas's attitudes stemmed from the Right rather than the Left. As far as Degas was concerned, utopia had evaporated when his father's bank collapsed. Having to make a living only reminded him of lost privilege. Certainly, Degas was passionately committed to his art: his obsession with scientific observation and novel techniques was unchanged by the sudden shift in personal fortunes. But even his contemporaries observed a nastiness in his wit and codifications of social distinctions. He could cheerfully thumb his nose at established propriety, as in his series on prostitutes. He was notoriously hard on his models, one of whom, Alice Michel, tells how he exploded when she tried to engage him in serious conversation:

What age is this that we are living in, Lord God! Everybody, even you models, come and talk about art, painting, literature, as if all they needed to know was how to read and write ... In days gone by weren't the common people more content without all this useless instruction they're given in schools? ... What an infamous century this is!

Degas is rejecting the notion of an art accessible to all, to which Pissarro was attracted and which the Third Republic fostered by introducing an art curriculum in state schools. This diatribe shows that views on art and politics are in the end inseparable. His political ideal lay in an inegalitarian past, with no glimmer of social change. In this, we might compare him to Renoir, who was also disturbed by egalitarianism, even though he had negotiated upward mobility through the profession of artist. Renoir lamented the effects of technology and feared the wrath of its worker victims. His visions were pastoral and idyllic, far from any hint of conflict or mechanization. For Renoir, in other words, conservatism meant protecting what remained of his hard-won standing.

The most notorious episode in Degas's politics involved his support of the army during the Dreyfus Affair. In 1894, a German military attaché was caught with secret information passed to him from the French. A wealthy Jewish army captain of Alsatian origin (the province ceded to Germany), Alfred Dreyfus, was summarily convicted of espionage based on a handwriting sample. At first, he had few defenders outside his family; he was demoted and deported to French Guiana. Two years later, the chief of French espionage, Commandant Picquart, discovered a letter from the German attaché to an aristocratic French officer of Hungarian origin, Count Esterházy. A sample of the latter's handwriting convinced Picquart of Dreyfus's innocence, and he demanded a revision of the court-martial, but Esterházy was acquitted and Picquart transferred to Algeria in 1898.

Dreyfus became a cause-célèbre that divided France and marked an entire generation. Among his most notable supporters was Émile Zola, whose article entitled 'J'Accuse', which appeared on the front page of George Clemenceau's liberal journal *L'Aurore* on 13 January 1898, is one of history's most famous political tracts. Renowned for a sense of justice since his defence of Manet, Zola was condemned to a year in prison and fined 3,000 francs. Even when false documents were found to have been added to the Dreyfus file, the army reaffirmed its sentence in 1899, and the forger, who committed suicide, was lionized by the Right. The battle had long since transcended the fate of a single man to pit defenders of tradition and military honour – all the more entrenched for its failures during the Franco-Prussian War in 1870–1 – against outsiders, *parvenus* and the Left. Dreyfus was not rehabilitated until 1906.

Pissarro recalled working on his city views (see 229) during anti-Dreyfusard disturbances. At one point, he was caught in a crowd shouting 'Death to Jews! Down with Zola!' We know he followed the Dreyfus affair closely, though because he was a Danish citizen he feared deportation if he signed a petition in support of the captain. The summary arrests of anarchists earlier in the decade certainly exacerbated his sense of vulnerability. He made financial contributions to the Dreyfus cause when he could but confessed that 'in spite of my preoccupations, I am obliged to continue working from my window as if nothing were happening'. His long friendship with Degas was broken off, and Degas began to attack his work. Monet, on the other hand, stayed in close touch with Pissarro and openly congratulated Zola for his stance, signing the pro-Dreyfus 'Manifesto of the Intellectuals' that was published in January 1898. Cassatt supported Dreyfus, too. But Renoir, as one might expect, was staunchly anti-Dreyfusard, and he reaffirmed his relationship with Degas, with whom he had recently organized Berthe Morisot's posthumous retrospective.

Renoir's anti-Semitism came from the old-fashioned provincial and working-class mistrust of an unfamiliar group reputed to control money and manipulate power. There, it was as endemic to the Left as to the Right. Since the 1880s, however, anti-Semitism in France had risen rapidly, fed by publications such as Édouard Drumont's weekly, *La Libre parole*. An illustration from this journal, *Jewish Virtues According to the Method of Dr Gall* (189), alludes to the 'scientific', racialist basis of anti-Semitism by evoking the early nineteenth-century physiognomist Dr Franz Gall. Degas had his housekeeper (190) read this journal to him aloud while he worked. In this context, Pissarro's drawing of *Capital* (see 188) is informative, for it shows that even he assimilated the association between Jews and capitalist finance – his banker has the long nose, thick lips, protruding ears and slouched posture of the Jewish stereotype. Pissarro himself looked Jewish (Cézanne once referred to him as the rabbi of Impressionism) and never hid his origins; but his radical politics placed him at a safe distance from moral characteristics that he considered ugly. In light of Pissarro's position, then, perhaps Renoir can only be accused of ignorance and gullibility.

Degas, on the other hand, had many Jewish associations, among them his schoolboy comrade Ludovic Halévy. Jews were prominent in his social circle; many of his family's cultured friends and his own private patrons, Albert Hecht, Charles Ephrussi, Charles Haas and Ernest May, were Jewish. Degas's anti-Semitism was therefore not only inexcusable, it must have come from deep-seated self-hatred, rendered all the more virulent by his personal hypocrisy. Bank scandals of the 1880s contributed to anti-Semitism; Degas may retrospectively have thought about the failure of his father's bank. But remembering it could only have led to anxiety over the degree to which his own family trajectory resembled that of Jews whose social status was based on money. Degas's vested interest in the infallibility of French institutions still dominated by an aristocracy to which his family aspired was a form of denial and separation from this vulnerable past.

But although the Dreyfus Affair was a defining moment for many Frenchmen, our interest must focus on how it sheds light on Degas as an Impressionist. A case in point is the exaggerated Semitic profile,

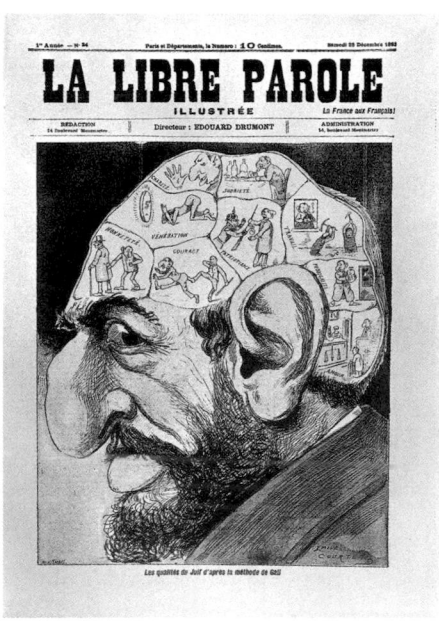

189
Émile Courtet,
Jewish Virtues According to the Method of Dr Gall, in *La Libre parole*, 23 December 1893. Photo-mechanical print; 38 × 28·5 cm, 15 × 11¼ in

190
Edgar Degas, The artist with his housekeeper, 1895

emphasized by a highlight on the nose, of the Jewish stockbroker and collector Ernest May in *Portraits at the Stock Exchange* (191). Bearing in mind how art constructs what comes to be called reality, we can understand how Degas's naturalism, based on racialist theories, perpetuated stereotypes of Jews and therefore served right-wing politics. Degas's comments on Ernest May imply precisely that upward social mobility he associated with Jews: 'He is a Jew ... He is a man who is throwing himself into the arts, you understand,' wrote Degas to Bracquemond, with whom he was to collaborate on a journal of prints (see Chapter 8). May, a successful financier, and the independently

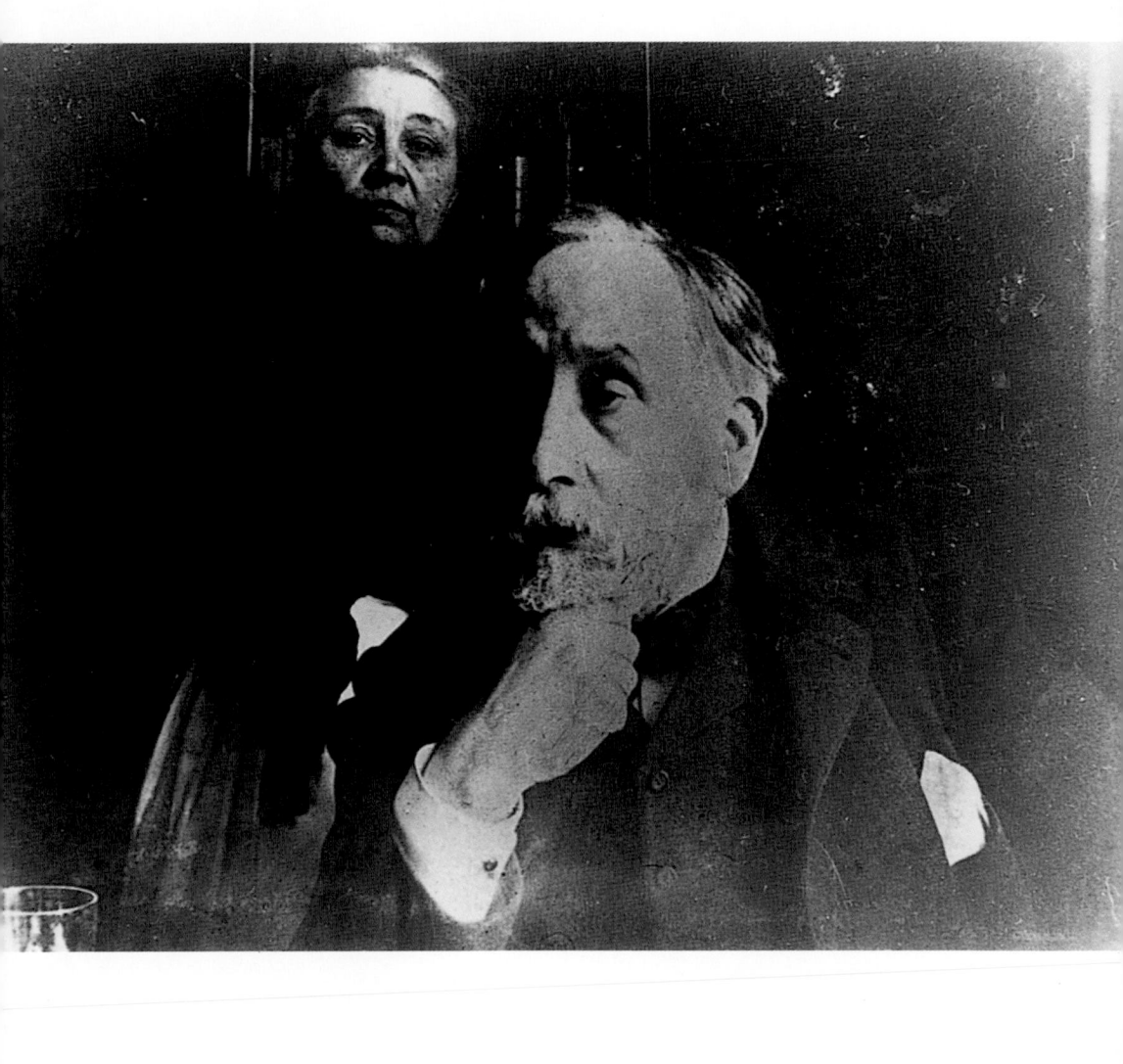

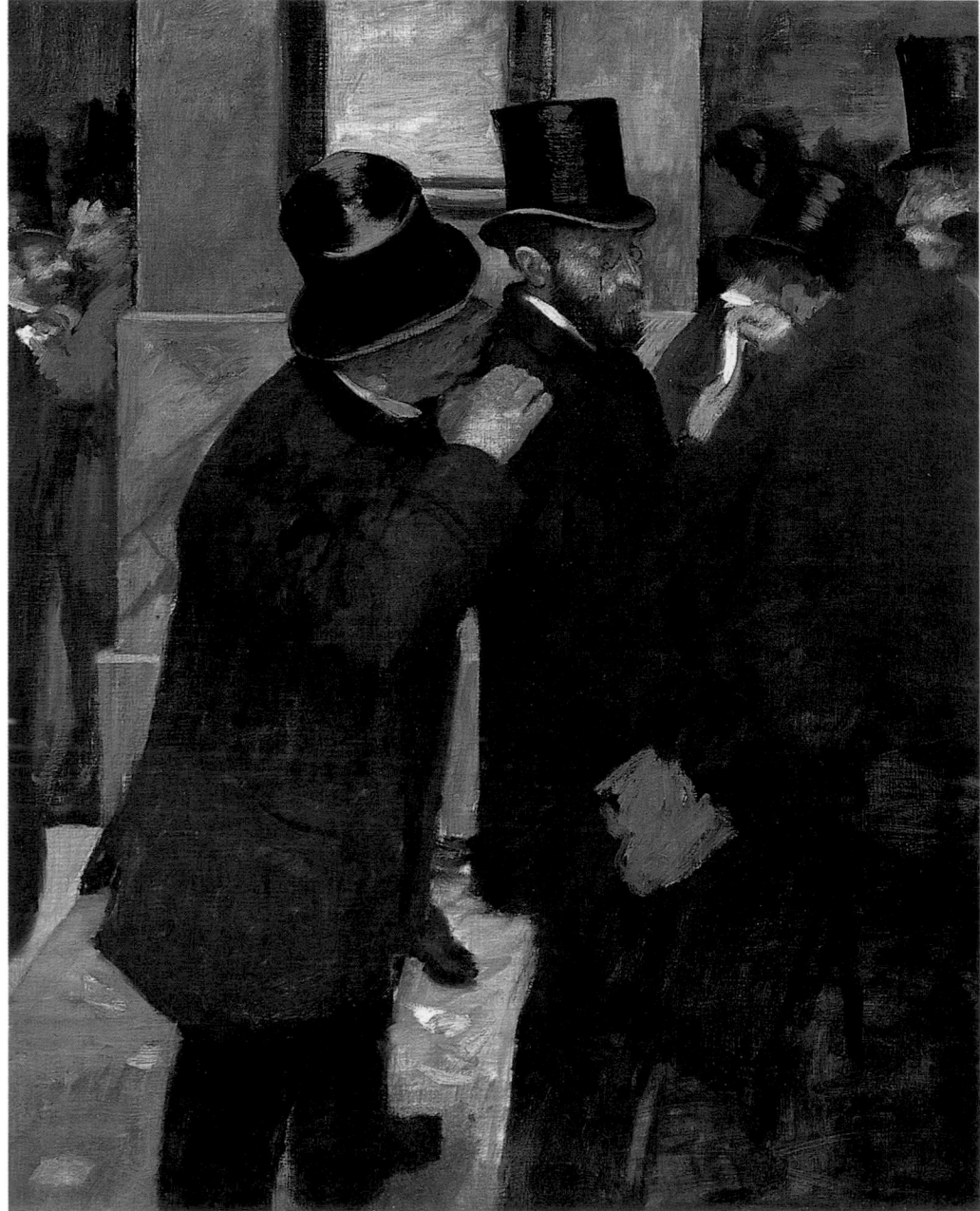

wealthy Caillebotte were going to provide the capital. In addition to Degas's unflattering treatment of May's features, the guarded whispers, secret spaces and blocked views purveyed by his composition imply something underhand about May's business. Linda Nochlin describes the picture's central gesture of 'confidential touching' as summing up the entire 'mythology of Jewish financial conspiracy'.

There is also the case of Degas's old school friend, the talented writer and librettist (for Georges Bizet's *Carmen*, 1875) Ludovic Halévy, whose stories of the Cardinal family Degas illustrated (see Chapter 5). In a

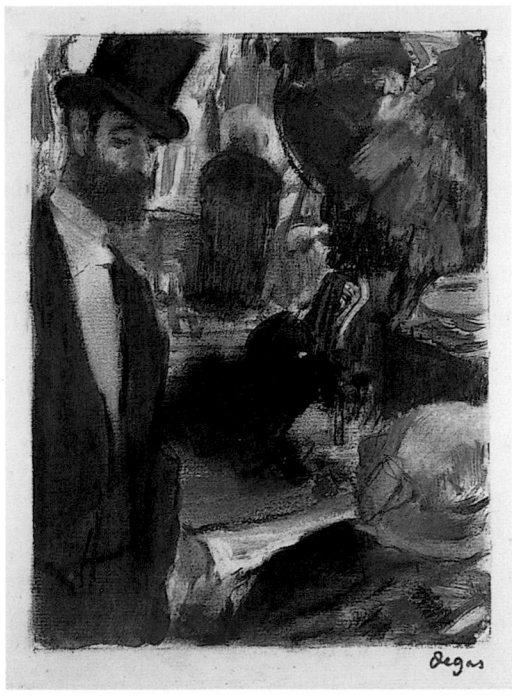

191
Edgar Degas,
Portraits at the Stock Exchange,
c.1878–9.
Oil on canvas;
100 × 82 cm,
39⅜ × 32¼ in.
Musée d'Orsay, Paris

192
Edgar Degas,
Ludovic Halévy Finds Madame Cardinal in the Dressing Room,
1876–7.
Monotype in black ink with red and black pastel, 1st state of 2;
21·3 × 16 cm,
8⅜ × 6¼ in.
Staatsgalerie, Stuttgart

pastel of *Ludovic Halévy Finds Madame Cardinal in the Dressing Room* (192) Degas accentuates the nose and elongates the ears, which combine with the tilt of Halévy's top hat to make him look a bit ridiculous. Far more damaging in another brothel monotype was Degas's profile of *The Procuress*, whose features explicitly link Jews to the flesh trade. Whatever Degas's intentions in such works, their basis in the racial distinctions of his time is of a piece with the social distinctions to which he was committed. Their underlying politics were divisive. As regards the

Halévys, of whom Degas made some superb photographs in about 1895 which still remain in the family, the break came in late 1897, immediately following the outbreak of the Dreyfus Affair in the press. Daniel Halévy's journal records Degas as 'very anti-Semitic' at a dinner party. Thereafter, Degas refused invitations and by Christmas had disappeared from their circle until after Ludovic's death in 1908.

The lesson in this sad tale may be summed up by the phrase with which Ernst Gombrich began his seminal *The Story of Art*: 'There is no such thing as art, there are only artists.' As the product of men and women, art partakes of the imperfect human world, no matter how hard we try to raise it higher. So when we examine art critically, we are not always reading personal politics (our own or the artist's) into it; we are recovering cultural attitudes that must inform our scrutiny of its portrayal of the world. For both Degas and Pissarro, the political aspects of their later careers help identify implicit political dimensions in earlier work. It would be reductive to turn their paintings or other Impressionist artworks into political allegories. Yet it is not enough to limit their politics to a mere context for what in such interpretations remain primarily aesthetic objects. Impressionist paintings are part of a cultural discourse that includes significant political meanings.

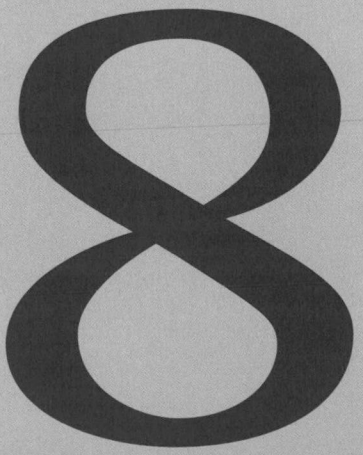

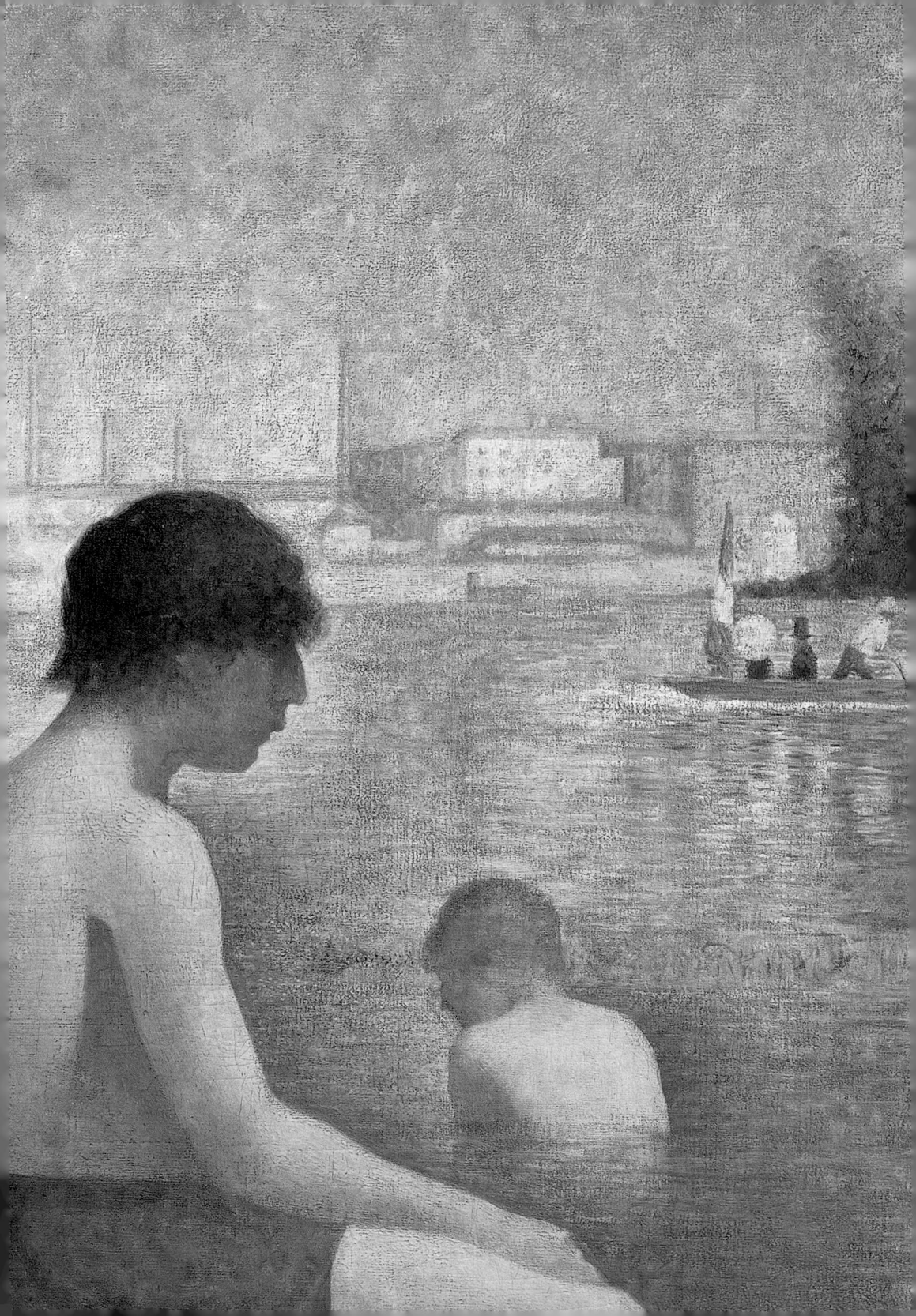

In the early to mid-1880s, there were changes to who participated in the Impressionist exhibitions, as well as important developments in style. Several factors contributed to what was more a reassessment than a crisis – the latter an exaggerated term that has entered the literature. With the gradual acceptance and economic success of Renoir and Monet, Impressionist exhibitions became less crucial to their exposure. With the onset of hard economic times in the late 1870s and early 1880s, they had everything to gain by looking beyond collective endeavours. Renoir could show at the Salon, Monet and Sisley with Durand-Ruel. In the meantime, Degas was introducing painters who tried to reconcile the novel techniques of the *plein-air* faction with their conservative training. Such developments were accompanied in Renoir's case by self-doubt and an increasing concern for his relationship to past art. Cassatt's work echoed the clear tonalities of fresco painting and her family groups evoked the theme of Madonna and Child. In Chapter 3, we saw Monet beginning to withdraw behind a strident defence of *plein-air* practice, assuming the mantle of true Impressionism in his interview with *La Vie moderne*. Yet he, too, sought renewal in his work, with novel structures and travels to new sites.

Finally, amidst this crumbling of solidarity, new voices claimed to re-found Impressionism on more objective grounds. The painter Georges Seurat (1859–91) and a group of young art critics attacked Impressionism as superficial and offered a scientific and theoretically inspired alternative that was called Neo-Impressionism. Among the Impressionists of the earlier generation, Pissarro was the only one who wholeheartedly converted to the new style, albeit briefly. He considered it a possible antidote to the earlier 'romantic' form of Impressionism. As a foil for the ideas and practices of the 1870s, then, the new rhetoric of the 1880s helped define Impressionism's parameters as well as to transform it.

193
Georges
Seurat,
*Bathers at
Asnières*
(detail of 204)

There had always been differences within Impressionism between the approaches exemplified by Monet and Degas. They eventually led to open conflict, as when in 1881 Caillebotte withdrew support after Degas continued to impose artists Caillebotte considered incompetent – such as Jean-Louis Forain (1852–1931), Jean-François Raffaelli (1850–1924) and Federico Zandomeneghi. The following year, it was the turn of Degas and friends, including Cassatt, to abstain. The ever-present Pissarro was rejoined by Monet, Sisley, Renoir and Caillebotte; Huysmans wrote that the 'real Impressionists' had returned. In simplest terms, the conflict seems to have been between landscape and figure painting, associated respectively with innovative versus conservative technical practices. But such divisions were never clear-cut. Chapter 4 examined how the combination of the figure with *plein-air* painting was a unifying theme in the Batignolles group of the late 1860s. And Renoir was never primarily a landscape painter. His studio practices and urban subjects, as in *The Ball at the Moulin de la Galette* (see 109), stood halfway between Monet and Degas.

Two other painters, Caillebotte and Marie Quiveron Bracquemond, developed a middle course in figure painting related to Renoir's. Caillebotte's *Paris Street: A Rainy Day* (see 21) is an especially good example. His choice of rainy weather was certainly original, and his subtle blue-grey lighting, the reflections caused by watery surfaces, and his sensitivity to atmosphere, as in the background where figures merge into the mist, fall completely within the *plein-air* ethos. Yet the limited range of colours in a city under cloudy sky preserves a more conservative look than the brightly coloured works of his main contemporaries. Caillebotte's painting also exhibited that rigorous geometry with which he was already associated and which connected him to Degas; it has powerful vertical and horizontal axes with a vanishing point almost at dead centre. In conveying the strict layout of the new Paris streets and the imposing bulk of recently built apart-ment blocks in his neighbourhood, Caillebotte also demonstrated respect for learned skills of conception and workmanship. The couple in the foreground look off to our left, as if plotting their itinerary or preparing to cross the busy street; unaware of being observed, they display that Impressionist sense of moment. Yet their powerful

194
Marie Quiveron Bracquemond,
On the Terrace at Sèvres,
1880.
Oil on canvas;
88 × 115 cm,
34¹⁄₂ × 45 in.
Musée du Petit Palais,
Geneva

sculptural presence signals Caillebotte's moderation between Monet's flattened, fragmented forms and the traditional solidity of Salon painting. His modernity was thus all the more persuasive to critics who appreciated an awareness of order and tradition.

Marie Quiveron Bracquemond's large paintings, which were shown in the fifth Impressionist exhibition of 1880, have not received the attention they deserve. Like Morisot, Bracquemond painted primarily within the confines of her family, where most of her works remain.

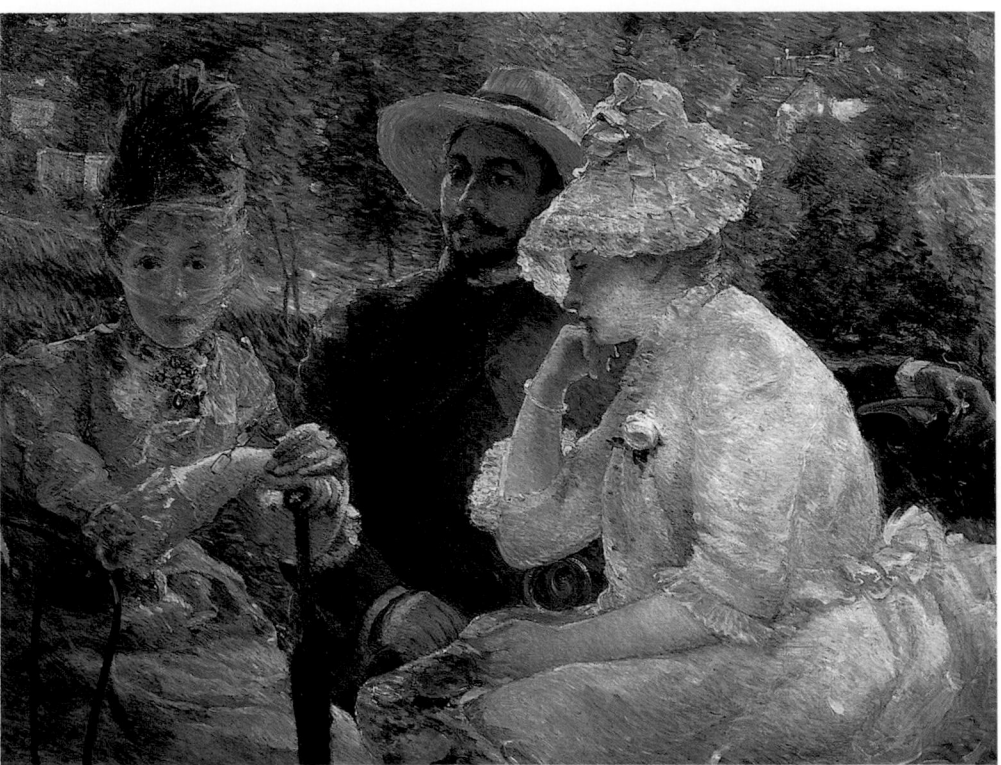

What is more, it appears that her printmaker husband, who was linked to Degas and opposed *plein-air* practice, may have felt threatened by her talents and forced her to give up painting for long periods of time. Yet Marie Bracquemond was acutely aware of the issues raised by Impressionism, of which she briefly effected some stunning resolutions. Her masterpiece is *On the Terrace at Sèvres* (194), which boldly if belatedly seizes the Impressionist theme of modern figures in sunlight. An attention to the fashions of the two women, posed

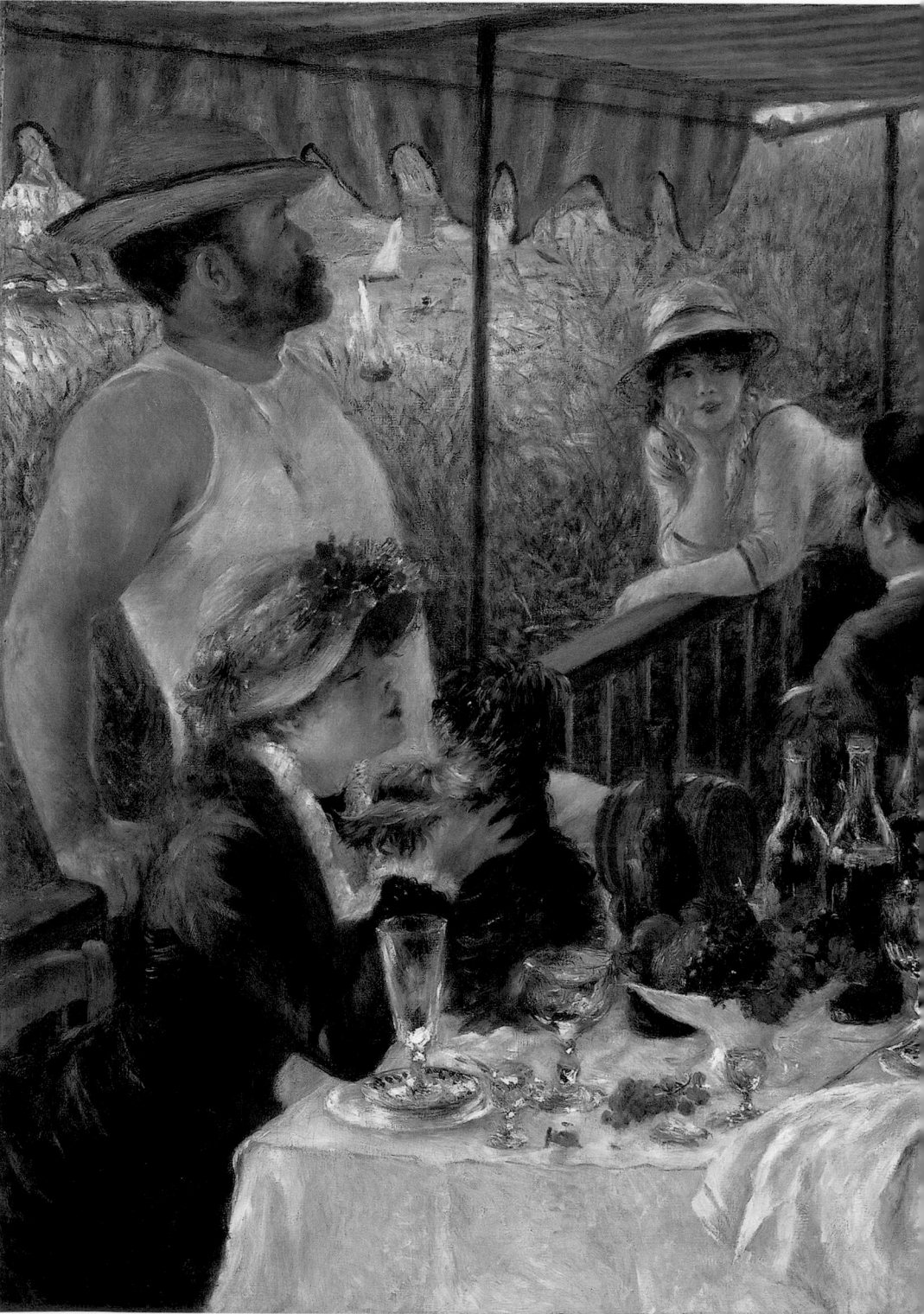

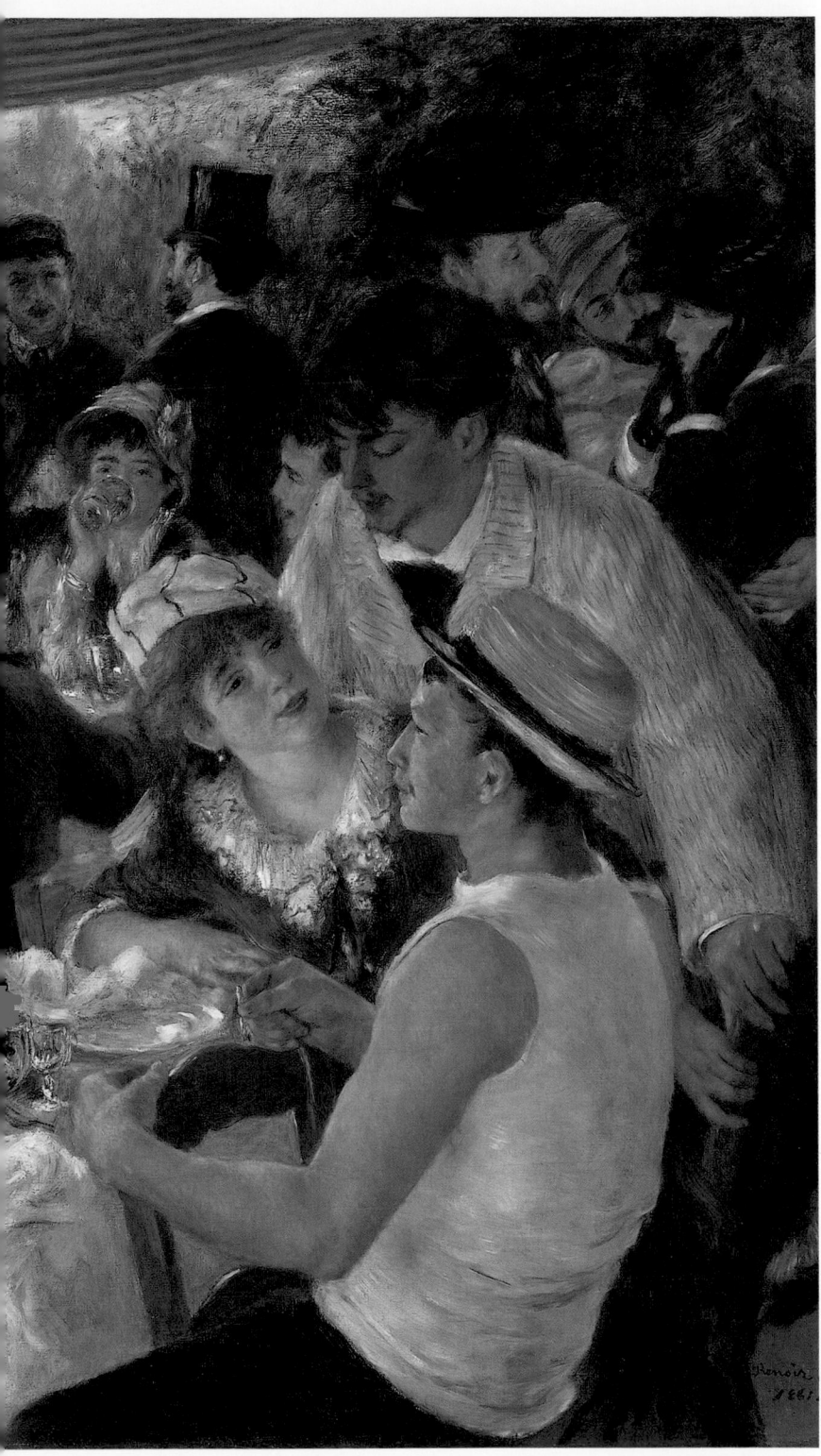

195
**Pierre-Auguste
Renoir**,
*The Luncheon of
the Boating Party*,
1880–1.
Oil on canvas;
130 × 175 cm,
51¼ × 68¼ in.
Phillips
Collection,
Washington, DC

by her unmarried sister Louise Quiveron, places her within the parameters of women's art, while her use of bluish shadow on the white dress and the backlighting on parts of the hat and ruffled cuff display *plein-air* concerns. The variety of poses, including the man's casually held cigarette, indicates receptiveness to Impressionist candour and instantaneity. At the same time, her strong sense of design (she trained under a pupil of Ingres), like Cassatt's, gives the composition a monumental feel comparable to Renoir's *Madame Charpentier and her Children* (see 110) of one year earlier.

Unlike Caillebotte and Marie Bracquemond's attempts to reconcile conflicting models within Impressionism while preserving some of the values from traditional training, Renoir's compromises were born of a combination of opportunism and self-doubt. With the Salon open to him from the late 1870s, and with the encouragement of his patron Charpentier, Renoir began to modify his style to suit the Salon public as well as his private clientele. His most important painting following the Charpentier portrait was *The Luncheon of the Boating Party* (195), in which he revisited the indoor–outdoor socializing of *The Ball at the Moulin de la Galette* (see 109) at the more refined location of the terrace of the Restaurant Fournaise at Chatou along the Seine.

It is sometimes said that Renoir was painting in response to an article by Zola of 1880, which lamented the Impressionists' failure to outgrow a makeshift style and challenged them to go beyond sketches. While filling the composition with all of his renowned colour, detail and ingratiating incident, Renoir now formed his figures with far greater solidity and distinctness from their background than before. The bare arms and shoulders of the two foreground oarsmen, the son of the restaurant owner Fournaise to the left and a youthful-looking Caillebotte to the right, announce his more muscular approach to form. At the same table, we recognize Renoir's mistress Aline Charigot and probably the actress Ellen Andrée, whom we know from Degas's *Absinthe* (see 158). At the centre is his model, Angèle, drinking a mug of beer. While these main characters and other figures are from Renoir's immediate artistic and bohemian circle, a few in the background testify to his upward mobility. The man talking with the woman leaning on the railing is Baron Barbier, a former cavalry officer, and the man in the top hat is Charles Ephrussi, a banker, sometime critic, and friend of Degas. The painting was quickly sold to Durand-Ruel.

On a trip to Italy in 1881, Renoir had begun studying Renaissance art. His sales now allowed him to travel in pursuit of a better understanding of the relationship between line (with which he was newly concerned) and colour. Delacroix, in whose footsteps Renoir travelled to North Africa, had emulated the Venetians – Renaissance painters with the cachet of Italian classicism but who were renowned colourists. But Renoir had also begun looking at Ingres, much admired by Degas, and it was his example he followed on a tour through Italian museums, where he studied the work of Raphael. He consulted Renaissance writings on art and began to write about it himself, claiming artists had lost touch with 'nature', by which he must now have meant something beyond *plein-air*. He later confessed to the art dealer Ambroise Vollard that he felt he 'had reached the end of Impressionism' at this time, and that he 'could neither paint nor draw'. Of course, success had also made him wary of Impressionism's revolutionary reputation (see Chapter 7). So now he was backtracking, as if he could belatedly acquire the formal training he had skipped as a young man in a hurry to produce goods that pleased.

Beginning in about 1883, Renoir's experiments with technique resulted in an even more accentuated change, sometimes called his Sour Period. The new style confirmed his direction towards more solid forms but placed heightened emphasis on draughtsmanship and conventional modelling. *The Umbrellas* (197) exhibits this change through its two-stage development. Conceived as one of several large paintings of modern life from about 1881, Renoir appears to have completed it only after a four-year hiatus. The painting echoes *The Three Graces* (196) by Marie Bracquemond, in which she used contemporary figures with parasols to evoke the mythological theme. (Renoir's references were not yet so explicit, but eventually he would follow her lead.) The figures in the right half of his foreground – a mother and her two daughters – are painted in the soft, rich, blended style of the late 1870s. By contrast, the umbrellas, the background and the figures to the left – a servant out shopping and an admiring fellow behind her – are modelled in a drier, tighter manner with duller colours and more systematic brushstrokes. The sharply defined edges of the market basket at the centre flaunt Renoir's new rigour. And the wonderful interplay of the arcs and points of umbrellas above the figures reiterate his new focus on linear geometry.

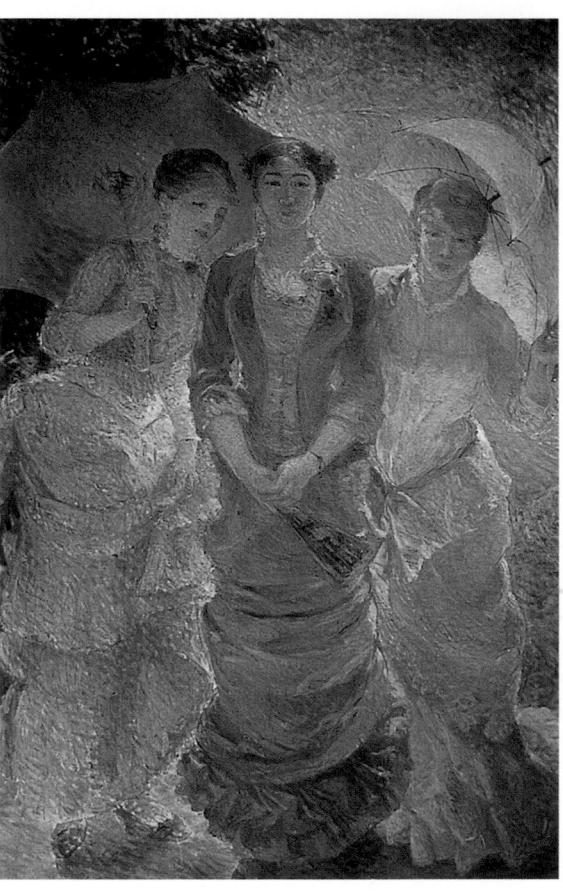

196
Marie Quiveron Bracquemond, *The Three Graces*, 1880.
Oil on canvas; 137 × 88 cm, 54 × 35 in.
Hôtel de Ville, Chemillé, Maine-et-Loire

197
Pierre-Auguste Renoir, *The Umbrellas*, c.1881 and c.1885.
Oil on canvas; 180·3 × 114·9 cm, 71 × 45¼ in.
National Gallery, London

The culmination of Renoir's effort was his large painting of *The Bathers* (198). Here, representations of the female nude (posed by the model Suzanne Valadon), under the pretext of a Mediterranean bathing scene, are virtually academic in their smooth outlines and polished finish. Only the landscape background preserves something of the old Impressionist spontaneity. His colours have a new brightness, reflecting both the brilliant light of the south and the clarity

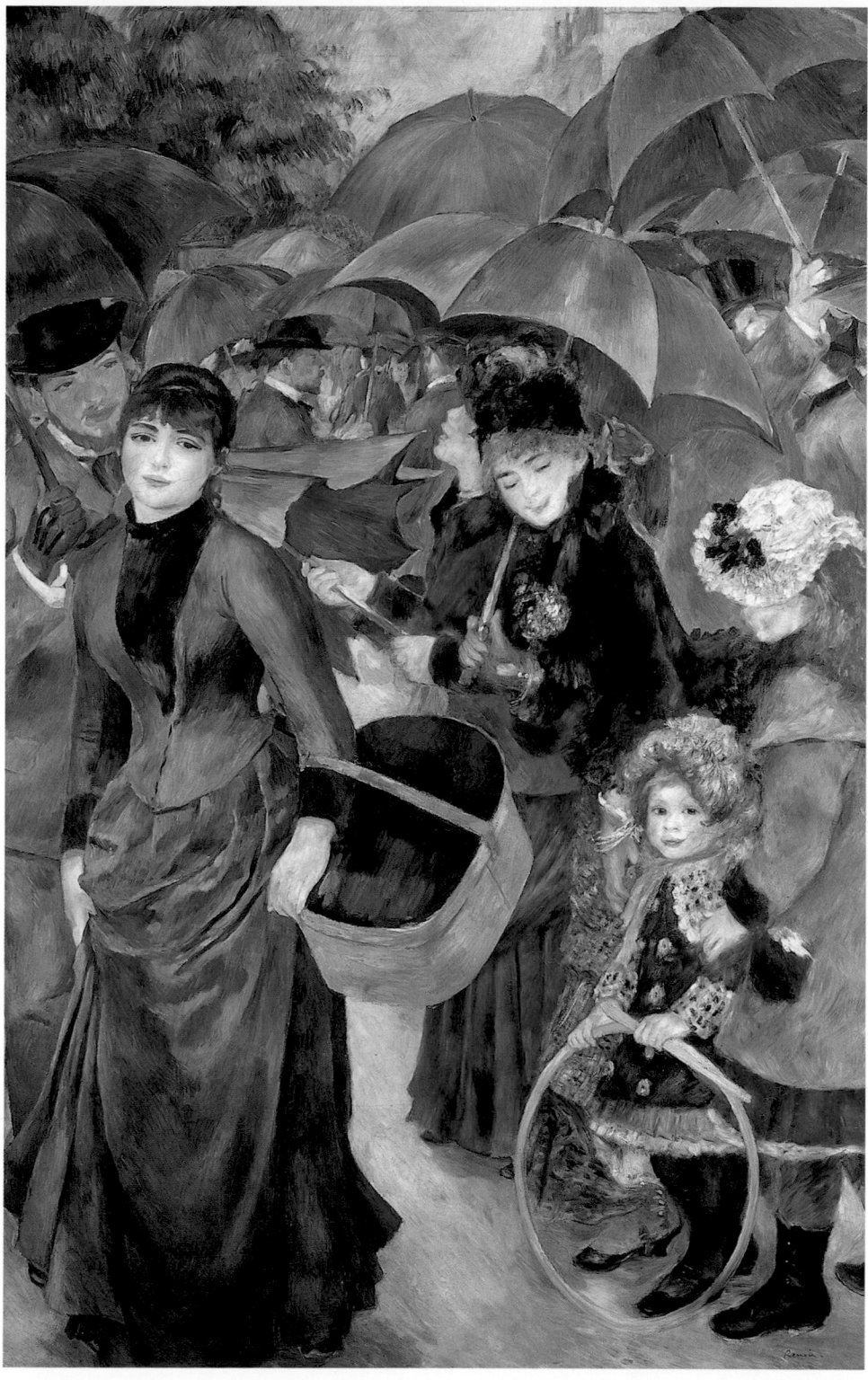

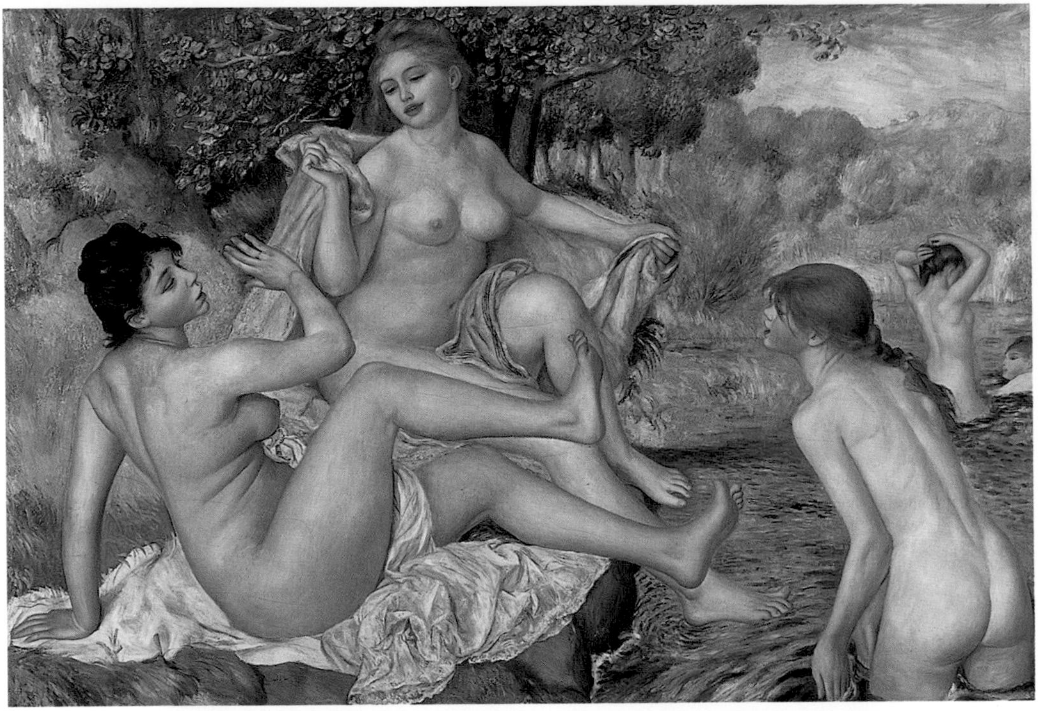

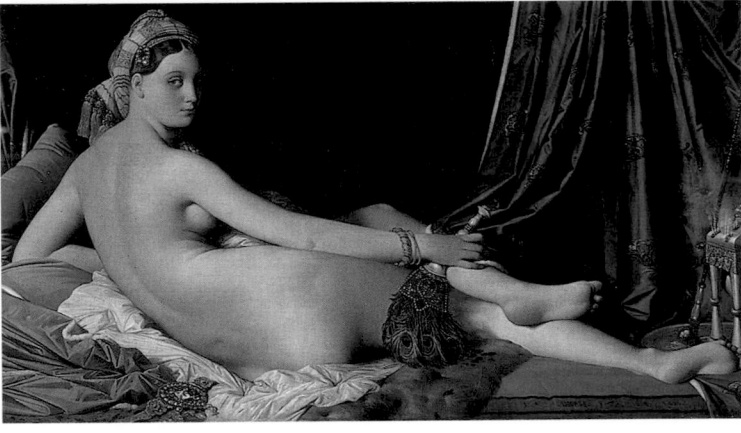

198 Above
Pierre-Auguste
Renoir,
The Bathers,
1887.
Oil on canvas;
117·7 × 170·8 cm,
46⅜ × 67¼ in.
Philadelphia
Museum of Art

199 Left
Jean-Auguste-
Dominique
Ingres,
*The Grande
Odalisque*,
1814.
Oil on canvas;
91 × 162 cm,
35⅞ × 63¾ in.
Musée du
Louvre,
Paris

of Italian fresco, in which pigments are painted directly into wet
plaster and fuse with the white ground in drying. Renoir prepared
his composition with careful studies, some of which emulate the line
drawings of Ingres. Indeed his figures allude overtly to Ingres's nude
poses: one, the famous *Bather* owned by the father of Degas's friend
Paul Valpinçon, has a three-quarter rear view similar to Renoir's
figure to the right; another, *The Grande Odalisque* (199), is echoed by

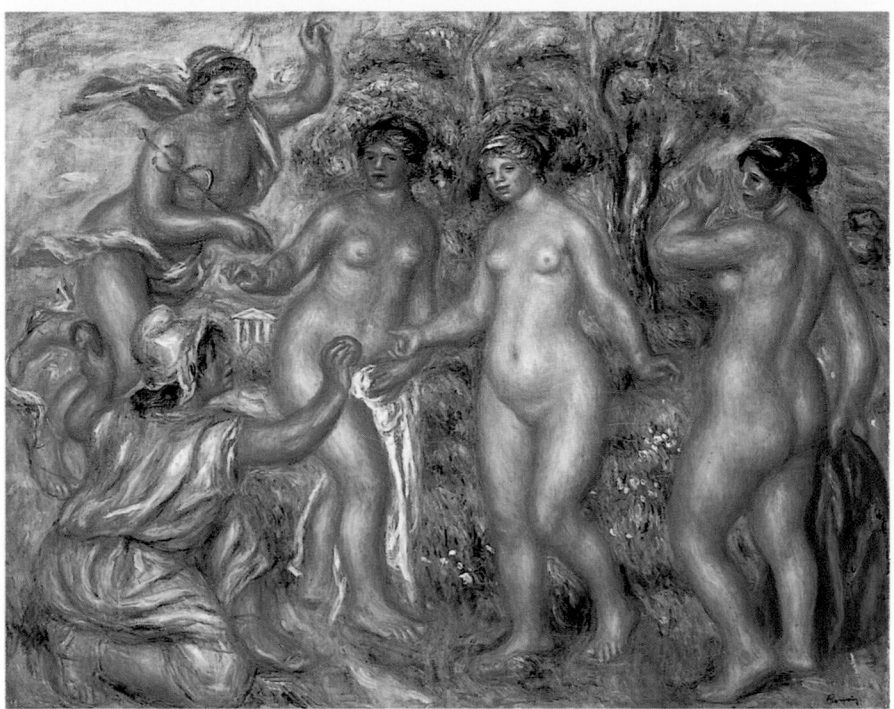

200
Pierre-Auguste
Renoir,
*The Judgement
of Paris*,
1914.
Oil on canvas;
73 × 92·5 cm,
28³⁄₄ × 36⁵⁄₈ in.
Hiroshima
Museum of Art

the twist of the nude in the foreground. The latter reminds us how Renoir's ideals coincided with Orientalist fantasies of available women – as in his harem scenes of the early 1870s (see 103).

With their active, playful poses, Renoir tried to preserve Impressionist spontaneity and freedom in his figures, but the result is contrived to the point of theatricality. Renoir termed the picture a 'trial for decorative painting', indicating his dream of decorating interiors in the tradition of Roman wall-paintings or Italian villas. This ambition evoked the widely respected classical painter, Pierre Puvis de Chavannes (1824–98; see 205), whose example, we shall see, interested the Neo-Impressionists. Durand-Ruel disliked Renoir's new style, so in 1887, Renoir exhibited *The Bathers* with his rival Georges Petit, with whom he had shown the previous year and whose stock of academic paintings gave him a more élite clientele. Renoir's compositional source for the painting was an eighteenth-century relief made by François Girardon (1628–1715) for the fountains of Versailles – an aristocratic pedigree if ever there was one. Eventually, Renoir backed

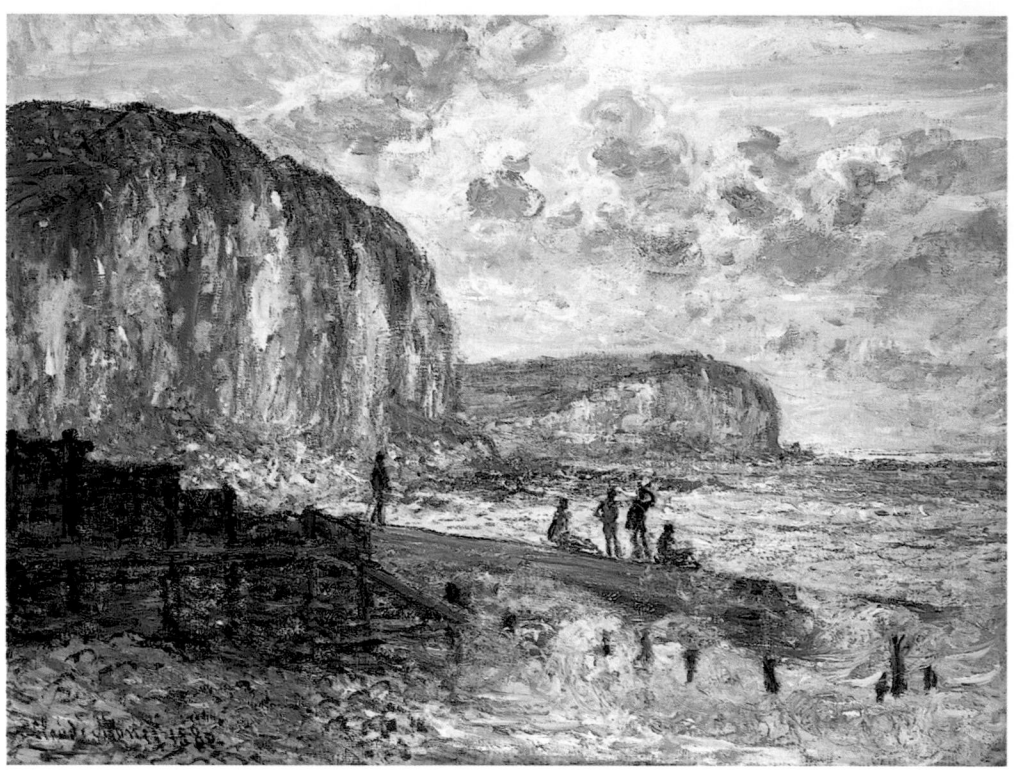

away from his reforms, but he continued to hanker for respectability through associations with the Old Masters. This yearning persisted through the late work, in which classical themes were too often stillborn into flaccid bodies evoking Peter Paul Rubens (1577–1640) set against Mediterranean backdrops painted like theatre flats (200).

Monet's reputed sympathy for Renoir's aims may reflect their companionship of 1883, when they travelled to the South of France together; they also coincide with Monet's own search for renewal. He began pursuing new experiences of scenery and weather conditions through travel around France (see Chapter 3). At the same time, he tried new compositional viewpoints and gave his forms greater monumentality. Compare the flattening and confused spatial relationships of his earlier *Cliffs of Les Petites Dalles* of 1880 (201), in which the mass seems to float above the wooden breakwater, to any of the later images of Normandy cliffs or rock formations, such as *The Manneporte (Étretat)* or *Cliff Walk at Pourville* (see 74 and 76). In the later

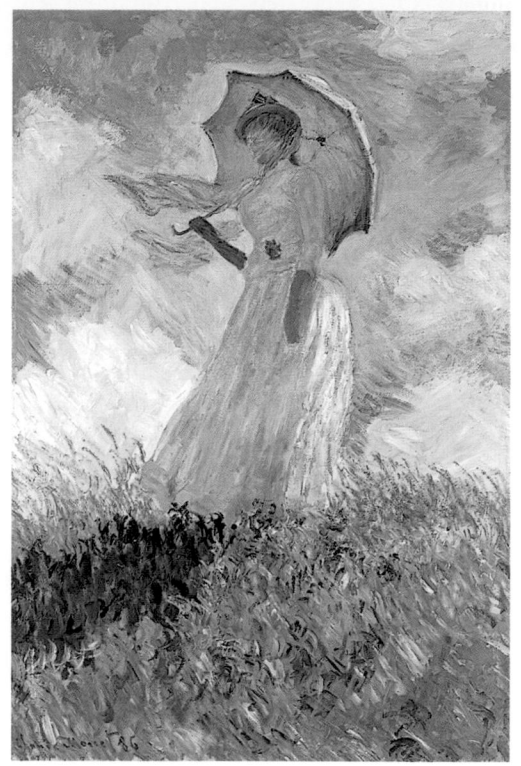

201
Claude Monet,
*Cliffs of Les
Petites Dalles*,
1880.
Oil on canvas;
60·5 × 80·2 cm,
23⁷⁸ × 31⁵⁸in.
Museum of
Fine Arts,
Boston

202
Claude Monet,
*Study of a
Figure Outdoors,
Facing Left*,
1886.
Oil on canvas;
131 × 88 cm,
51⁵⁸ × 34⁵⁸ in.
Musée d'Orsay,
Paris

paintings, Monet uses shadow and outlining reminiscent of Japanese
prints to create a powerful sense of volume. *Cliff Walk at Pourville*
also uses an abrupt juxtaposition between the large foreground motif
and distant background, a pattern again inspired by Japanese art.
Monet even returned briefly to the monumental figure, with his large
Study of a Figure Outdoors (202), posed by the young Suzanne Hoschedé
on the Normandy cliffs. Yet although the figure here is his principal
motif, we sense bright sunlight and brisk wind. Clearly, Monet's
efforts at solidification and renewal were framed within his overriding
commitment to *plein-air* landscape and techniques associated with it.
His response to dissatisfaction with his work was to reaffirm and
strengthen, rather than abandon, a direction long since pursued.

Pissarro's position in the early 1880s shows him, too, searching for
a firm basis for his practices, while redefining himself in response
to conflicts threatening the group. In Chapter 3 we left him moving
towards figure painting. In dialogues with his son, Lucien, who

was following his father's footsteps in becoming an artist, Pissarro found a new interest in theories and techniques that could help him orient his pupil and clarify his own foundations. Already, working with Cézanne in the later 1870s, he fostered the latter's development of a regularized brushstroke that has come to be known as 'constructive' (see Chapter 10). Pissarro's less methodical handling anticipated that development, as in the *Côtes des Boeufs at L'Hermitage* (see 96). Both eschewed the casual, sketch-like effects of a leisure-oriented style in favour of what they believed was a more serious, workman-like manner.

In the early 1880s, Pissarro renewed those experiments with paintings such as *Peasant Girl with Stick* (see 97). In this work, as Martha Ward suggested, the coarse, overlaid texture of Pissarro's heavily worked surface parallels the rough-woven cloth of peasant garments, making the painting a sympathetic embodiment of the rural aesthetic. Pissarro brings the figure close to the picture plane and compresses its setting so the background participates in an overall flattening. This slightly awkward spatiality and rugged relief of a built-up surface combine with an anti-heroic psychological moment – an absent-minded preoccupation with the mundane (a mere stick) – to produce what Pissarro characterized as a 'modern primitive' effect. He once counselled Lucien to look at Japanese art, Persian miniatures, Egyptian reliefs and Gothic sculpture. The weird positioning of legs in *Peasant Girl with Stick* may evoke the latter. Pissarro was clearly trying to reform his work in traditions opposed to the bourgeois ethos that Degas and now Renoir had come to represent. Implied in those efforts was a critique that explains Pissarro's conversion to Neo-Impressionism when it suddenly appeared.

This most powerful challenge to Impressionism came at the 1886 exhibition, which turned out to be the last one. It was made by two artists about twenty years younger than the Impressionists, Georges Seurat and Paul Signac (1863–1935), accompanied by Pissarro and his son Lucien, who became Seurat's disciples in the summer of 1885. The centrepiece of a special room devoted to the new work was Seurat's huge *Sunday Afternoon on the Island of La Grande Jatte* (203), a scene of summer leisure on one of the narrow islands running down the middle of the Seine northwest of Paris. The critic Félix Fénéon dubbed the new style Neo-Impressionism in an article of September 1886. His label suggested a renewed or reformed Impressionism and implied that the younger generation had seized its leadership. But rather than cultivating continuity with their predecessors, the Neo-Impressionists emphasized a break with what Pissarro called 'romantic' Impressionism and its re-founding in a new 'scientific' mode. Neo-Impressionism is indeed recognizably distinct from Impressionism and provides us, therefore, with a foil against which to establish the latter's limits.

Signac coined the term *chromo-luminism*, which had a scientific ring that corresponded to their interest in colour theory and optics. Seurat's origins in a family of investors and manufacturers surely predisposed him to combine institutional conservatism and utilitarian progressivism. He trained at the École des Beaux-Arts and with the Ingresque master Henri Lehmann (1814–82), spending much of his time there drawing academic life studies and strict copies after plaster casts of classical sculpture. On the side, he worked in a freer style concentrating on values of light and dark, and he studied artists whose techniques were colouristic – Delacroix, the Barbizon painters and, by the end of the 1870s, the Impressionists. Methodical and bookish, though equally ambitious and rebellious, Seurat accompanied his exercises with readings in art theory. He began with the famous treatise on complementary colours and reflections, *On the Law of the Simultaneous Contrast of Colours* (1839) by Michel-Eugène Chevreul, a chemist who worked for the national tapestry works (where different coloured threads must be juxtaposed since they cannot be mixed like pigment). By 1881 he supplemented Chevreul with others, including a translation of the more up-to-date *Modern Chromatics* (1879) by Columbia University professor Ogden Rood. Rood explained the discovery by the German scientist Hermann von Helmholtz of the difference between colour as rays of light and colour as solid pigment, emphasizing how the latter could never attain the former's intensity. (Mixing the three primaries, blue, yellow and red, as beams of light produces white, whereas mixing them as pigments produces black.)

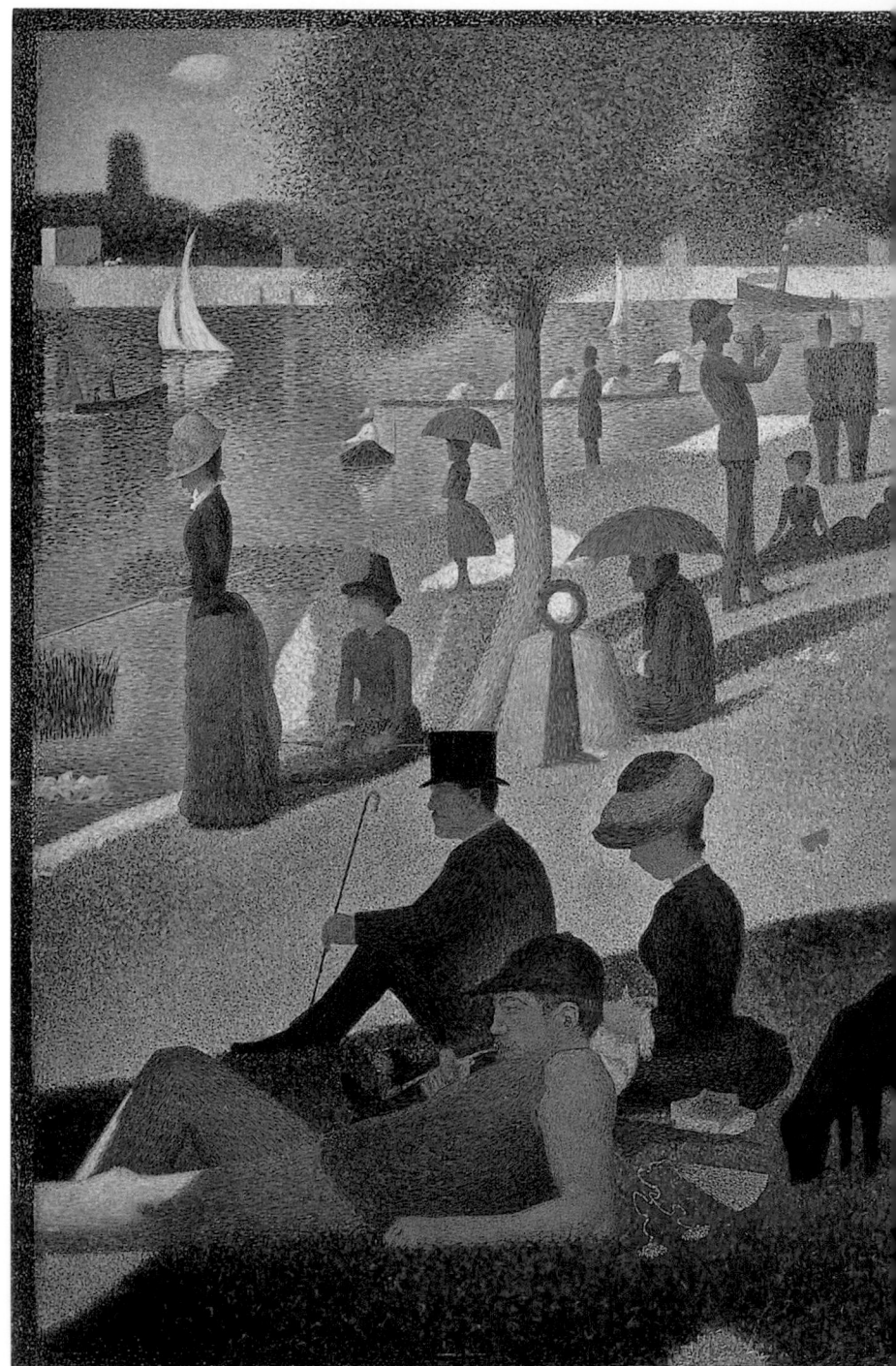

203
Georges Seurat,
*Sunday Afternoon
on the Island of
La Grande Jatte*,
1884–6.
Oil on canvas;
207·6 × 308 cm,
81³⁄₄ × 121³⁄₈ in.
The Art Institute
of Chicago

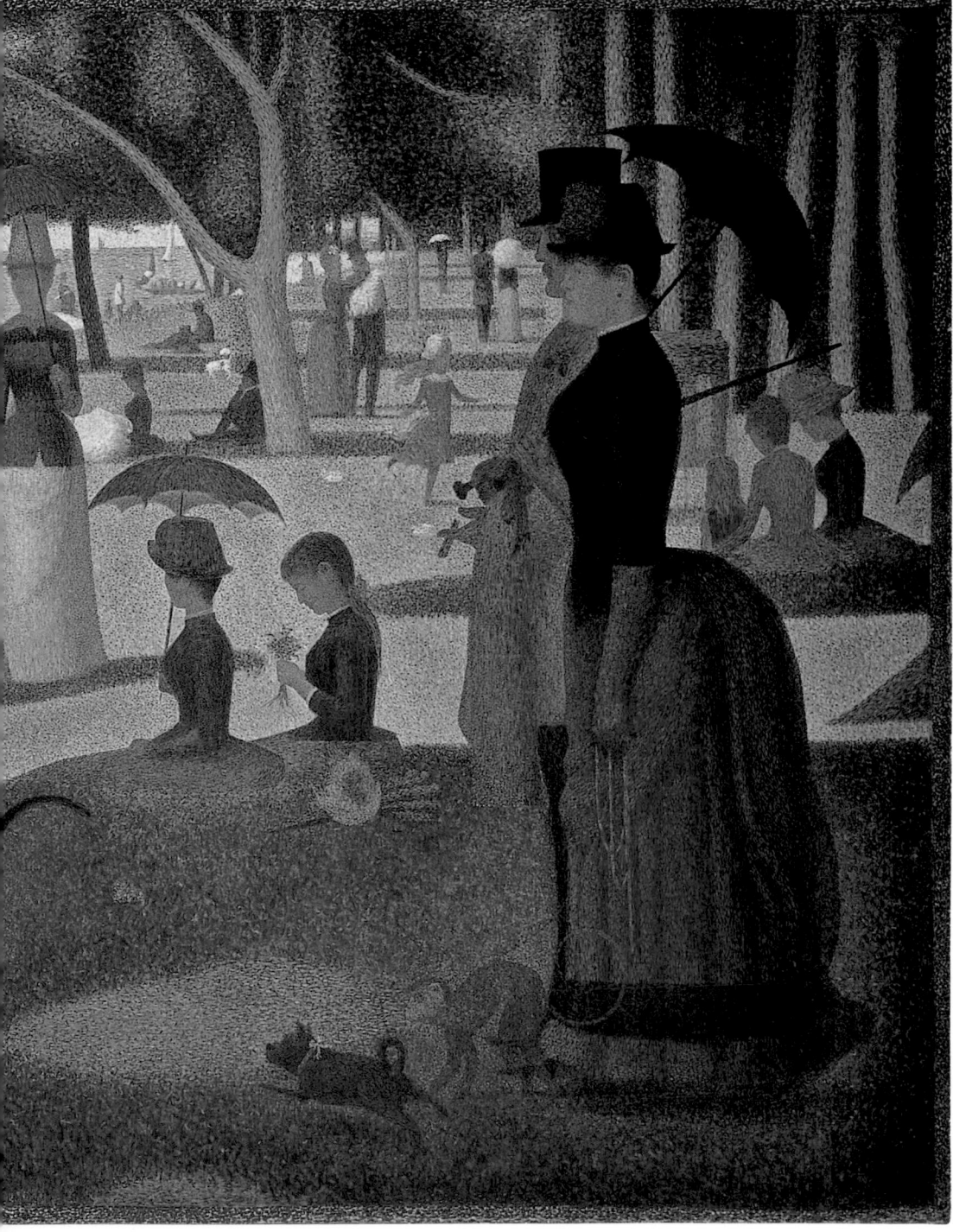

The display in *La Grande Jatte* (see 203) of what Seurat called 'optical painting' at the Impressionist exhibition of 1886, clarified what now became a startling contrast with the older generation. In an essay regarded as a Neo-Impressionist manifesto (though called 'The Impressionists in 1886'), Fénéon underlined Seurat's novelty by attacking previous treatments of colour as 'arbitrary' and imprecise. Seurat and his followers, he claimed, now divided tones 'in a conscious and scientific manner'. Fénéon compared *La Grande Jatte* to 'a patient tapestry', perhaps an allusion to Chevreul, but certainly a reference to careful craft. 'Here in truth,' he wrote, 'the accidents of the brush are futile, trickery is impossible.' His implication was that Impressionist technique was haphazard and intuitive, possibly inauthentic.

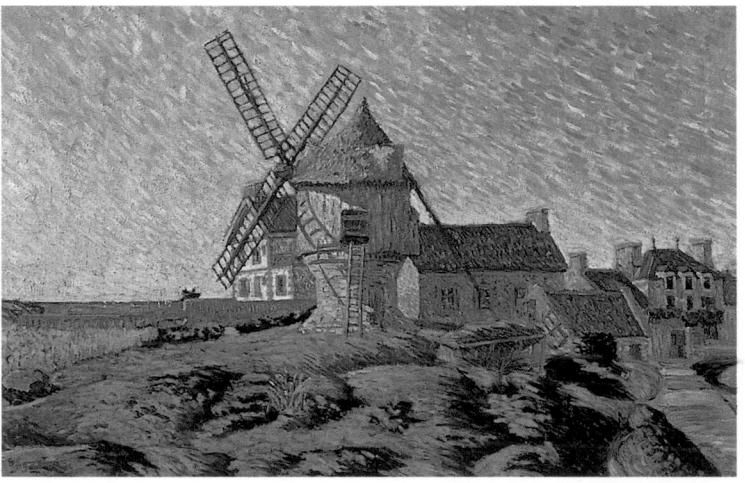

Even if there were trends within Impressionism with which Seurat was sympathetic (and made his association with some members of the group possible), there was also a bold development one could now trace at the exhibition itself. Signac's *Pierre Hâlé's Windmill, Saint Briac* (206) of 1884 merely uses a regularized Impressionist stroke, compared to the Pointillist system of his *Gas Tanks at Clichy* (207) of 1886. Signac had taken up Impressionist style in 1883, when he met Guillaumin painting along the Seine and saw Monet's show at Durand-Ruel's; then he befriended Pissarro, whose more methodical bent he found appealing. His shift from the traditional picturesque motif of the windmill at a seaside village to the harsh and brightly coloured industrial suburb of Clichy, indicates his adoption of Seurat's ostentatiously modern subject matter, as in the factories in the background of *Bathers at Asnières* (see 204), in addition to the dot-and-dash technique. The impersonality of the style seemed modern, too, for it implied that the practice of art was democratically accessible to anyone who simply followed the scientific recipe. In 1887, Fénéon claimed: 'This spotting of the canvas demands no manual skill, but only – only – an artistic and experienced vision!' It corresponded to both the dispassionate empiricism of Positivism and the implacable rationalism of modern labour. The seemingly wooden figures of *La Grande Jatte* appear frozen in time, the waters

206
Paul Signac,
*Pierre Hâle's
Windmill,
Saint Briac,*
1884.
Oil on canvas;
60 × 92 cm,
23⁵⁄₈ × 36¼ in.
Private
collection

207
Paul Signac,
*Gas Tanks
at Clichy,*
1886.
Oil on canvas;
65 × 81 cm,
25⁵⁄₈ × 31⁷⁄₈ in.
National
Gallery of
Victoria,
Melbourne

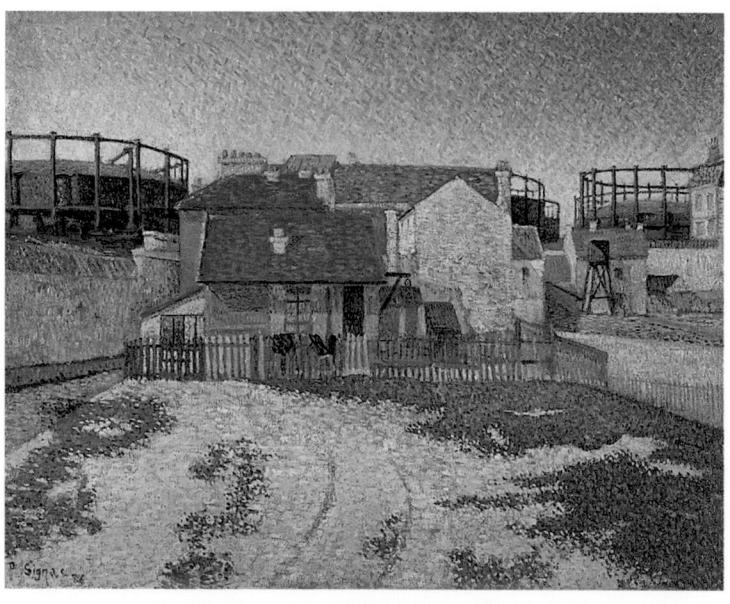

are stilled, Seurat's boats go nowhere. Everything suggests duration rather than spontaneity and the fleeting moment.

There was a rising critical attack on Monet's kind of Impressionism. For Fénéon, the new aim was 'to synthesize the landscape in a definitive aspect which perpetuates the sensation', rather than Monet's seizing of 'fugitive appearances'. The latter necessitated 'capturing the landscape in a single sitting', which amounted to superficiality, mere 'anecdotes', and made nature 'grimace to prove that the moment was indeed unique'. The Neo-Impressionist

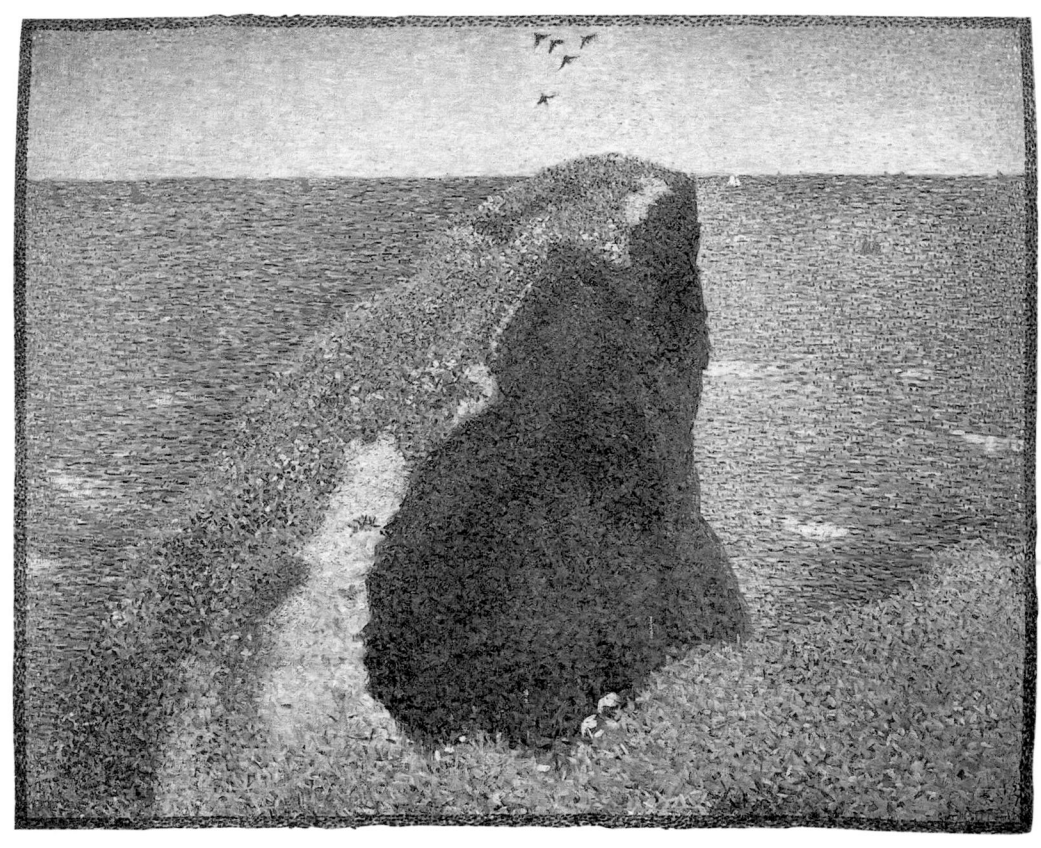

208
**Georges
Seurat,**
*Le Bec du Hoc,
Grandcamp,*
1885.
Oil on canvas;
66 × 82·5 cm,
26 × 32½ in.
Tate Gallery,
London

'synthesis', by contrast, sought a 'superior, sublimated reality', corresponding to deeper intellectual truth. An example of Seurat's direct challenge to Monet can be found in his coastal scenes, such as *Le Bec du Hoc, Grandcamp* (208), executed in the summer of 1885, though a painted border was added later. Seurat had never previously studied seascapes, but this cliff formation on the Normandy coast between Cherbourg and Caen boldly called forth *Manneporte (Étretat)* by Monet (see 74) and other of his Channel coast works. Seurat's motif without figures allowed him the concentration and simplicity necessary to bring his technique to the desired point. The mighty thrust of Le Bec du Hoc's ponderous shape seems so stilled and controlled by the atomizing overlay of dots and dashes that the flight formation of the tiny birds above it is a sufficient counterbalancing effect. It produces a sense of nature relentlessly subdued by human control.

The Symbolist writer and critic Gustave Kahn was attracted to Neo-Impressionism precisely because he, too, saw the new artists reaching beyond the surface of reality. Symbolism was the latest literary group, comprised primarily of poets, including Manet's friend Stéphane Mallarmé, Arthur Rimbaud and Paul Verlaine. The Symbolists opposed their world of inner subjective dreams and sometimes mystical metaphysics to Zola's empiricist and descriptive Naturalism. Kahn criticized Monet's work at Georges Petit's exhibition of 1887 as disunified because its execution varied according to the object or the distance from the foreground. 'The impression of M. Monet's paintings is not definitive,' he complained, by which he meant it was dependent on observation, which could vary at any time, rather than on insight. In 1886, Kahn usefully formulated the difference between Neo-Impressionism and Impressionism:

The essential aim of our art is to objectify the subjective (the externalization of the Idea) instead of subjectifying the objective (nature seen through the eye of a temperament).

The last part echoes the definition of art offered by Zola in 1865 (see Chapter 1). For Kahn, Impressionism originated in the external world (the objective), which each artist imprinted (subjectified) according to his personal make up (temperament). According to Kahn, the

Symbolist poets and the Neo-Impressionist artists wished to invert that relationship, giving primacy to the perception (Idea) held internally by the (subjective) mind of the individual, the artistic rendering of which into concrete form (externalization) produced an objectively existing representation. The art object, then, embodied the thought or analysis of the artist rather than a mindless copy of nature, however personalized the latter may have been. Of Monet, Fénéon complained: '[He] is a spontaneous painter; the word "impressionist" was created for him ... but, within him, there is nothing contemplative or analytic.' Impressionist perception corresponded to the eye without the exercise of memory or intelligence; whereas our human experience is always an interpreted one, from which we derive meanings.

The Neo-Impressionist argument combined a moralizing doctrine echoing the old academic preference for art displaying the exercise of reason with modern scientific concepts on the nature of human experience. The synthesis to which Fénéon referred combined many moments of experience in order to reach their essential common denominator in a newly made (synthetic) reality (the art object), 'superior' to the external world by infusing its representation with intelligent interpretation. Kahn wrote that the Neo-Impressionists wanted to 'give not just any old hour of the landscape, but its day-long silhouette'.

The socio-political dimension to Neo-Impressionist form was introduced through their connection to the charismatic 'psychophysicist' Charles Henry. Henry was one of those characters unique to French culture – the intellectual of the moment. He was a prodigy who began publishing at age nineteen, and gave public lectures on aesthetics in his apartment, the essence of which appeared in his brief *Introduction to a Scientific Aesthetic* of 1885. (Seurat copied passages from this book.) Linking theories on art to psychology, neurology and music, Henry formulated a mathematical relationship between visual forms, reduced primarily to lines and colours, and human emotions, simplified to pleasure versus pain. Henry drew on art history to define the social function of art, namely that the greatest art was that which fulfilled the perennial human quest for happiness.

Seurat and Henry's shared ambition was to use science 'to guide art towards harmony', a term referring to the social as well as artistic domain. This notion coincided with utopian theories dating back to the 1840s, in which art was held to embody an ideal vision for the future, and where the word 'harmony' referred to that ideal. From this role came the original connection between avant-garde art and politics. When in the preface to his *Salon of 1846* Baudelaire held that art was necessary to restore harmony to tedious bourgeois life, he was only half-ironically drawing on such theories. It is now known that Seurat sympathized with anarchism, hence with a utopian political vision based on principles of equality and decentralized authority. And so it may be suggested that his scientific aesthetics embody a social vision Charles Henry helped him define.

Since the Renaissance, the outdoors has often been the location for visions of ideal society, for it is the opposite of the urban confinement from which utopia (meaning literally 'no-place') is an escape. From the 1840s, artists with anarchist leanings had evoked classical times through costume and setting. The painter Dominique Papety (1815–49), follower of the anarchist philosopher Charles Fourier, conjured up such a world in his *Dream of Happiness* of 1842, as Signac was to in the 1894 painting, *In Time of Harmony*. We saw in the work of Pissarro that landscapes often betray the same nostalgia for a simple life that underlies many utopian urges. Seurat's paintings, however, infuse the sense of order and timelessness that pervades such classical imagery to a visibly modern setting with distinctly modern methods and patterns. It seems likely that *Bathers at Asnières* (see 204) shows male workers and shopkeepers on their traditional Mondays off; whereas *La Grande Jatte* (see 203) depicts the more familial Sunday holiday favoured by the bourgeoisie and Church. The two paintings, which were originally planned to be the same size (*La Grande Jatte* was later expanded by a painted frame), show opposing banks of the same river spot. The view from Asnières has a row of factories in its background, thus emphasizing the figures' absence from work; the view from La Grande Jatte dwells more exclusively on forms of relaxation and play. One of Seurat's literary supporters and an anarchist sympathizer, Paul Adam, wrote of *La Grande Jatte*: 'Even the stiffness of the people, the ready-made forms, help give the sound of modernity, the recall of our tight clothing, glued to the body, the reserved gestures, the British manner everywhere imitated.' For him, Seurat was mocking modern pretensions at the same time as he alluded to the possibility of harmony.

Whether or not we believe such aims can successfully coexist, Seurat's awareness of social customs and clothing, as well as class – its distinctness on Monday, its intermixing on Sunday – gave his pictures a form of authenticity we hardly suspect today. Seurat himself compared *La Grande Jatte* to the Parthenon frieze in Athens, which at the time was thought to represent the religious procession of Athenians renewing the sacred gown of the statue of Athena. That comparison bespeaks his ambition for an alternative to the public art of Puvis de Chavannes or the fantasies of Papety – one in which he would record the actual practices of contemporary culture yet in timeless harmonious form. But it also reveals the reactionary dimension to Seurat's modernism, for his supposedly objective formulas, social and artistic, placed constraints on freedom, hence their ultimate inadequacy for Pissarro.

Pissarro's conversion for a few years to Neo-Impressionism helps us measure its significance for Impressionism. Recalling his brief membership in the artist's union led by Alfred Meyer, it is fair to say politics was often a factor in his institutional choices. The Independents, where Seurat had been exhibiting and out of which Neo-Impressionism first emerged, were the spontaneous result of a group meeting of artists. This kind of effort had left-wing associations, and the artists obtained space in city-owned buildings through the efforts of some leftist city councillors. By contrast, the Impressionists' exhibitions were now held in private galleries, including the aristocratic milieu of Georges Petit. The Independents thus seemed to take over the democratic aims that once motivated Impressionist shows. So whether Seurat's conscious aims were actually political or not, one could link his style and methods to the Independents' democratic practices. Pissarro felt compelled to test their viability for himself.

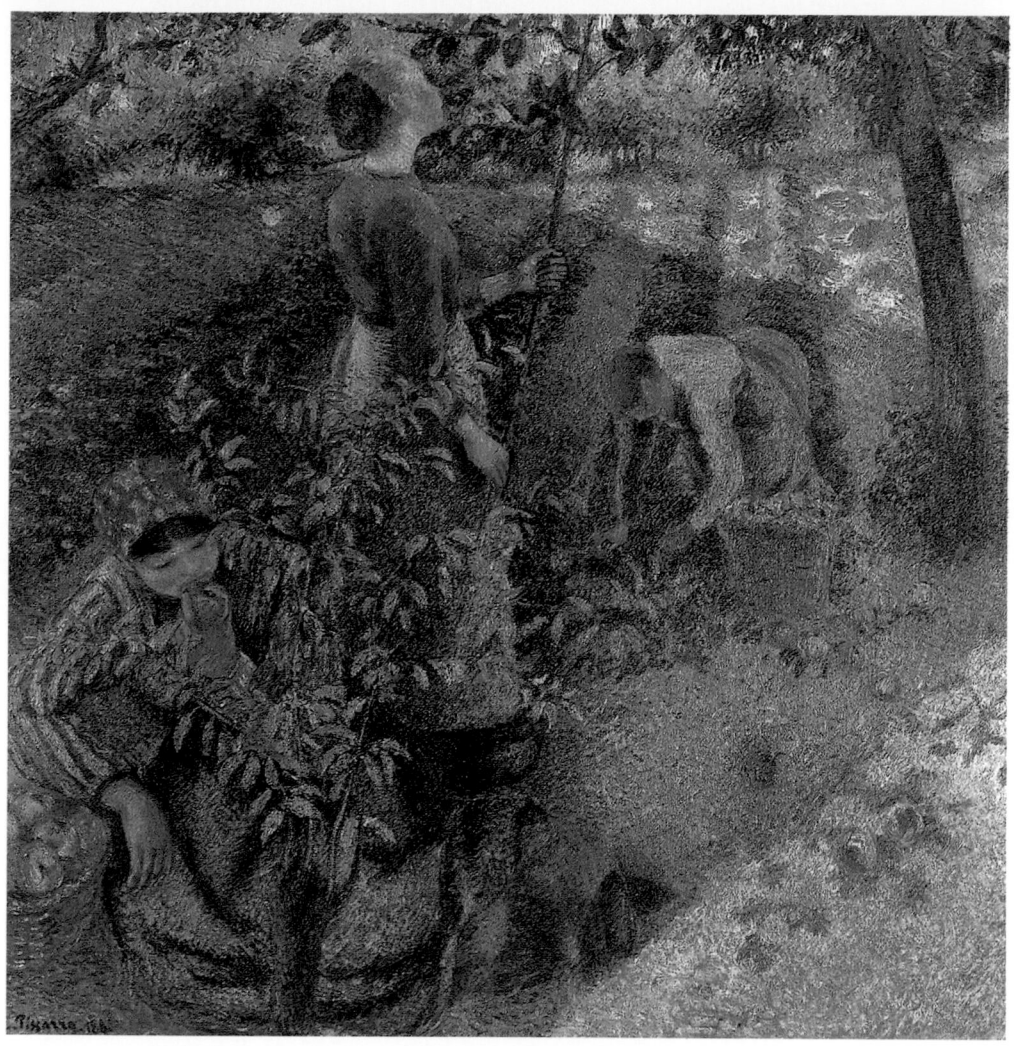

209
Camille
Pissarro,
Apple-Picking,
1886.
Oil on canvas;
127 × 127 cm,
50³⁄₈ × 50³⁄₈ in.
Ohara Museum
of Art,
Kurashiki,
Okayama

Pissarro showed a large painting called *Apple-Picking* (209) at the
Impressionist exhibition of 1886. Begun in 1882, this painting reveals
how the overlay of Seurat's dots upon its already established composition could produce an ostensibly mature work of the new style. In
other words, Seurat's initial impact lay in colour theory and technique
of execution. Pissarro's first major work conceived entirely within the
new method was *View from My Window in Cloudy Weather, Eragny* (210).
It adopts a simpler geometry than *Apple-Picking*, or even Signac's
Gas Tanks at Clichy (see 207), and is built up entirely of small, nearly
uniform, primarily vertical and horizontal dots and dashes. Pissarro

argued to Durand-Ruel, who lamented that the picture was unsaleable, that the painting bore a 'modern primitive stamp'. He combined ostensible opposites – the modern and primitive – suspended in unyielding tension. Through the painting's title, Pissarro gave it an autobiographical twist, personally committing himself to a continuing rural vision that was now declaratively modern as well. He thus remained consistent with his earlier work. The appeal of Neo-Impressionism lay in the hope it offered of correcting the nostalgic element in utopianism with unimpeachably progressive techniques.

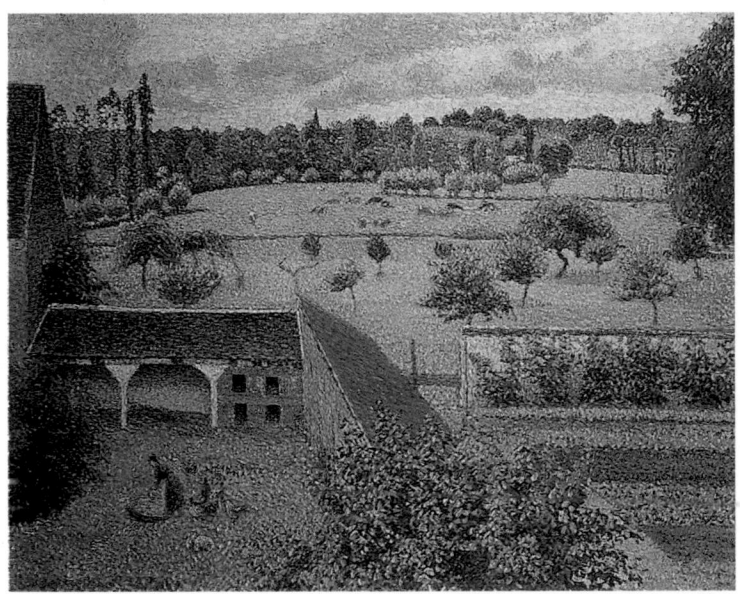

210
Camille Pissarro, *View from My Window in Cloudy Weather, Eragny*, 1886, reworked 1888. Oil on canvas; 65 × 81 cm, 25⁵⁸ × 31⁷⁸ in. Ashmolean Museum, Oxford

211
Georges Seurat, *Poseuses*, 1886–8. Oil on canvas; 200·6 × 251 cm, 79 × 98⁷⁸ in. Barnes Foundation, Merion, Pennsylvania

But Pissarro retouched the work two years later, adding more foliage in the foreground and softening colour in order to mitigate the painting's original stridency. His disillusionment had come quickly. For one thing, Seurat's own painting was moving away from engagement with Pissarro's outdoor brand of Impressionism. His studio scene, *Poseuses (Models)* of 1886–8 (211), seemed to engage issues similar to the bather paintings by the more conservative Degas and Renoir. Its poses (hence the title) evoke figures by Ingres and the academic practice of viewing the nude from different positions in the same composition. The indoor setting and controlled light were Seurat's answer to those who thought his system valid only for landscape. In addition,

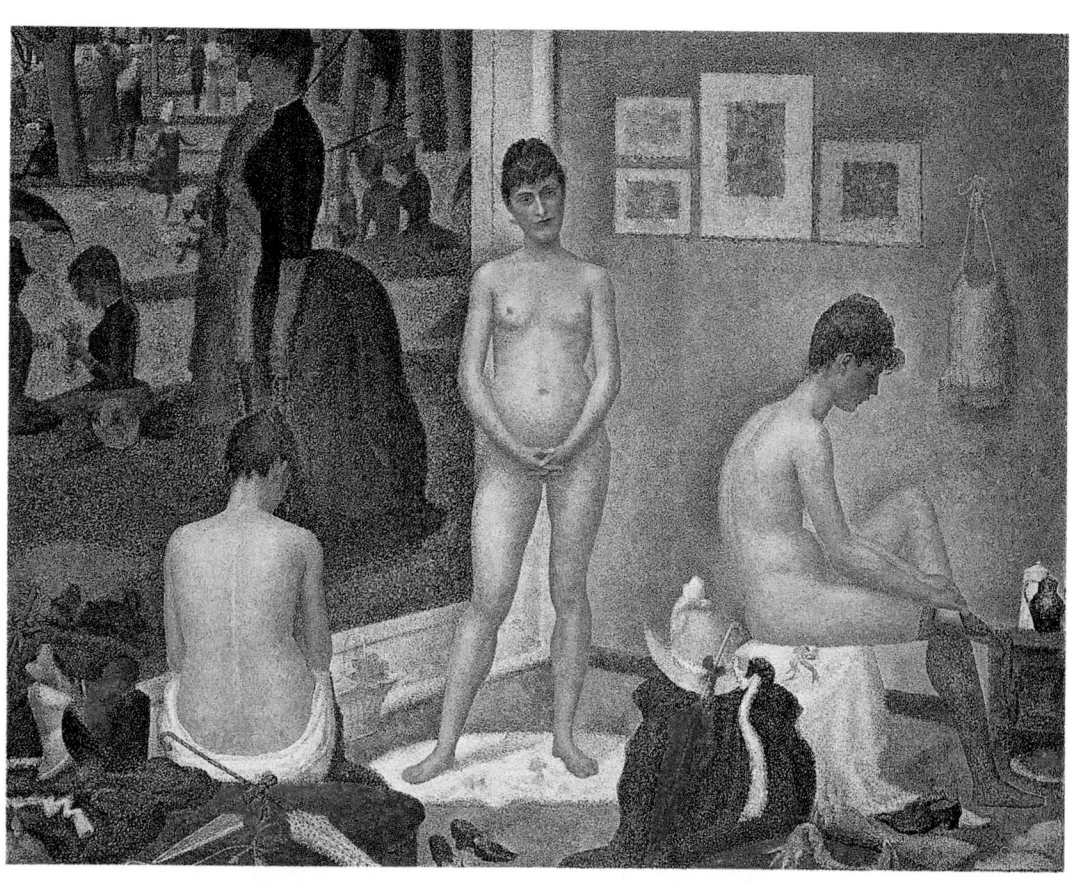

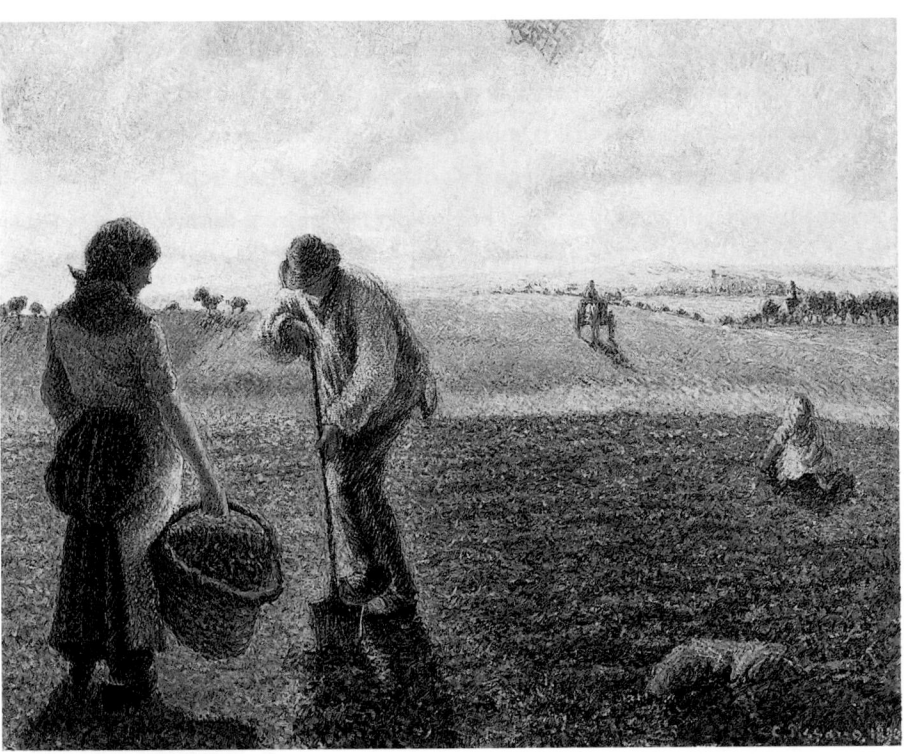

213
Camille
Pissarro,
*Peasants in the
Fields, Eragny*,
1890.
Oil on canvas;
64·3 × 80·4 cm,
25⅜ × 31⅜ in.
Albright-Knox
Art Gallery,
Buffalo

214
Claude Monet,
*Valley of the Creuse
(Sunlight Effect)*,
1889.
Oil on canvas;
65 × 92·4 cm,
25⅝ × 36⅜ in.
Museum of
Fine Arts,
Boston

brushstrokes and colour juxtapositions clearly evolved from Neo-Impressionism, Pissarro produced a glowing vision that instils his countryside with a timeless sense of wellbeing. Especially striking is the backlighting of the two principal figures, who cast shadows forward towards the viewer (paralleling the rising sun of anarchism on the cover for his *Social Turpitudes*; see 187). The heightened contrast of the sunlight near the dark forms of their lower bodies both creates a halo and corresponds to the optical principle of 'irradiation', again learned from Seurat. (The intensity of light and dark is strongest at the edges of contrasting forms.) Hence, through Seurat, Pissarro discovered new ways of rendering his perceptions – perceptions we recognize as grounded in an observable, though selected reality, while infused with the light of irrepressible political optimism. This mythic naturalism, which recalls Millet more than ever, appealed both to those who rejoiced in Pissarro's return to Impressionism and to the spiritually inclined Symbolists, such as Octave Mirbeau, whose interpretation of these paintings bordered on pantheism.

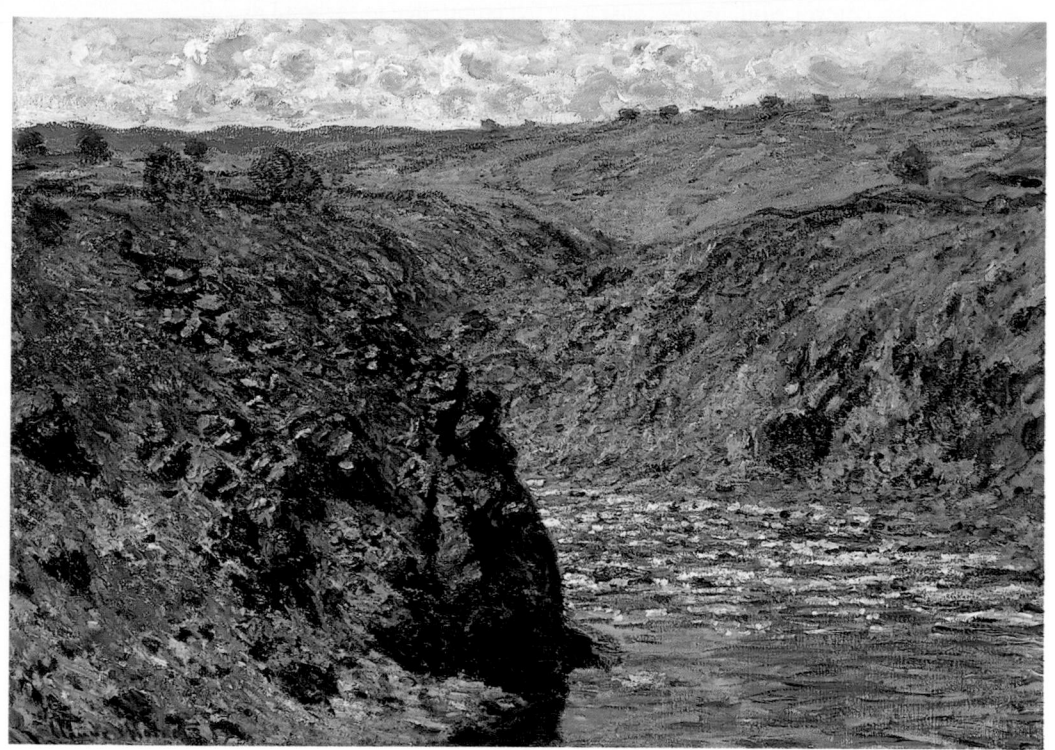

It remains finally, then, to ask what effect Neo-Impressionism may have had on Monet, the primary object of their attacks. We already saw him moving towards greater structural coherency in the first half of the 1880s, as he dug in his heels at the threatened takeover of Impressionism by Degas and his friends. Perhaps his brief return to the figure in 1886, as in *Study of a Figure Outdoors, Facing Left*, was prompted by *La Grande Jatte* (see 202, 203). Surely Neo-Impressionism contributed to Monet's series paintings, as well. Monet and Seurat both collected moments, and, whereas Seurat combined his many studies to produce an overall synthesis through a single monumental work, Monet's artistic monument to his experiences was the series.

Moreover, with Monet's Belle-Île paintings, there was a change of rhetoric. For one thing, Monet's letters and his links to the critics Mirbeau and Geffroy suggest reorientation towards the inner poetic experience sought by Symbolists. For another, Monet's view of himself as a hero doing battle with nature in the tradition of great sea painters may relate to feelings of resistance to forces in the art world beyond his control. Still, Monet must have felt compelled to respond to aspects of Neo-Impressionism that challenged his naturalist claims. Though he would never employ Seurat's system or pretend to be scientific, Monet developed smaller brushstrokes, bold geometries, novel colour juxtapositions and uninhabited landscapes, as in his painting (214) *Valley of the Creuse (Sunlight Effect)* – which compares interestingly with Seurat's *Le Bec du Hoc* (see 208). Its effects hover between his hallowed instantaneity and the sense of timelessness and permanence proffered by the new generation. Monet's response confirms that for Impressionism, Neo-Impressionism was not only a critique, but with its new emphasis and series of discoveries, an impetus for renewal.

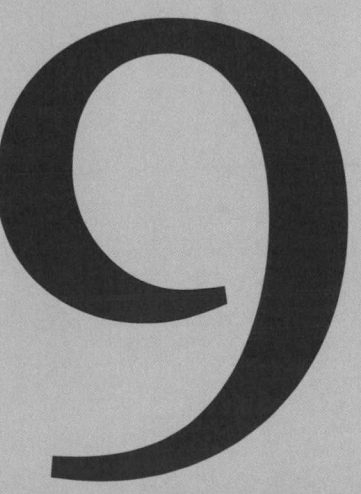

moved his company to this newer neighbourhood from across the river, where he had primarily sold stationery to a university clientele.

Fuelled by the booming economy of the 1860s, speculation spilled over into the arts, turning the market into an unregulated free-for-all with all sorts of overlapping positions and self-serving roles. Auctions became frenetic at the Hôtel Drouot, a salesroom often used by artists as a gallery, which opened halfway between rue Lafitte and the stock exchange. Prices were high enough to attract dealers, who doubled as art experts when they were not in their shops. Durand-Ruel took on silent partners: one of them posed as the owner of works auctioned in 1881; another suddenly called in loans when his bank failed in the crash of 1882, forcing the dealer to sell holdings quickly and making new purchases temporarily impossible. Respectable writers and historians, such as Armand Silvestre, Charles Blanc and Philippe Burty, were commissioned to write notes or introductions for exhibition or sales catalogues, often acquiring superb collections at the same time. The artists had already acted on their own behalf when in the 1860s they both submitted work to the Salon and discussed organizing alternatives collectively. The Impressionists' 1875 auction, held at the Hôtel Drouot, followed their independent exhibition of the year before. Though suggested by Renoir, the auction was less a novel act of desperation than a way of drumming up sales that had already been used by the previous generation.

Anne Distel has assembled a wealth of information about Impressionism's early collectors, revealing how chance meetings and youthful friendships more than planning affected their future. The earliest patrons were found mostly through family and friends. The ship-owning Gaudiberts of Le Havre commissioned one of Monet's large early full-length figures, the *Portrait of Madame Gaudibert*. The architect-brother of Renoir's painter-friend Jules Le Coeur got Renoir a commission for the town house of the Romanian Prince Bibesco. It was probably through the prince that Renoir met the Romanian homeopathic physician Georges de Bellio, an important future collector. Manet's relations with Théodore Duret began with a chance meeting in a Madrid hotel in 1865. The homeopathic physician and art collector Dr Gachet had moved to Auvers-sur-Oise in 1872 (see Chapter 4). By chance, he had treated Pissarro's mother and subsequently helped the young Camille and his family settle in nearby Pontoise. Auvers was already something of an art colony where Guillaumin and Cézanne briefly settled, near Daubigny, its best-known inhabitant. A chance meeting in 1872 of Guillaumin with his boyhood friend the chef Eugène Murer led to Murer's fine collection and his dinner-receptions featuring writers and artists. We know how Émile Zola, the boyhood friend of Cézanne, was part of the Impressionist circle in the 1860s (see Chapter 2). He was surely instrumental in introducing his publisher Georges Charpentier to their work. Charpentier and his wife, Marguerite, became avid collectors, and Madame Charpentier's weekly salon included Renoir and offered many contacts. In 1879 Monsieur Charpentier founded the journal *La Vie moderne*, which included articles on the painters they had begun to collect, and he opened his offices to exhibitions of their work.

As to artists supporting each other, Bazille played a crucial part in the early survival of Monet and Renoir (see Chapter 3). Henri Rouart, a successful industrial engineer, was a school friend of Degas and an amateur painter. Rouart both exhibited with the Impressionists and purchased many of their works. It was through him and Degas that Gustave Caillebotte joined the Impressionists. In the end, the superb collection of their works Caillebotte assembled, and eventually left to the state (which accepted them after extreme controversy), was as important a legacy as his own painted work.

Such stories of accidental discovery and friendship are typical of artists in the modern period. But they perpetuate the myth that genius will somehow be rewarded, isolating art from its material circumstances by minimizing the economic dynamics of both collaboration and individual enterprise. If one looks to progressive art movements since the first challenges to academic rules and government patronage under the French Revolution, one finds a pattern of grouping and bonding among young artists that served as a substitute for official status or family security. One thinks of Jacques-Louis David's atelier, the young Delacroix and Théodore Géricault (1791–1824) in the studio of Horace Vernet (1789–1863), Courbet and his comrades at the Brasserie Andler, and then later, after the Impressionists, the Nabis at Pont-Aven. Interestingly, Bazille, Caillebotte and Degas, the three unmarried male Impressionists, and the richest, thrust their social energies into the group. (Cassatt was quite active as well.) Pissarro was another central figure, and his role as mentor at Pontoise will be a topic in Chapter 10. The capacity of such relationships to reinforce the individual's self-confidence and sense of purpose cannot be underestimated. The point here is that such support invariably had an economic dimension, as the slightest examination of Impressionist correspondence reveals.

The three most commercially successful Impressionists, Monet, Renoir and Degas, however different from each other, shared an acute sense of business self-interest. For example, Renoir's large *Riding in the Bois de Boulogne* (216) was not a commission, but rather more like an advertisement calculated to impress the Salon of 1873. Typical of Renoir's approach to scenes of modern life, it was a double portrait – but of two unrelated figures, Madame Henriette Darras accompanied by the young son of the architect Charles Le Coeur. Madame Darras was the wife of an amateur painter and army captain who had commissioned portraits from Renoir in 1871. Surely Renoir hoped to attract clients and paint the children of the Darras's friends and others of their circle. The painting's relative finish and obvious evocation of aristocratic British sporting pictures exemplifies Renoir's desire to reconcile Impressionist concerns with more conservative tastes. Its uneasy stiffness is not far from Bazille's last efforts, which embodied similar contradictions. Refused by the Salon, the painting was eventually sold to Henri Rouart.

216
Pierre-Auguste Renoir,
Riding in the Bois de Boulogne,
1873.
Oil on canvas;
261 × 226 cm,
102³⁄₄ × 89 in.
Kunsthalle, Hamburg

In the belief that one sale leads to another, several artists in the first Impressionist exhibition showed works that were already owned. In Sisley's case, giving Durand-Ruel's name indicated his support and identified the place where the pictures were available. In 1876, all his works were listed as belonging to dealers – Pierre-Firmin (known as Père) Martin, Louis Latouche and Alphonse Legrand, a Durand-Ruel associate. For Degas, seven out of ten listed works in 1874 were already owned – but by collectors, not dealers – suggesting not only their saleability but feigning a successful artist's interest in exhibiting for its own sake rather than primarily for sale. (Monet and Renoir followed this example in 1876.) Degas's relationship to the market was always ambivalent; reality and appearances often conflicted.

Marilyn Brown has studied the most egregious example of Degas's early entrepreneurship, *Portraits in a Cotton Office, New Orleans* (217). For its subject matter, the painting focused directly on business – the cotton trade – an enterprise in which Degas had a personal and

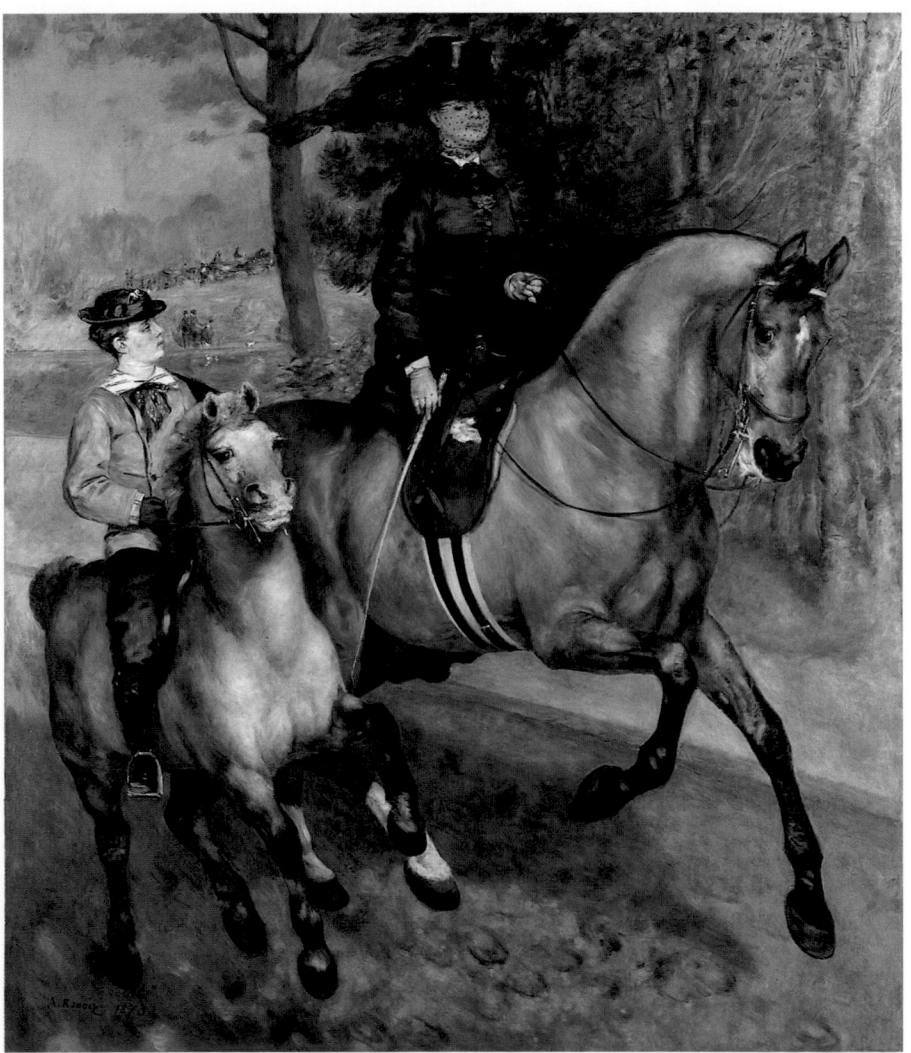

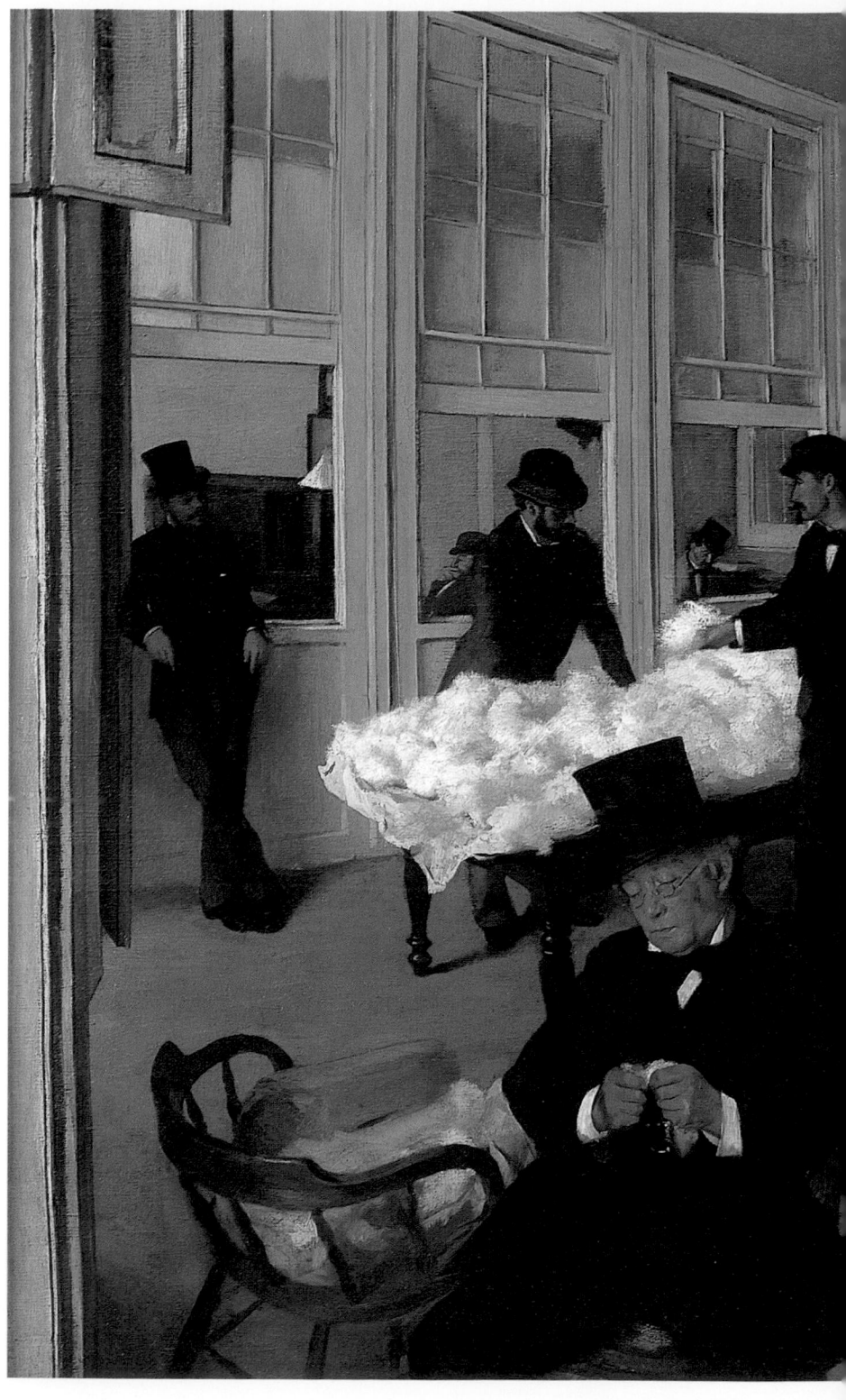

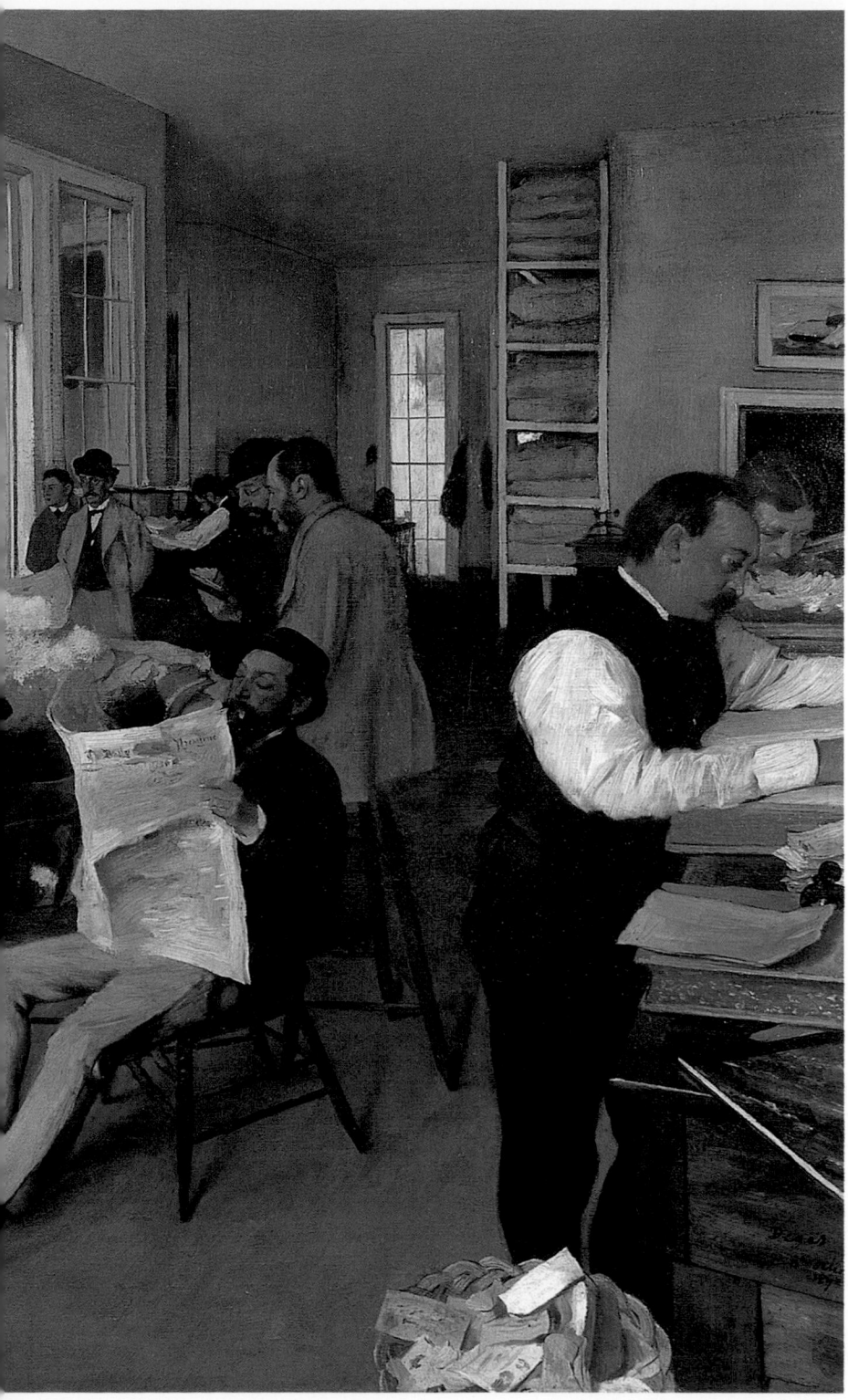

217
Edgar Degas,
*Portraits in a
Cotton Office,
New Orleans*,
1873.
Oil on canvas;
73 × 92 cm,
28³⁄₄ × 36¹⁄₄ in.
Musée des
Beaux-Arts,
Pau

financial stake. His uncle, Michel Musson, is in the foreground looking at a cotton sample; Musson's partners James Prestidge (seated on the high stool) and John Livaudais (to the right, studying a ledger) are present with the painter's brothers, Achille (leaning against the window to the left) and René (reading the newspaper near the centre). The two were sent to New Orleans to work with Musson, in whose firm Degas's father had invested large sums; Edgar travelled to New Orleans to visit them. (At the father's death, it was this foundering business that swallowed much of the family fortune.) The painter represents his brothers as distant, idle and indifferent to the productive activities in which the others are engaged. To a degree, Degas shared their diffidence, as if their aristocratic background made work distasteful. Yet Degas was also impressed by the practicality of Americans, and in emulation he proposed to his British friend James Tissot that *Portraits in a Cotton Office, New Orleans* would appeal to a certain collector in Manchester whose fortune was made in textiles. Hence, Degas directed this painting towards a particular target market. When that strategy failed, some supporters including Henri Rouart convinced the Friends of Art Society in the fashionable and progressive provincial town of Pau to purchase the picture for its newly founded museum in 1878. It was the first Impressionist painting to enter a public collection.

Manet's experiences exhibiting at Martinet's cooperative gallery (in which artists paid rent or the equivalent) and at the Salon des Refusés anticipated those of his younger colleagues. His encounters with Duret, Zola and Durand-Ruel helped lay the ground for their interactions with younger artists. The independently wealthy Duret, a Republican journalist, had been a supporter of Courbet's Realism, to which he was drawn in part through political sympathy. He and Manet shared an interest in Spanish Realism – hence their parallel travels – so Manet's hispanisizing works, from which Duret made purchases, had a special appeal. In 1867, Duret began writing art criticism; in 1868, Manet portrayed him in a full-length portrait (218) filled with references to Goya. By that year, Duret and Zola were also friends, and both defended Manet in the press. Then, in Britain during the Franco-Prussian War, Duret looked in at Durand-Ruel's

London gallery, where he happened to see a painting by Pissarro. We cannot determine whether Duret already knew Pissarro from the Café Guerbois, but from this time on he was a dependable supporter and advised the artist on what would sell. Probably through Pissarro, he met Monet, from whom he also purchased works. One after another, Duret met Renoir, Sisley and the others; through Zola he met Charpentier, who published some of his writings. Whenever the painters were in debt, they wrote to Duret, who arranged loans or purchases. He became a mainstay of their circle and also their

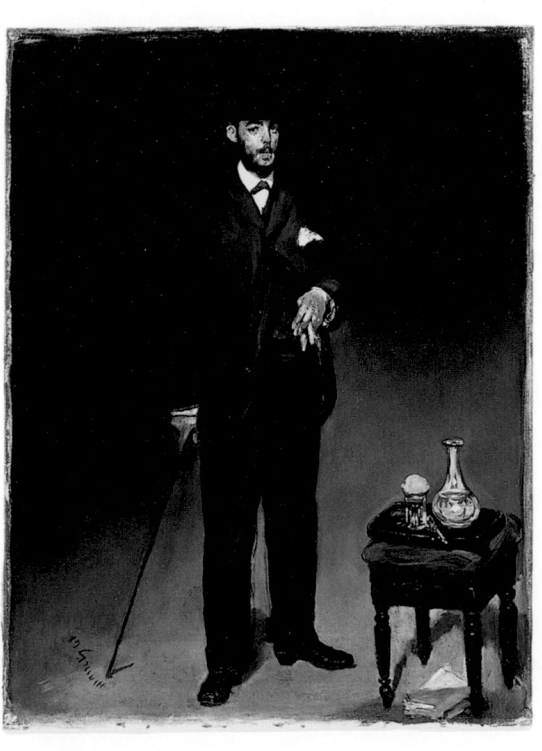

218
Édouard Manet,
*Portrait of
Théodore Duret*,
1868.
Oil on canvas;
43 × 35 cm,
17 × 13¾ in.
Musée du
Petit Palais,
Paris

chronicler, writing one of the earliest coherent interpretations of their art in his 1878 pamphlet, *Les Peintres impressionnistes*.

A very different kind of collector was the great baritone Jean-Baptiste Faure. An international opera superstar since the 1850s, he received astronomical sums for performances and began collecting paintings by Romantic artists and Barbizon landscapists. In 1873, as he acquired his first works by Manet, he sold off much of his earlier collection for over half a million francs. (For reference, the more expensive of his first Manets, *The Spanish Guitar Player* of 1860, cost 7,000 francs – earning Durand-Ruel 4,000 francs profit. By comparison, a modestly comfortable bourgeois income was 10,000 francs or above.) Thinking perhaps of retiring – he did so in 1876 – Faure's love of art merged with an investment strategy, which included circumventing dealers to purchase directly from artists. Sixty-seven canvases by Manet belonged to Faure at one time or another, including such key works as *Music in the Tuileries Gardens*, *Le Déjeuner sur l'herbe* (see 27 and 30) and *Gare Saint-Lazare*. Manet generously introduced Faure to

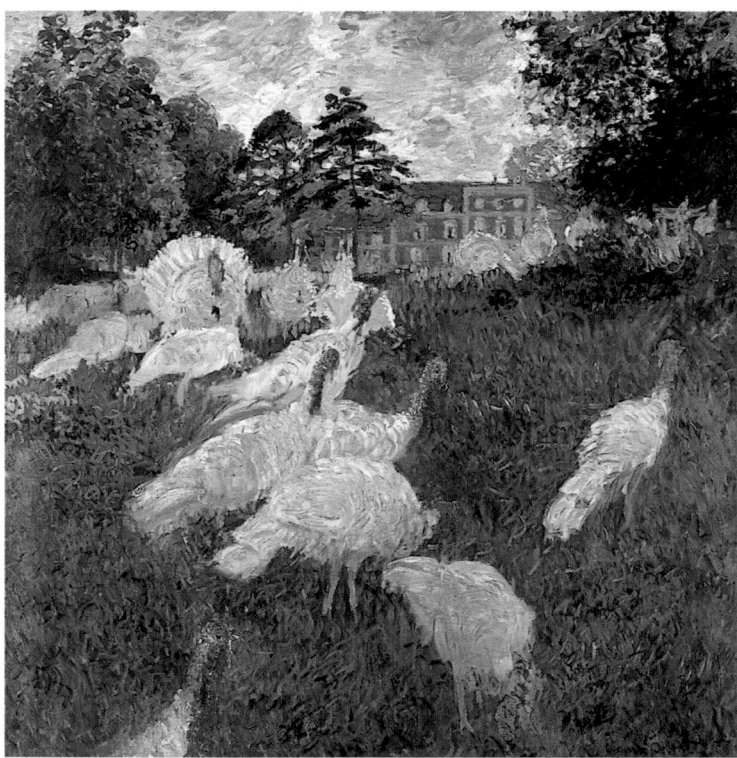

219
Claude Monet,
Turkeys,
1876.
Oil on canvas;
172 × 175 cm,
67³⁄₄ × 69 in.
Musée d'Orsay,
Paris

other members of the circle. Among Faure's favourites were Monet, who sold nineteen paintings to him between 1874 and 1877; Sisley, whom Faure took travelling to Hampton Court in 1874; and Degas, ten of whose works he owned by 1880. Faure had purchased Degas's *A Carriage at the Races* (see 117) from Durand-Ruel's London gallery in 1873. Perhaps that led to the commission for a version of *Dance Class at the Opéra* (see 123) the following year.

Faure held on to most of his collection for the long term. The unfortunate Ernest Hoschedé did not have that option. Son of a self-made fabric wholesaler, married to the daughter of a wealthy property developer and director of a department store, Hoschedé got used to little work and much ostentatious spending. Like Faure, he tried to speculate on works of young artists bought cheaply from Durand-Ruel, which he mixed with more established names from the Salon or the Barbizon School. Several times in the 1870s, Claude Monet visited the Château Rottembourg at Montgeron, inherited by Alice Hoschedé, for which he made four large paintings on commission in 1876–7. Their leisure themes included hunting, *The Pond at Montgeron* and the justly celebrated and highly unusual *Turkeys* (219). For at least two years, however, Hoschedé's financial situation had been unstable. While he continued buying paintings, some of which he never paid for, he tried to auction others, and he borrowed heavily from financiers to fund personal expenses. In August 1877, he finally went bankrupt. (It was as a result of this that Monet took in the family.) The Hoschedé sale of 6 June 1878 was a barometer for the new school's fortunes: it was too early to unload a large quantity all together, and the results were very poor. Monet's paintings sold for an average of 150 francs, Manet's for 583 francs, while three works by Renoir were all bought for 157 francs! Pissarro complained that low prices for his earlier works were depressing those of his current output.

In addition to Faure, Duret, De Bellio and a few others, including Durand-Ruel, who bought for stock, one of the most interesting collectors to benefit from the Hoschedé sale was the customs official Victor Chocquet. Unlike those for whom collecting was an aspect of conspicuous consumption, Chocquet was a devoted connoisseur who lurked around the auction houses in search of good buys and distinguished himself by his eye rather than his wallet. When he retired in 1877, Chocquet's annual salary was a mere 4,000 francs. Anne Distel points out that Chocquet and his wife had modest private incomes, but it was not until the death of Madame Chocquet's mother in 1882 that the couple became comfortable. Chocquet had begun collecting small works by Delacroix and Courbet in the 1860s. These were followed by Renoir and Cézanne, who might be considered their less expensive heirs and were to become Chocquet's long-term favourites. Renoir was the first to meet the collector, probably through the Impressionist auction of 1875. In that year, Chocquet commissioned portraits of himself and his wife. In both, Renoir represented the sitters in their apartment, with paintings by Delacroix hanging directly behind them.

Chocquet's friendship with Cézanne was durable, despite the painter's volatile character. Cézanne's portraits of him were among the most daring in the Impressionist style to date. All the Impressionists were grateful when, as the story goes, Chocquet attended each day of the third exhibition in 1877, to which he lent many pictures, defending them against hostility and proselytizing the recalcitrant. But though Chocquet was probably the most altruistic of Impressionism's collectors, one should not forget that taste in art is a highly subjective matter, requiring an investment of personal credibility as well as money. For any collector who promoted Impressionism, the satisfaction of supporting novelty converged with a natural desire to protect his or her assets.

One could add profiles of many other such collectors: Dr Paul Gachet will be mentioned again later in connection with Cézanne; the Charpentiers have been cited more than once, as has Eugène Murer; and Gustave Caillebotte has been regarded primarily for his contributions as an artist, although his financial support and activities as a patron were no less significant. But there remains one collector of enormous import who certainly deserves more attention. Louisine Elder Havemeyer was the first independent female collector of Impressionist art as well as the first American. Without her introduction to Mary Cassatt in 1875, who was ten years her senior, the international success of Impressionist painting might have been far less swift and glorious. Cassatt, the friend of Degas, first advised Miss Elder to buy a pastel by Degas, the 1876–7 *Ballet Rehearsal*, now in the Nelson-Atkins Museum of Art, Kansas City; then a Monet done during the artist's Dutch sojourn, *The Bridge, Amsterdam* of 1871, now in the Shelburne Museum, Vermont; as well as a Pissarro fan. It is true that her collecting did not begin in earnest until after her marriage to Henry O Havemeyer, the son of her father's partner in a booming sugar refinery, and the birth of their children. By the mid-1880s, however, Mrs Havemeyer had resumed her earlier interest in art. Durand-Ruel was also instrumental in American collecting. He opened a branch of his business in Boston in 1883 and in 1886 held an 'Impressionists of Paris' exhibition in New York, where the next year he opened a gallery that would become a mainstay of his firm. Following Louisine Havemeyer's death in 1929, a sizeable portion of her collection was bequeathed to New York's Metropolitan Museum of Art, including Manet's *Boating*, Monet's *La Grenouillère* and Degas's *Woman with Chrysanthemums* (see 44, 59 and 114).

At the heart of the popular mythology of the artist, which the Impressionist story represents for many today, lies the question of market influence. Were these artists ahead of their time, pursuing a singular vision and imposing their genius on a sceptical public? Or was their work, like any new product which eventually catches on in capitalist economies, responding to unsatisfied needs then manipulated by interested parties? There is enough truth in both views to chasten any believer in either myth or ideology. One of the most interesting examples of the interaction of personal vision and marketing is the development of one of later Impressionism's hallmarks, the painting in series. Certainly, Monet's paintings of grainstacks and Rouen Cathedral, like Sisley's pictures of the flooding at Port-Marly almost twenty years before, grew out of *plein-air* practices. But they were encouraged by a marketability related to their production in a manner resembling that of multiples, while still preserving uniqueness and originality. Focusing attention on a single motif heightened the impact of an exhibition, while offering individual collectors the security of buying into a sustained effort and (in number) a monumental work. Judging by remarkable sales figures and rising prices, collectors for whom Impressionism might still seem risky were more likely to buy paintings that were similar and related, though not identical, to works which others had already bought. No longer would artists invest so much in single large exhibition pieces, as had been the case for Salon painters hoping for government patronage, or even Renoir,

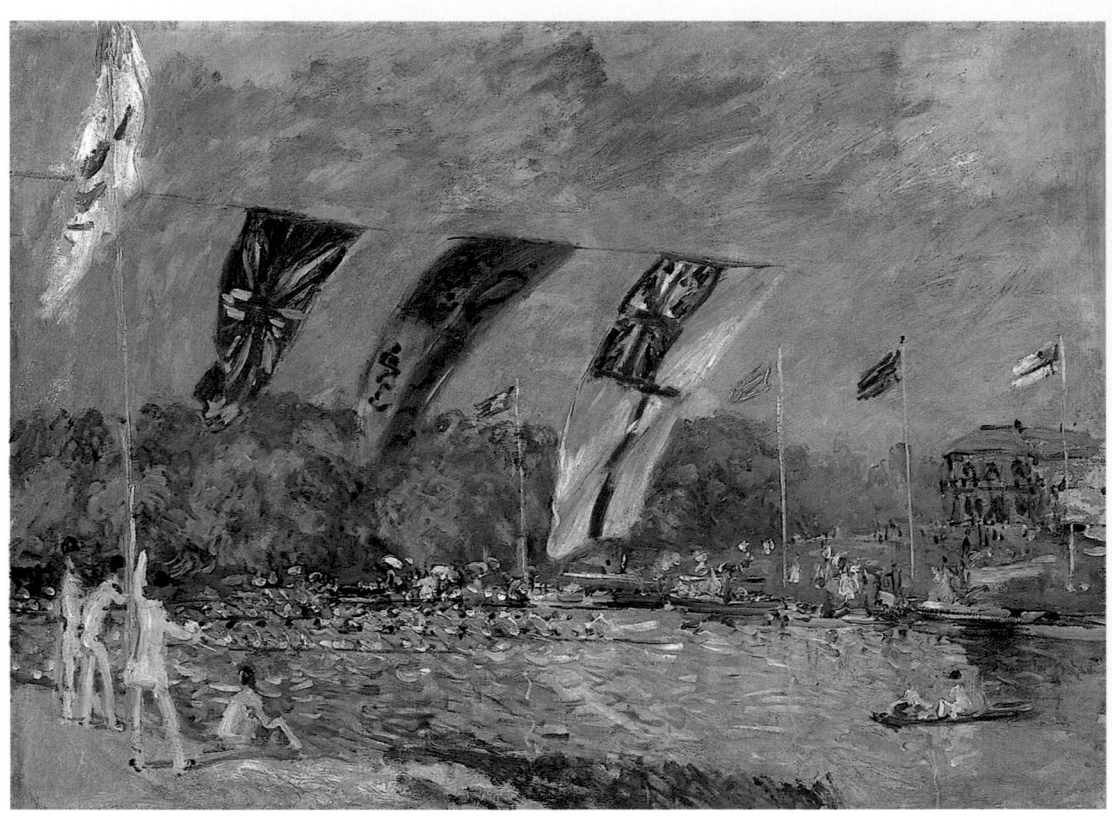

looking for impact at the Impressionist show of 1877 with *The Ball at the Moulin de la Galette* (see 109). So although series paintings had many precedents in the early years of Impressionism, the concept acquired its definitive expression within the market. The natural desire of artists to have their work widely known and highly valued converged with dealer strategies that produced huge profits and sellout shows.

Alfred Sisley's work of the 1870s provides two classic instances of the relationship between external circumstances and the genesis of painting in series. In 1874, Faure invited Sisley to accompany him on a trip to London, paying expenses in exchange for six of the paintings he would produce. Sisley did approximately sixteen views of the Thames in and around Hampton Court, most of them with sportsmen in rowing shells. *The Regatta at Molesey, near Hampton Court* (220) records one of the two annual regattas held in the area. Its rapid

220
Alfred Sisley,
*The Regatta at
Molesey, near
Hampton Court*,
1874.
Oil on canvas;
62 × 92 cm,
24¹₂ × 36¹₄ in.
Musée d'Orsay,
Paris

221
Alfred Sisley,
*The Wharf
During the Flood
at Port-Marly*,
1876.
Oil on canvas;
50 × 61·5 cm,
19³₄ × 24¹₄ in.
Museé des
Beaux-Arts,
Rouen

execution and loose handling suggest both a windy day and the event's excitement. Focusing on the English national passion for athleticism, these images of riverside leisure are unique within Impressionism for their British location and subject matter, yet they typify the movement's upper-middle-class, outdoor-pleasure orientation.

Sisley also did seven closely related views of the flooding of the Seine at Port-Marly in the spring of 1876. Whereas there were a variety of sites, angles and activities in the Hampton Court group, Sisley now concentrated almost entirely on a single location, with some nearly identical views. In the painting now in the Musée des Beaux-Arts in Rouen (221), we view the inn À St-Nicholas from across the flooded road, where stands the rival inn, Au Lion d'Or. In this picture, unlike its near twin at the Musée d'Orsay, a woman stands on planks laid across barrels in front of the door. Most of Sisley's views show skiffs ferrying people about. This unusual and newsworthy event offered the skies and water central to *plein-air* painting along the Seine, though with a special sense of solitude and awe for nature, giving the works an expressive power that echoes Romantic landscape and is unequalled in most of Sisley's other work. Their consistency makes the group a tightly interrelated series, with slight variations in vantage point or

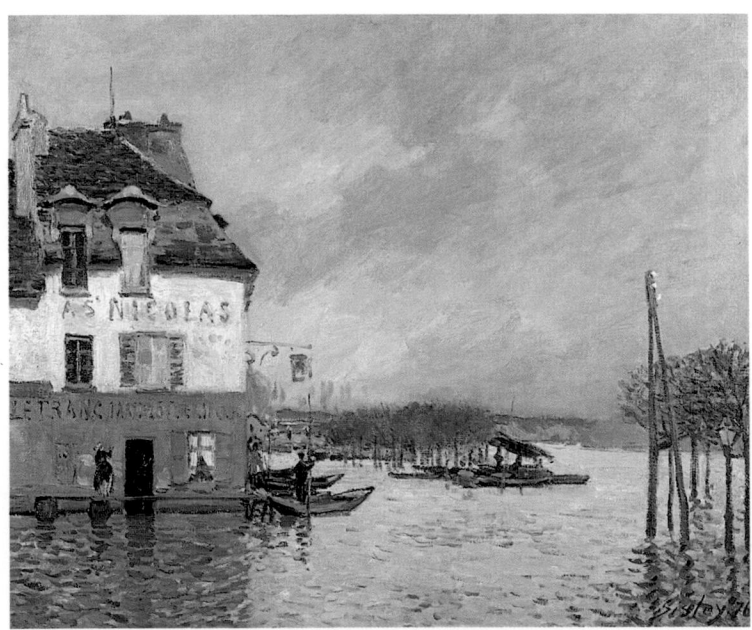

lighting, and cloud formations suggesting the passage of time. It is as if the temporary conditions of flooding – Impressionist transience *par excellence* – galvanized Sisley to document them closely. These paintings are very like groups of related works made by painters of old, such as the views of Venice by Canaletto (Giovanni Antonio Canal; 1697–1768) or those of Salisbury Cathedral by John Constable (1776–1837), distinguished by their focus on specific motifs or on events within a limited period of time. Sisley seized opportunities he might not have sensed were they before his eyes daily, or which would not normally have inspired such concerted labour.

Similar examples exist in Monet's work from the same period. His paintings of the Saint-Lazare station (see 71) are as coherent a set as Sisley's, perhaps even more so since Monet deliberately created the occasion by returning to Paris from Argenteuil for his campaign. On the other hand, the four views of the Tuileries made from Chocquet's window (see 182) exemplify the way patrons can create opportunities leading to a definable series. Among that group, some paintings seem like sketches for others. While it is natural for the *plein-air* painter to treat related motifs simply to explore available scenery more fully than a single view permits, each of these sample groups is bracketed by special circumstances that give them added specificity. It is hard to know whether marketing was a significant factor in their creation. Sisley listed only one of his Port-Marly flood series in the Impressionist exhibition of 1876. In 1877, by contrast, Monet showed eight of his twelve Saint-Lazare station views. Judging by the attention they attracted, his strategy was effective, for they were singled out from among the thirty-odd paintings he showed. Similarly, when he showed eight paintings of relatively uniform size from Belle-Île at Georges Petit's in 1887, critics noticed interrelationships that implied their creation as a series. The difference with his earlier work was that now most of his production was made during such campaigns, leading to what might be called a 'serial practice' even when scenes would be practically next door – as for his poplar and grainstack paintings. It did not hurt that Monet could sell such works *en bloc*, as he did with pictures done on the French Riviera in 1888. Ten of the Antibes series were bought by Theo van Gogh for the

Boussod et Valadon gallery. Several of Monet's colleagues attacked what they concluded was a commercial motivation underlying the series. They provided grist for the Neo-Impressionist mill of resentment towards the power of private dealers. It is true that some of the Antibes paintings repeated similar views, but they were distinguished by lights of different times of day – a traditional effect, but one which others admired as subtle and precise.

Aspects of the marketing of Monet are evident in the large retrospective he held with the sculptor Auguste Rodin (1840–1917) at Georges Petit's in 1889. This show, which assembled together more of his paintings than ever before, was timed to coincide with the Universal Exposition, with which the French government wanted to celebrate the centenary of the Revolution and hoped to display the accomplishments of French industry and arts. (The construction of the Eiffel Tower on the Champ de Mars was its most lasting accomplishment.) Courbet in 1855 and 1867, and Manet in 1867, had timed their one-man exhibitions similarly. For this show, Monet undertook a new campaign in the valley of the Creuse River (see 214), in the Massif Central, from which he produced some twenty-four views, fifteen of which would be among the 145-odd pictures at Petit's. For the first time, Monet hung all pictures of the same subject together, emphasizing their definition as an ensemble. With them were twelve Belle-Île paintings. Hence, about twenty per cent of the retrospective belonged to groups we now consider series. For the rest of his career, such groups would be increasingly dominant, and their success taught him effective exhibition strategies. For example, he would never again produce new work for a group show, bluntly informing Durand-Ruel in 1890 that he could organize it from his own stock if he wished. Monet sensed his growing power. For the grainstacks of 1891 he had received 3,000 francs apiece; all twenty-four of the poplars series were snapped up in 1892 for almost double that price. In 1895, he demanded 15,000 francs for each of his Rouen Cathedrals. When the dealer balked, Monet sold a few privately, then left on a trip to Norway. On his return three months later, Monet and Durand-Ruel organized a hugely successful one-man exhibition, which included the *Rouen Cathedral* series, priced at 12,000 francs each.

Before leaving for the Creuse valley, Monet had done a few paintings of the grainstacks behind his house at Giverny (222). When he returned to the motif in 1890, after a hiatus of nearly a year, he conceived his goal as a series. In a letter that year to Geffroy, he described his methods:

I'm grinding away, struggling stubbornly with a series of different effects (stacks) but at this time of year the sun sinks so fast that I can't keep up with it. I'm beginning to work so slowly that I despair, but the longer I go on, the more I see that it is necessary to work a great deal in order to succeed in rendering what I seek – instantaneity, above all the 'envelope', the same light spreading everywhere – and more than ever I'm disgusted with things that come easily in one go. I am more and more obsessed by the need to render what I experience.

Here, Monet finally uses the word 'series' to describe paintings of the same motif with different effects. Not that the word was never used before, but here it acquires particular significance combined with the concept of 'effect', meaning the sensation produced by certain sights on the viewer (see Chapter 1). The motif of the grainstack did not vary; rather, effects of light and instantaneity for which it was a vehicle was each painting's unique feature. Moreover, Monet refers to the struggle to record his 'experience' – a word implying something broader, more emotional and personal, than simply visual perception.

222
Grainstacks
behind Claude
Monet's house
at Giverny,
1905

In his thorough study of Monet's series, Paul Tucker has dispelled some of the myths surrounding their technical origins. The idea that they emerged as a quasi-scientific examination of sunlight at successive times of day corresponds neither to their vantage points, which are far from always identical, nor to the titles, which name different seasons and weather conditions, as well as times of day. For example, the superb *Grainstack (Snow Effect)* is a morning picture (see 225), as can be judged by the position of the sun. Another winter picture, *Grainstacks (Sunset, Snow Effect)*, cannot be from the same day, since both of its stacks have snow on them (224). Monet has also varied his point of view: a second stack is included, and the houses in the background have a different position. Other pictures represent summer effects or cloudy days. One of the most spectacular is *Grainstack (Sunset)*, in which the stack looms close to the viewer in burning reds,

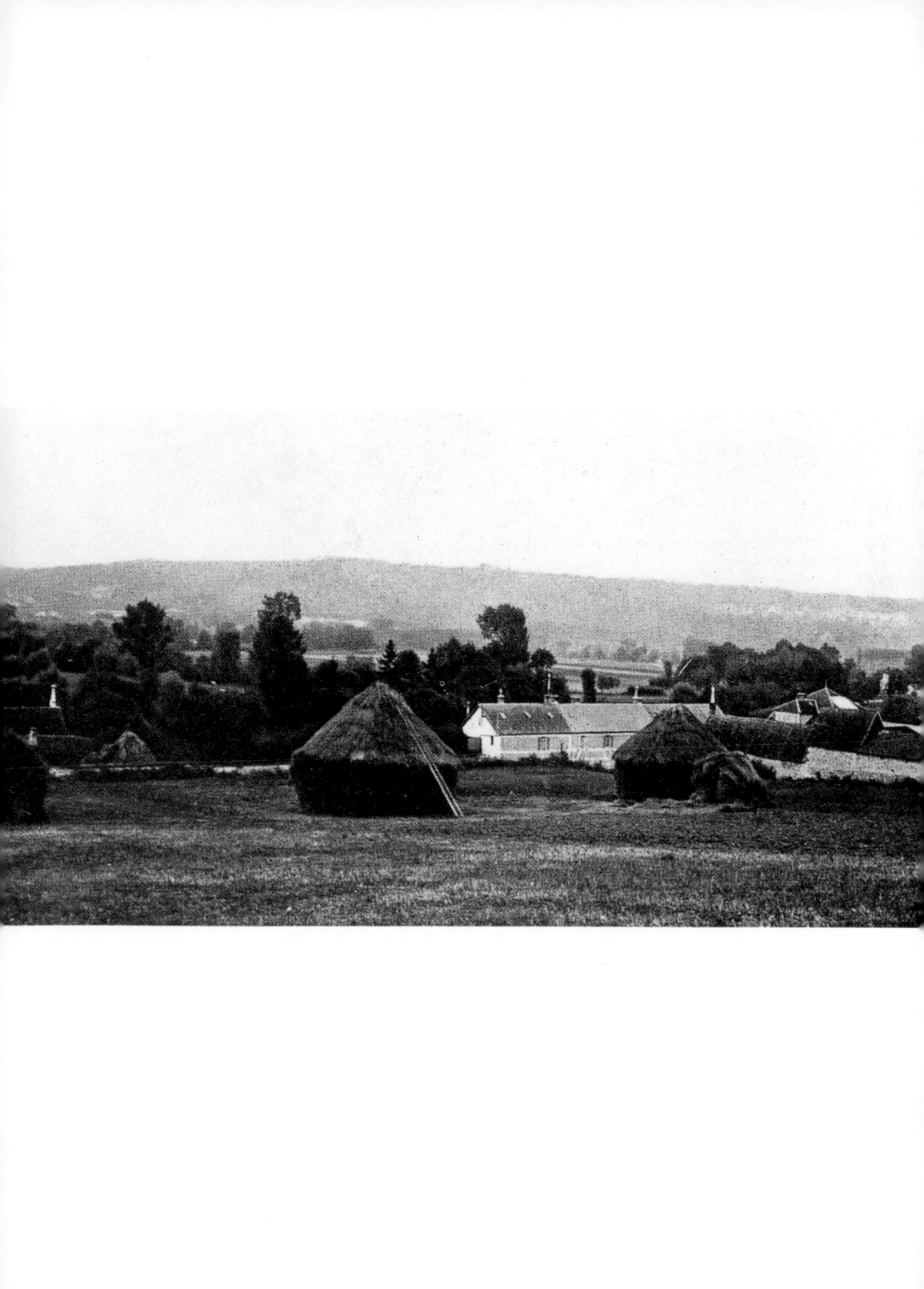

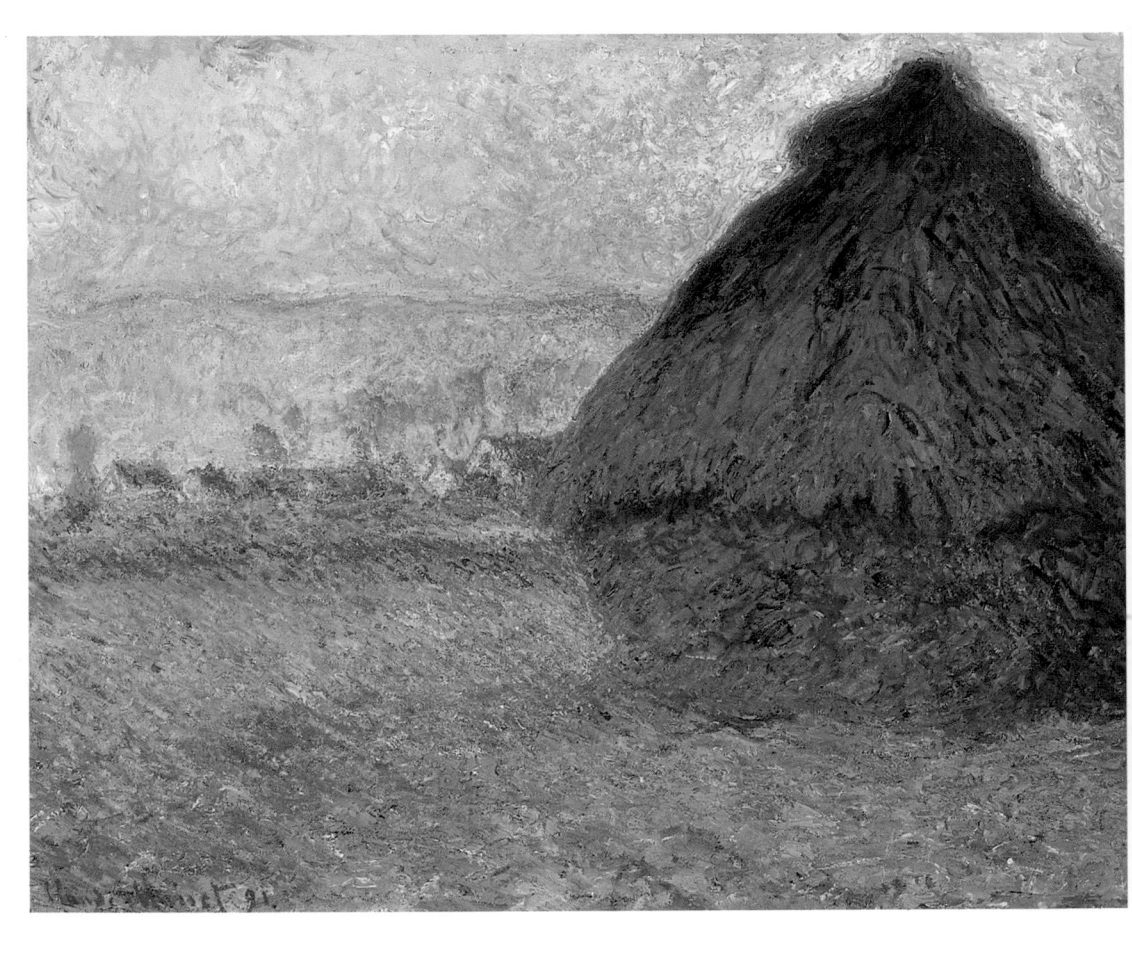

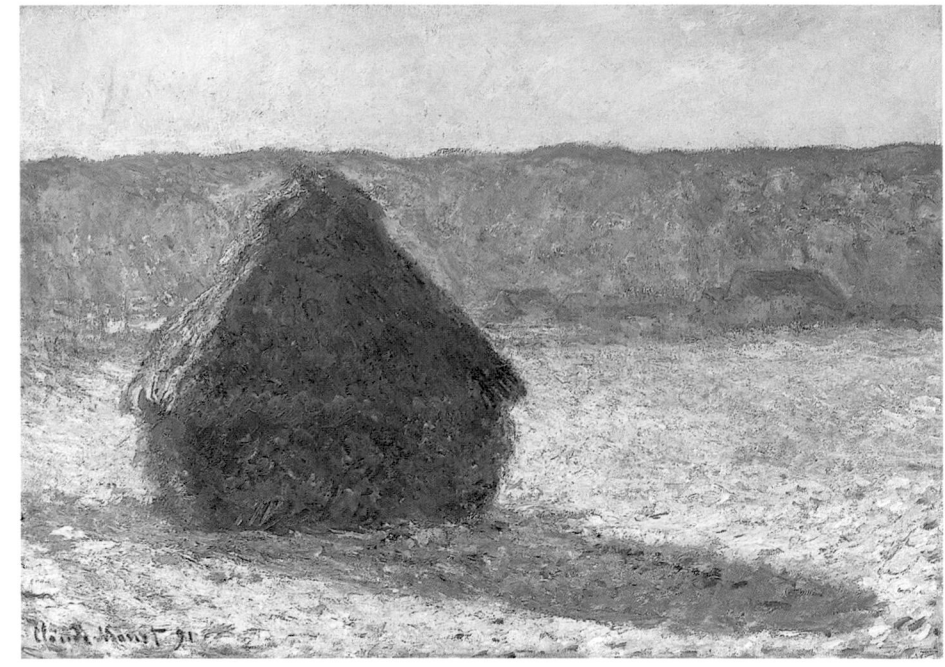

223 Opposite
Claude Monet,
*Grainstack
(Sunset),*
1891.
Oil on canvas;
73·3 × 92·6 cm,
28⅞ × 36½ in.
Museum of
Fine Arts,
Boston

**224 Above
right**
Claude Monet,
*Grainstacks
(Sunset, Snow
Effect),*
1891.
Oil on canvas;
65 × 100 cm,
25⅝ × 39⅜ in.
The Art
Institute of
Chicago

**225 Below
right**
Claude Monet,
*Grainstack
(Snow Effect),*
1890–1.
Oil on canvas;
65·4 × 92·3 cm,
25¾ × 36⅜ in.
Museum of
Fine Arts,
Boston

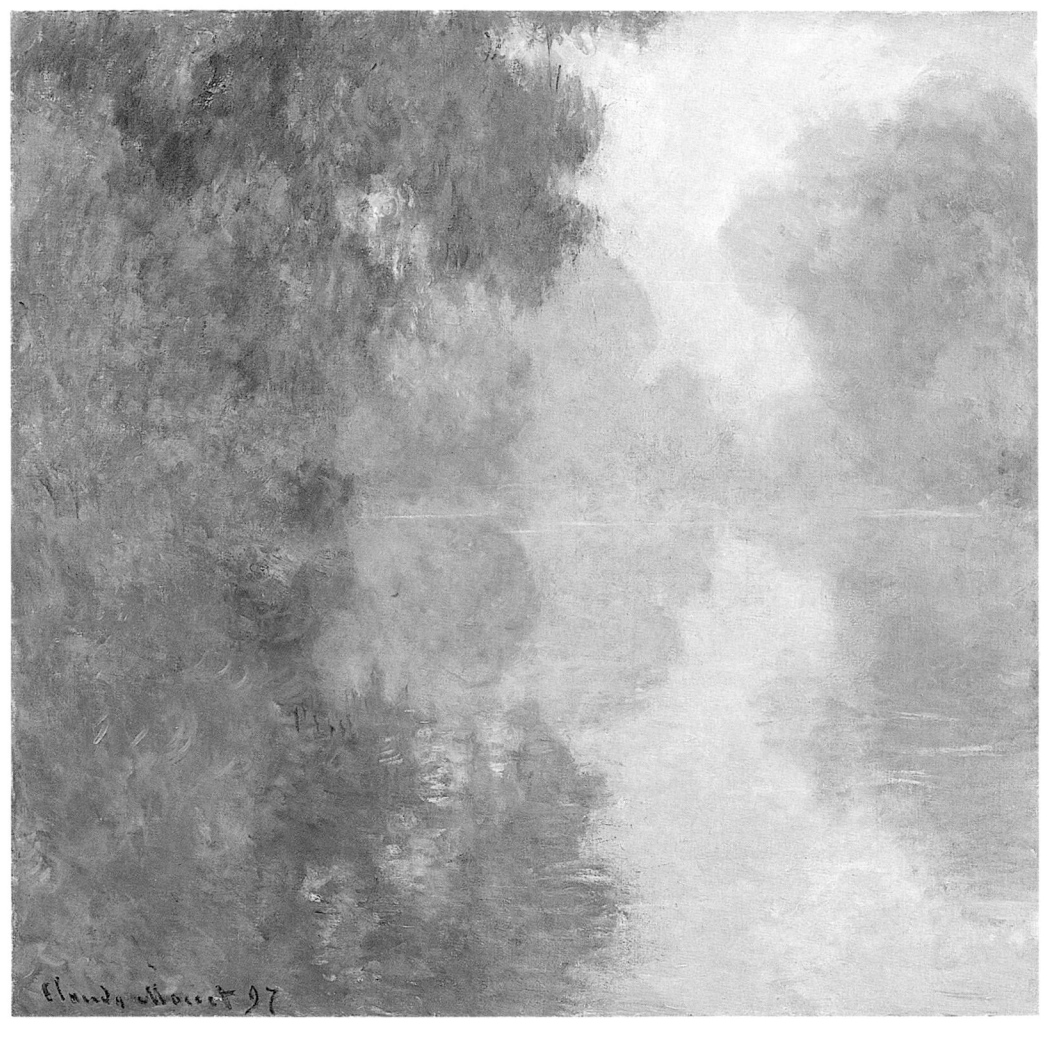

while its landscape setting runs almost the full spectrum from violet to white moving clockwise from the immediate foreground up and around to the sky (223).

While Monet certainly sought variety within the limited motif of the grainstack, there is nothing that suggests the careful sequentiality in either time or space of, for example, Degas's ten bather pastels of 1886. Only a much later series, *The Seine at Giverny, Morning Mists* (226), for which Monet awoke before dawn to be in his boat for sunrise (and for which the stretchers were reputedly numbered), might correspond to that concept. The myth undoubtedly grew out

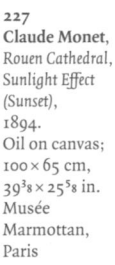

226
Claude Monet,
The Seine
at Giverny,
Morning Mists,
1897.
Oil on canvas;
88·9 × 91·4 cm,
35 × 36 in.
North Carolina
Museum of Art,
Raleigh

227
Claude Monet,
Rouen Cathedral,
Sunlight Effect
(Sunset),
1894.
Oil on canvas;
100 × 65 cm,
39³⁄₈ × 25⁵⁄₈ in.
Musée
Marmottan,
Paris

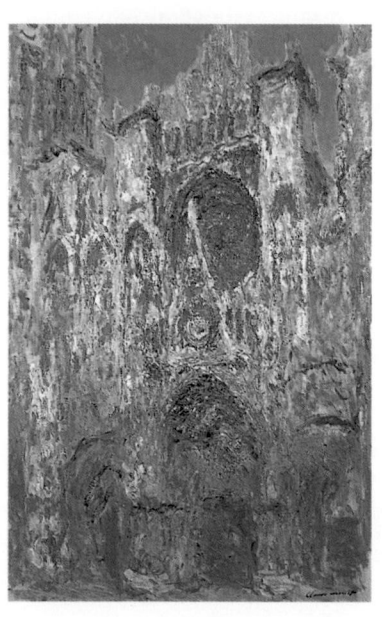

of Monet's own story about how one day the change in light was so striking that he had to stop work on a particular painting. Perhaps he sent his stepdaughter back to the house for another canvas, but other details that imply a regular system date from so long after the original incident that they are not credible. We do know, however, that Monet assembled paintings in his studio for reworking. For overall effect, he 'harmonized' them with each other, according to Geffroy. Although it never crossed his mind that the paintings should remain together, since private sales would have the opposite effect, at least when they were fresh they could make their impact as a decorative ensemble.

That the concept of series paintings was defined within an exhibition and marketing strategy should not deprive them of their power nor suggest the artist was any less sincere in his pursuit of equivalents for visual experience. To the contrary, a successful commercial strategy offered a secure framework for concentration on aesthetic and expressive issues. Nor should treatment of these thrilling works in a chapter on Impressionist collecting imply that marketing is their only or even primary meaning. The rhetoric surrounding them, orchestrated by Monet so that articles by critics of his choice appeared just prior to openings, stressed the artist's physical struggles and poetic achievement. There is certainly a ring of truth in claims that the grainstacks display 'the unceasing flow of changing sensations' or that the Rouen Cathedral paintings (227) reveal a 'colossal' 'phantom' filled with 'mysticism' and that Monet made 'stones vibrate' with vitality through his layered and heavily encrusted surfaces. Associations between the paintings and visionary states evoke Symbolist concepts of art and poetry, which heralded intimations of primal abstraction in later art. Their effects were sometimes compared to music. Monet himself asserted that he wished to paint 'as a bird sings'. It is as if the more art was exhibited as a commodity, the more its effects were called intangible and its portent philosophical – and the more the artist needed to believe in and act out a higher calling.

There are coherent series in the *oeuvres* of other Impressionists, as with Degas and Sisley. In the 1890s, Degas developed the sequential views he had begun with his bathers of 1886, either in single paintings, such as *Frieze of Dancers* of 1893–8, or in series, primarily of dancers (see Chapter 5). Sisley did a now mostly forgotten group of at least fourteen views of the old church at Moret, a series begun at least a year after Monet started his cathedrals. It was Pissarro who most completely adopted a serial practice comparable to Monet's, and with highly intriguing results, despite a very different focus on urban views rather than isolated motifs. Like Monet and Sisley, Pissarro had produced groups of paintings without at first conceiving of them as formal series. Among them were views of Rouen, from his visit to that city of 1883 (see Chapter 8). Pissarro was close to Monet and acutely aware of his development of series. But not until 1896, after enthusiastically viewing the Rouen Cathedral pictures, did he fully awaken to the potential for series paintings of city scenes. More than ever he was anxious to sell – to pay off debts, provide for his future and support his children, whose own artistic careers earned them little. Caillebotte's posthumous exhibition of 1894, where street scenes and balcony views drew favourable critical attention, encouraged Pissarro's interest. Other factors contributed to his choice, especially problems with his tear ducts that forced him to remain inside in all but the best weather. In the last ten years of his life, then, Pissarro produced over three hundred city scenes viewed from windows, in eleven different series. By 1903, at the age of seventy-three, he saw himself slaving away for his 'collectors'.

Looking out over the street or an urban river, one can watch a constantly moving spectacle without changing one's point of view. Rouen's industrial port along the Seine was Pissarro's first choice for a real series (228), pursuing more systematically a theme he knew well. A very different aspect of the city from Monet's ancient, grandiose cathedral, this place satisfied Pissarro's desire to maintain his own distinctness and remain loyal to his more modern, workaday character. Unlike Monet's late works, Pissarro's everywhere attest to observed human activity rather than concentrating so overtly on internal perceptions. Just as he explored rural labour as part of a value system he admired, Pissarro's emphasis in the majority of his Rouen views is productivity. Even most of Pissarro's Paris views, which correspond more to tourist sites, show the bustle of humanity, moving along boulevards in carriages and omnibuses or on foot in front of shops.

Pissarro's technique and his approach to composition are quite distinct from Monet's. Pissarro's small patches of paint relate more to the classic *plein-air* technique than the broad sweeps of underdrawing and heavily built-up layers that were evolving in Monet's paintings in the 1890s. Pissarro had backed away from the systematic Pointillism of the Neo-Impressionists, but he adopted some of their uses of colour to achieve vibrancy and to call attention to craft. Unlike Monet's geometrically simplified compositions, Pissarro's are complex and fragmented, and many of his figures seem individually observed so

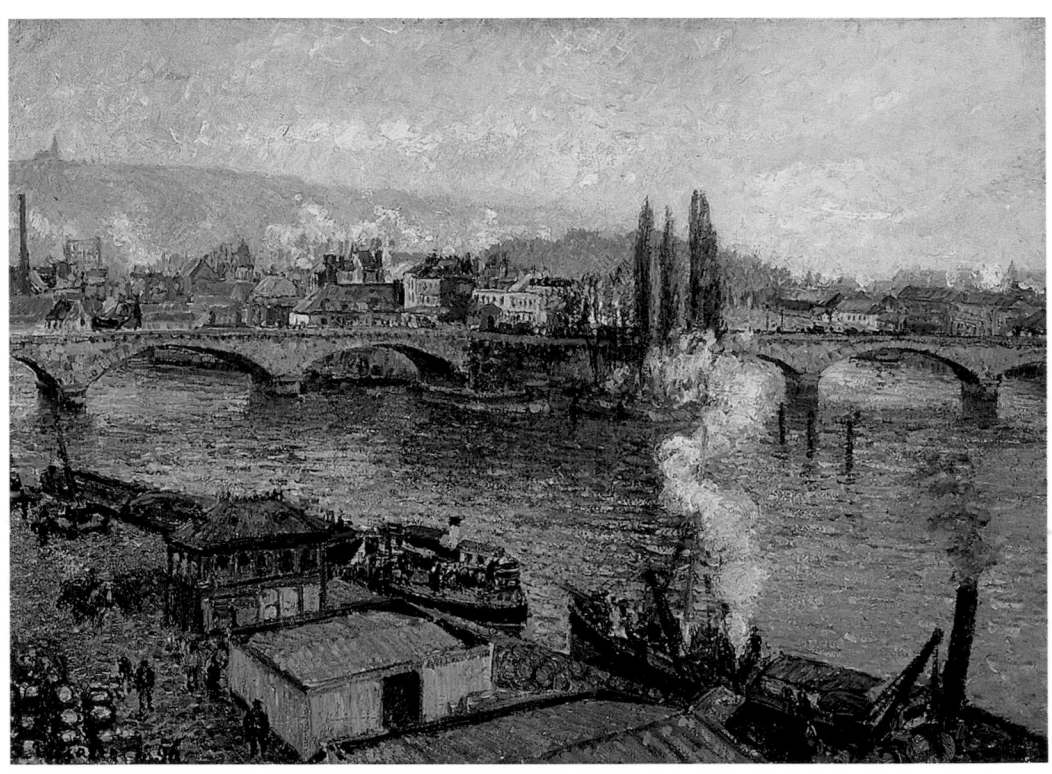

228
Camille
Pissarro,
The Stone Bridge
in Rouen,
Grey Weather,
1896.
Oil on canvas;
66·1 × 91·5 cm,
26 × 36 in.
National Gallery
of Canada,
Ottawa

as to reveal class or occupation, echoing his paintings of L'Hermitage or the market scenes of the early 1880s (see Chapter 3). In *La Place du Théâtre Français, Rain* (229), the traffic is comprised of tiny separate entities – conveying both the city's throbbing circulation and the individual's anonymity. Pissarro's atomistic dispersal of figures and events across his surfaces may thus be related to his anarchist beliefs. These paintings are politically different from Monet's, which use the absence of figures to imply a harmonious, vital and beneficent, if mysterious, world. Life in Pissarro's series is as hectic and down-to-earth as ever – paralleling his own intense effort and sense of isolation in the task he had undertaken of producing large numbers of multiple views. Although Monet's letters also reveal a comparable sense of struggle and exhaustion, the paintings do not. Yet nor do Pissarro's reveal the rote production and commercialism he had criticized in Monet's Antibes series. Maintaining a firm base in observation, yet predisposed to a certain conception of society, Pissarro no less than Monet reveals through the consistency of his variety a powerful creative consciousness at work.

In Monet's series, especially the poplars (231), geometric patterns and flattening produce an effect termed 'decorative' by contemporaries. This word, which is often now derogatory but emerged originally within Symbolist theory, referred to colours or shapes that went beyond descriptive function. Symbolists were seduced by words or forms that evoked dreams or revealed artistic self-consciousness. The abstraction within individual compositions – whether caused by Monet's simplifications or Pissarro's unfocused dispersal, dominates visual experience; the eye only later seeks closer examination of the parts. The same is true of the relationship between the ensemble and the individual canvas in a series of works. The primary impact of the whole is the cumulative result of repetition. Even to that degree, then, Pissarro's series, however peppered with urban and architectural detail, moves towards the new Symbolist aesthetic.

Impressionist prints deserve discussion for the further light they cast on the relationship of series to the market. Nearly all Impressionists produced prints, sometimes in considerable quantity and amazing

While different effects in print series were thus purely artistic creations, their naturalist look is nonetheless convincing. Hence, the print practices of Pissarro and Degas call into question once again the facile assumption that each effect of a painting from a series is tied primarily to observation. Although different moments certainly exist in nature – of which the *plein-air* artist would be acutely conscious – the strategy of individualizing multiples to enhance their value was an equally practised tradition of art.

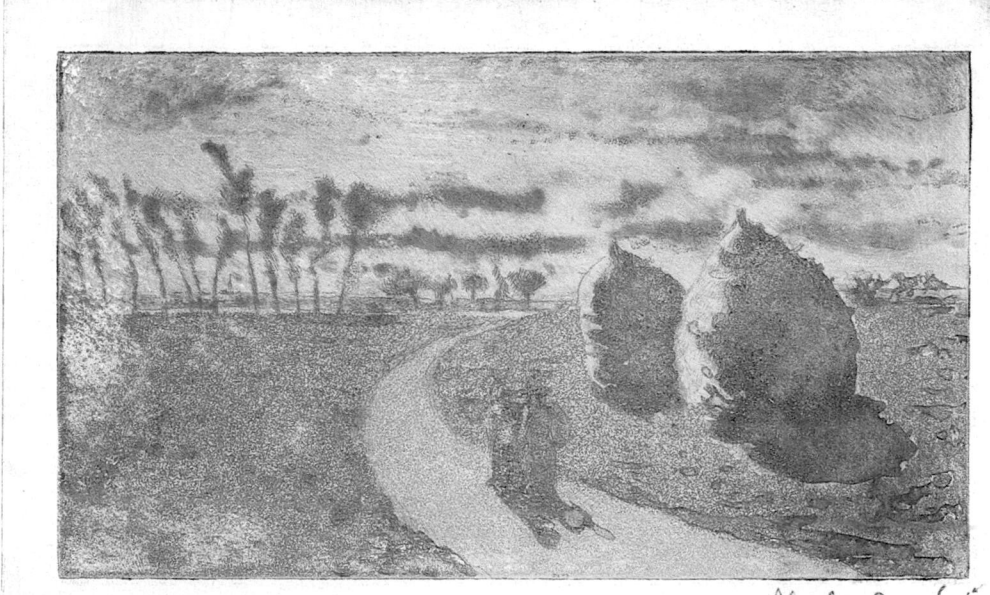

232
Camille
Pissarro,
*Twilight with
Haystacks*,
1879.
Aquatint with
etching and
drypoint in
green ink on
laid paper;
12·6 × 20·3 cm,
5 × 8 in.
National
Gallery of
Canada,
Ottawa

10

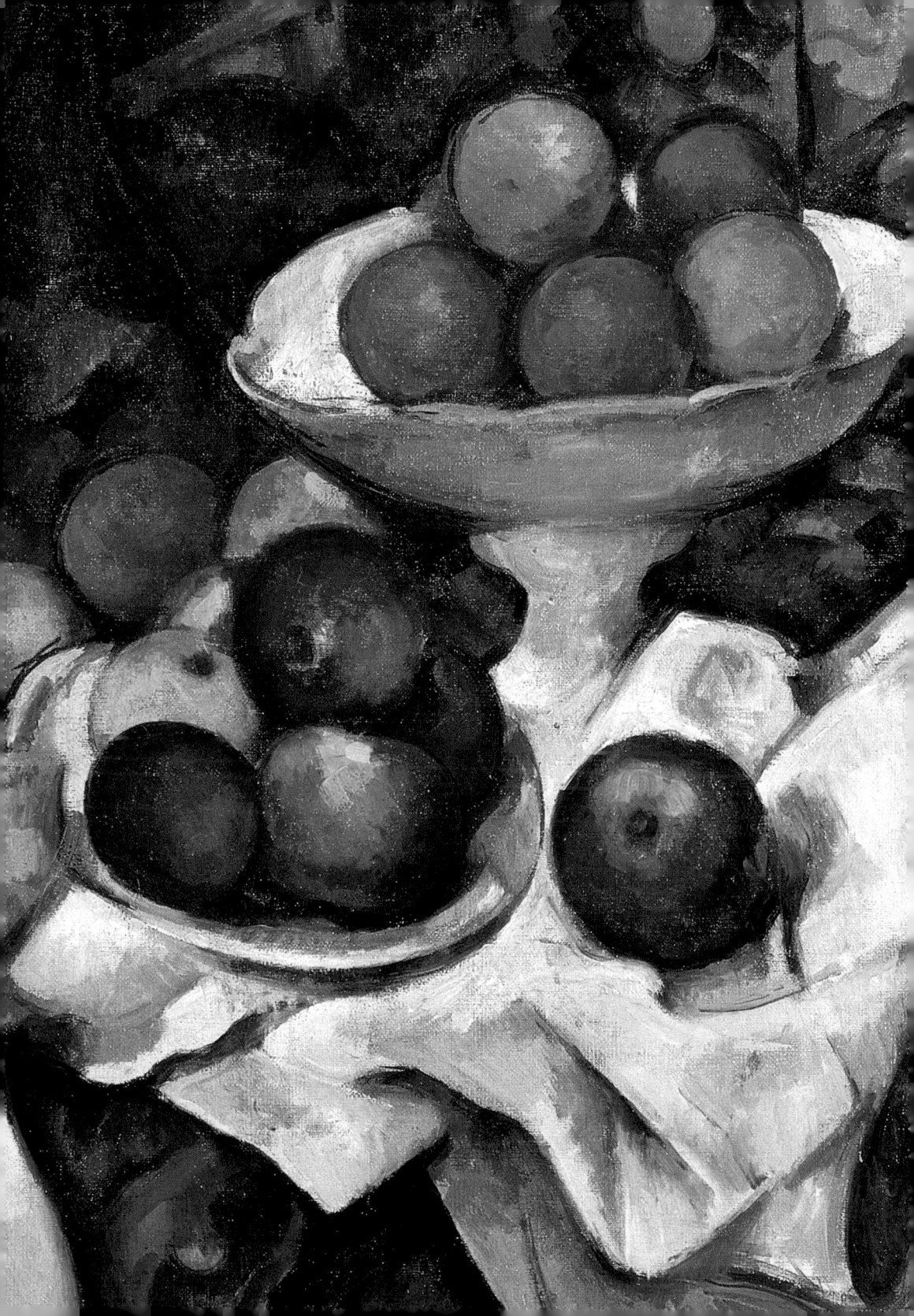

The career of Paul Cézanne brings into focus issues central to Impressionism, concerning both its definition, and how it developed over time. Cézanne generally kept aloof from his Impressionist peers, with the exception of Pissarro and Renoir, and his influence was slight until the 1880s. His work runs from early figure paintings emulating Delacroix, Courbet and Manet, to late *plein-air* series of Mont Sainte-Victoire. His maturity is usually placed in the 1880s, later than his colleagues, and he is often grouped within Post-Impressionism, a broad term invented after the fact to include painters as diverse as Cézanne, Van Gogh, Gauguin and Seurat. Post-Impressionism implies connections with Impressionism, but designates its aftermath. Most of the Post-Impressionists started in an Impressionist mode and defined their development in relation, often negative, towards it. None had been more deeply involved with Impressionism than Cézanne, and none so persistently respected its principles even while adapting to new concerns. Even Monet, who defined Impressionism for so many, appealed to Symbolist writers through his later work (see chapters 3 and 8); Cézanne's painting showed that potential early on. His Impressionism is therefore over-arching: firm in *plein-air* practices associated with naturalism while self-consciously asserting a personal vision. Cézanne was determined to achieve a convincing synthesis recognizing truths of both the eye and the mind.

Cézanne grew up with Émile Zola in the sunny southern town of Aix-en-Provence, less than twenty miles north of Marseille. These origins marked him, as did his family life. His father, a prosperous banker, was a stern and demanding patriarch whose overbearing influence, including resistance to his son's ambitions, certainly shaped the young artist's psyche. In 1861, Cézanne was finally allowed to leave for Paris, where Zola had already gone, with a mere 125 francs monthly stipend (the average worker earned about the same). By 1863, he had met Guillaumin and Pissarro at the Atelier Suisse, and was soon introduced to others. It was through him that Zola joined the circle and took on the defence of Manet's efforts. Like most members of Manet's group, Cézanne concentrated on figure painting until the early 1870s. We know through correspondence between Zola and his friends in Aix that Cézanne was considered both ambitious and erratic, powerful and tormented; he was moody and pathologically shy, easily offended and brusque.

His early style was dark, with heavy slabs of colour applied with a palette knife, as in *Portrait of Cézanne's Father Reading 'L'Evénement'* (the newspaper which published Zola's first articles on Impressionism; 235).

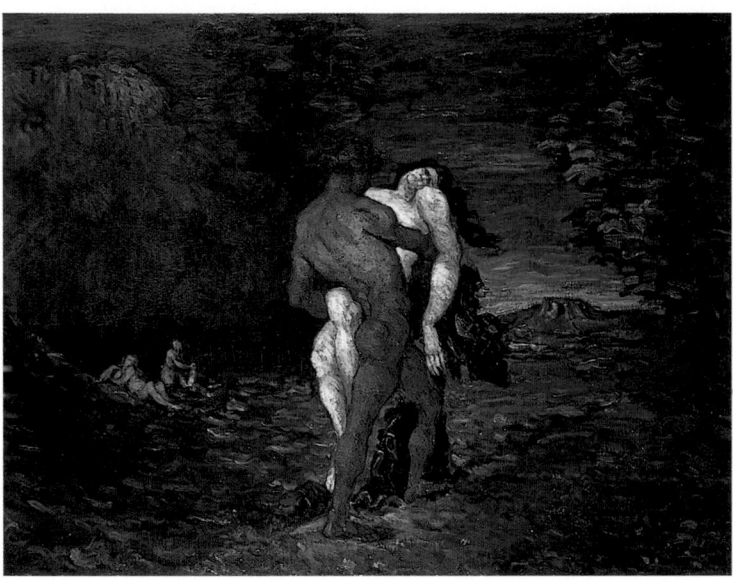

234
Paul Cézanne,
The Abduction,
1867.
Oil on canvas;
89·5 × 116·2 cm,
35¹⁄₄ × 45³⁄₄ in.
Fitzwilliam
Museum,
Cambridge

Its frontality and large size caricatured official portraiture, as its handling mocked academic finish. Cézanne later referred to this as his *style couillarde* ('ballsy style'), as if testifying to virility. His figure paintings often evoked violent sexual encounters – intriguing enough now to inspire psychoanalytic research. At that time, Cézanne's proclivities were certainly Baroque and Romantic, rather than Realist or modern. He was inspired by traditions resonant in the deeply Catholic Provençal culture, permeated, as evidenced by boyhood poems, with the lyricism of the regional bard Frédéric Mistral.

Cézanne's *The Abduction* (234) exemplifies his expressive use of colour and distortion of form as well as the importance of narrative. Mary Tompkins Lewis, who identified many of Cézanne's literary sources, found its theme in Ovid's story of Pluto and Proserpina – familiar reading for the classically educated youth. The painting's intense blue sky, rich oranges and greens echo the hues of Delacroix (see 19), whose death in 1863 provoked a resurgence of admiration. But its thick surface and overloaded brushwork (Cézanne abandoned the palette knife) go beyond Delacroix to the influence of Provençal painters such as Adolphe Monticelli (1824–86). Cézanne's *couillarde* style was the pictorial equivalent of a Provençal patois.

Cézanne made *The Abduction* in 1867 for Zola in the writer's house in the rue de la Condamine, the street where Bazille had his studio, not far from Manet's. Zola's defence of Manet and his followers was based on advocacy of Parisian modernity and working directly from nature. Judging from his work, Cézanne's problem was how to respond to such ideas without giving up commitments to private feeling or his Southern identity. At first, Gustave Courbet – man of the provinces *par excellence* – provided an answer, as implied in Pissarro's *Portrait of Paul Cézanne* (see 186). Ill at ease in Paris, Cézanne made a virtue of bohemianism and provinciality, growing his hair and leaving his beard untrimmed, while speaking in an exaggerated accent. He apparently refused to shake the elegant Manet's hand at the Café Guerbois under the pretext that 'I have not bathed for a week'.

The powerful *Portrait of Achille Emperaire, Painter* (236), which Cézanne defiantly submitted to the Salon of 1870, embodied his strategy. Emperaire, an artist he knew from Aix, was a dwarf whose large head, elongated hands and spindly limbs seemed the very antithesis of beauty – a caricature of 'Realism', so often dismissed as the art of the ugly. Dressing Emperaire in a house robe and long underwear was unseemly and deliberately provocative. Stylistically, the painting certainly evoked Manet, though in negative ways. Its shallow space and the frontality of the figure, painted in bold areas of colour outlined in black, refers to Manet's single figures of the 1860s, but substituting for his elegance and warmth a coarse, workman-like

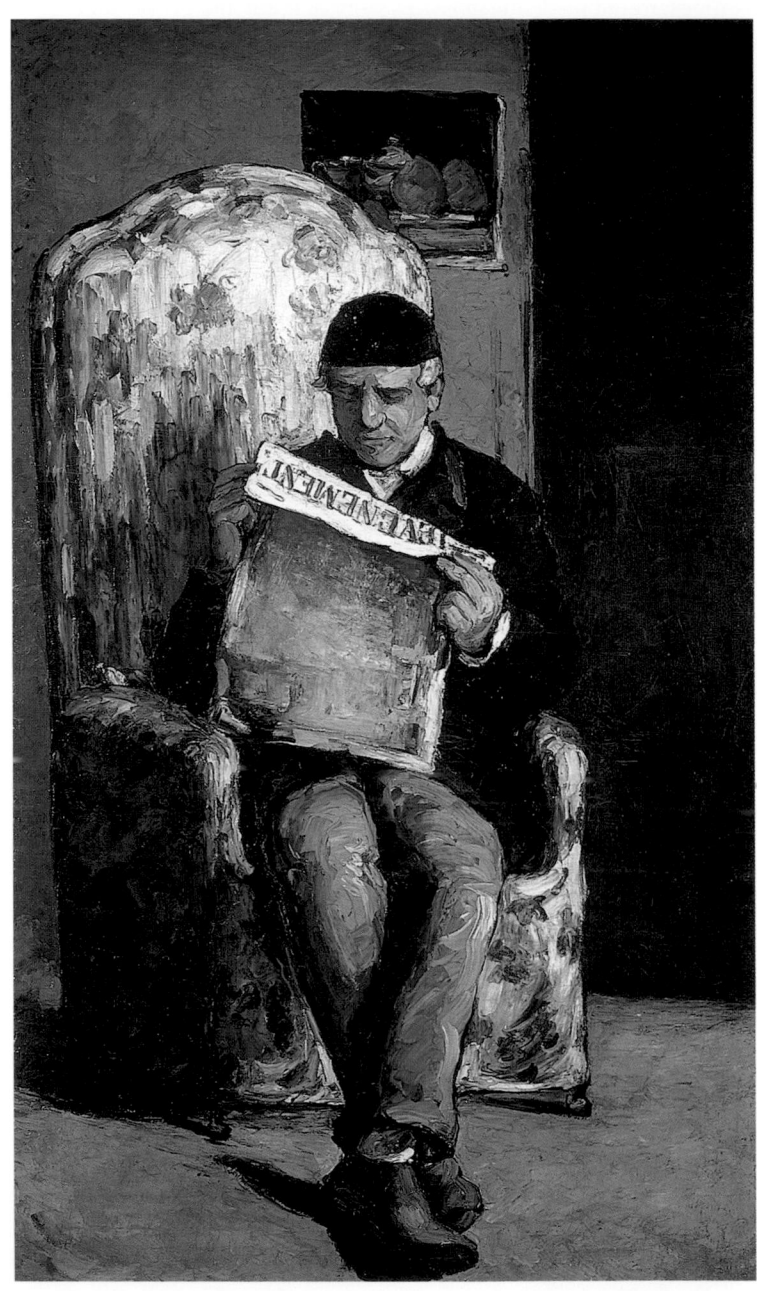

manner – again evoking Courbet. The stencilled lettering of Emperaire's name at the top of the painting echoes the news type in Cézanne's portrait of his father, as well as his assertive early signatures, suggesting an object of brute labour rather than Parisian chic. And instead of the urbane detachment of Manet's figures, Emperaire, with his wistful gaze and propped-up legs exudes a lethargy and fatalism far removed from the dandyish world of Paris boulevards.

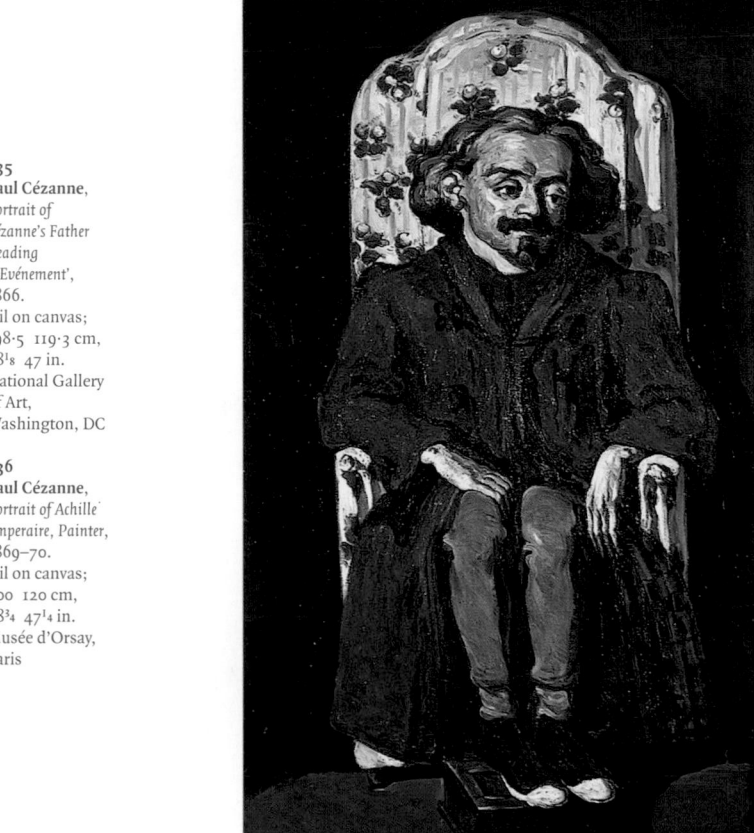

235
Paul Cézanne,
*Portrait of
Cézanne's Father
Reading
'L'Evénement'*,
1866.
Oil on canvas;
198·5 119·3 cm,
78¹⁄₈ 47 in.
National Gallery
of Art,
Washington, DC

236
Paul Cézanne,
*Portrait of Achille
Emperaire, Painter*,
1869–70.
Oil on canvas;
200 120 cm,
78³⁄₄ 47¹⁄₄ in.
Musée d'Orsay,
Paris

How was Cézanne's work related to Impressionism? Unlike Renoir and Monet, who quickly adapted to Parisian values, Cézanne could not paint a world he neither knew nor seemed able to adopt as his own. It would seem that the fragile self-esteem resulting from a domineering father forced Cézanne to compensate with a rigid, fortress-like identity. Cézanne made several paintings in direct response to two of Manet's seminal works. Yet the more Manet's example became compelling, the more Cézanne flaunted critical distance – to say nothing of his disdain for academic Salon art. The frequent awkwardness and incompleteness of his early works may have their origin in such negativity. For example, beginning in c.1868–70, Cézanne produced some paintings, including a *Temptation of Saint Anthony* and a *Pastorale*, which evoke Manet's *Déjeuner sur l'herbe* (see 30) and foreshadow his own persistent theme of bathers. They allude to visual fantasies of sexual availability and include a self-resemblant figure as the voyeur. Concurrently, Cézanne did some compositions showing a nude woman on display as in a brothel. He called one version of this scene *A Modern Olympia* (237) when it was shown at the first Impressionist exhibition of 1874. In this and another of the same title, a self-resemblant figure again contemplates a lavishly displayed courtesan, accompanied by flowers and a servant, evoking prostitution from contemporary literature as well as Manet's *Olympia* (see 34).

237
Paul Cézanne,
A Modern
Olympia,
1873.
Oil on canvas;
46 × 55 cm,
18¹⁸ × 21⁵⁸ in.
Musée d'Orsay,
Paris

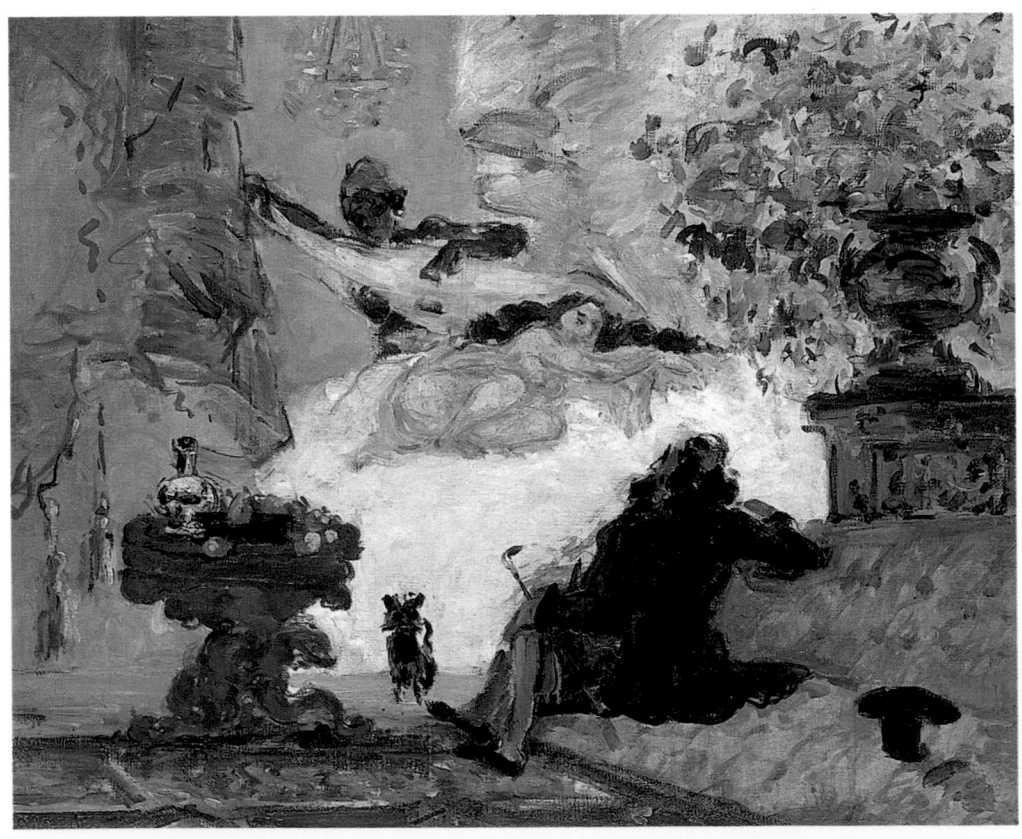

Cézanne's persistent inclusion of the self-portrait/observer is the principal difference (among others) from Manet's versions of such themes and offers the key to his commentary on them. For the staged Realism of Manet's painting, Cézanne substitutes a more ostentatiously personal art of self-conscious anxiety and desire, one that is literate as well as sexually vehement, if less pictorially suave. Manet, Cézanne once said, 'lacked temperament'. By contrast, in an interview of 1870, Cézanne claimed that he himself was the only one who dared to 'paint as I see, as I feel – and I have very strong sensations'. He later compared himself to the legendary Frenhofer of Balzac's *Unknown Masterpiece* (1832), the short story of an artist driven mad by inability to give form to his ideal. *A Modern Olympia*'s setting with its draperies and couch directly evokes Frenhofer's failed masterpiece. The autobiographical element is reinforced by Cézanne's liaison during these years with his model, Hortense Fiquet, whom he hid from his disapproving father, despite their eventual marriage and the birth of a son. Scenes like Manet's *Le Déjeuner sur l'herbe* and *Olympia* had defined early Impressionism. By remaking them his way, Cézanne insisted both on the subjective element in their visual-ization and on links to contemporary cultural debates, implying unsubtly that Manet's affectations of detachment (however we understand their origins in social unease) were either unauthentic or false. In his writing on Manet, Zola advocated, even more than modernity, the expression of an artist's temperament. In 1867, he affirmed: 'What interests me as a man, is humanity ... what touches me ... is to find in each [artwork] an artist, a brother, who shows me nature with a new face, with all the power or gentleness of his personality.' Zola's theories may well have originated with Cézanne; at the very least they were ideas the two of them had shared.

The range, variety and power of Cézanne's early paintings, which has barely been suggested here, shows the struggle and persistence of an ambitious artist groping for identity. Concurrent with the early 'expressionist' figure paintings, which he continued to paint until about 1872, Cézanne produced a number of still lifes and landscapes. As a youth in Aix, he took his painting materials on walks with Zola and their friends, a common practice in balmy Provence; in Paris, he learned to take *plein-air* painting seriously through Pissarro. In the late 1860s, we saw the Batignolles School (including Manet, Bazille, Renoir, Morisot, Sisley and even Monet) focused on figure paintings for the Salon. But Cézanne's relations with the group had never been especially warm or loyal. Only Pissarro, trained under Corot, and Sisley were as yet committed landscapists. During Cézanne's stays at the Jas de Bouffan, his family's estate in Aix, and then in L'Estaque, where he escaped from conscription with Hortense during the Franco-Prussian War, Cézanne turned increasingly to landscape.

Following the war, Pissarro, who was some ten years older than his Impressionist cohorts, became the central figure in what is sometimes known as the School of Pontoise. Cézanne's work there, at Pissarro's invitation, became the basis for what is often called an 'apprenticeship'. His attraction to Pissarro can be explained by the rural character of Pissarro's work, which was amenable to Cézanne's regional identity. We can also surmise that Cézanne was drawn to an older figure whose authority was unthreatening and whose lessons bolstered self-esteem. In 1874, he wrote to his mother: 'Pissarro has a high opinion of me, and I have a high opinion of myself.' The two collaborated with mutual respect (see 186 and 238).

Throughout Pissarro's correspondence one of the most repeated concepts is 'sensation', the word used by Castagnary to argue that Impressionist art went beyond surface perception (see Chapter 1) and cited by Cézanne in his 1870 interview in support of his pictorial daring. Indeed, as a 'cautionary example' of 'subjective fantasies' run wild, Castagnary pointed to the young Cézanne. By contrast, Pissarro found positive features in Cézanne's painful self-consciousness, while directing him away from the quasi-literary vehicles of narrative figure painting towards landscape. *Plein-air* painting was the place where truth to nature and to self converge. At the beginning of Cézanne's friendship with Pissarro, the latter was moving towards Monet's painting style of contrasting colours, although still adjusted for tonal unity. Cézanne's use of contrasts had a more expressionistic purpose, even in early landscapes, which are animated as much by sweeping movement as by bold colour areas in the early Impressionist mode. A fine example, probably inspired by Guillaumin's industrial views (Cézanne lived next to him in Paris for a while), is *The Railway Cutting* (239), an excavation outside Aix, with Mont Sainte-Victoire in the background. But collaboration with Pissarro convinced Cézanne of the need to sublimate extremes by making the act of painting itself a compelling practice. That is, he discovered through Pissarro how to make the immediacy of nature's visual impact convey personal ambition and intensity. Years later, Cézanne stated that 'I seek through painting': the *plein-air* dialogue between observation and representation became a means to experience the world as well as an instrument for self-expression.

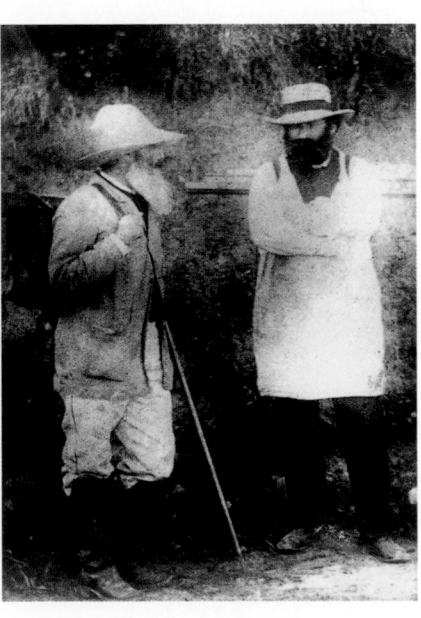

Cézanne consistently referred to himself as Pissarro's 'student'. Yet it is hard to find clear examples of painting the same motifs because Cézanne always refused to imitate others. An early landscape he considered successful enough to show at the first Impressionist exhibition demonstrates what he learned from the older painter as well as how they differed. *The House of the Hanged Man* (named after a local suicide; 240) falls into the category of roadside views, common in Impressionism, and of which Pissarro was a master. However, Cézanne's choice of a steep hillside with a rapidly descending road

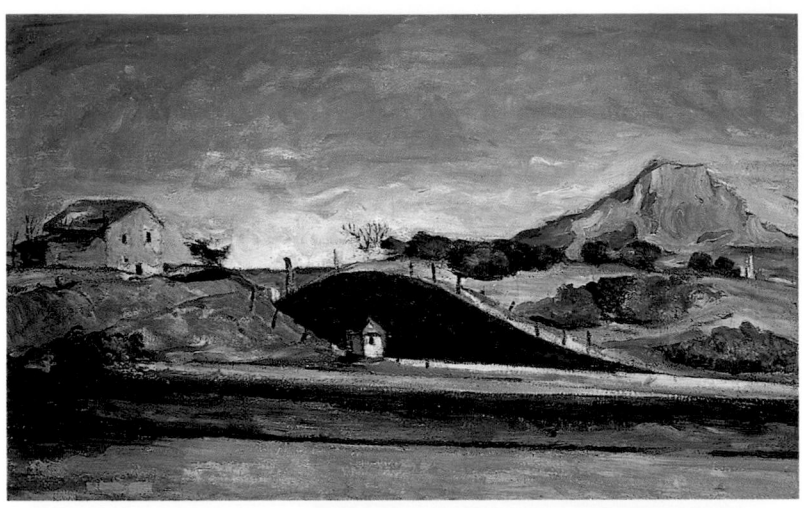

239
Paul Cézanne,
The Railway Cutting,
1869–70.
Oil on canvas;
80 × 129 cm,
31^1⁄$_2$ × 50^3⁄$_4$ in.
Neue Pinakothek,
Munich

240
Paul Cézanne,
The House of the Hanged Man, in Auvers-sur-Oise,
c.1873.
Oil on canvas;
55 × 66 cm,
21^5⁄$_8$ × 26 in.
Musée d'Orsay,
Paris

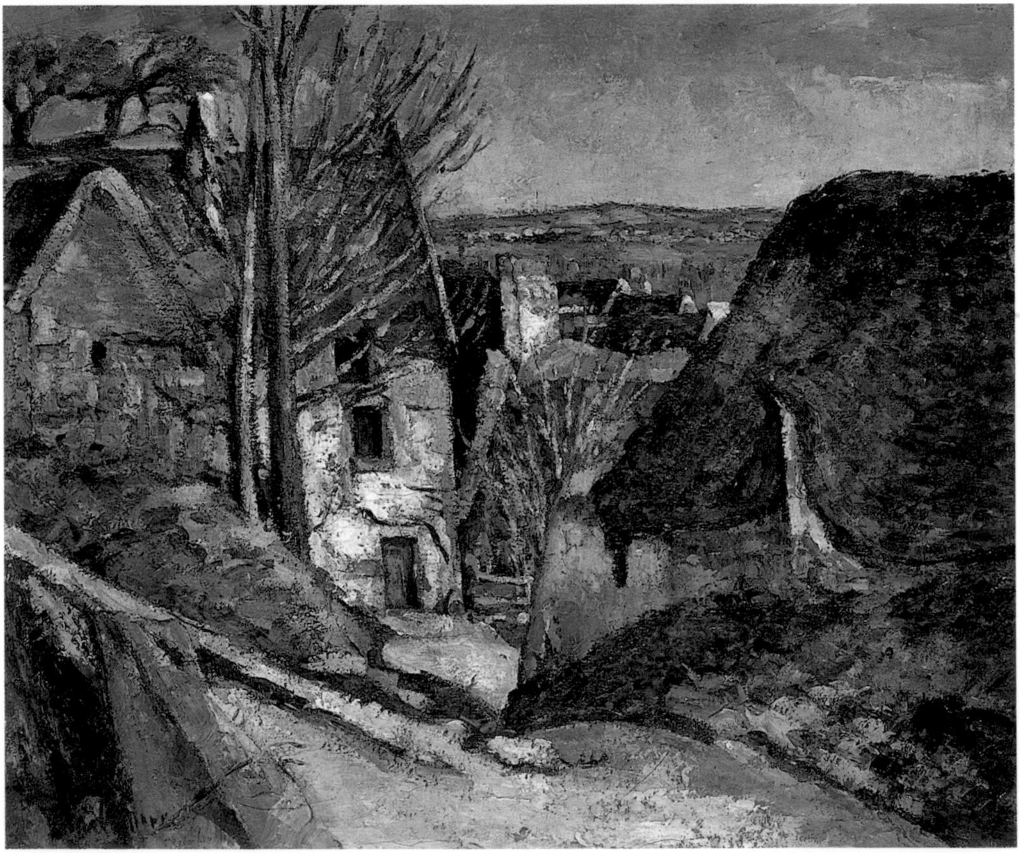

and his creation of a funnel-like space differs disconcertingly from the more level ground and flatter compositional effects of Pissarro (see Chapter 4). Technically, Cézanne has abandoned broad, thick strokes and bold areas of colour for the juxtaposed touches used by the *plein-air* painters. However, as exemplified by the greens to the left in his composition, they are often applied with a heavier hand than his colleagues. Favouring sculptural and spatial effects, Cézanne eschews the elegant transparency of Monet and his followers. While his small dabs signify *plein-air* directness, Cézanne's method included build-up and overpainting, processes associated with protracted thought and deliberate effort, rather than pure instinct and fugitive spontaneity. Finally, Cézanne's landscapes typically exclude figures, as if distancing his scenes from Impressionism's temporal specificity. When he paints figures in landscapes, they are never incidental, as they often seem in Impressionist landscapes; in his many bather compositions they serve to reflect upon the figure within nature.

Yet the figure is hardly absent from Cézanne's development of the 1870s. On the contrary, two models in particular were available to him for close scrutiny – himself and his wife. Some of the characteristics of his landscapes are also evident in figure painting in the late 1870s, for example, in a powerful *Self-Portrait* (241), which is undated and unfinished, hence (as with so many of his pictures) a study piece. Here, carefully juxtaposed patches of closely related hues create the modelled effect of traditional art. Cézanne has redeployed Pissarro's search for tonal unity for purposes of spatial and volumetric description. A focal point is the nose, for which Cézanne created what looks like a contour through shaped areas of paint. When grey, they signify the absence of form, just beyond the bridge, in order to distinguish it from the cheek behind. Here, Cézanne focused on problems quite different from his peers. Intensely studying the roundness of his balding head constituted a powerful act of self-encounter and emotional containment removed from the modern world, as it is represented in Impressionist paintings of specific times and places. Although appropriating techniques associated with direct observation of the moment and defiance of academic convention, he pared away their colouristic exuberance and fragmentation. Here, then, may lie an early example

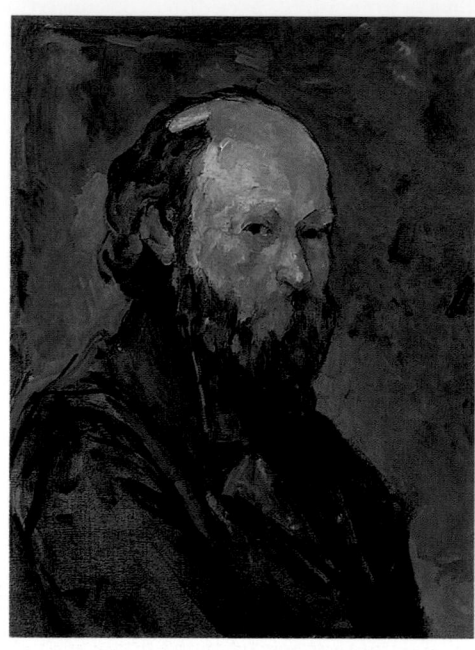

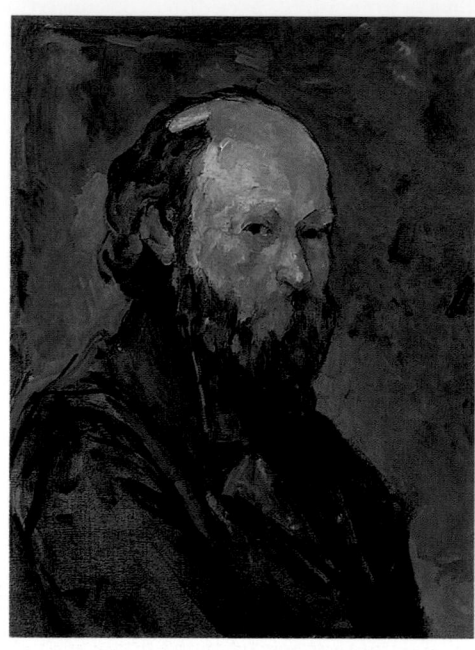

241
Paul Cézanne,
Self-Portrait,
c.1877.
Oil on canvas;
60·3 × 46·9 cm,
23³⁴ × 18¹₂ in.
Phillips
Collection,
Washington, DC

242
Paul Cézanne,
*Madame Cézanne
in a Red Armchair*,
1877.
Oil on canvas;
72·5 × 56 cm,
28⁵₈ × 22 in.
Museum of
Fine Arts,
Boston

of Cézanne's aim, stated later in life, 'to make of Impressionism
something solid, like the art of the museums'. Impressionism
provided the technique through which one could, as Cézanne was
also known to say, 'realize one's sensations' – translate experiences
derived from observation directly into concrete colour equivalents.

How different at first glance seems the brightly coloured portrait
of *Madame Cézanne in a Red Armchair* (242), with its interlocked forms
and flattened patterns, accentuated by wallpaper motifs, the blue-
green skirting board and the rectangle of window at the upper left.
Hortense's elegant blue smock, wide ribbon and striped silk dress
create a bold visual presence, even though her simple coiffure,
demure expression and folded hands suggest quiet and reserve.
Close examination reveals a patchwork of colour juxtapositions that
simultaneously convey breathtaking economy and a workman-like
construction. In the striped dress, which occupies nearly one third
of the picture area, the illusion of silk catching light coexists with a
sensation of coarse sculptural build-up to produce an effect that
combines skilful observation and wilful construction of form.
Similarly, Cézanne's bright colours echo the effects of Impressionist

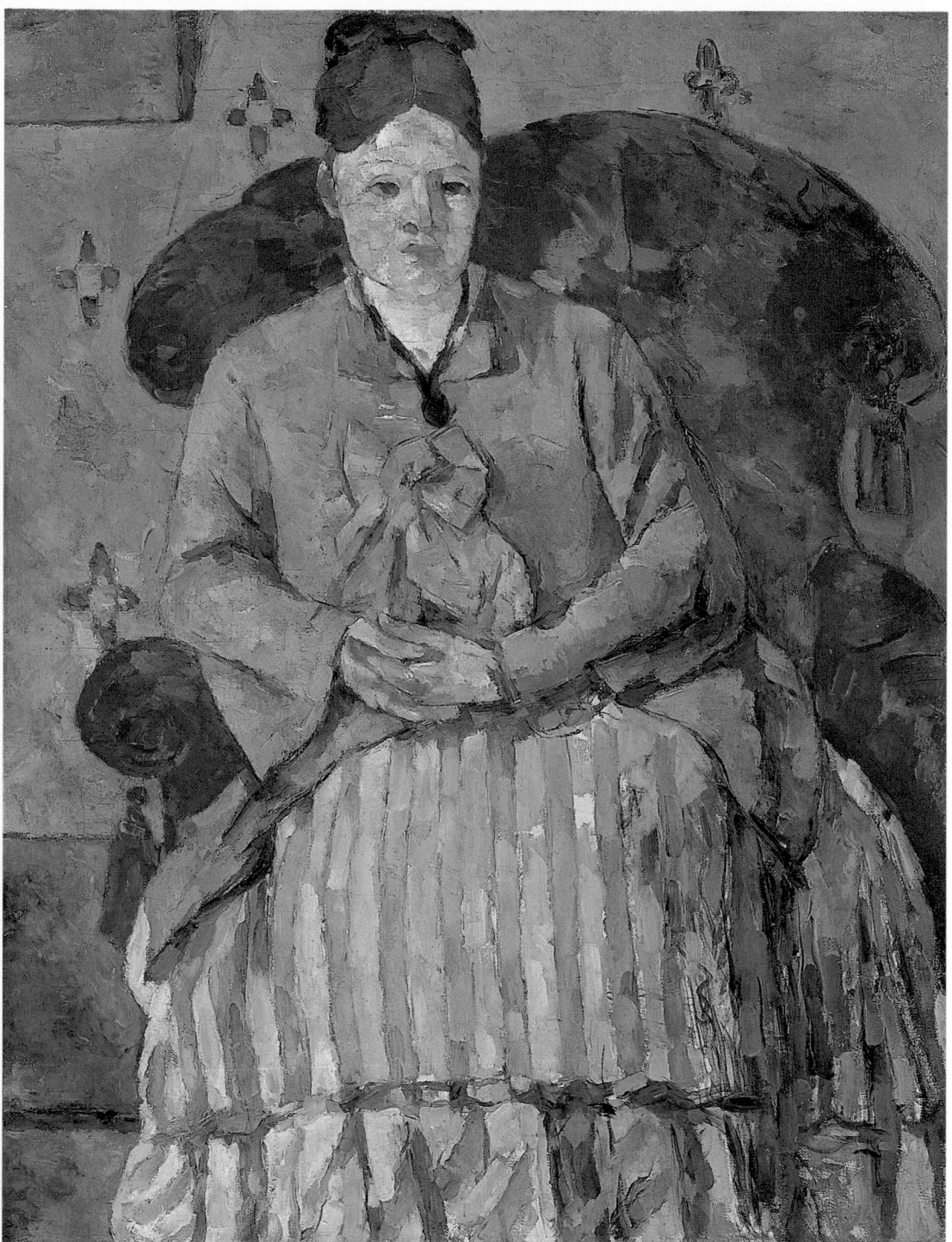

vitality, familiar by the mid-1870s, while determining abstract areas of studied design.

In the late 1870s, Cézanne began moving towards a more systematic brushstroke, labelled the 'constructive stroke' by art historian Theodore Reff. In *Turn in the Road, Pontoise* (243), series of short, juxtaposed parallel strokes, often changing in hue, are applied with a flat brush and usually positioned at angles to the surrounding area to construct larger patches. These ensembles of strokes imply planes in space while producing a simplification and abstraction that accentuate design. Their derivation from the hatching marks used in drawing and sketching reinforces our sense of the artist's direct contact with natural form, an effect enhanced by colour, which, though limited in range, is rich, subtle and immediate. Yet, at the same time, their reference to hand movement emphasizes the artifices of technique. In either case, they are a graphic device, through which Cézanne exercised a craftsman's control over any turbulent impulses that might remain within himself. The eye is led directly to the heart of the composition by the road, the rightward curve of which is picked up by a stone wall. Attention is concentrated in the middle ground, where a row of houses emerges from behind trees to the left, moving in deliberate procession across the field of vision. This methodical progression and Cézanne's systematic handling create a sense of mapping based on protracted observation, not limited to a single vantage point, with a concomitant effect of duration across time. Structural emphasis and spatial compression are especially pronounced where the painter overlaps colours which pertain to leaves, branches and houses, forms which are ostensibly separate spatially. One is constantly reminded of small acts of painting, yet the picture coheres as an image of the world.

Comparison with Pissarro's *Côtes des Boeufs at L'Hermitage* (see 96) shows how Cézanne has systematized a similar interweaving of forms in the middle ground to produce a far more consciously composed effect. We note the cerebral abstraction of Cézanne's grass, rocks, foliage and sky. The absence of figures confirms our sense of his withdrawn, solitary life. Like any *plein-air* landscape, *Turn in the Road* is thus an artificial construct derived from observation (as are most paintings), but it is one in which that status and our sense of the artist's personal comprehension now seem at least as significant as naturalistic effect. Similar interests lay behind Pissarro's experiments of the early 1880s and his attraction to Neo-Impressionism (see Chapter 8). In those developments, then, Cézanne was clearly a pioneer.

That Cézanne knew he was innovating is suggested by his fear that Paul Gauguin, who had joined Pissarro in Pontoise in 1879, would 'steal' his new technique – one which clearly differentiated Cézanne's work from the Impressionists of around 1880 at a time of general reassessment among them. Cézanne's powerful early influence over Gauguin is inescapable, exemplified by numerous works in which the latter used patches of parallel strokes, despite his brighter colours and greater flatness (244). Indeed, when Gauguin told his friend Émile Schuffenecker that art is an 'abstraction derived from nature', he could have been voicing ideas discovered in Cézanne's work. Their interaction suggests the porous borders between Impressionism and Symbolism, with which Gauguin is now primarily identified and which Monet approached through the increasing self-referentiality of his later work. The subjective element to the 'impression' or 'sensation' was always a potential; the emphasis in any dialogue between nature and self – pretending for the moment they are separable – may shift over time.

Crucial for understanding Cézanne's relationship to Impressionism is still life, a genre that he helped transform into a modernist paradigm, but which at the time was less marketable than landscapes or portraits. Cézanne did more of them than any of his peers, since he was little concerned with sales: for twelve years from 1877 to 1889, he exhibited almost nothing publicly. (He made more drawings than most Impressionists, too, except the traditionally trained Degas, and he did not always finish works or sign and date them even if complete.) His father's wealth allowed him to paint unhindered, a situation he accepted in spite of their difficult relationship. These conditions isolated him from the vicissitudes of modern life that were such a reality for the other Impressionists. So Cézanne's reluctance

243
Paul Cézanne,
Turn in the Road,
Pontoise,
c.1881.
Oil on canvas;
60·5 × 73·5 cm,
23⁷⁸ × 28⁷⁸ in.
Museum of
Fine Arts,
Boston

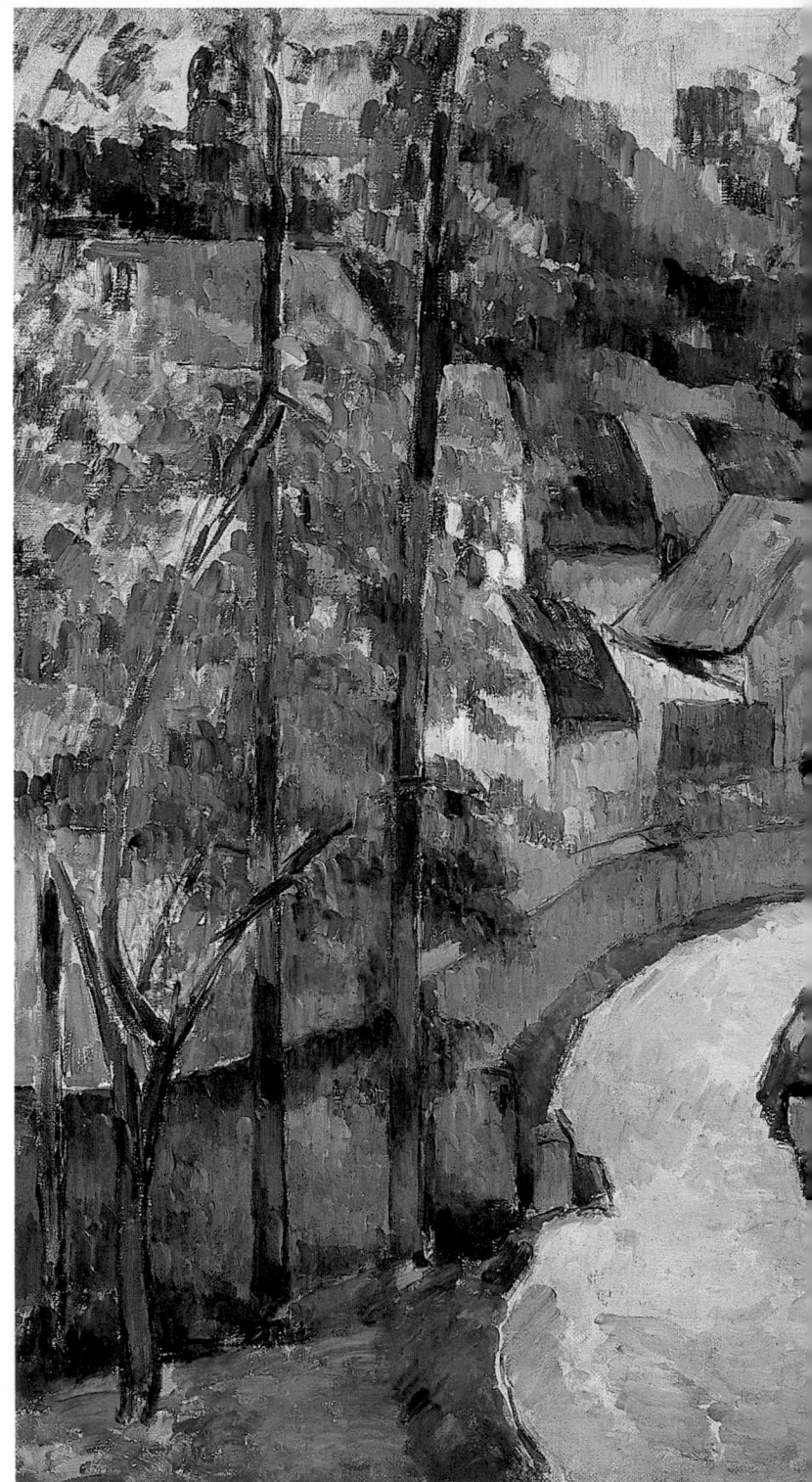

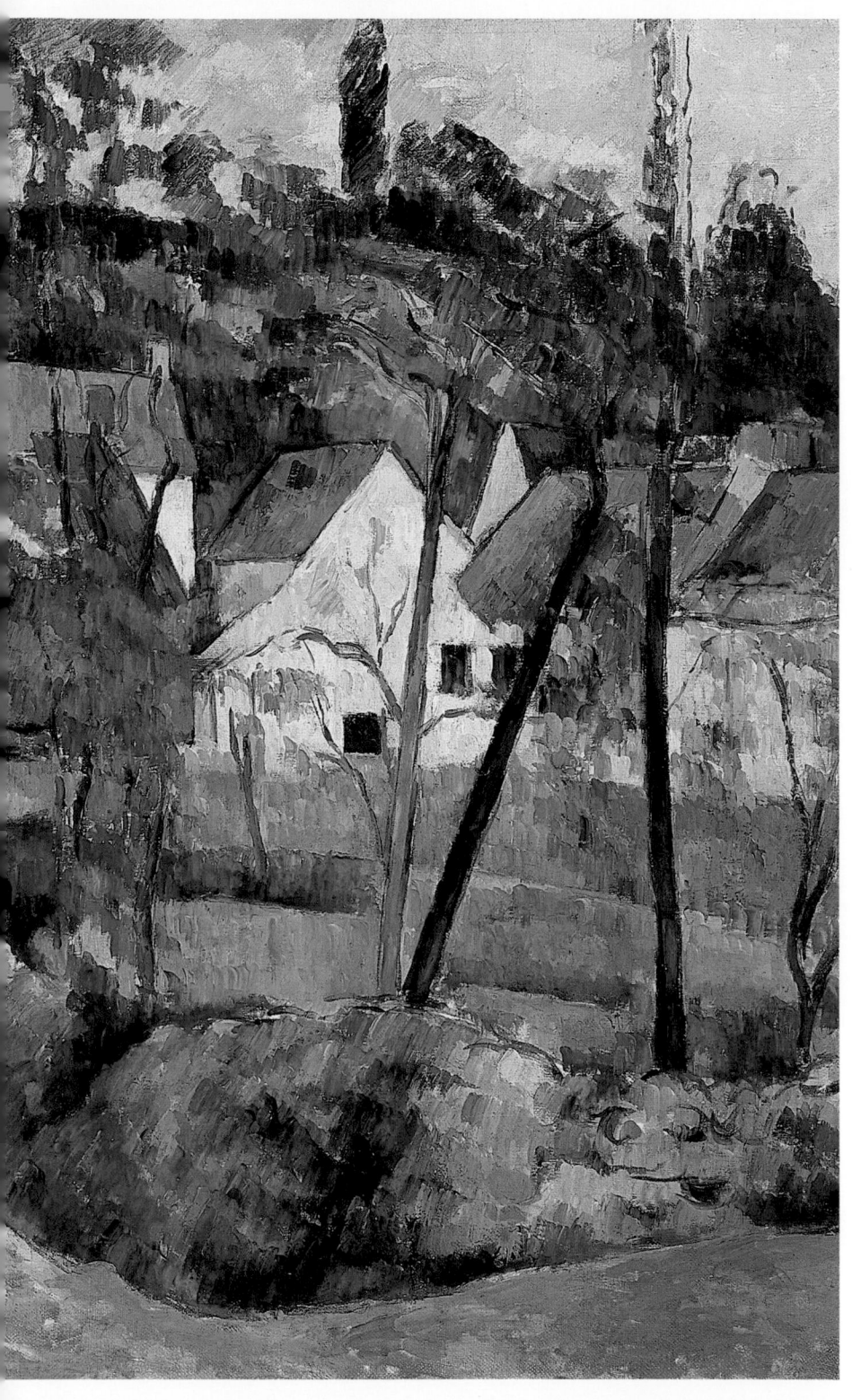

to broach modernity, his privacy and inwardness, may stem from unwillingness to expose the contradiction underlying his pose as workman-like outsider. The artificial and hermetic aspect of still life – a solitary studio practice – attracted him. Compositional arrangements the artist himself could predetermine removed accident as a factor in representation, yet in a way that respected observation.

In a landmark essay, the art historian Meyer Schapiro held that still life for Cézanne was a site of converging fantasies and aspirations,

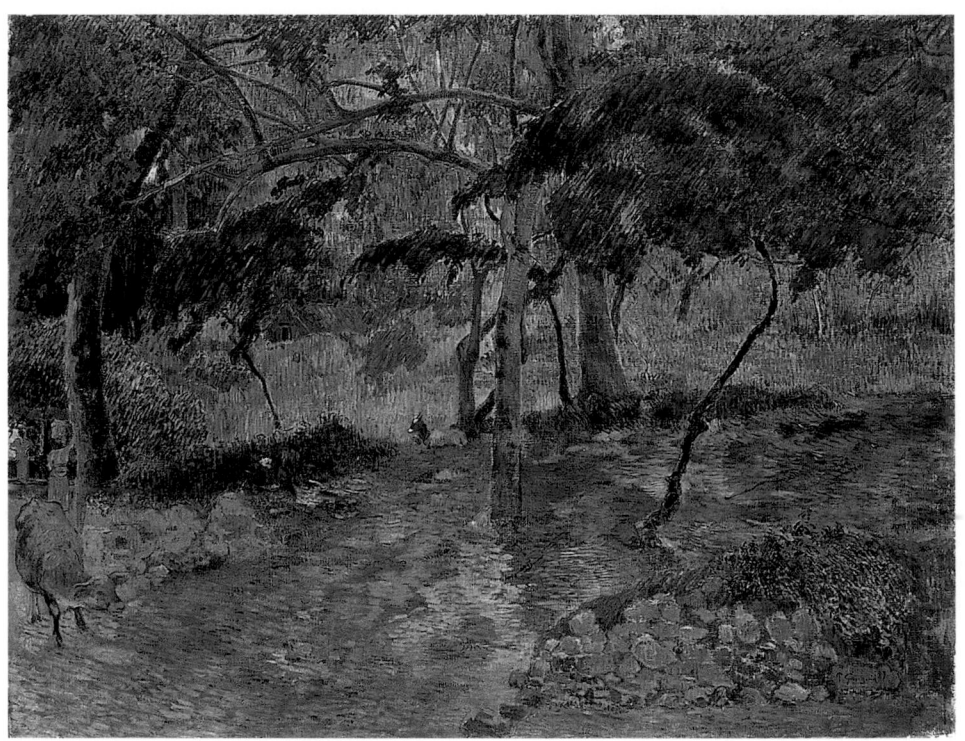

ranging from the erotic to the literary and philosophical. Citing the role of apples as offerings in classical myth and in rituals of love, Schapiro explained their prominence in Cézanne's still life – and their formal plenitude – as a displacement or transference of both physical desire and artistic ambition. Even if Cézanne's conscious programme was to eliminate those emotions he had flaunted in his early years, sublimation still informs the shape and meaning of his results. The painter's early still lifes feature primarily man-made objects in arrangements that echo Dutch art, with its tradition of symbolism. One early masterpiece of about 1870, *The Black Clock* (245), looks to the pictorial example of Manet (himself an admirer of the Dutch), though Cézanne as always painted far more thickly. He assembled an odd assortment of objects to create a mood of mystery and angst: the extraordinary seashell, like a living fossil with a voracious, red-lipped mouth, and Zola's handless modern clock evoke a transience and precariousness that contradict his domestic trappings of wealth and technology.

By the later 1870s, however, Cézanne used still life, like self-portraiture, as a vehicle for pictorial development. He probably turned to it in Pissarro's own house; Pissarro's *Still Life: Pears in a Round Basket* (246) could be a model both for Cézanne's reconception of still life as naturalistic rather than symbolic and for his simple, rigorous structures (though Pissarro's high-keyed colours maintain a primary relationship with the more decorative Monet and Renoir). Cézanne's *Still Life with Compotier* (247) is a central piece in this development, as its owner Gauguin, whose favourite it was and who reproduced it in the background of his *Portrait of a Woman* of 1890, must have understood.

244
Paul Gauguin,
*Martinique
Landscape:
The Pond*,
1887.
Oil on canvas;
90 × 115 cm,
35⅝ × 45¼ in.
Neue
Pinakothek,
Munich

Apples with their brilliant colours and repeated forms are Cézanne's focal point, with other objects framing, holding or standing by them, offering a comparison. In homage to the Dutch tradition he discarded, Cézanne placed a paring knife in the foreground. In Dutch paintings, such instruments doubled as symbols and illusionistic devices, projecting out towards the viewer to enhance both realism and precariousness. Here, the knife is fully embedded in the painting's surface, nearly touching the edge in a way that flattens the composition into a visibly pictorial structure rather than illusionistic opening. A similar effect is achieved at the very centre where what seems to be a shadow or a hole, which we might at first regard as indicating a corner or folding table leaf, extends vertically into the composition (a structural similarity to *Turn in the Road*; see 243). Connected to it by a napkin, the compotier's base picks up this axis and rises with curvaceous thrust from its hidden footing. The wallpaper oscillates between flat background and indeterminate space with floating foliage. Foreground and

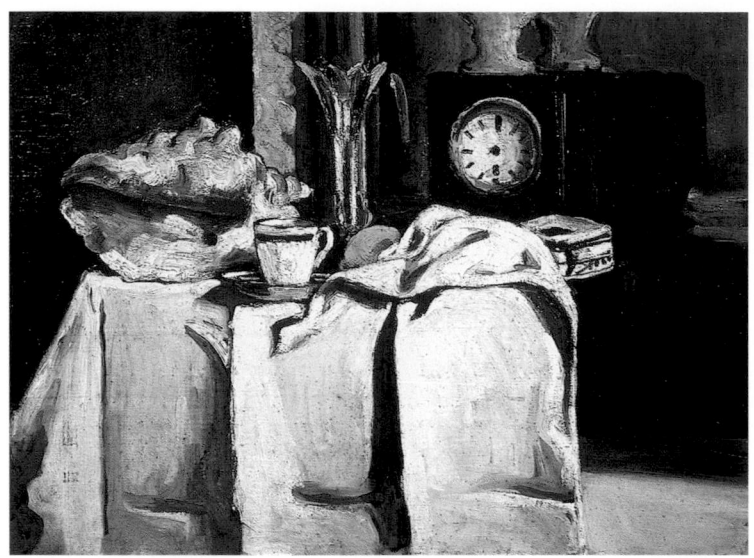

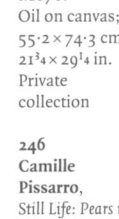

245
Paul Cézanne,
The Black Clock,
c.1870.
Oil on canvas;
55·2×74·3 cm,
21³⁴×29¹⁴ in.
Private
collection

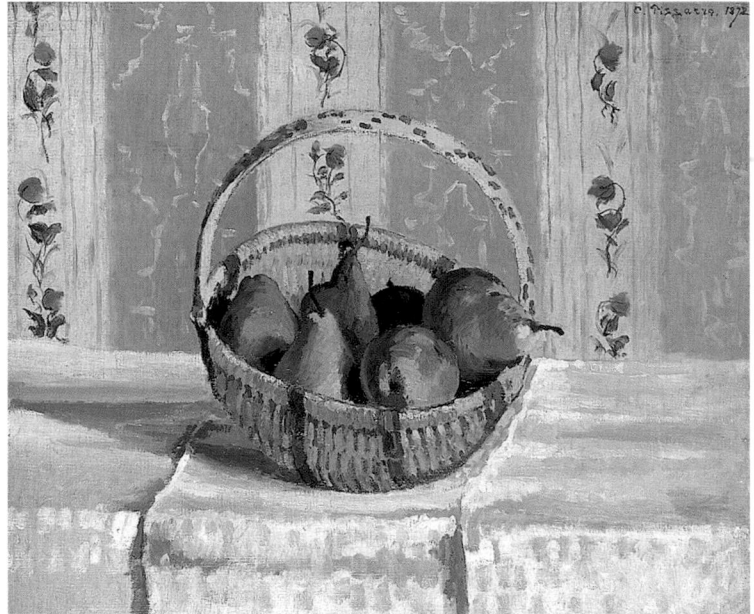

246
**Camille
Pissarro**,
*Still Life: Pears in
a Round Basket*,
1872.
Oil on canvas;
45·7×55 cm,
18×21⁵⁸ in.
Private
collection

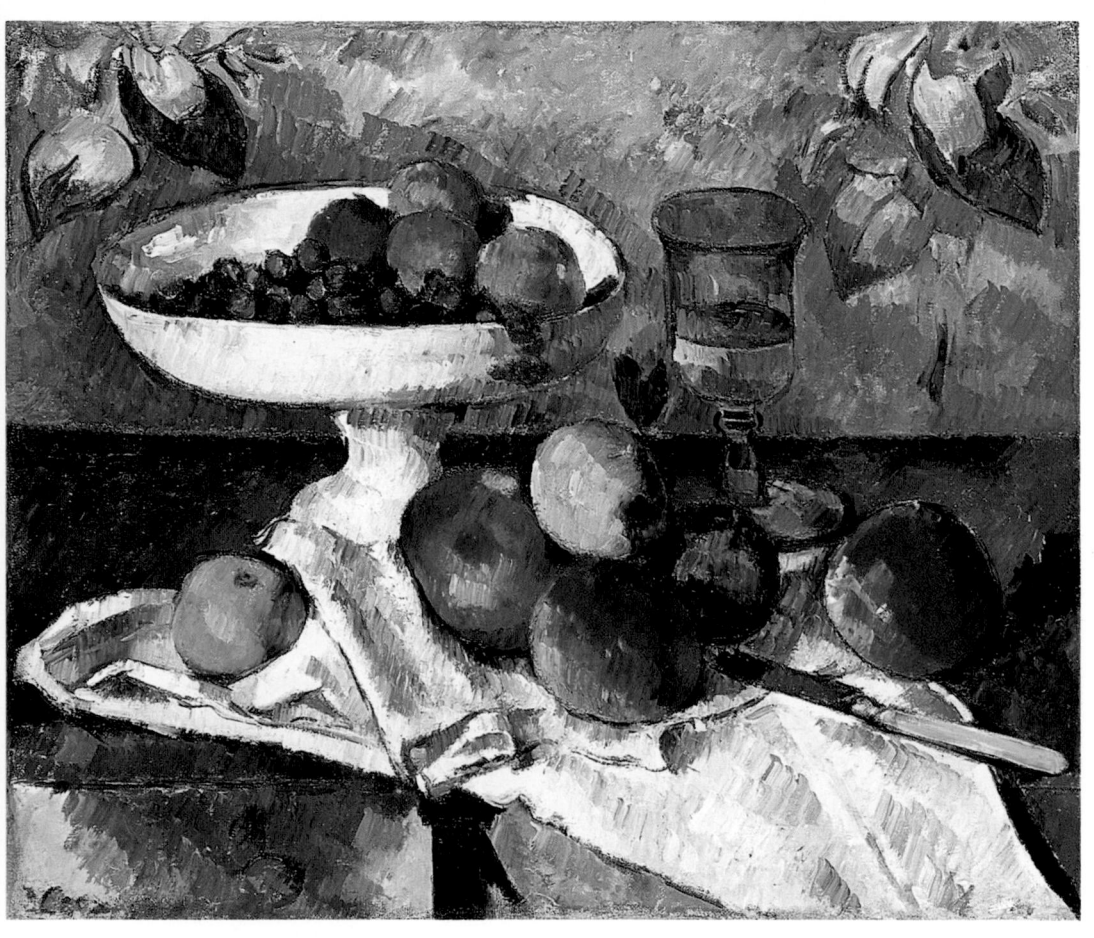

247
Paul Cézanne,
Still Life with
Compotier,
c.1879–82.
Oil on canvas;
46 × 55 cm,
18 × 21⁵⁄8 in.
Private
collection

middle ground are most effectively linked by the half empty glass to the right of the compotier, provoking a double-reading between flatness and volume, transparency and opaqueness. Much of the surface reveals the parallel hatchings we recognize as Cézanne's trademark. On the apples themselves, progressions of hue and modulations in angling contribute to the modelling effect. Yet one remains entirely conscious that they are constructed in paint, of a physical existence both emanating from and calling forth human attention. They are references to apples rather than apples themselves – removed from their context in reality as a natural food (defamiliarized, certain critics would say) to reveal the interdependence of their existence with our perception of them.

In Cézanne's still lifes, napkins and tablecloths seem arbitrarily arranged; the latter at once cradle the objects and yet often also execute their own perfectly unreasonable and exuberant display of folds and bunches (see 250), the purpose more pictorial than domestic. As such, they recall the drapery formations in Old Master figure painting. In *Still Life with Compotier*, rather than merely a cotton or linen cloth upon which the still life is arrayed – a role paralleling the painting's canvas support – the tablecloth is treated as a still-life object in its own right, one whose tactile surface and volumes (note how its shadows create sculptural relief) are among the most prominent ones within this work. Like the arrangement of the apples, this tablecloth is set for purposes of contemplation. Conjoining flattening effects of wallpaper and table-top with the putative roundness of fruit dish and wine glass, the still life becomes a hermetic or self-contained, sense-defying performance of perceptual acrobatics.

While our wonder at these relations substitutes for traditional narrative, we can nonetheless argue their basis in reality. Is not the tilting table, pressing objects forwards to our apprehension, merely the pictorial equivalent – call it 'lived perspective' – of our own attentiveness to middle ground and the multiple viewing points of protracted contemplation? Is it not the consequence of looking past objects in our path and ignoring peripheral regions in order to concentrate on the object of our intent? That related departures from so-called normative perspective might be found in Japanese art, folk imagery or the work of other Impressionists could only have encouraged Cézanne to find a use for them uniquely and disconcertingly his own.

That reciprocity between the eye (the 'I') and the object is, of course, the stuff of philosophy, here distilled from the original conundrum of Impressionism as both an objective and a subjective art. In academic circles, still life had been the lowest order of painting, for mere inanimate objects were thought incapable of evoking the grand human ideals of history, literature or metaphysics. Except for certain rare and gifted artists, still life was where novices honed their skills. Yet Zola had praised Manet's approach to figure painting as essays in the purely pictorial values of still life, which he considered untainted by the 'ideas' of narrative paintings that continued to be prominent at the Salon. Indeed, the only Impressionist to have practised still life as consistently as Cézanne was Manet. As a studio exercise *par excellence*, still life enabled the artist to narrow his focus to what is sometimes called pure painting – to seemingly neutral questions of form and representational technique, the grammar and linguistics of art. Yet Cézanne can also be said to come full circle, to the very fundamentals that constitute philosophy. For the still life object embodies nature as colonized by human perception, while still life arrangement thematizes human dominance by reference to manipulation. Phenomenologists, who study that which appears real to the mind, especially Maurice Merleau-Ponty, have written lengthy and enlightening texts on the processes of perception and representation evidenced through Cézanne. For Merleau-Ponty, still life was primordial. In his essay *Cézanne's Doubt* (1948), painting is a means to bridge physical distance and psychic anxiety created by questions about whether existence is anything but a mental state:

The painter recaptures and converts into visible objects what would, without him, remain walled up in the separate life of each consciousness: the vibration of appearances which is the cradle of things. Only one emotion is possible for this painter – the feeling of strangeness – and only one lyricism – that of the continual rebirth of existence.

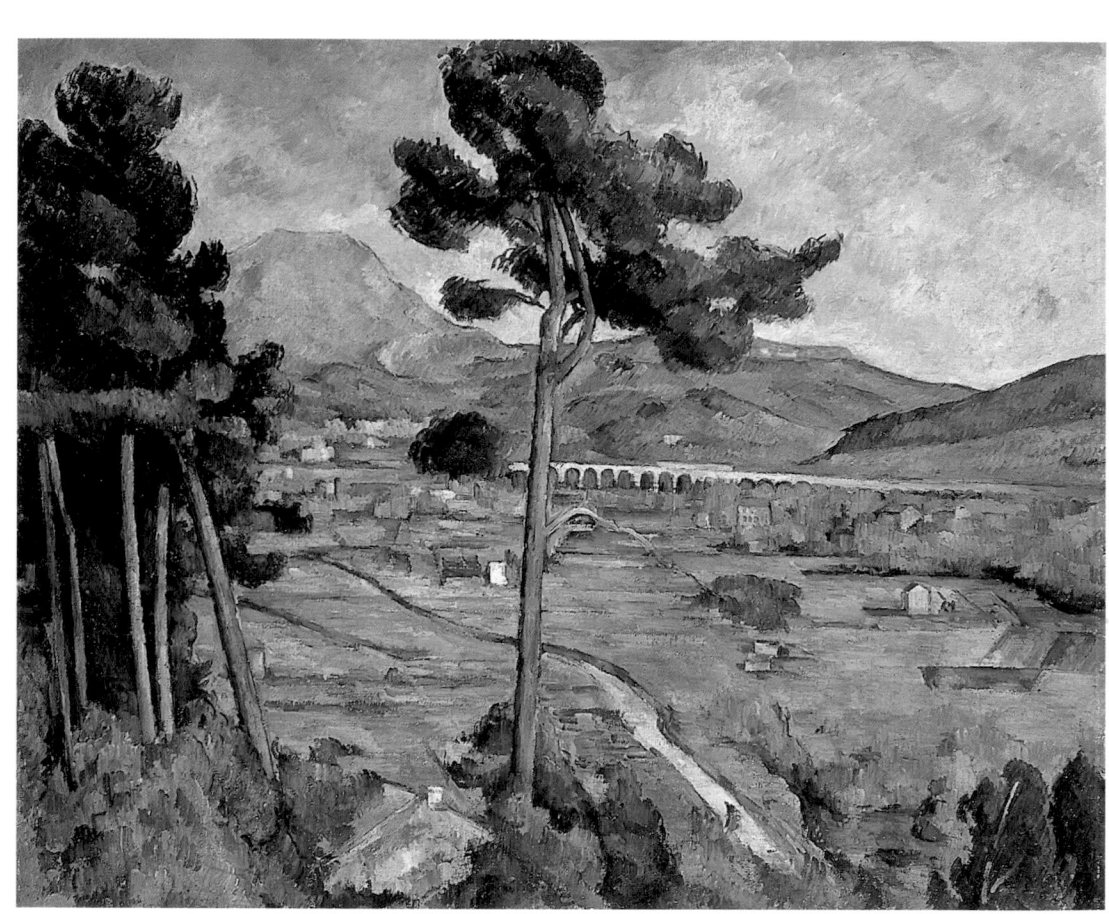

An unusual feature of this particular composition is the central pine, which extends nearly from the bottom all the way to the upper edge. Other, slightly later compositions were surveyed from farther down the slope and closer to the valley, with trees and branches framing rather than interfering with the view. In all of them, brushwork representing sky overlaps with foreground foliage, confusing spatial perception and flattening the whole. In our picture, this phenomenon (sometimes called *passage* in French) is especially prominent on the single branch about halfway up the trunk. In addition, along the complex right-hand outline of foliage there are briefly sketched black lines and exposed canvas that imply a lack of finish. One of the other paintings, now in the Courtauld Institute, London, has similar areas, and yet Cézanne signed it when he gave it to his friend Gasquet. Hence lack of conventional finish was no more bothersome for him than for other Impressionists. Indeed, the canvas contributes the beige of its ground preparation to Cézanne's palette while offering itself as a unifying element of overall design. With its powerful vertical overlying other geometric features of the composition, the central pine heightens tension between near and far. Combined with the strong horizontal of the viaduct, the tree forces everything to submit to the simple geometry of a cross. In addition, the shape and position of its head of pine needles implies the peak of a triangle extending from the lower corners. Hence the painting seems plotted along a rigorously traditional, even Renaissance conception of balance and symmetry, while it also reads as entirely unprecedented and authentically natural.

There is ample evidence for both readings. Scholars who have thought Cézanne was concerned primarily with underlying form have relentlessly traced similar geometries in many of his works. Others have systematically juxtaposed his compositions to photographs taken from identical locations. Yet, if we look to the Provençal land itself, with its origins in elemental time, these analyses are not mutually exclusive. Even in his own time, Cézanne was called the heir to Nicolas Poussin (1594–1665), the seventeenth-century French inventor of classical landscape. But he was also quoted by fellow artist Émile Bernard (1868–1941) in 1904 as saying one must 'become classical

248
Paul Cézanne,
Mont Sainte-Victoire seen from Bellevue,
c.1882–5.
Oil on canvas;
65·4 × 81·6 cm,
25³⁄₄ × 32¹⁄₈ in.
Metropolitan Museum of Art,
New York

again by way of nature, that is, by way of sensation'. Such statements contribute to the Cézanne legend, yet his classical ambitions are amply documented in youthful letters and evidenced through many works, particularly his bather compositions. *Bathers at Rest* (249), shown at the Impressionist exhibition of 1877, is one of the most complete and ambitious of his earlier versions of the theme. Judging by the number of studies for it, as well as the number of its figures reused in later compositions, the bathers theme was an overriding preoccupation throughout his career.

Bathing was an increasingly popular leisure activity in the nineteenth century, practised in public places suitably equipped as well as more isolated spots. The first Impressionist art scandal involved a bathing picture, Manet's *Le Déjeuner sur l'herbe* (see 30), originally titled *The Bath*. In Bazille's *Summer Scene (Bathers)*, a contemporary bathing group acquired a classical and utopian character (see 82). We know through many sources, including Cézanne's own drawings, that as a youth, he, Zola and other friends swam together in the Arc. His *Bathers at Rest*, like *Le Déjeuner sur l'herbe* a heterosexual scene, draws on all of these precedents, combining reality and fantasy, past and present. Its mountainous background suggests Mont Sainte-Victoire. Its central figure is close to a photograph on which Cézanne later based a famous single male bather of *c*.1885, now in New York's Museum of Modern Art. Figures to the left and right of it recall two from Bazille's scene. The composition also builds on numerous studies in which Cézanne tried figures of different sexes in these poses and experimented with placement of landscape elements. Cézanne's bather pictures respond thus to the still powerful status of figure painting and the age-old theme of man and nature, while they are rooted in nostalgia for a personal utopia associated with youth, sexual fulfilment and ancient Provence.

Cézanne certainly presents a very different model of the artist from the *flâneur* and the painter of modern life, so central to the modern aspects of Impressionism. These were moulds he never aspired to. He is closer to the solitary antisocial genius of Romantic myth or an 'Oriental mystic', as Gauguin, seeking connections with Symbolism,

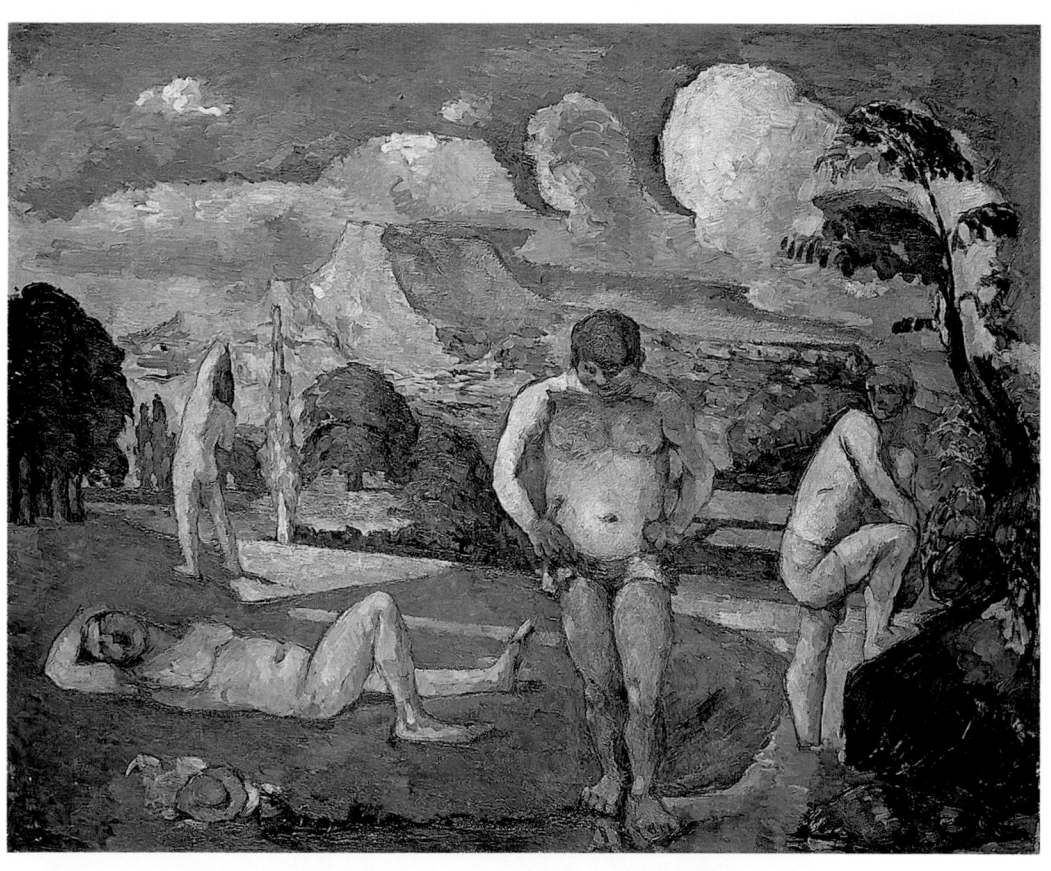

249
Paul Cézanne,
Bathers at Rest,
1876–7.
Oil on canvas;
82 × 101·2 cm,
32^{1}4 × 39^{7}8 in.
Barnes
Foundation,
Merion,
Pennsylvania

Cézanne's later work seems like the inevitable fulfilment of developments we have already discerned, as if irresistibly propelled by inner logic. Many of his later still lifes are exuberant, with a multiplication and varied distribution of objects, using complex patterned fabrics as their backdrop. *Apples and Oranges* (250) of the late 1890s has all the complexity of landscape, while staged on surfaces and against curtains reminiscent of *A Modern Olympia* (see 237) or a Renaissance reclining nude. It rivals the orientalizing Renoir, who was perhaps Cézanne's closest Impressionist friend after Pissarro, but who unlike Cézanne had no compunction about externalizing lust. Rather, it is an essay on abundance and plenitude addressed to appetite, though at a more deeply psychological than gastronomic level. Such a painting appears at first to contrast markedly with a new theme in Cézanne's work, *The Cardplayers* (251), whose simple composition and gravity overtly evoke the Italian Renaissance (another interest he shared with Renoir). All five of its versions are grandly classical essays in austerity. Based on studies of workers from the Jas de Bouffan who were paid a few francs to pose, these are the obverse of still lifes like *Apples and Oranges* for their revelation of Cézanne's reserve in confrontation with the living human figure. Yet not unlike the balanced forces in his still life, a deep sense of the cardplayers' stable concentration, almost somnolence, coexists with the tension preceding each player's approaching gambit. In the work of Jean-Baptiste-Siméon Chardin, Cézanne's great eighteenth-century predecessor in both still life and genre, the cardplayer theme had moral and philosophical implications, as in *The House of Cards* (252) of *c*.1737. It alluded to the frivolity of entertainments when faced with the fragility of life, likened to a house of cards – a theme paralleled by tobacco pipes and the ephemerality of smoke, also present in *The Cardplayers*. Following these traditions, Cézanne's gravity itself leads us to consider the 'hand' each of us is 'dealt' and how daily existence is comparable to a game of chance.

Such deeply conservative sources and meanings for Cézanne's work correspond to increasing age and solitude, as well as to his attachment to Provence. If both *Apples and Oranges* and *The Cardplayers* strike dissonant chords of primal desire and fear, their resolution may be sought in the late landscapes. The painter's habit of walking almost every day to familiar sites was itself a comforting ritual for him. Choices of topography lend credence to such interpretations, for he focused on places and motifs that reassure and shelter, places such as the Bibémus quarry, the nearby village of Le Tholonet, the so-called Château Noir (a group of houses built, despite their name, of the pale ochre Bibémus stone used throughout Aix since Roman times) and, of course, Mont Sainte-Victoire. These were places Cézanne knew and had explored since childhood. Their relative isolation, 5 km (3 miles) or so from Aix, provided an escape. Cézanne rented an outbuilding in the grounds of Château Noir to store painting materials.

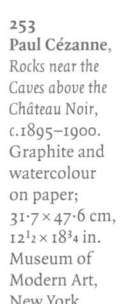

253
Paul Cézanne,
Rocks near the Caves above the Château Noir,
c.1895–1900.
Graphite and watercolour on paper;
31·7 × 47·6 cm,
12¹₂ × 18³₄ in.
Museum of Modern Art,
New York

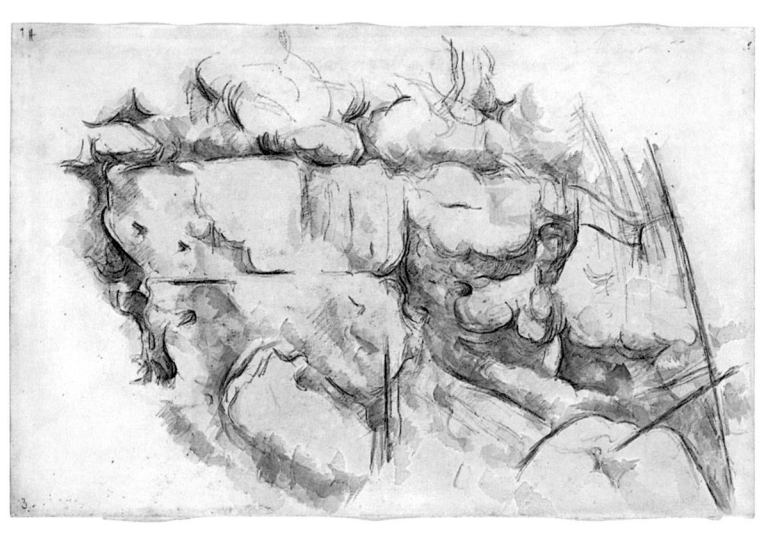

Beyond it were rock formations with caves used by prehistoric settlers. Cézanne made numerous watercolour studies (253) of their curious shapes. Despite the granite hardness of the rock's irregular façade, Cézanne's studies are lightly sketched in pencil and luminously coloured. His delicate application of nearly transparent patches of greens, grey-blues and light ochres reminds us that he continued to employ the Impressionist technique tied to immediacy of sensation. Our intimacy with his creative process, so openly direct, tentative and fragile, enlivens his motifs with far more than a sense of their physical existence. One divines an almost psychic exchange between nature and the artist, enhanced by the fragmentary isolation of the motif and the delicacy of the result. The harshest and most ancient forms seem alive for him.

Cézanne's late views of Mont Sainte-Victoire (254) must be understood within this context. The mountain looms distant, both defiantly and protectively defining Cézanne's enclosed world. As usual, there are no traces of the figure; even architectural elements are absorbed into what has become an animated array of colour patches approximating topographical patterns, expressing distance and embodying the substance of material form. In addition to these representational functions, the patches recapitulate the history of Cézanne's technique. Their frank brushstrokes echo the heavy Provençal pictorialism of his early years, channelled into his constructive stroke, while their flatness, openness and abstracted approximations relate directly to the subtleties of the late watercolours. Green patches in the sky recall foliage from 1880s scenes of the mountain, but here they also solo as pure colour recalling the valley below, design devices wilfully unifying the composition without overt reference to reality. The dialogue between man and nature enacted through artistic vision – and which is at the heart of those 'sensations' that define Impressionism – has here become art's dramatic theme. The artist's own creative process and the seeming life forces of Provence's primal earth converge in an image that teems with marks of animation as well as dialogue between the past and present. The geological strata of the mountain stone are rendered, as Kallmyer has suggested, with brushstrokes echoing the labour of prehistoric man shaping early flints and hatchets, of which many examples found nearby were reported by Cézanne's friend Marion. At the same time, with their painterly build-up flattening into abstract patterns, the late Mont Sainte-Victoires attain that visionary poetic dynamism beloved by the Symbolists in Monet's Rouen Cathedrals.

Nowhere are Cézanne's over-arching ambitions more apparent than in his late bathers. The largest version (255) was preceded by several others, which more explicitly take up the picnic theme from his early figure works. In these late paintings, the nudes are exclusively female and are far more integrated with the landscape than before. Cézanne creates a stage-like setting framed by an archway of trees, harkening back no doubt to his *Modern Olympia* (see 237) and related works. The bathers' simplified forms are grouped at the trees' bases and follow the axes of their leaning trunks. Cézanne's association between the two as harmonious and nurturing elements of nature is inevitable. The female nude in landscape looks back to antiquity and the Renaissance, while at the same time drawing on Cézanne's early and no doubt continuing sexual fantasies. The same fusion of motives underlies Renoir's *The Bathers* of 1887 (see 198). Opposed to the almost academic erotic naturalism of Renoir's figures, however, Cézanne's are transposed into the expurgated vocabulary of a cerebral and sublimating aesthetic.

Yet, in this largest, most abstract, and possibly unfinished version of the bather theme, Cézanne has introduced new elements that are autobiographical records of yearning as painful as in his early works. For the first time, one of his bather landscapes opens to a relatively natural setting with perhaps a village in the distance and a man and child standing at the shore looking directly outward. As in *A Modern Olympia*, a commentary on Manet's *Olympia* (see 34), Cézanne incorporates a viewer into his most ambitious bather composition. At the same time, he has virtually eliminated the black dog and still life with apples, which he repeatedly placed in the foreground of earlier versions as allusions to conflict between domesticity and temptation. Such tensions are resolved through the ultimately utopian vision, in which bodily freedom is equated with an ideal state of nature. This promised land across the river, from which one is always separated in nature, is the object of the desiring subject who finds it solely in his (the artist's) inner creative gaze.

Cézanne's paintings of bathers and of Mont Sainte-Victoire form the kinds of series that emerge from a concerted *plein-air* campaign and thematic fixation, with little concern for marketing strategy. Yet they were the works featured in the young dealer Ambroise Vollard's first Cézanne exhibition in 1895 and subsequent shows of 1904 and 1906. The revelation that the legendary hermit of Aix was the prolific author of works that embodied some of the most current

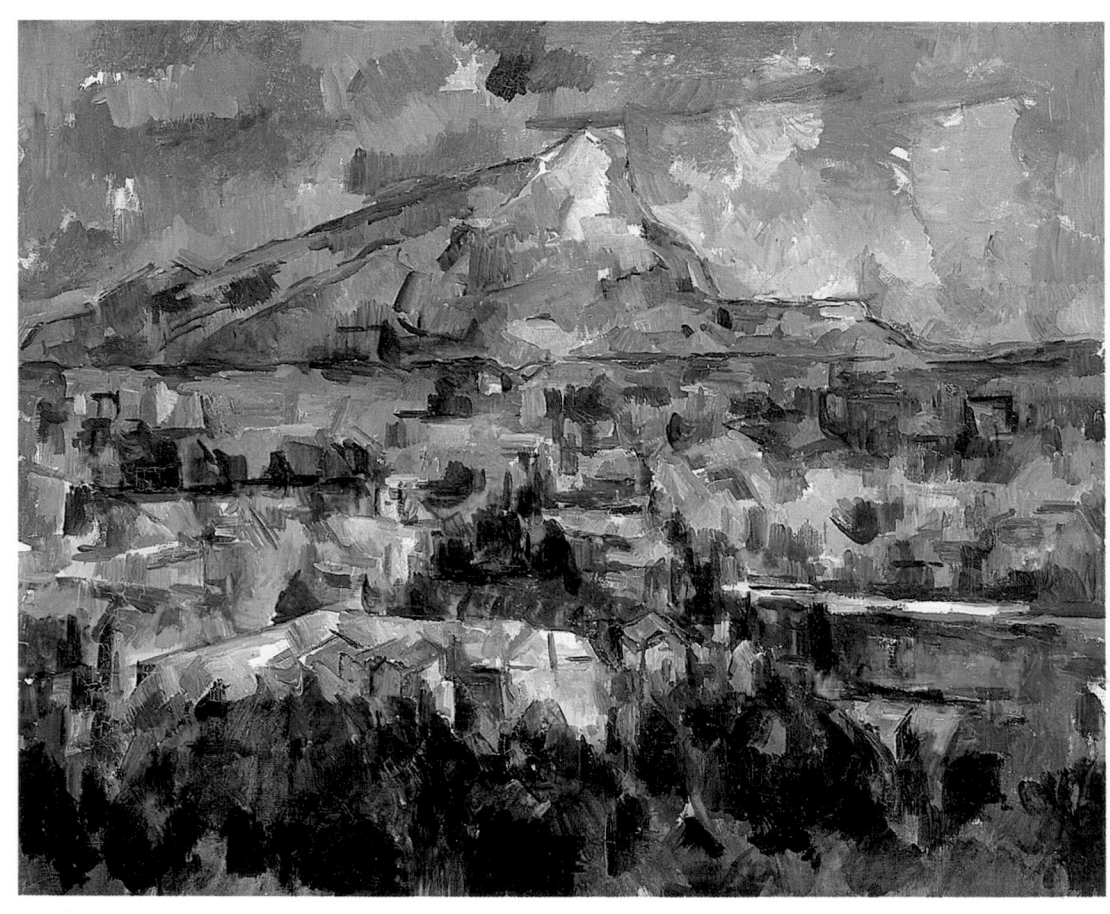

254
Paul Cézanne,
Mont Sainte-
Victoire,
c.1902–4.
Oil on canvas;
73 × 91·5 cm,
28³⁄₄ × 36¹⁄₈ in.
Philadelphia
Museum of Art

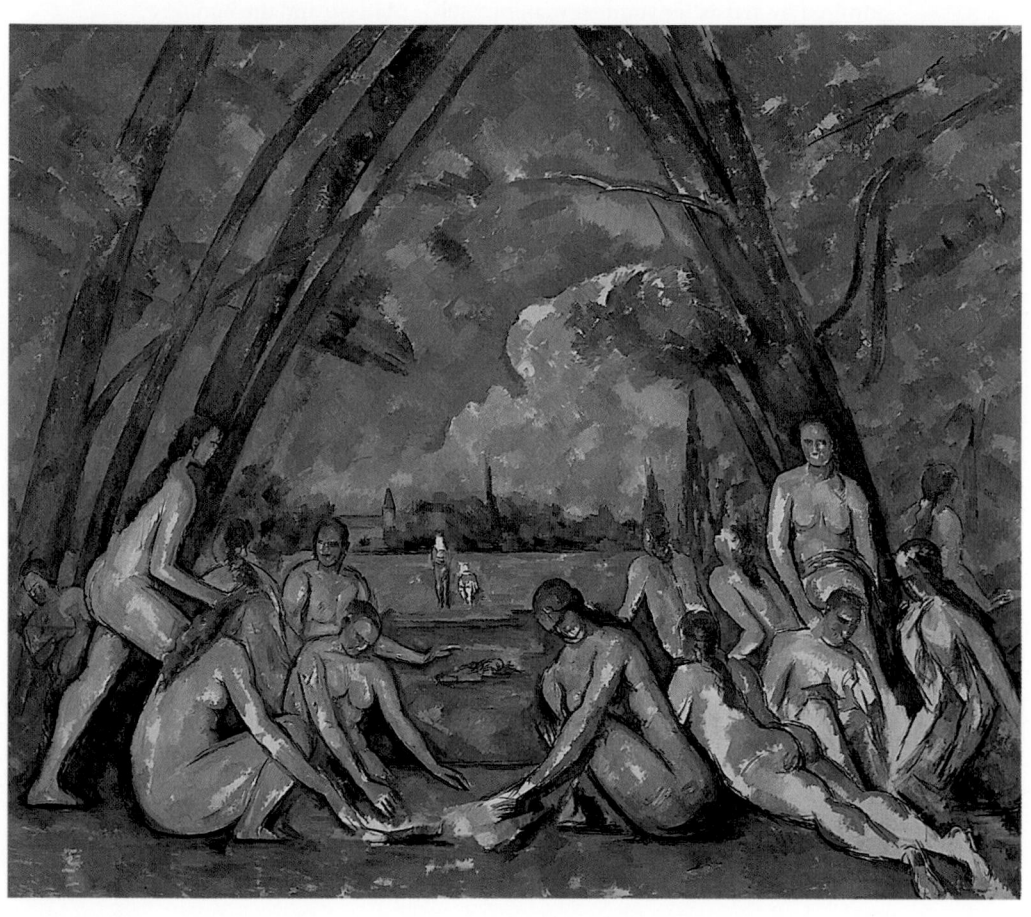

255
Paul Cézanne,
The Large Bathers,
c.1906.
Oil on canvas;
210·5 × 250·8 cm,
82⁷⁸ × 98³⁴ in.
Philadelphia
Museum of Art

artistic ideas suddenly placed him in the public eye as a topic of articles and interviews. Through all the verbiage, we discover that Cézanne himself remained essentially faithful to a few basic notions – the concept of 'sensation', a respect for nature, and loyalty to Pissarro, whom he called 'the father of us all'. He was exhibited with and admired by artists far younger than himself – Matisse and the budding Fauvist colourists, as well as Pablo Picasso (1881–1973) and Georges Braque (1882–1963), who drew on Cézanne's abstracting tendencies for Cubism. Insisting on both study of the world around him and preservation of personal vision, Cézanne drew from these two great opposing currents of the nineteenth century, recognizing truths in both. Thanks to his economic security and pride in being an outsider, he either defied or simply dispensed entirely with the institutional framework of Academy and Salon. Yet we should recognize the disengagement from social modernity that facilitated his aesthetic modernity. Justly called the father of modern art, his private fantasy and utopian visions inevitably combine nostalgia and revolt.

11

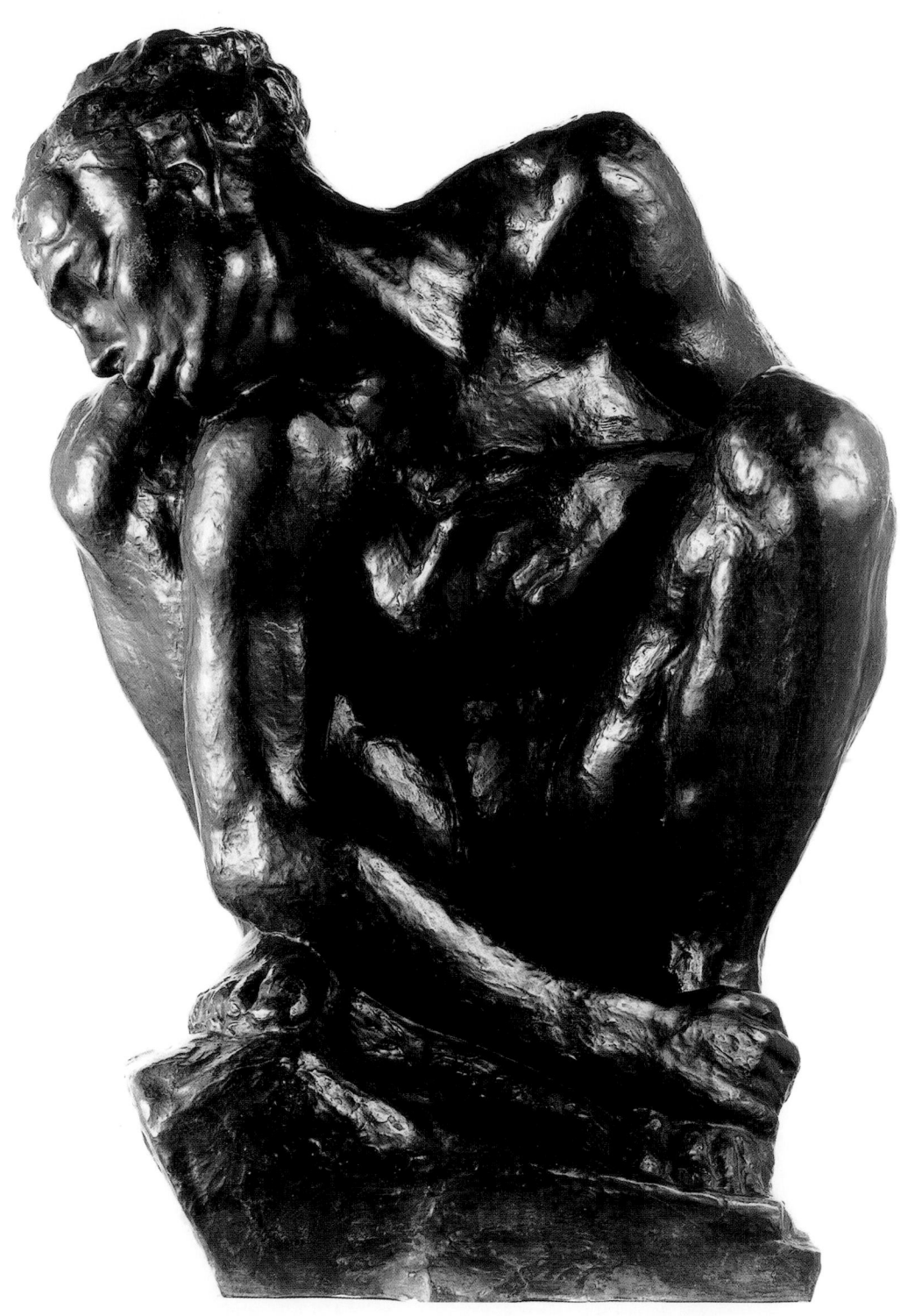

Impressionism – with its emphasis on naturalist landscape, on modern urban life and on the subjective dimension of art most evident in its later evolution – was a powerful development in art history and its legacy is wide-reaching. Not only did it raise questions that altered the assumptions of many French and other European painters, it also inspired trends in music and literature and drew loyal American practitioners to France. Even today, Impressionism exercises mass appeal that assures blockbuster museum exhibitions and is still present in currents of contemporary painting. Although it could sometimes be controversial in its early years, it was not nearly as universally despised as its later mythology would have it. There were important defenders, and it even tempted some conservative artists. As early as 1877, at least one critic discerned its influence at the official Salon. A few painters such as Bastien-Lepage (see 23) were using open, summary brushwork for landscape backgrounds, even when figures (still the dominant concern of academic painting) were handled more tightly.

In sculpture, the situation was more complex. Impressionist sculpture, by definition a figural art of solid form, was more closely related to the Realist current of Degas (see Chapter 5) and Caillebotte than to the *plein-air* ethos of instantaneity and light. Paul Gauguin, who exhibited several sculptures with the Impressionists, was directly inspired by Degas drawings, as we see in his 1881 figurine of a Parisienne out for a stroll (258, 259). Carving directly in the natural material of wood rather than using traditional marble or casting in bronze, he left tool-marks on surfaces as references to Impressionist technique and lack of finish. The monumental sculptor Auguste Rodin, whose large exhibition at Georges Petit's was concurrent with Monet's of 1889, is often associated with Impressionism, too. More committed to traditional subject matter than the Impressionists and working in conventional materials, Rodin nonetheless created a style that echoed painting's technical freedom in certain novel respects (256).

256
Auguste
Rodin,
*The Crouching
Woman*,
1882.
Bronze;
h.85 cm,
33¹₂ in.
Musée Rodin,
Paris

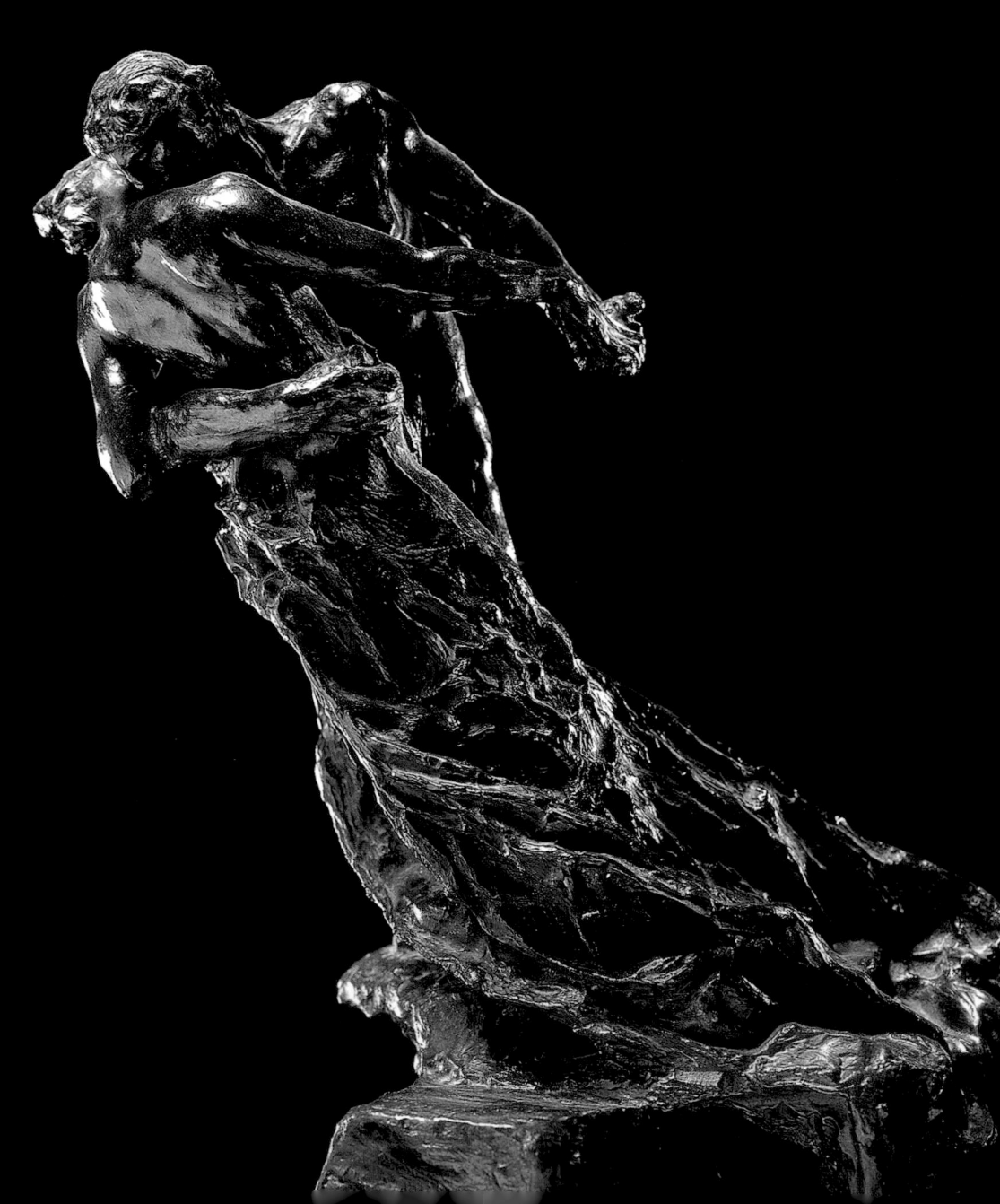

His surfaces often display light-catching complexity and suggestiveness that evoke rapid sketching in clay or plaster. In *The Waltz* (257) by the artist Camille Claudel (1864–1943), who had studied with Rodin and became his lover, lack of finish could also imply the emergence of form from matter. Paralleling Monet's late style, where cathedrals or waterlilies materialize out of shimmering mist or water, such effects were associated with mysticism or the dream-like states of Symbolist poetry.

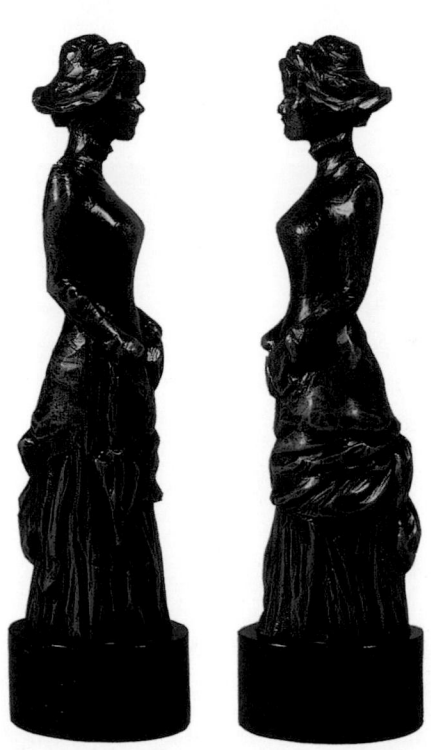

257
Camille Claudel,
The Waltz,
1893.
Bronze;
43·2 × 23 cm,
17 × 19 in.
Musée Rodin,
Paris

258–259
Paul Gauguin,
Two side views
of *Woman on a Stroll* or *The Little Parisienne*,
1880.
Wood
stained red;
h.25 cm,
9³⁄4 in.
Private
collection

Symbolist theory advocated the abstract effects of music, and this was the medium outside painting in which Impressionism had its most successful afterlife. An early orchestral composition by Claude Debussy, a symphonic suite called *Le Printemps* (*Springtime*) of 1887, was dismissed by his professors as 'vague Impressionism, one of the most dangerous enemies of works of art'. Debussy was already a friend of the young Symbolists, whose emphasis on evocation and organicism fit logically with music's non-representational means of expression. In a series of masterpieces beginning with *Prélude à l'après-midi d'un faune* (*Prelude to the Afternoon of a Faun*; 1894), evoking Mallarmé's poem, and culminating in the famous *La Mer* (1905), Debussy suggested the ebb and flow of nature. His effects were based on rich, sensuous harmonics and instrumental timbre rather than specific melody, and on fleeting, continuously changing and cyclical fragments rather than clearly structured, separable units. Debussy's music has been described as hypnotic and kaleidoscopic, evoking exotic and narcotic experience through its often oriental-sounding chords and arabesques. But the revelations of the visual arts were crucial for his conceptions. For the cover of *La Mer* (260) he used the Hokusai woodcut of *The Wave*, which had an early influence on Manet

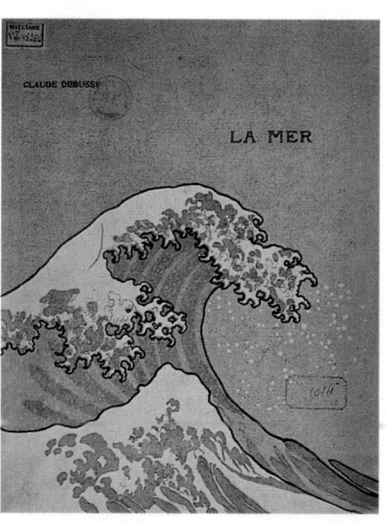

260
Cover for Claude Debussy's *La Mer* with Katsushika Hokusai's woodcut of *The Wave*, 1905. Bibliothèque Nationale, Paris

261
James Abbott McNeill Whistler, *Nocturne in Black and Gold, the Falling Rocket*, c.1875. Oil on canvas; 60·2 × 46·7 cm, 23³⁄₄ × 18³⁄₈ in. Detroit Institute of Arts

and Monet. Debussy's three *Nocturnes* (*Clouds, Feasts, Sirens*) of 1898 were said to be inspired by nearly abstract paintings of the Thames at night (261) by James Abbott McNeill Whistler (1834–1903). Titles such as 'Play of Waves', 'Estampes' (Prints), 'Veils', 'Reflections in Water', 'Fogs' and 'Footprints in Snow' deliberately evoked the visual. Though associated with Impressionism, Debussy himself claimed to be seeking 'realities', as he said, rather than mere impressions: 'Listen to the lessons of the wind passing and telling the history of the world.' Yet he also expressed pleasure when his music gave the feeling 'of not having been written' – evoking the spontaneity associated with Impressionist art.

With literary Impressionism, as it was called by its practitioners, we are faced with the very different medium of words. The densely descriptive prose of the expatriate American Henry James, who knew Impressionist art, and his British contemporaries Joseph Conrad and Ford Madox Ford, offers a fascinating contrast to the literary devices of Symbolist poetry and drama. Although committed Realists looking back to Balzac and Flaubert, James's group understood that reality is not the coherent realm implied by the omniscient voice of Realist narration. For them, the story to be told in literature was of discovery from within the inchoate mass of life's sensations. In reflections on Conrad, Ford held that life does not 'narrate, but [makes] impressions on our brains ... [In order] to produce ... an effect of life, [we] must not narrate but render impressions.' In 'On Impressionism' (meaning literary), his theoretical essay of 1913, Ford emphasized the rendering of visual sensations in language that could equally apply to painting. In his thinking, 'like so many views seen through bright glass', Impressionism was to convey 'the sort of odd vibration that scenes in real life really have'. James's emphasis on individual character and contrasting points of view as techniques for developing situations reflects his understanding of the subjective element in perception. For literary historian Paul Armstrong, their writing is marked by this 'heightened self-consciousness about the way in which any technique for rendering the world rests on assumptions about how we construe it'. The term Impressionism, then, as a successor to Realism in literature as well as visual art, carries a consciousness of the subjective element within it. But in contrast to Symbolist appeals to inner consciousness by circumventing external sensory data, literary Impressionism comes closer to the spirit of its visual forebears by favouring the empirical.

The heirs to Impressionism in painting were far less reflective about their work than those who followed them in other media, as if the artistic freedom hard won by earlier generations could be taken for granted. Impressionist painting seemed a completely natural, naïve practice, and its choices of subject matter now seemed value free. In France, painters like Van Gogh, Henri de Toulouse-Lautrec (1864–1901) and Pierre Bonnard (1867–1947) were inspired by and

262
Walter Richard Sickert, *Café des Tribunaux, Dieppe,* c.1890. Oil on canvas; 60·3 × 73 cm, 23³⁄4 × 28³⁄4 in. Tate Gallery, London

preserved certain aspects of the style while developing their own unique positions. Colour – meaning both Impressionism's technique of painting directly in colour and its usually brilliant palette – is the element that ties these three very different painters together. Fauvism, too, led by Henri Matisse, is certainly an outgrowth of the Impressionist legacy. However, French artists generally felt compelled to explore new realms, so that Impressionism was succeeded by a series of rapid developments towards expressionism and abstraction. Impressionism's naturalist basis appeared conservative compared to the currents which defined the modernist avant-garde.

Thus, after 1900, Impressionism in France was a continuing memory and a vital resource rather than an active movement (though Monet continued to paint until his death in 1926). It remained alive in other countries. In Britain, there was a modest Impressionist school, led by Walter Richard Sickert (1860–1942) and Philip Wilson Steer (1860–1942). Sickert, who studied first with Whistler, was led through him to meet Degas in France. He spent six years on the Continent, alternating between Dieppe (262) and Venice, painting in a style resembling Monet of the 1880s, though occasionally echoing

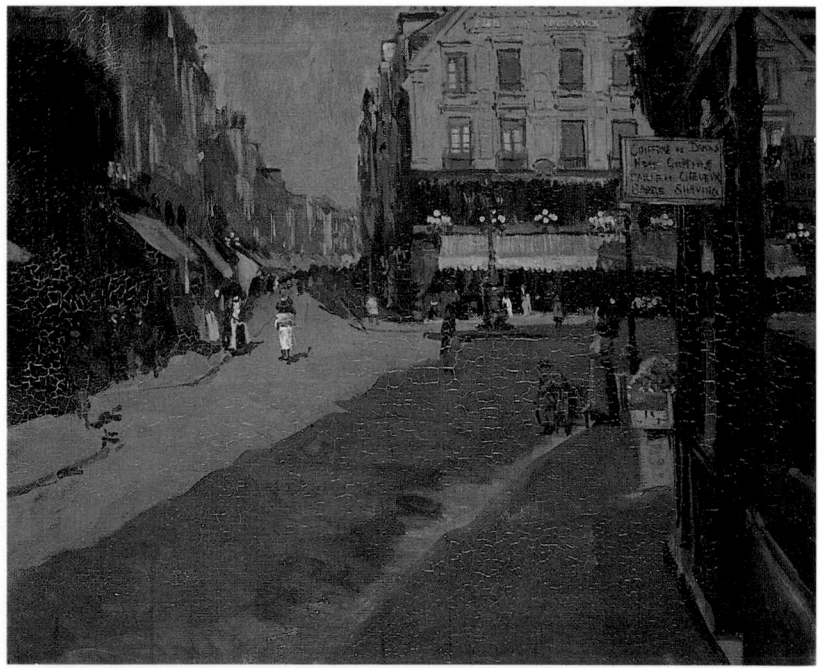

Degas's structures. Shortly after returning to London in 1905, Sickert founded the Camden Town Group with a number of other artists. Among its more prominent members was Lucien Pissarro, who moved to England from under his father's shadow in order to have an independent career.

By comparison, in the United States Impressionism nearly became a national style. Thanks to America's vast unspoiled scenic reaches and the pioneering spirit of its still youthful culture, landscape was already the dominant genre in the mid-nineteenth century. So-called Luminists and Tonalists, many of whom trained in Europe, painted in a Romantic spirit which at its most advanced looked stylistically to the Barbizon School. Two expatriate painters, Whistler and John Singer Sargent (1856–1925), the former a friend of Courbet and Degas, the latter of Monet, certainly understood Impressionism's aims. Degas even invited Whistler to join their exhibitions and shared Whistler's belief in the superiority of art over nature. Sargent was one of the first Americans to visit Monet in Giverny, where he executed some *plein-air* paintings. Both settled in England, where Whistler produced his daringly simple nocturnes (see 261), which stirred violent controversy, and Sargent pursued his career as a fashionable portraitist.

North America was far more sympathetic to Impressionism than any other place. Mary Cassatt and Louisine Havemeyer were among the first Americans to promote the style, but the role of Lilla Cabot Perry (1848–1933) was also instrumental. Born to one of Boston's first families and married to the grand nephew of Commodore Perry (who led the US naval expedition that opened up Japan in the mid-nineteenth century), she took up painting in France in the late 1880s. In 1887, she met Monet and for twenty years regularly visited Giverny, serving as a mainstay of the American colony there and as a conduit to Monet. By the late 1880s, many American painters sojourned in the village, gradually shedding their academic training for *plein-air* directness. Among the best-known to draw on such experiences was Theodore Robinson (1852–96), who first discovered Giverny in 1888 and entered Monet's intimate circle through the marriage in 1892 of Suzanne Hoschedé to his close friend, the painter Theodore Earl Butler (1861–1936).

Americans returning from France converted others, such as J Alden Weir (1852–1919) and John Henry Twachtman (1853–1902), whose training in Germany made them at first suspicious of outdoor work. By this time, of course, Neo-Impressionism and Symbolism formed a truer avant-garde; so perhaps Impressionism seemed safer. In the 1890s, there were numerous exhibitions of Impressionist works in the United States, and American disciples began holding shows of their own. They were eventually joined by William Merritt Chase (1849–1916) and Childe Hassam (1859–1935) in 1898 to found a society called The Ten or Ten American Painters.

Neither Hassam nor Chase met Monet directly, but they forged the most convincing versions of a truly American Impressionism. Tired of being viewed as pale imitators of the French, Americans began to value their national scenery and established a canon of places where they would paint, often in groups. Hassam was known for subtle views of American cities, especially Boston and New York (263), for which his vertical or square formats helped capture the scale of high buildings. The art colony became widespread in places like Cos Cob, Connecticut and Provincetown, Massachusetts, as well as the East End of Long Island, where Chase founded a summer art school (264). Perhaps the most lasting legacy of Impressionism lies in the association between painting and the sense of place which the establishment of such sites perpetuated. Around 1900, another group of American painters, calling themselves Realists, including Robert Henri (1865–1929), John Sloan (1871–1951) and George Bellows (1882–1925), declared their differences to Impressionism, claiming their urban motifs and darker palette as a separate trend. Although that split was always a potential within French Impressionism, the American Realists clarified it, viewing Impressionism as brightly coloured outdoor painting and a foil to their own. That definition has endured, and twentieth-century Impressionism has become the work produced in far-flung art colonies ranging from New Hope, Pennsylvania, to Laguna Beach, California, rather than in cities.

Impressionism paralleled early photographic developments and there are certainly resemblances. That there is virtually no such thing as Impressionist photography *per se* probably seems strange to those who view Impressionism primarily as the representation of modern life, which is what today's photographers are so good at recording. In their own time, however, photographs were thought to be lacking in what made Impressionism distinct: it was considered a mechanical art, whereas Impressionism was always linked to the personal. In retrospect, we realize that many aspects of nineteenth-century photography are tied to the individual artist-photographer; indeed

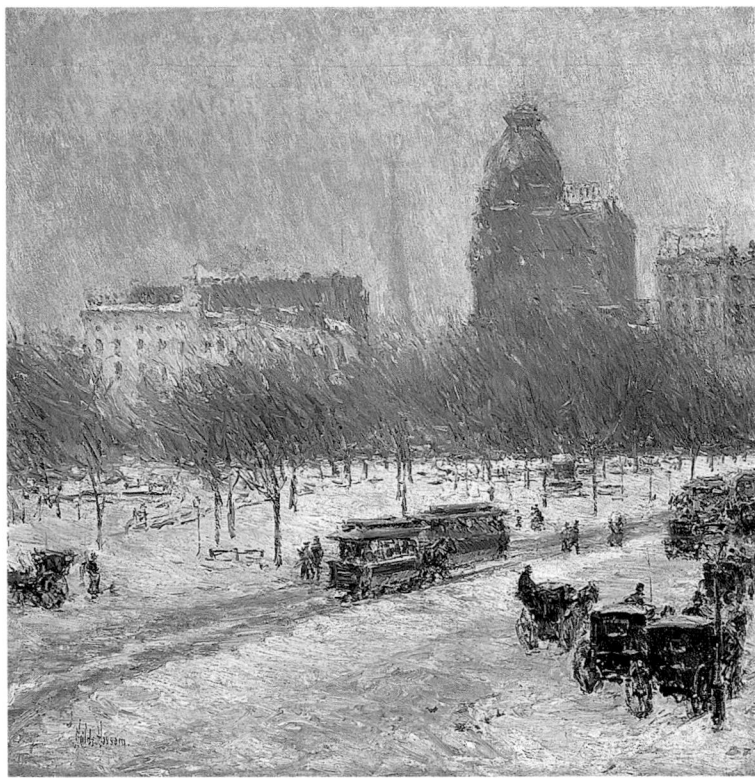

263
Childe Hassam, *Winter in Union Square*, 1894. Oil on canvas; 46.4 × 45.7 cm, 18¼ × 18 in. Metropolitan Museum of Art, New York

most had trained as artists and strove to preserve their integrity as such. Yet in the general perception, photography could never overlap with Impressionism, for it could never be more than a tool for any artist who prized freedom and imagination, as in Baudelaire's low opinion of the medium (see Chapter 1). Only Degas – the most realist of the Impressionists – experimented with photography, though never for public view. A picture showing Renoir and Mallarmé (265), with Degas reflected in the mirror (along with Julie Manet, in whose

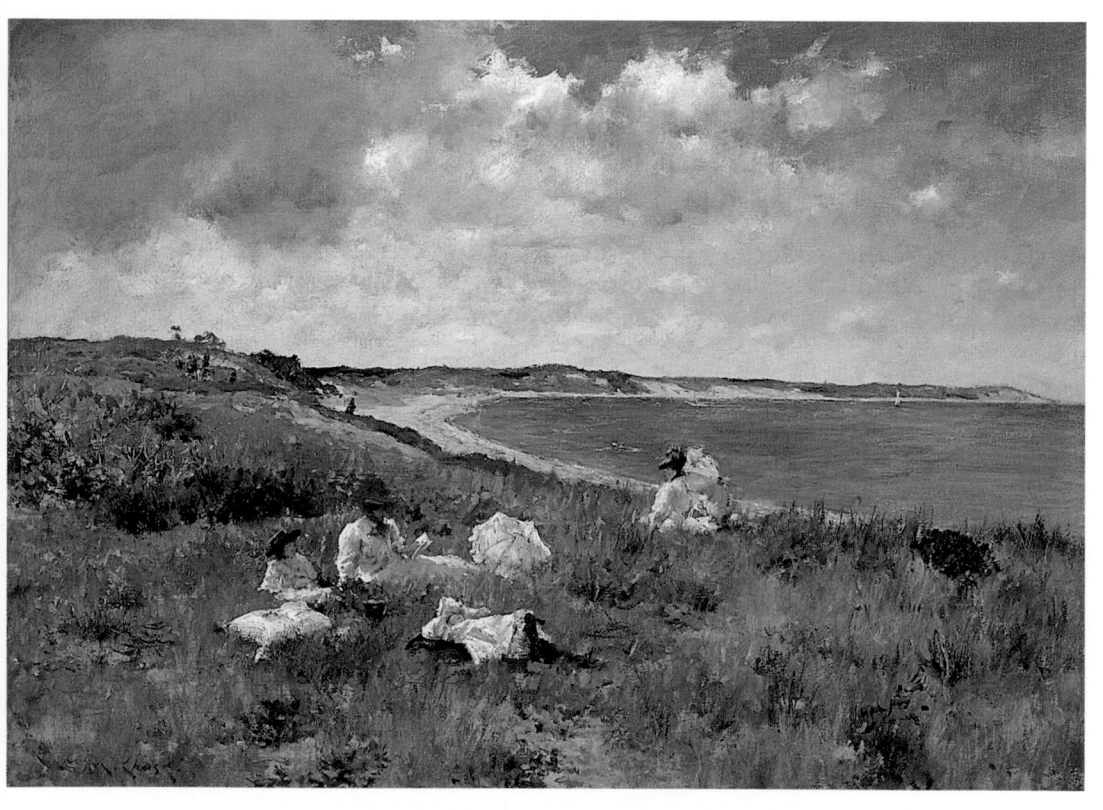

264
William Merrit Chase,
Idle Hours,
c.1894.
Oil on canvas;
64·7 × 90·2 cm,
25^1$_2$ × 35^1$_2$ in.
Amon Carter
Museum,
Fort Worth,
Texas

apartment the photograph was taken) suggests what Impressionist photography might have been (and what has sometimes been called Impressionist film of the 1920s would become). In retrospect, we can find parallels with landscape photographers such as Charles Marville (1816–79), the friend of Corot and Narcisse Virgile Diaz (1808–76), or the industrial photographer Édouard-Denis Baldus (1813–89), some of whose compositions show railway tracks or viaducts, as in an occasional work by Guillaumin. But Guillaumin is an exception, the

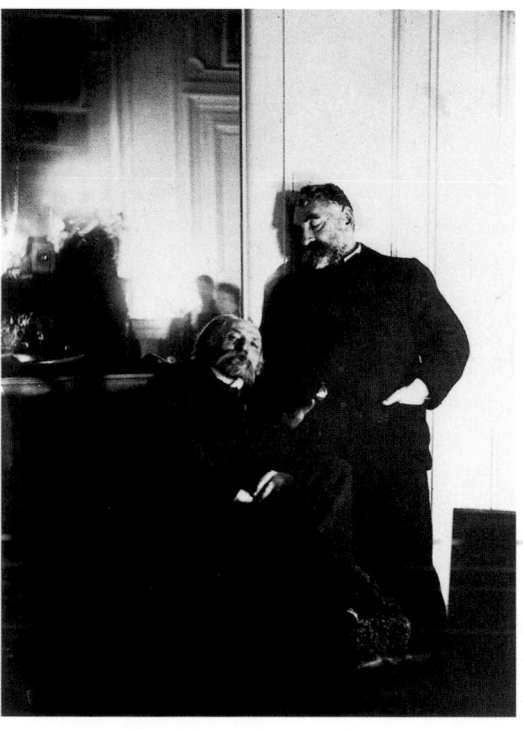

265
Edgar Degas, Pierre-Auguste Renoir and Stéphane Mallarmé, 1895

most industrially oriented of the Impressionists, and therein lies a point. Photography was rarely used to portray bourgeois leisure or express aesthetic joy. Its technical basis was deemed antithetical to processes art used to connote 'sensation' – personal vision and inner response. After the Romanticism associated with the Forest of Fontainebleau (see 13), landscape photography became mainly documentary, providing memories of distant travels or evidence for archaeology. How different from the American Impressionist ethos of summer resorts and leisure!

Although many of the Impressionists lived into the twentieth century, it was Post-Impressionism – the term coined by British critic and painter Roger Fry (1866–1934) – which seemed the most vital source of modernist developments prior to World War II. Fry and his 'formalist' followers believed that the most advanced art was that in which forms appeared consciously endowed with conceptual and expressive value. They found Impressionism's naturalist premises naïve and conservative compared to the succeeding generation of Van Gogh, Gauguin, Seurat and Cézanne. Only after World War II did Impressionism enjoy renewed status, but by then it came to be for reasons other than its naturalism. Claude Monet, who continued to work into the 1920s, was by that time considered a national treasure. With encouragement from his politician-friend Georges Clemenceau, who was elected prime minister in 1917, Monet created an entire room of waterlilies and weeping willows for the Orangerie, a building in the grounds of the Tuileries Garden, as a donation to the state. Following the logic of his artistic development, and perhaps his failing eyesight (he had had cataracts since 1912), Monet's late work became so brilliantly coloured and boldly brushed that to our late twentieth-century eyes it seems virtually abstract (266, 267). It has sometimes been cited as the harbinger of New York Abstract Expressionism, which after 1945 made its final break with the figural tradition. It happens that in the early 1950s, there was a revival of interest in Monet by the American avant-garde. The gesturalism of Jackson Pollock (1912–56; 268), which involved direct drawing in colour and dispersion of visual experience over the canvas surface, could have roots in Impressionism.

Tenuous though such specific visual links to Impressionism may be, there are perhaps more important conceptual ones that help us appreciate Impressionism's extraordinary survival. First, we saw how for succeeding generations the visual characteristics that could have interested Pollock defined Impressionism as an art of personal vision. Although its roots lay in naturalism, its lessons for the future lay in emotional responses, where artists' gestures signified the 'performance' of subjectivity. In American art, this phenomenon, transmitted also through European Surrealism, culminated in what was dubbed 'action painting', of which Pollock was the leading practitioner.

Second, through World War I and its aftermath, Monet's work served as both private refuge for an artist who increasingly abhorred the public world and as public expression of the continuing vitality of French culture. A similar idealistic quest for both personal meaning and universal power drove both the production and nationalistic reception of American abstraction during and following World War II.

Finally, the Impressionists were popularly recognized as artists who bonded socially and professionally as dissidents within a more conservative, sometimes hostile, artistic environment. Such formations are now considered the norm. Yet, like the Impressionists, virtually all artists seeking group solidarity do so to bolster their freedom

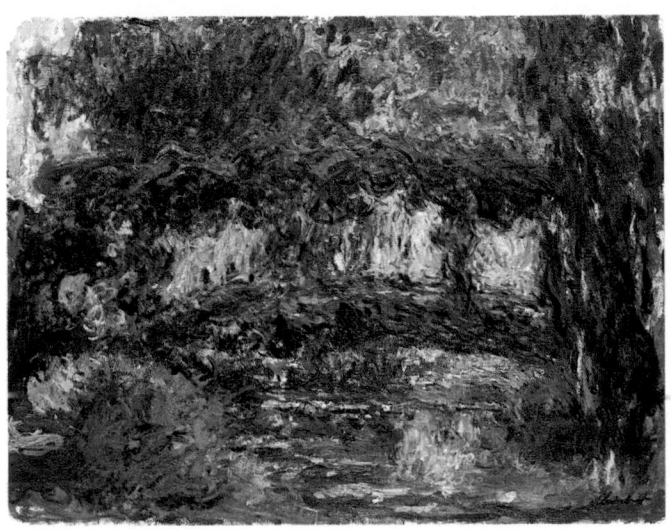

266–267
Claude Monet,
*The Japanese
Footbridge*,
c.1922.
Oil on canvas;
89.2 × 116.2 cm,
35⅛ × 45¾ in.
Minneapolis
Museum of Arts
Opposite
Detail

in what is still viewed romantically as the solitary enterprise of creativity. In that respect, the bars and cafés of Greenwich Village in New York, the Soho of both New York and London, and the art colonies of East Hampton on Long Island and St Ives in Cornwall, England, are direct descendants of the Café Guerbois, La Nouvelle Athènes and Pontoise. It is hardly surprising then that there are echoes of Impressionism in twentieth-century artists as different and distant as Philip Guston (1913–80), Sam Francis (1923–94) and Joan Mitchell (b.1926). The small markings and intense colours of Guston's abstract work evoke Impressionist fragmentation and optical intensity,

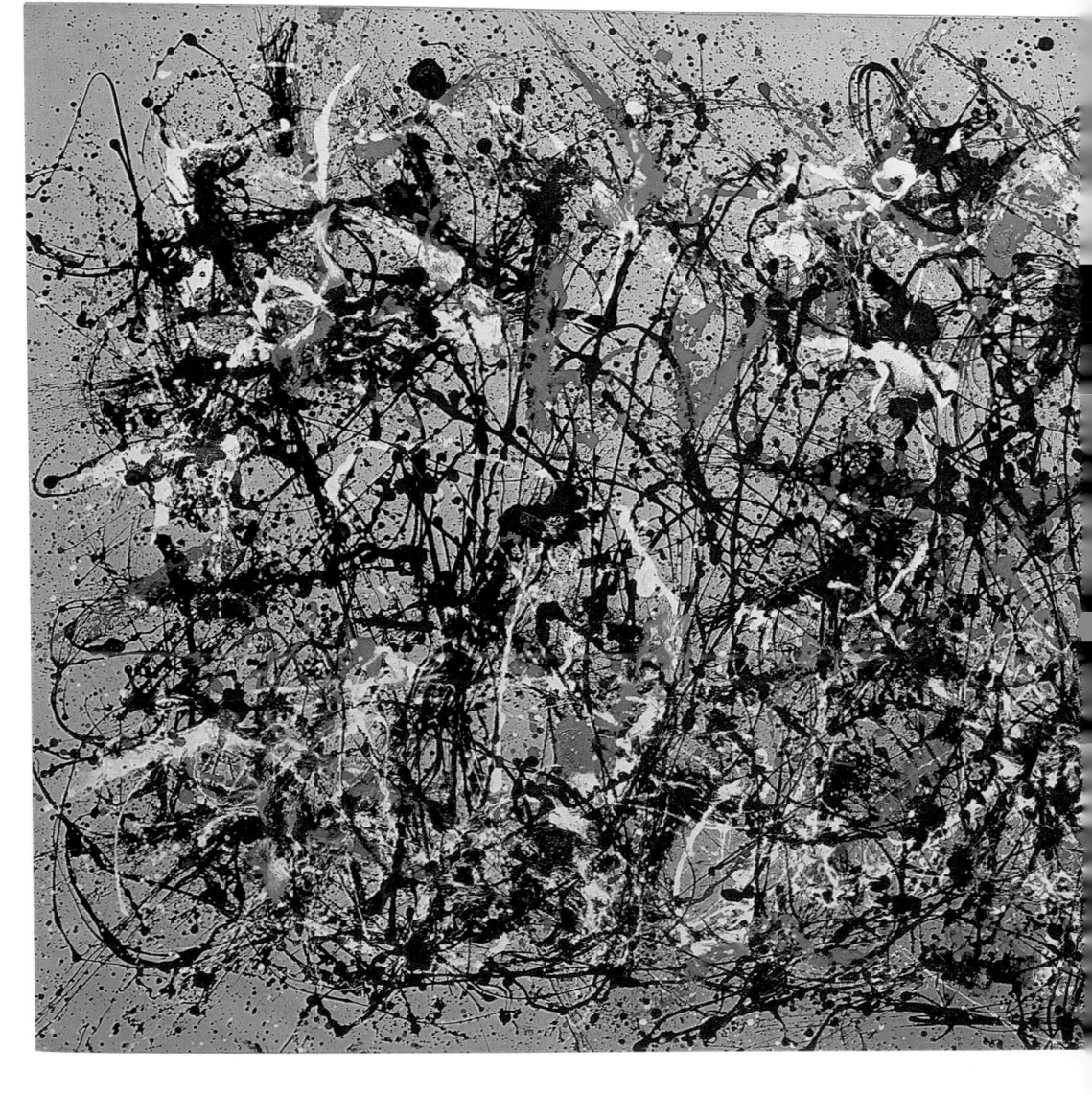

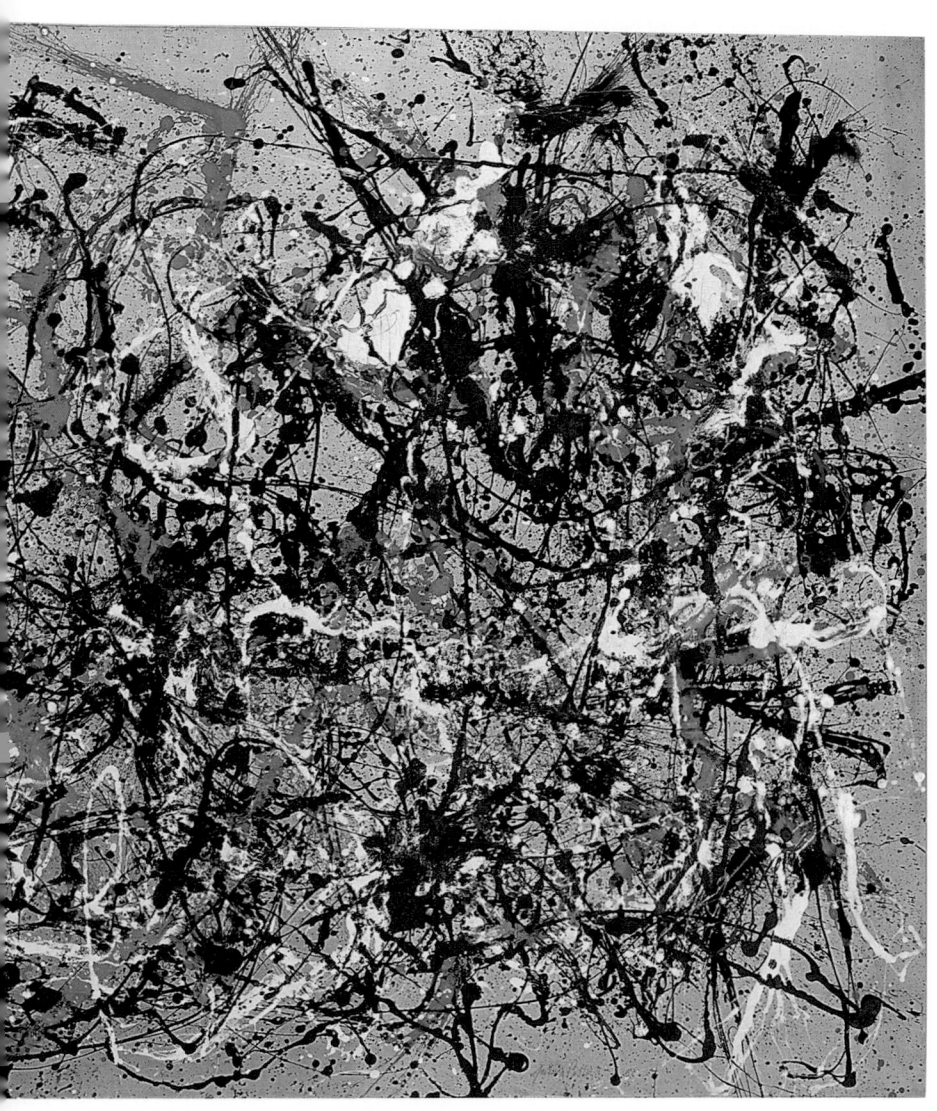

268
Jackson Pollock, *Autumn Rhythm (Number 30)*, 1950. Oil on canvas; 266·7 × 525·8 cm, 105 × 207 in. Metropolitan Museum of Art, New York

while Francis's organic colour flows suggest floral motifs often associated with Monet and those who painted in his wake. Joan Mitchell's large horizontal formats directly echo the Waterlilies, to the point where her Abstract Expressionism begins to look like 'Abstract Impressionism' (269).

Beyond art itself, there is no better testimony to the historical and symbolic value of such links than the current American presence in Giverny. Monet's home and studio, now the third most visited tourist site in France, was restored largely with American money, and the Musée Américain, with its collection of American Impressionism and its artist-fellowship winners in residence, has been a presence there since 1992. This huge investment in preserving and perpetuating Impressionism is paralleled by its unequalled prices in today's art market. With the exception of occasional masterpieces by Old Masters, nothing is a more reliable investment than an Impressionist work. To cite but one example, in July 1998, an anonymous buyer at Sotheby's in London paid nearly £20 million ($33 million) for Monet's *Waterlily Pond and Path by the Water* of 1900. The painting had been purchased for £4,500 ($7000) in 1954.

Underlying such success is the belief in both Impressionism's historical importance and its contemporary relevance. That is, links between Impressionism and contemporary taste go beyond its often pleasing look to something ultimately ideological. Impressionist art reassures us of associations between pleasure and freedom; it gives gratifying visual form to the idea that standing up for principles is a worthy pursuit. Although those principles were artistic, we take them to embody a broader notion of integrity we associate with a certain way of life. Even in the purest modernist criticism of, for example, 1950s American critic Clement Greenberg, the artist's single-minded devotion to problems of pictorial form embodies ideals of sacrifice and virtue that are widely inspiring. That relationship is not so different from Pissarro's utopian contention that artistic freedom serves as an example for society as a whole. The spontaneity and freedom associated with Impressionism are perhaps factors in its particular appeal for art lovers whose cultural background lies outside the Western

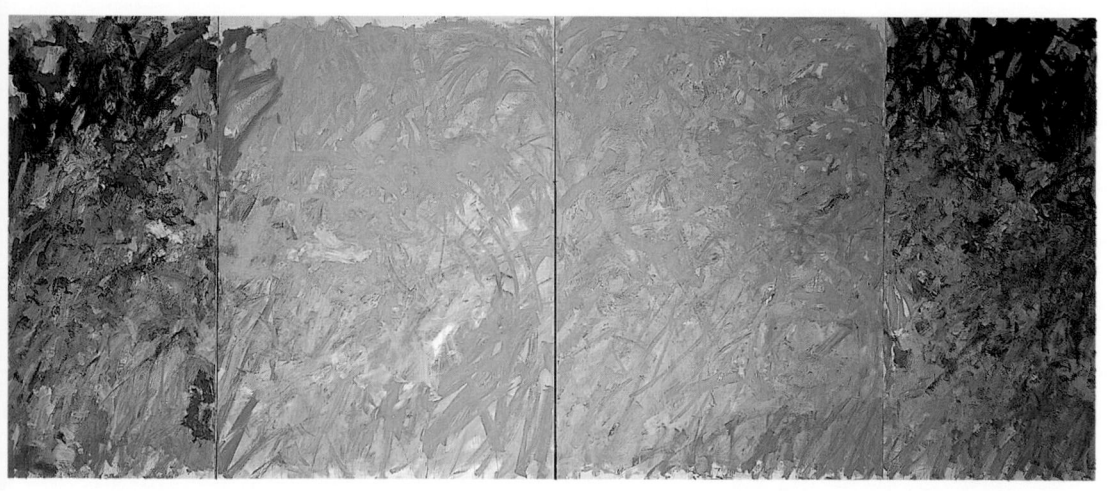

269
Joan Mitchell,
Chez ma Soeur,
1981–2.
Diptych,
oil on canvas;
279·4 × 660·4 cm,
110 × 260 in.
Robert Miller
Gallery,
New York

European tradition. The present-day passion for Impressionist art among the Japanese is a fascinating reversal of artistic exchange, given the influence of nineteenth-century Japanese prints on the movement. Surely, then, Impressionism's continuing popularity, phenomenal prices and box-office draw for museum exhibitions has to do with its ability to make people feel good both aesthetically and in terms of shared values. Its continuing power lies in its ability to reflect and reaffirm ideals which, even when regarded critically, still resonate today.

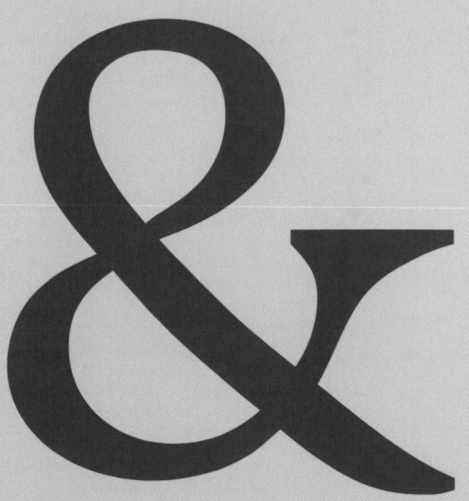

Academy Although the Royal Academy of Painting and Sculpture was destroyed during the French Revolution, the École des Beaux-Arts (Fine Arts School) inherited its institutional functions and its de facto control over the art world in the 1800s. It perpetuated conservative attitudes and styles associated with Classical antiquity, though it was inclusive enough to accept landscape, sketching and other progressive forms. Its idealistic theories favouring mythological, religious and historical subjects were increasingly opposed by painters committed to representing the natural and everyday world. Owing to its domination of government-sponsored exhibitions and awards, paintings by members were also regarded as 'official' art. It thus became a symbol of a corrupt establishment, and by the 1860s had lost much of its credibility among young artists.

Barbizon School A group of landscape painters centred around the village of Barbizon, near the Forest of Fontainebleau. The best-known members are Jean-Baptiste-Camille Corot, Charles-François Daubigny and Jean-François Millet. Considered precursors of **Realism** because of their truth to observation, nature for them was a refuge from urban life and an embodiment of virtue. Their painting, inspired by Dutch landscapes and the English painter John Constable, narrowed the technical gap between sketch and finished work – a direction that culminated in Impressionism.

Flâneur The word (from the French *flâner*, to stroll) used by **Charles Baudelaire** to refer to the urban man of leisure who takes pleasure in wandering through the crowd observing others. In *The Painter of Modern Life*, Baudelaire used the *flâneur* to exemplify the modern gaze, both intimate and distant, and acutely sensitive to social distinctions. The artistic equivalent was the sketch of manners, as in the work of Constantin Guys, which combined rapid sketching and accurate observation – a new formula for a naturalistic style that was eventually embodied by Impressionism.

Impressionist Exhibitions Eight independent exhibitions which began in 1874, although they were never officially called 'Impressionist'. Frustrated by refusals at the **Salon**, some future Impressionists began discussing an independent show in the late 1860s, but the plans were delayed by the Franco-Prussian War. In 1874, their idea was realized, though **Édouard Manet** refused to join because he believed the Salon was where an artist had to prove himself. The exhibitions were always held in the Grands Boulevards – the modern, central business district of Paris.

Naturalism In general, resemblance to nature, or a method or artistic style based on observation of nature. The word was used by **Jules-Antoine Castagnary** and **Émile Zola** in the 1860s and 1870s as a more neutral alternative to **Realism**. Castagnary linked it to the well-established and vital French landscape tradition, thereby providing Impressionism with a basis in non-controversial art. Zola used the term to denote his analytically descriptive writing style, making his treatment of volatile social themes appear scientific and dispassionate.

Neo-Impressionism A term invented by the critic Félix Fénéon in 1886 to designate a novel trend started by **Georges Seurat**. Seurat adopted a scientific approach to colour based on juxtapositions of unmixed pigments and systematic paint application – alternatives to the 'intuitive' Impressionist approach. His small dot and dash strokes came to be called Pointillism. The abstracting effect of his stylistic reform aimed at images of duration rather than the spontaneously observed moment of Impressionism. For this reason, the style is closely linked to **Symbolism**.

Paris Commune The socialist government of Paris from 18 March to the end of May, 1871. The Commune seceded from the **Third Republic** following the latter's capitulation to the Prussians after their siege of Paris. It refused to surrender and hoped to join in a federation of similar movements in other cities. The Commune ended when government troops overran Paris in a bloodbath, costing some 30,000 lives, more than those lost in the war with Prussia. These events marked France for years to come, establishing working-class socialism as the perceived enemy of national stability.

Peinture claire Literally, clear or light painting, meaning the technique of using high-keyed colours as ground preparations for canvases so as to heighten luminosity. Jean-Baptiste-Camille Corot was the chief practitioner in the mid-nineteenth century, although it had been used by painters of the Flemish, Dutch and British schools. It was associated with informal paintings done in *plein air* and was taken up by several Impressionists, especially **Claude Monet** and **Camille Pissarro**.

Plein-air Outdoor painting, originally referring primarily to sketches or studies for training or as the basis for more formal works. Its rise corresponded to the growing interest in observation of natural phenomena and **Barbizon School** landscapes in the mid-nineteenth century. Portable paint boxes and easels were developed to respond to the needs of outdoor painters. Not until the Impressionists were such paintings considered a final product for exhibition. **Claude Monet** is now regarded as the quintessential *plein-air* artist and the practice was at the heart of the aspects of Impressionism that he exemplified.

Positivism Belief in the primacy of facts and material phenomena in knowledge, and opposed to speculation about ultimate causes or origins. Specifically, the mid-nineteenth-century philosophical theory of Auguste Comte, who coupled such ideas with a schematic description of social evolution in phases, and a doctrine for reform that would ground politics in science so as to attain a final 'positive' and democratic phase. Hippolyte Taine applied these notions to art in the 1860s, arguing that each individual sees the world through a 'screen', which is formed by race, milieu and historical moment. **Émile Zola** was a follower, basing his novels on close observation and choosing social themes through which he hoped to reveal human nature in ways that would lead to social progress.

Realism In mid-nineteenth-century France, Realism denoted an artistic movement that aimed to produce objective representations based on impartial observation of everyday life. Realism was to be a measure of an artist's sincerity – of truth to his own vision rather than to one imposed by external authority. Realists assumed that naïve perception was a more or less objective process shared by all humans. Its most coherent development was in the art of **Gustave Courbet**, whose challenges to the authority of academic and official power had left-wing connotations. He linked the freedom of artists to the representation of their own times. Such ideas helped legitimize the Impressionists' painting of modern life.

Salon, Salon des Refusés At its founding in the seventeenth century, the Salon was the official exhibition showing paintings by members of the **Academy**. In the mid-eighteenth century, the Salon became a regular public event, though right to exhibit was limited to academicians, on grounds that their institution embodied the dignity of art as a humanistic practice. Others had to exhibit in their studios or in markets. With the French Revolution, this privilege was revoked and the Salon was thrown wide open, though after huge numbers of submissions a jury system was set up, dominated by academicians. Until the rise of private art dealers in the mid-nineteenth century, the Salon was the only place where artists could gain wider recognition and patronage. In the 1830s and 1840s, juries began refusing painters whose teachers were unknown or whose works did not conform to academic expectations. Resistance grew, with artists petitioning the state for more liberal juries and holding their own shows. Napoleon III finally agreed to a Salon des Refusés in 1863, in which every rejected work could be shown, though many withdrew, ashamed to be associated with artists deemed incompetent. Among the notable paintings exhibited, however, was *Le Déjeuner sur l'herbe* by **Édouard Manet**. The controversy over the Salon des Refusés aggravated the split between official art and the avant-garde.

Second Empire Following a *coup d'état* in 1851, Louis-Napoleon Bonaparte established the Second Empire, making himself Emperor and assuming almost dictatorial powers. The Second Empire saw the expansion of French industry and trade, with the Emperor taking the lead in lavish profligacy. Its militarized foreign policy, with campaigns in the Crimea and northern Italy, was meant to restore respect for France that had been lost at Waterloo. These policies failed when the Prussians attacked France in 1870 and quickly besieged Paris. The Empire collapsed with the declaration of the **Third Republic**.

Series In Impressionism, a series is a group of works very closely related by their subject matter and often by their composition, produced as part of a concerted campaign and exhibited together as a group. The first coherent series were paintings of rocks at Belle-Île by **Claude Monet**. Other famous series ensued, and the practice, which was convenient for marketing, was taken up by others in the group, notably **Edgar Degas** and **Camille Pissarro**. The fact that a single painter could produce different images of the same object stressed the subjective element in Impressionism and revealed a link with **Symbolism**.

Symbolism A literary movement mainly associated with French poets such as **Stéphane Mallarmé**, Jules Laforgue, Arthur Rimbaud and Paul Verlaine, as well as literary critics such as Albert Aurier, Gustave Kahn and Félix Fénéon, who also wrote about **Neo-Impressionism**. They rejected **Realism** and **Naturalism** in favour of recognition that all knowledge is subjective, and they believed the purpose of art was to express inner states of mind, sometimes mystical, rather than describe external reality. **Claude Monet** was admired by certain Symbolists because his later work seemed to exemplify such concepts.

Third Republic After the fall of the **Second Empire** in 1870, the Third Republic was established under the presidency of Adolphe Thiers. Immediately challenged by the **Paris Commune**, representatives of the new Republic fled to Versailles, where they eventually marshalled loyal troops which in May 1871 eradicated the Commune in a week-long attack. This act tainted the Third Republic for years as its three principal parties, Monarchists, Bonapartists and Liberal Republicans, each vied for legitimacy and proclaimed itself best guarantor of stability. The Third Republic was marked by intrigue and social conflict. Even with the eventual victory of the moderates, such conflicts continued until World War I. Ironically, this period is known as the Belle Epoque because of its prosperity and artistic efflorescence. The Third Republic survived until the Nazi occupation in 1940.

Universal Expositions International fairs held by governments to promote themselves politically and commercially. The first was held in London at the Crystal Palace in 1851. The French responded with a vast display of industry and arts in new buildings erected near the Champs Elysées in 1855. Thanks to the influx of tourists, artists were anxious to have their work exhibited. In 1855, **Gustave Courbet** set up a Realist Pavilion near the fairgrounds, and in 1867 both he and **Édouard Manet** had independent shows concurrent with the Exposition of that year.

Brief Biographies

Charles Baudelaire (1821–67) Poet, critic and author of the collection of poems *Les Fleurs du mal* (1857), which created a scandal in its time. He also wrote many essays on literature and visual art, including those on the **Salons** of 1845 and 1846, on his favourite painter **Eugène Delacroix**, and *The Painter of Modern Life* (1863), about the illustrator and watercolourist Constantin Guys. Baudelaire advocated the observation of modern life and was interested in caricature and illustration, the summary styles of which he linked to the rapid glance of the urban *flâneur*. His ideas influenced **Édouard Manet**, whom he supported in the early 1860s.

Frédéric Bazille (1841–70) Son of wealthy vintners and landowners from near Montpellier. Bazille went to Paris as a medical student but took up painting in the studio of Charles Gleyre, where he met several future Impressionists. He was introduced to the works of **Eugène Delacroix** and **Gustave Courbet** by his neighbour, the collector Alfred Bruyas, and his work combined the figural solidity of Courbet with Impressionist *plein-air* practices. Bazille was especially close to **Claude Monet** in the mid-1860s, when he shared a studio with him, as he later did with **Pierre-Auguste Renoir**. His studio in the rue de la Condamine in the Batignolles area was a rendezvous for the group in the late 1860s. He joined the meetings at the Café Guerbois and was among those who began planning independent exhibitions that would eventually start in 1874. However, Bazille enlisted in the army during the Franco-Prussian War and was killed in 1870.

Eugène Boudin (1824–98) A painter of beach scenes who became the mentor of **Claude Monet** in the late 1850s and early 1860s. He was a native of the coastal port of Le Havre, where he worked at a framing and picture shop that was patronized by certain members of the **Barbizon School** who came to paint on the nearby beaches in summer. Monet saw Boudin's works at the shop and acquired his commitment to *plein-air* painting through Boudin. Boudin sometimes exhibited with the Impressionists, but his bright palette, his age and his more traditional technique make him more of a transitional figure than a core member of the group.

Marie Quiveron Bracquemond (1840–1916) A painter who trained in the style of the **Academy** but strongly supported the Impressionists. She was exposed to Impressionism through her husband, the lithographer and etcher Félix Bracquemond, who had friends within the group and exhibited with them. She made a number of large works which combined aspects of *plein-air* practice with a traditional feeling for the figure. According to their son Pierre, her husband was jealous of her talent.

Except for her participation in the 1879, 1880 and 1886 **Impressionist exhibitions**, her art was rarely seen.

Gustave Caillebotte (1848–94) Son of a wealthy textile manufacturer, whose fortune he and his brother inherited in 1874. After training with the academic realist Léon Bonnat, Caillebotte became associated with the Impressionists through **Edgar Degas**, with whom he had the greatest artistic affinity at first. He began exhibiting with the group in 1876 at their second show, and he supported them enthusiastically until 1882. Caillebotte was instrumental in the organization of the **Impressionist exhibitions**, using his money to pay for frames, exhibition spaces, and to buy his friends' works at inflated prices. As a result, he acquired a splendid collection of Impressionist art, which he left to the French nation at his death. Most of the bequest was accepted, though not without controversy, and it now forms the core of the holdings at the Musée d'Orsay in Paris.

Mary Cassatt (1844–1926) Daughter of a prominent Pittsburgh businessman, Cassatt studied at Philadelphia's Pennsylvania Academy of the Fine Arts before travelling in Europe with her parents. There she met **Edgar Degas**, who persuaded her to join the **Impressionist exhibitions**, where she began showing work in 1879. Cassatt spent the rest of her life in France, and Degas remained a close friend. She bought works by Impressionists and encouraged her family and friends, most notably **Louisine Elder Havemeyer**, to do so as well. She was a sensitive portrayer of domestic scenes, and shared with Degas an interest in different techniques, working often in pastels and also making prints. In 1891 she made a highly original series of coloured etchings inspired by Japanese art.

Jules-Antoine Castagnary (1830–88) Liberal politician, lawyer and art critic from the Saintonge region of France. He met **Gustave Courbet** in 1860, defended **Realism** and then advocated **Naturalism** for its expression of both scientific and democratic attitudes. His response to Impressionism was ambiguous. Writing about the first exhibition, he formulated the difference between paintings that copied nature and those that responded to the sensations produced by nature upon the artist, using the word 'impression' to refer to the latter. In 1887, he became Minister of Fine Arts under the **Third Republic**.

Paul Cézanne (1839–1906) Growing up in the southern city of Aix-en-Provence, Cézanne began his studies in art against his wealthy father's wishes. His early friends included **Émile Zola** and others with literary and artistic aspirations. After following Zola to Paris in

1861, he studied at the Académie Suisse and joined the early Impressionist circle. Until the mid-1880s he alternated between the Paris region and the South. Following awkward yet powerful early works, many inspired by literary or religious themes, he began to work with **Camille Pissarro** at Pontoise in the early 1870s, concentrating on landscape and still life. Though he shared the Impressionist commitment to *plein-air* painting and exhibited with them several times, his ambitions were always informed by his Provençal roots and admiration of the classics. Thus, he pursued the idea of remaking the work of Classicist Nicolas Poussin 'after nature' and of solidifying Impressionism into something 'like the art of the museums'. In the 1890s, Cézanne began attaining critical success in exhibitions organized by the young dealer Ambroise Vollard, where his work influenced a new generation of artists led by Georges Bracque and Pablo Picasso.

Georges Charpentier (1846–1905) The successful publisher of Gustave Flaubert, **Émile Zola**, the Goncourt brothers and other literary realists and naturalists. He and his wife Marguerite were early and devoted patrons of the Impressionists, of whom their favourite was **Pierre-Auguste Renoir**. Charpentier founded the journal *La Vie moderne*, in which their art was often featured, and he held exhibitions of their work in an art gallery that was part of the journal's offices. During the Impressionist period, Madame Charpentier's soirees were an important meeting place for the artistic world of Paris.

Victor Chocquet (1821–91) A customs official and passionate art collector who began collecting works by **Eugène Delacroix** and **Gustave Courbet** with his meagre income, but eventually inherited substantial sums through his wife. Discovering the Impressionists at their 1875 auction at the Hôtel Drouot, he commissioned portraits from **Pierre-Auguste Renoir** and **Paul Cézanne**. He became notorious for his ardent support at their shows, especially when he defended them against criticisms he overheard at their exhibition of 1877. His collection contained over fifty Impressionist works at his death.

Georges Clemenceau (1841–1929) A militant Republican politician and leader of liberal forces within the **Third Republic**, he was a friend of **Édouard Manet**, who made at least two unfinished portraits of him in 1879–80. Clemenceau later befriended **Claude Monet**, whom he visited frequently in Giverny, writing an article on him in 1895. In 1898 Clemenceau's newspaper, *L'Aurore*, published 'J'accuse', the famous defence of Alfred Dreyfus by **Émile Zola**. Clemenceau was the French prime minister from 1906 to 1909 and from 1917 to 1920, and he used his influence to acquire Monet's Grandes Décorations for the state.

Gustave Courbet (1819–77) Leader of the **Realists**, he was the first artist of the avant-garde because of his unrelenting political and artistic opposition to establishment authority. His *Stonebreakers* and *A Burial at Ornans*, both exhibited in 1850–1, came to be associated with the left-wing revolution of 1848. Courbet set an example for Impressionism both through his art, which he based on common people engaged in everyday activities, and his independence from official institutions. In 1855, he held a private exhibition called 'Realism' across from the fairgrounds of the **Universal Exposition**. Accompanying the show was a manifesto in which he declared that art must represent its own times as seen through the eyes of the individual artist. In 1871, Courbet became deeply involved in the **Paris Commune**, for which he was later arrested and imprisoned.

Edgar Degas (1834–1917) Born to an upper-class banking family with claims to aristocratic lineage, Degas trained at the **Academy** and studied the Old Masters during a three-year period in Italy. On meeting **Édouard Manet** in the early 1860s, he entered the Impressionist circle and gradually discarded historical and literary subjects. Nonetheless, he retained his loyalty to many traditional principles, such as careful technical preparation for his pictures and the primacy of drawing. His imagery was the most urban of the Impressionists, and he disavowed landscape and *plein-air* painting in favour of realism and naturalism. Despite this, he was instrumental in sustaining the **Impressionist exhibitions**, which he missed only once. He also introduced other artists to the exhibitions, including **Gustave Caillebotte** and **Mary Cassatt**, but his recruitment of other less gifted and more narrowly **Realist** painters led to serious conflicts with his collaborators in the early 1880s. His fascination with craft led him to explore different media, including pastels and printmaking. Degas was fond of monotypes, which were the basis of many technically and iconographically original works. Horseracing and the ballet were favourite subjects, which he eventually evolved into **series**. Commercially successful, he collected art aggressively, including older masters, such as **Eugène Delacroix** and Jean-Auguste-Dominique Ingres, as well as his Impressionist peers. Politically conservative, he became estranged from many of his circle when later in life he revealed himself to be vehemently anti-Semitic during the Dreyfus Affair.

Eugène Delacroix (1798–1863) Painter of historical and literary subjects, leader of French Romanticism. His large paintings of the 1820s established Romanticism as an art of modern subjects and relatively naturalistic style, as opposed to the more traditional Classicism of his great rival, Jean-Auguste-Dominique Ingres. In this limited sense, he paved the way for **Realism** and Impressionism. However, for many artists and writers, Delacroix stood as a beacon for independence and artistic imagination in the face of both academic convention and photographic literalism. The Impressionists admired his loose handling of paint and expressive use of brilliant colour.

Paul Durand-Ruel (1831–1922) The most prominent art dealer to support the Impressionists, Durand-Ruel was head of a family art business, initially dealing primarily in **Barbizon School** and Romantic painters. He met **Claude Monet** and **Camille Pissarro** in 1871 in London, where in the following year he organized an exhibition that included several works by Impressionists. He was the first dealer to guarantee income to an artist in exchange for a percentage of his output. When he could, he would also make outright purchases when artists needed money. The **Impressionist exhibition** of 1882 was held in his gallery. Soon thereafter, surviving the bankruptcy of his financial backer, he began organizing one-man shows for Impressionist artists. He opened a gallery in New York in 1888.

Edmond Duranty (1833–80) A minor novelist and art critic who defended **Realist** art; publisher of the short-lived review *Le Réalisme* (1856). By the 1860s Duranty was a part of the early Impressionist circle. He was a friend of **Edgar Degas**, with whom he shared certain scientific attitudes and whose art was closer to the palette and technique of the earlier generation with which he had been associated. In 1876, he published an essay on Impressionism called *The New Painting*, which defended the young artists on grounds of their fidelity to observation of modern life and their development of new methods appropriate for its expression.

Théodore Duret (1838–1927) Republican politician, journalist and art critic. Duret's first connections to the art world were through **Gustave Courbet**, whom he knew in the early 1860s. In 1865, he met **Édouard Manet** in Madrid. His first article on art was published in 1867, and he collaborated with **Émile Zola** on a newspaper in the following year. Duret commissioned a portrait from Manet in 1868 and began collecting other Impressionist works in earnest in 1872, after meeting **Camille Pissarro**. In his essay *The Impressionist Painters of 1878*, Duret defended Impressionism as the natural heir to **Realism** and the **Barbizon School**. He also praised their innovative colour sensibility, awakened by Japanese prints, of which, thanks to travels to Asia, he was a connoisseur. Thereafter, Duret was forced by his father's death to take over the family business. While maintaining links to the art world, he was no longer so active.

Henri Fantin-Latour (1836–1904) A painter trained at the **Academy** but who quickly became associated with the early Impressionist group. Among his many portraits of the 1860s were two, *Homage to Delacroix* (1863) and *A Studio in the Batignolles Quarter* (1870), showing groups of artists and writers, including several Impressionists. His palette and sharp draughtsmanship aligned him stylistically with more conventional artists, and he never exhibited with the Impressionists. He is known today primarily for fresh flower still lifes whose beauty resides in their brilliant colours and traditional craft.

Paul Gauguin (1848–1903) The son of a French journalist and a Peruvian Creole, Gauguin was brought up in Peru and became an investment banker in Paris in 1872. After seeing the **Impressionist exhibition** of 1874, he began purchasing Impressionist works and decided to become an artist. He painted in Pontoise with **Camille Pissarro** and **Paul Cézanne**, whose influence his early works reveal, and he took part in the Impressionist exhibitions from 1878. Following the stock market crash of 1882, Gauguin found himself out of work

and devoted himself full time to painting. In 1884, his Danish wife and their children left for Copenhagen, which Gauguin visited twice without success either for his marriage or his art sales. As he matured as an artist in the mid-1880s, Gauguin began to incorporate the ideas of **Symbolism**. He became the leader of a colony of artists at Pont-Aven in Brittany, before travelling to Martinique and then later to Tahiti, where he eventually stayed for long periods.

Eva Gonzalès (1849–83) A figure painter who forsook her academic training to become the only student of **Édouard Manet** in 1867. In 1870, her *Little Soldier*, which echoes Manet's *Fifer Boy* of 1866, was purchased by the Musée du Luxembourg, which exhibited contemporary French art, possibly because her father was an influential literary figure. Paralleling Manet's development, her style loosened up in the 1870s, but her repertoire focused on the domestic.

Armand Guillaumin (1841–1927) Probably least known of the core Impressionists, Guillaumin was from a working-class family and had to study art in his spare time. In the 1860s, he worked for the Orléans Railway, then later got a job with the City of Paris which allowed him to paint by day. Until the 1880s his work was dominated by industrial scenes along the Seine river, which may have influenced **Paul Cézanne** and **Camille Pissarro**, whom he met at the Académie Suisse in 1861. The three of them experimented with etching at the house of Dr Gachet in Auvers-sur-Oise in the early 1870s. His vigorous brushstrokes and strident colour were more appreciated by Vincent van Gogh and the Fauves. Guillaumin was never commercially successful, but thanks to a large lottery prize in 1891, he attained financial security that enabled him to travel and devote the rest of his career to remote coastal landscapes and country scenes.

Ludovic Halévy (1833–1908) A school friend of **Edgar Degas** who became a dramatist, novelist and librettist for Georges Bizet's *Carmen* (1875) and operettas by Jacques Offenbach. In 1877, he collaborated on a play called *La Cigale* (*The Grasshopper*) satirizing the Impressionists, though despite this Degas helped design some of the sets. Soon after, his stories of the fictitious ballet dancers, the Cardinal sisters, inspired monotypes by Degas. Degas was a regular guest at his house and in the 1890s made photographs of him and his wife. Though raised as a Catholic, Halévy belonged to a prominent Jewish family. During the Dreyfus Affair, Degas's deep-seated anti-Semitism led to a break between them.

Louisine Elder Havemeyer (1855–1929) Daughter of a prominent Philadelphia family and a friend of **Mary Cassatt**, through whom she purchased her first Impressionist paintings even before her marriage in 1883 to Henry Osborne Havemeyer, head of the American Sugar Refining Company. Following the birth of their children and a trip to the Paris **Universal Exposition** in 1889, they began to collect Impressionist work in quantity. After her husband's death in 1907, she continued collecting and became a militant suffragette. She was decorated by the French government after donating a portrait of **Georges Clemenceau** by Édouard Manet to the Louvre. Her bequest of 1,972 items to the Metropolitan Museum of Art in New York formed the core of its now world-famous collection of Impressionist art.

Stéphane Mallarmé (1842–98) Poet, critic and teacher of English at a Paris lycée. Mallarmé was a close friend of **Édouard Manet**, whom he visited almost daily on his way home from school. His essay of 1876, 'The Impressionists and Édouard Manet', was an early and sophisticated analysis of Impressionism. Manet illustrated his translation of Edgar Allen Poe's *The Raven* (1875) and his *L'Après-midi d'un faune* (1876). He was also friendly with **Berthe Morisot, Pierre-Auguste Renoir** and **Edgar Degas**, who photographed him. The emphasis in his poetry on internal, dream-like experience, combined with self-consciously innovative structures and even arrangements of words on the page, made him a leader of the **Symbolist** literary movement. **Paul Gauguin** was among those who embraced his ideas for visual art in the 1880s.

Édouard Manet (1832–83) Born to a high-ranking magistrate of the **Second Empire** administration, sophisticated and debonair, Manet was considered by most Impressionists to be their leader, even though he refused to exhibit with them, believing that the **Salon** was where one must face the public. A student of the independent master Thomas Couture, he began his career with works that echoed Dutch and Spanish realism rather than the academic style still pre-eminent in France. Two enormously controversial works, *Le Déjeuner sur l'herbe* and *Olympia*, established his reputation as avant-garde radical. The former was refused at the Salon of 1863, but included in a special **Salon des Refusés** authorized the same year; the latter was shown at the Salon of 1865, when admission rules were liberalized. Manet helped to establish the Batignolles as an area for artists, and he was at the centre of gatherings at the Café Guerbois and elsewhere. By the early 1870s, his friendships, especially with **Berthe Morisot** and **Claude Monet** led to suburban visits and *plein-air* painting in a freely brushed style approaching their own. However, the pictures on which he expended greatest effort continued to feature the figure in urban settings, though he produced many still lifes, garden scenes and portraits of friends in the more casual Impressionist mode. Among his most exquisite works are small flower pieces produced under failing health before his early death.

Claude Monet (1840–1926) Born in Paris but raised in Le Havre, where his father was a dry goods dealer, Monet is the painter most synonymous with Impressionism. It was his painting of 1872, *Impression, Sunrise*, which led to the use of the term to characterize the work of several artists who showed with him at the first **Impressionist exhibition** of 1874. Monet began painting on the Normandy beaches, where he developed his commitment to *plein-air* painting. By 1869, when he worked with **Pierre-Auguste**

Renoir at La Grenouillère, he was concentrating almost exclusively on landscape, having more or less abandoned the interest in figure painting he had pursued after his first trips to Paris earlier in the 1860s. Following the precedent of the **Barbizon School**, he established residence outside Paris, but rather than choosing a rural retreat, he preferred the suburban environment of Argenteuil. His pictures of sailing boats there created a paradigm for Impressionism, but he continued to develop and explore, first by travel, then by the development of paintings in **series** of the same motif from related points of view or ostensibly under varying conditions. Monet eventually settled in Giverny, where in 1891 he purchased the property in which he created his splendid gardens, waterlily pond and Japanese footbridge. He was among the first Impressionists to become commercially successful, largely thanks to his collaboration with the dealer **Paul Durand-Ruel**. He was a generous supporter of his colleagues and friends, organizing the public fund-raising effort to purchase *Olympia* for the nation following the death of **Édouard Manet** and publicly supporting **Émile Zola** in the Dreyfus Affair. Late in his career, he made a series of large waterlily paintings commissioned by the French government through his friendship with **Georges Clemenceau**.

Berthe Morisot (1841–95) Daughter of a high-ranking civil servant, she and her sister Edma took drawing and painting lessons, eventually working under the **Barbizon School** painter Jean-Bapiste-Camille Corot. On meeting **Édouard Manet** in the Louvre through **Henri Fantin-Latour**, she joined his circle, adopting a style related to his, and posing for several of his pictures, including *The Balcony* of 1869. In 1874, she married Manet's brother Eugène, who encouraged her painting career. Against Édouard Manet's advice, she regularly participated with the **Impressionist exhibitions**, missing only in 1877 when her daughter was born. She worked within the limitations on women artists of her time and her social standing, focusing primarily on domestic scenes. Yet she developed an original and challenging personal style, based on long and loosely interwoven brushstrokes and high-keyed colours, and she displayed aspects of modern life to which male artists were not particularly sensitive. Rather than joining Impressionist café circles, which would not have been suitable to her station, she made her own house a place where Impressionists gathered. At her death, **Pierre-Auguste Renoir** and **Edgar Degas** organized a retrospective that attained considerable critical success.

Camille Pissarro (1830–1903) Born to Jewish merchants in St Thomas in the Danish (now US) Virgin Islands, he was educated partly in France but returned to St Thomas to enter the family business. There, he studied with the Danish painter Fritz Melbye, before returning to Paris in 1855 to commit himself exclusively to art. Oldest of the Impressionists, he worked with Jean-Bapiste-Camille Corot in the early 1860s, when he also met **Claude Monet** at the Académie Suisse and was soon introduced to the other artists in the circle of **Édouard Manet**.

Since he was not a French citizen, he had no military obligation and avoided the Franco-Prussian War by visiting relatives in London. There he encountered Monet, as well as the dealer **Paul Durand-Ruel**, who began to purchase his work. Pissarro was the only Impressionist to exhibit in all eight **Impressionist exhibitions**, and he was often instrumental in keeping the group together. Settling in Pontoise in the 1870s, he worked with **Paul Cézanne** and **Armand Guillaumin**, becoming leader of the so-called School of Pontoise, which **Paul Gauguin** later joined. They focused less on bourgeois leisure than the other Impressionists, and his own anarchism tended to idealize the peasantry rather than industrial society. Nonetheless, with Guillaumin, his works show the greatest acceptance of industrialization as subject matter for art. After moving to Eragny in 1884, he was the only core Impressionist to convert, albeit briefly, to **Neo-Impressionism**, to which he was attracted for its apparent scientific basis and democratic accessibility. In the 1890s, he followed Monet in producing **series** paintings, though his subjects were urban views from hotel windows rather than rural or garden scenes.

Pierre-Auguste Renoir (1841–1919) Born in Limoges, Renoir moved to Paris at the age of three, where his father, a tailor, hoped for a better living. In 1854, he was apprenticed to a porcelain painter, but in 1861 he began to attend the studio of Charles Gleyre, and the following year was admitted to the **Academy**. Although he exhibited a few works at the **Salon**, he painted frequently with Impressionists he had met at Gleyre's. In 1869, he worked with **Claude Monet** at La Grenouillère, where they developed their own characteristic Impressionist styles. Renoir was a great admirer of **Eugène Delacroix** and his favourite subject matter was women. His mistresses or amateur models, whom he met at cafés such as the Moulin de la Galette, were often the focus of his works. Through various friends, he obtained numerous commissions, especially for portraits, which dominate his work more than that of his peers. His successes eventually led to his return to the Salon in 1878, disqualifying him from the **Impressionist exhibition** of that year. Like Monet, he began to travel in the 1880s. However, at the same time he began revising his style in conservative ways, hoping to emulate the Old Masters. By 1884 he attained what has been called his 'Sour Period', with forms sharply defined by line, though still brightly coloured. In the 1890s, he settled near the French Riviera, where he did many sensuous pictures of young girls and Mediterranean landscapes.

Georges Seurat (1859–91) Painter who became the leader of **Neo-Impressionism**, he began exhibiting with the Artistes Indépendants, who formed in 1884, but in 1886 he and his followers had a room at the last **Impressionist exhibition**, where his most famous work, *Sunday Afternoon on the Island of La Grande Jatte* was displayed. Seurat trained at the **Academy** but was attracted by **plein-air** painting and the Impressionist commitment to modern life. He combined these pursuits with scientific interests in colour theory and developed a systematized

method of applying paint called Pointillism. Later he turned to representations of urban entertainment, for which he used increasingly abstract geometric structures. He died of an illness at age thirty-two. **Camille Pissarro**, along with his son Lucien, was briefly attracted to Seurat's theories, which he saw as an alternative to the individualistic bent of what he called 'romantic' Impressionism.

Paul Signac (1863–1935) Almost entirely self-taught, he began painting under the influence of **Claude Monet**, **Armand Guillaumin** and **Camille Pissarro** in the early 1880s. In 1884, he joined the Artistes Indépendants and met **Georges Seurat**, whose disciple he would become. He introduced Seurat to the **Symbolist** critics Félix Fénéon, Gustave Kahn and Paul Adam, who began writing about **Neo-Impressionism**. There is no better example of Pointillism than Signac's painting. In 1899, he published *From Eugène Delacroix to Neo-Impressionism*, in which he viewed the development of nineteenth-century art through the increasingly scientific use of colour. Like Pissarro, he was attracted to anarchist political theories.

Alfred Sisley (1839–99) Born in Paris of English parents, Sisley met several of the Impressionists at the studio of Charles Gleyre, where he studied in the mid 1860s. He worked primarily in landscape, accompanying his friends to the villages around the Forest of Fontainebleau. When he showed at the 1867 **Salon** he described himself as the student of Jean-Bapiste-Camille Corot. As he became closer to other Impressionists, his landscapes became more suburban than rural, resembling by the 1870s those of **Claude Monet** stylistically, though with a luminous unity echoing the **Barbizon School**. With some exceptions, such as a **series** done when he travelled with collector Jean-Baptiste Faure to Hampton Court in 1874, and another of the flooding at Port-Marly in 1876, his work hovered between that of Monet and **Camille Pissarro**. Of the main Impressionists, he is perhaps the most generic, though he had a sensitivity and craft sufficiently superb to permit financial survival, if not prosperity. His reticent personality prevented him from aggressive marketing, and he died without achieving as much recognition as his peers.

Émile Zola (1840–1902) Brought up in Aix-en-Provence, Zola was a childhood friend of **Paul Cézanne**. After moving to Paris, he entered the Impressionist circle and defended **Édouard Manet**. He was a prolific novelist and journalist who advocated a scientific approach to writing, dealing in his novels with contemporary social issues such as alcoholism, disease and prostitution. His novel *L'Oeuvre* (1886), about a struggling artist, ruptured his friendship with Cézanne. Zola was an ardent proponent of social reform and in his 1898 article 'J'Accuse' he attacked the French establishment over its conduct in the Dreyfus Affair. As a result, he was prosecuted for libel, fined and imprisoned, but the article eventually led to a retrial.

Key Dates

Numbers in square brackets refer to illustrations

Impressionism

A Context of Events
(primarily French,
unless otherwise noted)

1855	Edgar Degas enters the École des Beaux-Arts. Camille Pissarro arrives in Paris	
		1855 Universal Exposition in Paris. Gustave Courbet holds a one-man exhibition and publishes *The Realist Manifesto*
1856	Degas departs for a three-year stay in Italy. Claude Monet meets Eugène Boudin in Le Havre; Boudin introduces him to *plein-air* painting	1856 End of the Crimean War
1857	Édouard Manet travels in Germany, Holland and Italy	1857 Charles Baudelaire, *Les Fleurs du mal*
1858	Pissarro attends Académie Suisse. Pierre-Auguste Renoir gives up painting on porcelain	
1859	Monet moves to Paris and meets Pissarro at Académie Suisse. Manet's *The Absinthe Drinker* [25] is rejected by the Salon	1859 Britain: Charles Darwin, *The Origin of Species*
1860	Manet moves to the Batignolles area. Degas paints *Young Spartans Exercising*	1860 France and Britain sign a free trade treaty. USA: Civil War begins
1861	Manet meets Baudelaire and Edmond Duranty. Paul Cézanne and Armand Guillaumin join Académie Suisse, where they meet Pissarro	
1862	Manet comes into his inheritance, paints *Music in the Tuileries Gardens* [27] and meets Degas. Renoir, Frédéric Bazille and Alfred Sisley attend Charles Gleyre's studio. Renoir is admitted to the École des Beaux-Arts	1862 French troops sent to Mexico. Construction of the new Opéra, designed by Charles Garnier, begins in Paris. Victor Hugo, *Les Misérables*. Prussia: Bismarck becomes prime minister
1863	Napoleon III orders a Salon des Refusés; Marie Bracquemond, Cézanne, Manet and Pissarro exhibit works, Manet's *Le Déjeuner sur l'herbe* [30] causes a sensation. Manet marries Suzanne Leenhoff	1863 Ernest Renan, *Vie de Jésus*. Baudelaire, *The Painter of Modern Life*. Britain: First underground railway opens in London
1864	Renoir, Monet, Bazille and Sisley leave Gleyre's studio. A more tolerant Salon jury accepts paintings by Manet, Pissarro, Berthe Morisot and Renoir. Monet and Bazille work together in Normandy	1864 Edmond and Jules Goncourt, *Renée Mauperin* and *Germinie Lacerteux*. Mexico: Archduke Maximilian is crowned emperor
1865	Cézanne meets Pissarro at Académie Suisse. Manet shocks visitors to the Salon with his *Olympia* [34]. Degas, Renoir, Pissarro and Morisot are also represented. Renoir meets his model and mistress, Lise Tréhot	1865 USA: Abraham Lincoln assassinated. Civil war ends. Britain: Charles Dickens, *Our Mutual Friend*
1866	Pissarro moves to Pontoise. The Salon rejects works by Manet, including *The Fifer Boy* [40], but Morisot, Sisley, Bazille and Monet all have paintings accepted. Émile Zola begins publishing articles on Manet and other future Impressionists in *L'Evénement*. Mary Cassatt arrives in Paris	1866 Mexico: Withdrawal of French troops. Sweden: Alfred Bernhard Nobel invents dynamite
1867	Renoir's *Diana* [99] is rejected by the Salon jury. Manet opens a one-man show to run concurrently with the Universal Exposition	1867 Universal Exposition takes place in Paris. Courbet holds a show in his own pavilion. Mexico: Emperor Maximilian executed. Zola, *Thérèse Racquin*

Impressionism	A Context of Events

1868 The Salon accepts Manet's *Portrait of Émile Zola* [39], Bazille's *Family Reunion* [80], Monet's *Women in the Garden* [56] and Pissarro's *L'Hermitage at Pontoise* [96].
Henri Fantin-Latour introduces Morisot to Manet.
Monet, Renoir and Sisley join Manet and his circle at the Café Guerbois

1868 French laws restricting public meetings are relaxed.
Bibliothèque Nationale opens in Paris.
Russia: Peter Ilyich Tchaikovsky composes Symphony No. 1

1869 The Salon rejects Manet's *The Execution of the Emperor Maximilian* [176] because it is thought to be too politically sensitive. Eva Gonzalès becomes a pupil of Manet. Cézanne meets Hortense Fiquet

1869 Napoleon III institutes a more liberal regime with a parliamentary government. Empress Eugénie opens the Suez Canal.
Flaubert, *L'Education sentimentale*

1870 Manet and Edmond Duranty have a duel at the Café Guerbois; they soon become friends again.
Monet marries Camille Doncieux.
On France's declaration of war against Prussia, Renoir is called up and Bazille enlists.
While Paris is under siege Degas and Manet join the National Guard, while Cézanne avoids conscription by hiding in Éstaque with Hortense Fiquet. Monet and Pissarro move to England with their families, where first Monet and later Pissarro meet the art dealer Paul Durand-Ruel. Cassatt returns to the USA. Bazille is killed in action

1870 France declares war on Prussia.
Napoleon III abdicates following French defeat at Sedan. The Third Republic is proclaimed, led by Adolphe Thiers. Prussian forces besiege Paris

1871 Manet is among the fifteen artists included in a federation of artists set up under the Commune.
Pissarro marries Julie Velley in London. He returns to France to find his home looted and many of his paintings stolen or destroyed.
Monet moves to Argenteuil

1871 France defeated by Prussia. With support from the National Guard, Parisians take over the government of Paris, declaring a socialist Commune on 18 March. Government troops attack Paris in May. Nearly 30,000 Parisians are killed in the suppression of the Commune

1872 Durand-Ruel builds up his collection of Impressionist works.
Degas arrives in New Orleans.
Cézanne joins Pissarro in Pontoise

1872 France's economy booms and the French government pays off the huge indemnity imposed by Germany after the Franco-Prussian war

1873 Cézanne stays in Auvers-sur-Oise with Dr Gachet.
Monet meets Gustave Caillebotte.
The Société Anonyme des Artistes, including all the future Impressionists, is formed to organize group exhibitions

1873 The reactionary Marshal MacMahon is elected president.
France is struck by an economic crisis.
Zola, *Le Ventre de Paris*.
Britain: Death of Napoleon III

1874 First Impressionist exhibition. Louis Leroy coins the phrase 'Impressionist' in a review of the show. Morisot marries Manet's brother Eugène.
Sisley travels in England with the collector Jean-Baptiste Faure and paints at Hampton Court [220]

1874 Child labour outlawed.
Photography becomes cheaper with the production of bromide plates.

1875 The Impressionists hold an auction at the Hôtel Drouot, with disappointing results

1875 Constitution for the Third Republic is ratified

1876 Second Impressionist exhibition.
Duranty publishes the first book on the Impressionists, *La Nouvelle peinture*

1876 Mallarmé, *L'Après-midi d'un faune*.
USA: Alexander Graham Bell invents the telephone

1877 Pissarro and Alfred Meyer establish L'Union as an alternative to the Impressionists. Cézanne, Guillaumin and Pissarro leave the group before the opening of their exhibition, which is a failure.
Third Impressionist exhibition.
Georges Rivière publishes *L'Impressionniste, journal d'art*.
Ludovic Halévy writes *La Cigale*, a satirical comedy about the Impressionists

1877 President MacMahon dissolves the chamber of deputies and appoints a Royalist cabinet.
Zola, *L'Assommoir*.
Switzerland: Death of Courbet.
Britain: Queen Victoria proclaimed Empress of India

1878 Degas's *Portraits in a Cotton Office, New Orleans* [217] is bought by the Friends of Art Society in Pau.
Cézanne's allowance is halved when his father finds out about the birth of his son Paul.
Following his bankruptcy, Ernest Hoschedé's Impressionist collection is auctioned at Hôtel Drouot, with bad results. Monet provides a home for the Hoschedé family

1878 Universal Exposition opens in Paris.
First French Congress for Women's Rights.
Death of the artist Charles-François Daubigny

	Impressionism	A Context of Events
1879	Degas frequents the Cirque Fernando. Georges Charpentier launches *La Vie moderne*. Fourth Impressionist exhibition. Renoir's *Madame Charpentier and her Children* [110] is well received at the Salon. Monet paints *Camille on her Deathbed* [73]	**1879** Following MacMahon's resignation, Jules Grévy becomes president. Formation of the French Socialist Party. USA: Thomas Edison invents the electric light bulb
1880	Fifth Impressionist exhibition. Cézanne, Monet, Renoir and Sisley do not take part. Monet has one painting accepted by the Salon, where his work appears for the last time. Degas produces monotypes for Halévy's *La Famille Cardinal*	**1880** An amnesty is declared for exiled or imprisoned Communards. Public education is made available for girls. Zola, *Nana*
1881	Sixth Impressionist exhibition. Degas exhibits *The Little Fourteen-Year-Old Dancer* [127]. Caillebotte joins Cézanne, Monet, Renoir and Sisley in refusing to take part. Pissarro, Cézanne and Paul Gauguin paint together in Pontoise; Cézanne returns to Aix-en-Provence in the autumn. The ailing Manet is awarded the Légion d'honneur	**1881** Control of the Salon is transferred from the Ministry of Fine Arts to the Société des Artistes Français. Under the new system, any artist who has had work accepted by the Salon can elect the jury. Léon Gambetta becomes prime minister. Russia: Assassination of Tsar Alexander II. Britain: Henry James, *Portrait of a Lady*
1882	Seventh Impressionist exhibition. Manet's *A Bar at the Folies-Bergère* [47] is shown at the Salon, as are works by Cézanne and Renoir	**1882** A Courbet retrospective opens at the École des Beaux-Arts. Union Internationale bank crashes in Paris
1883	Deaths of Manet and Gonzalès. Monet moves to Giverny. First exhibition of Impressionist paintings takes place in the United States in Boston, followed by an 'art loan' show in New York, where William Merritt Chase and others contribute Impressionist works. This marks the beginning of widespread American interest in the movement	**1883** France's financial situation improves. Édouard Delamare-Debouteville invents the petrol-engined car. Zola, *Au bonheur des dames*. USA: First skyscraper built in Chicago. Germany: Friedrich Wilhelm Nietzsche, *Thus Spake Zarathustra*. Britain: Death of Marx
1884	Manet retrospective at the École des Beaux-Arts. Monet paints in Bordighera in Italy	**1884** The Société des Artistes Indépendants is founded in Paris
1885	Monet exhibits works at Georges Petit's Exposition Internationale. Morisot begins hosting soirees. Pissarro meets Paul Signac and Georges Seurat	**1885** Zola, *Germinal*. Charles Henry, *Introduction to a Scientific Aesthetic*. Death of Victor Hugo
1886	Seurat paints *Sunday Afternoon on the Island of La Grande Jatte* [203]. Pissarro begins painting in a Pointillist style. The eighth Impressionist exhibition is dominated by Neo-Impressionist works by Seurat, Signac and Pissarro. Cézanne receives his inheritance. Zola publishes *L'Oeuvre*, which ruptures his friendship with Cézanne	**1886** Bonaparte and Orléans families are banished from France. The right-wing General Boulanger becomes French Minister of War
1887	Monet, Pissarro, Renoir and Sisley exhibit at Petit's Exposition Internationale	**1887** Grévy resigns as president of France. Construction of the Eiffel Tower begins in Paris
1888	Durand-Ruel opens a gallery in New York. Monet refuses the Légion d'honneur. Pissarro contracts an eye infection that will persist for the rest of his life	
1889	Cézanne, Manet, Monet and Pissarro exhibit at the Universal Exposition. Monet starts a collection to buy Manet's *Olympia* [34] for the Louvre. Pissarro finishes his *Social Turpitudes* [187, 188]	**1889** The Eiffel Tower is finished in time for the Universal Exposition held in Paris to celebrate the centenary of the French Revolution. General Boulanger flees to Belgium after the French government issues a warrant for his arrest on the charge of treason
1890	Monet begins painting his grainstack series [223–225] in Giverny. Renoir is awarded the Légion d'honneur	**1890** Death of Vincent van Gogh
1891	Monet's grainstack series is exhibited at Durand- Ruel's gallery, to huge acclaim.	**1891** Gauguin travels to Tahiti for the first time. Deaths of the painter Johan Barthold Jongkind

Year	Impressionism	A Context of Events
	Pissarro undergoes an eye operation that prevents him from working outdoors. Guillaumin wins 100,000 francs in the lottery. Death of Georges Seurat	and the poet Arthur Rimbaud. Britain: Thomas Hardy, *Tess of the d'Urbervilles*
1892	Monet begins painting his Rouen Cathedral series [227]; his Poplar series [231] is exhibited at Durand-Ruel's gallery. In May Monet marries Alice Hoschedé. Pissarro visits his son Lucien in London	1892 Zola, *La Débâcle*. François Hennebique invents reinforced concrete. Germany: Rudolf Diesel invents the diesel engine. Russia: First performance of Tchaikovsky's *The Nutcracker*
1893	Pissarro contributes to the anarchist journal *La Plume*. Monet starts creating his water garden at Giverny	1893 Panama Canal corruption trial takes place in Paris. Germany: Edvard Munch paints *The Scream*
1894	Death of Caillebotte. His collection of Impressionist paintings is bequeathed to the state. Théodore Duret's collection is auctioned at Hôtel Drouot; Monet's *Turkeys* [219] attracts the highest bid	1894 The anarchist Félix Fénéon is arrested after bombings in Paris and elsewhere. Captain Alfred Dreyfus is convicted of treason. Claude Debussy composes *L'Après-midi d'un faune*, inspired by Mallarmé's poem
1895	Monet travels to Norway. On his return to Paris, a hugely successful one-man show is held at Durand-Ruel's gallery. Cézanne has a show at Ambroise Vollard's gallery. Death of Morisot	1895 Germany: Wilhelm Conrad Röntgen discovers X-rays. Britain: H G Wells, *The Time Machine*
1896	A Morisot retrospective and a Pissarro exhibition take place at Durand-Ruel's gallery	1896 Russia: First performance of Anton Chekhov's *The Seagull*
1897	Exhibition of Sisley's work at Petit's gallery. The Caillebotte bequest is hung at the Musée du Luxembourg. Degas breaks off his friendship with the Halévy family following the Dreyfus affair. Monet starts his series of paintings of the Seine near Giverny [226]	1897 Mathieu Dreyfus discovers that Major Esterhazy is the true author of the document that incriminated his brother Alfred. Belgium: Universal Exposition held in Brussels
1898	Sisley applies for French citizenship. Monet has a very successful exhibition at Petit's gallery	1898 Esterhazy is acquitted of treason. Colonel Henry admits forging evidence against Dreyfus and commits suicide. Zola exposes the scandal in 'J'Accuse', his famous open letter to President Faure. Deaths of Mallarmé and Boudin
1899	Death of Sisley	1899 Dreyfus is found guilty again at a retrial, but is subsequently pardoned and released
		1901 Britain: Death of Queen Victoria; she is succeeded by Edward VII
1903	Death of Pissarro	1903 Death of Gauguin. Britain: Death of James Abbott McNeil Whistler
1904	Cassatt is awarded the Légion d'honneur. An entire room at the Salon d'Automne in Paris is devoted to Cézanne's paintings	1904 Russia and Japan declare war
1906	Death of Cézanne	1906 Dreyfus is awarded the Legion d'honneur
1907	Manet's *Olympia* [34] is exhibited at the Louvre	
		1914 Beginning of World War I (to 1918)
1917	Death of Degas	1917 Russian Revolution
1919	Death of Renoir	
1922	Death of Durand-Ruel	
1926	Deaths of Monet and Cassatt	1926 Japan: Coronation of Emperor Hirohito. Britain: General Strike. John Logie Baird makes first television transmission
1927	Monet's *Grandes Décorations* cyclorama opens at L'Orangerie in Paris	1927 Joseph Stalin becomes leader of the USSR

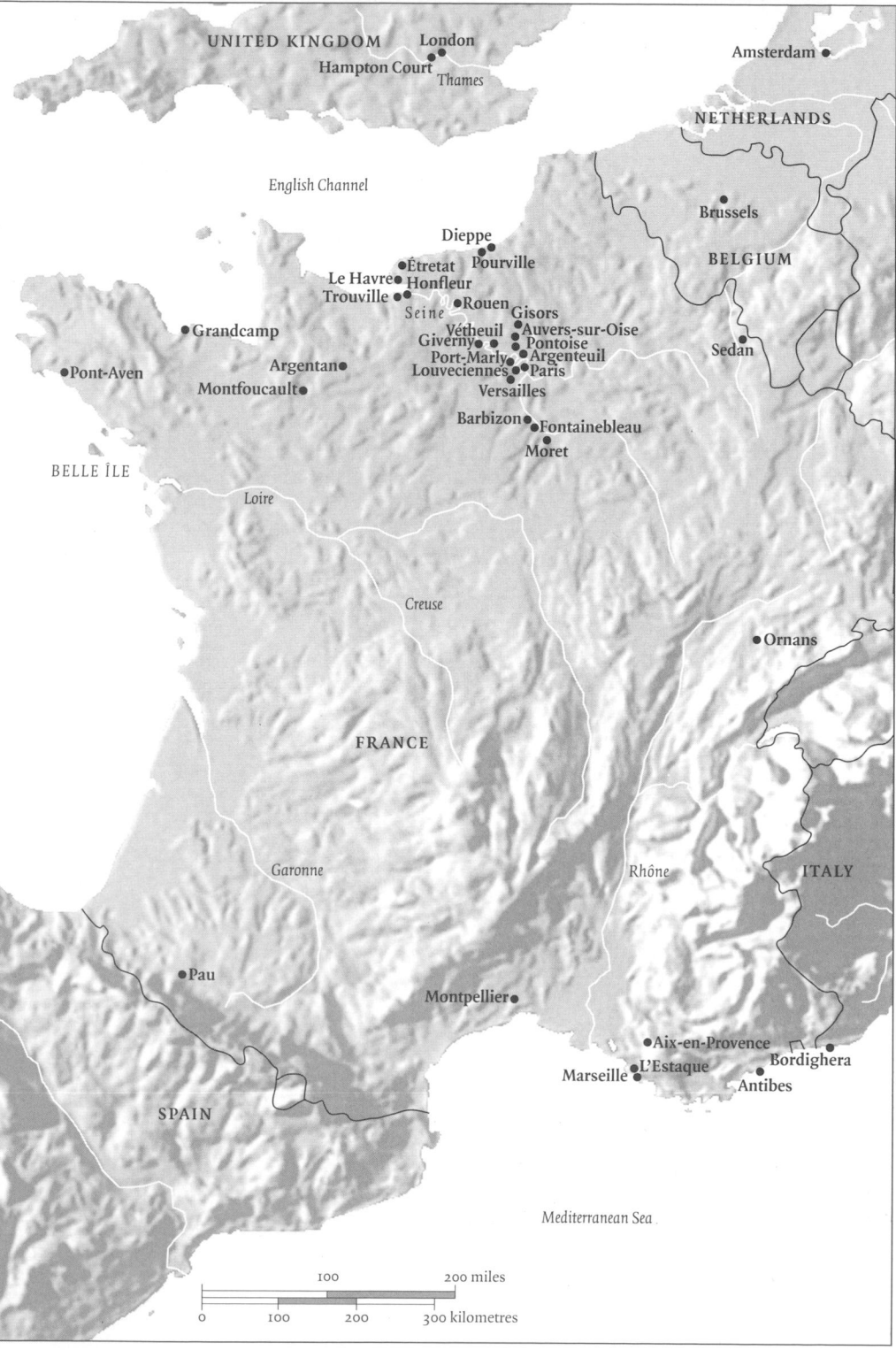

Further Reading

General

David Bomford et al., *Art in the Making: Impressionism* (exh. cat., National Gallery, London, 1990)

Richard R Brettell et al., *A Day in the Country: Impressionism and the French Landscape* (exh. cat., Los Angeles County Museum of Art, 1984)

Anthea Callen, *Techniques of the Impressionists* (London, 1982)

Francis Frascina et al., *Modernity and Modernism: French Painting in the Nineteenth Century* (London and New Haven, 1993)

Robert L Herbert, *Impressionism: Art, Leisure and Parisian Society* (London and New Haven, 1988)

Charles S Moffett et al., *The New Painting: Impressionism 1874–1886* (exh. cat., The Fine Arts Museums of San Francisco, 1986)

John Rewald, *The History of Impressionism* (4th revised edn, London and New York, 1973)

Gary Tinterow and Henri Loyrette, *Origins of Impressionism* (exh. cat., Metropolitan Museum of Art, New York, 1994)

Lionello Venturi, *Les Archives de l'Impressionisme*, 2 vols (Paris, 1939)

Chapter 1

Charles Baudelaire, *Art in Paris, 1845–1862*, ed. by Jonathan Mayne (London, 1965)

—, *The Painter of Modern Life and Other Essays*, ed. by Jonathan Mayne (London, 1965, 2nd edn, 1995)

Jonathan Crary, *Techniques of the Observer: On Vision and Modernity in the Nineteenth Century* (Cambridge, MA, 1990)

Michele Hannoosh, *Baudelaire and Caricature: From the Comic to an Art of Modernity* (University Park, PA, 1992)

David H Pinkney, *Napoleon III and the Rebuilding of Paris* (Princeton, 1958)

Jane Mayo Roos, *Early Impressionism and the French State, 1866–1874* (Cambridge, 1996)

James H Rubin, *Courbet* (London, 1997)

Anthony Sutcliffe, *The Autumn of Central Paris: The Defeat of Town Planning, 1850–1970* (Montreal, 1971)

Judith Wechsler, *A Human Comedy: Physiognomy and Caricature in 19th Century Paris* (Chicago and London, 1982)

Chapter 2

Carol Armstrong, *Manet/Manette* (New Haven and London, 2002)

Marilyn Brown, *Gypsies and Other Bohemians: The Myth of the Artist in Nineteenth-Century France* (Ann Arbor, MI, 1985)

Françoise Cachin et al., *Manet, 1832–1883* (exh. cat., Metropolitan Museum of Art, New York, 1983)

Timothy J Clark, *The Painting of Modern Life: Paris in the Art of Manet and his Followers* (New York, 1985)

Bradford Collins (ed.), *Twelve Views of Manet's Bar* (Princeton, 1996)

Michael Fried, *Manet's Modernism and the Face of Painting* (Chicago, 1996)

Anne Coffin Hanson, *Manet and the Modern Tradition* (New York, 1977)

Eunice Lipton, *Alias Olympia: A Woman's Search for Manet's Notorious Model and her Own Desire* (New York, 1992)

Theodore Reff, *Manet and Modern Paris* (exh. cat., National Gallery of Art, Washington, DC, 1982)

James H Rubin, *Manet's Silence and the Poetics of Bouquets* (London and Cambridge, MA, 1994)

Paul Hayes Tucker (ed.), *Manet's 'Le Déjeuner sur l'herbe'* (Cambridge, 1998)

Juliet Wilson-Bareau, *The Hidden Face of Manet: An Investigation of the Artist's Working Processes* (exh. cat., Courtauld Institute Galleries, London, 1986)

—, *Manet, Monet: The Gare Saint-Lazare* (exh. cat., National Gallery of Art, Washington, DC, 1998)

Émile Zola, *Mon Salon, Manet, Ecrits sur l'art*, ed. by Antoinette Ehrard (Paris, 1970)

Chapter 3

Kermit Champa, *Studies in Early Impressionism* (New Haven, 1973)

Nicholas Green, *The Spectacle of Nature: Landscape and Bourgeois Culture in Nineteenth-Century France* (Manchester, 1990)

Robert L Herbert, *Monet on the Normandy Coast: Tourism and Painting, 1867–1886* (New Haven and London, 1994)

John House, *Monet: Nature into Art* (New Haven and London, 1986)

Steven Z Levine, *Monet, Narcissus, and Self-reflection: The Modernist Myth of the Self* (Chicago and London, 1994)

Carla Rachman, *Monet* (London, 1997)

Paul Hayes Tucker, *Monet at Argenteuil* (New Haven and London, 1982)

—, *Claude Monet: Life and Art* (New Haven and London, 1995)

Daniel Wildenstein, *Claude Monet: biographie et catalogue raisonné*, 5 vols (Lausanne and Paris, 1974–91; 2nd revised edn, *Monet, or the Triumph of Impressionism*, 4 vols, Cologne, 1996)

Chapter 4

Richard R Brettell, *Pissarro and Pontoise: The Painter in a Landscape* (New Haven and London, 1990)

— et al., *Camille Pissarro, 1830–1903* (exh. cat., Hayward Gallery, London; Grand Palais, Paris; Museum of Fine Arts, Boston, 1980–1)

François Daulte, *Frédéric Bazille et son temps* (Geneva, 1952)

Anne Distel and John House, *Renoir* (exh. cat., Hayward Gallery, London, 1985)

Frédéric Bazille and Early Impressionism (exh. cat., The Art Institute of Chicago, 1978)

Frédéric Bazille: Prophet of Impressionism (exh. cat., Musée Fabre, Montpellier; Brooklyn Museum, New York, 1993)

Christopher Lloyd (ed.), *Studies on Camille Pissarro* (London, 1986)

Diane Pittman, *Bazille: Purity, Pose and Painting in the 1860s* (University Park, PA, 1998)

Joachim Pissarro, *Camille Pissarro* (New York, 1993)

— and Stephanie Rachum, *Camille Pissarro: Impressionist Innovator* (exh. cat., Israel Museum, Jerusalem, 1994)

Jean Renoir, *Renoir, My Father* (London, 1962)

Ralph E Shikes and Paula Harper, *Pissarro, His Life and Work* (New York, 1980)

Richard Thomson, *Camille Pissarro: Impressionism, Landscape and Rural Labour* (London, 1990)

Nicholas Wadley (ed.), *Renoir, A Retrospective* (New York, 1987)

Fronia E Wissman, 'The Generation Gap', in Kermit Champa *et al.*, *The Rise of Landscape Painting in France: Corot to Monet* (exh. cat., Currier Gallery of Art, Manchester, NH, 1991), pp.64–77

Chapter 5

Carol Armstrong, *Odd Man Out: Readings of the Work and Reputation of Edgar Degas* (Chicago, 1991)

Jean Sutherland Boggs *et al.*, *Degas* (exh. cat., Ottawa and New York, 1989)

Marilyn Brown, *Degas and the Business of Art: A Cotton Office in New Orleans* (University Park, PA, 1994)

Anthea Callen, *The Spectacular Body: Science, Method and Meaning in the Work of Degas* (London and New Haven, 1995)

Hollis Clayson, *Painted Love: Prostitution in French Art of the Impressionist Era* (New Haven, 1991)

Richard Kendall and Griselda Pollock, *Dealing with Degas: Representations of Women and the Politics of Vision* (New York, 1992)

Eunice Lipton, *Looking into Degas: Uneasy Images of Women and Modern Life* (Berkeley and Los Angeles, 1986)

Theodore Reff, *Degas, The Artist's Mind* (New York, 1976)

Chapter 6

Kathleen Adler and Tamar Garb, *Berthe Morisot* (Oxford, 1987)

Norma Broude, *Impressionism, A Feminist Reading: The Gendering of Art, Science, and Nature in the Nineteenth Century* (New York, 1991)

—, 'Degas's "Misogyny"', in Norma Broude and Mary D Garrard (eds), *Feminism and Art History: Questioning the Litany* (New York and London, 1982), pp.247–69

Anne Distel *et al.*, *Gustave Caillebotte: Urban Impressionist* (exh. cat., The Art Institute of Chicago, 1995)

Teri J Edelstein (ed.), *Perspectives on Morisot* (New York, 1990)

Tamar Garb, *Women Impressionists* (Oxford, 1986)

—, 'Renoir and the Natural Woman', in Norma Broude and Mary D Garrard (eds), *The Expanding Discourse: Feminism and Art History* (New York, 1992), pp.295–311

—, *Sisters of the Brush: Women's Artistic Culture in Late Nineteenth-Century France* (London and New Haven, 1994)

Anne Higonnet, *Berthe Morisot: A Biography* (New York, 1990)

—, *Berthe Morisot's Images of Women* (Cambridge, MA, 1992)

Nancy Mowll Matthews, *Mary Cassatt: A Life* (New York, 1994)

Linda Nochlin, 'Morisot's Wet Nurse: The Construction of Work and Leisure in Impressionist Painting', in *Women, Art, Power and Other Essays* (New York, 1988)

Griselda Pollock, *Mary Cassatt* (London, 1980)

—, *Vision and Difference: Femininity, Feminism and Histories of Art* (London, 1988)

Kirk Varnedoe, *Gustave Caillebotte* (New Haven and London, 1987)

Chapter 7

Albert Boime, *Art and the French Commune: Imagining Paris after War and Revolution* (Princeton, 1995)

Eugenia W Herbert, *The Artist and Social Reform in France and Belgium, 1885–1898* (New Haven, 1961)

Linda Nochlin, 'Degas and the Dreyfus Affair: A Portrait of the Artist as an Anti-Semite', in Norman Kleeblatt, *The Dreyfus Affair: Art, Truth and Justice* (exh. cat., Jewish Museum, New York, 1987)

Jane Mayo Roos, 'Within the "Zone of Silence": Manet and Monet in 1878', *Art History*, 3 (1988), pp.372–407

Chapter 8

John G Hutton, *Neo-Impressionism and the Search for Solid Ground* (Baton Rouge, LA, 1994)

Robert L Herbert, *Neo-Impressionism* (exh. cat., Guggenheim Museum, New York, 1968)

— et al., *Georges Seurat, 1859–1891* (exh. cat., Metropolitan Museum of Art, New York, 1991)

Joel Isaacson, *The Crisis of Impressionism, 1878–1882* (exh. cat., University of Michigan Museum of Art, Ann Arbor, 1979)

John Leighton and Richard Thompson, *Seurat and the Bathers* (London, 1997)

Linda Nochlin, 'Body Politics: Seurat's Poseuses', *Art in America* (March 1994), pp.70–7, 121–3

Michael R Orwicz, 'Anti-Academicism and State Power in the Early Third Republic', *Art History*, 4 (1991), pp.571–92

Paul Smith, *Seurat and the Avant-Garde* (London, 1997)

Martha Ward, *Pissarro, Neo-Impressionism, and the Spaces of the Avant-Garde* (Chicago, 1996)

Michael Zimmerman, *Seurat and the Art Theory of his Time* (Antwerp, 1991)

Chapter 9

Anne Distel, *Impressionism: The First Collectors*, trans. by Barbara Perroud-Benson (New York, 1990)

Ann Dumas et al., *The Private Collection of Edgar Degas* (exh. cat., Metropolitan Museum of Art, New York, 1997)

Marc S Gerstein, 'Degas's Fans', *Art Bulletin* (March 1982), pp.105–18

Nicholas Green, 'Circuits of Production, Circuits of Consumption: The Case of Mid-Nineteenth-Century French Art Dealing', *Art Journal* (Spring 1989), pp.29–34

—, 'Dealing in Temperaments: Economic Transformation of the Artistic Field in France during the Second Half of the Nineteenth Century', *Art History*, 1 (March 1987), pp.59–78

John Klein, 'The Dispersal of the Modernist Series', *Oxford Art Journal*, 1 (1998), pp.121–35

Michel Melot, *Impressionist Prints* (London and New Haven, 1996)

Joachim Pissarro, *Monet and the Mediterranean* (exh. cat., Kimbell Art Museum, Fort Worth, 1997)

Splendid Legacy: The Havemeyer Collection (exh. cat., Metropolitan Museum of Art, New York, 1993)

Paul Hayes Tucker, *Monet in the 90s: The Series Paintings* (exh. cat., Museum of Fine Arts, Boston; Royal Academy of Arts, London, 1989–90)

Cynthia A White and C Harrison, *Canvases and Careers: Institutional Change in the French Painting World* (Chicago, 1993)

Chapter 10

Nina Athanassoglou-Kallmyer, *Cézanne and Provence: The Painter and His Culture* (Chicago 2003)

Cézanne (exh. cat., Philadelphia Museum of Art; Tate Gallery, London, 1996)

Lawrence Gowing et al., *Cézanne: the Early Years 1859–1872* (exh. cat., Royal Academy of Arts, London, 1988)

Mary Louise Krumrine, *Paul Cézanne: The Bathers* (exh. cat., Kunstmuseum, Basel, 1989)

Mary Tompkins Lewis, *Cézanne's Early Imagery* (Berkeley and London, 1989)

John Rewald, *Cézanne: A Biography* (London and New York, 1986)

—, *The Paintings of Paul Cézanne: A Catalogue Raisonné* (New York, 1996)

William Rubin (ed.), *Cézanne: The Late Work* (exh. cat., Museum of Modern Art, New York, 1977)

Meyer Schapiro, *Paul Cézanne* (New York, 1962)

—, 'The Apples of Cézanne: An Essay in the Meaning of Still Life', in *Modern Art: Nineteenth and Twentieth Centuries: Selected Papers* (New York and London, 1978), pp.1–38

Richard Shiff, *Cézanne and the End of Impressionism: A Study of the Theory, Technique and Critical Evaluation of Modern Art* (Chicago and London, 1984)

Chapter 11

Paul B Armstrong, *The Challenge of Bewilderment: Understanding and Representation in James, Conrad, and Ford* (Ithaca, 1987)

Jean Barraqué, *Debussy* (Paris, 1962)

Paul Bordwell, *French Impressionist Cinema* (New York, 1980)

Thomas C Folk, *The Pennsylvania Impressionists* (Cranbury, NJ, 1997)

William H Gerdts, *American Impressionism* (New York, 1984)

—, *Lasting Impressions: American Painters in France, 1865–1915* (exh. cat., Musée Américain, Giverny, 1992)

André Jammes and Eugenia P Janis, *The Art of the French Calotype* (Princeton, 1983)

Maria Elisabeth Kronegger, *Literary Impressionism* (New Haven, 1973)

Susan Landauer et al., *California Impressionists* (exh. cat., Georgia Museum of Art, Athens, GA, 1996)

Kenneth McConkey, *British Impressionism* (Oxford, 1989, repr. London, 1998)

Christopher Palmer, *Impressionism in Music* (New York, 1974)

Peter H Stowell, *Literary Impressionism: James and Chekhov* (Athens, GA, 1980)

Paul Hayes Tucker, et al., *Monet in the Twentieth Century* (exh. cat., Museum of Fine Arts, Boston; Royal Academy of Arts, London, 1998–9)

Barbara H Weinberg et al., *American Impressionism and Realism: The Painting of Modern Life, 1885–1915* (exh. cat., Metropolitan Museum of Art, New York, 1994)

Arthur B Wenk, *Claude Debussy and Twentieth-Century Music* (Boston, 1983)

Impressionism

Index

Numbers in **bold** refer to illustrations

Acknowledgements

The bibliography I have provided gives some indication of the many scholars to whom any book on Impressionism is indebted. I would especially like to single out one of my first professors of undergraduate art history, Robert L Herbert, and a number of his former doctoral students at Yale, now first-rate art historians: Richard Shiff, Paul Tucker, Anne Higonnet and Richard Bretell. In addition, Carol Armstrong, T J Clark, Anne Distel, John House, Nina Athanassoglou-Kallmyer, Linda Nochlin and Theodore Reff are all colleagues whose work deserves special mention. I am also grateful to the staff at Phaidon Press for their extraordinary patience and collaboration. Pat Barylski, Julia MacKenzie, Ros Gray, Giulia Hetherington and Jo Carlill contributed more than they may suspect. Without them this book would not have seen the light of day.

J H R

This book is dedicated to my students, who've taught me what matters in the writing of art history.

Photographic Credits

AKG, London: 11, 148, 172, 183; Albright-Knox Art Gallery, Buffalo, NY: A Conger Goodyear (1940) 213; Allen Memorial Art Museum, Oberlin College, Ohio: 54; Amon Carter Museum, Fort Worth: 264; The Art Institute of Chicago: Charles H & Mary F S Worcester Collection (1964) 21, Mr & Mrs Lewis Larned Coburn Memorial Collection (1933) 76, Mr & Mrs Martin A Ryerson Collection (1933) 89, gift of Walter S Brewster (1951) 167, Helen Birch Bartlett Memorial Collection (1926) 203, Mr & Mrs Potter Palmer Collection (1922) 224, gift of Misses Aimée & Rosamond Lamb in Memory of Mr & Mrs Horatio A Lamb 225; Art Resource, New York: 189; Artothek, Peissenberg: 67, 121, 139, 176, 216, 239, 244; Ashmolean Museum, Oxford: 210; Baltimore Museum of Art: George A Lucas Collection 86; Barnes Foundation, Merion, PA: 211, 249; Bibliothèque Nationale, Paris: 75, 168, 178, 222, 260; BPK, Berlin: 45; Birmingham Museums and Art Gallery: 90; Bridgeman Art Library, London: 46, 133, 149, 150, 182, 194, 227, 245; British Museum, London: 118, 175; Christie's Images, London: 68, 127; Chrysler Museum, Norfolk, VA: gift of Walter P Chrysler, Jr 155; Courtauld Institute Galleries, University of London: 47, 156; Detroit Institute of Arts: gift of Dexter M Ferry Jr 261; Archives Durand-Ruel, Paris: 231; Fitzwilliam Museum, University of Cambridge: 234; Galerie Nichido, Tokyo: 69; Galerie Schmit, Paris: 143; Giraudon, Paris: 3; Glasgow Museums: Burrell Collection 51, 120; Harvard University Art Museums: bequest of Meta & Paul J Sachs 38, bequest from the collection of Maurice Wertheim 71, gift of Mr & Mrs F Meynier de Salinelles 82; Hiroshima Museum of Art: 200; Jean-Loup Charmet, Paris: 265; Kharbine-Tapabor, Paris: 145; Metropolitan Museum of Art, New York: Rogers Fund (1937) 12, purchase Howard Gilman Foundation and Joyce & Robert Menschel Gifts (1988) 13, bequest of Mrs H O Havemeyer (1929) Havemeyer Collection 14, 42, 44, 59, 114, 124, 248, gift of Mr & Mrs William B Jaffe (1955) 22, purchased with funds given or bequeathed by friends of the museum (1967) 57, bequest of William Church Osborn (1951) 74, bequest of Ralph Friedman (1992) 92, gift of George F Baker (1916) 104, Lesley & Emma Sheafer Collection, bequest of Emma A Sheafer (1973) 107, Wolfe Fund (1907) Catharine Lorillard Wolfe Collection 110, bequest of Mrs Harry Payne Bingham (1986) 126, gift of Paul J Sachs (1916) 136, gift of Mrs Charles Wrightsman (1986) 169, bequest of Stephen C Clark (1960) 251, gift of Miss Ethelyn McKinney in memory of her brother Glenn Ford McKinney (1934) 263, George S Hearn Fund (1957) 268; Minneapolis Institute of Arts: William Hood Dunwoody Fund 229, bequest of Putnam Dana McMillan 266; Mountain High Maps © 1995 Digital Wisdom Inc: 437; Musée Bonnat, Bayonne: 205; Musée de Brou, Bourg-en-Bresse: 95; Musée des Beaux-Arts de Rouen: 161, 185, 221; Musée du Petit Palais, Geneva: 171; Musée Fabre, Montpellier: 81, 106; Musée Gajac, Villeneuve-sur-Lot: 164; Musée Marmottan, Paris: cover; Musée Rodin, Paris: 256, 257; Museum of Art, Rhode Island School of Design: gift of Mrs Murray S Danforth 65; Museum of Fine Arts, Boston: 201, bequest of John T Spaulding 91, 243, Arthur Gordon Tompkins Residuary Fund 117, Hayden Collection 153, 154, Juliana Cheney Edwards Collection 214, 223, bequest of Robert Treat Paine II 242; Museum of Fine Arts, Houston: John A & Audrey Jones Beck Collection 88; Museum of Fine Arts, Springfield, MA: James Philip Gray Collection 93; Museum of Modern Art, New York: 116, Lillie P Bliss Collection 253; Museum Thyssen-Bornemisza, Madrid: 141; National Gallery of Art, Washington, DC: Chester Dale Collection 99, 151, photo Richard Carafelli 26, photo Bob Grove 103, gift of Mrs Horace Havemeyer in memory of her mother-in-law Louisine Elder Havemeyer, 48, Widener Collection 49, Ailsa Mellon Bruce Collection 144, Collection of Mr & Mrs Paul Mellon 154, 159, 162, 235, Andrew W Mellon Collection 252; National Gallery, London: 19, 27, 61, 72, 85, 96, 140, 165, 184, 186, 197, 204; National Gallery of Canada, Ottawa: 228, 232; National Gallery of Victoria, Melbourne: 207; North Carolina Museum of Art: purchased with funds from the Sarah Graham Kenan Foundation and the North Carolina Art Society (Robert F Phifer Bequest) 226; Norton Simon Foundation, Pasadena: 101, 163; Ny Carlsberg Glyptotek, Copenhagen: 25; Oskar Reinhart Collection, Winterthur: 160; Philadelphia Museum of Art: Henry P McIlhenny Collection in Memory of Frances P McIlhenny 113, 166, Mr & Mrs Carroll S Tyson Collection 198, John G Johnson Collection 212, George W Elkins Collection, 254, purchased with the W P Wilstach Fund, 255; Phillips Collection, Washington, DC: 195, 241; Photothèque des Musée de la Ville de Paris: 16, 20, 29, 55, 122, 218; RMN, Paris: 4, 7, 9, 10, 15, 23, 30, 33, 34, 37, 39, 43, 53, 56, 62, 64, 66, 70, 73, 78, 80, 83, 94, 97, 100, 105, 109, 112, 123, 125, 132, 134, 135, 137, 138, 147, 158, 170, 181, 191, 199, 202, 217, 219, 220, 236, 237, 240, 250; Robert Miller Gallery, New York: Estate of Joan Mitchell 269; Roger-Viollet, Paris: 128, 179, 190, 238; Santa Barbara Museum of Art: bequest of Katherine Dexter McCormick in memory of her husband Stanley McCormick 77; Scala, Florence: 5, 35, 36, 40, 52, 60, 63; Solomon R Guggenheim Museum, New York: Thannhauser Collection gift of Justin K Thannhauser (1978) 84; Staatsgalerie, Stuttgart: 87, 192; courtesy of the State Hermitage Museum, St Petersburg: 119; Statens Konstmuseer, Stockholm: 1; Sterling and Francine Clark Art Institute, Williamstown, MA: 18; Tate Gallery, London: 208, 262; Toledo Museum of Art: 115; photo Malcolm Varon, New York, © 1998 247; Ville de Chemillé, Maine et Loire: 196; Wallraf-Richartz Museum, Cologne: 102; Wildenstein Institute, Paris: 146

Phaidon Press Limited
Regent's Wharf
All Saints Street
London N1 9PA

Phaidon Press Inc.
180 Varick Street
New York, NY 10014

www.phaidon.com

First published 1999
Reprinted 2001, 2004
© 1999 Phaidon Press Limited

ISBN 0 7148 3826 8

A CIP catalogue record for this book is available
from the British Library.

All rights reserved. No part of this publication
may be reproduced, stored in a retrieval system
or transmitted, in any form or by any means,
electronic, mechanical, photocopying, recording
or otherwise, without the written permission of
Phaidon Press Limited.

Typeset in Quadraat

Printed in Singapore

Cover illustration Claude Monet, *Impression,
Sunrise*, 1872 (see pp.10–11)